WE ARE MADE *of* STORIES

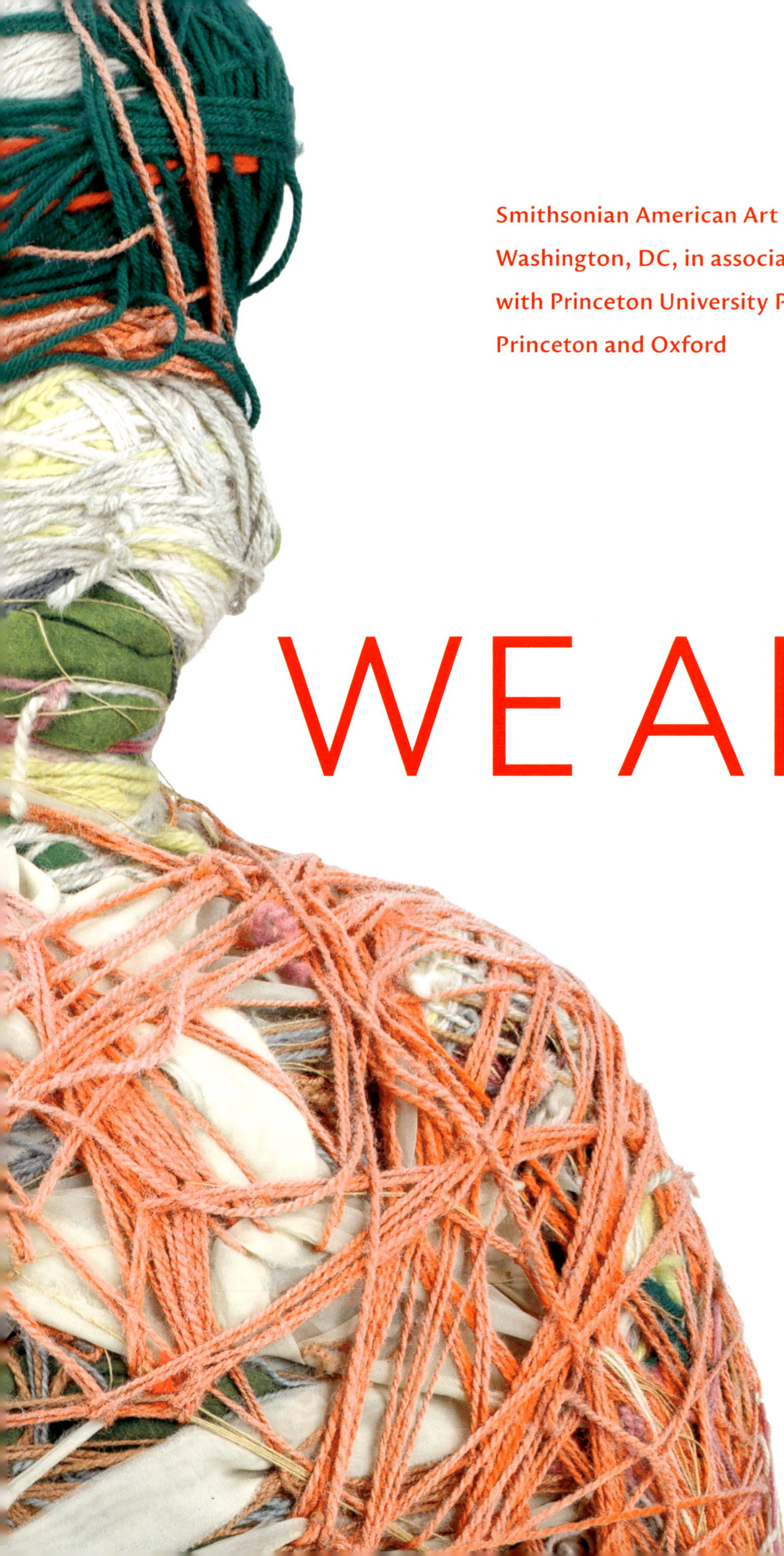

Smithsonian American Art Museum,
Washington, DC, in association
with Princeton University Press,
Princeton and Oxford

WE ARE MA

LESLIE UMBERGER

introduction by

Douglas O. Robson

DE *of* STORIES

Self-Taught Artists in the Robson Family Collection

WE ARE MADE *of* STORIES

Self-Taught Artists in the Robson Family Collection

Published in conjunction with the exhibition of the same name, on view at the Smithsonian American Art Museum, Washington, DC, July 1, 2022, through March 26, 2023.

Produced by the Publications Office, Smithsonian American Art Museum, Washington, DC, americanart.si.edu.

Tiffany Farrell,
Interim Director of Publications

Mary J. Cleary, *Senior Editor*

Denise Arnot, *Designer*

Richard Sorensen, Aubrey Vinson,
Permissions and Image Coordinators

Maria R. Eipert, *Curatorial Assistant*

Magda Nakassis, *Proofreader*

Kate Mertes, *Indexer*

SAAM Smithsonian American Art Museum

PRINCETON
press.princeton.edu

Published by the Smithsonian American Art Museum in association with Princeton University Press, Princeton and Oxford, press.princeton.edu.

The Smithsonian American Art Museum is home to one of the largest collections of American art in the world. Its holdings—more than 43,000 works—tell the story of the United States through the visual arts and represent the most inclusive collection of American art of any museum today.

It is the nation's first federal art collection, predating the 1846 founding of the Smithsonian Institution. The Museum celebrates the exceptional creativity of the nation's artists, whose insights into history, society, and the individual reveal the essence of the American experience.

Image details: cover: Philadelphia Wireman, *Untitled*, Cat. 66; inside covers: Dan Miller, *Untitled (DM 1024)*, Cat. 119; p. 2: Judith Scott, *Untitled (Medicine Bottle)*, Cat. 96; pp. 4–5: Leroy Person, *Untitled*, Cat. 57; pp. 6–7: Joseph E. Yoakum, *Devils Back Bone, in Mt Messa Near Trinadad Colorado*, Cat. 39; p. 8: Edwin Lawson, *Fashions 1899*, Cat. 110; p. 44: Jon Serl, *Texas Scene*, Cat. 100; p. 52: Justin McCarthy, *Marie Prevost*, Cat. 102; p. 66: Sister Gertrude Morgan, *Fan* (recto), Cat. 47; pp. 150–51: Judith Scott, *Untitled (JS 39)*, Cat. 97; pp. 194–95: Dan Miller, *Untitled (239_2016)*, Cat. 120.

Philadelphia Wireman: p. 142 (clockwise from top left): Cats. 66, 67, 71, 59, 64, 63, 69, 72; p. 143 (clockwise from top right): Cats. 70, 65, 73, 68, 61, 62, 60

Cataloging-in-Publication Data, Library of Congress Control Number 2022011542

ISBN 978-0-691-24042-8 (softcover)
ISBN 978-0-691-24384-9 (ebook)

Typeset in Mr Eaves Sans, Dunbar Tall, Proza and printed on Opus Matte.

Printed in Canada by Friesens Corporation

10 9 8 7 6 5 4 3 2 1

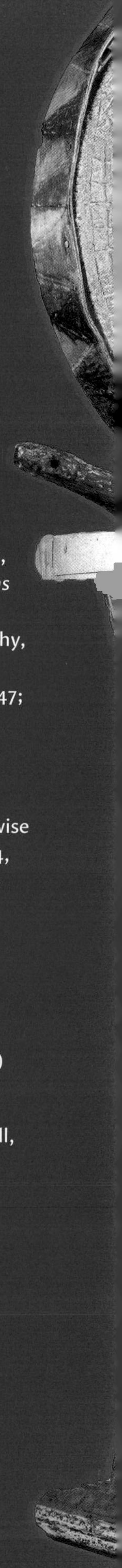

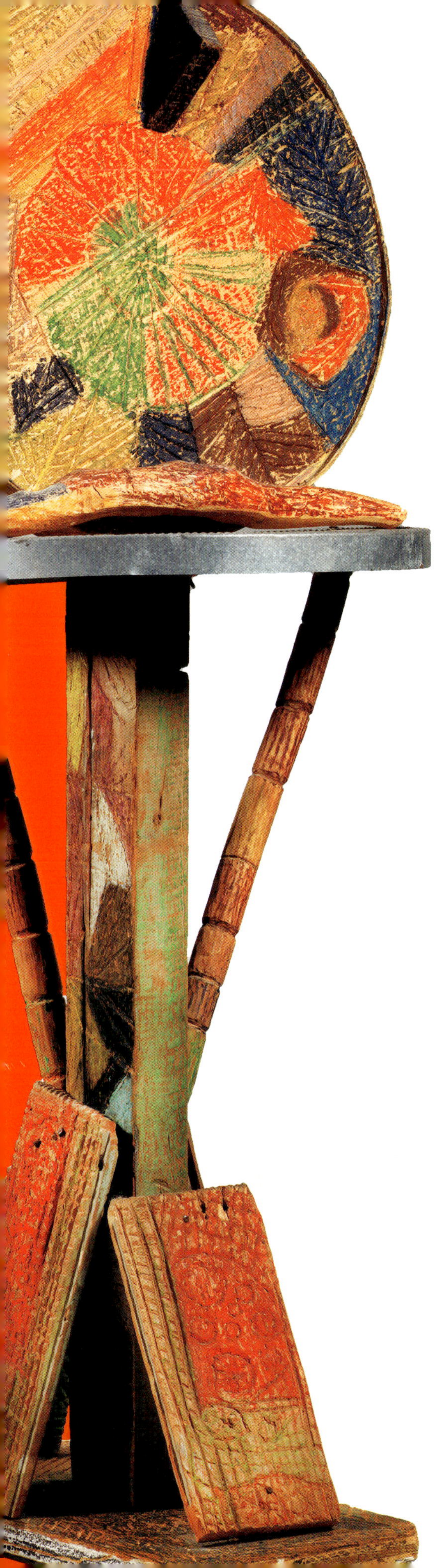

CONTENTS

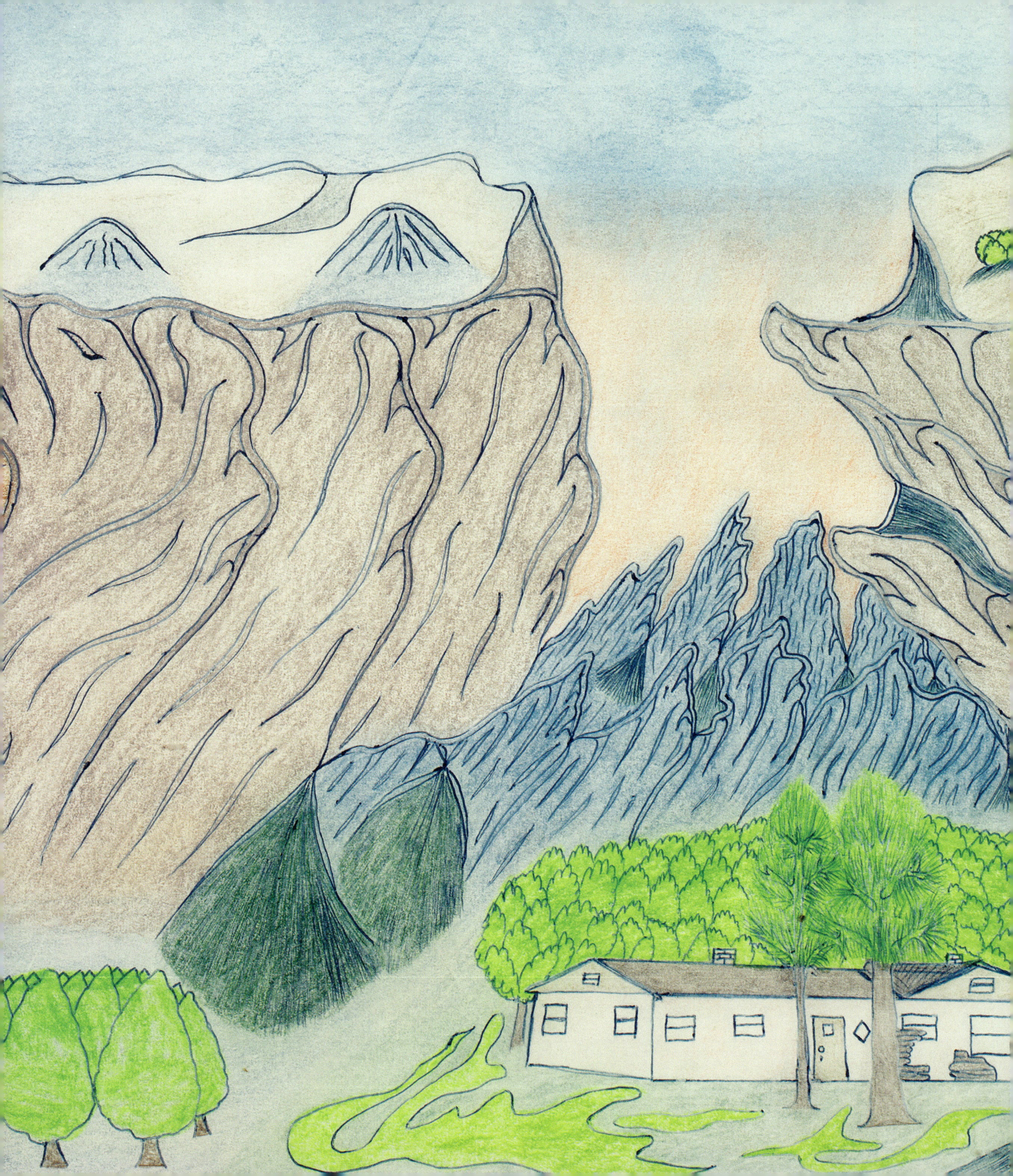

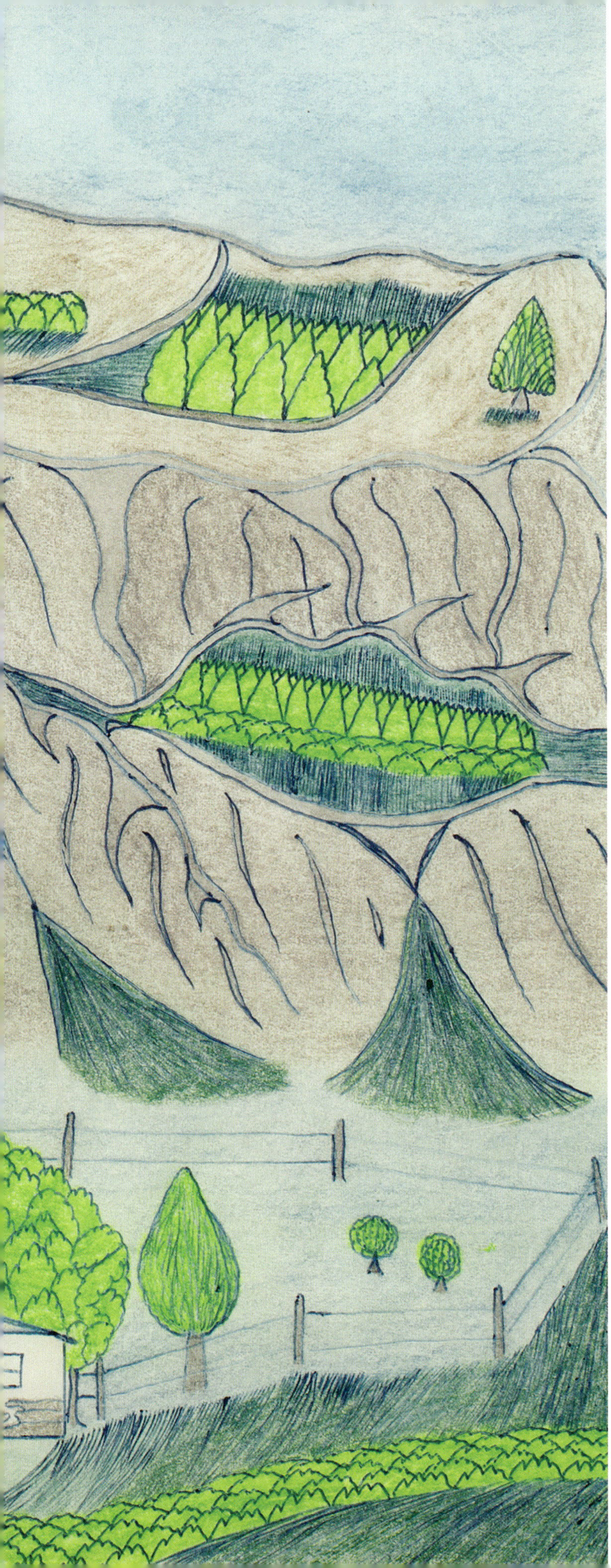

WE ARE MADE *of* STORIES

Self-Taught Artists in the Robson Family Collection

is organized by the

Smithsonian American Art Museum

Generous support has been provided by

Herbert Waide Hemphill Jr.
American Folk Art Fund

Shaun and Andy Block

Steven Czekala

James and Catherine Denny

Sheila Duignan and Mike Wilkins

Travis Marquette and Sean Kosofsky

Rumsfeld Family Fund

Jeff Rosensweig and Natalie Allen

Share Fund

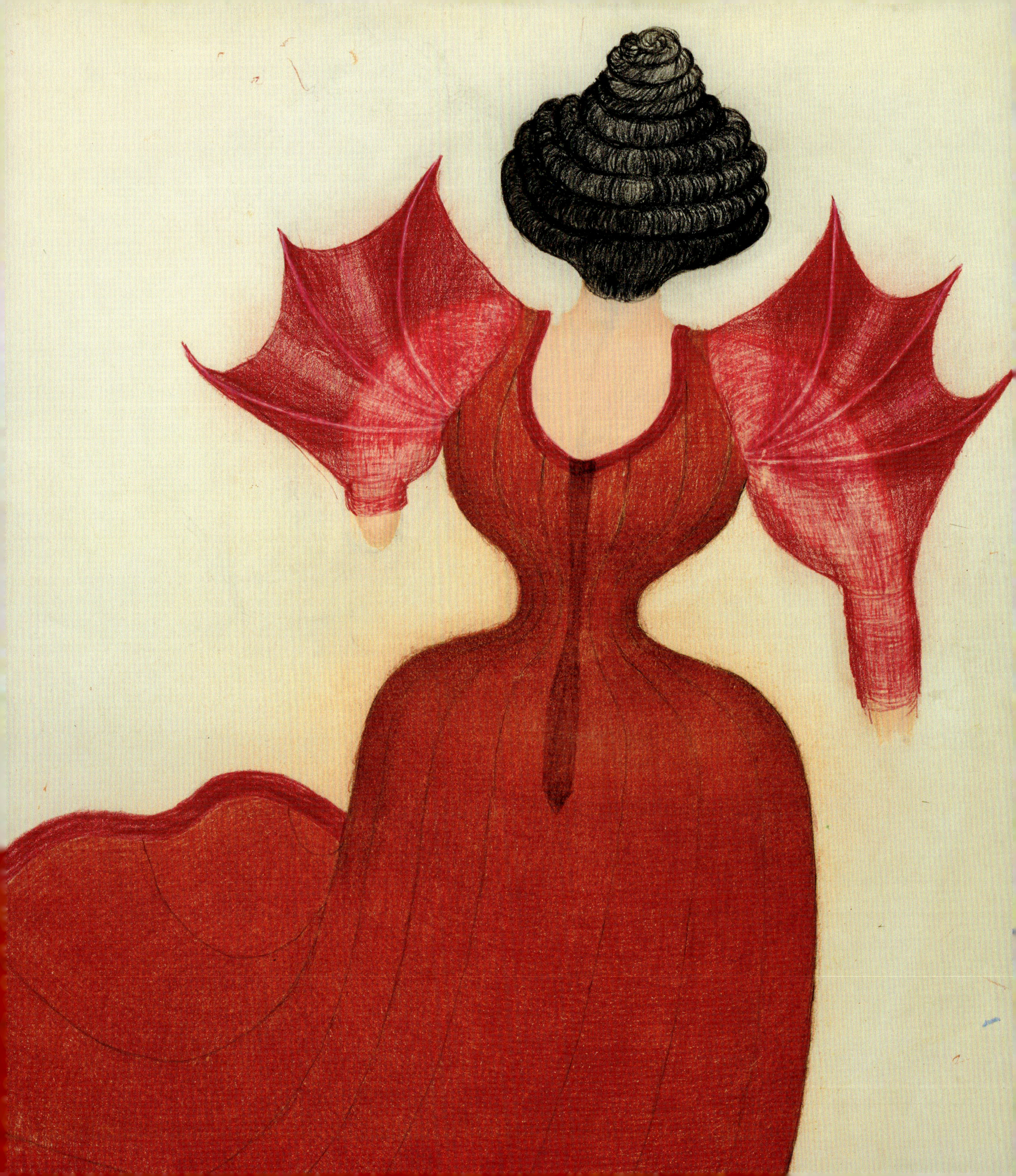

DIRECTOR'S FOREWORD

We Are Made of Stories presents a timely look at artists, collectors, and this present moment of racial reckoning in America. Featuring more than one hundred artworks, the catalogue and exhibition examine the extraordinary lives of forty-three self-taught artists in the Robson Family Collection, and the collecting journey of Margaret Z. Robson, a labor of love that her son Douglas O. Robson has carried into the present. The project invites conversations around inclusion and diversity now central to both public discourse and the daily work of arts organizations. By focusing on the personal stories of the artists, in tandem with the art that powerfully conveys these narratives, *We Are Made of Stories* confronts issues of marginalization that extend far beyond parameters of "self-taught" versus "academically trained."

The Robson family has been of inestimable importance to the Smithsonian American Art Museum's collecting strategies in this field. In 2016, Doug gifted the Museum ninety-three works from his late mother's collection, amplifying one of the most significant holdings of self-taught art in any museum in the United States. He has since donated another major artwork and has promised an additional thirty-two pieces; together, these 126 artworks, which are the focus of the catalogue and show, will compose the Robson Family Collection at the Smithsonian American Art Museum. In 2018, Doug generously endowed the Margaret Z. Robson Symposium Series, which will further a mission that Margaret and SAAM shared: to strengthen scholarship on, appreciation of, and equitable representation for self-taught artists. Like philanthropists Abby Aldrich Rockefeller and son Nelson before them, this mother and son collecting pair have brought this infinitely expansive world into even greater view.

In his introduction to this volume, Doug Robson offers an insightful window into his mother's formative years and, later, their life as a family, as Margaret and husband John started collecting in the 1970s. A product of the upper Midwest, Margaret understood the meaning of hard work and naturally connected with people from all walks of life. She became passionate about self-taught artists and was decades ahead of many public collections in recognizing the ways in which their art told important stories and exposed inconsistencies in the American Dream—an ideal she cherished but increasingly realized was available to some more than to others. What animated her collecting ethos was an abiding belief in the value of every person's point of view, the conviction that the lives and creativity of untrained artists following their own path were the democratic ideal writ large. For Margaret, that value transcended labels of "folk," "self-taught," or "outsider," and put her in touch with an astonishing and increasingly diverse array of people: Black, white, immigrants, the neurodiverse, individuals who challenged social conventions and strata, and whose artworks confound easy assumptions and stereotypes about what self-taught art "should" look like, and what being "self-taught" really means.

Leslie Umberger, SAAM's curator of folk and self-taught art, pens an essay that seeks to boldly reframe what we think art is, to recalibrate our understanding of self-taughts and of the labels and language that for decades have defined, and disfigured, dialogues about their work. She delves into the complex stories of artists forgotten and celebrated, with a view that the personal is political in the history of self-taught artists in the United States. She offers a concise overview of their growing prominence over the course of the twentieth century, with generous profiles for many of the artists in the installation and an examination of how, with the help of dedicated collector-advocates, their work has reshaped the art world.

Leslie examines early museum paradigms for presenting folk and self-taught, nascent strategies that simultaneously showcased and immured the art, and maps the art's gradual if fitful inclusion in public collections. Featured artists range from those whose identities were lost to time, to Nellie Mae Rowe, a Georgia native known for her exuberant pastel and crayon drawings, and whose home-yard Playhouse joyfully reclaimed an early life etched with deprivation and announced self-definition, at any age, as one's true work. From Judith Scott, whose fiber sculptures offered a portal to an expressive agency denied to her as a woman born with Down Syndrome and later becoming deaf as well; to Bill Traylor, born enslaved in Alabama around 1853, who began drawing and painting in his late eighties and created bold, abstracted images that attest to the brutal realities of life in the Jim Crow South. From the Philadelphia Wireman, an artist whose real name we may never know, but who left behind a powerfully enigmatic body of work that holds and offers clues about identity and culture, and charts one individual's daily existence through assemblage; to Calvin and Ruby Black, who together crafted a colorful and theatrical family that brought vivacity and visitors to their California outpost—and many more.

She brings us into the present with a look at artist Dan Miller, whose drawings and paintings bridge lifelong communication challenges inherent to autism, and who first captivated Margaret and later became one of the living artists that Doug most actively supports. With each artist profile, Leslie weaves a stunning canvas of inner realities made visible through art. What emerges in her essay is a clear-eyed recognition of Art in all its diversity and social backgrounds, indelible portraits of originality and material assertions of identity, all framed by history and a staunch advocacy for their rightful place in museum collections.

The Smithsonian American Art Museum has understood that rightful place since 1970, when it acquired James Hampton's *Throne of the Third Heaven of the Nations' Millennium General Assembly* (see Figs. 1, 2, pp. 63, 64). Hampton—janitor by day, artist by night, and full-time spiritual devotee—created his resplendent *Throne* in a rented carriage house, where he labored for fourteen years but never finished it. A multipiece sculpture made from aluminum and gold-colored foils and papers, metal, wood, glass, and found objects, Hampton's *Throne* was a visionary pursuit, one man's physical expression of faith and hope for eternal salvation. In the 1970s, the same years Margaret and John Robson began their collection, SAAM became one of the first museums to display and interpret artworks by artists who, like Hampton, followed their own path and learned through personal practice. Decades later, these kindred visions would unite with Doug's 2016 gift, bringing even greater light and appreciation to this field.

I am profoundly grateful to the extraordinary staff at the Smithsonian American Art Museum for its dedication to our important national mission, especially since March 2020, when the Smithsonian temporarily closed its museums in response to the COVID-19 pandemic, and for their work on *We Are Made of Stories*. As always, many departments contributed their talents, including conservation, curatorial, development, education, exhibits, external affairs and digital strategies, publications, and the registrars and collection managers, who have made so much possible. I greatly appreciate all they did, on-site and remotely, to bring the installation and exhibition catalogue to fruition.

I especially thank Douglas Robson for his family's unstinting support of self-taught artists, over time and at SAAM, and for his passionate participation in this important project. Doug's collection manager, Caitlin O'Meara, effectively joined the SAAM staff in making sure every detail was attended to and every goal was met, for which we are most grateful. In producing this important catalogue, Leslie Umberger has focused once again on scholarship and the community, twin concerns beautifully realized in *We Are Made of Stories*. I salute Leslie for her dedication to the field and for building SAAM's collection in thoughtful and important ways. Special thanks go to curatorial assistant Maria R. Eipert, senior editor Mary Cleary, exhibition designer Sara Gray, publication designer Denise Arnot, and interpretation strategist Kelly Skeen for being the points of connection and direction for the larger SAAM team. I offer my deepest appreciation and admiration to the artists themselves, who continue to inspire us with their vision and persistence, realized in the incomparable artworks we cherish. Their singular stories remind us of the inherent dignity of all lives, and that creativity abides in all quarters.

Stephanie Stebich

The Margaret and Terry Stent Director
Smithsonian American Art Museum

This catalogue and exhibition celebrate a major gift of artworks to the Smithsonian American Art Museum from Douglas O. Robson, given in memory of his mother, Margaret Z. Robson, and his father, John E. Robson.

FAR & WIDE /

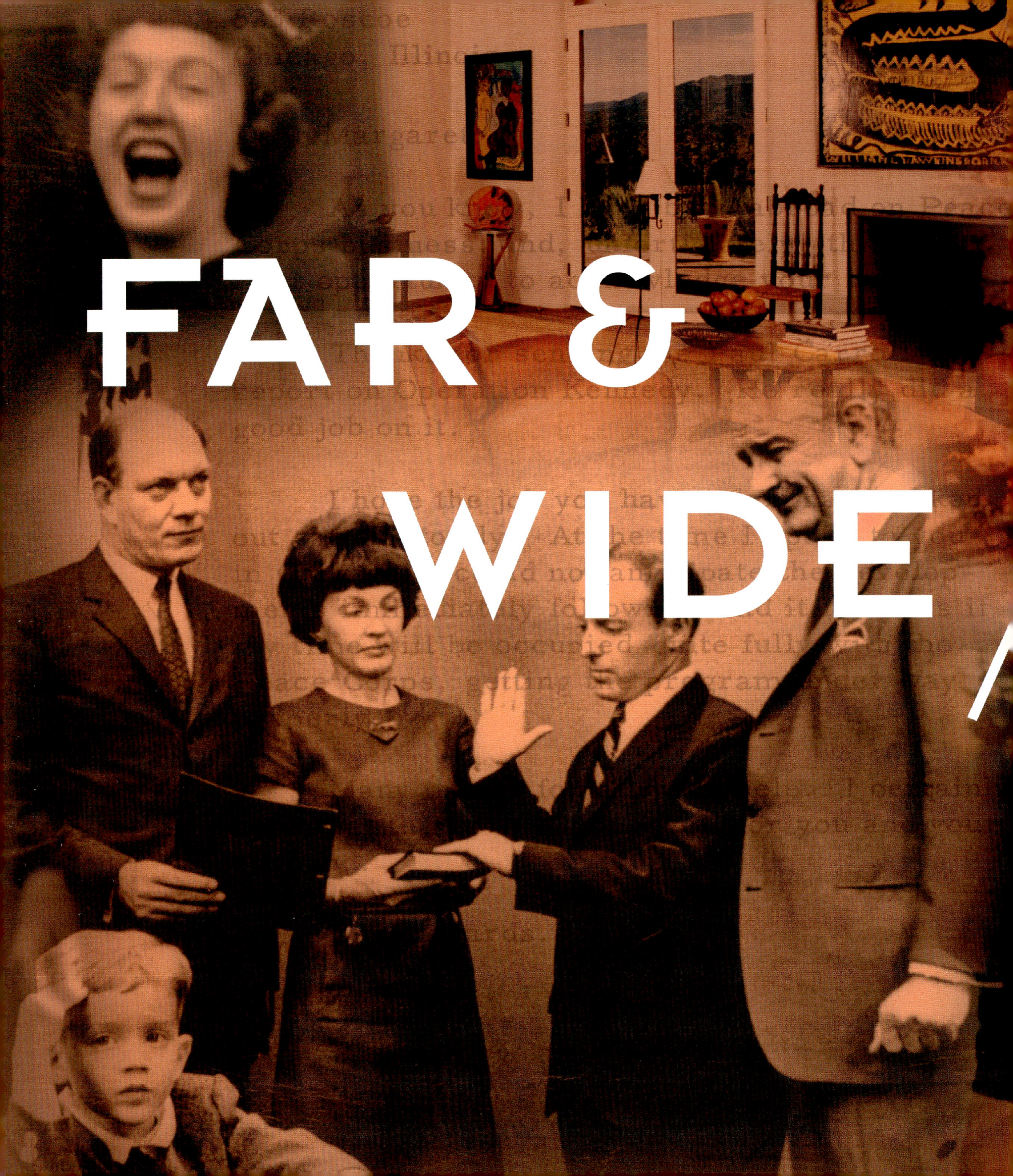

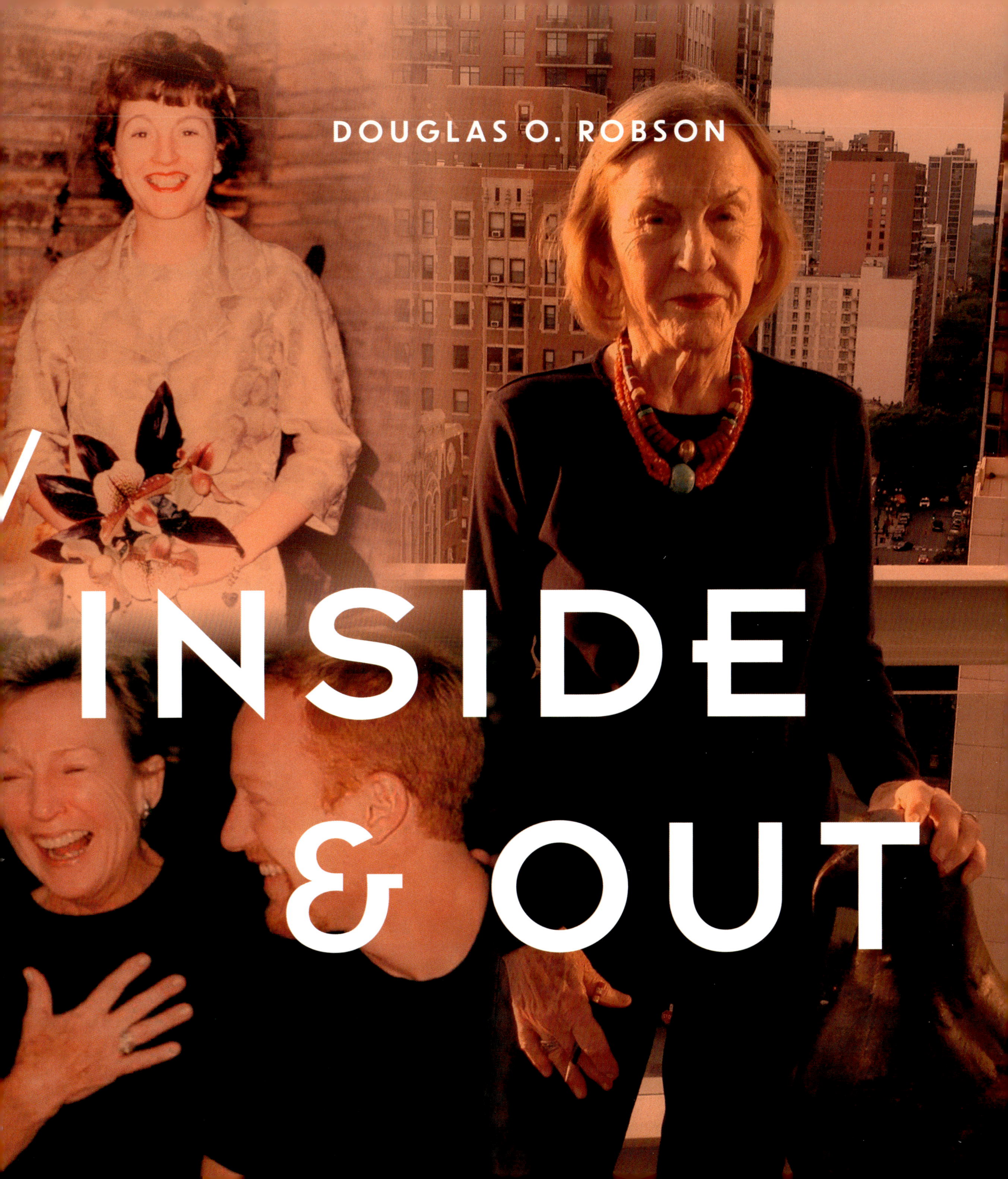
DOUGLAS O. ROBSON
INSIDE
& OUT

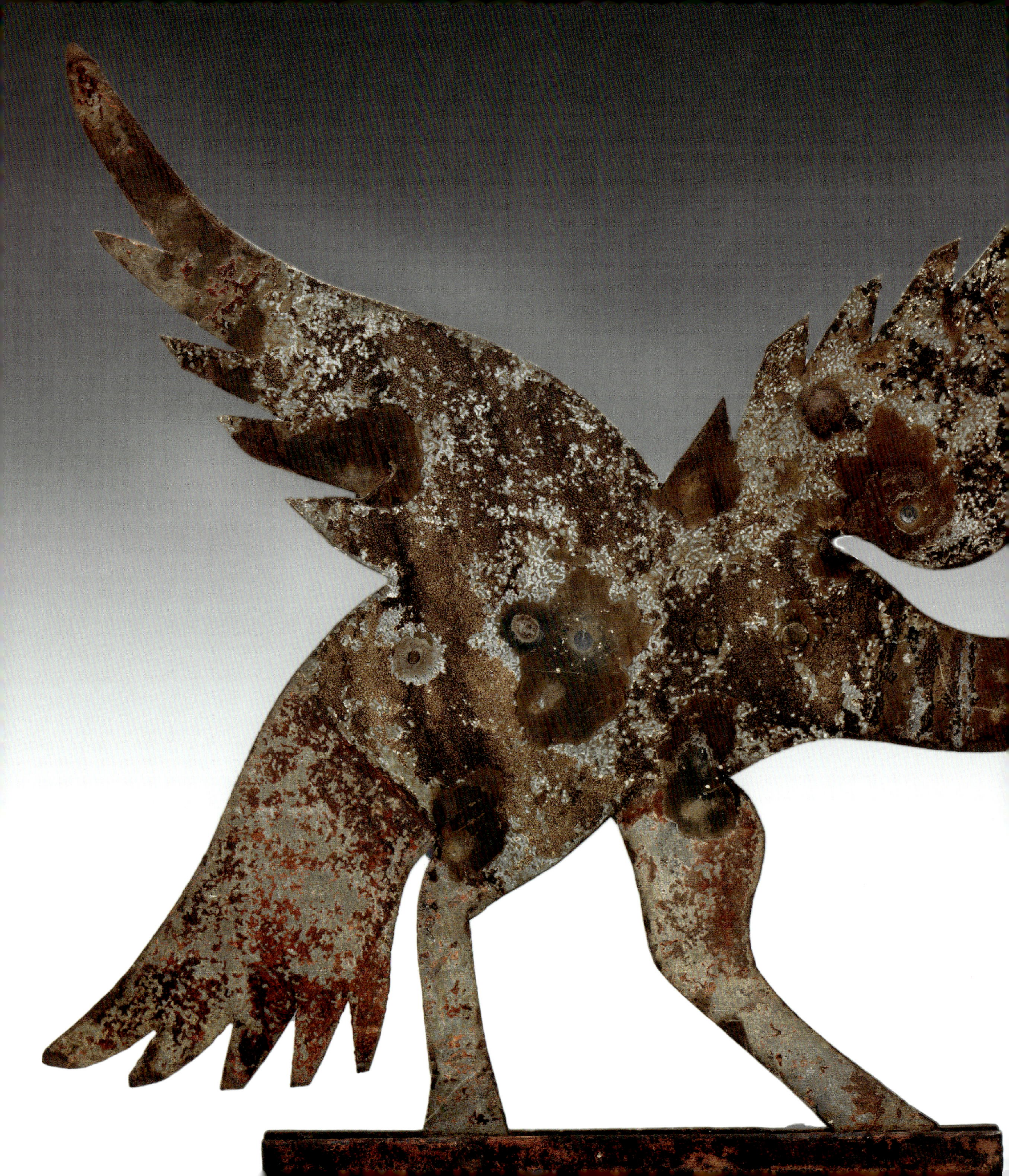

A JOURNEY WITH ART

REMEMBERING MARGARET ZUEHLKE ROBSON

It is impossible to predict what someone will hold close to their heart—why some things become cherished as others recede from view. Filtered through a kaleidoscope of perspective, experience, emotion, intention, spirituality, and psyche, every object becomes a puzzle piece to a mottled inner existence, with one foot in the world of the maker, another in the world of the person who later valued and saved it, and the nexus of that creative force sometimes offering a more profound understanding when considered together. Therein lies the mystery and surprise of the collector's vision.

My mother, Margaret Elizabeth Zuehlke, was full of surprises, as a person and eventual collector. Born in 1932, she grew up in rural Minnesota in the 1930s and 1940s, during the lean years of the Great Depression. Her divorced mother taught piano to provide for Margaret and her three older siblings (Fig. 1). They weren't poor, but they lived close enough to the poverty line to know want. As a young girl, Margaret survived on licorice gum and Shirley Temple movies (Fig. 2).

Catholicism and small-town mores shaped her formative years, providing a potent underpinning of stricture, superstition, and shame. A single-parent household in that era was often viewed with pity and judgment. This hardscrabble upbringing in Faribault—just south of Minneapolis—where she and her siblings shucked corn for extra money and Margaret later worked at a canning company, didn't expose her to much beyond what she might have learned in school or seen at the local movie theater. As a regular churchgoer and a product of Catholic schools, it seems likely that Margaret's exposure to arts and culture was limited to the religious art and iconography she encountered. She was hardly primed to become an art collector (Fig. 3).

Margaret did collect people. All stripes. This theme infused her life. Her world would expand dramatically in the decades ahead, but she steadfastly remained as conversant with blue-collar tradesmen as with heads of state. Early on, she harnessed an ability to connect with people at any station in life. She took a genuine interest in everyone. She asked questions. She had real affection and respect for the tradesmen and service providers in her life, often giving them endearing sobriquets such as "Art the Carpenter" or "Polly the Faux Painter." Their craftsmanship grew important to her. The world she sought to inhabit placed high value on personal creativity, often rooted in frugality but never lacking flair, and on people who were adept at using tools and materials close at hand rather than purchased. Process, as well as product, mattered.

"Margie," as some called her, majored in business and economics, graduating from the University of Minnesota in 1954. Afterward, she relocated to Chicago, where she began a successful and somewhat trailblazing career in banking. She was one of the early women executives in a prefeminist society, holding what the *Chicago Daily Tribune* called, in a 1958 article about her, "a 'man's' job"; the *Chicago Sun-Times* later featured a piece as well (Fig. 4).[1] These years before

Fig. 1. Margaret with her siblings, Faribault, Minnesota, ca. 1930s; left to right: Mary, Margaret, Jim, and Tom Zuehlke **Fig. 2.** Margaret (right) and her childhood best friend playing dress-up in Margaret's grandmother's wedding gown, late 1930s **Fig. 3.** Margaret, graduation day, Faribault High School, Minnesota, 1950 **Fig. 4.** *Chicago Sun-Times* article highlighting Margaret as a woman entering the male-dominated profession of banking, February 7, 1959. Photos by Jack Lenahan

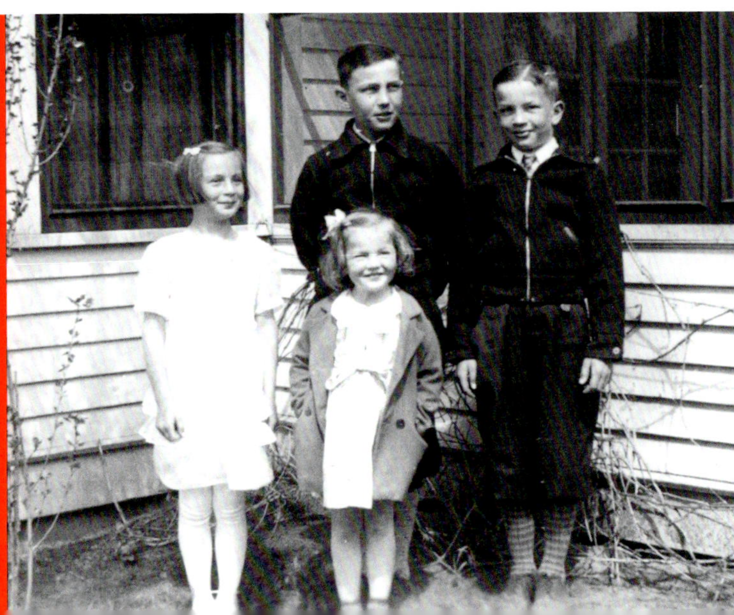

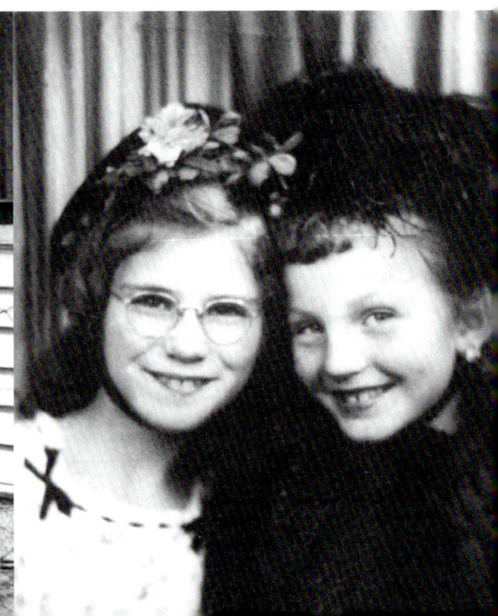

she met my father are little known to me. They were, however, punctuated with secrets, loss, and grief—themes that would shadow-shape Margaret's outlook on life. I discovered, only after my mother died, that she had put her first child up for adoption before she married my father. Three decades later, she would lose a second to an accidental overdose. A third child would come out as gay, which produced in my mother an attendant loss of expectations. What became a prominent, conventional existence on the surface often shielded complexities that later inspired deeper interpretations.

The presidential nomination of John Fitzgerald Kennedy captivated Margaret, whose enthusiasm and organizational acumen were quickly noticed—certainly by Sargent Shriver, who became a personal friend and tapped her to run a key district in the campaign. My mother left her banking career to join "Operation Kennedy" in 1960, serving as executive director of Citizens for Kennedy-Johnson. She interacted with Kennedy and his family firsthand, including JFK's sister Eunice, who had married Shriver in 1953. Margaret was with them all in Hyannis Port on election night (Fig. 5).

Less than a month after Kennedy was elected this country's first Catholic president, Margaret Zuehlke married my father, John Edwin Robson (Fig. 6). They had met two years earlier when residing in the same Chicago apartment building. As the story goes, my father made frequent pretense of bumming household goods like salt and sugar from Margaret and her roommates—until my mother suggested he summon the courage to ask one of them out. Margaret's connection to Shriver, who kick-started the Peace Corps in 1961 and ran on the Democratic ticket as the vice presidential candidate in 1972, lasted several years into her marriage. Their correspondence reveals her efforts to help him get the Peace Corps off the ground, including recommending personnel and organizing conferences. Their affiliation tailed off over time, but the impact of these formative experiences remained a lasting source of self-confidence for Margaret.

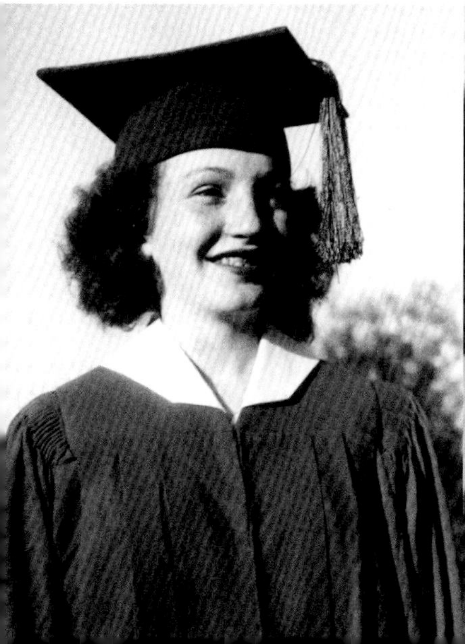

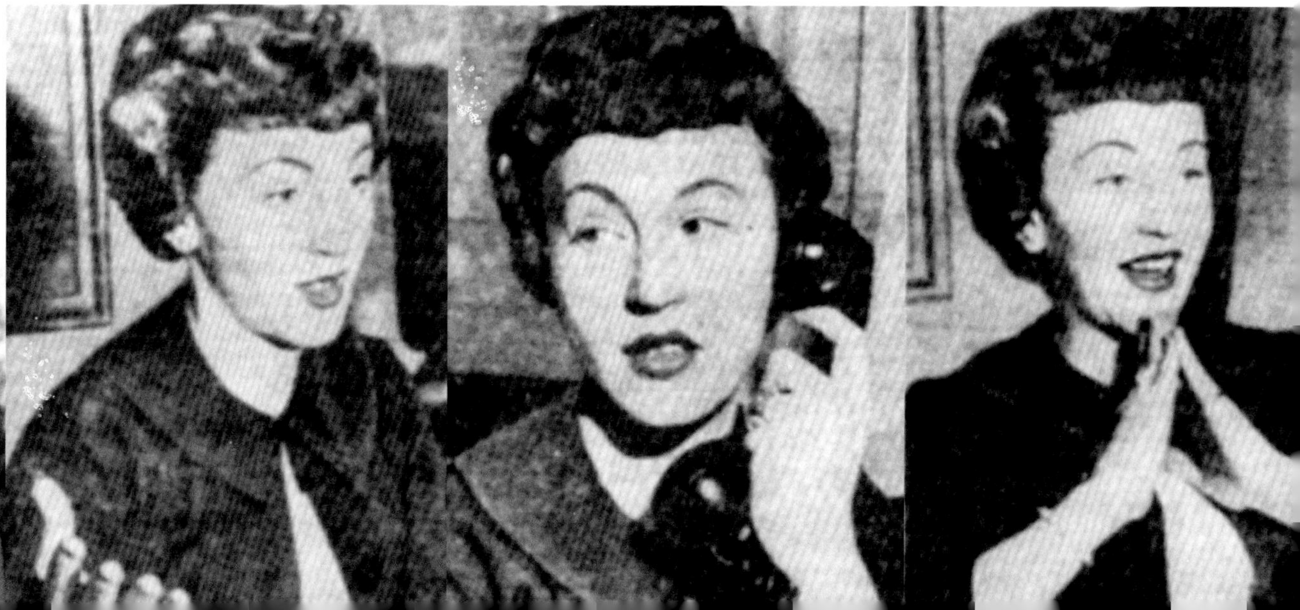

MARRIAGE

I don't know how my mother felt about giving up her professional identity for marriage and motherhood, not to mention the constraints those roles entailed in the 1960s. I do know she threw herself into these new responsibilities with gusto and excelled in the details of domestic life. My brother, Matthew, was born in 1962; I followed in 1965. My father, a Yale-educated, Harvard-trained lawyer and nonpracticing Jew from the Chicago suburbs, bore the burdens of a young attorney with ambitions. He busted his backside while my mother took the reins at home, raising the children and managing the household. Whatever career aspirations she harbored were set aside. She never returned to full-time employment, and domesticity became her default creative outlet (Fig. 7).

In 1966, my father's decision to leave his law firm and take a post in the Lyndon B. Johnson administration set their lives on a new trajectory. It was the first of several government positions he would hold, the subsequent posts all served under Republican presidents (Fig. 8). Between Washington stints, my father worked variously as a lawyer, business executive, and academic, oscillating between the private and public sectors for decades. Our family moved frequently between Washington, DC, and Chicago, living also in Atlanta, San Francisco, Santa Fe, and finally back in Chicago, where my mother spent the final two years of her life.

How did art fit into this itinerant equation? It had unassuming beginnings. John and Margaret revered the American democratic experiment. Every Fourth of July, my father read the Declaration of Independence aloud at the breakfast table to whoever was present. They had come of age in the 1950s, when the United States emerged from World War II as the preeminent economic and military superpower. The country had a new self-confidence and far-reaching optimism. In the art

Fig. 5. Margaret talking with John F. Kennedy on election night, Hyannis Port, Massachusetts, November 8, 1960 **Fig. 6.** Margaret and John Robson on their wedding day, Chicago, 1960 **Fig. 7.** Robson family, late 1960s; from left: Matthew, Margaret, John, and Douglas **Fig. 8.** Surrounded by his family, John Robson (center) is sworn in as chairman of the Civil Aeronautics Board by Supreme Court Associate Justice William H. Rehnquist for President Gerald R. Ford (far right), at the White House, April 1975

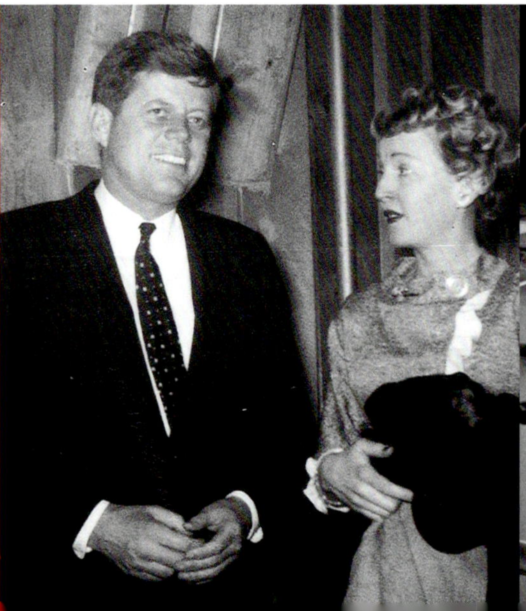

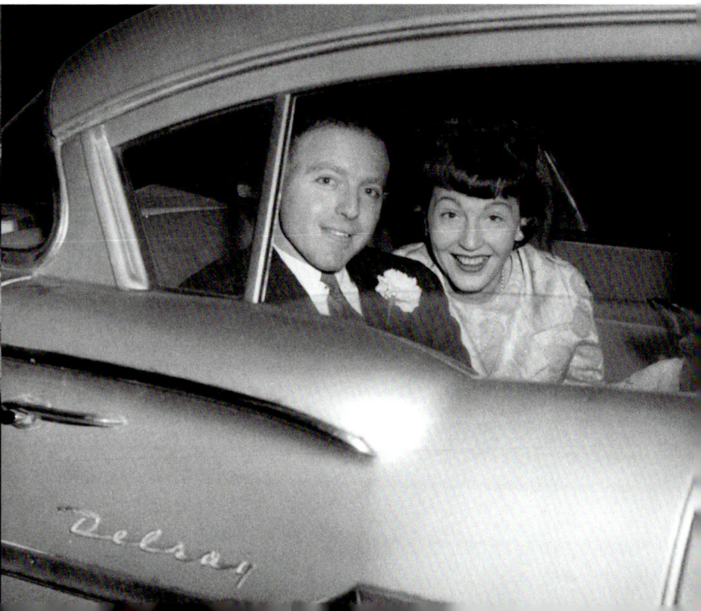

world, New York asserted its growing prominence with the rise of abstract expressionism, as artists Jackson Pollock, Willem de Kooning, Mark Rothko, and others tilted attention away from Paris.

Those artists were too avant-garde for my parents' taste—and frankly out of their price range. By inclination or circumstance, their early collecting telegraphed patriotism, and veered toward the folksy and accessible (**CAT. 1**). In those early days, my father played a substantial role in their collaboration. The antiques and Americana they used to furnish their home reflected the almost preordained, white-shoe environment in which they lived. This gradual amalgamation of handmade objects and antiques mirrored my parents' lives and characters. They were predictable people with midwestern roots that appreciated the enduring form and function of everything from a rusted weathervane to fly-fishing rods and reels (accumulated from another shared endeavor). Reflecting on it now, I wonder if discovering art together served an unspoken and subconscious purpose during their forty-year marriage: it helped transcend their political, religious, and socioeconomic differences, providing an emotional bridge that preserved their independence.

A seminal, early influence on my mother was a DC socialite named Martha Bartlett, wife of Pulitzer Prize–winning columnist Charles L. Bartlett.[2] The couple's claim to fame was introducing John F. Kennedy to Jacqueline Bouvier—though it was Martha who had first made Bouvier's acquaintance. Raven-haired and covered in freckles, Martha was the epitome of preppy. The Bartletts lived nearby, and Martha decided to take my mother, a Washington neophyte, under her wing to help her navigate life "inside the Beltway." This education ranged from dinner party tips to decorating advice to social networking. I believe this association solidified my mother's interest in American antiques, which dovetailed with the burgeoning patriotism in the Robson household.

The 1960s and 1970s likewise coincided with my mother's on-the-job training as a hostess for the insiders with whom my parents began to fraternize. During these and later Washington

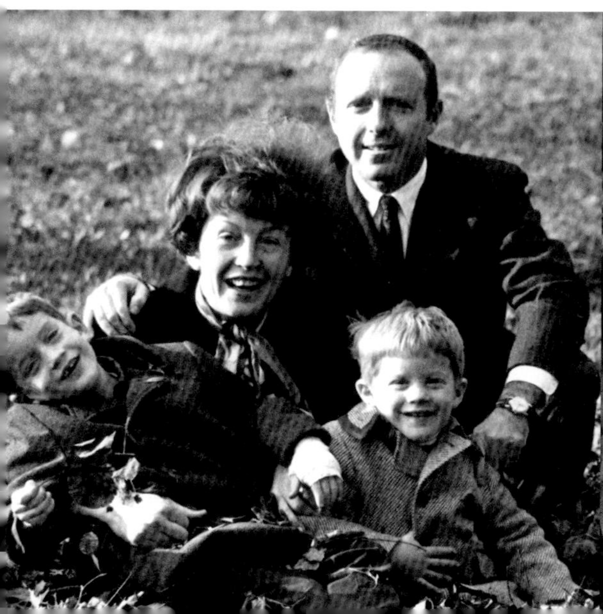

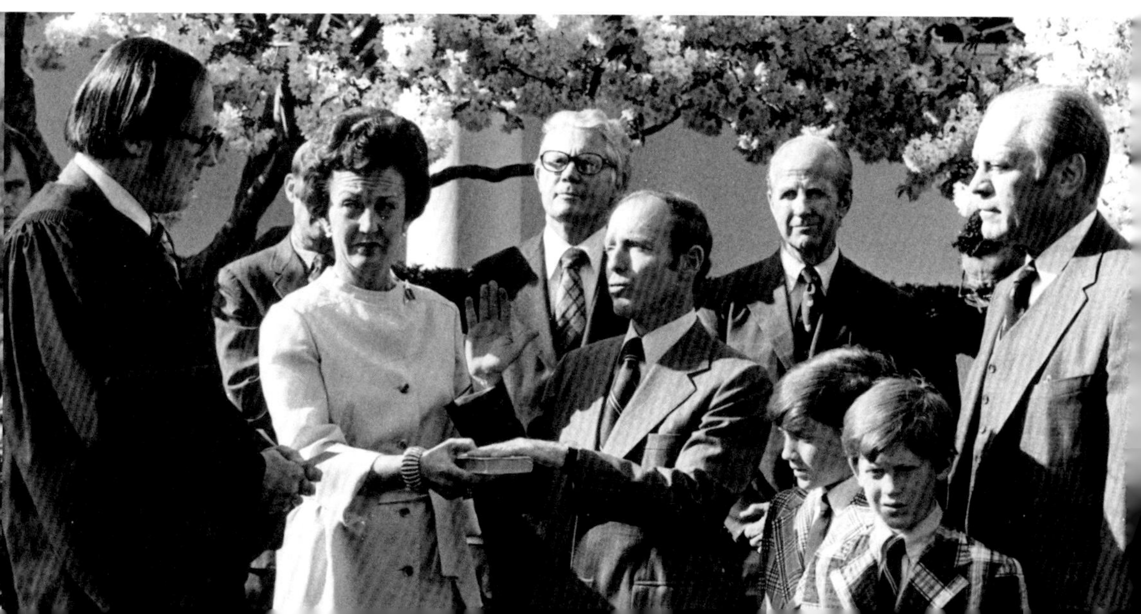

iterations, my mother threw elaborate, largely home-cooked dinner parties for top journalists and elected officials, vice presidents, Supreme Court justices, the head of the Federal Reserve, and many others.

In the holiday season, Margaret transformed our kitchen into a makeshift peanut brittle factory. She would order pounds of raw peanuts, large bags of sugar, and other ingredients, followed by a monthlong process from Thanksgiving to Christmas, during which my mother slathered the fragrant, sticky substance across the kitchen counters to cool. The result was a homemade treat that she mailed or delivered to friends and dignitaries around the world, including President Johnson. The whole process was ambitious, industrious, and disruptive, which presaged the same leanings that drove her collecting.

As she melded into the milieu of high society, Margaret never shed the small-town sensibility that grounded her character (Fig. 9). She developed her own kind of sophistication, one that would blend urbanity with commonsense pragmatism. Her well-regarded dinner parties were hands-on: she cracked and roasted the nuts, shopped for the delicacies, set the tables, and picked and arranged the flowers. A true midwesterner, she pulled off corn husks herself, as she had as a child. With increasing skill as the years went on, she could pull off one hell of a dinner party (Fig. 10).[3]

EARLY COLLECTING

My childhood memories of art collecting were of parent-only excursions to go "antiquing" in the mid-1970s, when we lived in Chicago. Antiquing was becoming more mainstream at this time; my parents took road trips to rural Illinois, Michigan, Wisconsin, and Indiana. Dressed in blue jeans and flannel shirts (or something equally comfortable and utilitarian), my parents would gleefully stake out small-town shops or roadside stands. The objects they returned with—

Fig. 9. Margaret Robson (right), early 1970s **Fig. 10.** Margaret Robson featured in "How to Throw a Party That Works," *Chicago Magazine*, December 1980 **Fig. 11.** The Robson home in Santa Fe, New Mexico, 2011, showing artworks, including Stephan W. Polaha's carved wooden eagle (**CAT. 4**) and Elijah Pierce's *Elephant* (**CAT. 42**), on the table in the foreground **Fig. 12.** Margaret with cast-iron eagle sculpture (**CATS. 2, 3**) in Chicago, 2013

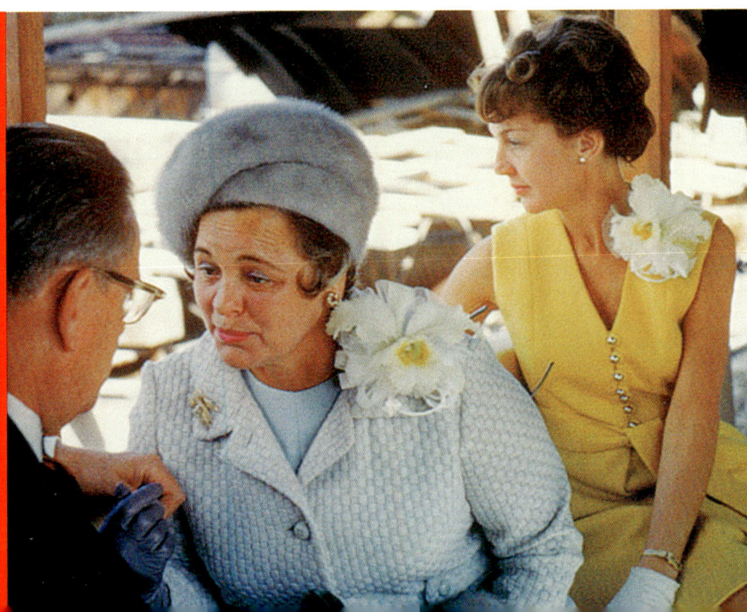

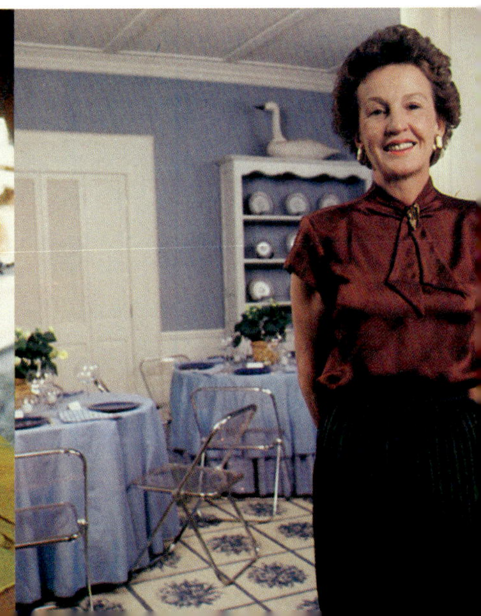

furniture, quilts, weathervanes—slowly populated the living room and common areas of our home, offsetting the staid chintz slipcovers and curtains with character and color.

These missions remained regular events during turns in Washington and elsewhere as well. Happenstance discoveries and an eclectic aesthetic, shaped in large part by those early forays into small-town America, persisted and came to define my mother's collection, from a pair of large cast-iron eagles from the White Eagle Oil Company to Stephan W. Polaha's carved wooden figures, to walking-stick snakes and more (Figs. 11, 12; **CATS. 2–4**).

Yet gradually, their collecting expressed something else, something multidimensional and primal. It reflected a more informed and complex understanding of the society in which they lived. It represented a comfort with their own identity as well as a subtle aversion to the parameters of custom and a willingness to embrace difference. They were a hard-to-categorize couple—on the one hand, extremely conventional, but in art, increasingly beyond definition.

It was in the late 1970s, with our lives back and forth between Chicago and Washington, when my parents became acquainted with Carl Hammer and his then wife, Trish.[4] Hammer was dabbling in antiques and teaching high school in the Chicago suburbs, having not yet committed to running a full-time gallery. "We were exchanging ideas and the folk movement was altering," recalls Hammer. "We were working from the antiques world and trying to put it into a contemporary art context."[5]

As their interests expanded beyond antiques and Americana, my parents became increasingly drawn to the stories of artists, as well as the expansive array of reasons they had made what they did. One of the first such artworks my parents acquired was by an artist who would enthrall them for years to come. It was around 1983 when they purchased a pencil drawing by Bill Traylor, which he had made in the late 1930s (**CAT. 5**). Traylor, who had been born enslaved in rural Alabama, took up drawing and painting in his late eighties, devising spare but compelling

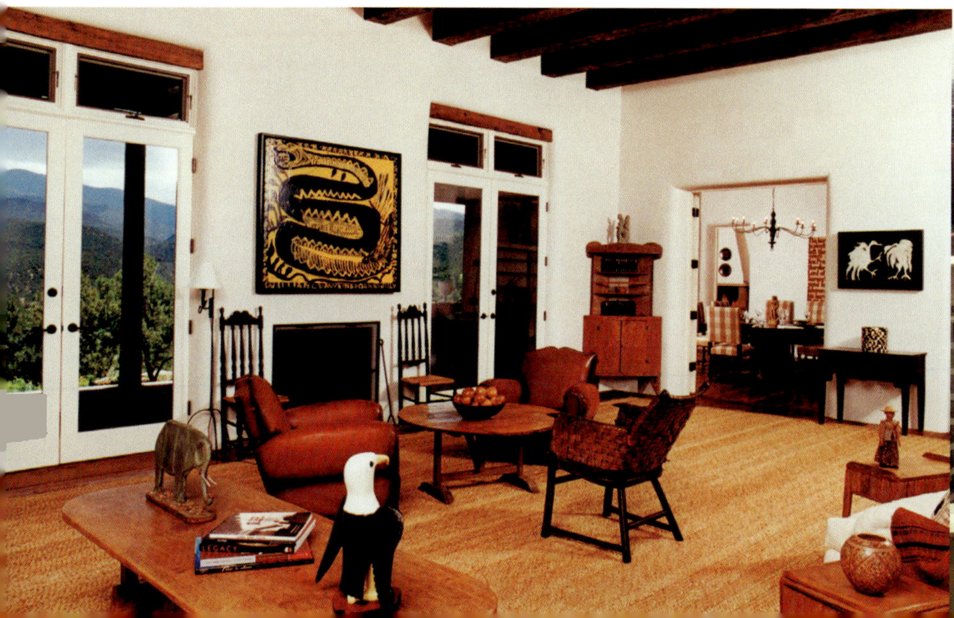

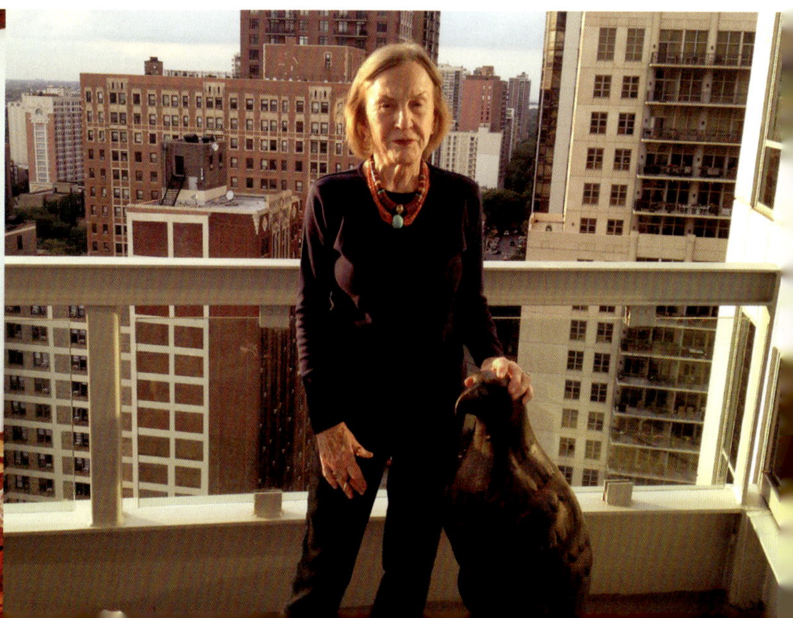

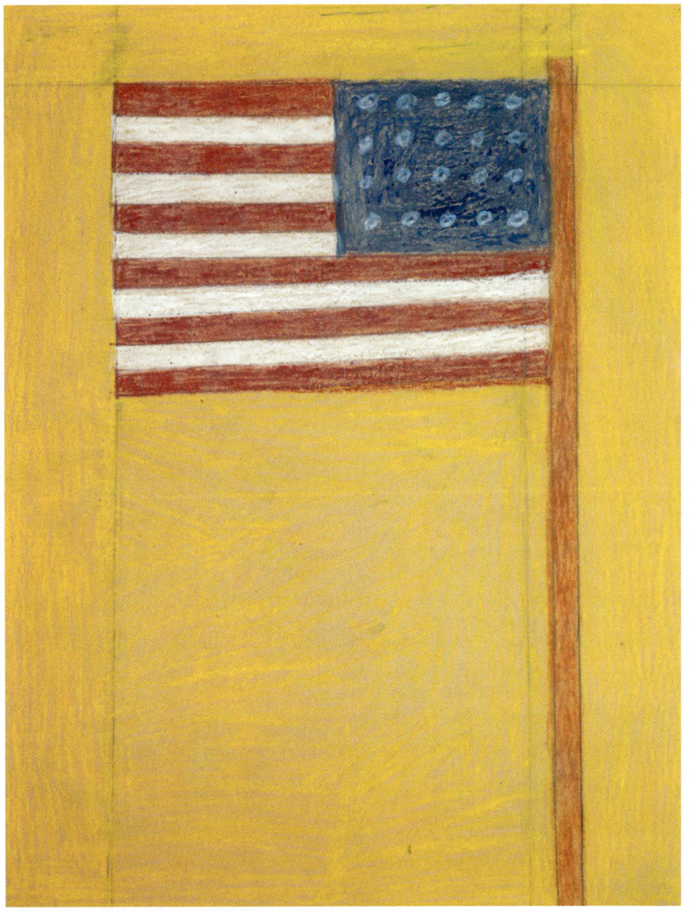

narratives to tell his own story. Traylor's intense, abstract configurations on discarded pieces of cardboard revealed both late-life industry and a unique vision that struck a powerful chord for my parents. Was it Traylor who awoke in them a critical understanding of that universal human impulse to transcend the limits of identity through creation?[6]

Gradually, their art collection became a shared means of expression, a way both to inject beauty and pleasure into daily life and to live with thought-provoking and expectation-thwarting objects and images. Across the country, notions about art and artists were expanding, and as curator Leslie Umberger details in this volume, museums and individual collectors were waking up to an untapped wellspring of creativity that extended well beyond the mainstream.[7] For collectors, passions were percolating, many fueled by the 1982 exhibition at the Corcoran Gallery of Art, *Black Folk Art*

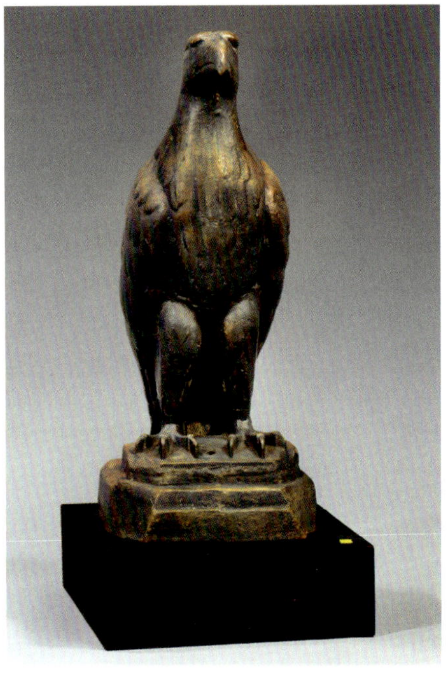

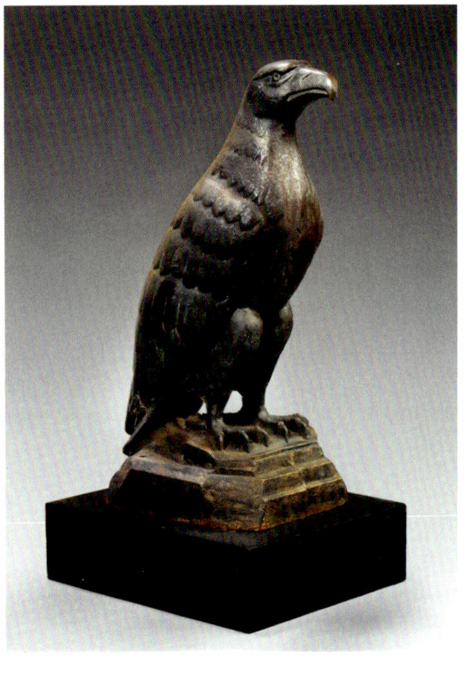

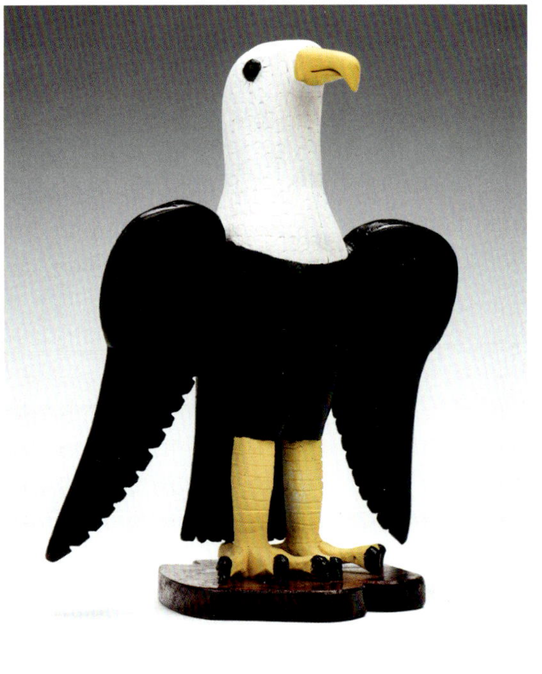

CAT. 1.
Eddie Arning
Untitled (American Flag)
ca. 1964

CAT. 2.
Unidentified artist
Untitled (Cast Iron Eagle from White Eagle Oil Company)
ca. 1920

CAT. 3.
Unidentified artist
Untitled (Cast Iron Eagle from White Eagle Oil Company)
ca. 1920

CAT. 4.
Stephan W. Polaha
Eagle
ca. 1975

CAT. 5.
Bill Traylor
Untitled (Mule, Dog, and Scene with Chicken)
July 1939

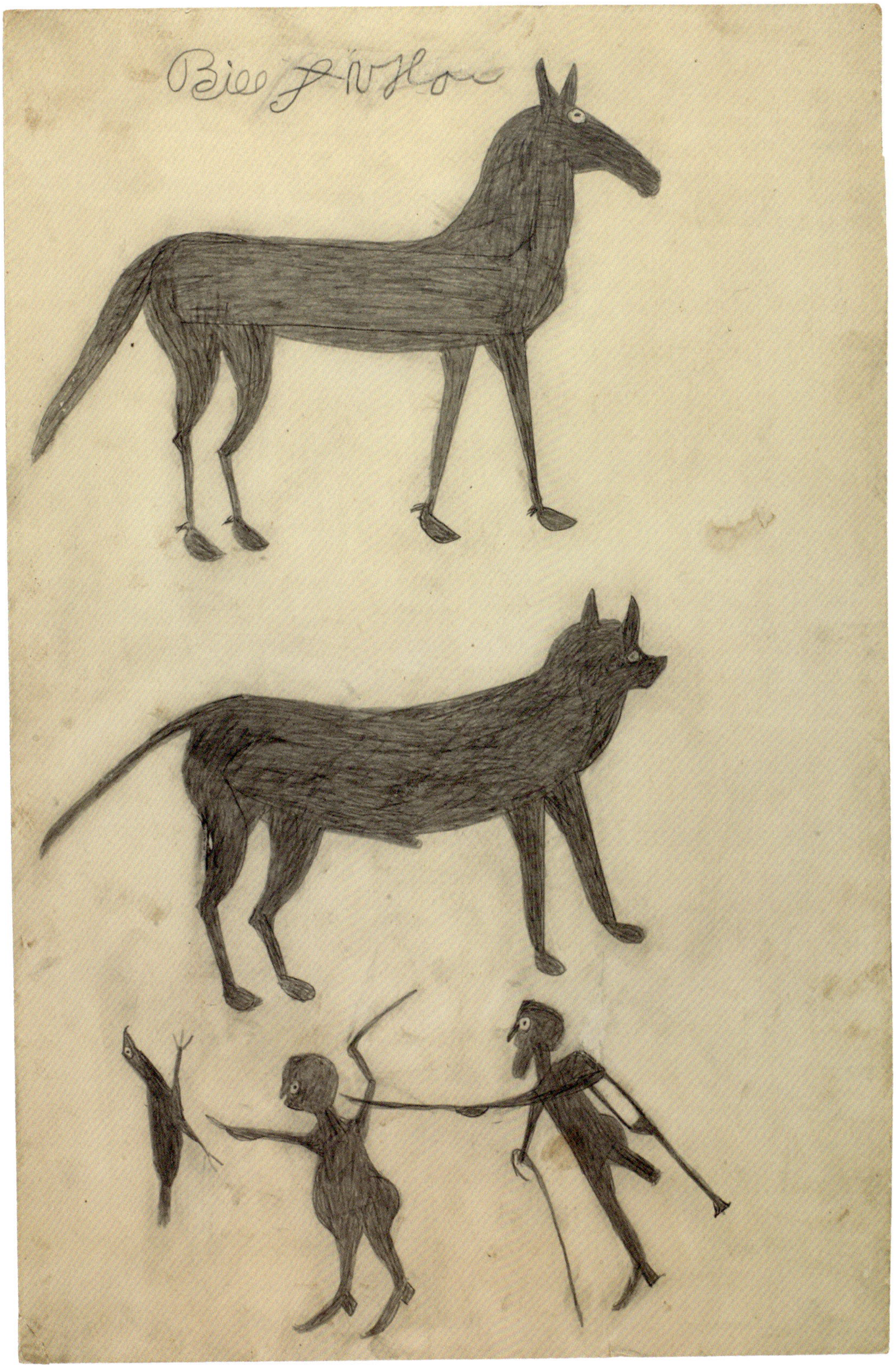

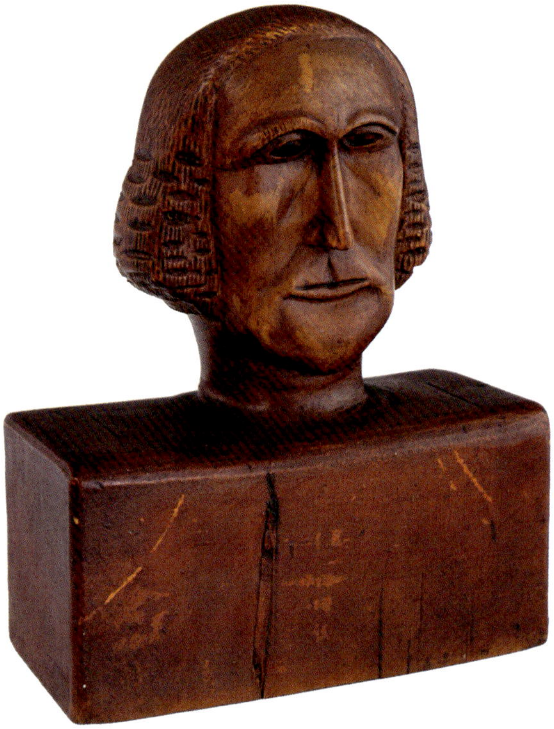

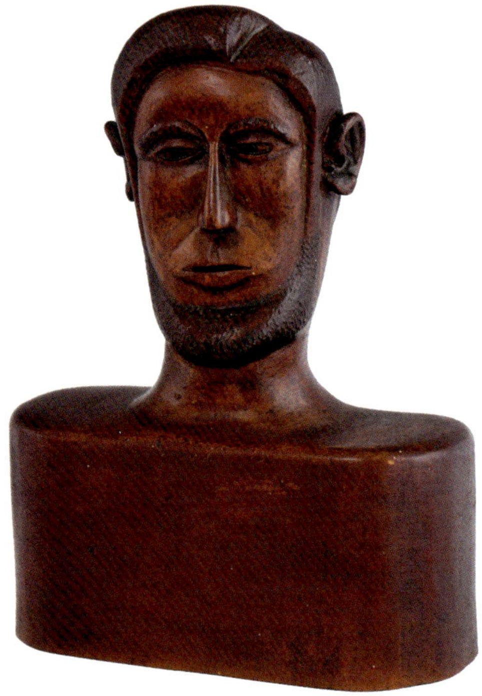

CAT. 6.
Ulysses Davis
George Washington
ca. 1940s

CAT. 7.
Ulysses Davis
Lincoln
1940

CAT. 8.
Ulysses Davis
Where Life Comes From
ca. 1950–90

in America, 1930–1980, which most certainly influenced my parents. By the time our family relocated to Atlanta in the late 1980s, my parents—increasingly my mother on her own—were connecting with various "pickers," such as Georgia-based Jimmy Allen.[8]

Allen turned Margaret on to the work of woodcarver Ulysses Davis. Becoming interested in Davis signaled another early inflection point at which my mother markedly pivoted from decorator to connoisseur—from gravitating toward tradition-based objects to those that, instead, expressed highly unique visions. An African American raised in rural Georgia, Davis, a barber by trade, carved exquisite objects. His creations embody the storytelling atmosphere inherent to the southern barbershop, ranging from quotidian to wild without ever owing anyone an explanation. An artist like Davis, whose subjects ranged from portrait busts to phallic totems and beasts of lore, was a perfect bridge (**CATS. 6–8**). If social norms had largely scripted much of my mother's life, the realm of collecting was improvisational theater, free-form and uncontained. "She loved the off-ness of it," says longtime friend and interior designer Berta Shapiro (Fig. 13).[9]

Subsequent moves from the South back to the mid-Atlantic and then to the West Coast amplified my mother's interest in the creativity she saw from region to region. She started to attend auctions and work regularly with galleries such as Phyllis Kind, Ricco/Maresca, and Cavin-Morris.[10] She collected works by European artists, including the Swiss painter, writer, and musician Adolf Wölfli and Italian artist Carlo Zinelli, both figures in art brut, whose stories and artworks were compelling in equal measure (**CATS. 9, 10**). But it was artists from her own country that drew her in a more meaningful way. Margaret's stalwart belief in liberal democracy and individuality served as a through line to her expanding collecting vision. "I think she really believed in the ideal of 'America' as an expansive and democratic place," says Shari Cavin, who has run Cavin-Morris Gallery in New York with her husband, Randall Morris, for more than three decades. Cavin recalls Margaret collecting works that reflected this Stars and Stripes inclination, notably by Jon Serl (see **CAT. 100**), but with her own take on what that meant:

> *Jon Serl was eccentric, and extremely individualistic, but for Margaret, this was part of a bigger idea—that unique and true selves were more important than adherence to norms or ideals. Serl said he started to paint because he was trying to capture a grittier American life before World War II. He felt that the texture of the country became homogenous after World War II; it was flattening out. His paintings were a way of honoring what American individuality meant, before advertising and the desire for possessions turned the country bland. He championed the underbelly of America. I think she picked up on that, the paradox of a postwar national identity that superficially promoted individuality but in reality, rarely embraced anyone that veered too far off the path of "normalcy."*[11]

While living in the Bay Area in the 1990s, Margaret learned about Creative Growth Art Center, the innovative studio for developmentally disabled artists.[12] She became an instant supporter and early collector of work by artists including Judith Scott, Donald Mitchell, and Kerry Damianakes.[13] Her instincts were bold. "Margaret was one

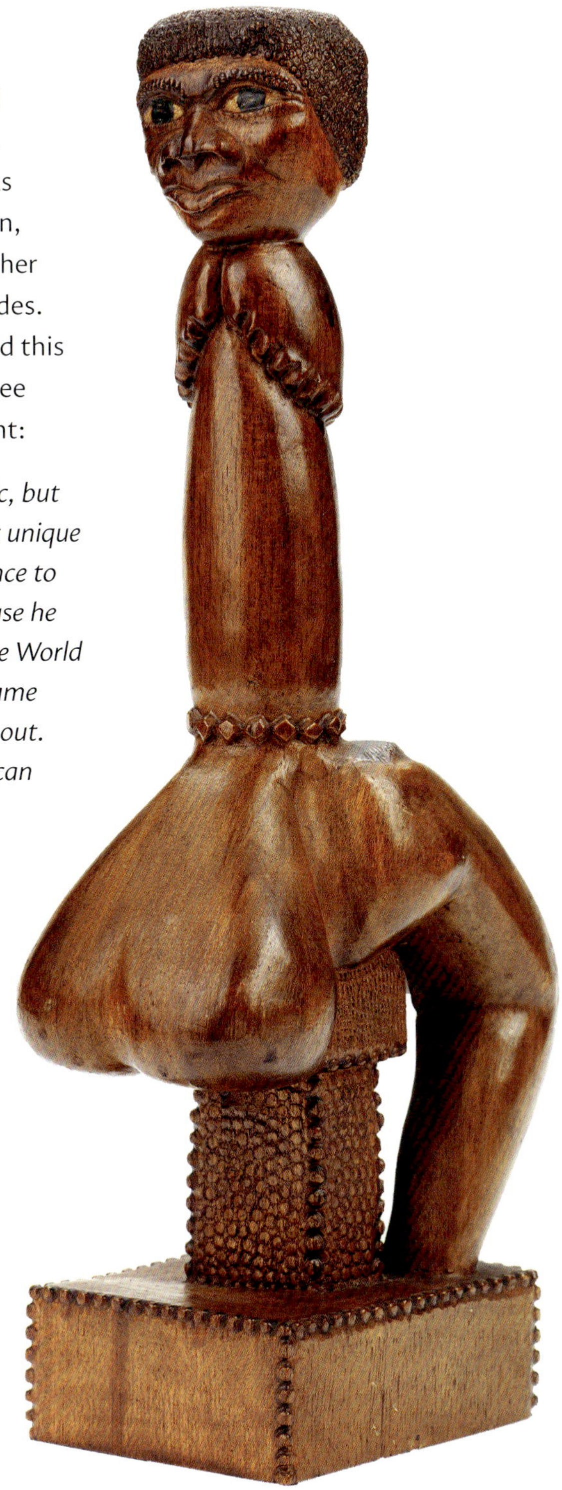

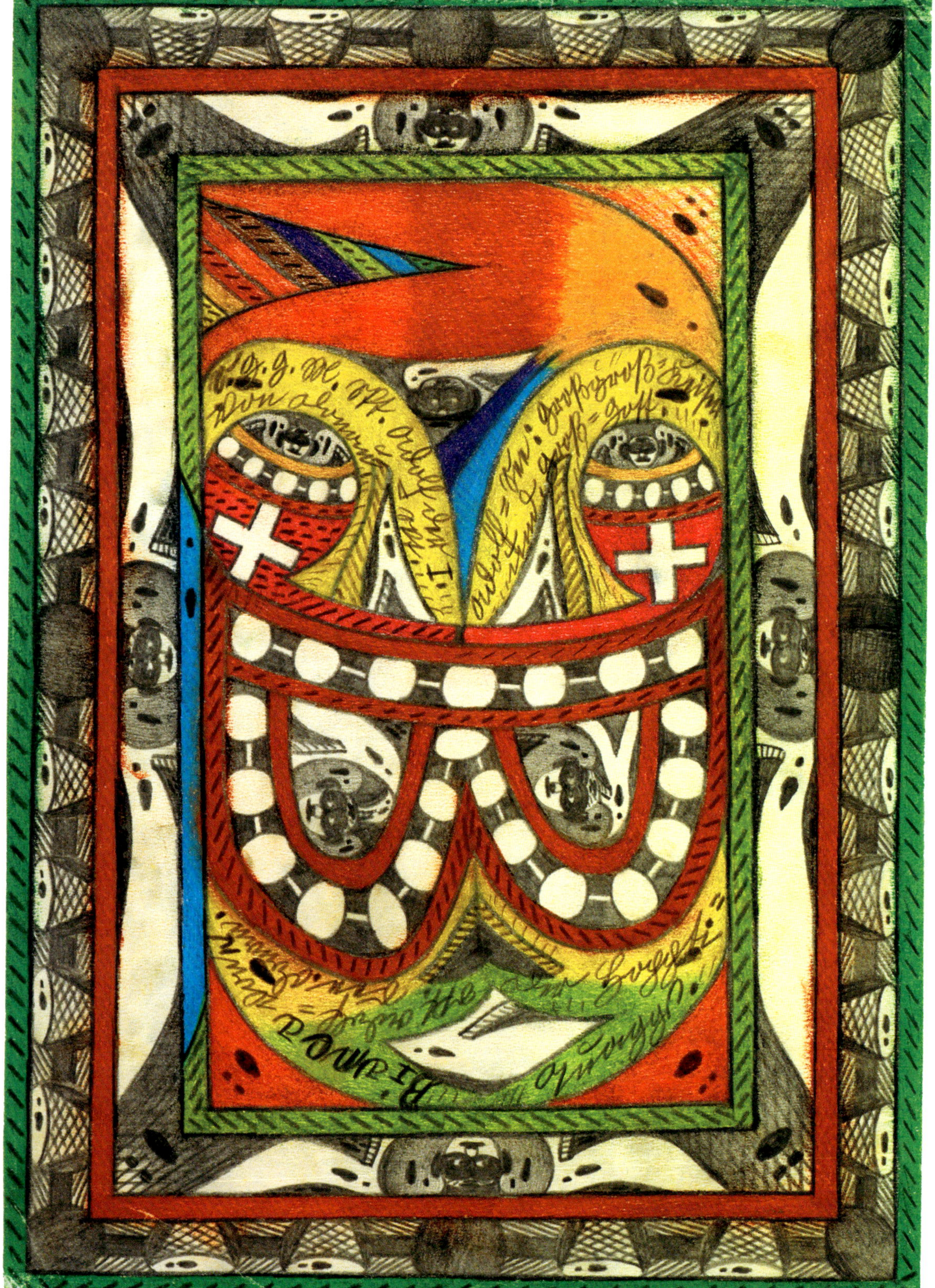

of the first with Judith Scott's work to say, 'I'm buying this,'" recalls Tom di Maria, the longtime face of Creative Growth who now serves as its director of external relations. "Judith was barely a blip on the map at that time. It's hard to remember how gutsy that was."[14]

Scott was afflicted by the genetic disorder Down syndrome; this, in addition to being deaf, severely limited her means for language or other modes of communication. The environment at Creative Growth allowed Scott to defy these constraints. She spent her days making three-dimensional pieces, layers of wrapped, multicolored fibers that both shrouded and teased objects trapped inside. Scott's mental isolation made her flowing abstractions all the more complex, confounding, and, to many, utterly dismissible. Her sculptures prompted profound questions about the meaning of art, the role of the maker's identity and intentions, and, ultimately, the human need to communicate by any means possible. My mother was instantly riveted by Scott and her creative drive—sensing, decades before many others did, the importance of this artist, who challenged every possible convention for contemporary art.

Di Maria remembers that Margaret also championed his early efforts to position Creative Growth at art fairs—a tack not always met with open arms by established galleries.[15] "She understood that this moment [the late 1990s] was a fundamental shift in how outsider artists could be seen and collected," he says. "She had a contemporary outlook. . . . [Margaret] wasn't afraid to dive in with artists, either; I remember an interaction with her and Dan Miller where he was spelling out words and she was just fascinated. She wanted to get in there and get her hands dirty."[16] Di Maria's impression of Margaret was that of a woman who wasn't captivated by "white cube" gallery types and felt confident taking risks without second-guessing herself.[17] "It was a fun time, an adventure, and she didn't need someone to tell her what was interesting," he recalls. "She liked to champion the underdog. Maybe she saw herself as an underdog in relation to the art world."[18]

FULL STEAM AHEAD

It was during this fin de siècle period in San Francisco that my mother demonstrated how much her perspective had broadened, seeing beauty even in the increasingly prevalent and poignant handmade signs of the homeless; it further contextualized her appreciation of the work of self-taught artists and spoke to her growing awareness of creativity as a powerful and ever-present force. These objects also resonated with her curiosity in fringe and ephemera—in this case the most utilitarian of artistic endeavors from people spanning the fiercely independent to those in urgent need of help: one moment to catch the eye, solicit aid, or trigger an ironic smile of a passerby.

Artistic expression entered Margaret's life in unexpected ways, especially when it could illuminate voices that might otherwise go unheard. Social consciousness and detours from expectation became

CAT. 9.
Adolf Wölfli
Blatt Aus Heft #15
1917

CAT. 10.
Carlo Zinelli
Untitled
(recto/verso)
September 26, 1968

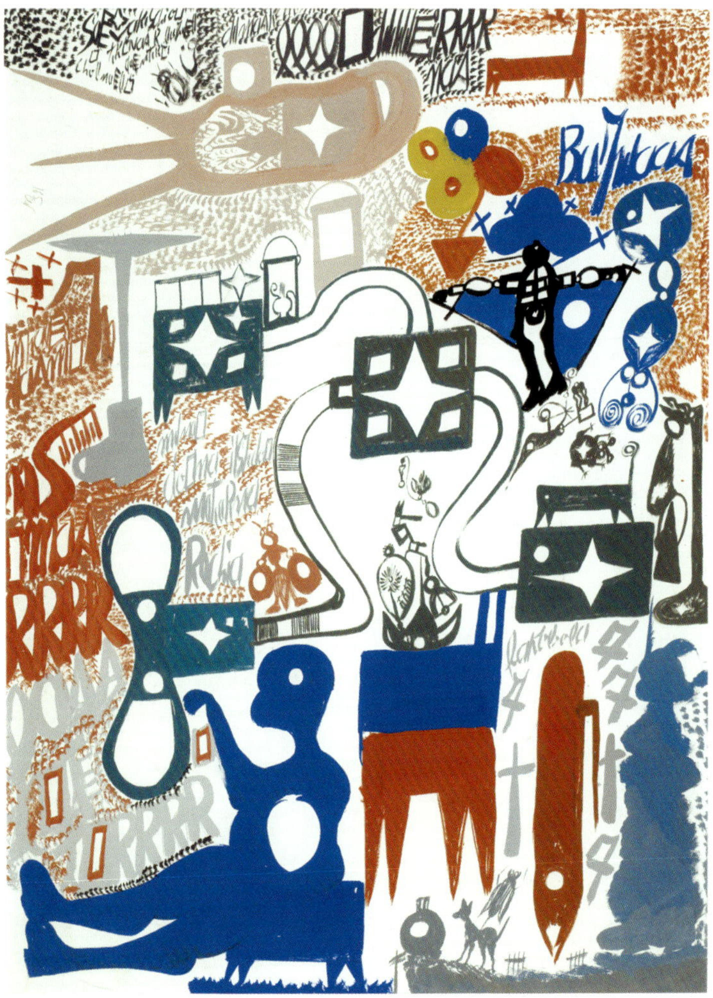

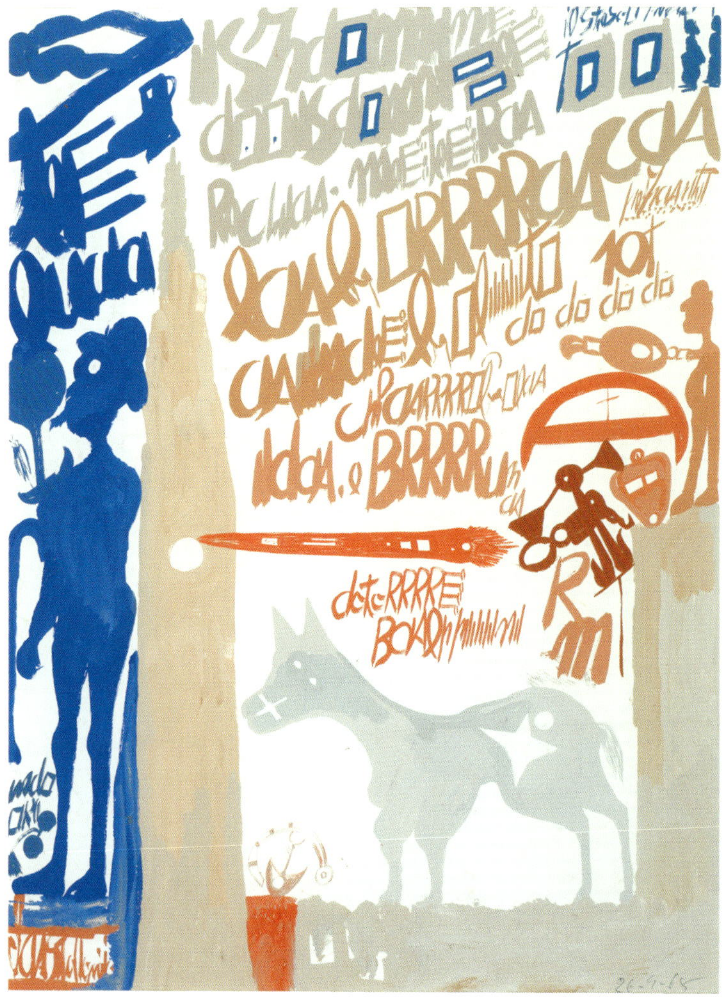

another connective arc of her collection. Long-standing friend and art lover Richard Sinkoff saw her character as one that ultimately dovetailed perfectly with her collecting endeavor: "She had a great deal of empathy for people who stood outside society."[19]

Yet three decades into collecting, my mother and father didn't think of themselves as art insiders, even as their collection grew. "We are *not* collectors," my father is quoted as saying in a 1999 book describing how people live with their art. "To be a collector sounds pretentious.... These paintings are part of our life....I think that it is the humor and earthiness in them that I like more than anything."[20]

When my father died in 2002, art became my mother's raison d'être. It focused her energies. It crystallized her own personal journey. She still engaged with her established social sphere, but like many of the artists she may have identified with, she resisted pigeonholing forces. She had already left her small-town upbringing for the big city. She married a Jew, despite a habituated sense of Catholicism. Her children challenged mainstream trajectories and her own expectations—from musical tastes to sexual orientation. To her credit, she attended Grateful Dead concerts and accompanied me to gay pride parades. She responded to her life and familial experiences—and grew. Outwardly, my mother developed strong but varied political affiliations at different times in her life, but she could be hard to pinpoint. More than anything, she was independent. Cavin, the gallerist, remembers this spirit in the way Margaret responded to the "extraordinary individuality" of artists, "that spirit that says, 'I must make this, I am here, this is who I am.'"[21]

To Margaret's disappointment, she had no grandchildren, but compensated with a tapestry of relationships with younger adults and godchildren. Art became her progeny. At some point after my father's death, I became aware that my mother didn't really *collect* art—she cohabitated with it. Art was her paramour, her intimate. It provided an ongoing and vibrant conversation. "She often talked about how to live with the art," says Brooke Davis Anderson, who worked closely with Margaret during her curatorial tenure at the American Folk Art Museum in New York.[22]

To wit: My mother called a carved figure by Calvin and Ruby Black by name—*Gladys*—and seemed to have a running dialogue with her (see **CATS. 111, 112**). A mummy-like sculpture by Judith Scott hung somewhat ominously in her bedroom—a circadian reminder of the secret value of objets trouvés (**CAT. 11**). She placed a weighty, outdoor-scale, limestone birdbath by William Edmondson in the center of her Chicago apartment, where she bestowed upon it two utilitarian functions: to conceal a pipe opening in the floor, and as a delicate staging ground for her unopened mail. An eight-foot-tall self-portrait of Howard Finster towered in the vestibule, like a friendly sentry (see **CATS. 31, 86**). She delighted in stuffing chili peppers into a carved wagon with mules (made by an unknown artist) as the centerpiece for her "chili pepper" dinner parties

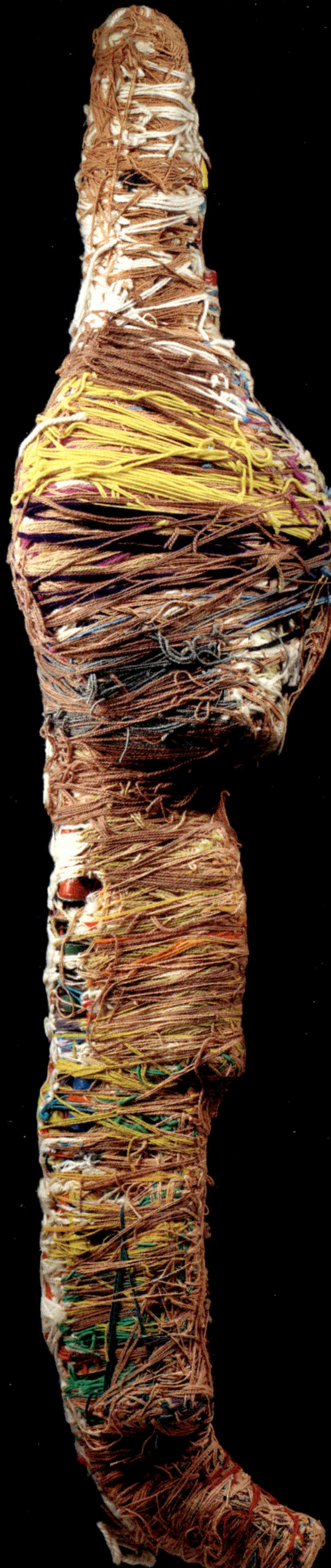

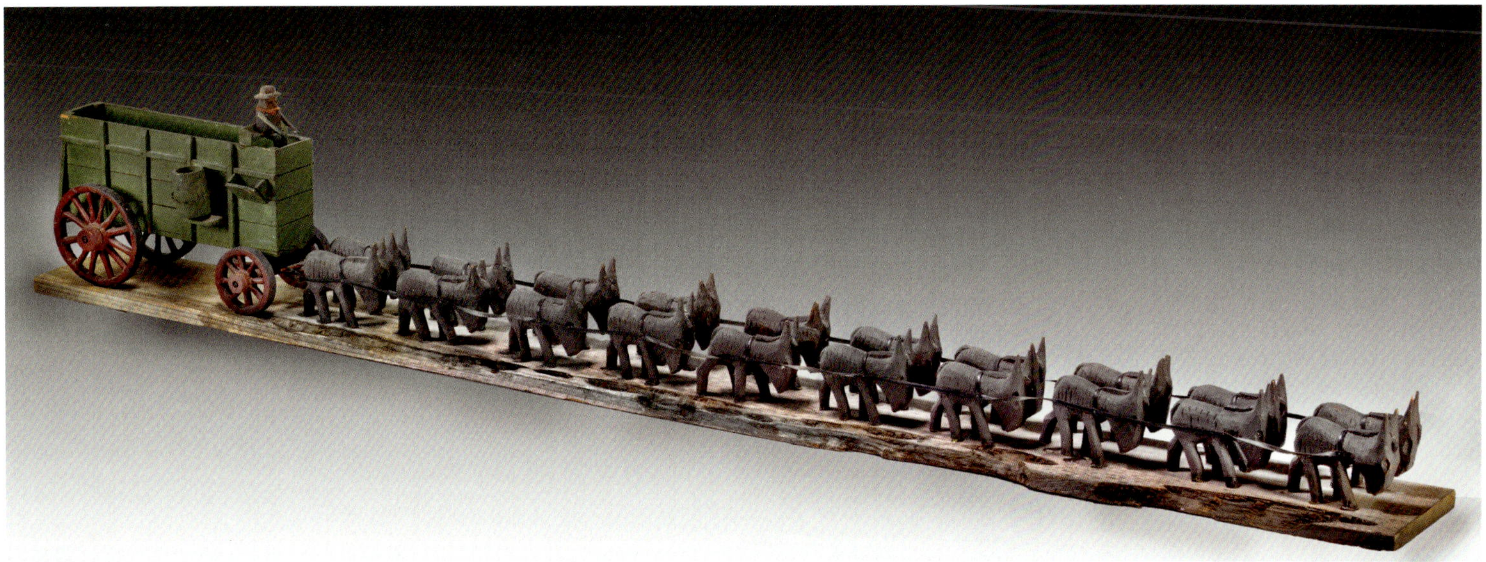

in Santa Fe (**CAT. 12**). There was a joy and gentle irreverence in the way she employed the artworks that surrounded her. They were friends and family.

Ultimately my mother extended her interest in art and artists beyond collecting. She was a staunch advocate for the loosely defined genre encompassing folk, self-taught, and differently abled artists. She supported galleries, sat on museum boards, and was known for attending any and all lectures and symposia.[23] In the last years of her life, my mother supported the self-taught ecosystem with gifts to museums, including the Art Institute of Chicago, the John Michael Kohler Arts Center in Wisconsin, and Atlanta's High Museum of Art.[24] "She was relentless as a patron," remembers Anderson, who further notes that while collectors of self-taught art were not uncommon by the 1990s, it was rare for a patron to also realize the critical need for scholarship in this area—and act on it. "She had a way of community-building that almost no one in the outsider art world was doing."[25]

By the time my mother died, she had created in her home small tributes to artists who had transformed their own humble, personal surroundings into special places: a cluster of items from Howard Finster's Paradise Garden; a bold mixed-media construction by Wisconsin artist Simon Sparrow that explodes like a glitter bomb in one's eye; and the whimsical but irresistible pile of cast-iron railroad spikes—each one hand-painted with dots and tiny faces—from the Michigan art environment of Albert "Kid" Mertz (see **CATS. 58, 87–91, 113**). Margaret placed equal value on works by little-known artists and those who became, in the late twentieth and twenty-first centuries, "blue-chip" sellers, such as Chicago's Henry Darger, and Martín Ramírez, who died alone in a state hospital in California. Religion and Americana remained themes that drew her, from Eddie Arning's drawing *Untitled (American Flag)* to David Butler's *Untitled (Mary with Baby Jesus)* (see **CATS. 1, 37**). Anyone opening a closet door to discover her trove would have been mesmerized by its eclectic depth.

CAT. 11.
Judith Scott
Untitled
1994

CAT. 12.
Unidentified artist
Untitled (Twenty Mule Team)
20th century

FAMILY AFFAIR

In 2014, at age eighty-two, my mother died rather unexpectedly. She hadn't formulated a specific plan for her now more than hundred-object collection.[26] Like a newborn dropped at my doorstep, it was something I didn't think I was prepared to nurture. Over the years, my mother had, of course, baited my interest by declaring (in that provocatively ironic way of hers), "Someday you're going to have to deal with all this." I wondered: Was it a puzzle she'd bequeathed to help me piece together her life? She had offered me little direction, either verbally or conceptually, about how she wanted it carried forward. Perhaps she expected it to speak for itself, to channel something she couldn't fully articulate, a Judith Scott sculpture writ large.

What could I draw upon? Beyond my mother's influence, I trace personal art edification back to my undergraduate days at Yale—notably, Vincent J. Scully Jr.'s dazzling lectures that canvased prehistoric times to the Renaissance, and Robert Farris Thompson's flailing "guerilla scholarship" orations on New York mambo ("Master T," as we knew him), which included guest appearances from the likes of Keith Haring, best known for his graffiti-inspired drawings, which adorned New York's subway stations in the 1980s.[27] Otherwise, I formed my artistic education mostly by osmosis, absorbing a rudimentary foundation for collecting simply by exposure. Everything my mother surrounded our family with impacted me over time, from Chicago artist Joseph E. Yoakum's luminous landscape drawings to the compelling root figures Bessie Harvey made in her adopted home state of Tennessee. I attended museum exhibitions, both with and without my mother. Before and after her death, I waded into the water and began to acquire artworks, mostly by artists from the Bay Area, where I live. My own association with Creative Growth, during and after the time our family lived in California, provided connective tissue to artists

Fig. 13. Margaret Robson (left) and Berta Shapiro, mid-1980s
Fig. 14. Laura Craig McNellis, 1992; photo by Libba Gillum
Fig. 15. Douglas with his mother, Margaret, Santa Fe, New Mexico, 2005; photo by Scott Saraceno
Fig. 16. Douglas in his San Francisco home with Judith Scott's *Untitled (Medicine Bottle)* (**CAT. 96**), 2021; photo by Scott Saraceno

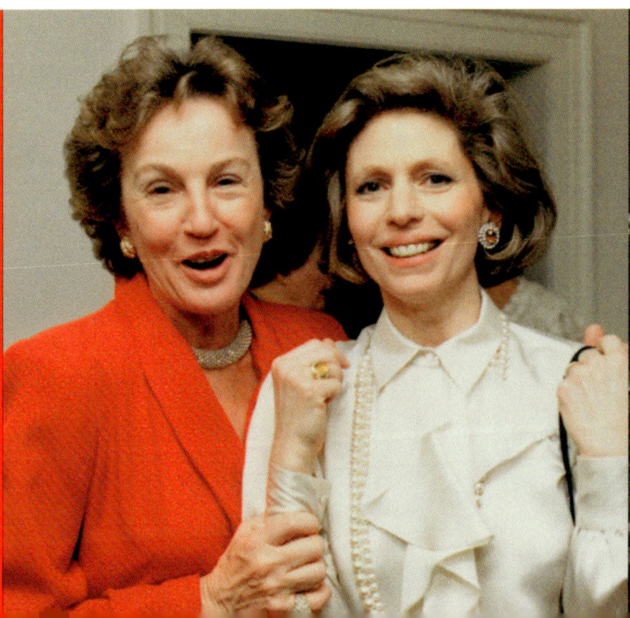

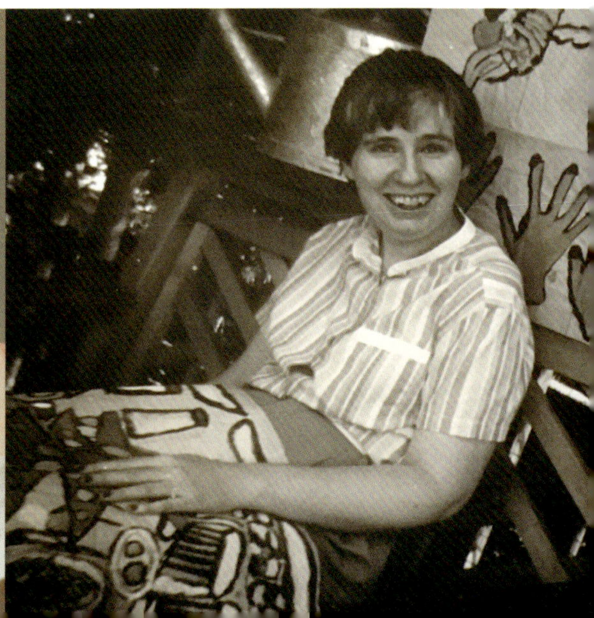

my mother had exposed me to early on, particularly Judith Scott and Dan Miller, whose intense paper drawings became my first acquisitions from the Oakland-based studio-cum-gallery.

The learning curve accelerated exponentially after my mother died. My profession as a sportswriter hadn't positioned me particularly well for art connoisseurship or caring for and crafting a collection. Thus began a more intense process of delving into the realm of self-taught art and artists, to better understand and manage the array my mother had cared so much about. I read. I reached out. Almost without warning, I realized that I was both responsible for and energized by carrying my mother's torch forward.

Practically speaking, I didn't have the space or the wherewithal to make use of or manage the ongoing stewardship of so many artworks, and I knew that the legacy of the artists who had made them should factor into the fate of these objects. I decided to place most of the collection in the care of the Smithsonian American Art Museum (SAAM) in Washington, DC, and to promise to the Museum a number of works that were important to me personally, that I still wanted to live with. This made sense, and more importantly, it felt right. My family had connections to Washington; I had spent some of my childhood there, and I knew the Smithsonian's reputation as a world-class art institution. But SAAM was also a pioneer—the first major art institution to embrace self-taught makers, to regularly include their work in the Museum's galleries and position it as an important element of American art, not as the work of "lesser" makers. It seemed the ideal place for buttressing scholarship, the ongoing care the artworks would need, and a far-reaching public embrace of art beyond the mainstream.[28]

In the ensuing years, I suppose I honed my own eye. I tapped into knowledgeable resources—curators such as Brooke Davis Anderson and Leslie Umberger; gallerists including Shari Cavin, Carl Hammer, and Frank Maresca; visionary advocates like Tom di Maria; as well as other art

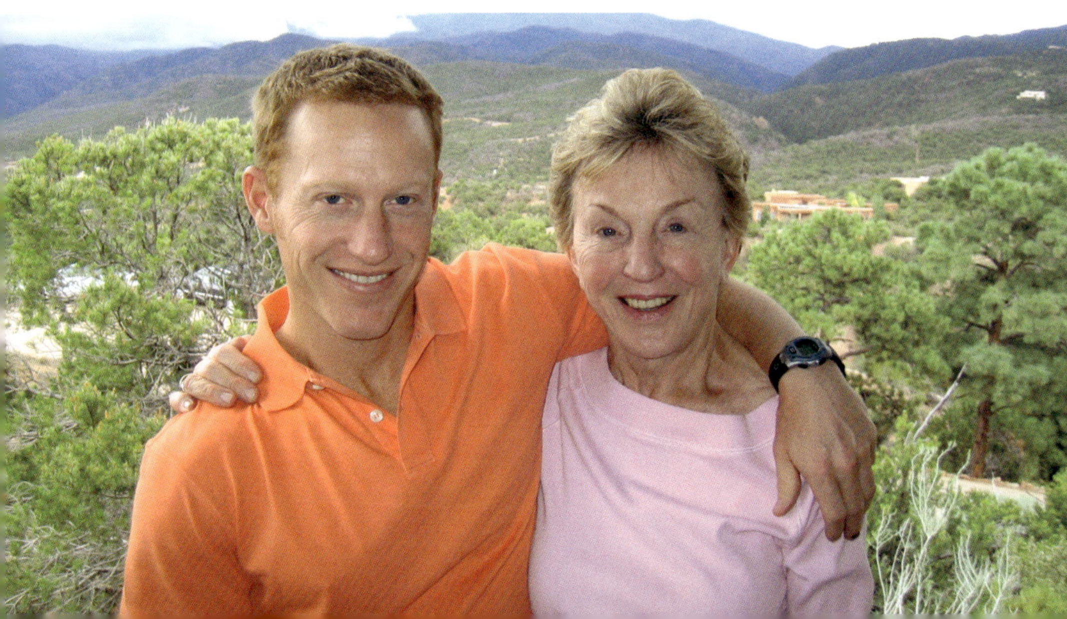

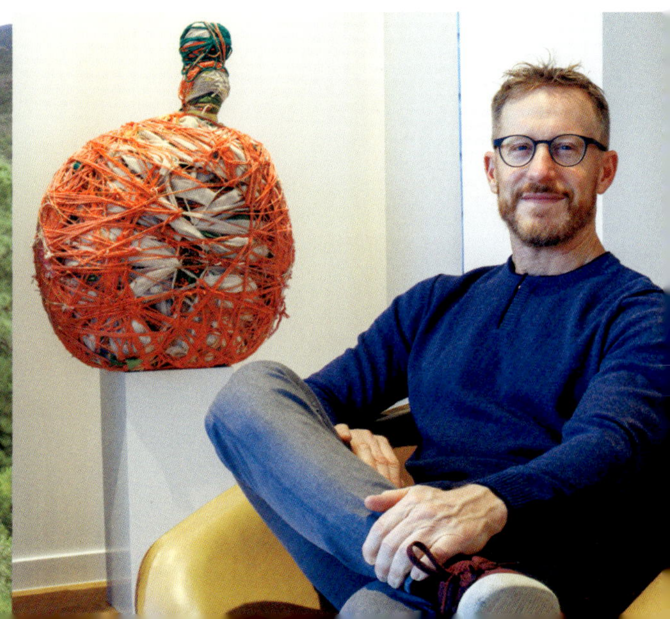

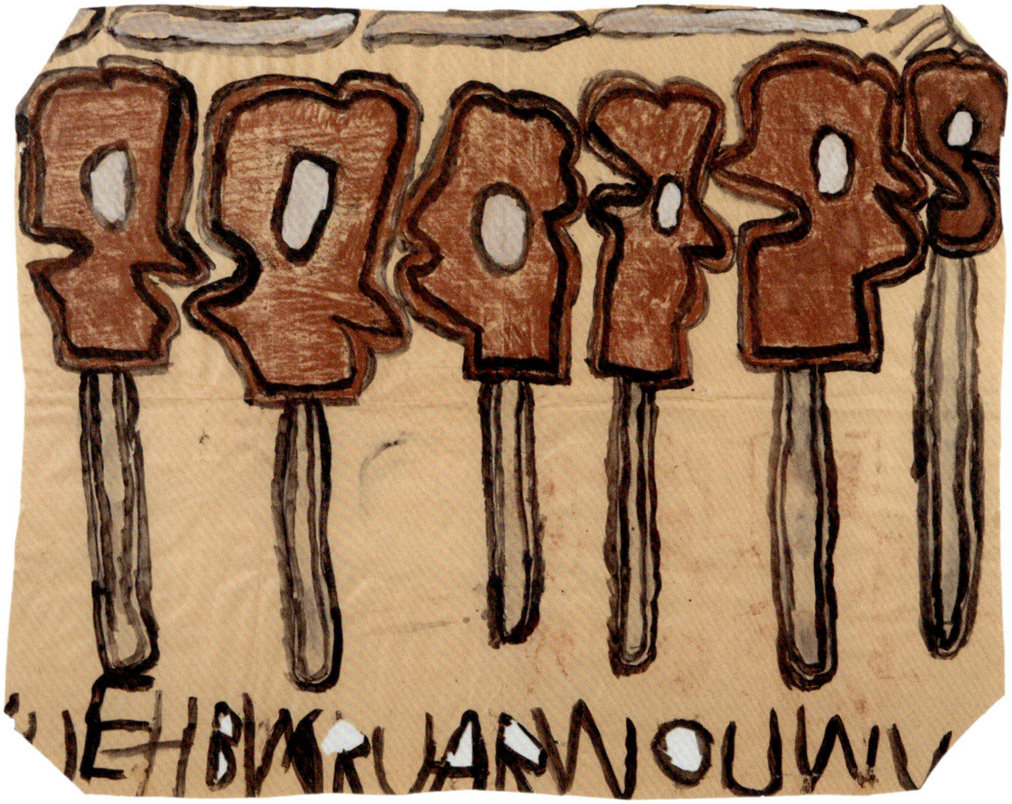

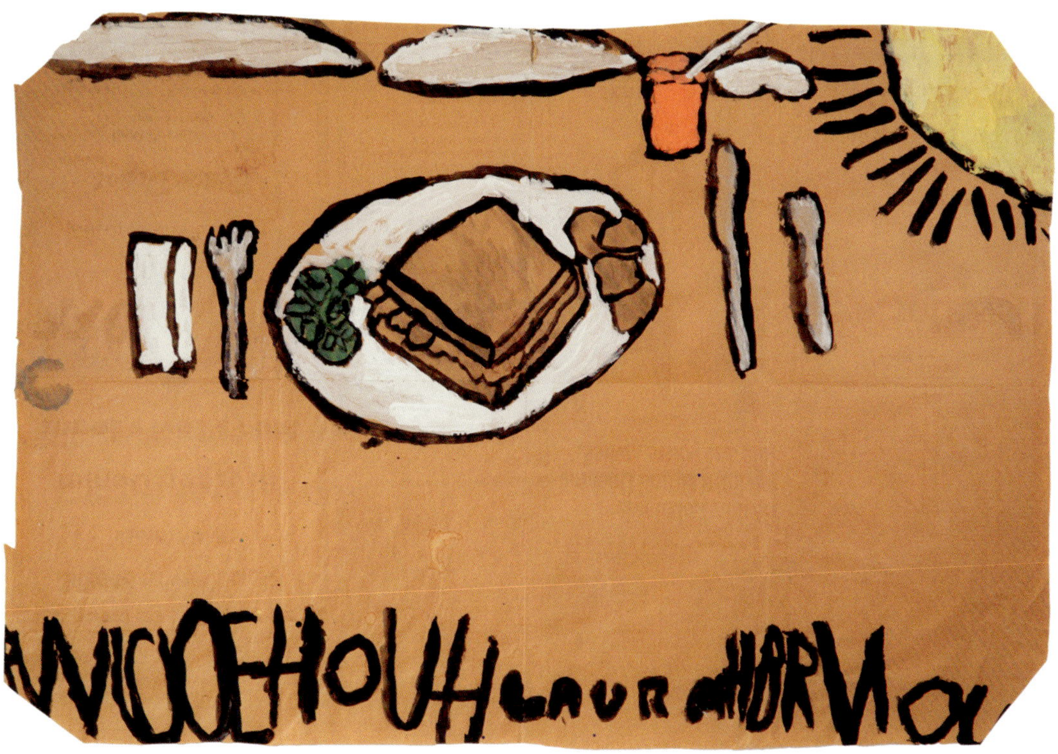

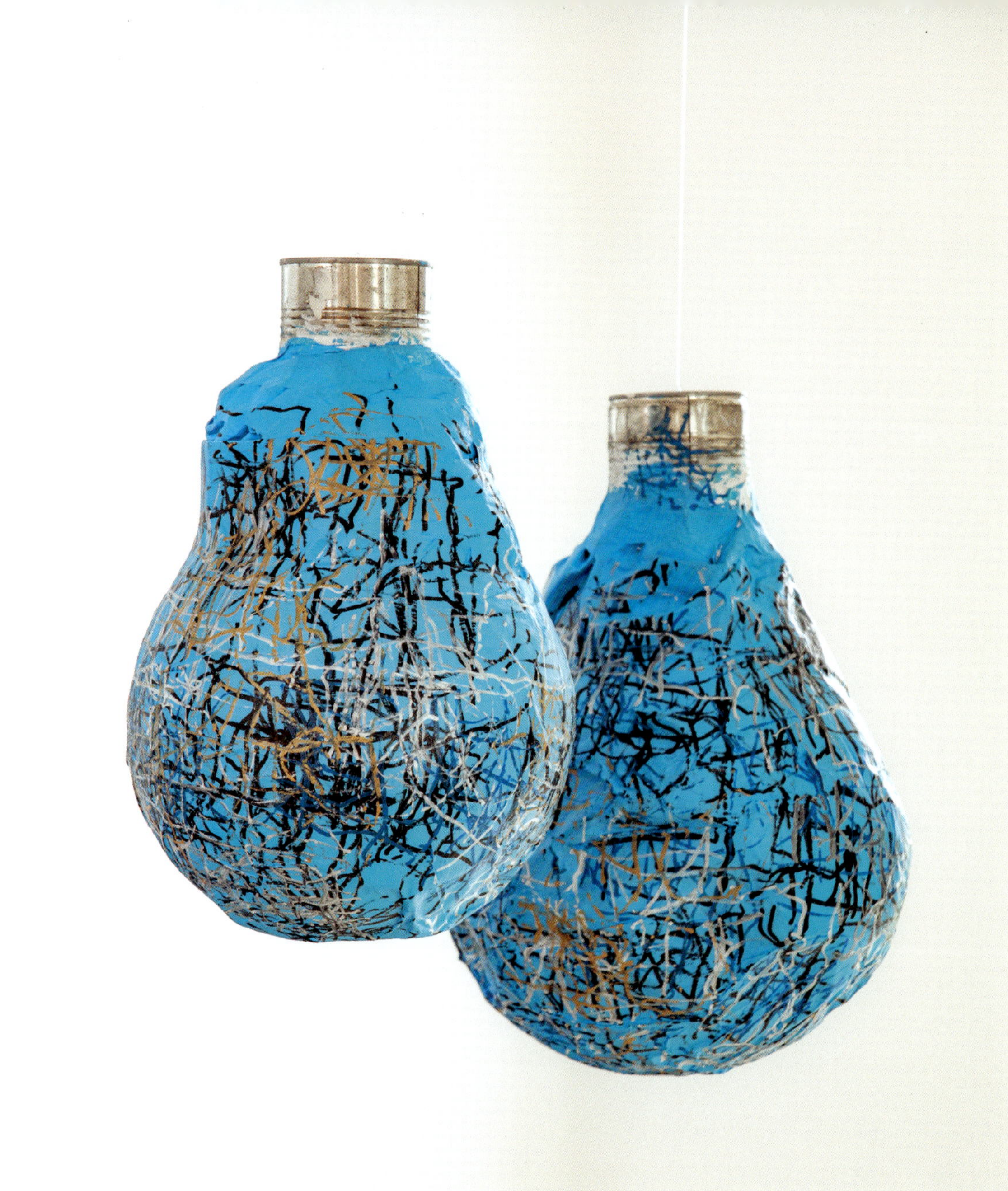

CAT. 13.
Laura Craig McNellis
Untitled (Fudgesicles)
ca. 1982

CAT. 14.
Laura Craig McNellis
Untitled (White Plate with Sandwich)
ca. 1982

CAT. 15.
Dan Miller
Untitled (DM 847)
2016

CAT. 16.
Dan Miller
Untitled (DM 848)
2016

collectors and passionate supporters of self-taught artists I've met along the way. The ongoing input of consultant Caitlin O'Meara, who worked with my mother near the end of her life, has proven invaluable.[29] I continued to collect artists my mother had cared about, such as Judith Scott and Dan Miller, but also discovered artists and works that spoke to me and that she adored, including Tennessee native Laura Craig McNellis (born 1957), who is on the autism spectrum and developed a painting practice when she was very young (Fig. 14; **CATS. 13, 14**).

If family lineage drew me to art beyond the mainstream, my own engagement is personal and entirely voluntary. Whether by the daring eccentricity of William Hawkins, the urgency of Dan Miller (**CATS. 15, 16**), Nellie Mae Rowe's driving need to define herself and live creatively, or the intellect and precision of Achilles G. Rizzoli, I am moved in many facets. I respect the craftsmanship and clever reimagining of discarded materials. I value the singularity of vision that can arise from blurred circumstances. I love the diversity that encompasses a tapestry of emotions and ideas—from skillful, goofy, and ingenious to joyous, reflective, and defiant. In a word, unabashed.

I need to feel some visceral connection to a piece. It must petition my senses, and not only visually. If known, the artist's life—the lived experience that shaped that object or image into being—inestimably enhances the experience of encountering that work, as I believe it did for my mother. Grasping the human component of the story adds a critical layer of historical, emotional, and intentional context. When I connect with a piece of art, it usually evolves over time, changing as I do, providing new pleasures or perspectives.

Few in my personal sphere are familiar with the artists that interested my mother. This has created opportunities to educate and share, although, increasingly, it's not uncommon for friends and guests at my home to recognize an artwork by better-known artists like Henry Darger or Bill Traylor. These artists have been encroaching on the mainstream contemporary art scene, particularly during the last two decades, as amply evidenced in media coverage, major museum exhibitions and acquisitions, and blue-chip gallery interest.

As with my mother, it's impossible to predict how this artistic journey will unfold, what objects I will continue to hold dear. I have no precise destination in mind. I hope to complement what she achieved in her collecting and fold my own sensibility into the mix, a generational dovetailing of sorts (Figs. 15, 16). My focus will likely center on artists from the United States, not necessarily those born in this country, but more essentially, those whose lives and works powerfully embody a unique American experience. I realize, as I believe my mother did, that so much of the American story remains untold—and that what happened in this country at earlier moments can help us make sense of where we are today. The compelling visual language that Margaret collected, and that I now collect and care for, remains a whisper but is growing in amplitude. Making these artists heard is increasingly important in political winds that can shift in a moment. In times when difference and artistic expression stand on less firm ground, the artists in the Robson Family Collection are beacons of resistance and potential. Often operating on the margins of convention—economically, socially, neuro-diversely—they defy the constraints that hem so many in. I value these distinct perspectives, these unique intonations. I hope this journey leads me to a greater appreciation of the artists I know, and to a discovery of new voices I have yet to hear.

NOTES

1. Joanne Knoch, "Women in Business," *Chicago Daily Tribune*, October 25, 1958. In a similar article, the *Chicago Sun-Times* noted Margaret was the only woman to complete the "College Men's Training Program" at the Continental Illinois National Bank & Trust Co., where she worked; Bette Scanlon, "How One Woman Carves Bank Career," *Chicago Sun-Times*, February 7, 1959.

2. Richard Goldstein, "Charles L. Bartlett, Journalist and a Kennedy Matchmaker, Dies at 95," *New York Times*, February 20, 2017, https://www.nytimes.com/2017/02/19/us/charles-l-bartlett-dead-journalist-kennedy.html. Bartlett won the Pulitzer Prize in 1956 while at the *Chattanooga Times*. As with many women married to important men in that era, less is known of his wife, Martha, who is cited in the article as first "befriending" Jacqueline Bouvier before the couple introduced her to JFK in Washington's clubby circles.

3. Jane Salzfass Freiman, "A Strategy for Entertaining: With Organized Planning and Informal Style, Chicago's Margaret and John Robson Produce a Convivial Dinner for 12 Friends," *Cuisine*, May 1982, 38–42, 72, 74, 76, 78.

4. My family first moved from Chicago to Washington, DC, in 1966, when my father went to work for the Johnson administration and eventually took the post of undersecretary at the Transportation Department. We returned to Chicago in 1970, where my father continued to practice law; moved back to Washington in 1975, where he became chairman of the Civil Aeronautics Board; returned to Chicago in 1977, where my father was COO at the pharmaceutical firm G. D. Searle & Co.; relocated to Atlanta in 1987, where my father became dean of the Goizueta Business School at Emory University; returned to Washington in 1990, where my father became deputy secretary of the Treasury; moved to San Francisco in 1993, where my father joined the boutique investment banking firm Robertson Stephens; and in 2001, returned to Washington, where my father became chairman of the Export-Import Bank of the United States. After his death in 2002, my mother lived in Washington and then moved to their second home in Santa Fe around 2006. In 2012 she returned to Chicago.

5. Carl Hammer, interview with the author, August 30, 2018. Carl and Trish Hammer opened Hammer & Hammer Folk Art Gallery in Chicago in 1979. The business became Carl Hammer Gallery around 1984; it is still in operation under that name today.

6. Traylor's use of discarded, often soiled pieces of paper and cardboard might have aided my mother in seeing the comprehensiveness of an artist's personal journey as an inherent part of the artwork. Many years later, Margaret undertook a collection-within-a-collection of signs and depictions made by homeless people on whatever scraps of paperboard they could find. Although these signs are dramatically different than Traylor's autobiographical imagery, a palpable connection exists between these disenfranchised makers: circumstances impelled them to create. Traylor recorded the brutal truth of life for Blacks in segregated Alabama; others gave voice to another searing reality: the basic human need for food and shelter. For both, the deceptive simplicity of their creations conveys a deeper, lived complexity.

7. In her essay in this volume, Leslie Umberger discusses the history of American self-taught art as a growing phenomenon in the larger art world.

8. Jimmy Allen was based in Atlanta and called a "folk-art scout extraordinaire" by the *New York Times* in 1995. For more information on Allen, see Lynda Roscoe Hartigan, "From the Sahara of the Bozart to the Shoe That Rode the Howling Tornado: Collecting Folk Art in the South," in *Let It Shine: Self-Taught Art from the T. Marshall Hahn Collection* (Atlanta: High Museum of Art, 2001), 58; and Patricia Leigh Brown, "42,000 Miles a Year on the Antiques Track," *New York Times*, November 9, 1995.

   While workaholism had always permeated my father's multifaceted career (see note 4, above), his transition to academia at Emory, in 1987, represented a significant leap. My mother continued to branch out on her own in this period, serving, remarkably, on the Georgia State Boxing Commission. A 1987 article on her appointment describes how my father was too busy to serve, so my mother stepped up: "He was approached to go on the boxing commission, and his commitments are tremendous at this point, and I asked him, if he didn't have time, would they consider me?" Margaret Robson, quoted in Duane Riner, "Newcomer Appointed to State Boxing Board," *Atlanta Constitution*, March 29, 1987.

9. Berta Shapiro, interview with the author, August 23, 2018.

10. Phyllis Kind (1933–2018) opened Phyllis Kind Gallery in Chicago in 1967, specializing in old-master prints before finding her niche representing Chicago artists, trained and untrained. In 1975 Kind opened a second branch in New York's SoHo district; in 1998 she closed the Chicago branch. The New York branch moved in 2006 to Chelsea and remained open until Kind retired in 2009. Ricco-Johnson Gallery, created by Roger Ricco and Elizabeth Johnson, began in SoHo in 1979 and became Ricco/Maresca Gallery when Ricco formed a new partnership with Frank Maresca in 1985. It has moved over the years from Tribeca, back to SoHo, and finally to Chelsea in 1997. Roger Ricco retired in 2017 and the gallery is run today by Frank Maresca. Cavin-Morris Gallery has been run by the married team of Shari Cavin and Randall Morris since 1985, having worked privately for several years before opening their first gallery space in Tribeca. The gallery moved to SoHo in 1992 and to Chelsea in 2006, where it remains today.

11. Shari Cavin, interview with author, January 14, 2019, and emails with author, April 22, 2021.

12. Creative Growth was established in Oakland, California, by Elias Katz and Florence Ludins-Katz in 1974, as a creative work space and commercial gallery outlet for adults with physical and developmental disabilities. The Katzes' mission was both therapeutic and creative, and also public: the art was meant to be offered for sale. In 1978 the studio moved to a storefront with an adjacent gallery in Oakland after receiving a grant from the National Endowment for the Arts—the first of its kind for people with disabilities. Four years later, Creative Growth relocated to a twelve-thousand-square-foot former automobile repair shop in downtown Oakland, where its studio, gallery, and offices have been since 1982. The Robson family lived in San Francisco from 1993 to 2001 and Margaret encountered Creative Growth around 1997–98. See also Nathaniel Rich, "A Training Ground for Untrained Artists," *New York Times Magazine*, December 16, 2015, https://www.nytimes.com/2015/12/20/magazine/a-training-ground-for-untrained-artists.html.

13. Artists Donald Mitchell and Kerry Damianakes are not featured in this exhibition or catalogue, *We Are Made of Stories*.

14. Tom di Maria, interview with the author, September 5, 2018. Di Maria served as director at Creative Growth from 2000 to 2018; he currently serves as director of external relations.

15. For more on the entry of Creative Growth into the commercial market for self-taught artists, and the sociopolitical implications of di Maria's work, see Leslie Umberger's essay in this volume, pp. 189–90.

16. Di Maria, interview.

17. The "white cube" gallery aesthetic, with its white walls and spare, boxy interior museum spaces, grew out of the rise of abstraction in modern art in the early twentieth century. In later decades, the white-cube paradigm came under criticism, notably by Brian O'Doherty in the 1970s. See Brian O'Doherty, *Inside the White Cube: The Ideology of Gallery Space* (1976; repr., Santa Monica, CA: Lapis Press, 1986).

18. Di Maria, interview.

19. Richard Sinkoff, interview with the author, July 30, 2018.

20. Estelle Ellis, Caroline Seebohm, and Christopher Simon Sykes, *At Home with Art: How Art Lovers Live with and Care for Their Treasures* (New York: Clarkson Potter, 1999), 159.

21. Cavin, interview.

22. Brooke Davis Anderson, interview with the author, November 11, 2018. Anderson was founding director and curator of the Contemporary Center at New York's American Folk Art Museum from 1999 to 2010. She currently serves as the inaugural executive director of the VIA Art Fund in Boston.

23. Margaret participated in many forms of public service, primarily in the fields of health, art, and historic preservation. She was a member of the board of directors of the Northwestern Memorial Foundation in Chicago and a trustee of Northwestern Memorial Hospital (1979–84). From 1987 to 1990, she served on the Georgia State Boxing Commission. She was a member of the board of directors of the American Folk Art Museum in New York (1998–2007), the Santa Fe Art Institute (1995–2002), and the College of Saint Benedict (1996–97), Saint Joseph, Minnesota. She was a board member of the President's Advisory Council on Historic Preservation (1992–97) and on the Names Project (AIDS Quilt) board of directors (1993–96). From 2002 to 2005, she served on the Defense Advisory Committee on Women in the Services (DACOWITS), as well as the Vice President's Residence Foundation (2001–9). She also served on the board of the Foundation for Self-Taught Artists, Philadelphia (2006–9), and was a member of the President's Committee on the Arts and Humanities (2002–9). She served as a trustee for the American Folklife Center, Library of Congress, from 2010 to 2014.

24. Leslie Umberger, curator of folk and self-taught art at the Smithsonian American Art Museum, first met and worked with Margaret Robson in her capacity as senior curator of exhibitions and collections at the John Michael Kohler Arts Center, Sheboygan, Wisconsin (1998–2012).

25. Anderson, interview. In 2000 the American Folk Art Museum, New York, acquired a large group of Henry Darger paintings and all his writing from Kiyoko Lerner, the widow of Darger-discoverer Nathan Lerner. In 2001 the museum formed the Henry Darger Study Center at its former home on West Fifty-Third Street. As part of these efforts, my mother funded a Darger Study Center Fellowship (2007–9).

26. In the last years of her life, my mother culled her collection, as a natural evolution of her aesthetic sensibility and because she wanted to downsize her living space. It was important to her to donate to a wide variety of institutions; placing the right piece with the right home mattered. She donated works by Felipe Archuleta, David Butler, Ken Grimes, William Hawkins, Lonnie Holley, Clementine Hunter, Nellie Mae Rowe, Charlie Willeto, and Albert Zahn to museums across the country, including the Art Institute of Chicago; the High Museum of Art in Atlanta, Georgia; New Jersey's Newark Museum of Art; the John Michael Kohler Arts Center in Sheboygan, and the Milwaukee Art Museum, both in Wisconsin; the Mingei International Museum in San Diego; and the Wheelwright Museum of the American Indian in Santa Fe. She sold select artworks via galleries, including works by William Hawkins and Henry Darger.

27. Vincent J. Scully Jr. (1920–2017) was Yale's Sterling Professor of the History of Art and Architecture; Robert Farris Thompson (1932–2021) was the Colonel John Trumbull Professor of the History of Art and Professor of African American Studies, also at Yale University in New Haven, Connecticut.

28. In 2016, I donated ninety-three works of art — thereafter known as the Margaret Z. Robson Collection — to the Smithsonian American Art Museum, and made a promise of many additional works. This project is named in honor of both my mother's collection at SAAM and the works from my own collection that are promised to the Museum: The Robson Family Colletion. In 2018, on the occasion of a major exhibition at SAAM, *Between Worlds: The Art of Bill Traylor* (September 28, 2018–April 7, 2019), curated by Leslie Umberger and featuring five artworks by Traylor from the Margaret Z. Robson Collection and one from my collection, I formally endowed a symposium series, also in my mother's name, to be held at SAAM on an ongoing basis and for which the Traylor symposium was the inaugural event.

29. Caitlin O'Meara started working with Margaret in 2012 as her personal assistant after meeting her through Carl Hammer Gallery. She is an independent art consultant and the owner of O'M Consulting, LLC.

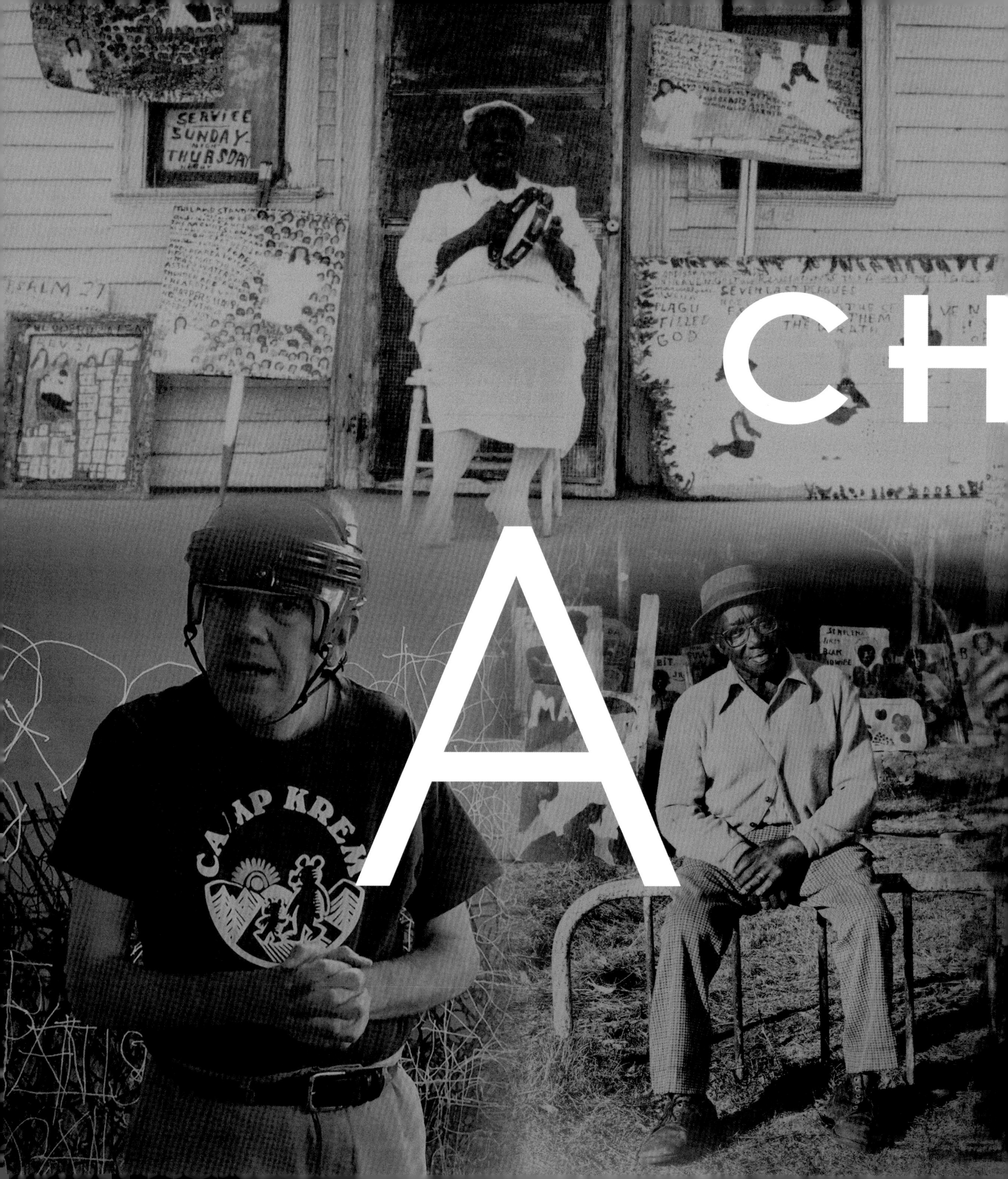
SERVICE
SUNDAY
THURSDAY
PSALM 27
SEVEN LAST PLAGUES
CH
A

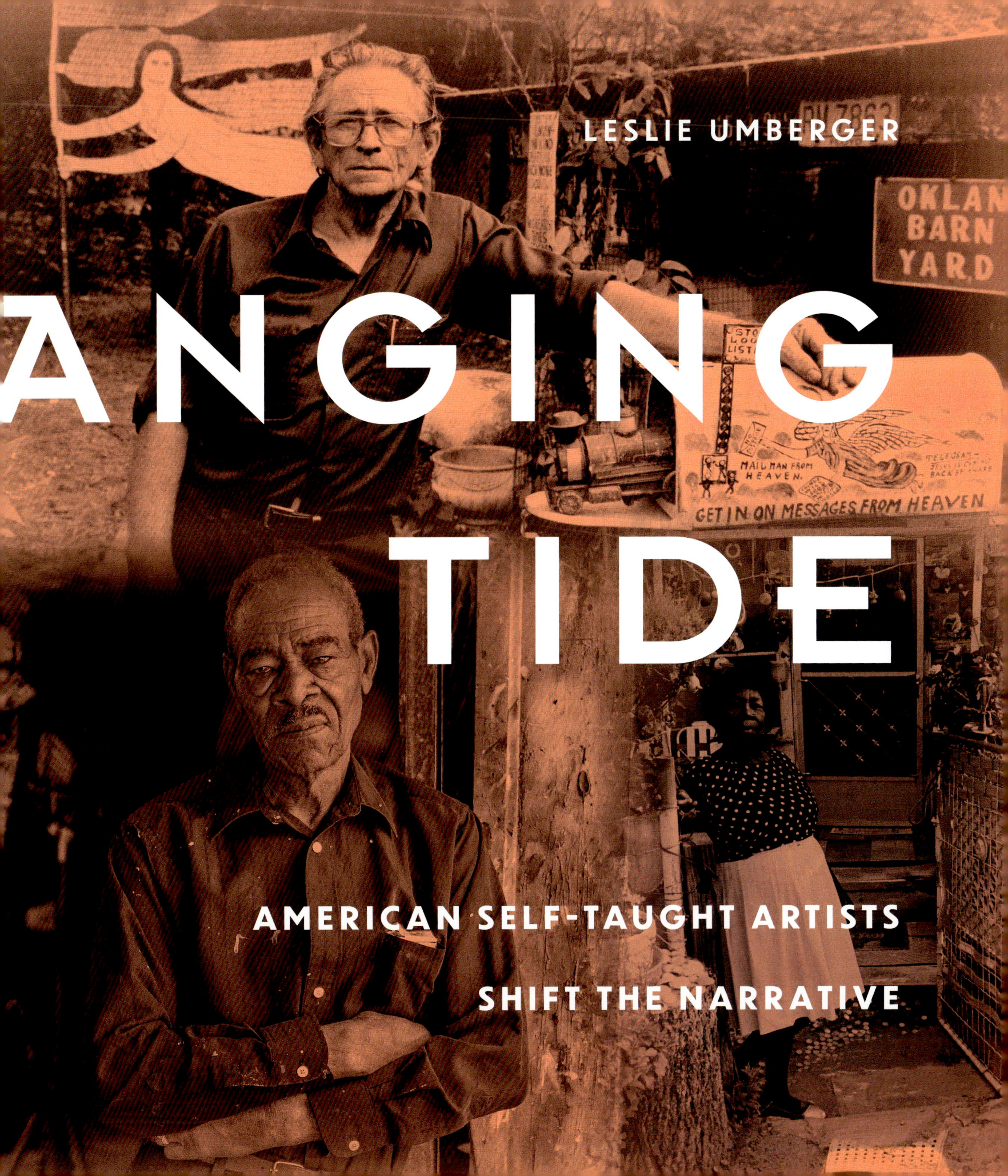

LESLIE UMBERGER

ANGING TIDE

AMERICAN SELF-TAUGHT ARTISTS SHIFT THE NARRATIVE

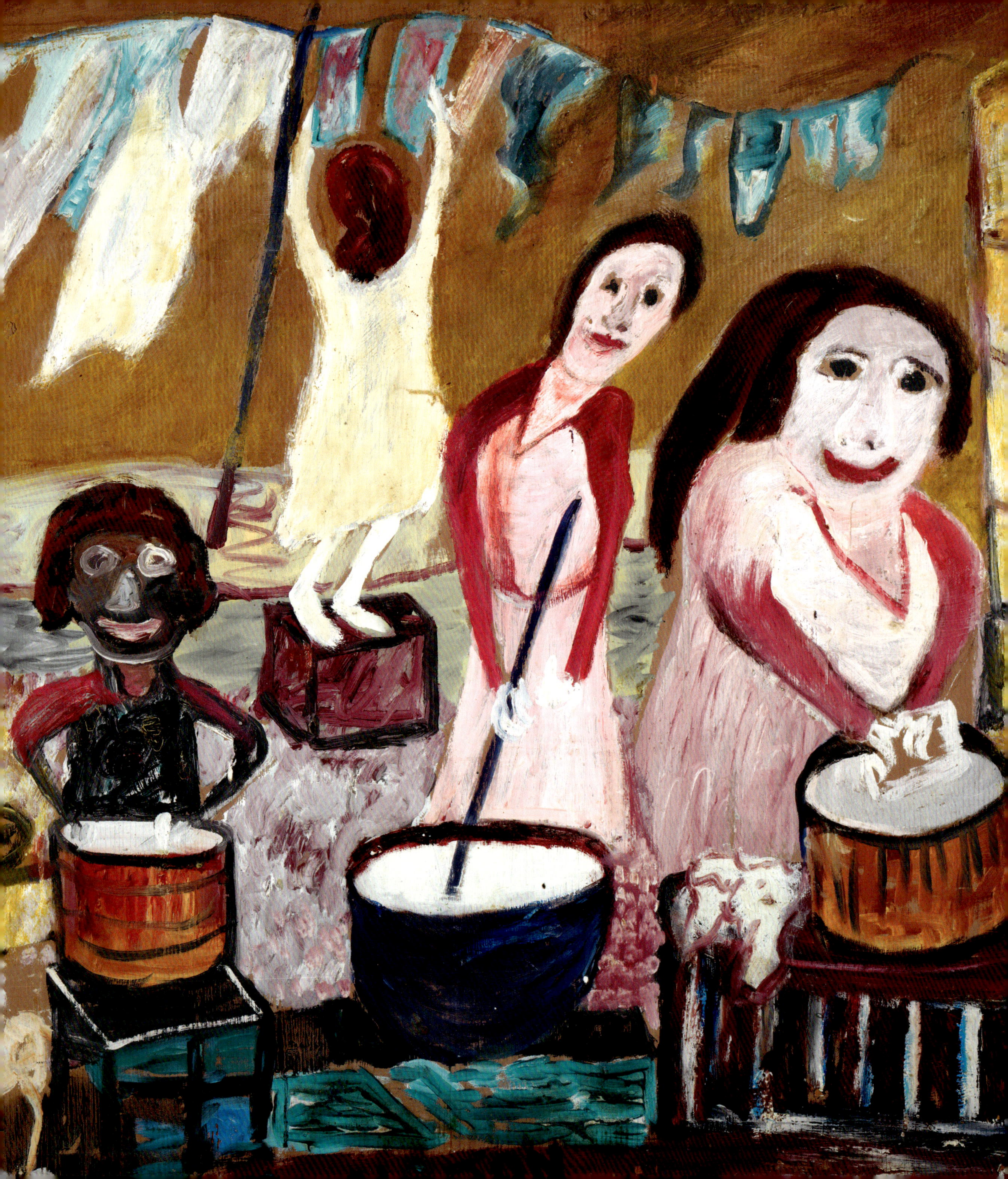

THE ROBSON FAMILY COLLECTION

Ocean tides have long offered a metaphor for flux: fury and calm, fortune and famine, life and death. Unstoppable and formidable, they are a force to be reckoned with. Yet the notion of coming change, something moving inexorably in one direction, has proven particularly apt as a framework for social change, a reversal of what was once considered the norm.

The beginning of the twentieth century in the United States was a time of reinvention—not only for the country but also for the diverse citizenry who together wove its fabric. After the agonizing years of the Civil War, Reconstruction proposed an egalitarian nation, but deeply ingrained ways lastingly thwarted the advance of this goal. Amid the turmoil and struggle that kicked off the last century, artists from every region, every culture and ethnic background, and every degree of ability increasingly asserted their right to voice their views, define personal spaces and places, and attest to their own self-worth and creative perspective.

Through forty-three artists, born over a span of a hundred years, *We Are Made of Stories: Self-Taught Artists in the Robson Family Collection* explores the ways in which artists, and the pioneering collectors who recognized the value of their work, brought lasting change to the face of American art.[1] The exhibition and catalogue center on artists whose creative output drew the attention of Margaret Z. Robson between the late 1980s and her death in 2014. Robson believed that these artists reflected a truly diverse nation of makers and that their singular bodies of work expanded the boundaries of American art in important ways. The Smithsonian American Art Museum blazed a new trail in 1970, showing and collecting material by individuals who challenged conventional notions of art and the identity of artists, and supporting makers who were untrained and marginalized from the mainstream for myriad reasons, decades before their mainstream recognition. In 2016, her son Douglas O. Robson donated the Margaret Z. Robson Collection to the Museum, uniting these kindred spirits. Doug Robson has continued to support an expansive vision of art, and this project incorporates additional artworks from his collection, which have been promised to SAAM.

BATTLE FOR THE SOUL OF A NATION

Only a small contingent saw the consequential possibility of a global pandemic before it was upon our world, in the early days of 2020. COVID-19 suspended normalcy, forced a remove from family, friends, and colleagues, and inflicted loss and havoc on an inestimable scale. The ongoing disruption of in-person engagement also prompted many to connect online more than ever before and in almost equal degrees with people far away as to those in their own communities. But as museums shuttered and scrambled to move online to remain relevant, another pandemic, simultaneously aged and contemporary, refused to be ignored. “Once again, we struggle to make sense of the senseless. Once again, we bear witness to our country’s troubled history of racial violence,” Lonnie G. Bunch III, secretary of the Smithsonian Institution and founding director of the Smithsonian’s National Museum of African American History and Culture, said in the wake of the killings of George Floyd, Ahmaud Arbery, Breonna Taylor, and far too many others.[2] As the Black Lives Matter movement roared into the foreground, the issue of long-standing, pervasive institutional racism also reached a boiling point. Policing practices have drawn the sharpest criticism, but cultural institutions have been similarly confronted with a long-overdue reckoning with foundational identities, from colonial pillaging to ongoing imperialistic cultural preferencing.

The year 2020 put museums and the entire cultural sector into a stark “before” and “after” moment, but a paradigm shift in American art was in the making long before that. “History is a guide to a better future and demonstrates that we can become a better society,” Bunch observed.

"But only if we collectively demand it from each other and from the institutions responsible for administering justice."[3] For too long and in too many instances, art museums have hewed to the preferences of mainstream culture and shied away from a leadership role on the frontier of social equity. The art that Margaret Z. Robson collected, sometimes with her husband, John, sometimes on her own, and that she inspired her son to appreciate and collect as well, is rooted in ideals of the civil rights era and feels especially relevant now. As this exhibition and publication were being developed, the death of George Floyd consumed the country. His family, his community, and the national and international public watched and listened to see if, this time, a Black life would be valued in America. When his death was judged by a jury of his peers to be wrongful and criminal, a community member said with emotion: "Everybody saw it—but still, you're sitting back thinking, you know, it's back to the Rodney King days—everybody saw that too, but those cops got off. . . . This is a new day, this is something different—finally!" A reporter covering the crowds the day the verdict was announced reflected, "This is the beginning of something better."[4]

/ / /

The works of art in the Robson Family Collection give voice to people who faced challenge, oppression, and often extreme marginalization in their lifetimes, but by leaving their imprint in the form of art, moved the needle toward a more enlightened age, a more humanistic moment. This project amplifies unique perspectives and argues that multivocality is essential for a full and genuine picture of America. It looks at the myriad hurdles constructed by an elite mainstream art world, and the rewards of playing the long game—the collective ground gained by artists who asserted their personal view of the world and told their own story. Journalist Margaret Renkl recently reflected on her own journey to really understanding what was necessary, noting, "When I was in a graduate writing program back in the mid-1980s, it was a cultural commonplace to believe that a writer's social responsibility included giving voice to the voiceless. We understand now the error of that thinking. Nobody is voiceless. There are only people whose voices are not heard."[5]

We Are Made of Stories presents a flexible framework for the many viewpoints encompassed within the Robson Family Collection, honoring the personal vision and experience of each individual artist, in tandem with that of the supporters who connected with the objects and images they made. As Doug details in the preceding essay, "Far & Wide, Inside & Out," his mother collected people as much as she collected the art they made, and inasmuch embodied an endeavor that was humanistic at its core. Margaret came from humble beginnings—there was nothing in her upbringing that destined her to be an art collector. But she did grow up with egalitarian ideals and possessed an inherent ability to value individuals, as well as the qualities and skills that made them unique, and the stories that contained their experience. With her husband, John E. Robson, Margaret shaped a collection that, as Doug puts it, first "telegraphed patriotism, and veered toward the folksy and accessible." Over time, especially as Margaret became the primary vision behind the collection, the objects that drew her acknowledged a more complex reality, a country whose history was far less straightforward, beset with paradoxes, and not always ideal. Margaret's collecting journey mirrors, in many ways, the dawning of a larger awareness and acceptance in the United States, particularly between the late 1980s and early twenty-first century, that the role of self-taught artists was not insignificant or passing but reflected the soul of the nation in real and meaningful ways.

Doug also notes that his parents' views were likely impacted by the exhibition *Black Folk Art in America, 1930–1980*, which opened at the Corcoran Gallery of Art in Washington, DC, in 1982 and traveled to seven venues over two years.[6] The exhibition featured twenty African American self-taught artists, arguably none of whom were "folk," or tradition-based—but a grounded framework for the genre of artists therein did not yet exist. Although their practices had roots in communal traditions and folkways, their art was about personal vision and lived experience, and asserted selfhood. A number of now-prominent artists were included in the Corcoran show, including Bill Traylor. Traylor was little known before that exhibition, but he made a big (posthumous) splash with his thirty-six featured paintings and drawings, including one on the catalogue cover.

Margaret and John acquired their first work by Traylor in May 1983, from the Carl Hammer Gallery in Chicago—another foresighted advocate for this artist. It is an early pencil drawing showing a scene with a mule, a dog, and a man hitting a woman, perhaps in dispute about a hen (see **CAT. 5**). Whether it was Traylor alone or the twenty artists in *Black Folk Art* that, more broadly, impacted the Robsons' views, it was likely this moment, as Doug recalls in his essay, that prompted their turn toward artists who "transcend[ed] the limits of identity through creation," and used art to make a personal record, and to navigate a challenging world. A few years later, John and Margaret began to collect the work of Ulysses Davis, who was also included in the Corcoran show. Unlike Traylor's works, Davis's carved wood sculptures are not narrative, but his complex array of subjects—spanning the straitlaced patriotic to the wild exotic—arguably came to embody their collecting journey.

Jane Livingston and John Beardsley, the organizers of *Black Folk Art in America*, may have imperfectly defined the art and artists they brought together, but they astutely identified an area of artistic production that was both powerful and obscure. By uniting twenty untrained African American artists born between 1853 and 1926, they put a spotlight on makers whose families had come up through enslavement, across the American South and Atlantic coast—the Black Atlantic South—and whose lives had been shaped by an intense cultural shift in the United States. These artists had immersed themselves in creativity during the first decades in which African Americans had the space and personal agency to do so, and their artistic practice—in the rare instances it was recognized at all—was severely marginalized on fronts of both race and social class.

As Margaret grew as a collector and understood the relevance of the artists' lives in the art they had made, she frequently attended exhibitions and symposia on self-taught artists and was increasingly involved with museums that supported this art. She appreciated SAAM's long-standing interest in nonmainstream artists, and I visited her at her Chicago home not long after becoming the Museum's first dedicated curator for folk and self-taught artists. By the time of Margaret's death, in 2014, SAAM had evolved considerably since it first acquired works by untrained and differently abled artists, understanding the need both for transformative scholarship in this area and for further diversifying its collection. Media coverage for self-taught artists had become commonplace, yet major art museums that included such a diversity of artists in their programming remained the exception; rarer still were those that backed a genuine commitment to expanding the canon by adding self-taught artists to their collections, challenging outmoded interpretive constructs, and dedicating time and resources to the care, study, and exhibition of their work. Much remained to be done toward bridging the divide between advocates who believed this material was valid and important, and institutional gatekeepers who could not reconcile the irony of including artists they had worked so long to keep out.

As Stephanie Stebich notes in her foreword to this volume, SAAM has argued, since 1970, that such artists are not only relevant but are indeed key to the story of art in America. They appear in every section of the Museum, sometimes in thematically organized galleries elucidating the different roads that self-taught artists traveled, in other instances situated in conversation with their creative peers across the board. Today, the tide has finally turned and the last of the holdouts—institutions that have defined the elite center of the art world—have given in to the idea that communally trained and self-taught artists are a legitimate part of art history.[7]

Of the forty-three artists highlighted in *We Are Made of Stories*, over half were born in the nineteenth century. Close to half were African American. Only two are living. Some remain unknown to us, while others lived to see their work compete in blue-chip markets. They all faced challenges of being recognized as artists, and each raised important questions about the power of language and categories, and how humanity regularly defies simple encapsulation. Whether a lot or a little is known about these makers, the artworks speak to individual ways of experiencing and seeing the world, and recording one's place in it. These creative individuals, and the allies who supported them—collectors, other artists, curators, academics—refuted the mandates laid out by the art-world mainstream and argued for an array of art canons over a single monolithic one, turning the tide once and for all toward a more diverse representation of makers. It is important to note at the outset of this essay, that as critical as these allies of self-taught artists have been, too often they—and the roles they played in the "discovery narratives" for marginalized makers—have disproportionately overshadowed the artists and the transformative power of the art itself. This project foregrounds the creativity of artists and the power of art, while both acknowledging and scrutinizing the support networks that encompassed and accompanied their histories.

The following sections offer lenses through which a diverse constellation of nonmainstream makers can be aligned with select streams of impact.[8] Section two, "Momentum: The Unstoppable Rise of American Self-Taught Artists," situates these creatives against the larger backdrop of American art in the first part of the century, when the division between untrained and professional artists was stark, as were the social hierarchies that often governed the path artists had to take. As the art explored in this project was made primarily in the second half of the twentieth century, "Momentum" is offered not as a deep exploration of this early era but as a starting place for understanding the historical baggage and the vestigial assumptions that have accompanied the untrained into the present. Section three, "Becoming Visible: African American Artists Make Their Mark," follows individuals whose experience is inextricably linked to the Black vernacular tradition, African Americans who drew on transatlantic family memories, beliefs, and folkways and made independent, powerfully original bodies of work in the mid- to late twentieth century; they used art as a declarative tool, and made cultural visibility an action item. Collectively, these autonomous practices came together and shaped one of the most forceful streams of creativity in the United States. Section four, "Gamechangers: Pivotal Artists Within a Shifting Paradigm," looks at a short list of artists whose unique and robust oeuvres were transformative in particular ways, and whose advancing historical moments synthesize in discomfiting truths the human propensity to name, categorize, and dehumanize difference. Many additional artists would have been appropriate to this section, but highlighting bodies of work that attracted exceptionally widespread attention for enormously varied reasons emphasizes several key factors: the immense power of individual artistic vision and the ability of artists of all kinds to impact the world; the ways in which each artist's experience deserves singular apprehension and context over reductive and dysfunctional categories of minimalizing their worth; and how faulty vehicles for "othering" fail in the face of transformative art. The final section, "A Breaking Wave," touches on artists who, together with those discussed in earlier sections, embody the heart and soul of *e pluribus unum*: out of many, one. They made artworks that were known, celebrated, and preserved in widely varying degrees, but share in having conveyed extraordinary drive and vision; they reveal the ongoing need for scholarship and recognition of artists who may lack the agency to draw attention to themselves, but lack nothing in terms of creative contributions to the cultural fabric of our nation. Central to *We Are Made of Stories* is the position that artists transform our world through their stories and by offering multiple lenses and portals, but that their contributions may be lost without allies who unite to see, honor, save, respect, and share these invaluable efforts and points of view, and work toward a kinder, more inclusive future.

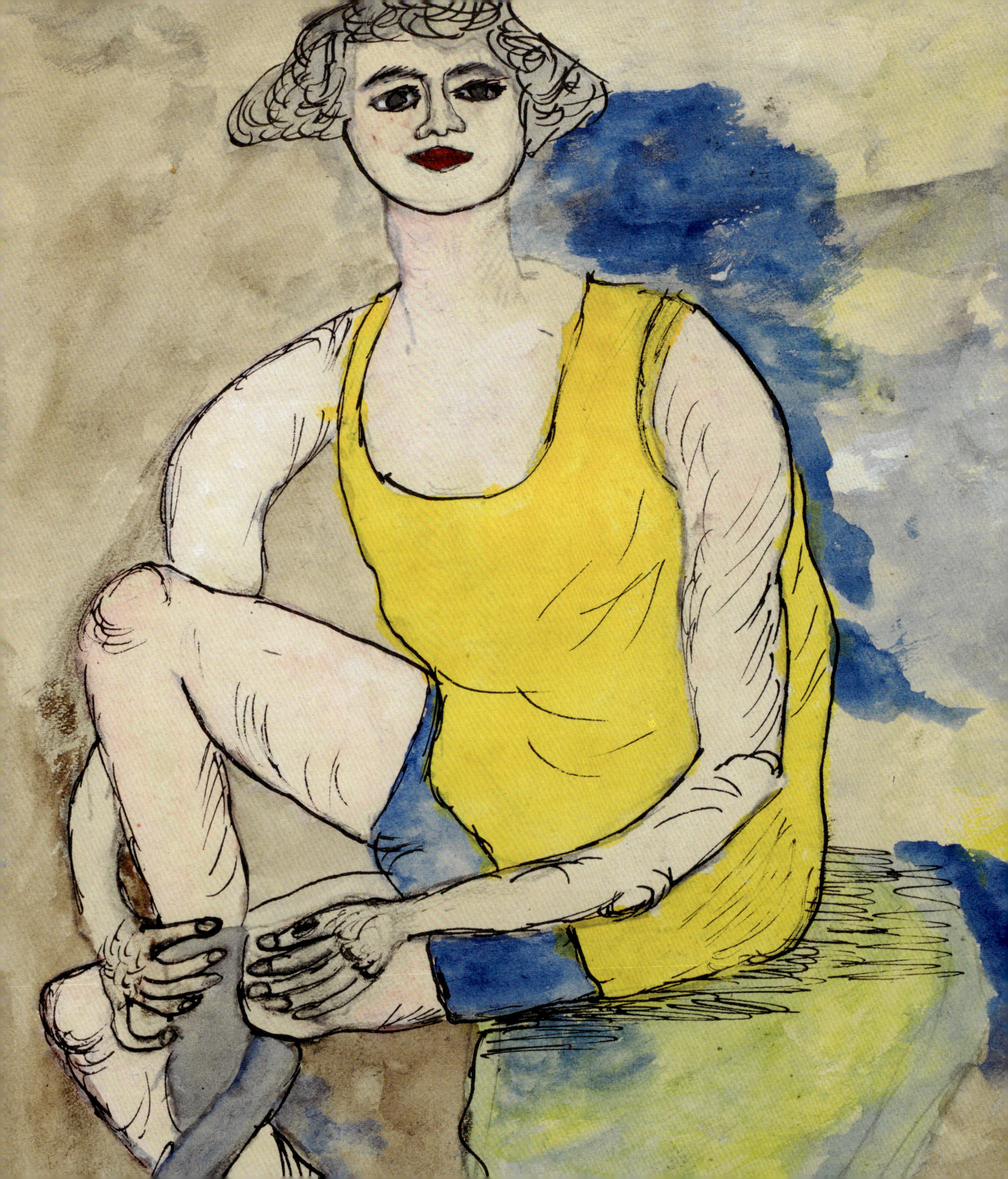

MOMENTUM / THE UNSTOPPABLE RISE OF AMERICAN SELF-TAUGHT ARTISTS

The history of artists who learned and made work in their homes and communities rather than in academic settings is not easily encapsulated. Nor should it be, as these makers derive from a far greater array of humanity than those who shaped the canon of Western art. The terms "folk" and "self-taught," often given to such artists, are not interchangeable; the former refers to artists who learned foremost through traditional or communal modes, the latter to those whose path was predominantly a singular one. Arguably, all artists grow over time, learn in multiple ways, and are incalculably affected by the era, place, and culture that backdrop their lives. Whether a body of work favors tradition, autonomy, or formal training, it is essential to consider the balance of factors evidenced in the work before attempting to describe the artist. Because fine art canons were literally built on elitism—celebrating the premier artists of globally dominant cultures—it has been a long journey toward an art world that reflects a wide universe of makers, instead of a narrow selection.

Many would argue that any number of the long-standing labels and categories for classifying art and artists have reached their expiration dates. But the increasingly diverse art world of today is rooted in a history of dueling factions that might reduce to this: the empowered versus the underclass.[1] The use and appeal of these labels will continue to diminish and fade in the twenty-first century, but the lives discussed herein were all heavily impacted by our society's stratification and ways of categorizing art and artists.[2] Today, the art world still favors the mighty, but the demographics of agency have changed over time, not only on frontiers of sex and race but on those of social class, physical ability, and neurodiversity as well. Artists like Dan Miller, discussed in section five, are celebrated for revelatory bodies of work, but they also stand on the shoulders of artists who refused to be silenced, and have become increasingly appreciated within a larger sphere thanks to the many advocates who saw the cultural richness of art beyond the mainstream. Machinations over what to call, and the best ways to show, consider, promote, and historicize art by untrained artists continue, and many books have examined these issues at length, collectively revealing the fortitude of the art canon. These concerns expose both the sacredness of the inner realm and the considered strategies of the gatekeepers—for, as critic and philosopher Arthur C. Danto has observed, being part of the art world means knowing how to play a "language game," wherein added qualifiers always signify disparity.[3]

THE ROAD

Few naming debates have drawn as much fervor and media attention as the tangle of labels meant to disassociate untrained artists from their professional, mainstream peers. But even as the balance begins to tip in favor of inclusion, and self-taught and differently abled artists are encountered at museums more often and in more meaningful ways, the art world remains an abidingly exclusive place. The artists featured in *We Are Made of Stories* each played a role in a collective march toward equity. With bodies of work rooted in personal journeys and autonomous learning paths, they demonstrate how art can be at its most powerful when it reveals the world through the eyes of another and prompts active empathy. This exhibition, and its accompanying catalogue, chronicles the gathering momentum of self-taught artists in the United States, beginning around the mid-twentieth century and following that journey into the present. This history is distinct from parallel journeys overseas, although significant moments of impact and cross-pollination between Europe and America are discussed.[4]

Numerous books have documented the evolution of "Early American Folk Art," a genre historically centered on popular material that transmitted nationalistic zeal and an American Dream spirit, and a construct that supported the collective aims of European immigrants and

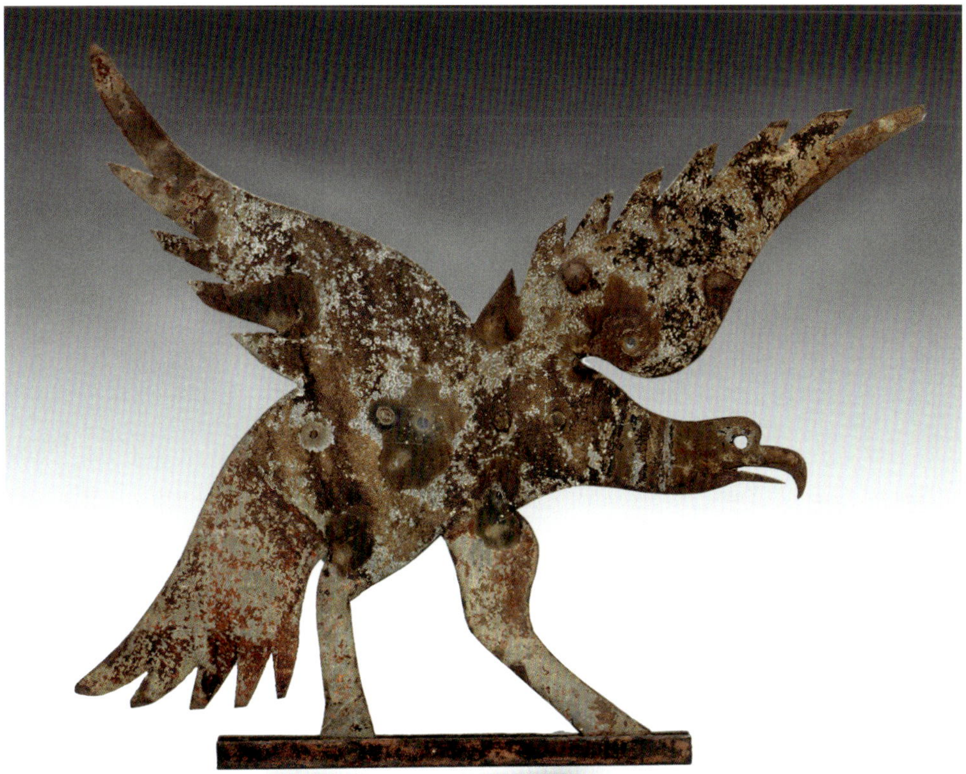

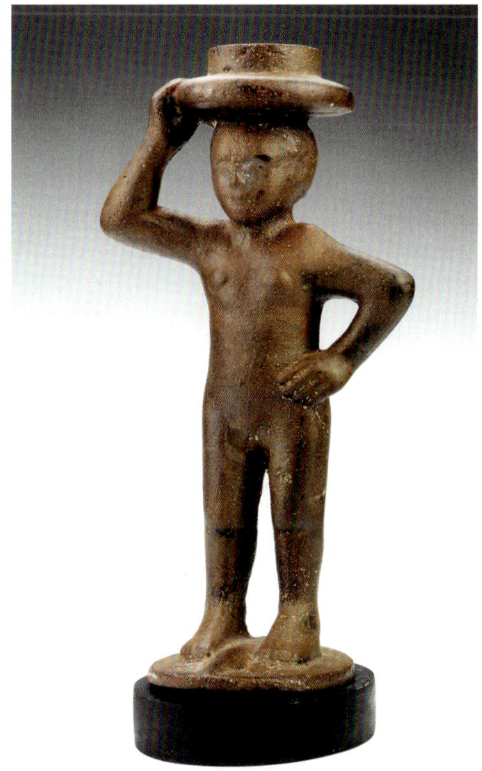

CAT. 17.
Unidentified artist
Untitled (Eagle Weathervane)
ca. 1875

CAT. 18.
Unidentified artist
Untitled (Figure with Hat)
late 19th or early 20th century

their descendants (**CAT. 17**). European colonization of the Eastern Seaboard began in the early seventeenth century, with the Spanish in Florida, the Dutch in New York and New Jersey, the Swedes and Finns in Delaware, the Ulster Scots in Appalachia, the Germans along the mid-Atlantic, and the English in Virginia and Maryland, as well as the English Puritans in New England and the English Quakers in Pennsylvania, and increasingly the British and French in the South.[5]

The colonial era reveals certain roots of this project but occludes the fuller picture—for the fabrication of an "American" identity required that European immigrants be united in shaping idealistic narratives that overwrote and displaced Indigenous nations and prospered at the expense of enslaved human beings, whose works play a major role in an encompassing picture of American art. In the early days of her collecting, it is fair to surmise that Margaret Robson embraced notions of "American" and "Americanness" but increasingly thought about the paradoxes enmeshed in such fabulations. She was drawn to objects that channeled a sense of American individualism (**CAT. 18**), but over time her collecting journey traced a path toward awareness, and an active embrace of the nuanced ways in which individuality extends beyond race and sex into complex realms including social agency, spirituality, gender, and physical and mental ability.

We Are Made of Stories includes many artists who were born in the nineteenth century, but, with the exception of a few objects made in the nineteenth century by unidentified artists, it was nearly halfway through the twentieth before these artists began to openly express creative natures,

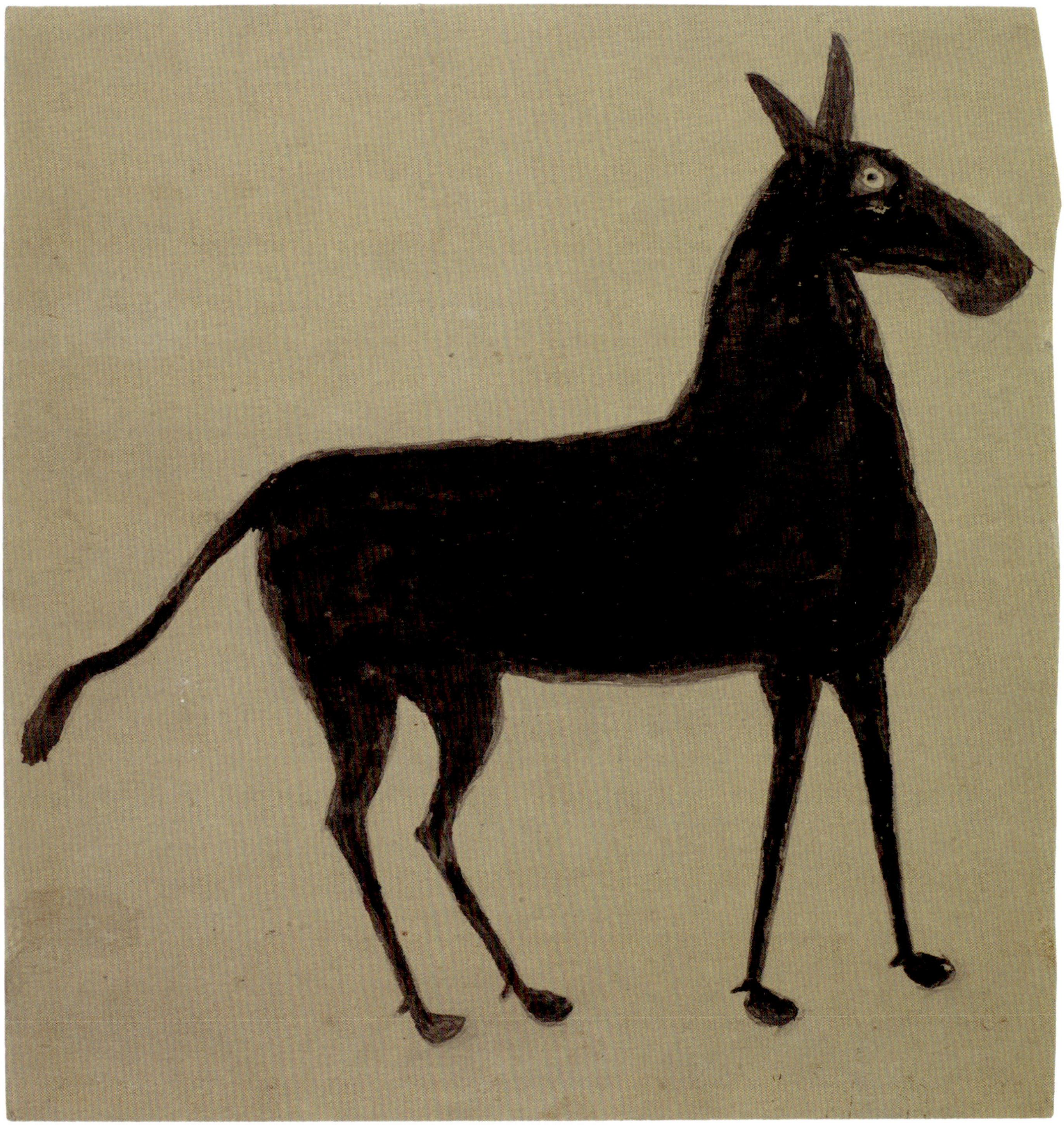

CAT. 19.
Bill Traylor
Untitled (Mule)
December 1939

and still later before any would enjoy widespread recognition. These makers had roots in the old world but flourished in a new day; many did not live to witness the sea change they helped effect. This section offers important context from the first half of the twentieth century but is necessarily succinct, in favor of the artworks by known artists in this project, the earliest of which date to the late 1930s (**CAT. 19**).

American folk art—the material that would prompt a long-standing national ambivalence for the art of the common man—emerged in the early days of the republic, with communally trained artisans or craftspeople and work that was often utilitarian or decorative in nature (**CAT. 20**). This expansive realm of quotidian production bridging "folk art" and "craftwork" was seen in contrast to "fine art," sculptures and paintings made by trained professionals and held in esteem as refined, rarefied, and inherently valuable. Folk art became increasingly fashionable among certain collectors in the early twentieth century, when, given the preponderance of unknown makers connected with works from this period, it seems that they placed high value on objects but very little on artists of the underclass—which in this context is an admittedly sweeping classification, but meant to clearly distinguish artists and patrons of power and privilege from members of the middle, working, impoverished, and enslaved castes. The most prized folk art objects inadvertently intersected with a modern art aesthetic. But distinctly inferior positioning for this material, in relation to the work of the trained upper class, would rein until the last decades of the twentieth century, when hierarchical structures at last began to crumble.

In the 1920s, collectors regarded folk art as appealingly fresh, pure—imbued with an ineffable American spirit and democratic ideal. The subtext of naivete and accidental charm was all-important: nothing dark, broody, or indicative of real personal struggle would be appreciated for decades. While trained artists including Thomas Cole, Thomas Eakins, and Albert Pinkham Ryder had more latitude for exploring murkier realms, the art world expected untrained artists to toe a sunnier line, with works radiating American positivity regardless of how their society treated or viewed them. Painter and photographer Charles Sheeler, one of the early modernists who regarded unschooled artists as foundational to American art, noted that this simple and wholesome art showed "something of the character of the people of the time in which it was produced"; he described, however naively, the uplifting spirit that the working class was expected to exude, while taking entirely for granted the factors of white privilege that frame his perception.[6]

The kind of objects Sheeler spoke of, and that prominent collectors including Edith Gregor Halpert, Abby Aldrich Rockefeller, and Electra Havemeyer Webb admired and collected, spanned the range of "Americana." Shaker furniture, decoys, weathervanes, hooked rugs, and other items were shown at the Whitney Studio Club in 1924, in an exhibition called *Early American Art*, organized by artist Henry Schnakenberg, together with Juliana Force, the club's director who was also a prominent folk art advocate. "Foundational" or not, the ways in which these artworks were routinely severed from the social and personal histories of their makers reveal an era in which the collecting class—professional artists, curators, and collector-patrons alike—dwelled on a loftier tier than the material culture that informed and inspired them, and was comfortable with the artists, particularly female makers, being "anonymous."[7]

The 1930s was a decade of momentous change, the Great Depression colliding with America's Great Migration, during which some six million African Americans chose self-definition over ongoing oppression in the South and moved their families north, east, and anywhere they could.[8] This period of mass human movement began before the First World War and extended through the 1960s, but, in the buildup to the Second World War, it overlapped with President Franklin Delano Roosevelt's New Deal social programs, including the Federal Art Project (FAP), created in 1935. Holger Cahill was the director of the FAP, a program that aimed to bring art to community spaces via art centers, classes, exhibitions, and commissions.[9] These initiatives, which offered jobs to artists, blurred the lines between fine art and paid commissions. Cahill was among the first to clearly articulate a position for folk art within a broader art hierarchy, showing what a democratized artistic sphere might look like with an exhibition he organized in 1932 for the Museum of Modern Art (MoMA) in New York: *American Folk Art: The Art of the Common Man in America, 1750–1900*. The exhibition proffered a double-edged sword that proved exceptionally durable; simultaneously celebratory and belittling, it hailed the work for being a breath of fresh air, but also foregrounded its naivete and underclass tarnish. With this project, self-taught artists entered the upper echelon of art, but did so under framing devices that decisively ghettoized them therein.

The case of French self-taught painter Henri Rousseau, a working-class artist who was simultaneously feted and mocked, in the early part of the twentieth century, by Pablo Picasso and others who promoted and took inspiration from him, is often mentioned as a prime example of condescension and compliment being served on the same plate. In her 2018 exhibition at the National Gallery of Art in Washington, DC, *Outliers and American Vanguard Art*, curator Lynne Cooke addressed a long and complex history of relationships between trained and untrained artists in both Europe and America, a phenomenon that was ubiquitous, if rarely mutually beneficial. Cooke described MoMA's founding director Alfred Hamilton Barr's decade-long campaign "to establish a division or tributary of modern art based in the work of what he called the 'modern primitive'" as inestimably influential but admittedly flawed.[10] The demeaning label of "primitivism" —applied as a counterpoint to sophistication even when used as an ironic critique of elite culture—was particularly offensive when referring to the work of Black artists, hearkening as it did to

CAT. 20.
Unidentified artist
Untitled (Swan Decoy from Delaware)
ca. 1920

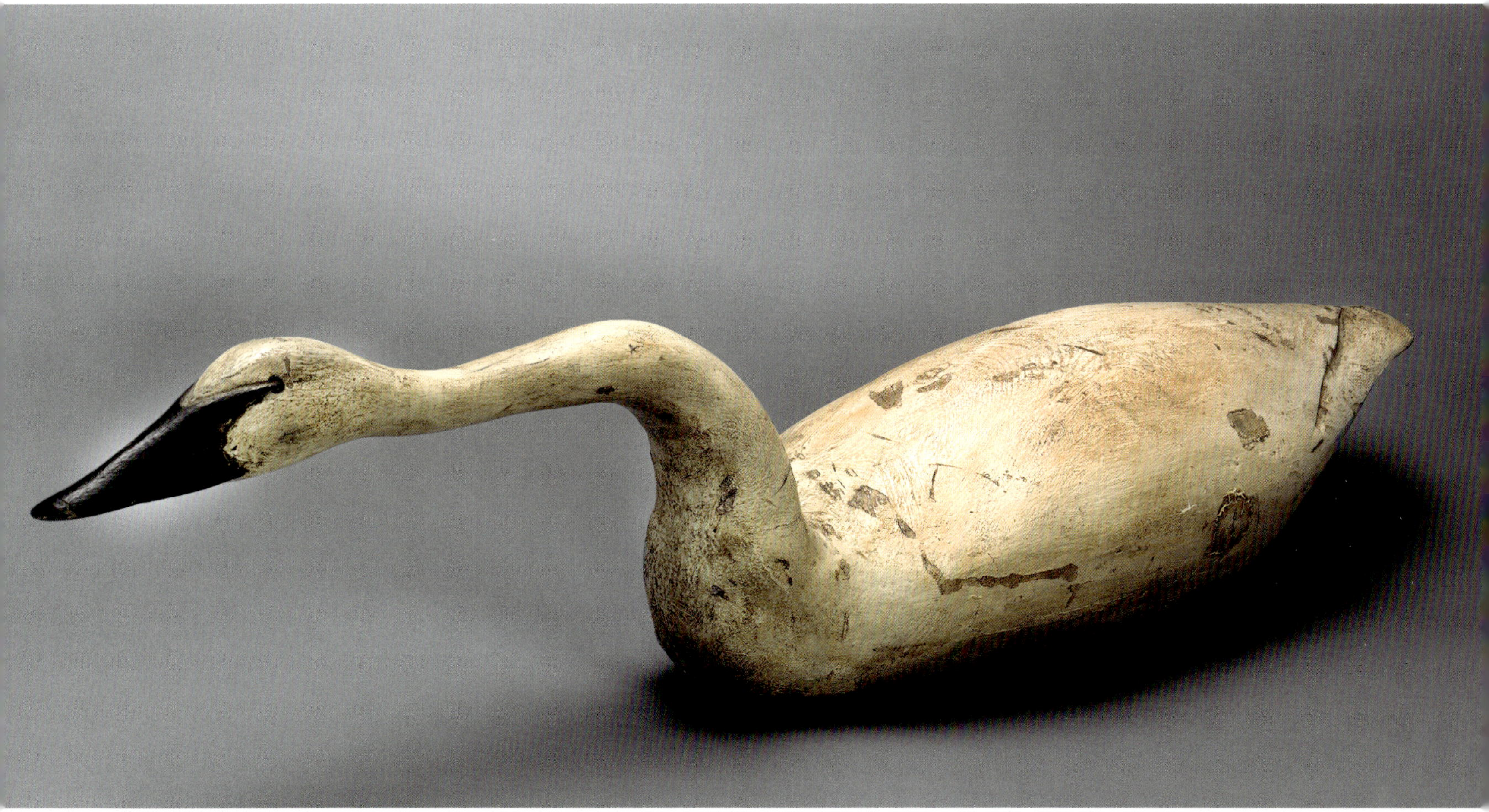

antebellum stereotypes and undercutting evocations of the defiant, educated, and modern "New Negro." When, in 1937, William Edmondson became the first African American and the first self-taught artist to have a solo exhibition at MoMA, it was a groundbreaking moment on both fronts.[11] But to the chagrin of professional Black artists striving for recognition—not only personally but in representation of a sophisticated intellectual class—Edmondson was positioned as a living relic, an unassuming leftover from days of old, and inadvertently emblematic of an art world that was not prepared to fully accept Black artists on equal footing with their white counterparts.[12] The museum's press release described him as "prosperous for a Negro," and "simple, almost illiterate, entirely unspoiled, and happy in his work." "For scholars familiar with the packaging of black artists by the white art world in the interwar era, nothing in Edmondson's story will come as a surprise," art historian Jennifer Jane Marshall has observed. "It was common for white curators to emphasize a black artist's humble, working-class origins, especially to promote the narrative of an artist pursuing creative self-fulfillment against the odds."[13]

In 1938, African art specialist Robert Goldwater published *Primitivism in Modern Painting*, a volume exploring the exploitative relationship between modern artists in Europe and their non-Western and primitive subjects. The book includes a chapter, "The Modern Primitives," in which Goldwater considered living self-taught artists. He saw his chapter title not as an oxymoron but as a niche describing makers who were modern, inasmuch as they used creative means to express boldly individualized notions of selfhood and the world at large, yet "primitive" in terms of social rank and "civilized" status.[14] The same year, Barr and Cahill collaborated, with Dorothy C. Miller, on another MoMA exhibition, *Masters of Popular Painting: Modern Primitives of Europe and America*, drawing the problematic framework of "modern primitives" into a still broader conversation.[15]

As curator Katherine Jentleson details in *Gatecrashers: The Rise of the Self-Taught Artist in America*, Cahill, in his catalogue essay, embraced this as a midcentury rubric that would mark a lasting differentiation between preindustrial, tradition-based handcrafts—folk art—and paintings and sculptures by living, self-taught artists. He, like Goldwater, dubbed these autodidacts "modern primitives," and cast makers who, via their art and their personal stories, embodied the American spirit and unwittingly conjoined a bygone age with a living tradition.[16] Presenting an array of working-class players including John Kane, Edward Hicks, and Horace Pippin, Cahill offered this perspective on art by amateurs as a direct challenge to the standards and achievements of the high art world. Building on these frameworks still further, in 1941 Barr dedicated a suite of rooms at MoMA to *Modern Primitives: Artists of the People*, an installation that ultimately sent mixed signals on the aims and achievements of reconciling the status of untrained artists within one of the world's most prominent art museums.[17] With an emphasis on working-class makers over ethnic or racial equity, Cahill and Barr had both asserted conflicting ideas—that the art was on a par with any, but that the artists' achievements were accidental; they were preservationists of national nostalgia and notions of a simpler time more than active participants.

Sidney Janis, a collector and art dealer, further promoted living, working-class artists with his 1942 book, *They Taught Themselves: American Primitive Painters of the 20th Century*. Janis presented a more ethnically diverse array of makers than Cahill had, placing greater emphasis on the class and character of the artists themselves and effectively laying the groundwork for an identity-based category of art. The publication's table of contents lists each painter's name, along with her or his primary occupation or default label, as if to emphasize that art was not, in any case, the maker's profession. Janis's entries include the following: "William Doriani, Opera Singer," "Anna Mary Robertson Moses, Farm Wife," "Hazel Knapp, Former Invalid," "Horace Pippin, Disabled War Veteran (Negro)," and "William Samet, Inmate, Dannemora Prison." This tactic would feed, in the 1980s and after, the American version of "outsider art," an unwieldy rubric that ultimately created a false unity among disparate makers and too often put biography in front of artistic practice. Nevertheless, *They Taught Themselves* lauded autonomous, self-defined creativity over traditional or communal practices, and argued that "self-taught" spanned a more encompassing and "satisfactory" category. Janis reviewed and rejected terms, including nonprofessional, Sunday painter, popular painter, painters of the people, instinctive, naive-primitive, autodidactic, and folk artist, saying of the last that the name "implies a person who makes rural or peasant art and directs his efforts to objects made primarily for use."[18]

But even when folk art began to morph and grow as a field, and became "institutionalized" with the founding of the Museum of Early American Folk Arts (now the American Folk Art Museum) in New York in 1961, what often came to mind for many was primitivized, white, material culture objects and images that, as art historian Wanda Corn described it, "expressed a desire for an imagined blood relationship to a national past."[19] Herbert "Bert" Waide Hemphill Jr., an avid collector and cofounder of the Museum of Early American Folk Arts, shook up staid notions of folk art by furthering Janis's assertion that living, working-class artists were making some of the most interesting and original art anywhere. In his 1970 exhibition, *Twentieth-Century Folk Art*, Hemphill explored folk art as a living tradition rooted in craft practices but also revealed a sphere of production that extends well beyond painting. He and coauthor Julia Weissman published a related book in 1974, *Twentieth-Century American Folk Art and Artists*, which acknowledged an ongoing struggle with naming or defining the artists, but described his own grounding principle as this: "If there is one characteristic that marks folk artists, it is that for them the restraints of academic theory are unimportant, and if encountered at all, meaningless. In effect, the vision of the folk artist is a private one, a personal universe, a world of his or her own making."[20]

Many credit Hemphill with the rule-breaking "anything goes" ethos that—despite his own frequent use of the term "folk art"—clearly distinguished tradition-based artists from those who learned on their own and for whom innovation and personal vision reigned. Hemphill influenced generations of collectors, but the 1970s was a moment in which many people were seeing things in a new light. The civil rights movement saw significant social change, but it also revealed the vastness of the cultural divide. The violence against peaceful protestors and the assassinations of iconic figures fueled national anger and unleashed civil unrest. The Black Power movement challenged the efficacy of nonviolent protest and encouraged Black Americans to celebrate cultural identity and ethnicity; in tandem with sister movement Black Is Beautiful, it emphasized cultural pride and aesthetics rooted in African heritage and beliefs, rejecting white-culture stereotypes designed to demean and demoralize.[21] Civic outrage escalated in the Vietnam years, and art in the United States broadened to include myriad concerns and peoples, including "lowbrow" art forms like comics, assemblage, tattoos, and lowrider cars. Suddenly, the vernacular did not telegraph poverty and naivete so much as cool alternative narratives and original vision. As art from what was once considered the bottom of the cultural barrel became increasingly celebrated, the mainstream canon, by contrast, appeared repressed, unoriginal, and racist.[22]

It was in this same era that SAAM acquired James Hampton's *Throne of the Third Heaven of the Nations' Millennium General Assembly* (Figs. 1, 2). When Hampton, an African American from South Carolina who followed the Great Migration to Washington, DC, in 1928, passed away in 1964, he left behind an unfinished project he had begun years earlier—sporadically in the 1930s and with greater focus after 1950. But Hampton's death coincided with an institutional moment at SAAM, when staff were thinking more broadly about "American art," who makes it, and the role museums play in perpetuating bias in issues of race and class.

Hampton worked as a janitor in a government building but aspired to preaching to his own congregation from a resplendent pulpit. *The Throne of the Third Heaven* is the devotional piece Hampton made toward the fulfillment of his spiritual vision. With almost two hundred foil-covered components, the complex installation filled a carriage house that he had rented expressly for its construction. When *The Throne* came to light after the artist's death, it drew the attention of artists and curators alike. Although Hampton's creation was little understood at the time, SAAM acquired the full array in 1970 and put the central section on view.[23] Between 1972 and 1976, this condensed version of *The Throne* toured to the Abby Aldrich Rockefeller Folk Art Museum in Virginia, the Walker Art Center in Minneapolis, New York's Whitney Museum of

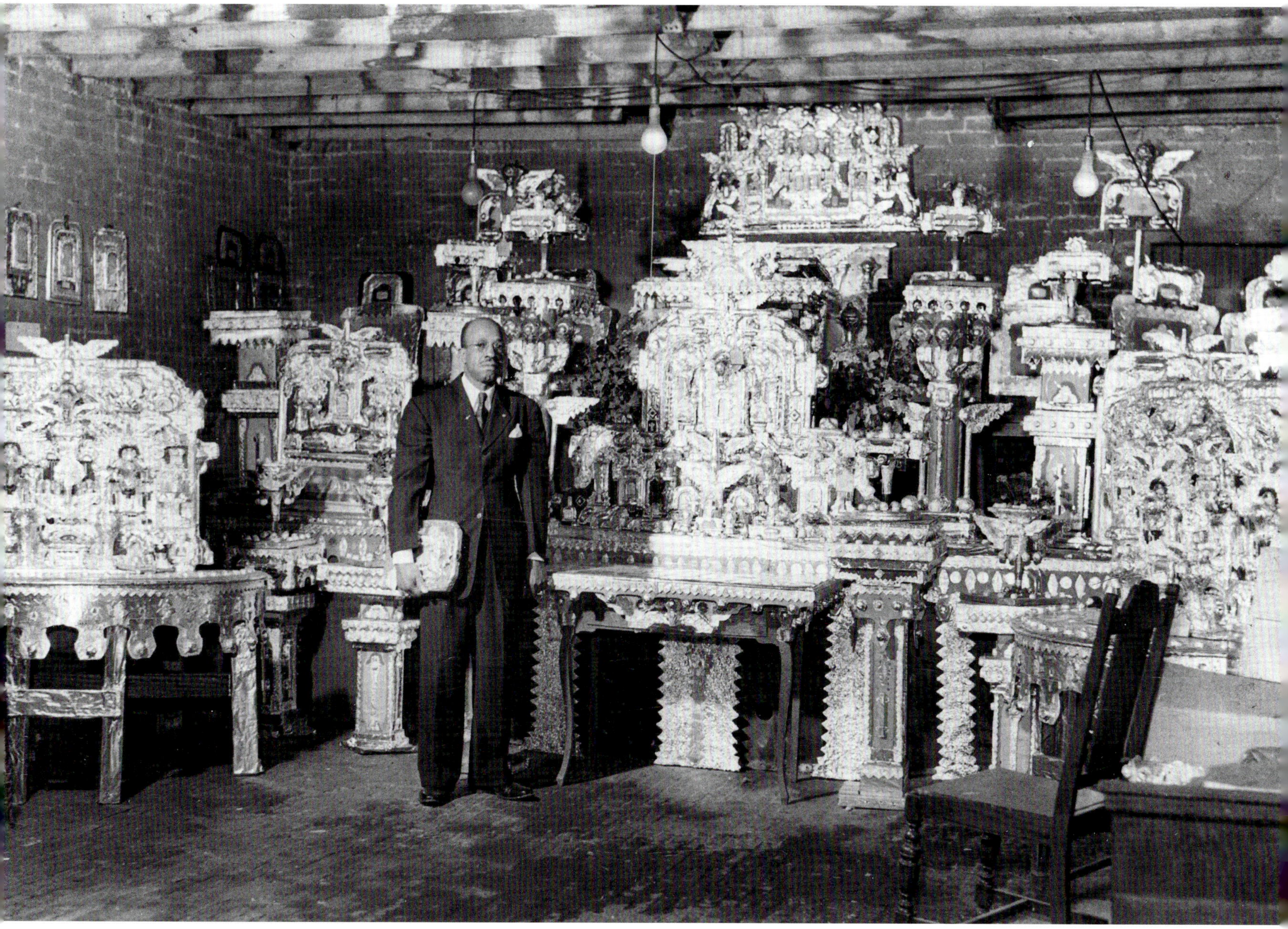

Fig. 1. James Hampton with *The Throne of the Third Heaven of the Nations' Millennium General Assembly*, ca. 1960–64; unknown photographer. Courtesy of the Smithsonian American Art Museum

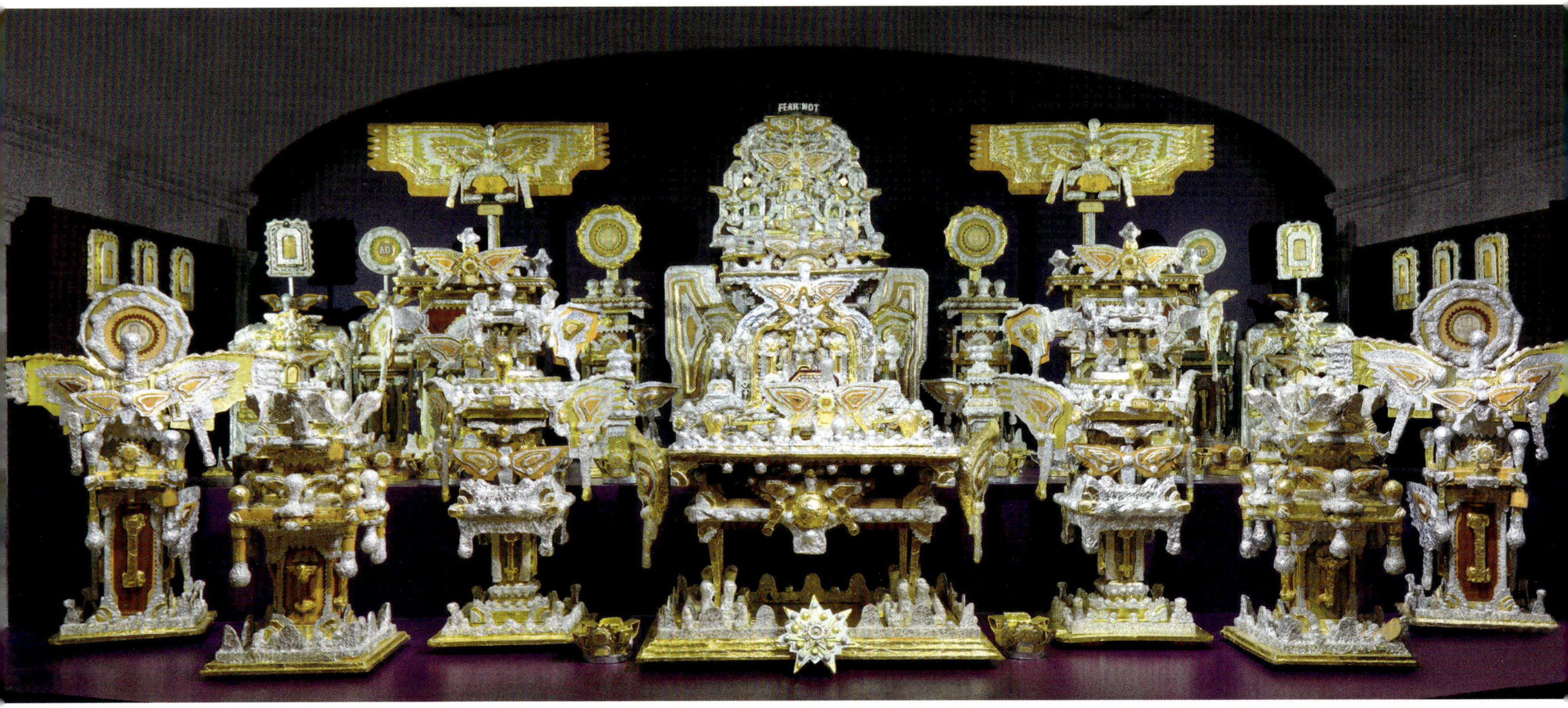

Fig. 2. James Hampton, *The Throne of the Third Heaven of the Nations' Millennium General Assembly*, ca. 1950–64, mixed media, dimensions variable. Smithsonian American Art Museum, Gift of anonymous donors, 1970.353.1–.116

American Art, and the Museum of Fine Arts, Boston. And as mentioned previously, Hampton's work reached still greater exposure after elements of it were included in the 1982 exhibition *Black Folk Art in America, 1930–1980*, at the Corcoran, alongside the artworks of nineteen other Black artists born between 1853 and 1926, all of whom had either been enslaved or were the progeny of the enslaved.

ARRIVALS

The events highlighted above are not a comprehensive history but a confluence of moments, small streams flowing into a longer and deeper river. By the time of Hampton's inadvertent foray into the limelight and the Corcoran show, African American vernacular practice was gaining ground across the country. Native American, Latinx, and European American self-taught artists became increasingly visible along similar timelines, but Black artists became prominent in a forceful and collective way in the late twentieth century.[24] Even if in fraught ways, William Edmondson and Horace Pippin had broken ground at MoMA, in 1937 and 1938, respectively. Although they were uncommon in drawing the mainstream gaze as they did, these artists were ultimately part of something far larger—an unspoken, unorganized, vernacular movement dating back to the forced immigration of Africans, which gained momentum and ever-firmer footing in the nineteenth century and beyond. It is this creative wellspring that moved into the light and gained institutional legitimacy with the installation of Hampton's *Throne* at SAAM, and then spilled more fully into national view with *Black Folk Art in America*.

The dominance of Black artists within the larger sphere of self-taught art is particular to the United States, and it is notable that their art composes roughly half of the Robson Family Collection. Doug Robson's observation that his mother, Margaret, enjoyed human beings as much as she collected art highlights an important shift from earlier collecting models. And in fact, Margaret's collecting journey—increasingly empathetic, individualized, and radically encompassing—mirrors an overarching development of this field in the United States. She had a keen understanding of the connectivity between maker and object, and by respecting and saving the art, she honored the artists and their lives. The following sections provide distilled accounts for select artists in the Robson Family Collection, whose work both Margaret and subsequently Doug collected, and whose artistic projects were instrumental in effecting indelible change in the long game of American art. For artists of color, born around the turn of the century, allies with greater social agency played an important if not uncomplicated role. Too frequently, such allies positioned themselves as heroes in the rescuer/discoverer role, diminishing the creative agency of the artists and the power of their work. Undeniably, however, these advocates were instrumental in promoting a wider recognition within a white-dominated society and art world. As often as not, empowered allies acknowledged and honored the aesthetics and worldviews of less empowered artists, and chipped away at making the social norm of intolerance, unacceptable. Over time, classism and ableism became similarly understood as additionally complex marginalizing factors. The artists who faced these, often inhumane, challenges had powerful and unique visions to share; slowly, and with the help of an army of indefatigable supporters, their important contributions are now recognized as integral to a more honest and replete picture of the art of our time.

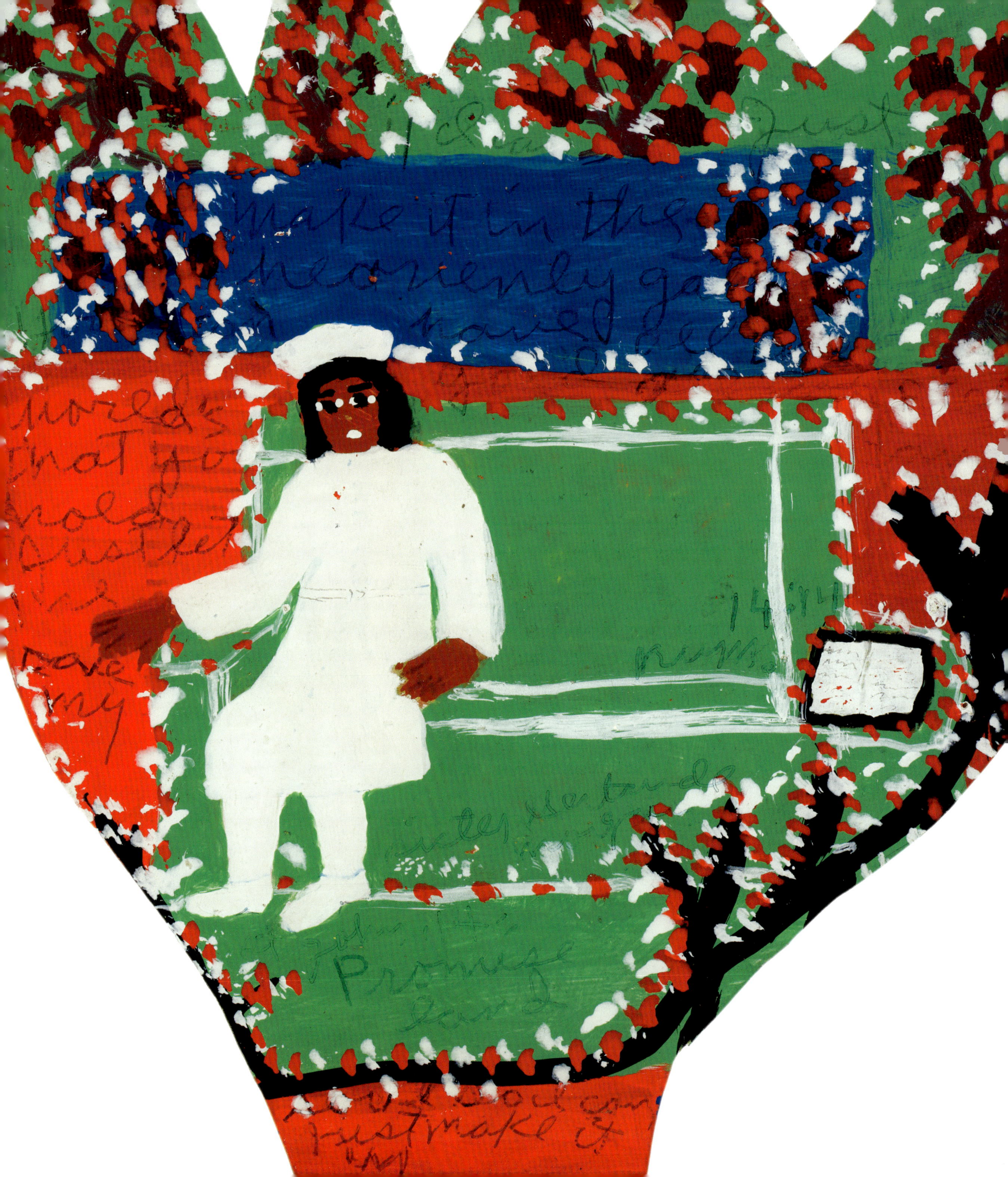
make it in the
heavenly
that yo
hold
Promise
land
Just make it

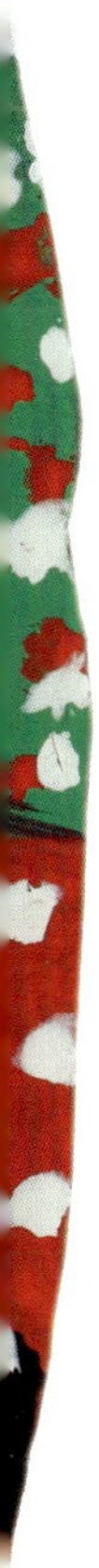

BECOMING VISIBLE / AFRICAN AMERICAN ARTISTS MAKE THEIR MARK

Between the late nineteenth century and the present, self-taught Black artists became actively visible in the United States—both to white mainstream society and to one another. From the earliest moments that Black Americans sought to reclaim suppressed cultural identities and openly express their aesthetics and beliefs, untrained artists were marginalized along lines of race and social class. Yet within and despite an exclusionary environment, creative individuals asserted selfhood and conveyed the Black experience through visual traditions that expressed highly personal views, and linked Africa with the Americas, and the past with the present. These artists made autonomous bodies of work and, before the late 1970s, infrequently knew or knew of one another. Collectively, however, their work draws from wellsprings of history and culture rooted in Africa and its diaspora, which survived and fluidly reshaped the Black Atlantic South, and eventually suffused the United States along the paths of the Great Migration.

The concept of "becoming visible" is about collective actions that staked a claim for a distinct cultural worldview and aesthetic as unique, valid, and American; mainstream white recognition was never the goal. This framework foregrounds centuries of white suppression of Black American visual practices and aesthetics. It also establishes art-making and homemaking as forms of personal resistance that comprehensively resulted in a more widely seen, understood, and respected visual culture. Among the earliest such efforts to survive in the form of artworks and a known maker entails the story of enslaved potter David "Dave" Drake (ca. 1800–after 1870).

Drake's experience occurred almost two hundred years after the first Africans were forcibly brought to the East Coast of the United States. The population from which he descended included countless individuals who creatively retained ancestral customs and cultures in the shadows of forced assimilation. Free Black artisans including the silversmith Peter Bentzon (ca. 1783–after 1850) of Philadelphia and cabinetmaker Thomas Day (ca. 1801–1861), who was born into a free Black family in North Carolina, made exquisitely crafted items that rivaled any.[1] But before 1863, the year of Emancipation, it was not easy for people of African descent to break away from enslavement and join the ranks of free communities. Legal freedom could be granted, earned, or purchased, and people variously joined or were born into such communities. Communally trained craftsmen such as Bentzon and Day reveal an important historical component of Black artisanry in America, yet it should be noted that skin color and mixed-race lineage played a powerful role in caste-based opportunities, while the preponderance of African American makers remained entrenched within a racially oppressive system.

Among enslaved African Americans, records of individualized creative practice are far rarer. As interest in and awareness of the work of enslaved laborers increases, information will undoubtedly come to light about heretofore unknown makers. At present, it is with Drake that the story of expressive art by identified Black artists in the United States effectively comes into view.[2] Drake was born around 1800 and lived, enslaved, in the Edgefield District of South Carolina. This region gained acclaim for the production of alkaline-glazed stoneware vessels, which prior to the early 1800s had to be imported from the northern states or Europe. This industry owed its success in large part to slave labor, and, although there were white potters as well, Drake would become renowned for strong, graceful, and often massive turned stoneware jars, some of which held as much as forty gallons of meat or grain.

Drake's well-earned reputation as a master potter may have allowed him more latitude than other enslaved potters. It is notable that Drake was conventionally literate, having learned English reading and writing in South Carolina, which had outlawed these skills for Black Americans with the 1834 Anti-Literacy Act.[3] Unlike many of the oppressed, who hid knowledge from white owners,

Drake defiantly proclaimed his by signing his name and inscribing his stoneware vessels with notes, dates, and comments such as "I made this jar," or pithy couplets that reflected his mental acuity as much as they did his state of mind. Ultimately, Drake left behind an amazing and unique autobiographical account, at a time and place where the enslaved were far more likely to die without a clear record. Declaring his identity and authorship, before and during the Civil War and under the country's most stringent anti-literacy laws, was exceedingly dangerous and uncommon. Drake's inscribed jars are relatively rare, and not included in the Robson Family Collection, but his determination to refute anonymity by signing his name, and to push back against literacy suppression by adding lines of verse, alert us to a coming change—a Black refusal of the racist status quo that would grow stronger with each passing year.[4]

With the exception of several objects by unidentified makers from the late nineteenth and early twentieth centuries, the artists discussed in this section began making work as early as the 1930s and came into wider recognition in the 1970s and 1980s. It was in the late twentieth century that museums first began to recognize the practice of self-taught African American makers as a valid component of American art, and contextualize it as a visual lingua franca of the Black Atlantic—a common language of ancestral heritage. Influential events, including SAAM's acquisition and installation of James Hampton's *Throne* in 1970 (see Figs. 1, 2, pp. 63, 64), and the Corcoran Gallery of Art's *Black Folk Art in America, 1930–1980* exhibition in 1982, prompted a groundswell of interest from scholars and collectors and the unstoppable rise of artists who made large, powerful bodies of work despite the mainstream art world's general dismissiveness of its value.

IDENTITIES ONCE KNOWN

Before Emancipation, objects made by African Americans—free or enslaved—were more likely to survive if they had some utilitarian value. Although the identity of the person who made an elegant coiled-snake trivet, from the Robson collection, has been lost to time, its style and subject offer possible insights into its past (**CAT. 21**). Two important exhibitions organized by UCLA's Fowler Museum—*Sacred Arts of Haitian Vodou* (1995) and *Striking Iron: The Art of African Blacksmiths* (2018)—showed blacksmithing's deep and rich history in Africa and its diaspora. As the curatorial team of *Striking Iron* explained: "In Africa south of the Sahara, iron figures prominently as a medium that activates spiritual power. The blacksmith—as master of the transformative processes of making iron into culture's tools, weapons, and poetic accoutrements—is often charged with making the very objects used to invoke, represent, and mediate deities and other mediums of supernatural agency. He is called upon to enhance humanity's ability to survive and thrive."[5]

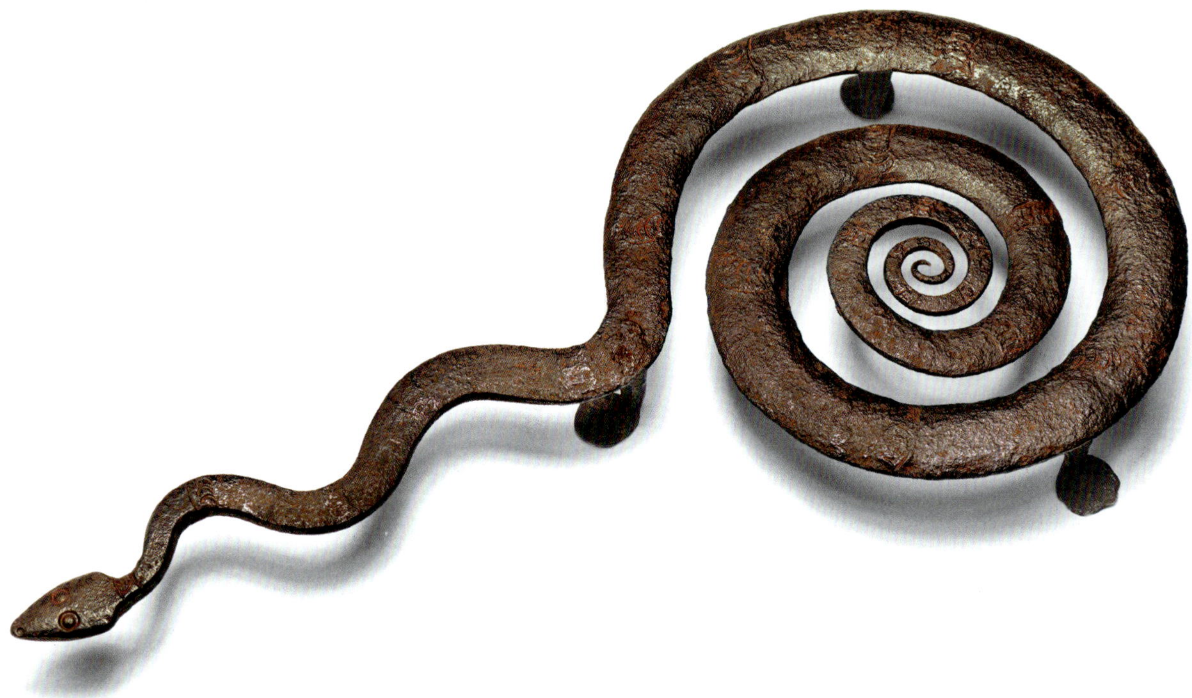

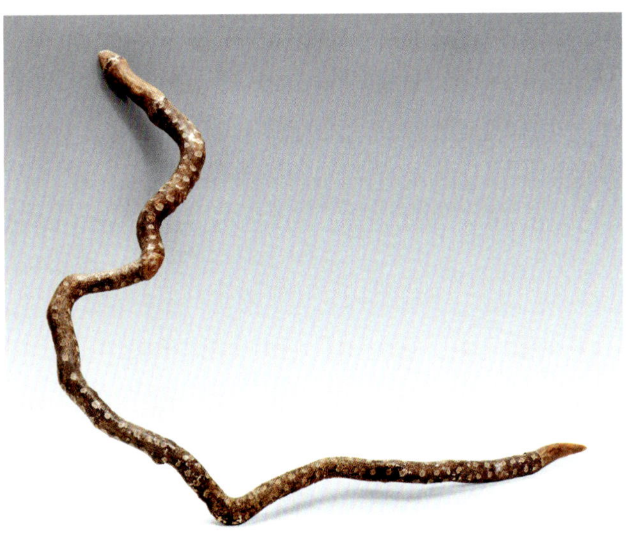

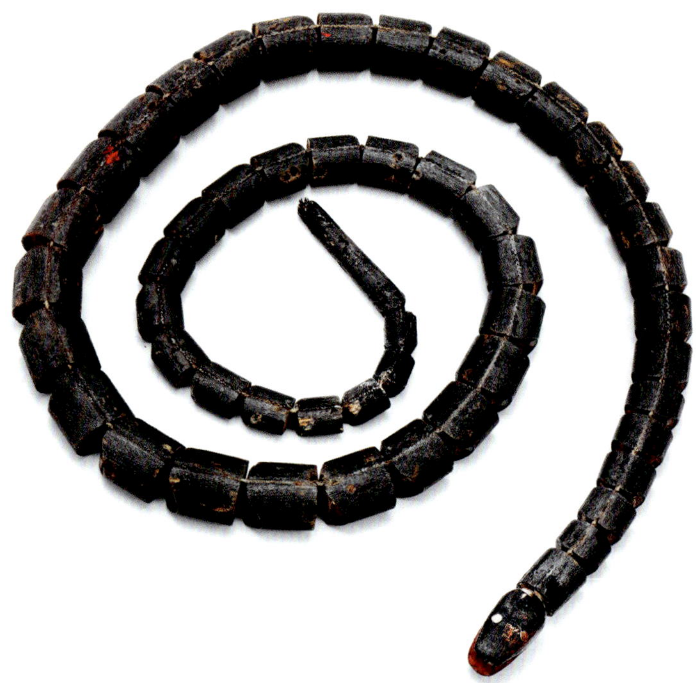

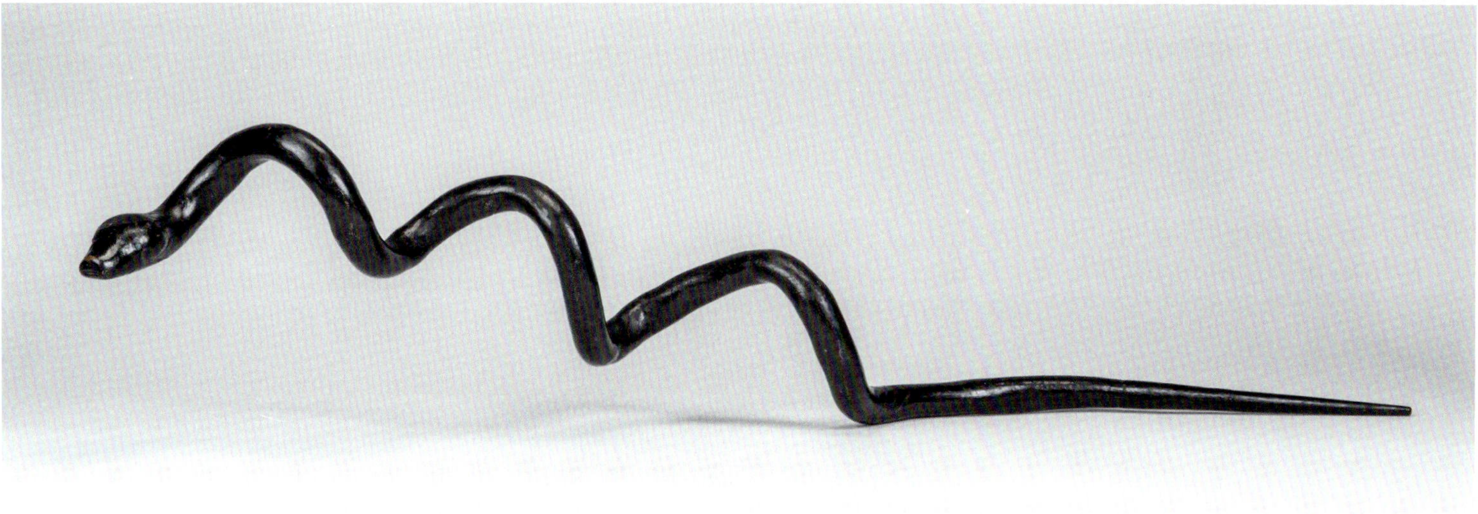

CAT. 21.
Unidentified artist
Untitled (Snake Trivet)
late 19th or early 20th century

CAT. 22.
Unidentified artist
Untitled (Root Snake)
20th century

CAT. 23.
Unidentified artist
Untitled (Articulated Snake)
20th century

CAT. 24.
Unidentified artist
Untitled (Snake)
20th century

While it is uncertain whether the maker of the snake trivet was African American, blacksmithing remained a prominent trade skill for Black makers in the United States, both before Emancipation and after, and the symbolism embodied in both the material and act of shaping it lends credence to this possibility. From Africa to Haiti to the American South, snakes are powerful characters in belief and lore, from the Haitian *loa* Damballa—the creator of life—to prominent characters in southern folklore and conjure culture, where a coiled snake in spring was a portent of ill fate.[6] Snakes abound in both folklore and in rural arts, from canes to articulated toys to sculptures inspired by the gnarled tree roots they often evoke. Snakes are ubiquitous throughout rural America, but in the South, where venomous varieties are more common and particularly in earlier times when snakebites were more perilous than in modern society, the fear these reptiles evoked was both real and symbolic—the fate that awaited unseen in the grass (**CATS. 22–24**). The elegantly coiled snake comprising the sturdy trivet might have been designed for the neat way the animal's form could support a hot pan, but also possible is that the coiled form—ready to bolt or strike—passed a wordless hex from maker to user.[7]

Another intriguing piece from the Robson collection reveals a more common form of African American artistry from the late nineteenth or early twentieth century, an inlaid memory jug (**CAT. 25**). Arts and crafts dedicated to preserving personal and familial memories spiked in popular practice in the late nineteenth and early twentieth centuries and were common parlor pastimes for homemakers. But the crafts practiced by the well-to-do generally reflected their status, from fine floss and fabrics in crazy quilts and embroidery to upscale mementos in memory jugs and the like—items in which keepsakes cohere into a memorial object.[8]

In African American practice, memory work reflected something very different. For centuries, enslaved African Americans practiced discreet forms of creative and cultural customs that, in various ways, retained their cultural identity in a country that was not their chosen home. Discretion was a means of spiritual survival, as white supremacists aimed to extinguish bonds to Africa that might unite the enslaved. The graveyard was a place where memorial traditions were more tolerated; objects made or placed there had a better chance at survival. Robert Farris Thompson has charted the ways in which Kongo-Angola traditions that survived in America included graves embellished with the last-used belongings of the deceased, as such items might be "charged with emanations, traces of the spirit."[9] On tombs, charms act as both memento and sacred medicine, using decorative or useful fragments of the material world to remember the deceased on earth, and to guide and honor the spirit. Shells and glass bottles were important memorial objects as well—small interworld spaces wherein the soul's immortal presence could linger and dwell.

Anyone who has kept a keepsake for the potency of its memories knows the transporting power objects can hold. After the Civil War and into the twentieth century, memory jugs survived as a means of remembrance. Such personal works were not valued as art objects, and the identities of the makers usually became detached from the item, leaving the circumstances behind the creation of individual memory jugs to be gleaned by future beholders. But the profusion of mementos encrusted onto crockery conveys vestigial messages about the beliefs and customs of their makers, and the stoneware memory jug from the Robson collection offers the history of a life through more than 275 objects pressed into its claylike outer layer: bone, buttons, stones, shells, doll fragments, beads, tiny glass bottles, a miniature skillet, a tooth (extracted by its roots), a thimble, a crab claw, a glass eye, a metal file, broken pieces of ceramic, an Aunt Jemima button, and more.

Much of the material culture predating the early twentieth century—from items rooted in trades and utility to domestic crafts and decorative or commemorative objects—is still recorded as being by "Anonymous," as if the maker had chosen to have their identity hidden or forgotten. It is more accurate to say that the identities of such makers were once known, known to those who cared about them—but lost long before any collector, preservationist, or historian took an interest. What is also embodied in terms like "anonymous" is a marked distinction between creative makers from poor or working-class communities and their affluent counterparts, for whom records were invariably better kept. Art or material goods made for personal use or the home, particularly those made by women, were not valued as "art," and in the case of "folk artists" whose names successfully remained attached to their artworks, almost all were white and male painters or sculptors.

CAT. 25.
Unidentified artist
Untitled (Memory Jug)
ca. 1890–1920

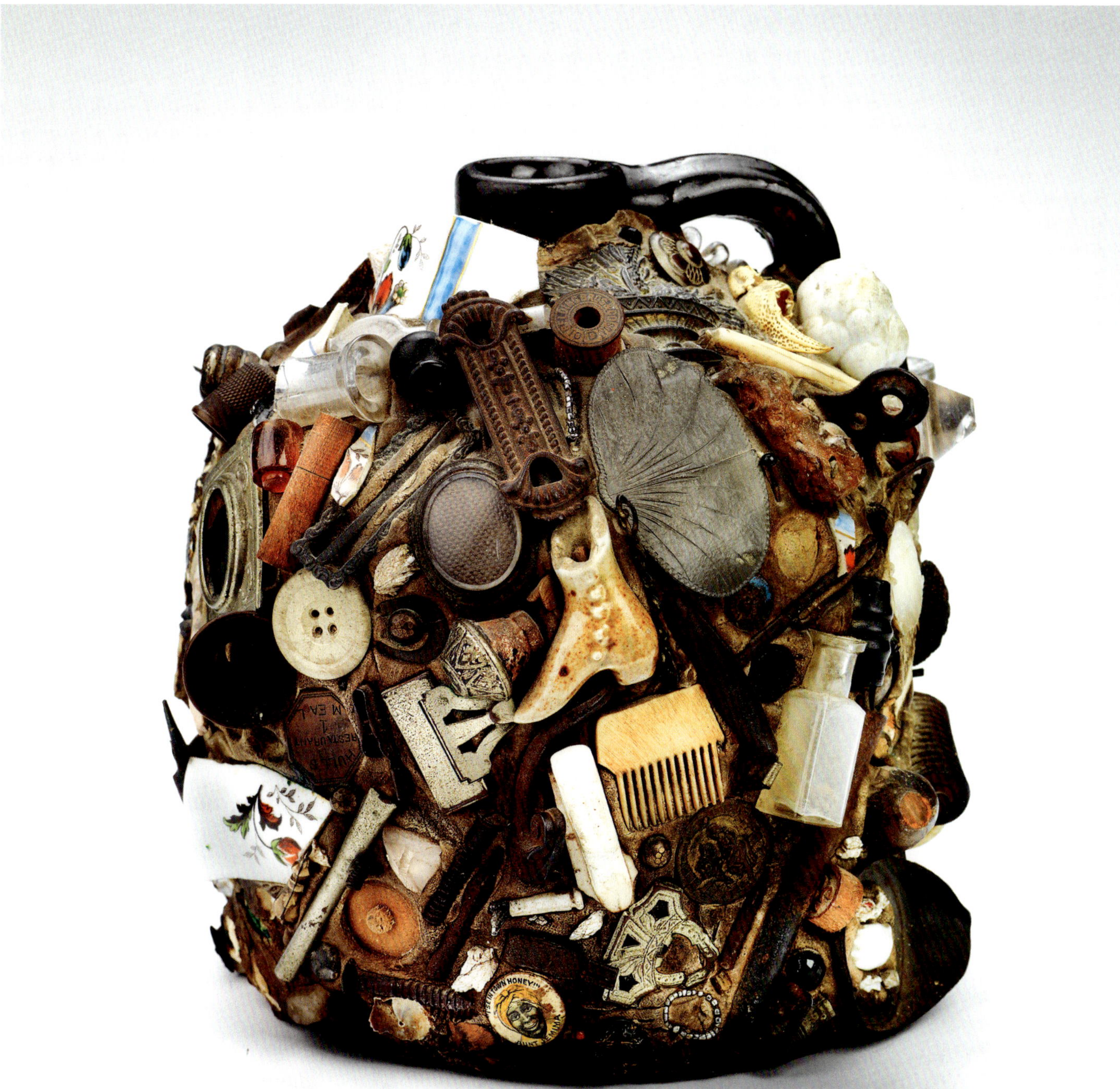

BILL TRAYLOR (ca. 1853–1949) / WILLIAM EDMONDSON (1874–1951)

As noted, enslaved Black people practiced covert forms of creative and cultural practices and activities —spirituality, dance, commemoration and grave-marking, hairstyles, foodways, and more—from their first arrivals in the Americas. But it was not until after Emancipation that African Americans were able to express themselves more openly and apart from creative skills in the employ of a trade. Still the process was slow and set back profoundly by the backlash of Reconstruction, which would define the early and mid-twentieth century. It was during this later, equally if not even more perilous era that another keystone American artist lived and worked, **BILL TRAYLOR** (Fig. 3). Traylor was born about fifty years after Dave Drake, around 1853 in rural Alabama, where he remained most of his life. Like Drake, Traylor was born enslaved. But Traylor was still a child when the Civil War ended and Emancipation was formally enacted, making the foundation of Traylor's life and time dramatically different than Drake's.

Being emancipated did not mean an easy or even truly free life. Whereas Drake learned and honed a valuable skill while enslaved, Traylor's field-laboring family had limited choices. Their mobility was hampered by a lack of formal education, financial dependence on the family that had enslaved them, and the oppressive culture of Alabama, where white landowners united to maintain their labor force via tactics spanning paid employment and free housing to intimidation and retribution for those who considered leaving. When the legal institution of slavery ended in 1865, empowered whites devised alternative systems for thwarting African American agency in insidious ways. Although Traylor would witness radical change for African Americans over the course of his lifetime, the experience in real time was arduously slow, and the personal rewards, for him, were few.

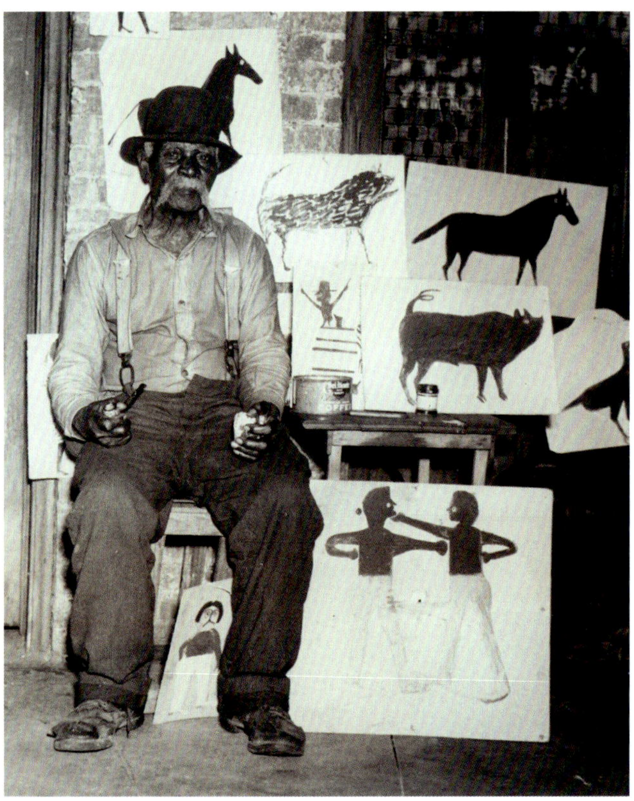

Fig. 3. Bill Traylor, June 1940, unidentified photographer, ACME Newspaper Inc. Courtesy of Judy A. Saslow

In the late 1920s, following the death of Traylor's third wife and the northward and eastward migrations of most of his children, and when the physical strain of farmwork became more than he could manage, he moved into the Alabama capital of Montgomery. For some years, Traylor supported himself with lighter work and occupied a rented room. In his final decade, he relied on the support of people in the segregated Monroe Street Black Business District, where he began to create a visual record of his experience. His drawings and paintings employed graphic ingenuity and poetic radicalism to describe moments spanning the banal and horrifying. He depicted racial hierarchy through armed overseers and barefoot workers, and used animals to mirror human character and the dynamics of power. He captured moments of levity: drinking, dancing, diving in the river. And he recorded the violence that saturated his world: people being clubbed, hunted like prey, or hanging from the trees. Without art-world suggestion or influence, Traylor pictured his community in optimistic, urban, and upward scenes, a world apart from the inhumane plantation experience: African Americans finely dressed in patterned prints and power-radiating colors, shopping, walking with children or pets, carrying books, preaching, arguing—living, but not working.[10]

As a former slave, hobbled by age and decades of hardship, Traylor was not valued by his society, and, for the most part, neither were his pictures. It is thanks to a small group of progressive white artists, who met Traylor in Montgomery and saved his artwork between 1939 and 1942, that Traylor is known to us at all.[11] He did not live to see his project regarded as anything important, but he decided to tell his own story, in his own way, at a time and in a place when any perceived critique of white society or the subtlest of insubordinations could have cost him his life. He ultimately made more than a thousand artworks describing a lifetime that spanned slavery, the Civil War, Emancipation, Reconstruction, and the long, brutal aftermath of Jim Crow segregation.

Traylor glimpsed the dawn of a rising Black culture in the urban hub of Montgomery, something Drake did not live to see. Although Traylor never learned to read or write in conventional English, he had the visual literacy of a master. He understood that just as the white man's written pages were opaque for him, the pictorial language he knew would be illegible to white culture—but not to his own. In his chase scenes, such as an untitled work in SAAM's collection (Fig. 4), he encoded the story with subtle markers of hierarchy: the chaser wears a hat and brings a hunting hound; the man fleeing is the sole figure painted in the color black—he runs with the rabbit, an African American folk symbol of the prey animal that survives by being smart and fleet of foot. The black/Black figure and rabbit move under the accompaniment of flying birds, symbolizing their quest for freedom. And in works like the iconic *Untitled (Seated Woman)* from the Robson collection, Traylor shows a Black figure comfortably at rest, arms akimbo and chin up, striking a pose of defiance and pride (**CAT. 26**).

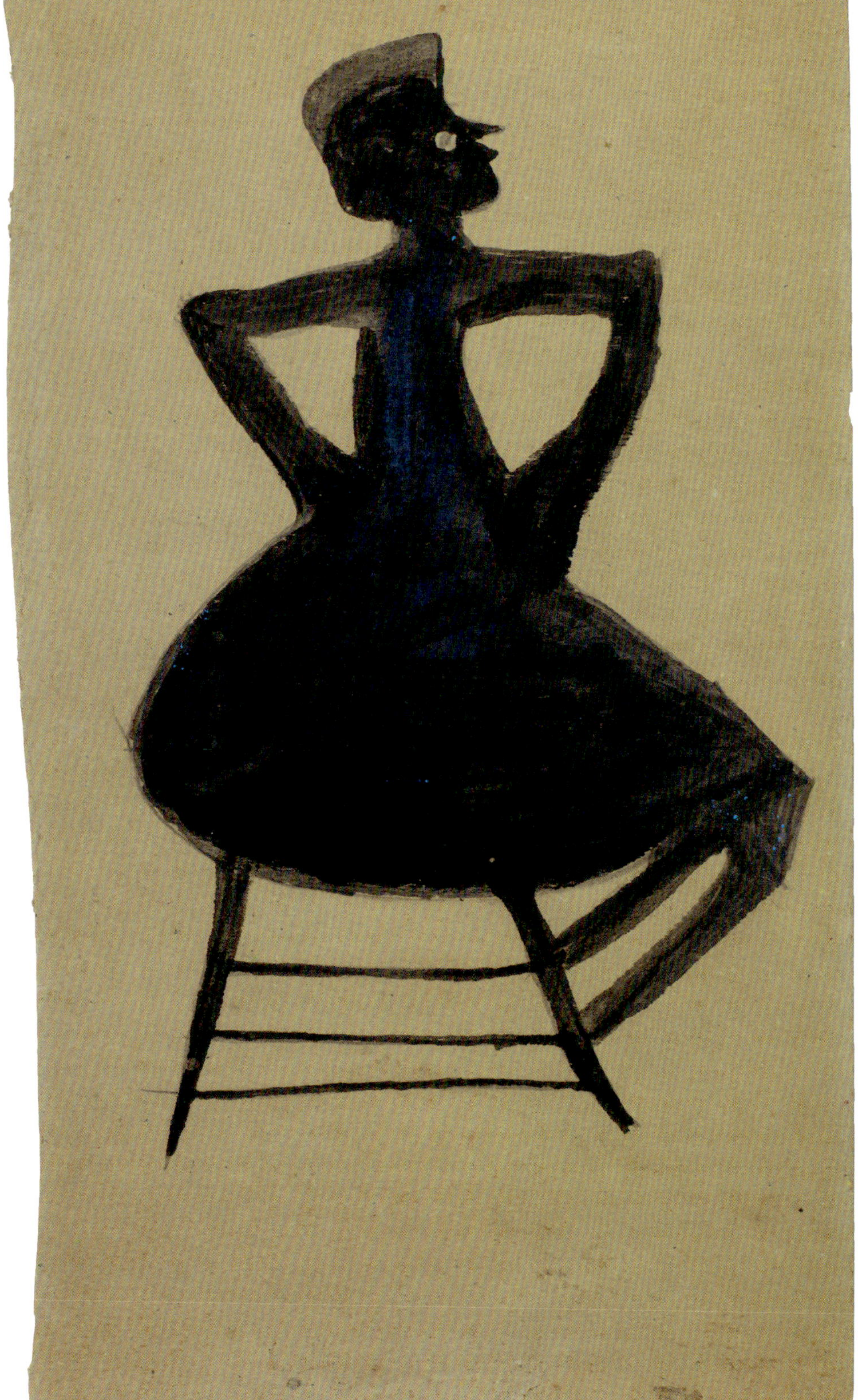

Fig. 4. Bill Traylor, *Untitled (Chase Scene)*, ca. 1940, pencil and opaque watercolor on paperboard, 7 × 13 ¼ in. Smithsonian American Art Museum, Gift of Micki Beth Stiller, 2015.25

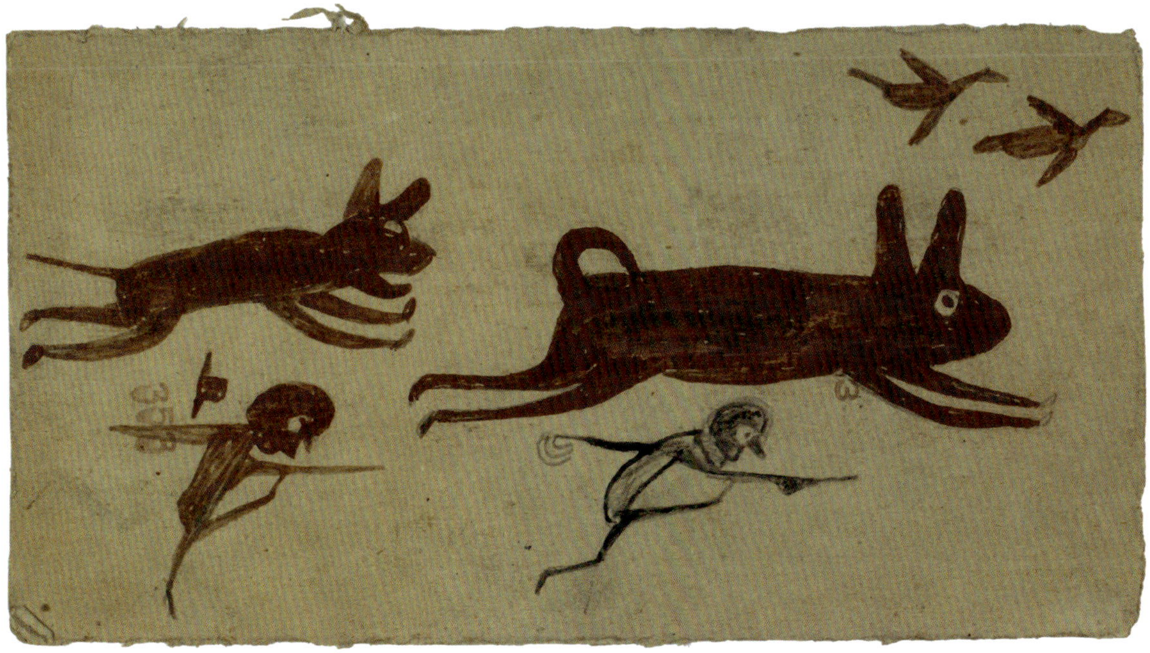

Fig. 5. Installation, *Black Folk Art in America, 1930–1980*, the 1982 exhibition organized by the Corcoran Gallery of Art, Washington, DC

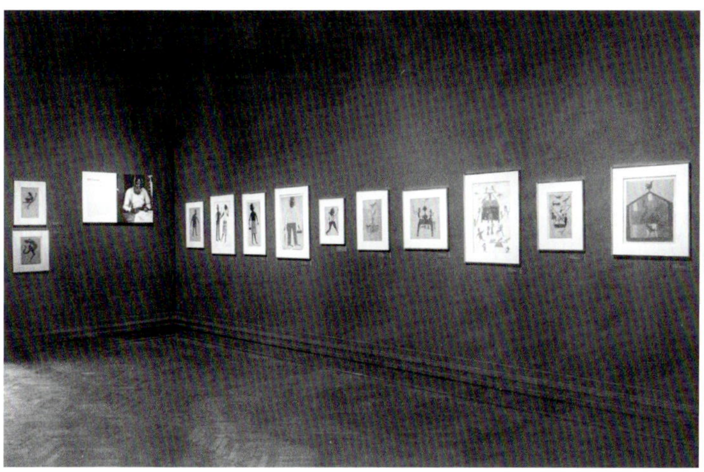

As art historian Grey Gundaker and others have explored, the white concept of literacy—who could read what in what way—can be overly reductive. "Institutionally backed Roman script literacy," she notes, undervalues vernacular visual and oral literacy, which fall outside of accepted scriptural practices but play equally important roles, particularly in situations where conventional literacy was suppressed.[12] Paradoxically, such myopic views may have played a role in why many of Traylor's images were saved and he escaped retribution for them. He was conventionally illiterate and perceived, in turn, as a person lacking wisdom and intellect. Traylor's artworks were presumed to be simplistic reflections of ignorance, instead of the layered and biting records they actually were. His deftness with images allowed Traylor to play with flexible narratives braided with metaphor, metonymy, and allegory—strategies that bestowed a safeguarding veneer onto subversive imagery that alternately asserted cultural pride and revealed deep-seated rage. Almost a hundred years after Dave Drake was inscribing his vessels, conventional literacy and personal agency for Blacks were still hot-button issues in the American South; individualized expression like Traylor's, if read clearly for the ways in which it poked at a racially fraught past, would have been unequivocally dangerous. Traylor's subordinated life meant he understood how to navigate a white-ruled world. Since his private thoughts and views, if openly expressed, would imperil him, he largely kept them hidden. He may not have conceptualized being an artist in a predetermined or conventional way, but Traylor's choice to bear witness and represent the people of his community in the midcentury

CAT. 26.
Bill Traylor
Untitled
(Seated Woman)
ca. 1940–42

CAT. 27.
Bill Traylor
Untitled (Man in Blue and Brown)
ca. 1940–42

CAT. 28.
Bill Traylor
Untitled (Drinker in Chair)
ca. 1939–42

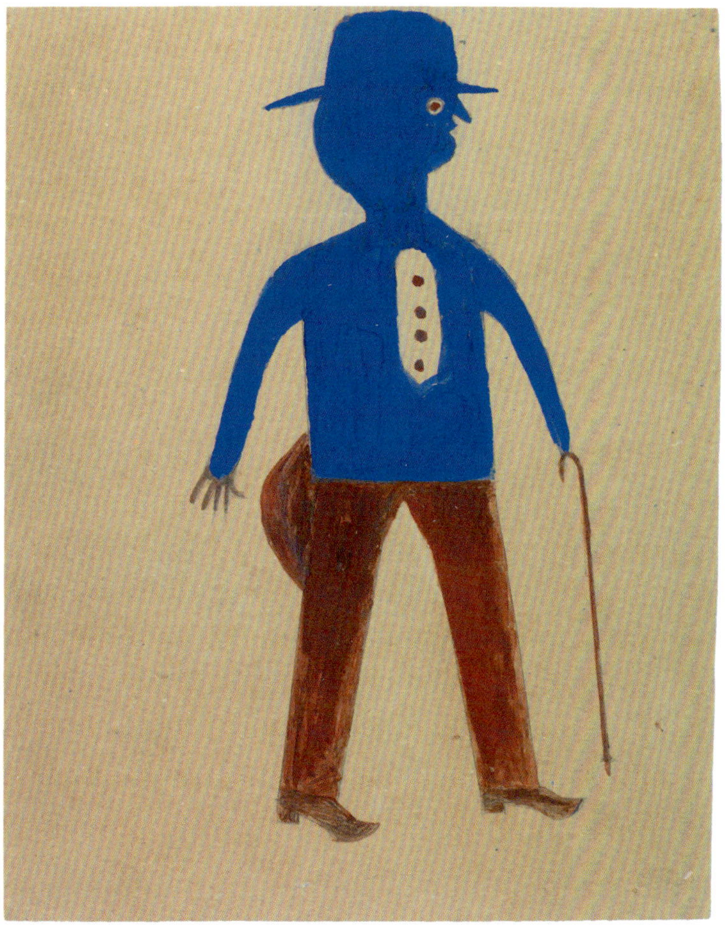

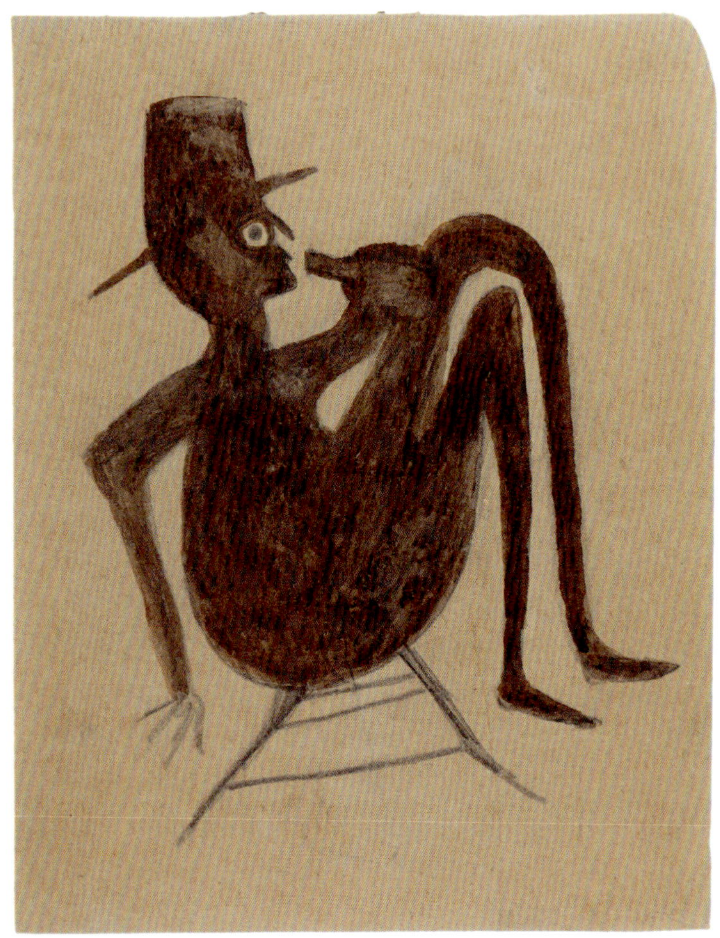

CAT. 29.
Bill Traylor
Untitled (Spotted Cat with Two Eyes)
ca. 1939–42

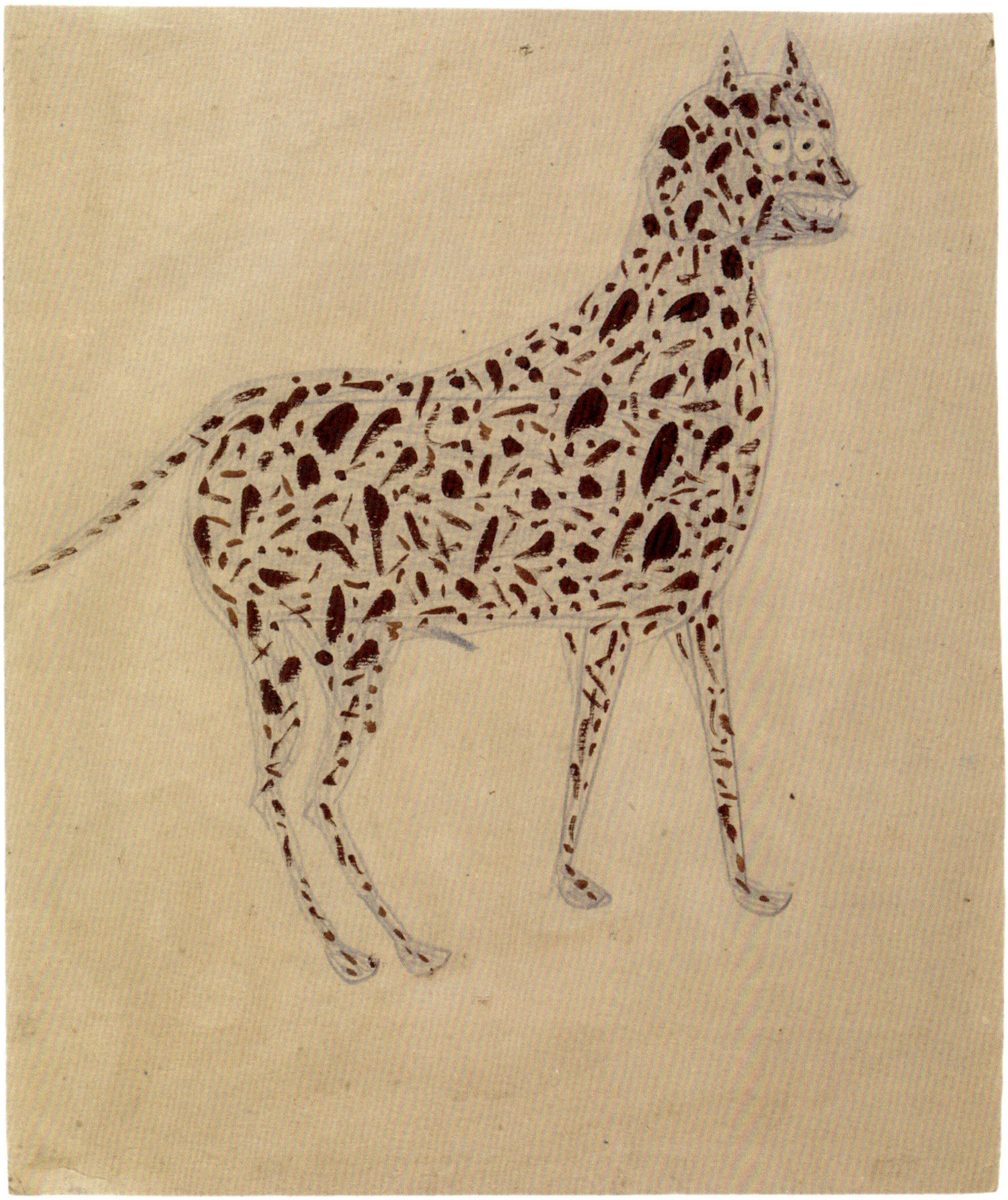

heartland of Jim Crow marks a crucial juncture—a point at which autonomous Black American makers begin to openly shape expressive practices that were not handed-down traditions or utilitarian crafts, but entirely their own (**CATS. 27–30**).

As the only formerly enslaved Black artist known to have made a body of images pertaining to his time and place, Traylor's body of work is both unique and pivotal. His extant work, made between 1939 and 1942, would not gain widespread appreciation until he was prominently featured in the Corcoran show *Black Folk Art in America*, thirty-three years after his death (Fig. 5). But Traylor's determination to stake a claim and refute invisibility foreshadowed a surge in African American vernacular creativity and identity reclamation. Traylor's worldview was grounded in extreme oppression, a critical distinction from trade-based artisan work, communal modes, and the visual expressions of European American self-taught artists. *Black Folk Art in America* may have imprecisely framed Traylor's practice as "folk art," but as noted above, the exhibition revealed the coming wave of self-taught African American artists who determined to make themselves visible as self-directed creative individuals—whose roots were in another world but who, as American citizens, refused to have their aesthetics or beliefs defined by others. This concept of being visible—as an act of resistance and self-determination—of declaring selfhood and cultural connectivity in this land became increasingly manifested in the yards and homes of African Americans, from quiet details in homemaking to bold arrays of remaking personal worlds. With the generations after Traylor's—the progeny of the enslaved—this phenomenon would move further out of the shadows and demand attention.

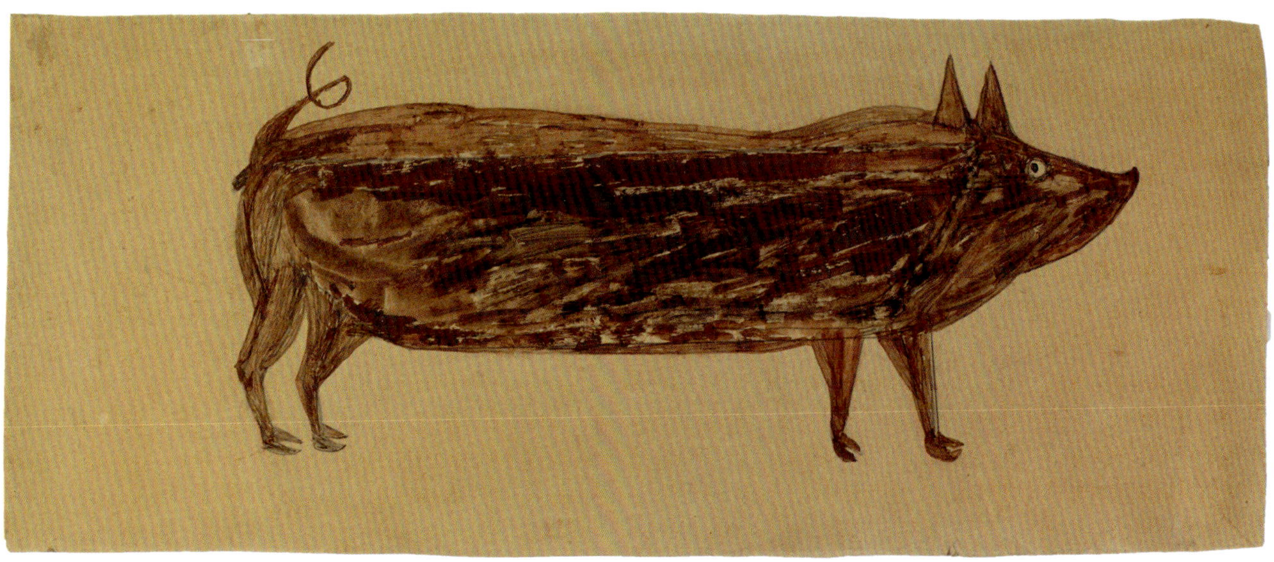

CAT. 30.
Bill Traylor
Untitled (Brown Pig)
April 1940

Fig. 6. Louise Dahl-Wolfe, *William Edmondson, Sculptor, Nashville*, 1937, gelatin silver print, 9 ½ × 8 ⅜ in. Collection Center for Creative Photography

Fig. 7. William Edmondson, *Crucifixion*, ca. 1932–37, limestone, 18 ⅛ × 11/6 ⅛ in. Smithsonian American Art Museum, Gift of Elizabeth Gibbons-Hanson, 1981.141

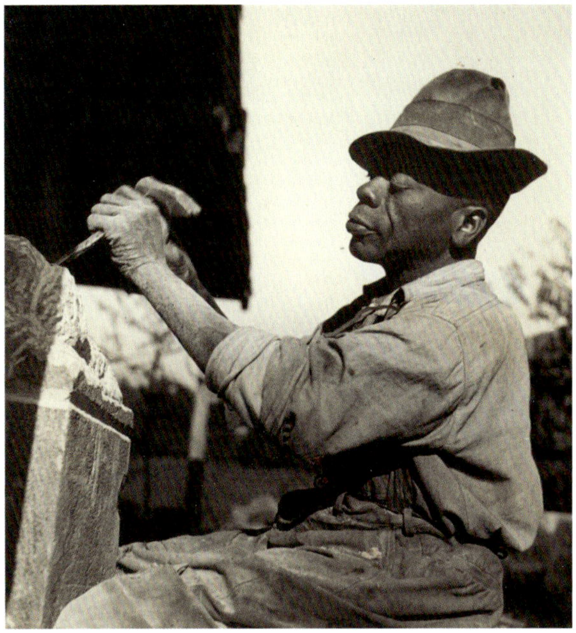

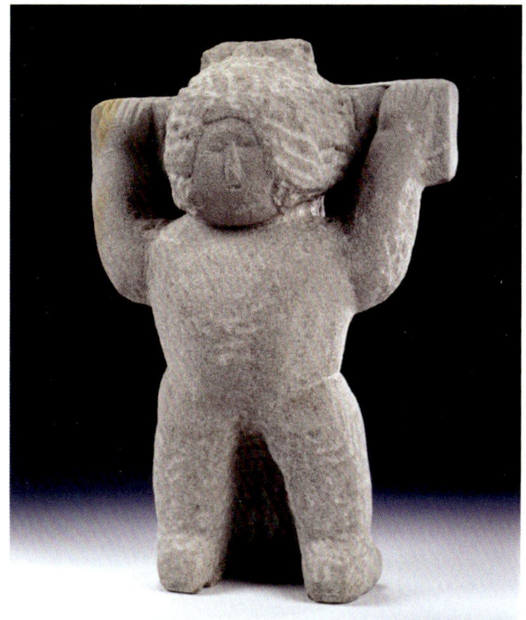

Born in 1874 on a plantation near Nashville, Tennessee, where his father had been enslaved and not far from where his mother had been, **WILLIAM EDMONDSON** became the earliest born of this next generation to make a name for himself via his art (Fig. 6). Edmondson was recognized by the art world a bit ahead of his forefather Bill Traylor, when, as noted earlier, he became the first person of African descent—trained or untrained—to feature in a solo exhibition at New York's Museum of Modern Art (MoMA). After his father died around 1889, Edmondson's mother moved him and his siblings into Nashville. Edmondson never married and continued to live in that house, with his mother and an unmarried sister. Between the mid-1920s and mid-1930s, Edmondson experienced a series of hardships that collectively had a profound impact. He suffered the loss of his mother in 1924, and just a few years later his brother died as well. Financial strain related to the relocation of the hospital he worked at and the larger machinations of the Great Depression added further burdens in an already hard time.[13]

Edmondson held a variety of jobs, but, after an injury working the rail lines, he sought lighter and more stationary work, and it was likely during a subsequent stint working for a stonemason that he found his calling, starting his own stonecutting business around 1932.[14] Limestone was native to the region and plentiful enough to be used even for roadside fencing. As Edmondson's physical strength deteriorated, he was increasingly confined to work he could conduct from home; he gathered discarded pieces from streets and fields and made tombstones and yard ornaments to sell.

CAT. 31.
William Edmondson
Untitled (Bird Bath with Figures), two views
ca. 1932–40

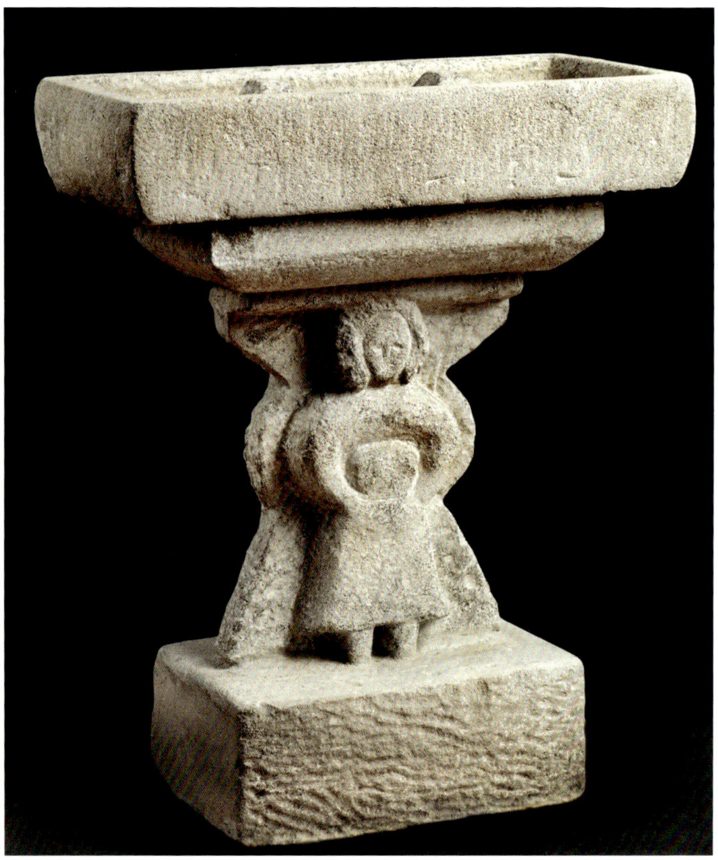

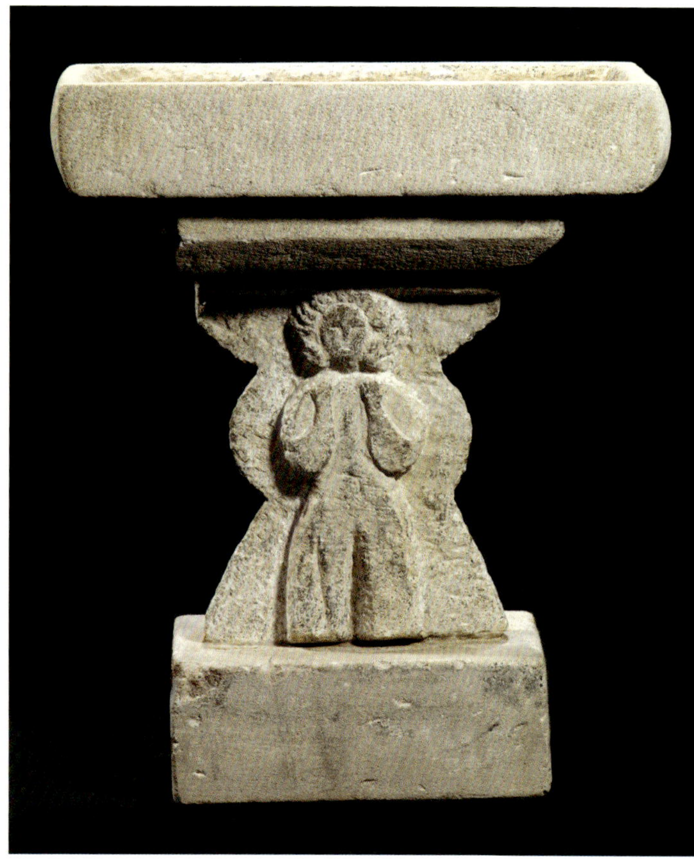

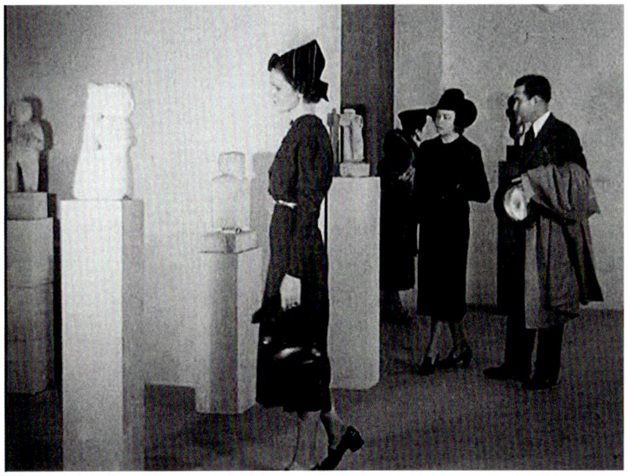

Fig. 8. Installation view of *Sculpture by William Edmondson*, presented at the Museum of Modern Art in New York, 1937; film still from *New York*, Pathé Gazette, December 20, 1937

When his endeavor became better known, community members brought remnants of limestone for him to use. Edmondson lacked proper masonry tools but learned to carve and shape rectangular and three-dimensional forms, as well as relief patterns and words, using a plain hammer and railroad spikes. His skill grew organically, from rudimentary inscribed grave markers to elegant birdbaths and animal forms (**CATS. 31, 32**). He made spiritual works—crucifixes (Fig. 7), angels, and what Robert Farris Thompson has called "birds of the Holy Ghost." Considering Edmondson's many birds, Thompson explains, "His two doves suggest the story of Noah's Ark, while his numerous single birds suggest the dove that descended during the time that Jesus was baptized by John the Baptist."[15] But mourning doves are also associated with sadness and loss for the haunting cooing sound they make, and Edmondson may have seen them as symbolically appropriate to the grave markers he made. His figural works are often his most poignant, tributes to everyday heroes, including teachers in the African American community, signaled through the books they carried (**CAT. 33**).

Curator Edward M. Puchner notes that, in 1934, Edmondson experienced evangelical conversion, which included spiritual visions that redirected his identity to being that of a man aligned with God. "Conversion transformed past suffering into active resistance to an oppressive and difficult society. These benefits were no less true for Edmondson, who turned to the church at a time of hardship, loss, and transition." Puchner contends that, for Edmondson, stone carving metaphorically enacted the freeing of one's soul from the threat of damnation, and that whether his subjects appeared religious or secular in their subject matter, they comprehensively emerged from the sermons of the Black church, and symbolize issues of morality, redemptive suffering, and civil protest.[16]

In 1935, Sidney Mttron Hirsch, a faculty member at the George Peabody College for Teachers, noticed Edmondson's carving-filled yard. He brought students and artist friends, including Louise Dahl-Wolfe, a fashion photographer at *Harper's Bazaar*. Her magazine declined to publish her photographs of an African American and his work. Thomas Mabry Jr., a Clarksville, Tennessee, native then serving as executive secretary at MoMA, connected Dahl-Wolfe with his museum's director, Alfred Barr, who took an interest.[17] Barr, capitalizing on a growing American interest in what many were calling "primitive and folk art," subsequently organized the small, ten-piece exhibition *Sculpture by William Edmondson* in 1937 (Fig. 8).

Edmondson attributed his work to divine guidance, eschewing personal vision or credit for what he made. Throughout the Jim Crow era, Nashville's white press indoctrinated the

CAT. 32.

William Edmondson

Untitled (Bird)

ca. 1937

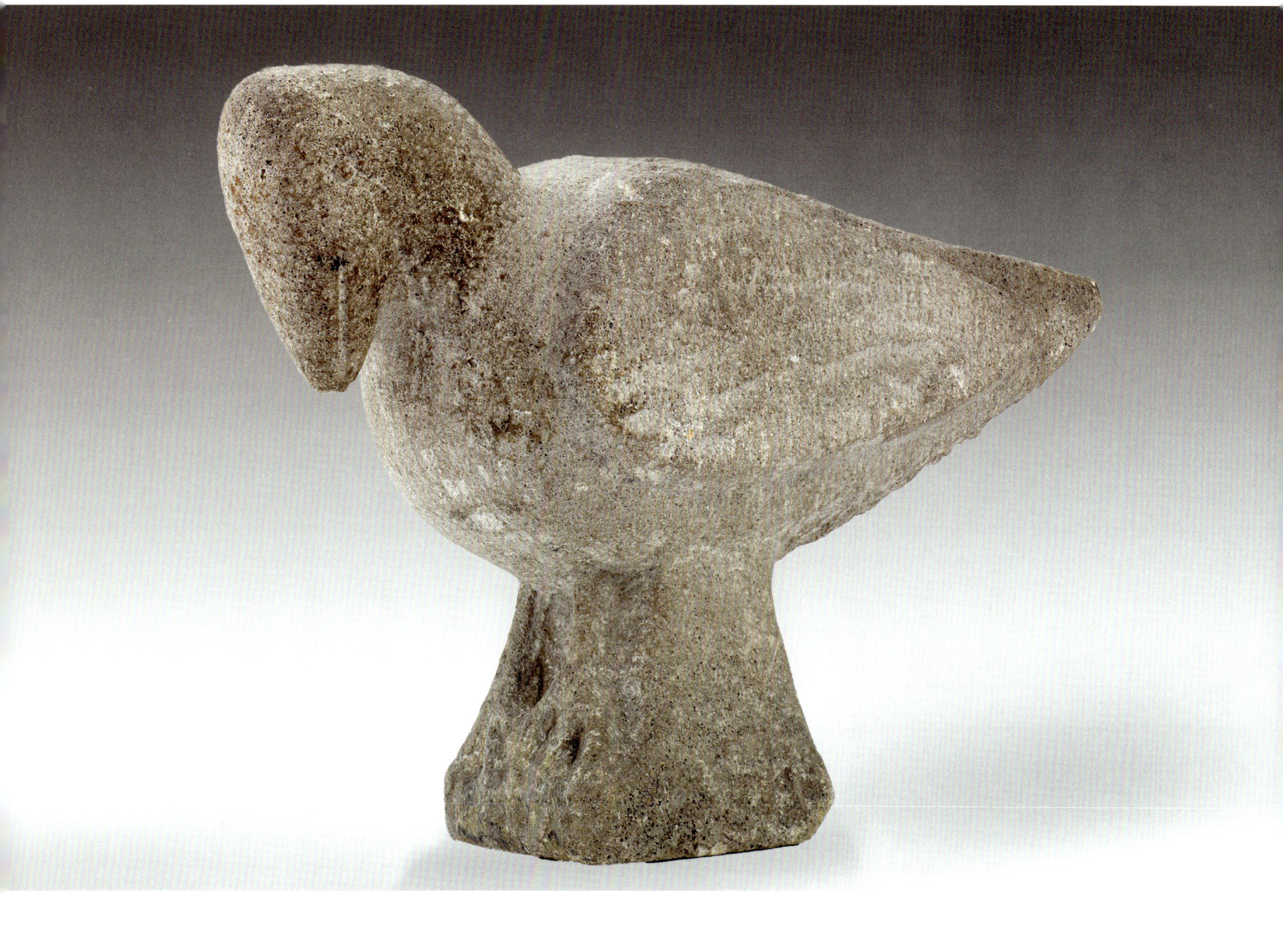

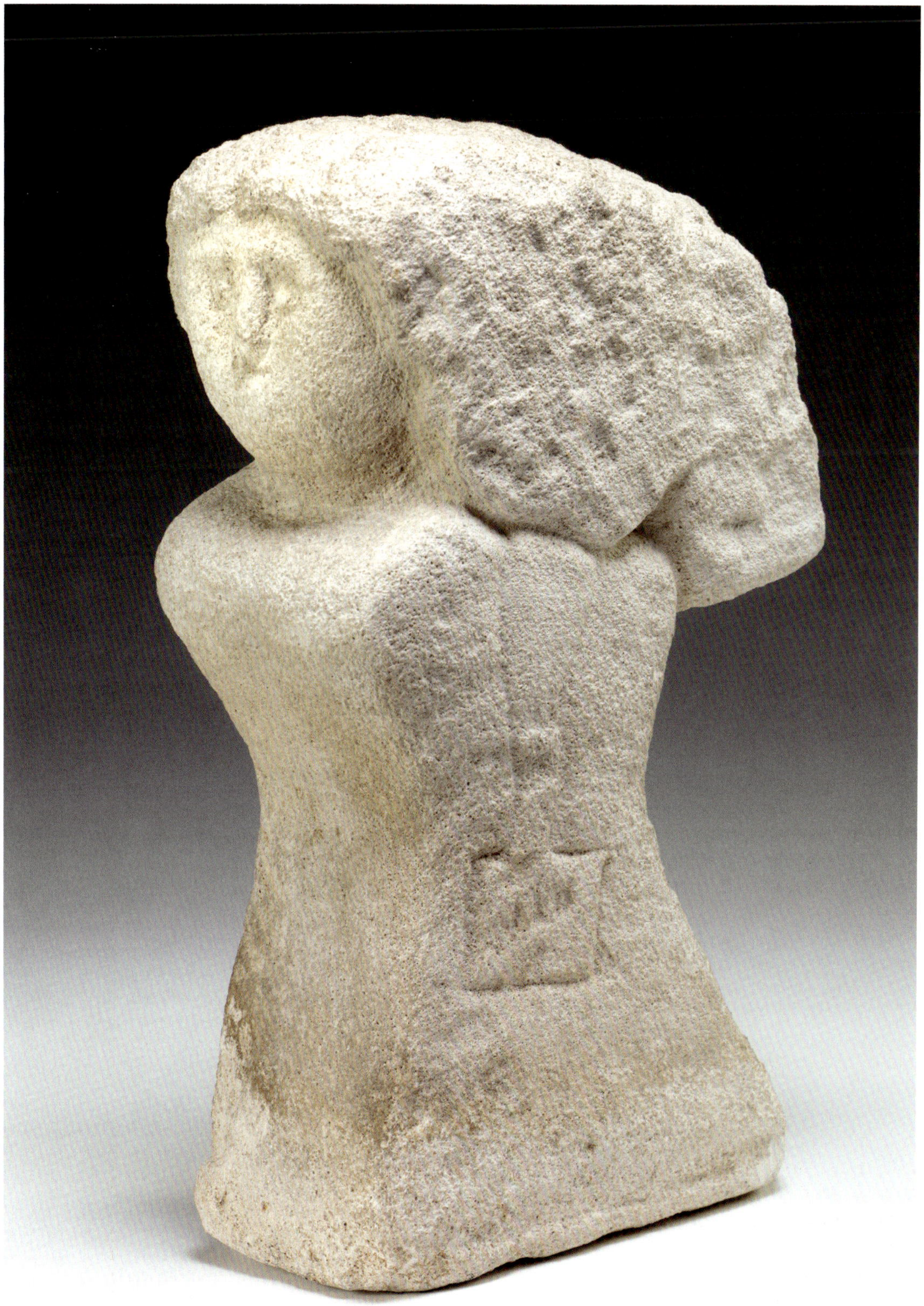

CAT. 33.
William Edmondson
Untitled (Teacher)
ca. 1932–40

community with beliefs that Blacks were inferior in all things social and cultural, so local attention being paid to Edmondson was frequently undergirded by the notion that his work was crude and unsophisticated, and astonishing just in terms of its very production. The backdrop of spirituality complicated the work for Black and white viewers alike. Many worried that Edmondson's "God-inspired art" hearkened to southern stereotypes of ignorant and superstitious African Americans—which white scholars and trained African American artists had different reasons for wanting to distance themselves from. This factor drove both interest and refutation of Edmondson's work, depending on the beholder's point of view. Recognized Black artists and scholars at Nashville's Fisk University, including Aaron Douglas and James Weldon Johnson, held Edmondson and his art at a remove, believing white interest in his work was simply a vehicle for framing Black artistic enterprise as unrefined, primitive, or only accidentally interesting.[18] Artist Romare Bearden and journalist Harry Henderson asserted that Edmondson's carvings were "impressive and attractive," but also that the artist's proclamations of spiritual visions reflected his understanding of "what people expected a black man to say," and played to a commercial interest in effectively dealing with white people.[19] Katherine Jentleson, however, has pointed out that important Black figures, such as Alain Locke and James A. Porter, supported Edmondson in various ways, even if that support sometimes reflected ambivalence.[20] John Michael Vlach, a white scholar specializing in folklore and African American folklife, offered important grounding information about Edmondson's work in the context of African American traditions of mourning, burial, and remembrance in the early 1990s.[21] Nevertheless, Puchner argues that, too often, scholars undervalued the complex factor of spirituality in Edmondson's work, preferring to sidestep the thorny issue of religion and favor instead its formal modernist appeal.[22]

Barr's response to Edmondson's inherently powerful work may indeed have been genuinely positive, but it is impossible to separate a formalist, aesthetic response from the accompanying romance of Edmondson's story and identity—which dovetailed perfectly with the mainstream white public's increasing nostalgia for a simple, racially hierarchical existence and thirst for art objects and images that seemed plain, simple, and pure. Whether Edmondson or another Black artist should have been the first to earn a solo show at MoMA is a conversation in itself, but it is fair to say that Edmondson was chosen for paradoxical reasons.

Although Edmondson was twenty-one years younger than Bill Traylor, Traylor preceded the younger man in death by only two years. Edmondson's work, heavily rooted in traditions of gravestone carving and spirituality, yet personalized in subject and style, hovers between folk and self-taught art to a far larger degree than that of Traylor, who departed more distinctly from communal skills to make a body of work based entirely in memories and experience. Still, the conjoined prominence of these two artists would dovetail with a surge in creative output in the African American community and blaze a very specific trail.

CLEMENTINE HUNTER (ca. 1886/7–1988) / DAVID BUTLER (1898–1997)

Clementine Hunter and David Butler were born in the waning years of the nineteenth century in Louisiana—a place as reluctant to let go of the antebellum era as any. **CLEMENTINE HUNTER**'s grandmother was enslaved but identified as Creole, as her father had Irish and Native American ancestry. She was born Clemence Reuben, at Hidden Hill Plantation, near Cloutierville, and briefly attended Catholic school as a girl. Around the turn of the century, Hunter's family moved to Melrose Plantation, in Natchitoches Parish, to work as sharecroppers (Fig. 9). Clementine's work on Melrose included hoeing rows for corn, picking cotton, and harvesting sugarcane. In the late 1920s, she moved from field work to cooking and cleaning in the Big House.

Joseph Henry made his family the third in a succession of Melrose owners in 1884, and, when he died, the estate passed to his son. John Hampton Henry and his wife, Cammie, undertook a major restoration of architectural structures on the property and expanded the Big House. They also moved historical log cabins from the area onto their land. When John died in 1918, Cammie maintained the agricultural work at Melrose, but also made it a retreat for visiting artists and writers. When Hunter, then in her fifties, found some paints left by one such artist, she began the work for which she is known today. As art historian Stacy Morgan notes, Hunter's life was "long on manual labor and short on formal education."[23] But Hunter was a keen observer of life, and she began painting stories she felt historians overlooked—primarily the labor, leisure, and spirituality of the Black community in central Louisiana's Cane River country.

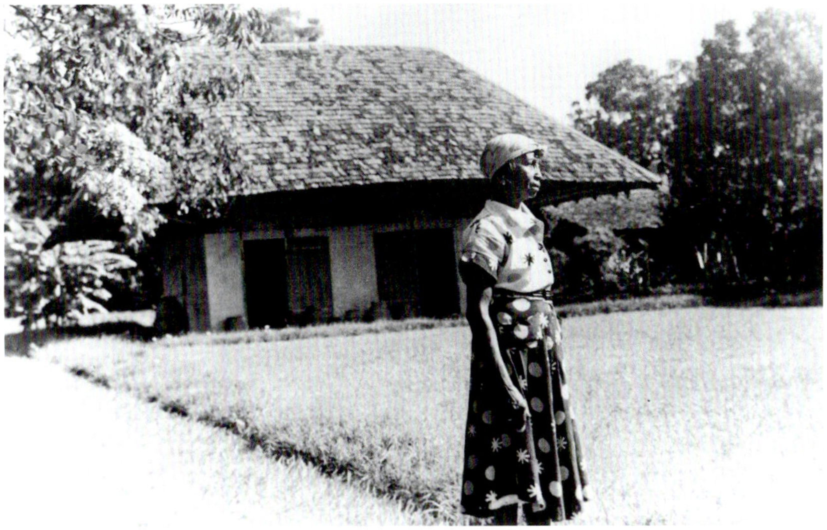

Fig. 9. Clementine Hunter at Melrose Plantation, outside African House, Natchitoches Parish, Louisiana; photograph by Carolyn Ramsey

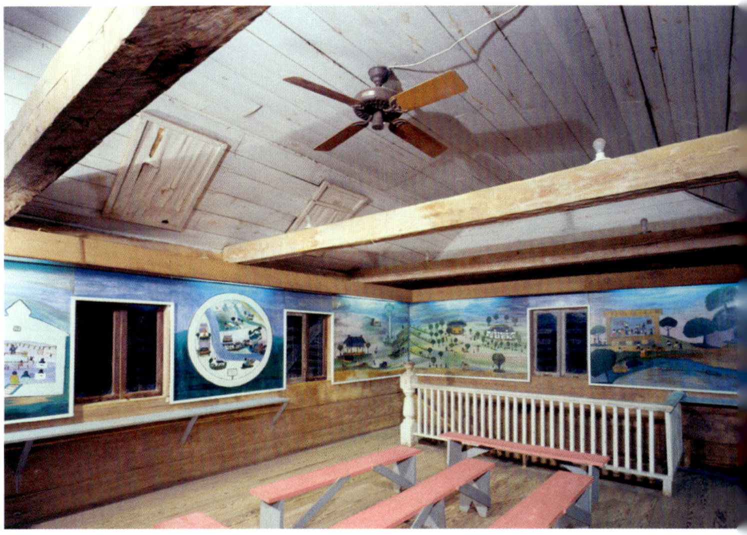

Fig. 10. Interior view of Clementine Hunter's murals at African House, Melrose Plantation, Natchitoches Parish, Louisiana. Library of Congress, Prints and Photographs Division

CAT. 34.

Clementine Hunter

Untitled (Magi Bearing Gifts)

ca. 1970–80

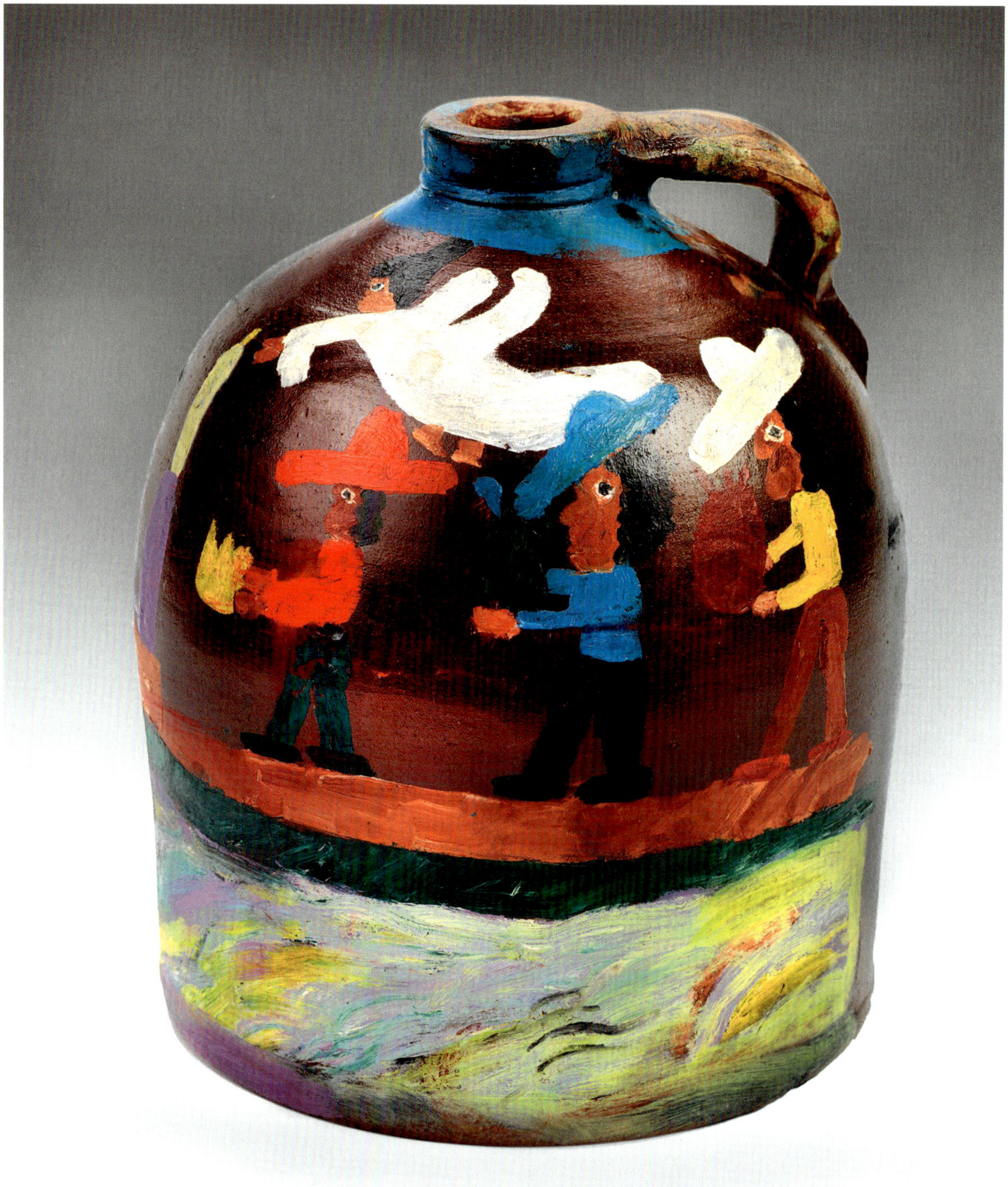

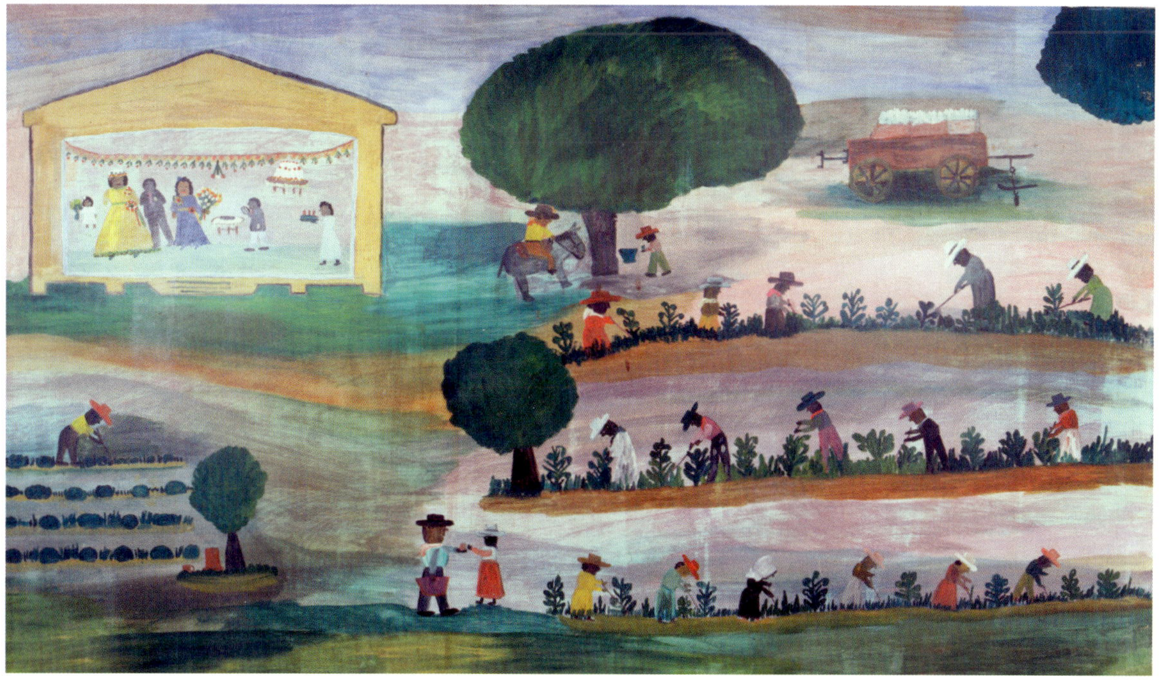

Fig. 11. Elevation view of Clementine Hunter's mural *Wedding*, at African House, Melrose Plantation, Natchitoches Parish, Louisiana. Library of Congress, Prints and Photographs Division

Stacy Morgan notes that Hunter was born and buried as a Catholic but felt the heavy pull of the Baptist Church for much of her adult life, carrying within her a multifaceted spiritual and ethnic identity that is clearly conveyed in her imagery. She made a number of pictorial quilts, which show in appliqué some of the notable buildings at Melrose, including the Big House, Yucca House, and the so-called African House.[24] Hunter painted variously on board, ceramic jugs, washboards, window shades, and other household items (**CAT. 34**). She became widely recognized, thanks in large part to François Mignon, a New York writer who came to Melrose in 1939, and then stayed on as a "permanent guest." Mignon helped Cammie Henry keep a history of Melrose and its guests, and after her death, he managed tours and entertainment for visitors, increasingly promoting Hunter and her work as central facets of the historic plantation.[25] Mignon lived at Melrose under what was later discovered to have been a false identity, but his understanding of Hunter's project and its importance was keen. Lee Kogan, a scholar and former curator at the American Folk Art Museum in New York, said of him, "Mignon's role in furthering Hunter's success cannot be overstated. A person of unusual ability, he created a fictitious identity for himself, a romanticized vision of Melrose, and an artistic persona for Hunter. This does not detract from her artistic talent and drive."[26]

Hunter was a prolific painter, making thousands of small works for sale. Among her most celebrated works, however, are nine room-size murals painted in 1955, inside the building called African House. By then, Hunter had been painting at Melrose for some fifteen years and had established an array of favored themes.[27] The murals show historical scenes of plantation life, including the planting of spring crops, a baptism, a wedding, wash day, harvest day, a honky-tonk—where adults play cards, drink, and dance—the pecan harvest, and a funeral (Figs. 10, 11). In the final panel, *The Last Surviving Slave, Uncle Israel Sudduth*, Hunter painted a scene in which yesterday's horse and buggy contrasts with an airplane and an automobile—the changing times. Throughout her body of work, Hunter's images reveal the omnipresent role of church in the southern Black community, the rich everydayness of life, the cycle of life that touches and unites every living thing, and the journey across earth and time toward the heavenly beyond.[28]

Coauthors Art Shiver and Tom Whitehead note that by midcentury, when Hunter was recalling these scenes from an earlier era, plantation life had changed dramatically. The Great Migration and the Second World War spurred change across the nation, from the movement of Black Americans out of the South—toward more lucrative work and freer and more self-affirming lifestyles—to the ways in which machines increasingly mitigated the massive labor force once needed to run plantations like Melrose. African American women were, notably, the predominant subjects in Hunter's work, and she portrayed them as strong, caring, capable people who give foundation to their entire community.

Hunter was born either late in 1886 or early in 1887, and lived for over a hundred years. Anna Mary Robertson Moses, better known as Grandma Moses, was born in 1860 and also lived to see more than a century of change in the United States. The two women also had in common their

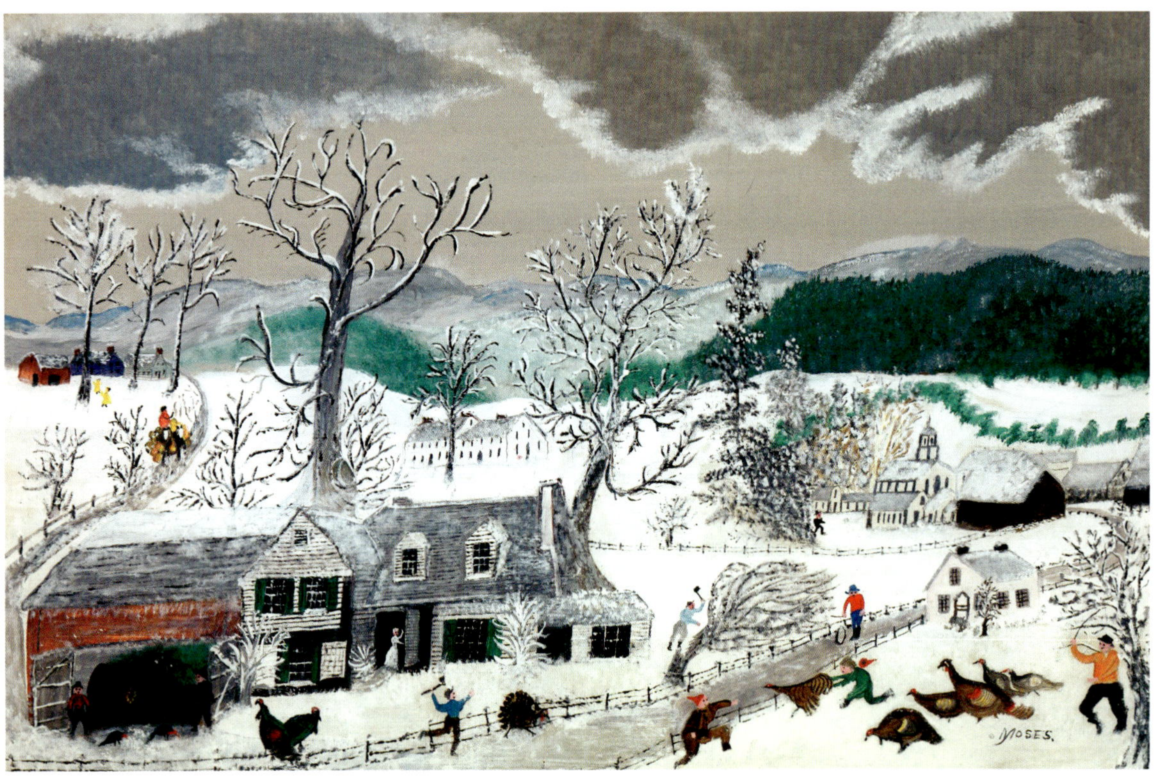

Fig. 12. Grandma Moses, *Turkeys*, 1958, oil on pressed wood, 16 × 24 in. Smithsonian American Art Museum, Gift of the Kallir Family in memory of Otto Kallir, 2017.34.1

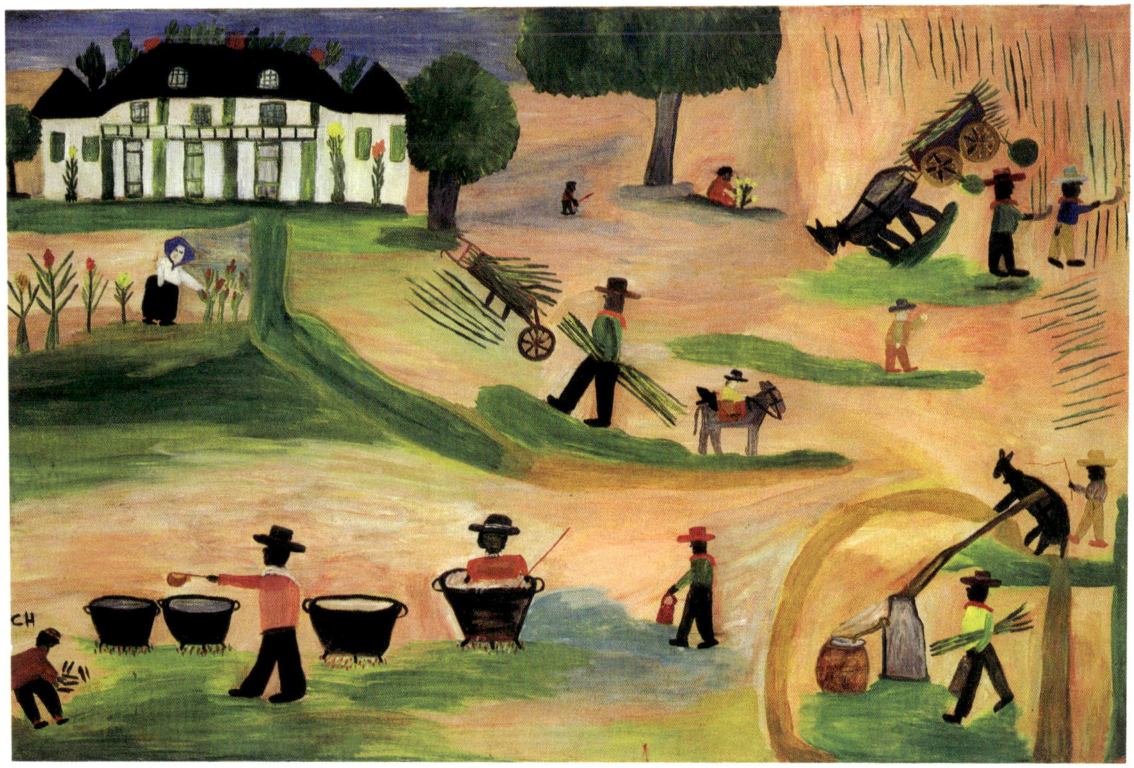

large bodies of painted "memory work" showing farm life, the incessant labor and communal centrality of women, and their personal recollections of seismic shifts over the course of their long lives. Beyond their notable commonalities, the paintings each woman made reveal different Americas. For Moses, it was rural life in Virginia and upstate New York, where work and life were hard—but the pursuit of happiness was unrestrained by racial oppression (Fig. 12). For Hunter it was life in the Deep South, on a large plantation that, even well after Emancipation and the creative environment that arose at Melrose, could not help but remain symbolically attached to a landscape of African American trauma and pain. As curator Alice Rae Yelen has noted, when artists like Hunter were growing up in the agrarian South, poverty was all they knew.[29] Black Americans dominate Hunter's scenes, in dramatic contrast to the memory work of white artists and, as Hunter had noted, too often the historians as well. Curator and art historian Elaine Y. Yau has observed that Hunter's depictions of Creole women in Louisiana, wearing tignon headscarves, evoke the complicated multicultural histories of the region but also indicate that Hunter identified with strong, historical Black women such as Marie Thérèse Métoyer (called Coincoin). Her son Louis Métoyer, the founder of Melrose, was among Coincoin's descendants, and the legendary matriarch looms large in the Cane River region. Coincoin was a freed slave in colonial Natchitoches who became a landholder, planter, entrepreneur, and slaveholder. Her status as both freedwoman and enslaver complicates her legacy, but Coincoin's endurance and independent success solidified her as an icon of female self-determination, and her personal agency likely informed Hunter's views on what was possible.[30]

Fig. 13. Clementine Hunter, *Sugar Plantation*, n.d., oil on academy board, 48 × 72 in. Courtesy of Ben and Jeanette Jaffe Family Collection

Although Hunter's imagery largely sidestepped overt social commentary, Yau and Yelen agree that, in her own way, Hunter put her views on record.[31] In the undated painting *Sugar Plantation*, Black laborers process sugarcane, work that includes cutting, hauling, and boiling the cane in huge cast-iron pots (Fig. 13). In one cauldron, an African American figure boils with the sugar—while the white woman near the Big House gathers flowers. In another painting, made in 1945, Hunter depicted a human-scale bronze statue that had been raised in the 1920s in Natchitoches, formally called *Uncle Jack* but better known as "Monument to the Good Darky," a name drawn from its inscription, which reads: "Erected by the City of Natchitoches in Grateful Recognition of the Arduous and Faithful Service of the Good Darkies of Louisiana. Donor, J. L. Bryan, 1927."[32] Journalist Nick Sacco has reproduced the text that was read aloud at the statue's dedication ceremony: "The faithful and devoted service rendered by the old Southern slaves, in working and making crops and taking care of the [white] women and children, while their masters were away for many years, fighting to keep them in slavery, has never been equaled."[33] The statue showed an African American man tipping his hat in a submissive pose—a racist memorial of the antebellum South. It became a symbol of bigotry in the civil rights era and in 1968 was pulled down by Black activists and thrown into a nearby river.[34]

Hunter's paintings reflect her personal experiences and memories as they intertwined with the history and changing circumstances of Melrose over time. When the plantation was sold and its contents—including a number of her artworks—were put up for auction in 1970, Hunter watched and subsequently made paintings in response to those events as well. In the last decade of her life, the agency and independence Hunter had long envisioned in her imagery was actualized, when the sales from her art enabled her to buy a house trailer and depict that place, humble but hers, as home.

DAVID BUTLER was a very different artist than Hunter but, like her, had a complex identity rooted in African American culture, regionally flavored with African folkways and beliefs (Fig. 14). Butler, and other African Americans across the South, blended Christian beliefs with folk practices to create spaces that felt self-determined and protective in a world that was often harsh and unpredictable. He was born in Good Hope, Louisiana, not far from New Orleans. His mother, a Baptist minister, instilled in him a dedication to scripture, spirituality, and tradition.[35] Also like Hunter, his life was long on manual labor and short on education, but a serious work injury when he was sixty-four caused him to live thereafter on disability benefits.

When his wife died six years later, in 1968, Butler bought a small house and tried to keep it cheerful and enlivened with a flower garden. But when the upkeep was more than he could manage, Butler began fashioning a garden of pounded, cut, and painted forms from roofing tin, often with articulated or spinning parts. The tiered layers and cutout shapes animated the array

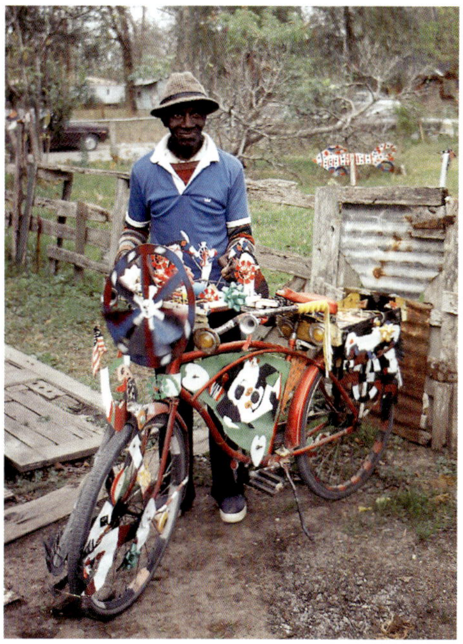

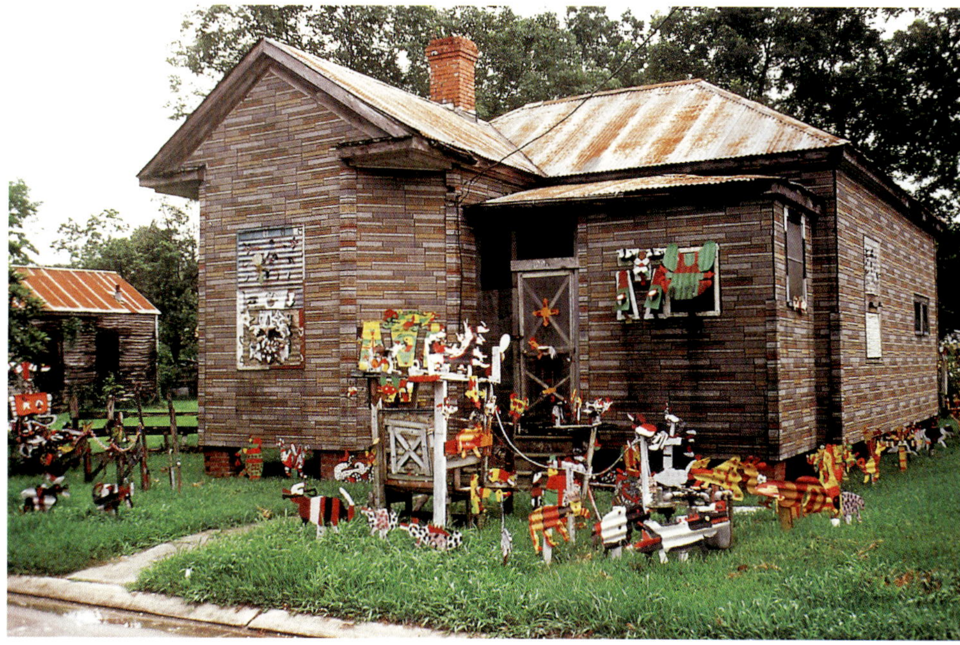

Fig. 14. David Butler with his bicycle, 1982; photograph by Richard Gasperi

Fig. 15. David Butler's house, Patterson, Louisiana, 1983; photograph by John Geldersma

as wind and sunlight toyed with his installation (Fig. 15). Butler built one of the premier examples of a "yard show": embellished homes and personal surroundings that honor the spirits and ancestors through symbolic shapes and colors, physical or visual motion, often using recycled objects that, through metaphor or metonymy, evoke relationships and flexible meanings across time and place.[36]

He added detail to his scenes and figures with bread ties, buttons, bike reflectors, ribbons, light bulbs, and other found objects. His sculptures fuse biblical imagery with characters from his dreams. Among his unique creations are window screens, panels of steel into which he cut scenes (**CATS. 35, 36**). As sunlight moved across Butler's yard, the cut patterns created a shadow puppet-like moving story inside his home. Richard Gasperi, a New Orleans art dealer who worked closely with Butler for many years, recalled: "[Especially] remarkable were the windows, which were covered with the 'screens,' as we called them. Inside, they made the house very dark, but the negative spaces appeared white and the positives very dark, with no colors discernible. It was very dramatic, and quieting, as in a church with stained glass."[37]

Butler's aesthetic was singular and powerfully inviting. He brought to life a wild array of creatures, some distinctly animal or human, sometimes hybridized or highly dreamlike. He fluidly merged the spirituality of the African diaspora—notably in the distinct flavors of Louisiana—with Black Christianity, as comfortable with water spirits as with tributes to Mary and Jesus

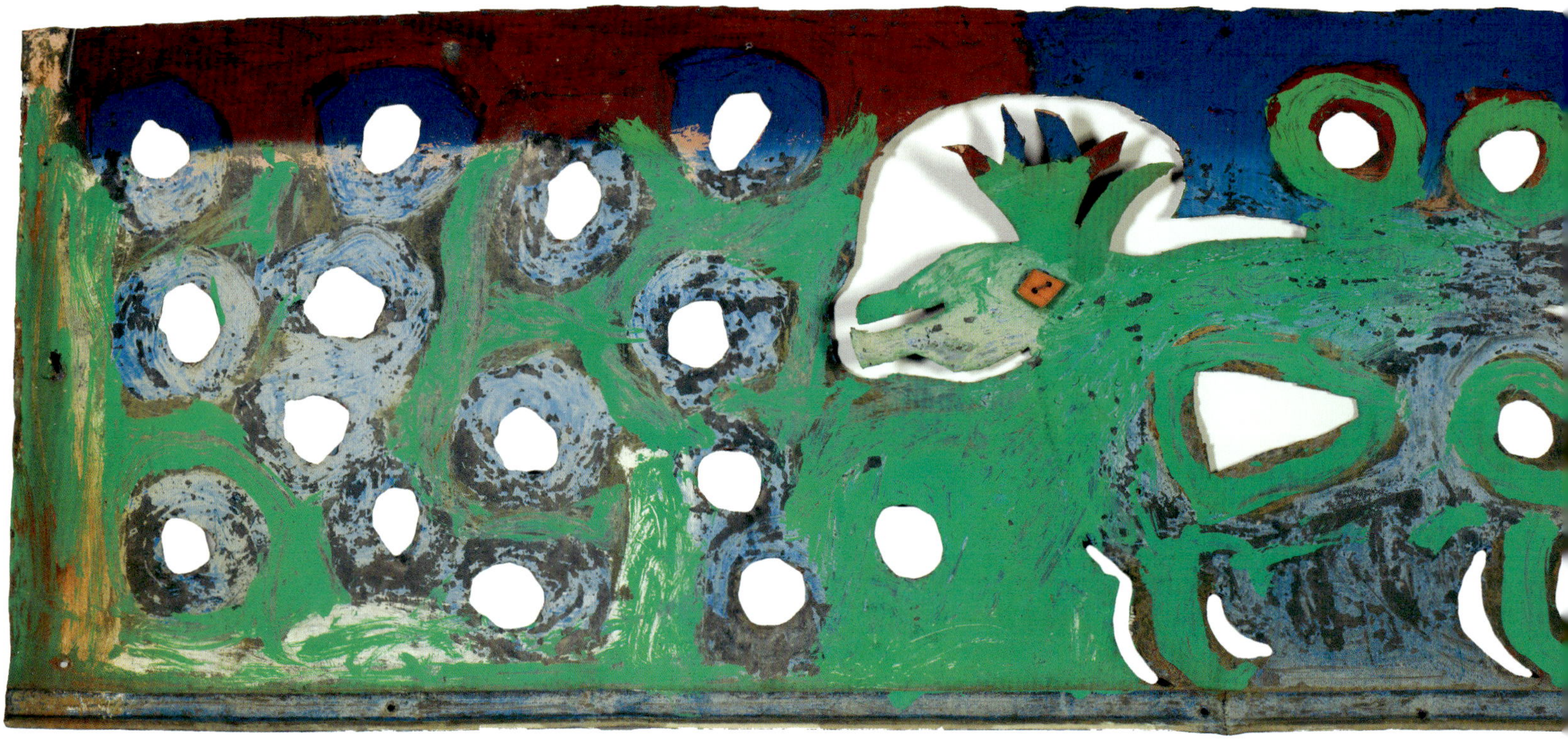

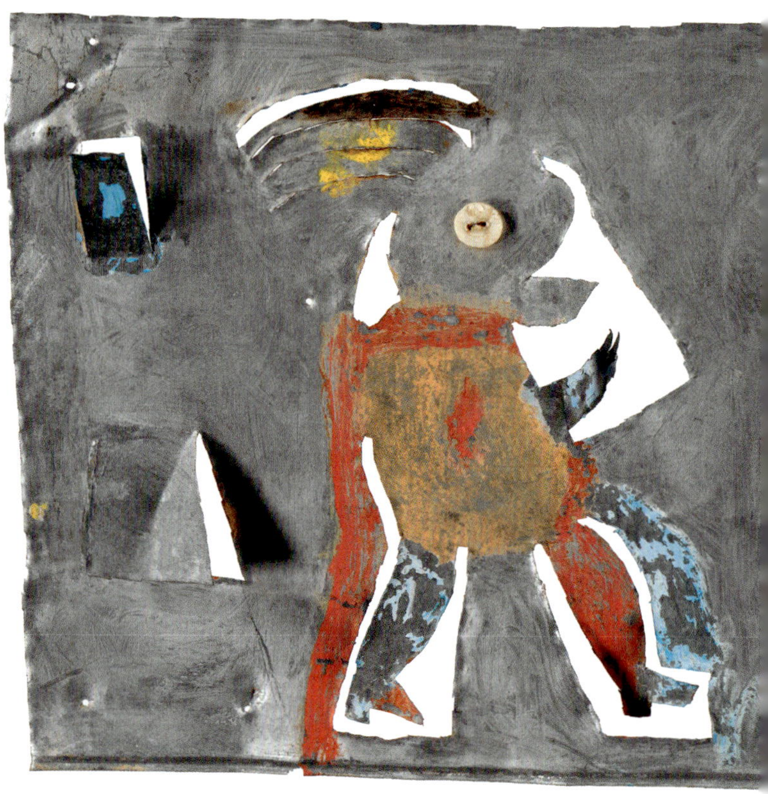

CAT. 35.
David Butler
Untitled (Reindeer)
1965

CAT. 36.
David Butler
Untitled (Three Wise Men and a Goat)
1965

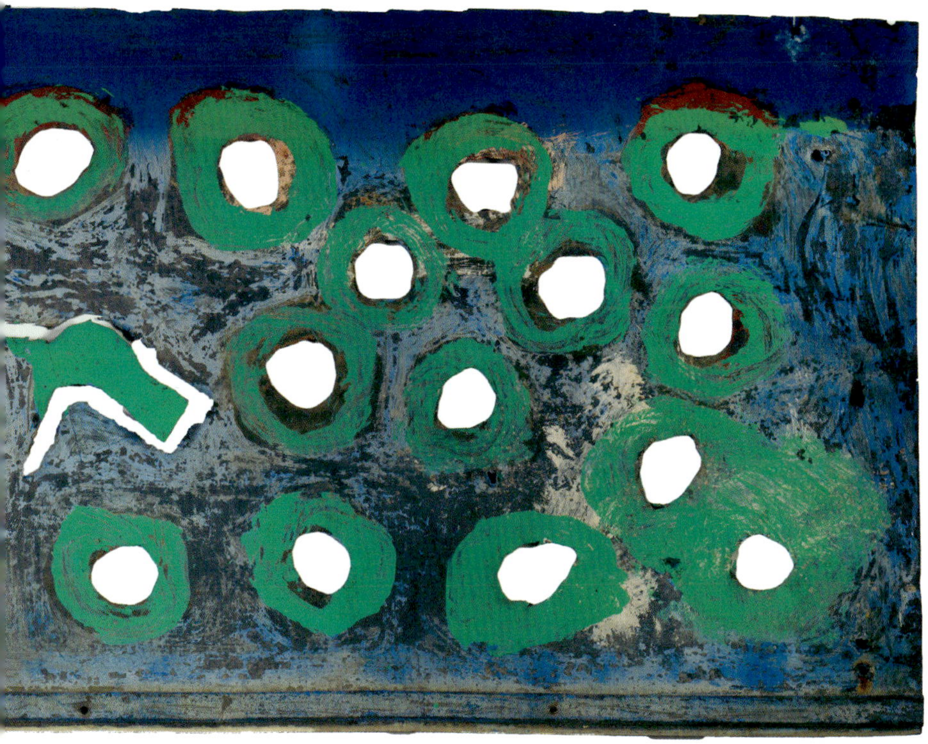

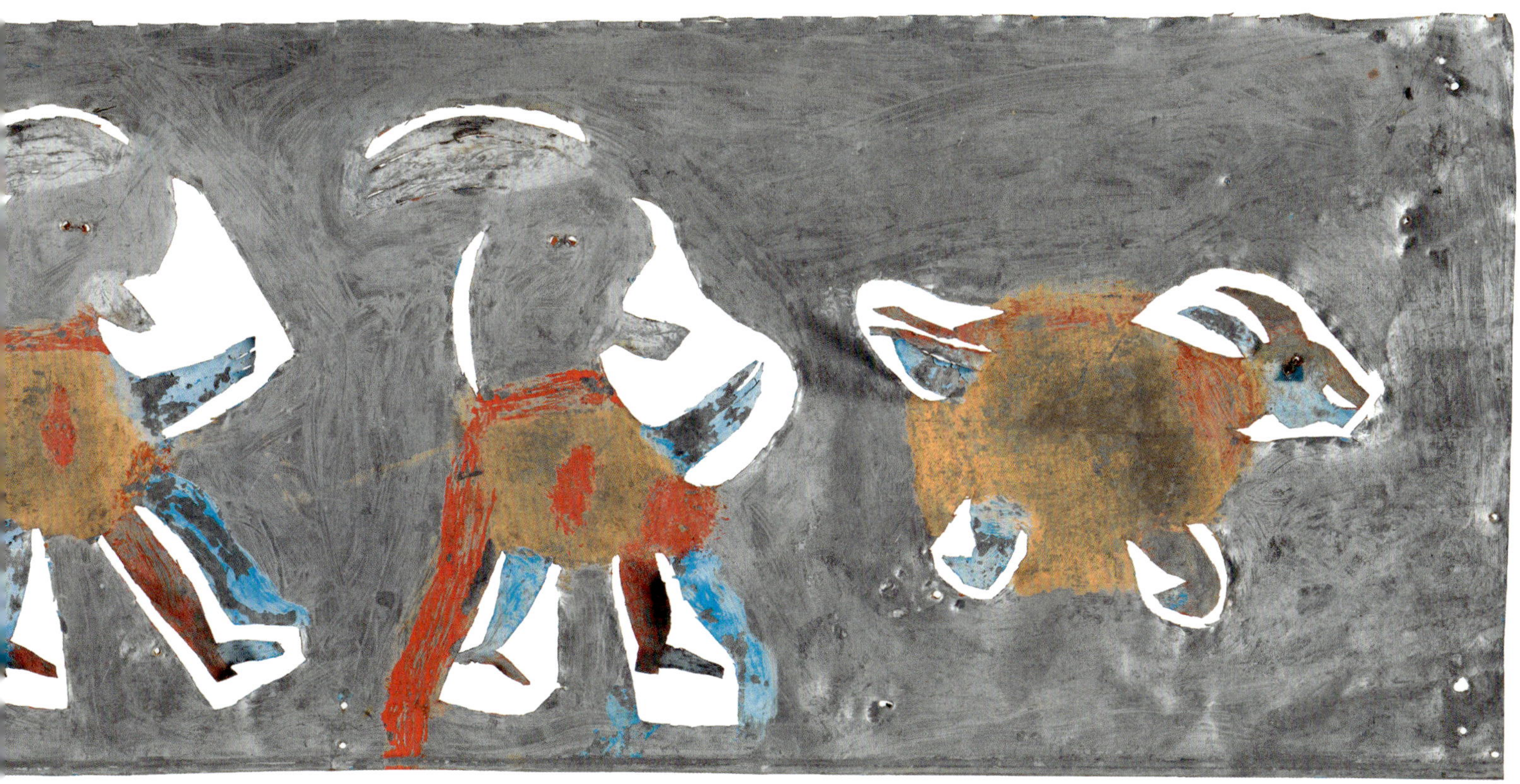

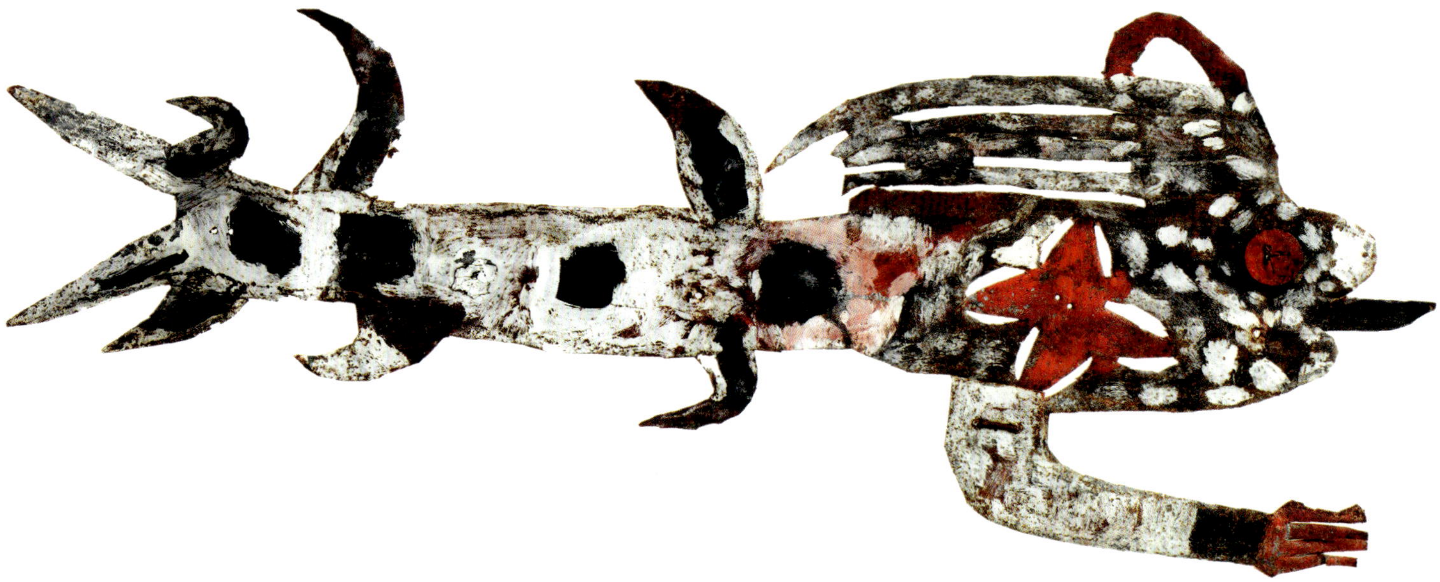

Fig. 16. David Butler, *Untitled (Very Old Mermaid)*, ca. 1968, paint on tin, 12 × 30 ½ in. Smithsonian American Art Museum, Museum purchase through the Luisita L. and Franz H. Denghausen Endowment, 2014.6.1

(Fig. 16, **CAT. 37**). Curator William A. Fagaly met Butler in the early 1970s and organized an exhibition of his work at the New Orleans Museum of Art in 1976. Fagaly introduced Butler and his work to Jane Livingston, which led to his inclusion in the 1982 Corcoran show. Gasperi and Fagaly have both recalled Butler as a person who had highly personal reasons for making art; he never wanted to be famous and only reluctantly parted with the things he made.[38]

Central to Butler's project was immersion, cohesion, and the creation of an alternate and insular world. Individually, his sculptures conveyed an unparalleled creative vision but collectively, they created an atmosphere of protection and equilibrium. Gasperi noted that by the time the Corcoran show opened, enthusiastic collectors had already begun to deplete the environment, often failing to grasp that the sculptures needed one another as much as Butler needed them. Butler's lifetime, rooted in a culture wherein Black Americans were expected to be submissive to whites even in amicable situations, put his personal need to create a private world and accommodate the desires of visitors at odds. His story came to embody powerful lessons on social imbalance and the sometimes conflicting goals within preservation.[39] Ultimately, Butler's sculptural practice remains emblematic of the home environment/yard show tradition of the Black Atlantic South, a physical manifestation of personal beliefs, Louisiana culture, and spiritual vision.

CAT. 37.
David Butler
Untitled (Mary with Baby Jesus)
ca. 1970–80

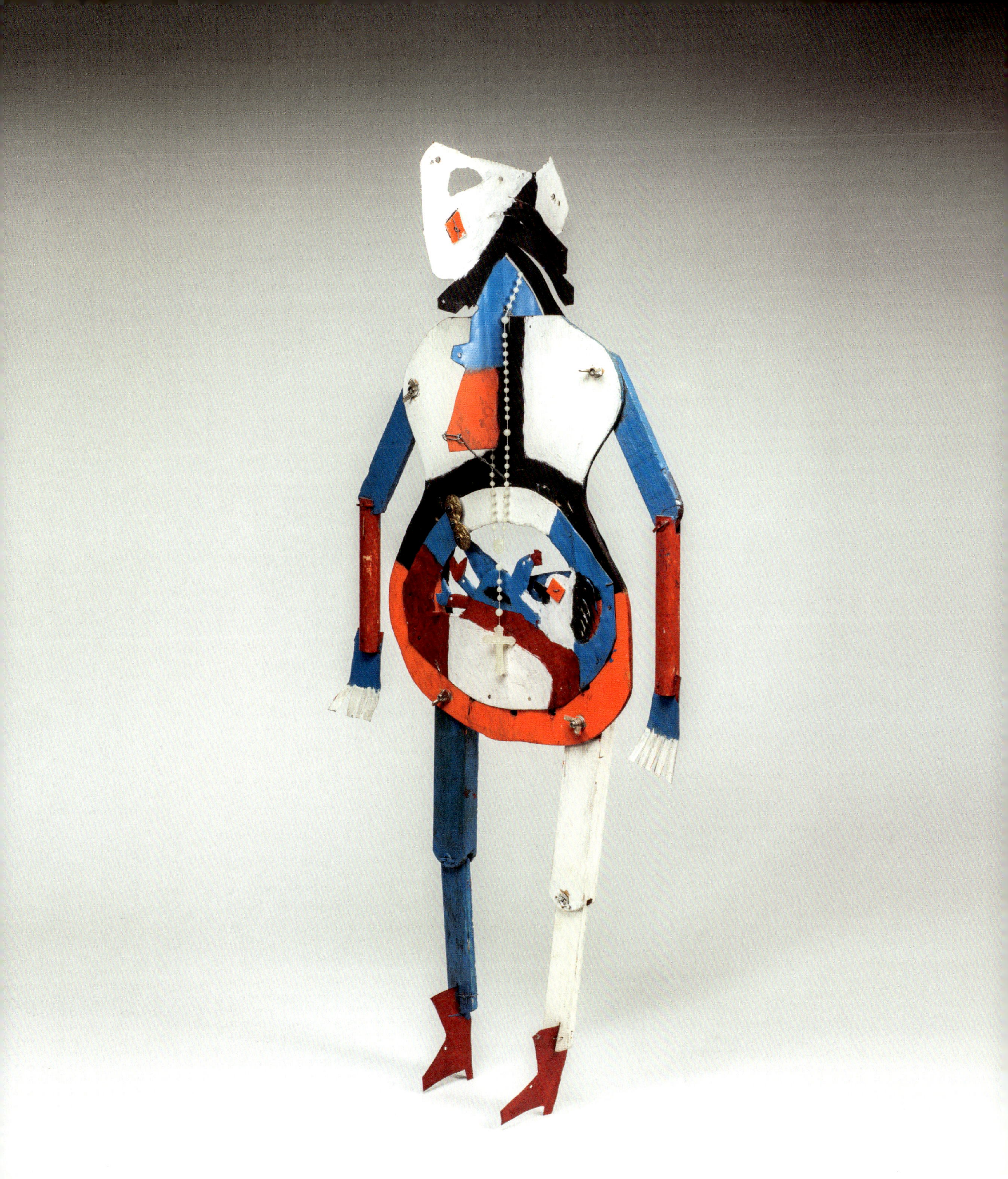

JOSEPH E. YOAKUM (1891–1972) / **ELIJAH PIERCE** (1892–1984) / **WILLIAM HAWKINS** (1895–1990)

Joseph Yoakum, Elijah Pierce, and William Hawkins evidence some of the ways in which the Black Atlantic world moved into the North and East through the Great Migration. All carried with them vestiges of the previous century and used art to assert themselves as creative and self-directed individuals. Yoakum shaped his practice around an internal desire to be valued beyond his identity—both in the way he saw himself and the way others perceived him. Pierce was driven by a mission to share the faith that drove and empowered him. Hawkins dreamed up a world in which imagination and creative play were all the equipment that life required.[40] Yoakum's adult life and the body of work he made in Chicago would have enormous influence on the mainstream artists he met and came to know in the 1960s and 1970s, and the ripple effect he had on art history writ large is hard to fully gauge. Pierce and Hawkins, from Baldwyn, Mississippi, and Union City, Kentucky, respectively, both came to reside in and be recognized for their art in Columbus, Ohio, where they too had an impact on the schooled artists—mostly white—they met and engaged with over time. For all three, the lives they established in the urban North allowed them to regularly sell their art, and become influential in lasting ways.

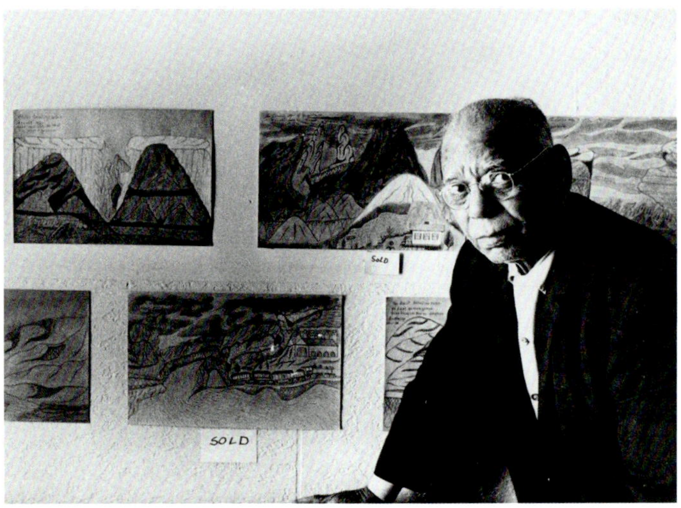

JOSEPH E. YOAKUM began making drawings in his home on the South Side of Chicago around 1962, but it was not until about 1967 that his work became more widely known (Fig. 17).[41] Yoakum became best known for a large body of highly abstracted landscape drawings made in the last decade of his life. The places Yoakum drew were rooted in real geography but contained a high degree of fabrication as well, mapping the landscape of his memory and aspirations. His artworks were done most often in colored pencil and ballpoint pen, in a style that embraced a disorienting flatness and with coloration that hewed only loosely to the confines of reality (**CATS. 38–41**). Yoakum would capture the attention of a number of influential Chicago figures, including art professors at the School of the Art Institute of Chicago (SAIC) and the artists who came to be known as the Hairy

Fig. 17. Joseph E. Yoakum at the Chicago coffee shop The Whole, 1967; unidentified photographer. Archives of American Art, Smithsonian Institution, Whitney Halstead papers

Fig. 18. Joseph E. Yoakum and visitors in front of his East 82nd Street apartment on the South Side of Chicago, 1968. From left: Lorri Gunn, Karl Wirsum (holding daughter Ruby), Roger Brown, Yoakum, Philip Hanson, and Christina Ramberg. Art Institute of Chicago, Institutional Archives, Whitney Halstead Papers

Fig. 19. From left: Whitney Halstead, Joseph E. Yoakum, and Ray Yoshida, ca. 1969. Art Institute of Chicago, Institutional Archives, Whitney Halstead Papers

Who, or the Chicago Imagists, who collected his art and variously channeled Yoakum's vision into their own (Figs. 18, 19).

Yoakum led an itinerant life before settling in Chicago, and tended to offer oblique accounts of his life. Documentation shows that he was born in Missouri in 1891 and traveled extensively while working with the circus, before he settled in Chicago around 1929 or 1930.[42] His family history indicates African American and Cherokee heritage, but Yoakum's own story was that he was a Window Rock Navajo.[43] In the Art Institute of Chicago's 2021 catalogue *Joseph E. Yoakum: What I Saw*, curator Mark Pascale explores the complexity of identity for Yoakum, and the artist's inclination to distance himself from reality in favor of something idealized.

It was the professional artists that Yoakum befriended in Chicago who would offer most of the accounts of Yoakum's art and life there. His voice is captured in letters and brief remarks he made to them or to the press, but Pascale acknowledges that bringing Yoakum into focus, through the white lens he was most frequently seen, poses a number of challenges. The last five years of Yoakum's life were momentous, from a chance encounter to a quick succession of exhibitions, gallery representation, and the acquisition of his work by multiple museums.[44] It was John Hobgood, a professor at Chicago State College, who in 1967 first noticed the drawings on view in Yoakum's storefront window and stopped to introduce himself. Hobgood put Yoakum in contact with Harvey Pranian, who owned a coffeehouse/community gathering spot and gallery, The Whole. From there, Pascale charts the fast-moving chain of events and encounters that brought Yoakum into the SAIC-based group of artists that included Roger Brown, Whitney Halstead, Jim Nutt, Ray Yoshida, and others. The unhesitating interest these artists had in Yoakum can be largely attributed to an SAIC culture that actively sought to diversify "world art."

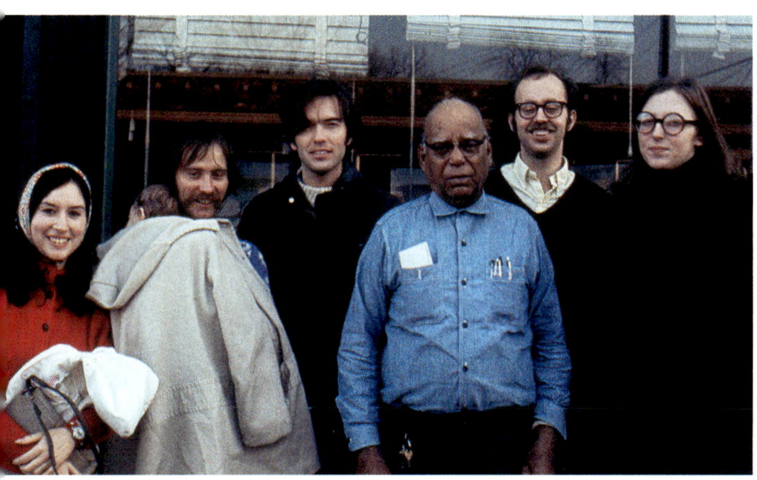

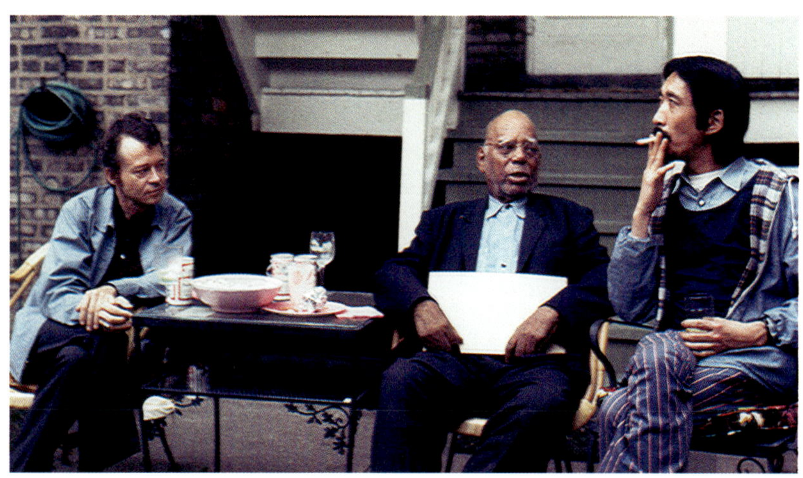

CAT. 38.
Joseph E. Yoakum
Mt Jemel in Medicen Mtn Range
Near Cheyenne Wyoming
on Larime River
ca. 1960

CAT. 39.
Joseph E. Yoakum
Devils Back Bone, in Mt Messa
Near Trinadad Colorado
1966

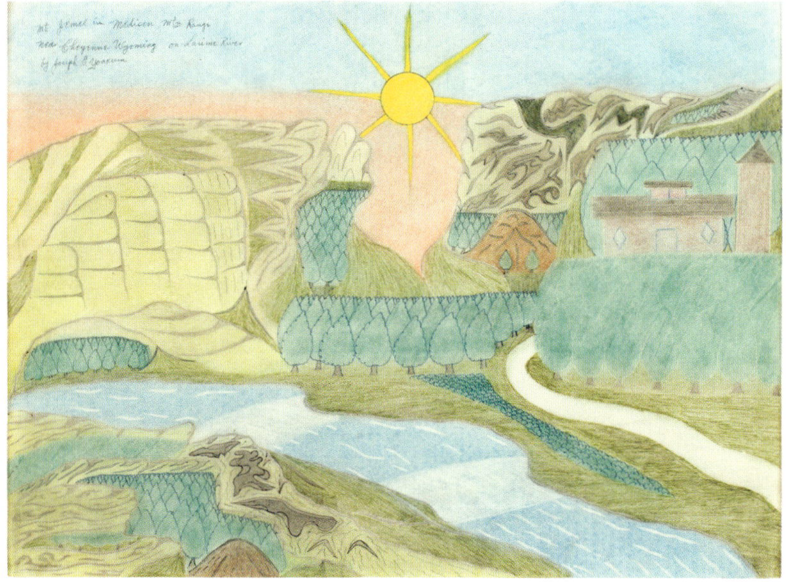

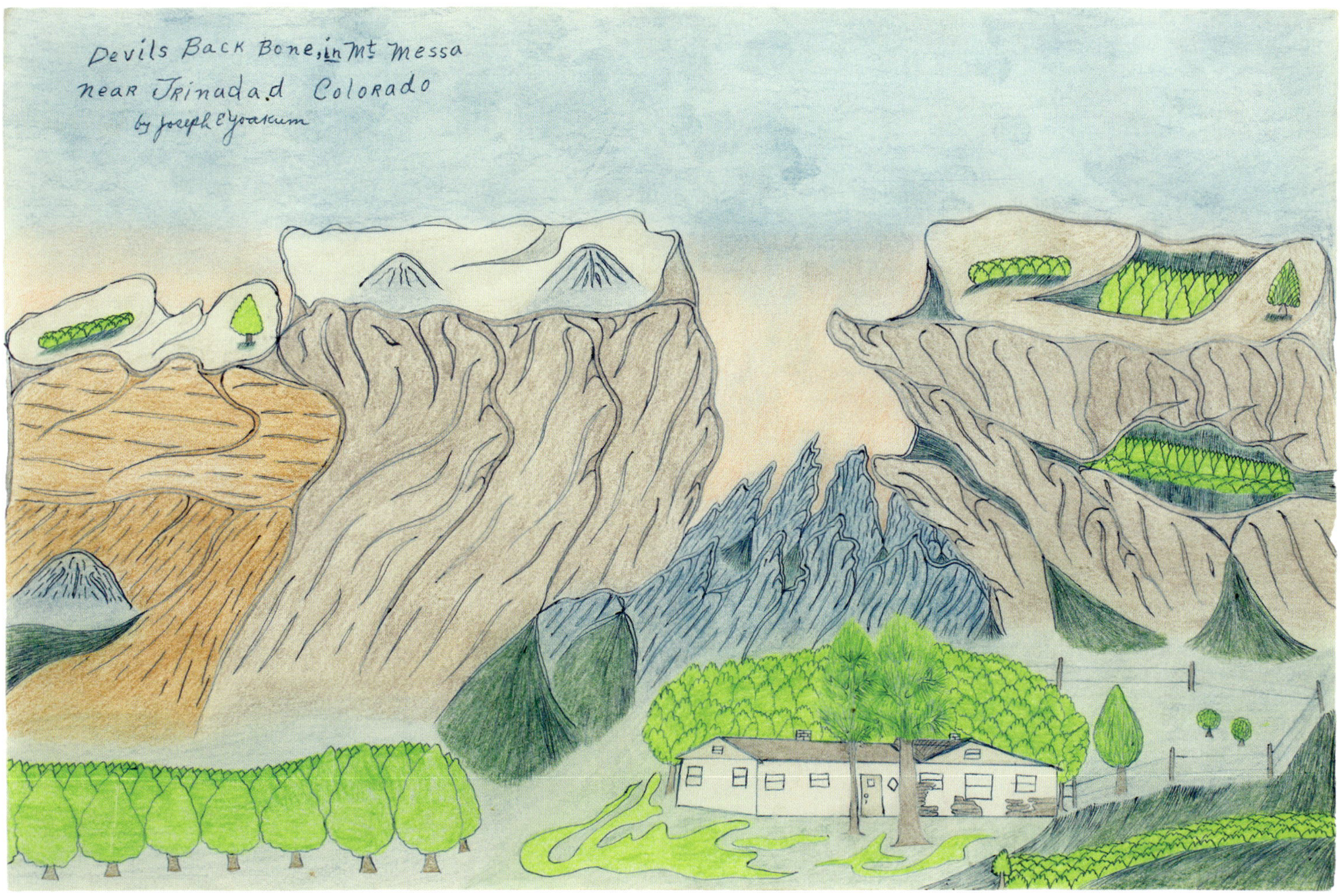

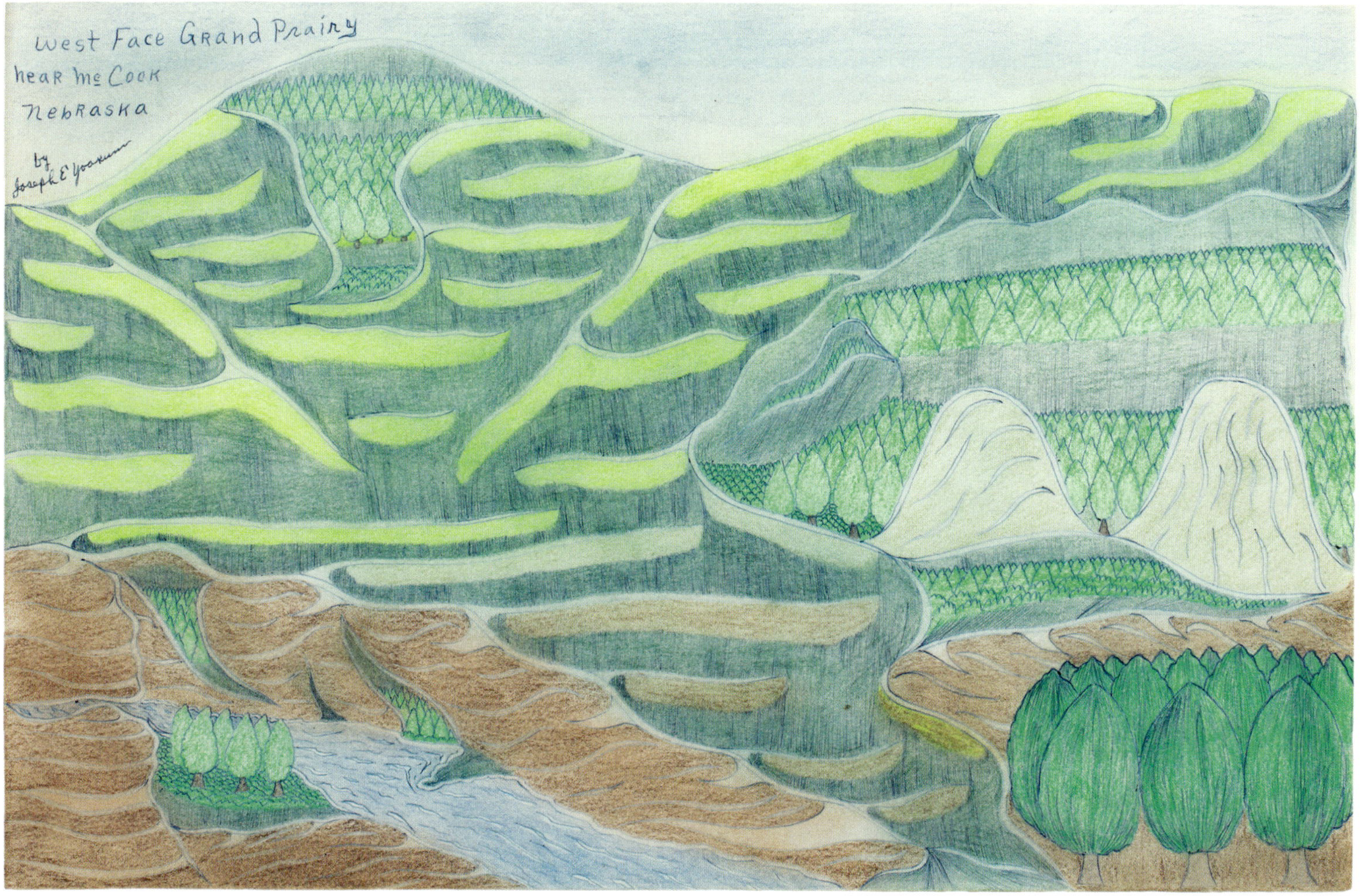

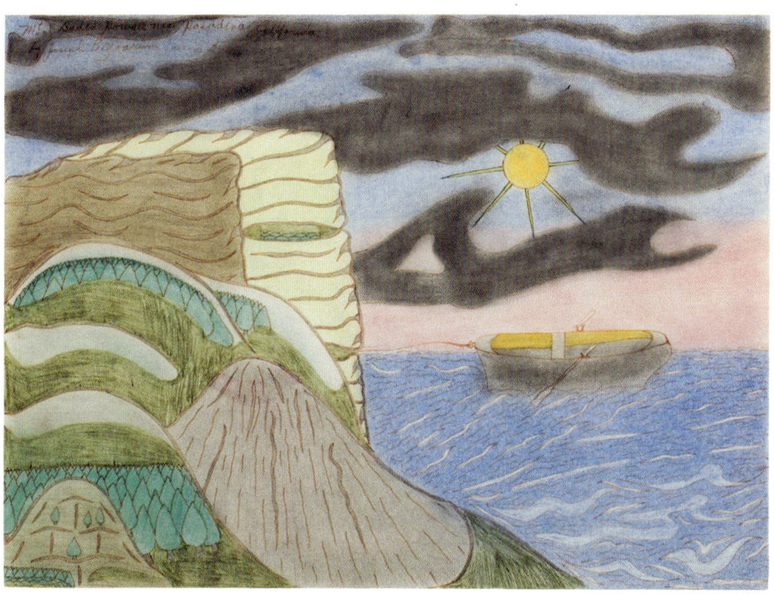

CAT. 40.
Joseph E. Yoakum
West Face Grand Prairy Near McCook Nebraska
1966

CAT. 41.
Joseph E. Yoakum
Mt. Baden Powell Near Pasadena California.
1969

Halstead, an SAIC professor, had been a student of Kathleen Blackshear, who in turn had been a student of Helen Gardner—author of the widely used world-art textbook *Art Through the Ages*, an influential volume that gave context to the art of Africa, the Middle East, and other global cultures that were generally omitted from university presentations of "art history." Gardner was careful not to position world arts in primitive contrast to the refined arts of the Western canon, and bestowed value on spiritual and cultural imperatives as well as those that were academically driven. Gardner's impact on the greater art culture of the upper Midwest is inestimable; her texts and teachings inspired multiple generations to revere the unconventional and the underappreciated, and to honor the validity of all points of view. The Imagists blended these tenets into a unique Chicago flavor, and in turn, made enthusiasm for the work of self-taught artists a major facet of the region's collective identity. Pascale explains: "Today the term *Chicago Imagism* evokes an irreverent attitude and various, largely figurative styles incorporating the vernacular, the comedic, and the grotesque."[45]

Halstead and artist Jim Nutt helped Yoakum sell his work beginning in the late 1960s, and Halstead facilitated a solo exhibition of Yoakum's work at the Whitney Museum of American Art in 1972, a full decade before he was included in *Black Folk Art in America*. Perhaps ironically, Yoakum's many art-world supporters admired him in the context of non-belonging and iconoclastic outsiders, when what Yoakum wanted most was to disassociate from a lineage of oppression and perceived inferiority and be recognized as an artist of vision. Not unlike professional African American artists including Augusta Savage and Charles White, Yoakum wanted recognition as a successful artist beyond his racial identity. He was uncomfortable with enthusiasm that foregrounded his biography—the very "up from nothingness" he wanted to leave far behind him. Pascale quotes the artist as pleading, in a letter to Jim Nutt, not to "advertise me as a negro," gleaning that Yoakum feared that being known as an African American would result in social exploitation and financial under-compensation.[46]

Art historian Nancy Thebaut has argued, however, that in the end, it is the particular way in which Yoakum's art speaks for itself—apart from his racial identity or life story—that resulted in the artist's abiding acclaim. "Attempts to identify a 'true' account of Yoakum's past can actually, then, do a profound disservice to the way that Yoakum seems to have intended his work—and himself—to be understood," she observes. "Instead, it is primarily through the mere act of looking at Yoakum's landscapes and portraits that his work and meaning and important place in art history come to the fore. The strange forms, rich patterns, and subtle traces of his artistic process act as rewards for the attentive viewer."[47] Yoakum referred to his drawings, predominantly highly stylized, imaginative landscapes, as "a spiritual unfoldment."[48] In his mind, he traveled a world of sensuous colors and soft, undulating topographies. Yoakum insisted that the places he depicted were inspired by real life and travels. But as curator Esther Adler has pointed out, his landscapes are filtered through degrees of reminiscence, spiritual transcendence, and the desire to roam freely in a country that put extreme limits on Black travelers.[49] Ultimately Yoakum's worldscapes invite viewers to places beyond the literal; they seduce one into their midst and invite the willing to explore places wherein the "real world" seems increasingly abstract.

ELIJAH PIERCE was a lay preacher who understood the power of making his sermons visible, which he did by carving parables, moral tales, and tributes into bas-relief wood panels (Fig. 20). From childhood Pierce felt like he did not belong in the rural Deep South plantation setting of his youth. In addition to his callings to preach and to carve, Pierce believed he needed a viable trade to steer him clear of farming life, and he apprenticed as a barber when he was still a boy. He ultimately braided this trio of vocations into a life's work. He barbered in Baldwyn when he was a teenager, and then spent a time living itinerantly and seeing the country. This span included a period in Chicago, where he met Cornelia Houeston; the two moved to her hometown of Columbus, Ohio, in 1923, and married.[50] In Columbus, Pierce worked in several barbershops before finally opening his own in the 1950s, replete with a room that could serve as a gallery for his carvings.

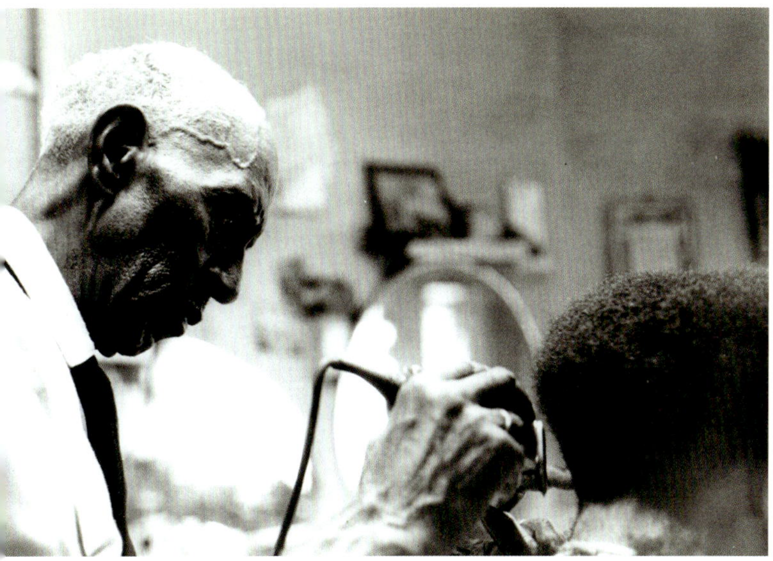

Fig. 20. Elijah Pierce shaving Harry Hight, ca. 1974; photograph by Kojo Kamau. Courtesy of the Archives of the Columbus Museum of Art, Ohio

Filmmaker Jeffrey Wolf was a student at Ohio State University (OSU) in Columbus, and met Pierce in 1971, when his carvings were on view at the university art gallery. The two became friends, and over the years Wolf documented Pierce's work in photographs and films (Fig. 21, **CAT. 42**). Wolf recalled: "During the late 1920s, Pierce carved a small elephant as a gift for Cornelia's birthday. She liked it so much that he promised her an entire zoo. For Pierce, these individual animal carvings had their own story. They represented either the beasts from the Book of Genesis, or creatures from the folktales of Pierce's youth."[51]

Pierce's "carved sermons" most clearly represent his oeuvre. Wolf explains that the artist intended his narrative carvings to serve as visual aids for religious instruction. "Pierce and his wife Cornelia would set up shop at county fairs wearing robes and using school pointers to preach the meaning, morals, and parables in the works [Fig. 22]. The images and the way they were laid out are reminiscent of illustrated bibles, popular in the 1930s and '40s."[52] Betsa Marsh gave a similar account, noting that "[Pierce] believed God had given him the

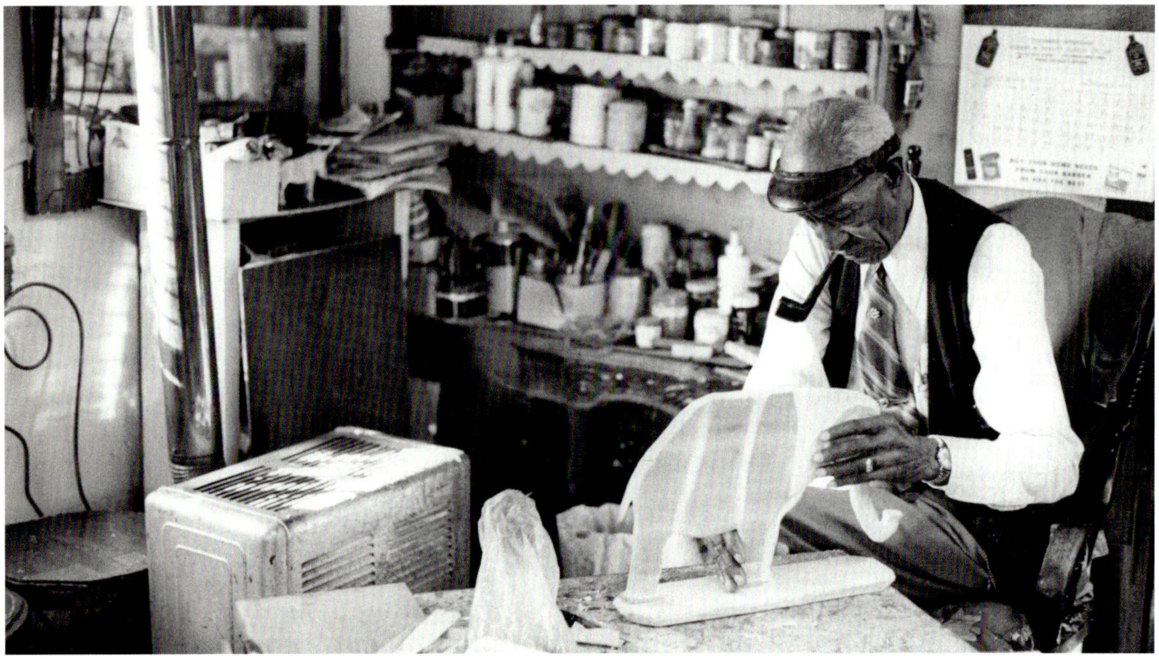

Fig. 21. Elijah Pierce and *Elephant* (Cat. 42), ca. 1978. Collection of Jeffrey Wolf and Jeany Nisenholz-Wolf

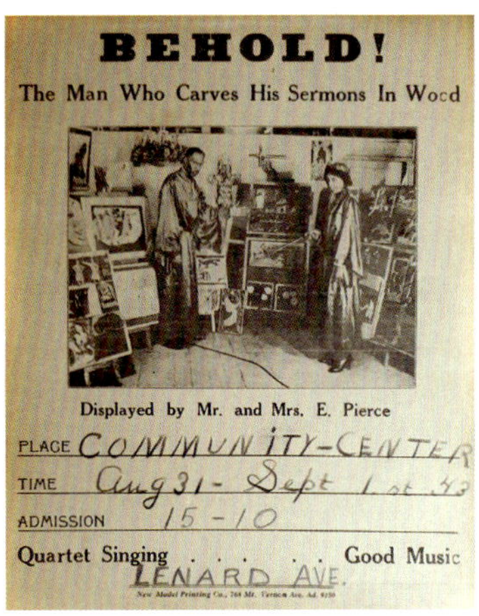

Fig. 22. "Behold! The Man Who Carves His Sermons in Wood," poster for the Pierces' itinerant art display with handwritten inscription, 1943. Collection of Jeffrey Wolf and Jeany Nisenholz-Wolf

talent to carve, and that his life's purpose was to make 'every sermon I never preached.'"[53]

Curator Nancy Ireson asserts that Pierce took an active role in shaping his own life, that he sought recognition, and that, when his reputation grew, he felt empowered to use his voice. "Pierce knew his art had social value and saw that, in concert with his actions, his art could create change."[54] She notes that Pierce refused to sell some of his best work, including his *Book of Wood*, an oversize bas-relief carved "book" illustrating scenes from the life of Christ, begun around 1932.[55] Years before any institutions took interest, Pierce told a journalist he had refused offers to sell this major work to individuals, but noted he would feel differently if the work would go somewhere the public could see it: "for a museum or something like that—well that would be different," he said.[56] The Columbus Gallery of Fine Arts (now Columbus Museum of Art) organized *Elijah Pierce, Woodcarver* in 1973, and subsequently came to hold the foremost collection of Pierce's art when it purchased, after Pierce's death in 1984, the entire contents of his barbershop gallery, from his third wife, Estelle Greene Pierce.[57]

CAT. 42.
Elijah Pierce
Elephant
ca. 1978

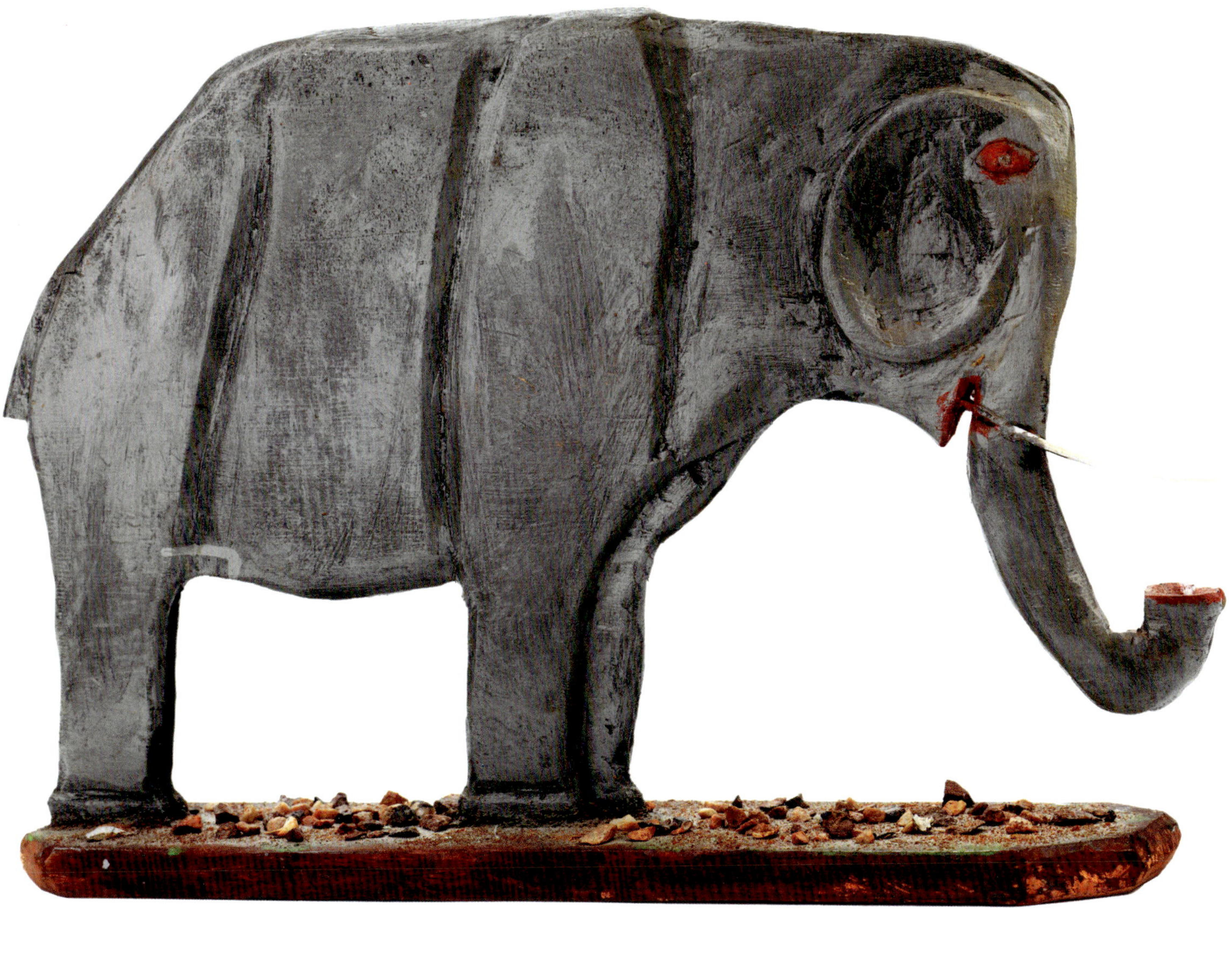

When Pierce was included in the Corcoran's *Black Folk Art in America*, his work was seen in the context of other Black artists who, in the words of Professor Sampada Aranke, invoked "a Black radical tradition" as an expression of freedom and independence. "Not only was the Black Church a central and steady place for gathering in an otherwise segregated and crises-driven landscape," she pointedly argues, "but ministers preached with constancy about the humanity of Black Americans and the promise of a freedom from the pains, violences, and traumas of this world."[58] Aranke hits upon the element of faith as a complex and critical issue, a double-edged sword that simultaneously enabled many artists' persistence and marginalized their practice from the mainstream. Pierce would be among numerous self-taught African American artists who reinvented the Bible in their own cultural image and vested belief in the proverbial guidance that "your gifts will make room for you."[59]

WILLIAM LAWRENCE HAWKINS was also driven by his artistic nature from a young age. As was true for most Americans of color in the late nineteenth and early twentieth centuries, Hawkins's early years were not easy or ideal (Fig. 23).[60] His mother died when he was little, and Hawkins and his brother were raised on their grandmother's farm near Lexington, where never-ending work took priority over schooling. But the farm provided for their needs, and their community was more tolerant of racial difference than many. Hawkins was proud to be of mixed ethnicity, identifying as having African and Native American ancestry, and believed that "all things good" came from having a multicultural heritage.[61] Hawkins had an artistic inclination early on, and often drew the animals from the farm. When he moved to Columbus, Ohio, at twenty-one, he was equipped with a variety of practical skills but few that he could easily parlay into an income. He took on a wide array of jobs but always found innovative ways of supplementing his earnings—including selling paintings and drawings he had made. Accounts from those who knew him describe his sharp mind, which, in tandem with curiosity, ingenuity, and significant ambition, set Hawkins on a unique path.

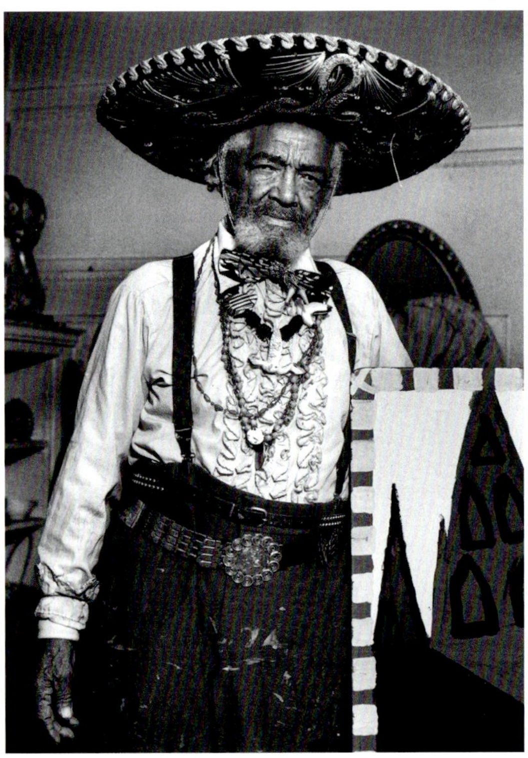

Fig. 23. William L. Hawkins, early 1980s; photograph by Chas Ray Krider

CAT. 43.
William Hawkins
Demolition of St. Mary's Church, Boston
1986

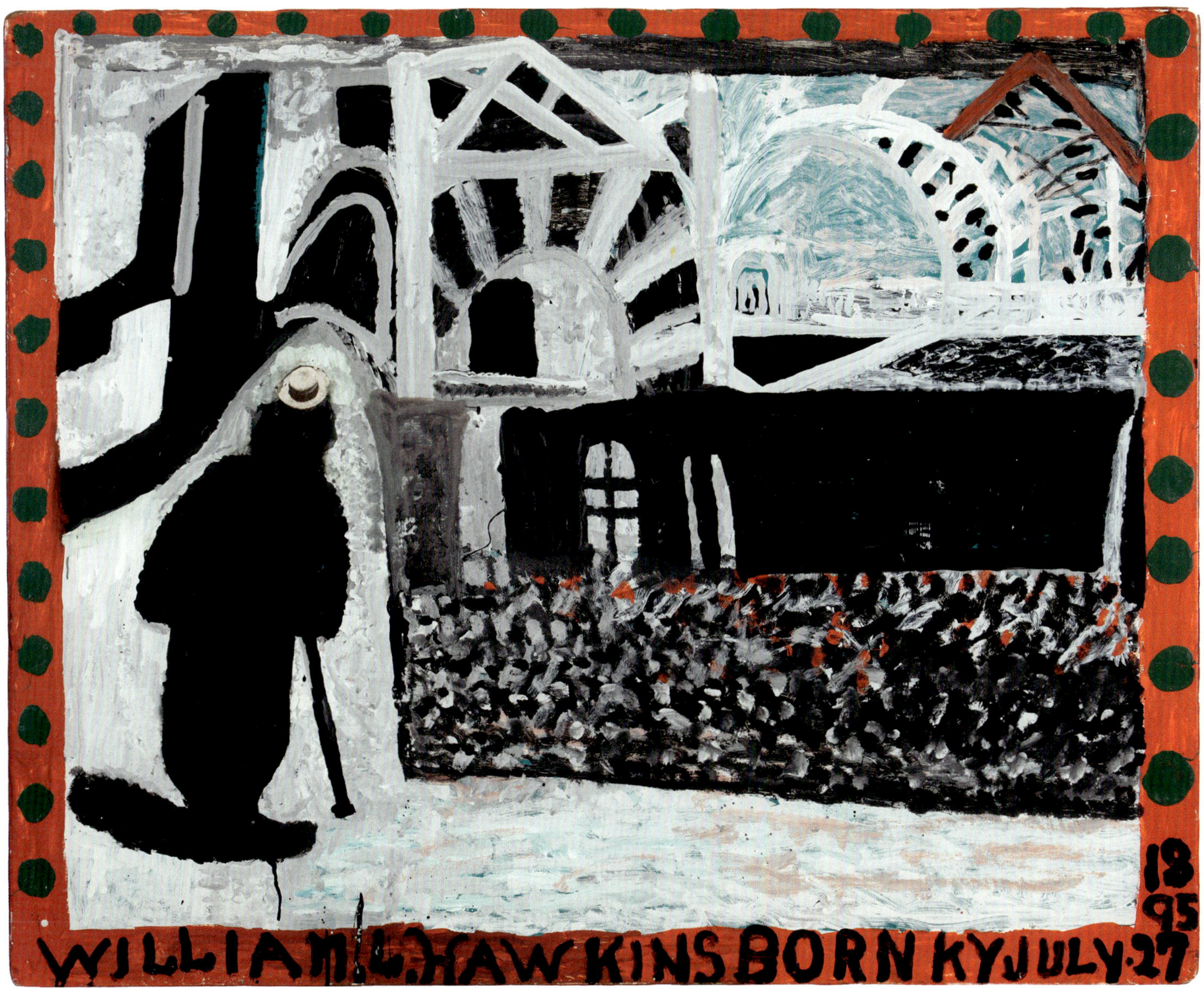

CAT. 44.

William Hawkins

White Dog

1988

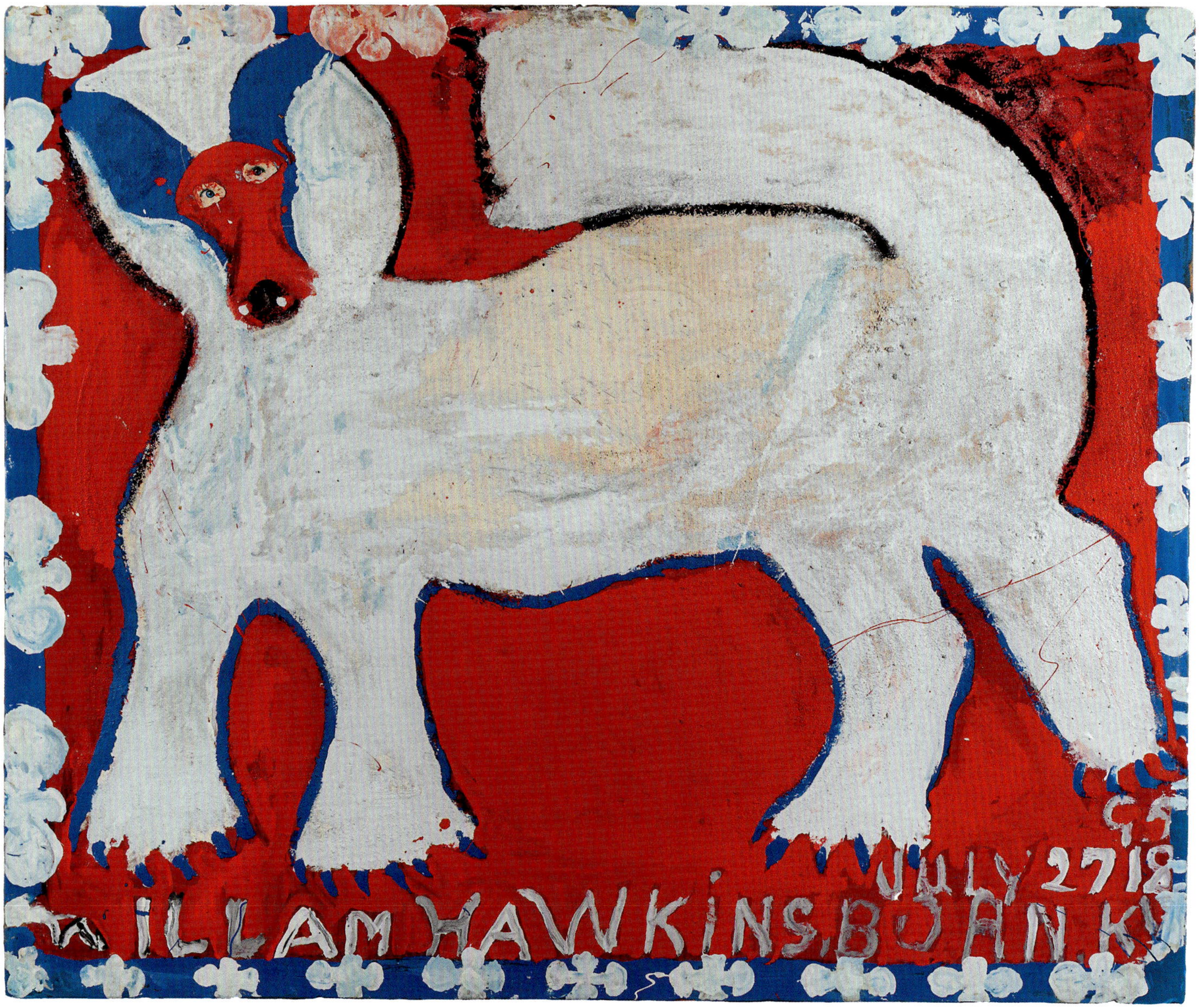

Hawkins's painted and collaged imagery drew on a number of topics, a favorite among them being the urban landscape. He made portrait-like tributes of buildings he felt had significance, places that had hosted important events in US history. In *Demolition of St. Mary's Church, Boston* (**CAT. 43**), Hawkins chronicles the destruction of a historic nineteenth-century Catholic church that had served the North End community as both place of worship and cultural center; it was demolished in 1977 to make way for new apartment buildings. The foreground figure wearing a collaged-in hat links the loss of the building to a concrete human experience. Gary J. Schwindler, who befriended and supported the artist, notes that almost all of Hawkins's paintings began with photographs or illustrations from the media. He kept his clippings in a "legendary" suitcase —an archive from which Hawkins extracted subjects, and literally plucked pieces of reality, employing fragments of the printed world to anchor his highly expressive images to moments within lived time.[62]

Hawkins's lifelong affinity for animals is evidenced in his many images of them, and he became adept at capturing their inherent characters using exaggerated color and distorted physiognomy. His deft use of photo collage adds surprising touches of realism, as in *White Dog*'s arresting blue-eyed gaze (**CAT. 44**; see detail, pp. 260–61), and he became known for boldly inserting Black figures into pivotal religious scenes such as the Last Supper, a theme he revisited numerous times. Hawkins had a knack for rendering the mythic at an everyday, human scale, and although he was only minimally literate in a conventional way, he emblazoned his works with his name and birth date (William L. Hawkins. Born KY July 27 1895), in keeping with Dave Drake's and Bill Traylor's assertion of authorship.

Susan Mitchell Crawley has explored the powerful role imaginative play had in Hawkins's creative path, art serving as an uninhibited space for personal growth. "In the play-space, which is both real and not real, in which we shed the limitations of our finite beings even as we retain our sense-bound existence," she explains, "Hawkins suffused his art with play in a lavish array of forms. He made the trying out of possibilities a fundamental aspect of his practice as he worked in a series. This exuberant man—always aware that he was performing for an audience, always investing in producing for them the most astonishing spectacle—fashioned an alternative world of joyous vitality and heightened experience."[63]

Hawkins had begun selling his artworks around Columbus in the 1930s and 1940s, but it was in the 1970s that he began to focus on his art. In the late 1970s, Lee Garrett, a sculpture graduate from OSU with a studio on Columbus's east side, met Hawkins, who lived and worked in the same neighborhood (Fig. 24). Impressed by the visual power of Hawkins's paintings, he encouraged him to work larger and seek a bigger audience. Garrett persuaded Hawkins to enter his paintings

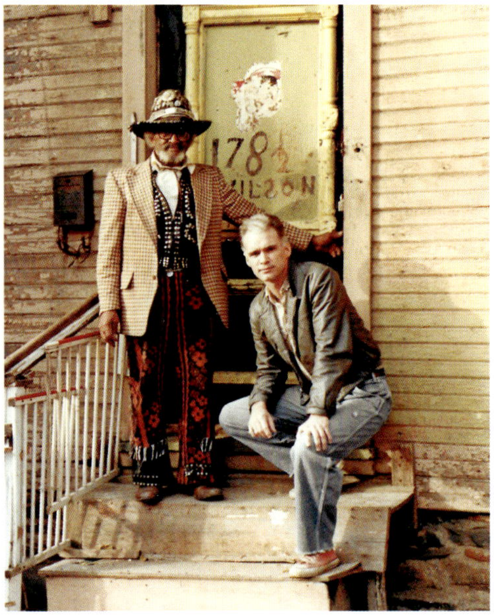

Fig. 24. William Hawkins and Lee Garrett, ca. 1980; photograph by Michael Noland

at the state fair in 1982 and helped him secure an exhibition at Roger McLane's Ohio Gallery that same year.[64]

The lives and experiences of William Hawkins and Elijah Pierce, two African American artists residing and working in the same midsize midwestern city, had striking overlap but remained distinct. In a recent essay charting these parallel existences, Barbara R. Nicholson and Deidre Hamlar write: "Born in log cabins on farms in the rural South in the 1890s, both Hawkins and Pierce started making art at an early age and found their ways—in 1916 and 1923, respectively, to reside on Columbus's east side. Through appreciation and recognition by local admirers in the 1970s and 1980s, each would come to prominence on the local and national art scenes. Both Hawkins and Pierce lived past ninety years old, continuing to develop their work up to the time of their deaths."[65]

From there, the coauthors chart the many differences that gave nuance and character to each man's life and experience, noting: "These two major players of the Columbus art world met only once, in the winter of 1983, one year before Pierce died."[66] Painter Michael Noland, who knew them both well, perceived a marked difference in their characters. "Elijah Pierce was Gandhi and William Hawkins was like Muhammad Ali," he said. While they never became friends, Hawkins and Pierce were united by the supportive community centered at Ohio State University, and by a significant moment in which a rising number of young white artists were questioning the tenets and effects of formal training and academic hierarchies.[67]

NELLIE MAE ROWE (1900–1982) / SISTER GERTRUDE MORGAN (1900–1980)

Nellie Mae Rowe and Sister Gertrude Morgan were both born in the last year of the nineteenth century and, along with Inez Nathaniel-Walker (1911–1990), were the only women on the twenty-artist roster for the Corcoran exhibition.[68] Female artists have always faced unique challenges, but, while professional women in the arts worked hard for and achieved recognition, their untrained counterparts were recognized far more rarely, and self-taught women of color have remained at the bottom of a deeply entrenched hierarchy.[69] The African American women included in the Robson Family Collection—Rowe, Morgan, Clementine Hunter, and Bessie Harvey—should be

Fig. 25. Melinda Blauvelt, *Nellie Mae Rowe, Vinings, Georgia*, 1971, printed 2021, silver gelatin print, 24 × 20 in. Gift of the artist, High Museum of Art

considered all the more exceptional for their refusal to be daunted, and for finding personal footholds in a society that rarely valued their experience and point of view.

Positioning these women within the context of a history that undervalued them even more starkly than it did their male counterparts presents a number of challenges. We can scarcely imagine how many untrained female artists went entirely without notice or advocacy during their lifetimes, and how many bodies of work were entirely lost. The women encompassed in *We Are Made of Stories* had circumstances and allies that resulted in our appreciation of them today, yet endeavors in the present must contend with the fact that the documentation of their lives, work, and views is less replete than that of male contemporaries. Beyond the fact that their art was less likely to survive, there are fewer interviews, essays, and photographs, and less film footage; they were rarely the subject of solo exhibitions and, until very recently, few have been the focus of renewed or in-depth scholarship.[70] Like other artists discussed in this section, each of these women played an important role in moving the needle and became "gamechangers" in their own way. They are discussed in this section for the important alignment between their endeavors and their historical moment, although Nellie Mae Rowe's ever-rising acclaim is contextualized in the following section as well, where she, like Bill Traylor and William Edmondson, also rightly belong.

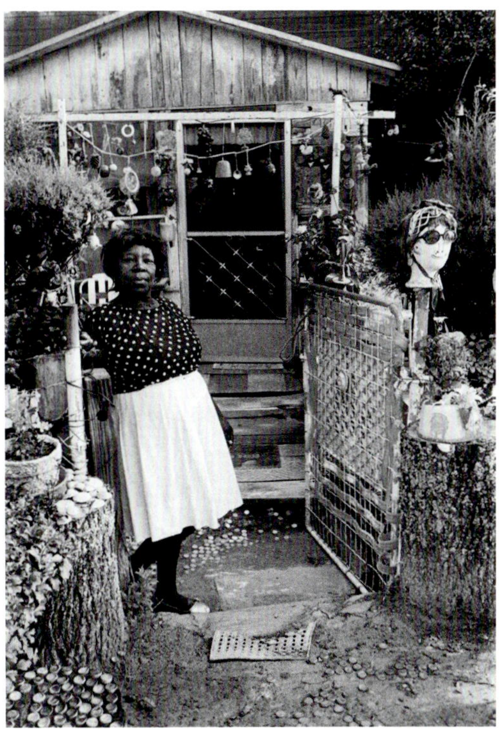

NELLIE MAE ROWE (née Williams) was the daughter of a formerly enslaved man and a woman born the year of Emancipation in Fayette County, Georgia (Fig. 25). Like her peers in the Corcoran show, her life was shaped by segregation, poverty, and ongoing oppression, but this reality would come to inform the art she made in a very particular way. When Rowe was sixty-eight, she turned her time and attention to a creative practice grounded in repossessing a stolen youth and asserting pride and self-worth.

According to Rowe herself, she was born on July 4, 1900—a date redolent of independence and fresh starts. In the High Museum of Art's 2021 catalogue, curator Katherine Jentleson acknowledges that—as was often the case with African Americans of Rowe's generation—the records for her birth year are inconclusive. Nevertheless, Rowe's assertion of it being Independence Day and a year on the cusp of a new century tells us a great deal about the way in which she self-identified. One contributor to the catalogue, filmmaker Ruchi Mital, explains that in a recent documentary on Rowe, her team chose not to probe the four-year discrepancy in birth year found in the census, but to honor the artist's word. "In the measurable distance of four years between these two facts is an immeasurable truth: we are made of stories. It's the story that matters, the story that reveals, and the story that evolves....What is more interesting is the truth that the conflicting narratives and memories reveal."[71]

Rowe labored as a child, married young, was widowed twice, and worked much of her adult life as a uniformed "domestic" in white households. When her second husband died in 1948, Rowe was alone for the first time. She owned the home they had shared, and some artworks from the late 1940s indicate that Rowe began to revisit her creative nature at this time, although it was not until about 1968 that she really began to reshape her life in earnest.[72] Nineteen sixty-eight was a pivotal year in the United States, with the assassination of Dr. Martin Luther King Jr. and the passage of a second civil rights law, but Rowe may have been particularly impacted by the victory, that year, of Shirley Chisholm—the first Black woman elected to the United States Congress—and the vocal and visible ways in which Chisholm urged Black women to rebel against the "dual oppressions of patriarchy and racism."[73]

Rowe was deeply spiritual and considered her artistic creativity as a God-given way to convey her commitment and gratitude.[74] She also understood that the lack of improvisational playtime as a girl had caused lasting trauma, and she spoke about her need to recover the lost child within herself. She said of that turning point: "I've worked my days, now I want to play these other days out."[75] But Jentleson points out a misogynist disparity between the positive reception of play and playfulness in the work of certain white male artists and its negative positioning for women like Rowe. "Agency is granted to artists from Paul Klee to Mike Kelley, their reinvention of the expressive visual forms that characterize youthful art or their embrace of childhood objects like stuffed animals seen as an active return," she explains. "But for nearly a century, the self-taught artist's relationship to childhood has been characterized as unsophisticated, a state of arrested development producing styles that are only accidentally similar to the work of their trained modernist peers."[76]

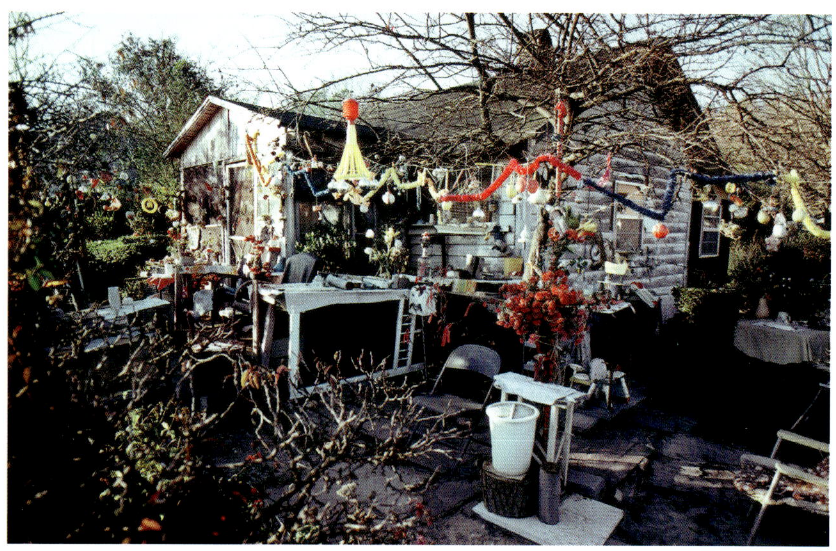

Fig. 26. Nellie Mae Rowe's house, Vinings, Georgia, 1971; photograph by Lucinda Bunnen

Regardless of who approved or did not, Rowe gradually transformed her property into an enriched realm she called her "Playhouse," populated with large dolls she had made and clothed (Fig. 26).[77] She cut the bushes into topiary forms and hung bottles, plastic flowers, toys, and a myriad of found objects in the trees, bringing

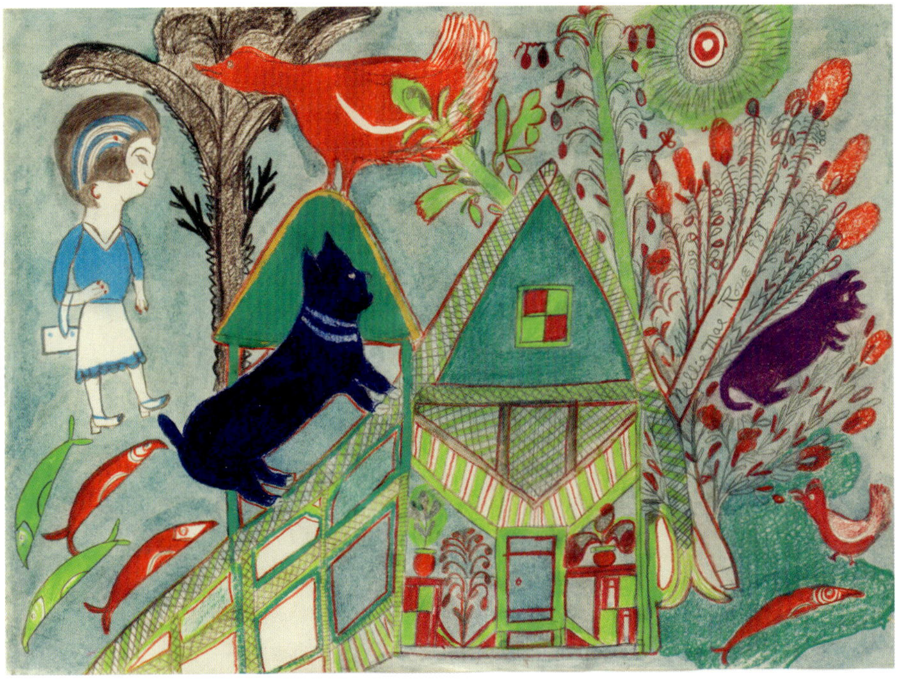

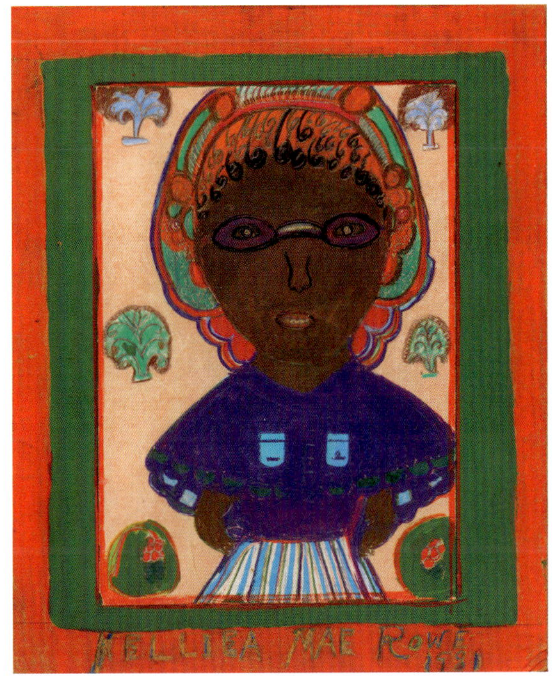

Fig. 27. Nellie Mae Rowe, *Shopping in Vinings, Georgia*, 1981, watercolor, crayon, and graphite on paper, 18 ⅞ × 23 ⅝ in. Smithsonian American Art Museum, Gift of Josh Feldstein, 2019.53.2

Fig. 28. Nellie Mae Rowe, *Self-Portrait*, 1981, crayon and paint on cardboard and artist-made frame, 20 × 16 in. Smithsonian American Art Museum, Museum purchase through the Luisita L. and Franz H. Denghausen Endowment and the American Women's History Initiative Acquisitions Pool, administered by the Smithsonian American Women's History Initiative, 2021.29.8

a heightened animation to her yard as things tinkled in the breeze and glinted in sunlight. The depth and richness of the Black vernacular aesthetic was embodied in Rowe's multivalent, unfixed way of celebrating joy and bounty. Curator Kinshasha Holman Conwill has noted, "The American South…is the soil in which much of Black vernacular culture was planted and cultivated," explaining that the complex conditions of slavery merged with African and Caribbean spiritual, musical, and other cultural roots, generating what the literary critic Houston A. Baker Jr. has called "a forceful and indigenous American creativity."[78]

In addition to enriching her Playhouse yard, Rowe made vivid mixed-media drawings of hybridized creatures and African American women enmeshed in color and abundance, consistently depicted as proud, creative individuals brimming with kindness and love (Figs. 27, 28). In answer to a society that rarely depicted Black women in works of art and too often cast them as demeaning stereotypes in the ubiquitous imagery of popular culture, Rowe took control of her own narrative by making images of Black beauty and joy—a radical act of selfhood. She depicted friends, neighbors, and herself in drawings and hand-colored photographs that telegraph individual style and cultural identity, and convey a world in which personal difference and the unexpected embody the richness of life. Ultimately, Rowe pushed back against a life of degrading work and uniformed facelessness with highly original images picturing a symbolic and lush alternative to a harsh reality. She relished the ability to transform one small part of the planet into a space that felt welcoming, protective, and nurturing, to create beauty where there had been none—even if the means for creating that beauty was not in accord with the conventions of white decoration and homekeeping.

Rowe had grown up in a cultural atmosphere ruled by dictums of "racial etiquette," white-ese for codes of subservient behavior that African Americans were expected to adhere to, with harsh

CAT. 45.

Nellie Mae Rowe

Nellie on Blue

ca. 1978–82

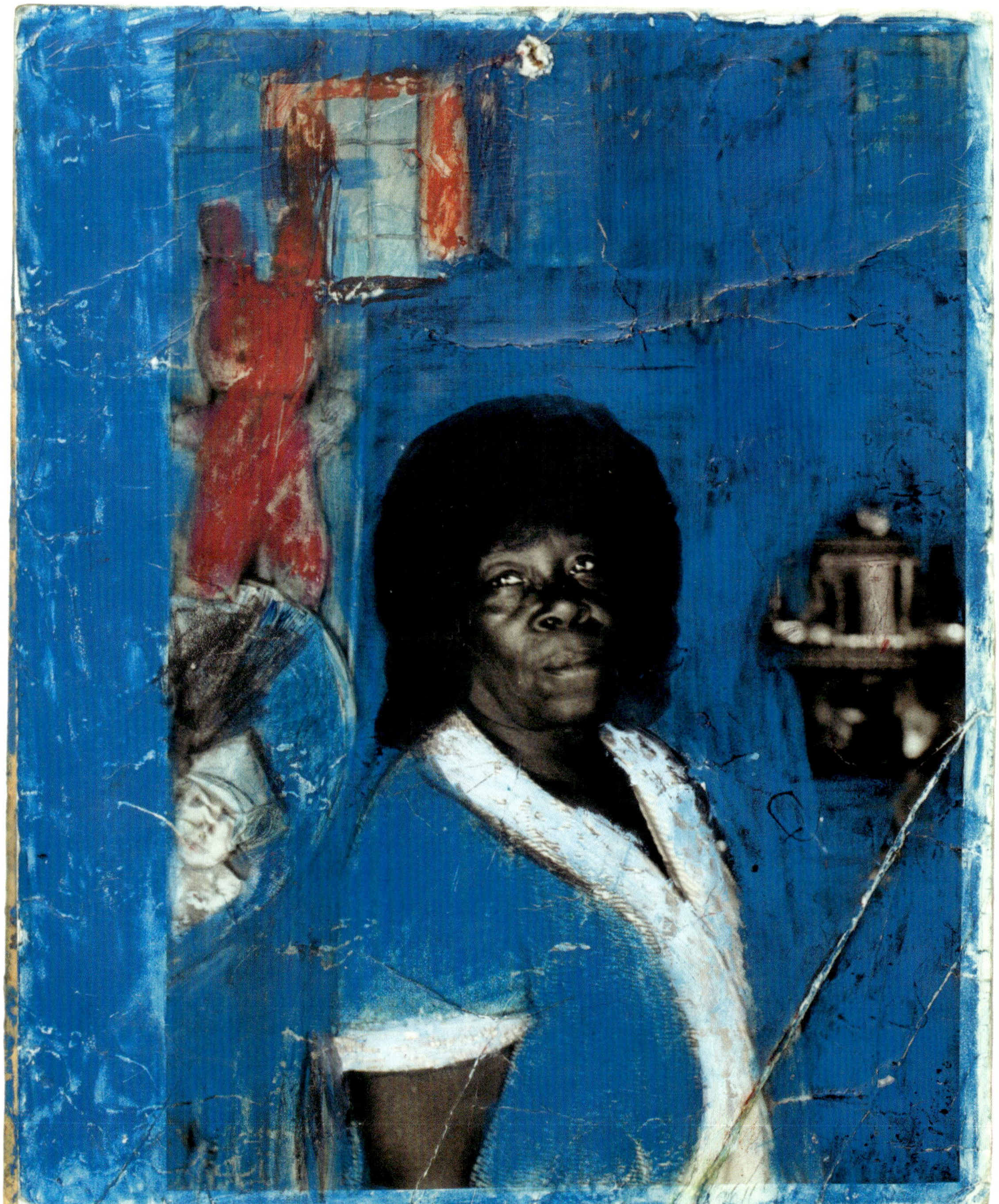

CAT. 46.

Nellie Mae Rowe

Nellie Mae Seated on Bench

ca. 1980

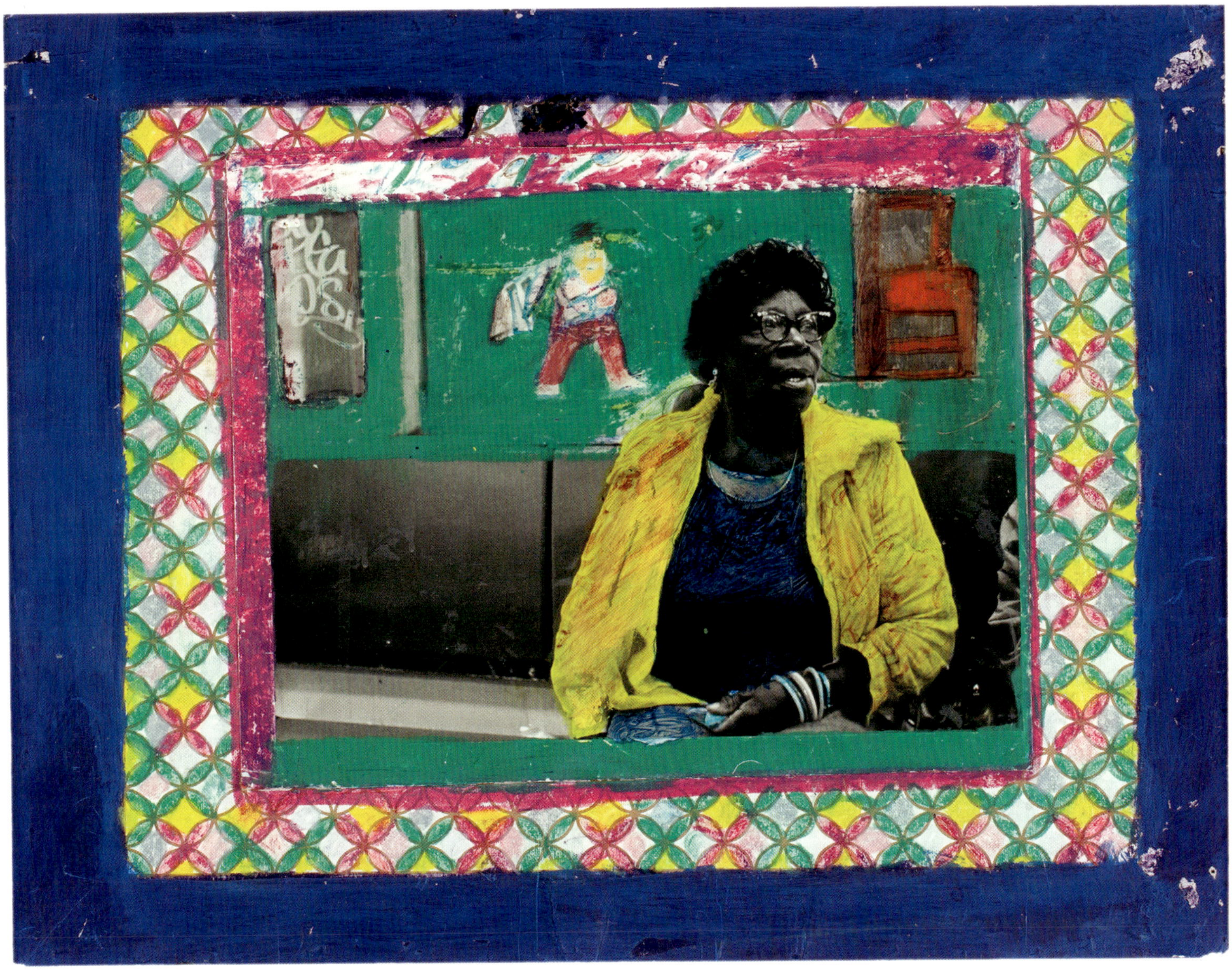

repercussions for those who did not. As Rowe transformed her home and yard, particularly in this predominantly white Atlanta suburb, and as a Black woman whose life overlapped the peak years of lynching in the Deep South—she would have understood that she walked a line between acceptable norms and perilous transgressions. Indeed, Rowe's aesthetic practices—which were above all else an assertion of her Black, female identity—were often judged as overly eccentric or distasteful. For pushing the limits of white tolerance she suffered the backlash—derided as a conjure woman or hoodooist and harassed by vandals. She recalled: "Everyone used to be so mean to me around here....They throw rocks and knock my window out, rocks all up against my house, firecrackers and everything and old rotten eggs all over my house....See, I kept my things hanging outdoors in the trees....They thought I was a hoodoo or something like that."[79]

In the 1970s, Rowe's yard increasingly attracted attention, especially after the *Atlanta Journal-Constitution* published an article and photographs about Rowe.[80] People started to visit, among them the collector Herbert Waide Hemphill Jr., who signed her guest book, purchased some of her drawings, and may have played a role in her inclusion in an exhibition at the Atlanta Historical Society, *Missing Pieces: Georgia Folk Art, 1770–1976*.[81] In 1978, Rowe met Judith Alexander, an Atlanta collector and dealer. Alexander was taken with Rowe's ebullience and energy, and the two formed an important friendship. Rowe had gradually become viewed as an artist, a creative person in her community. Her kind nature and determination to focus on joy over trauma played a large part in her evolving reception, although Rowe herself, who often turned to God for guidance when people were cruel, thought the meeting with Alexander might have been a heavenly intervention: "I kept on tolerating and talking with the Master until everything was all right," Rowe recalled. "I prayed and asked God, and he moved it."[82] Working with Alexander, Rowe sold her art regularly and, by the end of the 1970s, had been in exhibitions at Judith Alexander's Atlanta gallery, and the Parsons-Dreyfuss Gallery in New York. For the exhibition in New York, Rowe traveled with Alexander, her dealer's niece, Judith Alexander Augustine, and Atlanta artists Virginia Warren Smith and Lucinda Bunnen, who took many of the photographs that Rowe would later transform with drawn embellishments (**CATS. 45, 46**).[83] Jentleson has made the salient point that these two women enjoyed an unusually reciprocal relationship—that Rowe impacted Alexander as much as vice versa. Knowing Rowe changed the trajectory of Alexander's gallery focus and, overarchingly, her entire life.[84] Rowe's career was cut short by her death, in 1982, but she was aware of the appreciation her work was garnering. That year, she enjoyed a solo exhibition at Spelman College and saw her work published in the Corcoran's *Black Folk Art in America* catalogue. And although she was too ill to accept, she was honored by an invitation from First Lady Nancy Reagan to design a Christmas card for the White House.[85]

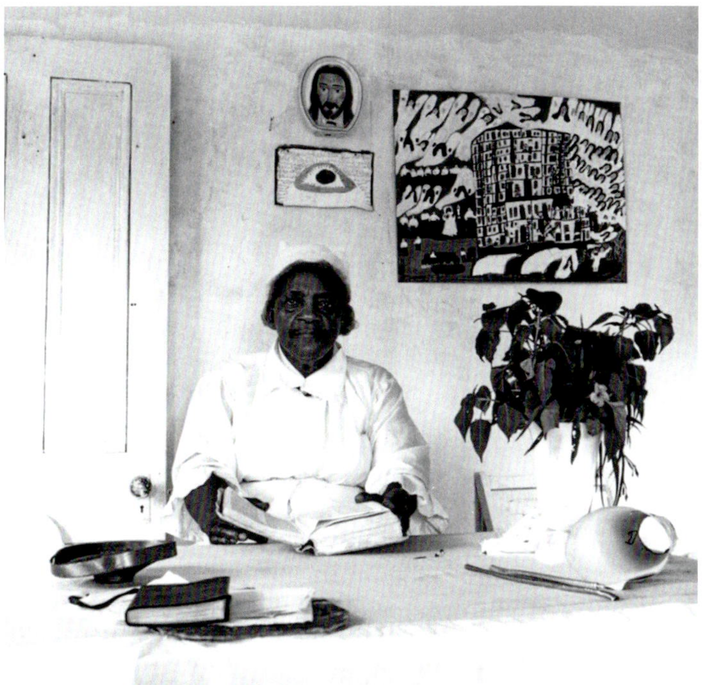

Fig. 29. Sister Gertrude Morgan in her prayer room at the Everlasting Gospel Mission, New Orleans, Louisiana, 1973; photograph by Guy Mendes

SISTER GERTRUDE MORGAN, in the tradition of Elijah Pierce, saw art as a vehicle for evangelism (Fig. 29). Morgan was born in Lafayette, Alabama, and as a teenager moved with her family to Columbus, Georgia, where she began attending the Rose Hill Memorial Baptist Church. Morgan married as a young woman, but a series of revelations between 1934 and 1939 instilled in her the conviction that God had called her to pursue a devout lifestyle and preach his gospel.[86] She first left home in 1938, working for God and caring for orphans in Opelika, Alabama, and elsewhere before arriving in New Orleans in 1939. Morgan banded with some other women in a practice of the Holiness and Sanctified movement, which did community work and encouraged music and dance as expressions of faith.

Some twenty years later, Morgan experienced another revelation: to live as a bride of Christ and use drawing and music as "tools for her ministry," as William A. Fagaly has described her artistic practice. She ceased wearing the black dress and white collar that had been her standard for many years, and donned from then on all-white garments to symbolize her spiritual union. Fagaly notes the clothes themselves ranged from actual wedding gowns to nurse's uniforms, the latter suiting her image of herself as a spiritual healer. In one painting Morgan wrote: "And that's Dr. Jesus there, and that's me standing next to him, his faithful nurse. Nurse? That's right! When I go to people's bedsides, I'm there to nurse their spirits. Amen!"[87]

In a rented house in the Lower Ninth Ward, Morgan created the Everlasting Gospel Mission, with a bright white prayer room and a front-porch gallery for her hand-painted signs and biblical imagery. She held Bible readings in the morning and hosted meetings in the prayer room several times a week, receiving guests on a regular basis. The space had no air conditioning, and Morgan made and painted paper or cardboard fans to help her congregants bear the heat during her services (**CAT. 47**). "The Everlasting Gospel Mission was a very personal mission, and Sister Gertrude Morgan had her own preaching style," Fagaly notes. "She was never ordained by a church, she was a self-proclaimed Sister. Her religious expression held a certain amount of autonomy and spontaneity. But her practices were rooted in gospel traditions of the Baptists and the Holiness movement."[88] Elaine Yau notes, however, that titles such as "sister" and "mother" were names

CAT. 47.

Sister Gertrude Morgan

Fan (recto/verso)

ca. 1970

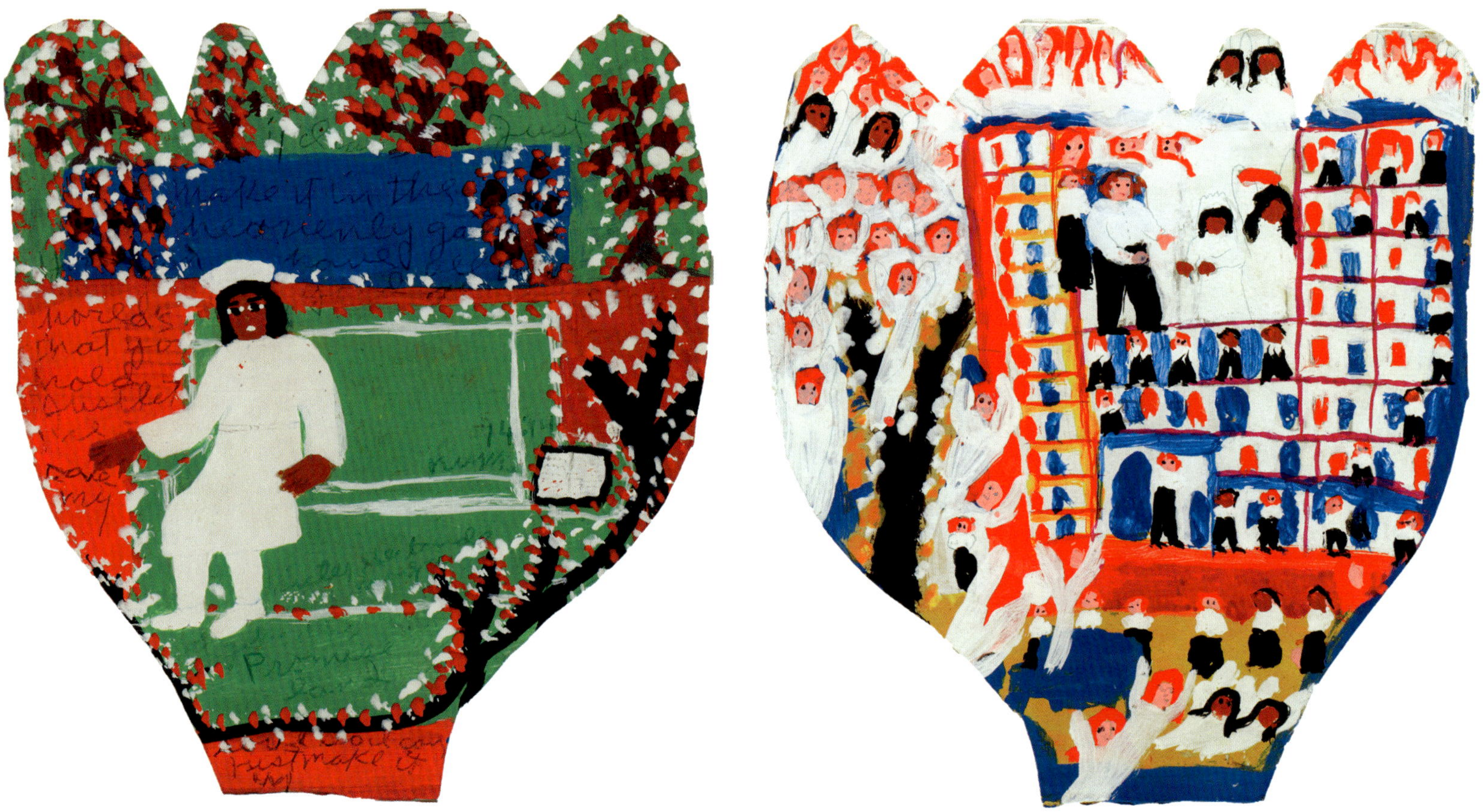

used to indicate religious kinship and hierarchy within congregations, and Morgan's ongoing use of "Sister" traces back to the first mission she served in, and importantly connects her to the ways in which Black religious culture honored an individual's sanctified journey with the divine.[89]

Morgan's art gave color and form to passages of scripture from the Old and New Testaments, and served as visual aids for her own gospel services. Morgan depicted herself singing, playing the piano, or preaching God's word through one of her handmade and painted paper megaphones. The backgrounds of her paintings, like her own surroundings, were frequently a bright white and depicted Morgan or angels doing God's work. In tandem with her own image, Morgan's paintings are often imbued with a copious amount of text—scripture, sermons, the Word—flowing endlessly like a river. Like Rowe, Morgan felt her art was a divine gift, but the two artists were worlds apart when it came to how they interpreted this gift and what to do with it. For Rowe it was a path of self-actualization; Morgan, on the other hand, believed that she was the conduit of God's very will. In a letter to curator Regenia A. Perry in 1972, Morgan wrote, "Now God uses me here in the Prayer Room he gives me Revelation's and a few days later he give me scripture what the Prophecy was and where it came from. O god move's in a mysterious way."[90] Not unlike William Edmondson, and the Reverend Howard Finster, discussed in the following section, "Gamechangers," Morgan's extraordinary spirituality contributed to a layered marginalization. "Her religious devotion was so acute as to be considered abnormal and eccentric and to put her at a certain remove from society," Fagaly notes.[91] But, just like Finster, Morgan saw interest in her and her work as a means to spreading the Word; if people found her compelling, that could only benefit her cause.

It was E. Lorenz "Larry" Borenstein, an art dealer in the French Quarter, who began to sell Morgan's art around 1960, after encountering her while she was preaching. Borenstein was a capable manager and marketer, and his sales of her work allowed her to keep her mission running. Morgan often did musical performances at his gallery, and he connected her with collectors and curators to ensure her way forward. Morgan gained international attention when she was featured in the September 1973 issue of Andy Warhol's *Interview* magazine, which Yau argues suited its "trendsetting readership" despite the devout Black musician/painter's apparent incongruity within a mix of articles about movie stars and glitterati.[92] "One could say Morgan fascinated precisely because she was a 'nonartist' artist, reinforcing the kind of paradoxes than ran through Warhol's art and the quixotic artistic identity he fashioned for himself," Yau explains.[93] She believes that it was this very identity, and Morgan's genuine lack of interest in professional growth or commercial pursuits, that made her so compelling as African American self-taught artists moved increasingly into the public eye. Morgan would become central to many of the era's debates about whether a visual practice like hers—so fully enmeshed in life and spirituality—was really "art" as the Western canon

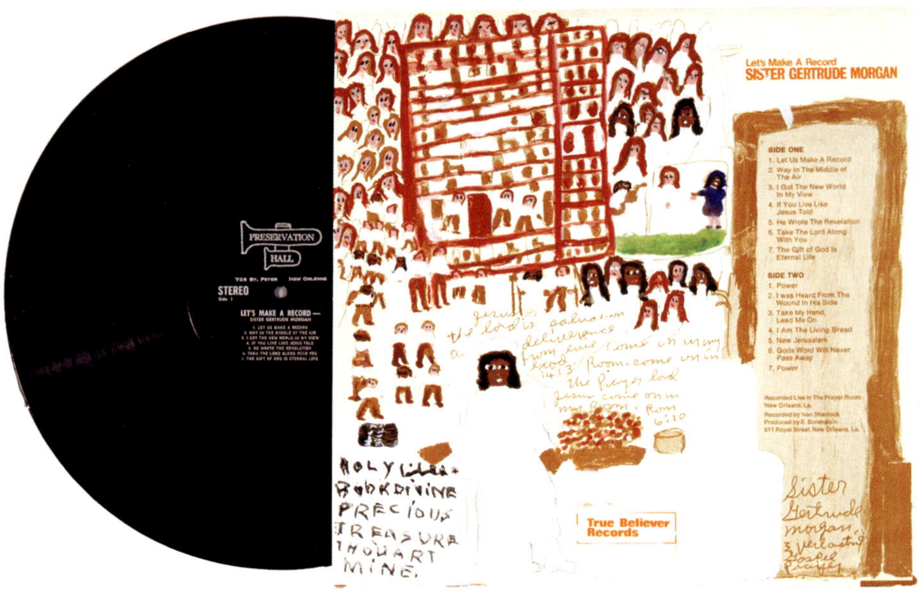

understood it, or if it was more appropriately considered as a cultural artifact. But, for Morgan, these concerns were beside the point; it was the mission that mattered, and her full embrace of visual media and sound technologies is conveyed in what Yau has called "the rapturous emotion and forms that shaped Morgan's sanctified dialogues."[94]

Similarly untroubled by concerns of the art canon, *New York Times* music critic Ben Ratliff, reconsidering her 1971 recorded album *Let's Make a Record* in 2004, in conjunction with Fagaly's exhibition *Tools of Her Ministry: The Art of Sister Gertrude Morgan* at New York's American Folk Art Museum, made a rich and direct assessment of Morgan's talent (Fig. 30). Instead of dwelling on the novelty of her persona, Ratliff observed that the immediacy and charisma Morgan conveyed were truly powerful—key traits that gave her creative efforts an entirely beguiling human candor.[95] Michael Kimmelman's art review for the same exhibition similarly credited her directness, emphasizing the way in which Morgan employed text for both its meaning and its visual impact. "Untutored but full of an uncanny grace, her paintings were meant as teaching aids to spread the Word of God, and words, thousands of them, increasingly took up every spare millimeter of space in her pictures. They flowed, stream-of-consciousness like, in rapt and incantatory style, which was also how she spoke.... [The art's] plainspoken ecstasy gives it an aura. You don't have to be religious to appreciate the inborn eloquence, both formal and literary; you only have to accept that painting, when it comes from the heart and is so clearly genuine, can lift the soul."[96]

In this last remark, Kimmelman identifies an important, unifying factor in the art of both Rowe and Morgan: that the power of art—in all of its visual, aural, and enveloping sensory modes—uplifts the soul and engenders an environment of well-being rooted in humanity and positivity. Early in 1974, Morgan reported to Borenstein that the Lord had told her to stop

Fig. 30. Sister Gertrude Morgan, *Let's Make a Record*, 1971, tempera, acrylic, and pencil on paperboard; vinyl. Album cover: 12 ⅜ × 12 ½ in. Smithsonian American Art Museum, Gift of Chuck and Jan Rosenak, 1981.136.5A-B

making art and turn to poetry.[97] Morgan died in 1980, two years before she was selected for inclusion in the *Black Folk Art in America* exhibition. Yau contends that the long-term impact of Morgan's art cannot be separated from her cultural beliefs and a confluence of timely phenomena, including the postwar revival of jazz, an increased social agency for African American believers within Sanctified religion and culture, the widening acclaim for Black musical performance, the inclusive spirit of New Orleans's French Quarter, and an expanding interest in untrained artists that was inextricably linked to the collective force of African American vernacular culture. "Out of this matrix, Morgan forged an indelibly powerful, personal artistic life for herself that persists in her paintings and recordings."[98]

SAM DOYLE (1906–1985) / ULYSSES DAVIS (1913–1990)

Sam Doyle and Ulysses Davis independently created large bodies of art along the Lowcountry coast spanning South Carolina and mid-coastal Georgia and made their public debuts in the *Black Folk Art in America* exhibition at the Corcoran. Doyle lived most of his life on the Sea Island of St. Helena, where he painted portraits, real and mythical, of his Gullah community and historic figures. Most notably, Doyle celebrated and documented the accomplishments of his fellow Black Americans, understanding that these histories were rarely recorded by white historians and that they would otherwise disappear. Davis became a woodcarver of exceptional skill, shaping artworks ranging from bas-relief pictures to portrait busts to creatures drawn from an imaginative mythology. Doyle and Davis followed individual visions, yet both artists were grounded in faith, patriotism, honored heritage, and history, and depicted a diverse array of characters spanning the straitlaced and the unconventional.

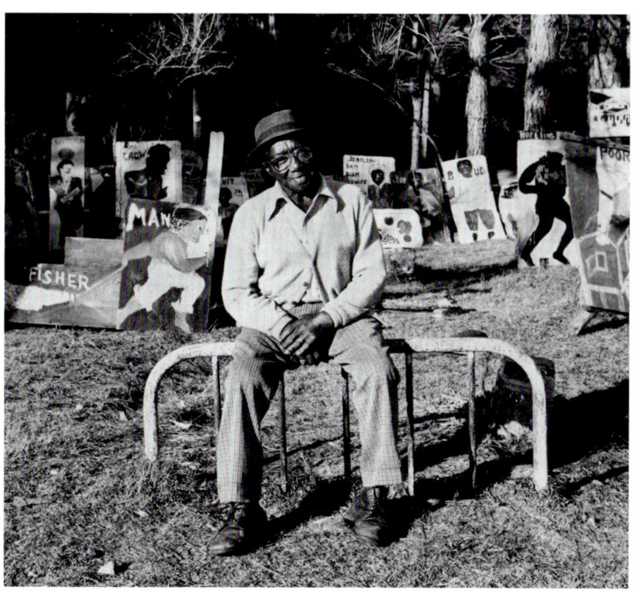

Fig. 31. Sam Doyle, St. Helena, South Carolina, 1985; photograph by Roger Manley

The Sea Islands of the Lowcountry, where enslaved peoples farmed fields of rice, indigo, and cotton on expansive plantations, gave rise to Gullah culture. **SAM DOYLE** was born into this rich amalgamation of African and Caribbean influences and creolized language which, by then, had grown strong over the course of three centuries (Fig. 31). The region was liberated in the early days of the Civil War, and Northern missionaries established the Penn School on St. Helena, named in honor of Quaker philanthropist William Penn, to benefit the newly emancipated citizens. After the war, the US government sold plantation land that had been abandoned by Confederate owners, much of which was purchased by freedmen.

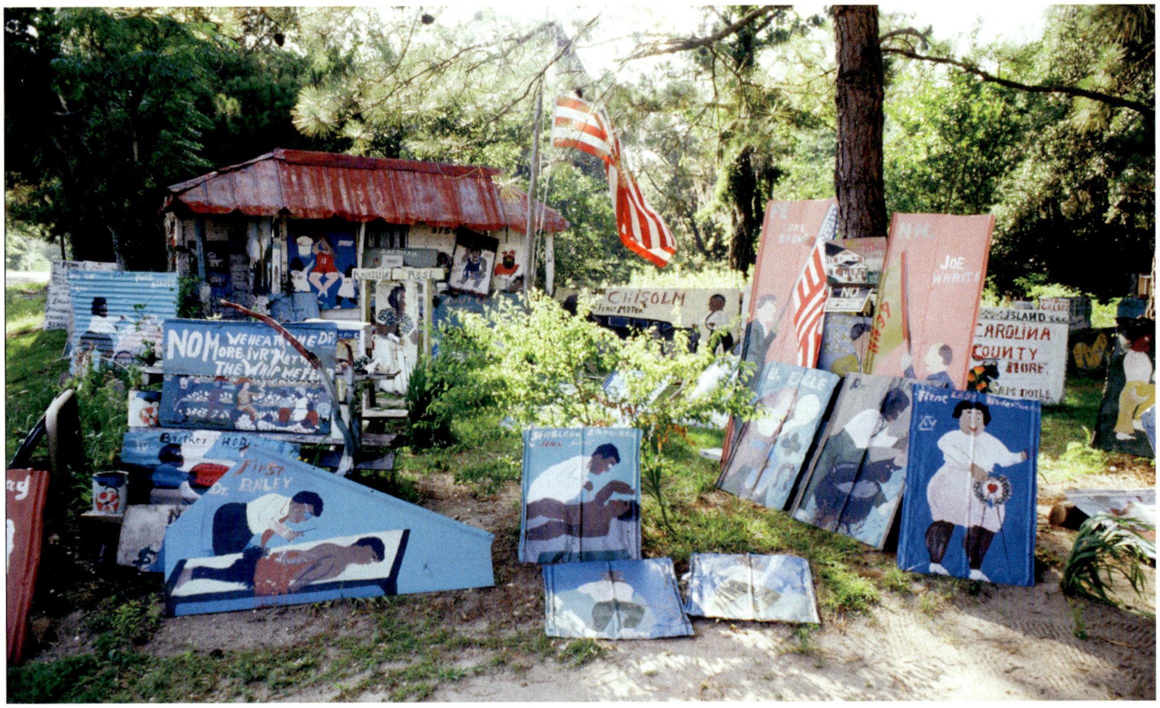

Fig. 32. Sam Doyle's yard, St. Helena, South Carolina, 1985; photograph by Roger Manley

Doyle's life was steeped in the folkways and beliefs of a people who relied little on mainstream white culture and retained a strong connection to their ancestral roots. He attended the Penn School as a boy, learned about the region's history and developed his interest in art, but family circumstances demanded that he leave school after the ninth grade. Doyle was twenty-one before the island was connected to the mainland by bridges. It was in the 1970s, after living and working in several nearby places and locales, marriage, children, and separation from his wife, that Doyle retired and began his art project in earnest.[99]

Although he made sculptures as well as paintings, Doyle was best known for his painted portraits made on sheets of roofing tin. "He blended ancestral Gullah lore and his devout Baptist faith into a rich multicultural impasto," explains Gordon W. Bailey, expert on and longtime advocate for Doyle's work. "Two series, *Penn* (school) and *First* (achievement or event), commingled with his folkloric works and clearly established Doyle's mission to honor Gullah culture and, more generally, African American advancement. Through the years, the museum-like display that overflowed the yard of his small, two-story house and adjacent workshop evolved into the St. Helena Out Door Art Gallery"[100] (Fig. 32). Doyle's apprecitions were wide-ranging. He honored war veterans and fighters for civil rights including Abraham Lincoln, Robert Smalls, John F. Kennedy, Robert F. Kennedy, and Rev. Dr. Martin Luther King Jr., and acknowledged the achievements of community members, including his brother James Doyle, St. Helena's first Black

CAT. 48.
Sam Doyle
F. Capers
ca. 1970–83

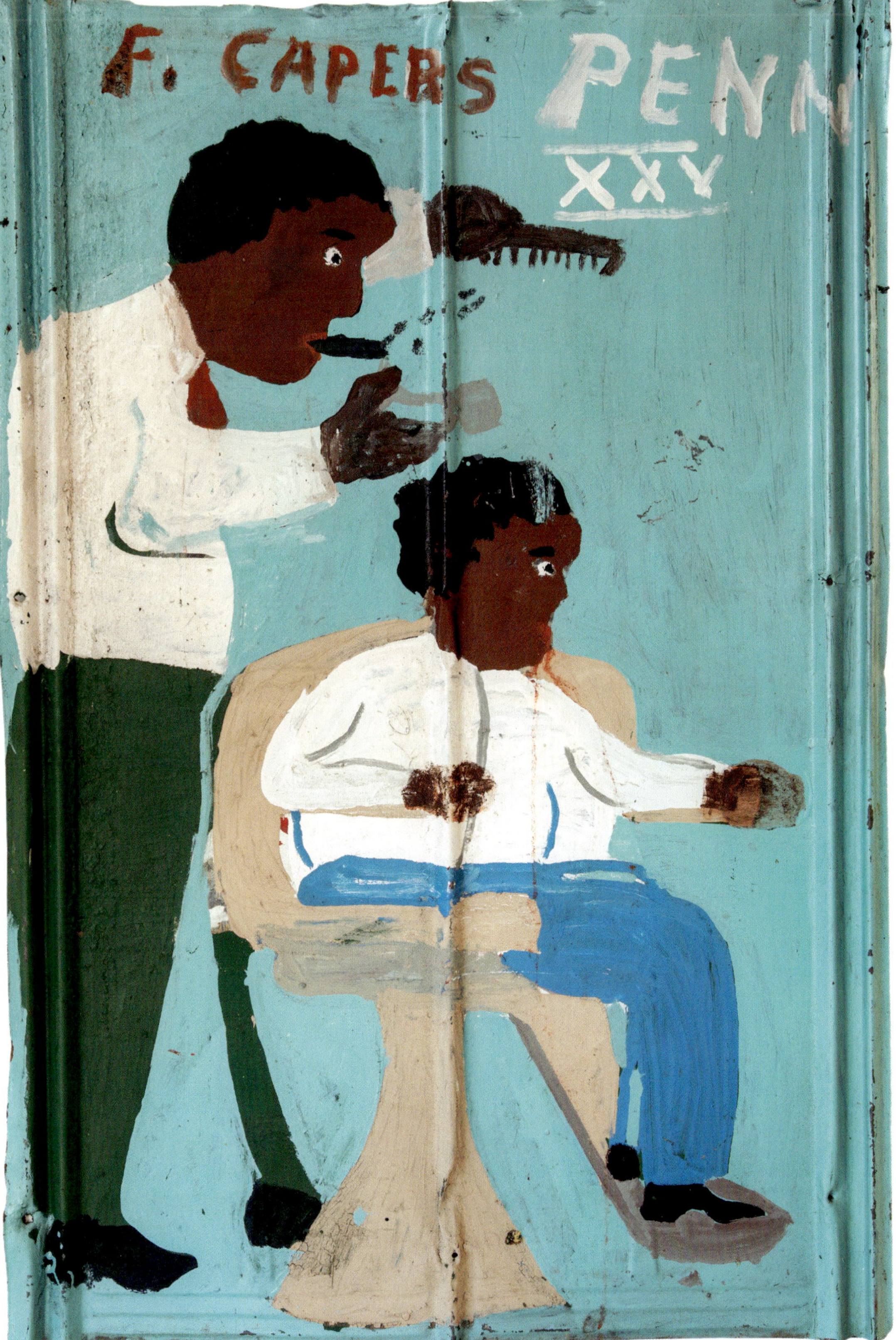
F. CAPERS PENN
XXV

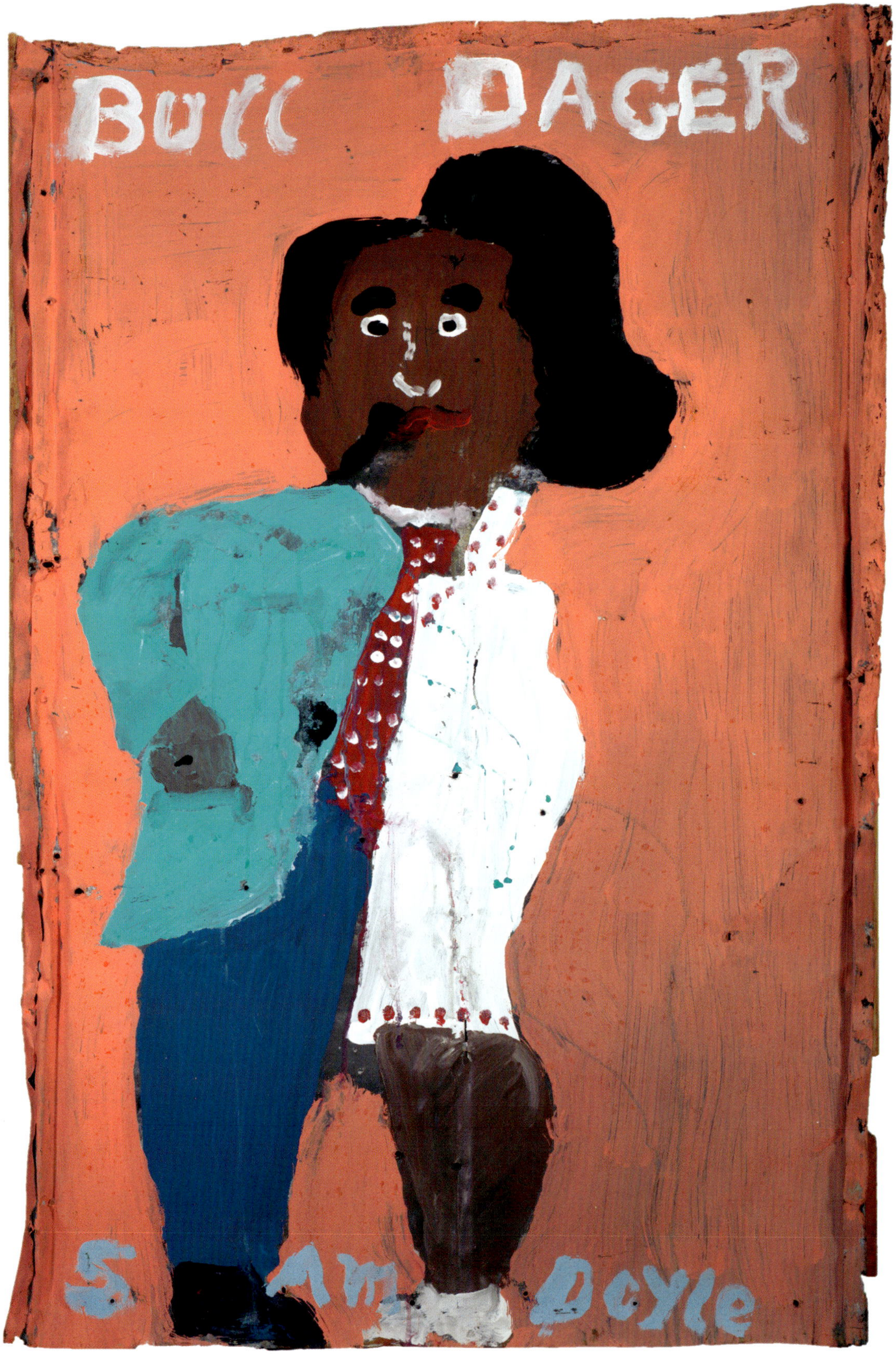
BULL DAGER
SAM DOYLE

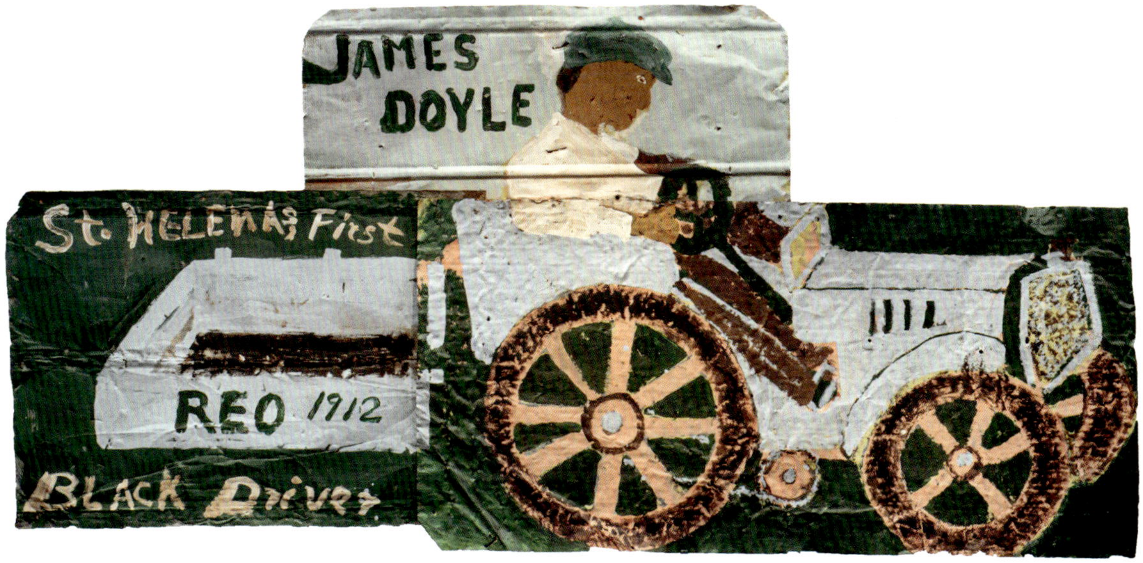

Fig. 33. Sam Doyle, *James Doyle, St. Helena's First Black Driver*, ca. 1982, house paint on metal roofing panels, overall: 43 ½ × 86 ⅛ × 5 in. Smithsonian American Art Museum, Gift of Chuck and Jan Rosenak and museum purchase through the Luisita L. and Franz H. Denghausen Endowment, 1997.124.13A-C

driver, and Frank Capers, a respected barber and one of the islands first openly gay residents (Fig. 33, **CAT. 48**).[101] Among his most dynamic images are those visualizing haints—spirits from Afro-Caribbean legend and lore—including *Jack O Lanton*, and root practitioners, *Dr. Buz* and *Dr. Crow*, who drew on traditions of conjure and hoodoo to heal and protect the islanders. His sociopolitical paintings confront the brutality of slavery and the lasting fallout of racism in America and hot-button topics never daunted him.[102] Doyle was known to say, "That's natural, man!," reflecting his ease with subjects that others might have found uncomfortable, such as sexual identity and gender fluidity. Among such portrayals are *Bull Dager* and other depictions of, as the artist described them, individuals who are "sometimes a woman, sometimes a man" or who thwarted mainstream conventions or straightforward presentations of identity (**CAT. 49**).[103]

Doyle's title for this piece reflects what is now clearly understood to be pejorative slang for an African American, masculine lesbian, but overarchingly his portrayals reflect inherent respect for those who remained true to themselves and revealed inner strength.[104] In the painting, we see a figure split—quite literally and not naturally—down the center. The left side conveys a feminine appearance through a white dress and poufed, bobbed hair; the right, a mustached, masculine character in a trouser suit. Doyle regarded the sexual inclinations, gender identities, and self-presentations of individuals as part of what made them unique. Whether he makes reference to someone specific here is unknown, but Doyle's tendency to feature an individual's name or nickname on his portrait-tributes, and to capture a degree of likeness in them, suggests this may be a more generalized reflection on the expansiveness of people he knew and encountered, and perhaps the notion that personal identity need not be fixed.[105] Sharon P. Holland, professor of English and African American studies and sexuality studies, has observed, "Doyle is forever playful, mixing nomenclature and caricature to get us to think about our own situatedness."[106]

CAT. 49.
Sam Doyle
Bull Dager
ca. 1980

Bull Dager's engaging theatricality invites reflection on and empathic acceptance of individuality, our own and others'. William Arnett, a writer and collector from Atlanta, Georgia, believed that Doyle's depictions often worked on more than one level and consistently celebrated people as complex beings, pointing out that Doyle's multiple tributes to Frank Capers depicted the islander not only as a successful businessman, but as a proud gay man, and as a colorful local character.[107]

For Doyle, painterly precision took a back seat to recording the humanity and history of his community, the admirable and the questionable, the mythic and the quotidian. "Doyle painted our presence, our enslaved history, our American history," artist and designer Hylan Booker has observed. Booker, citing Doyle's influence on Jean-Michel Basquiat, who was an admirer and collector of Doyle's art, went on to say, "His [Doyle's] Gullah lore, with its African shadow, guides us outward, giving lines of reference, making a world visible, tangible, naming the dreams, tagging the darkness. Doyle is our witness, our voice, our griot. He created art that does more than arouse—it reveals."[108] Marquetta L. Goodwine, Queen Quet, elected chieftess and spokes-person for the Gullah/Geechee Nation, has described Doyle's effort succinctly: "It is a complexity of simplicity we have here. There is a depth and multiplicity of meanings behind the simplest of expressions; you don't have to dress it up, it comes across sharp and clear."[109]

ULYSSES DAVIS grew up a bit farther inland, in Fitzgerald, Georgia (Fig. 34). He took up carving as a boy, having to make—as many children did in that era—his own toys. Like Elijah Pierce, he began barbering as a boy as well, but he learned this skill primarily on his own, practicing and learning on the heads of willing neighbor-hood boys. He later apprenticed as a railroad blacksmith, which took him to Savannah in 1942. But when car travel and highways dis-placed the passenger rail lines, he fell back on barbering, opening his own small shop. Also like Pierce, Davis reserved part of his space for woodworking, making and restoring furniture, and carving whenever time allowed. He learned the skills of whittling, from the ubiquitous walking cane to more sophisticated challenges such as the "ball in cage," a technique that, among whittlers, shows the journey of time-honored, acquired skills, in this case one in which the practiced removal of wood, bit by

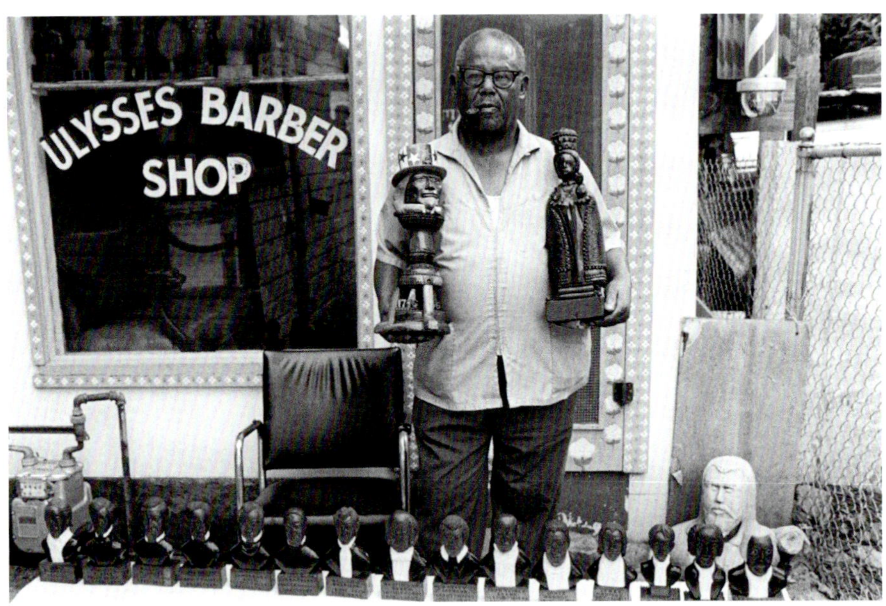

Fig. 34. Melinda Blauvelt, *Ulysses Davis Outside His Barbershop*, Savannah, Georgia, 1981

CAT. 50.
Ulysses Davis
Sputnik
ca. 1957

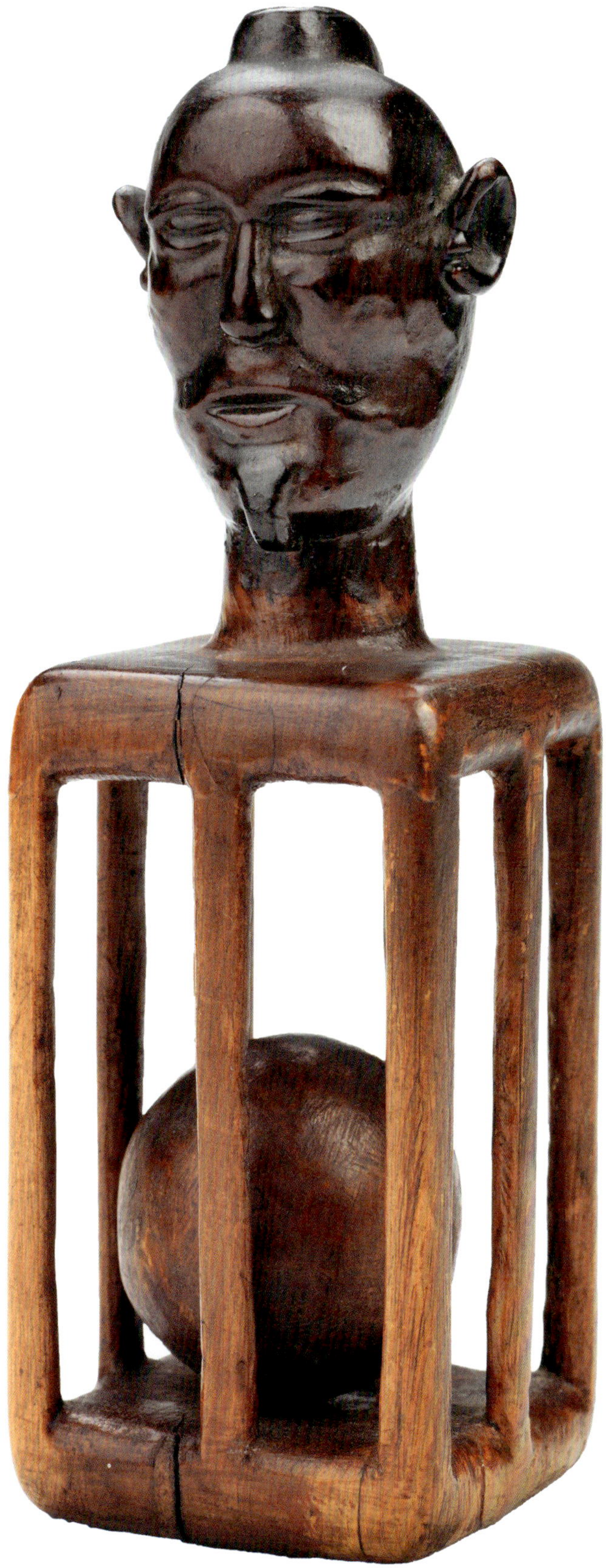

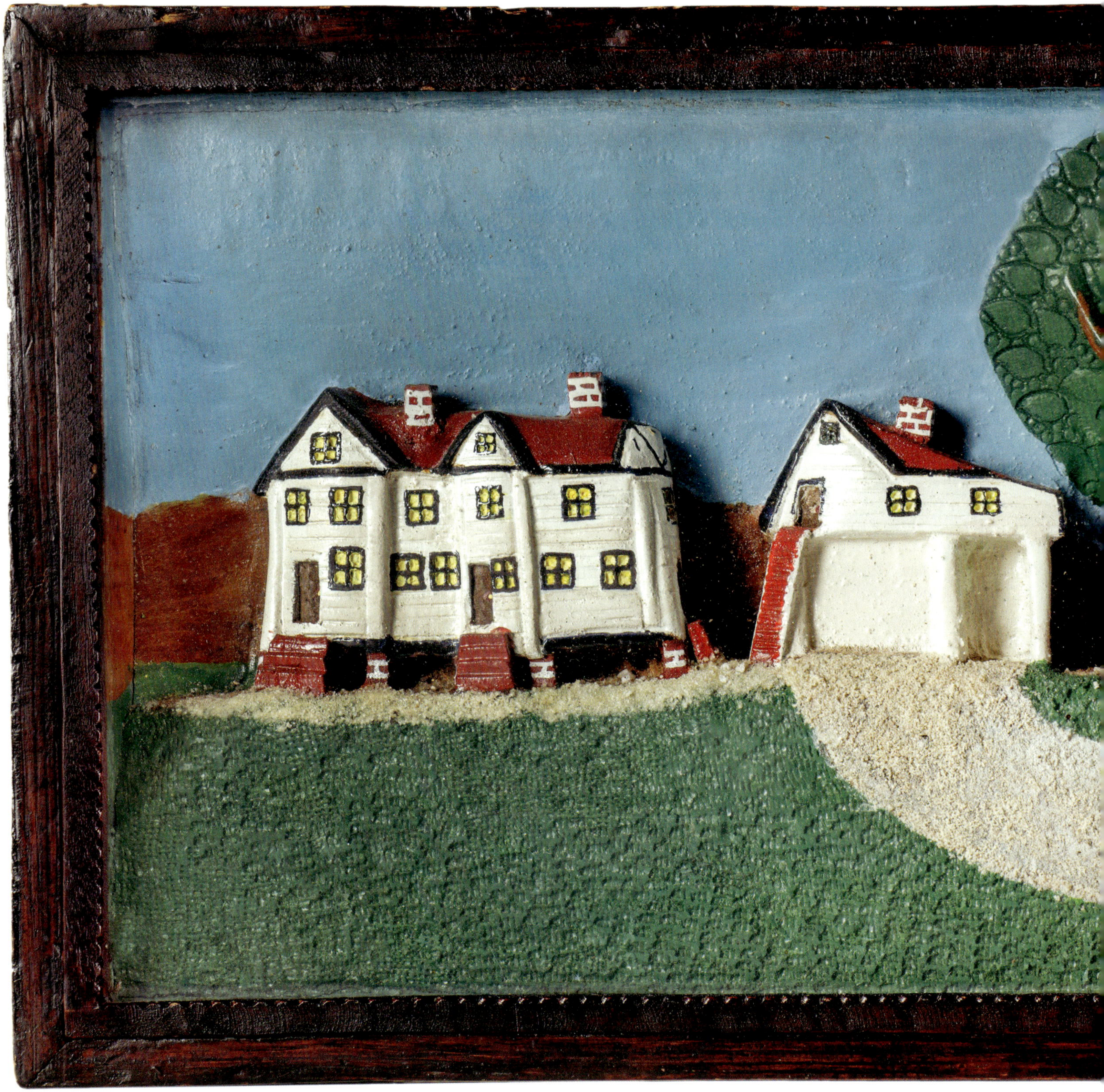

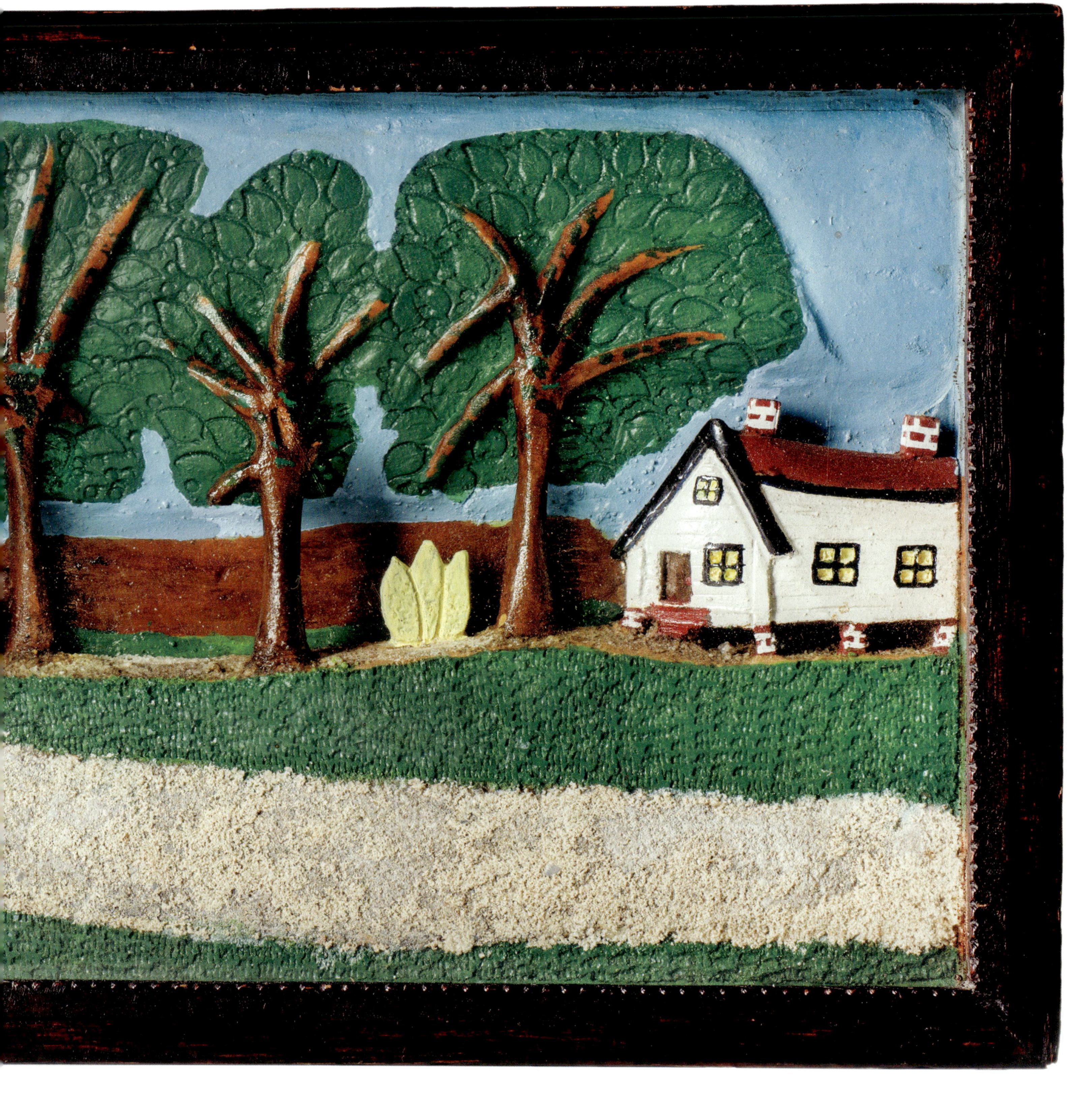

preceding pages

CAT. 51.
Ulysses Davis
Untitled
1942

CAT. 52.
Ulysses Davis
Strong Man
ca. 1950–90

CAT. 53.
Ulysses Davis
Headhunter
ca. 1950–90

CAT. 54.
Ulysses Davis
Untitled
ca. 1950–90

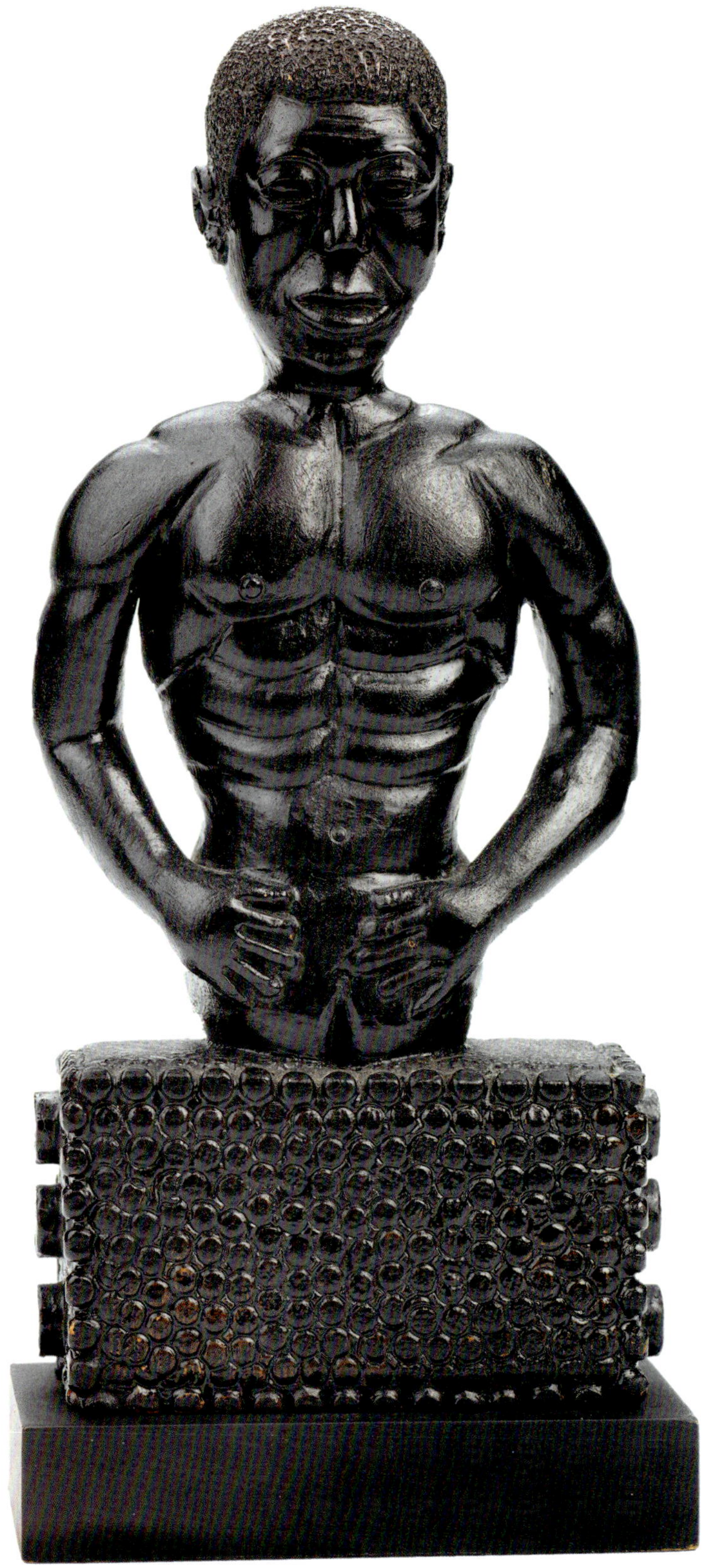

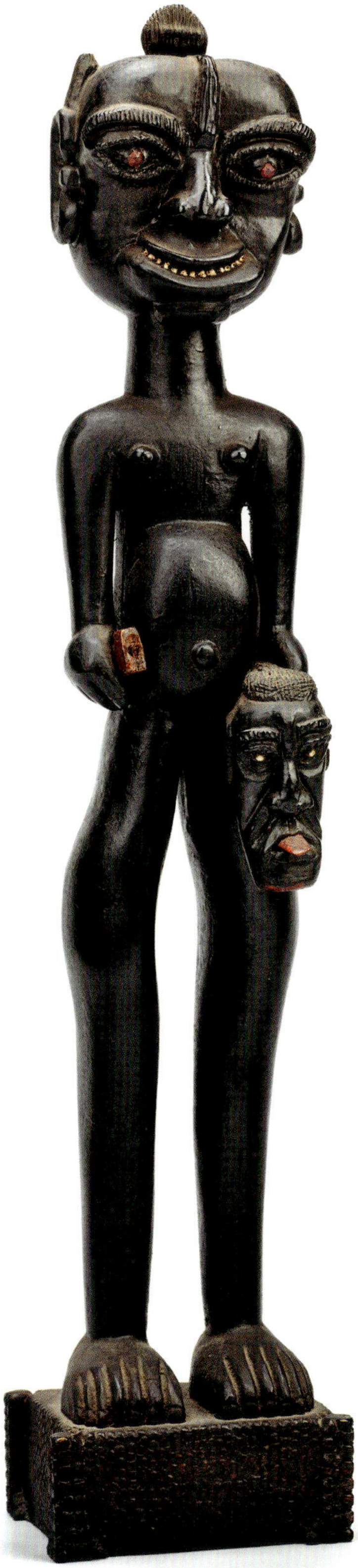

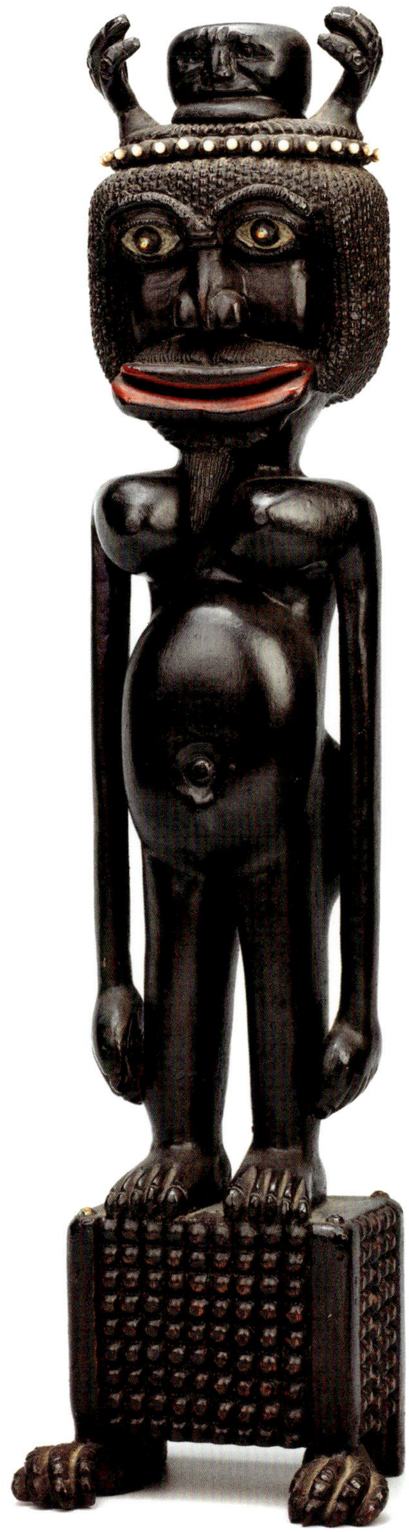

bit, results in a sort of visual magic trick—a sphere trapped inside a rectangular cage (**CAT. 50**). Davis's carvings most often featured the natural colors of wood, sometimes embellished with painted details. In an unusual piece from 1942, Davis presented a scene of houses, carved in deep relief, set within a boxlike frame, painted, and hung like a work on canvas (**CAT. 51**). Among Davis's favored treatments was to saturate his finished carvings with shoe polish for a dark, smooth, and glossy surface (**CAT. 52**).[110]

Before the end of Jim Crow segregation in the United States, barbering was among a handful of independent professions open to African Americans. More than simply a place of autonomy for the owner, however, like Black churches and beauty salons, barbershops served as a community hub. "During the era of Jim Crow, black men had few spaces where they could congregate and deliberate freely and with a sense of privacy," historian Quincy T. Mills explains.[111] Mills notes that in the nineteenth century, when Black barbers serviced white men, they were seen as servile. But in the twentieth century, especially with the rise of neighborhood barbershops like Davis's, Black barbers "emphasized the artistry in their work to groom a respectable blackness," becoming pivotal figures in what he calls the terrain of "grooming race."[112]

Susan Mitchell Crawley observed the paradox in Davis's oeuvre: "His work united opposing tendencies in carvings that manifested his faith through solemnity and parody, demonstrated intense love for America and deep pride in his African heritage [**CATS. 53, 54**], and explored subject matter ranging from traditional depictions of leaders to the most outlandish creatures his extraordinary imagination could conceive."[113] Davis's most expansive undertaking was carving bust portraits of all the US presidents (see Fig. 34, p. 126). While individual bust portraits of George Washington, Abraham Lincoln, and Frederick Douglass were carved around the 1940s (see **CATS. 6, 7**), Crawley believes he began the bust series sometime in the early 1970s, with a different version of George Washington, and continued the matched group based on a schoolbook featuring the presidential portraits—stiffly posed and similarly dressed. The earlier busts show an elegant but developing style, unpainted with plain bases, but details such as eyes and hair color distinguished with darker tones of varnish. In the later series, Davis presents the presidents clad in black suits, white shirts, and black ties, which he painted, leaving the wood color of the head its natural shade, sometimes glossed with shoe polish. Additionally, he carved their names, dates of tenure, and sequence number. The 1970s Washington bust stands apart for the stark contrast between the white hair and the darker hue of the wood, raising the question as to whether Davis was intentionally playing with representations of white icons.[114]

Davis was known to be particular about the wood he used; sometimes he made do with found scraps, but, for the more carefully planned pieces, he acquired and used finely grained hardwoods,

CAT. 55.
Ulysses Davis
Uncle Sam
1976

CAT. 56.
Ulysses Davis
Untitled (Cane)
ca. 1950–90

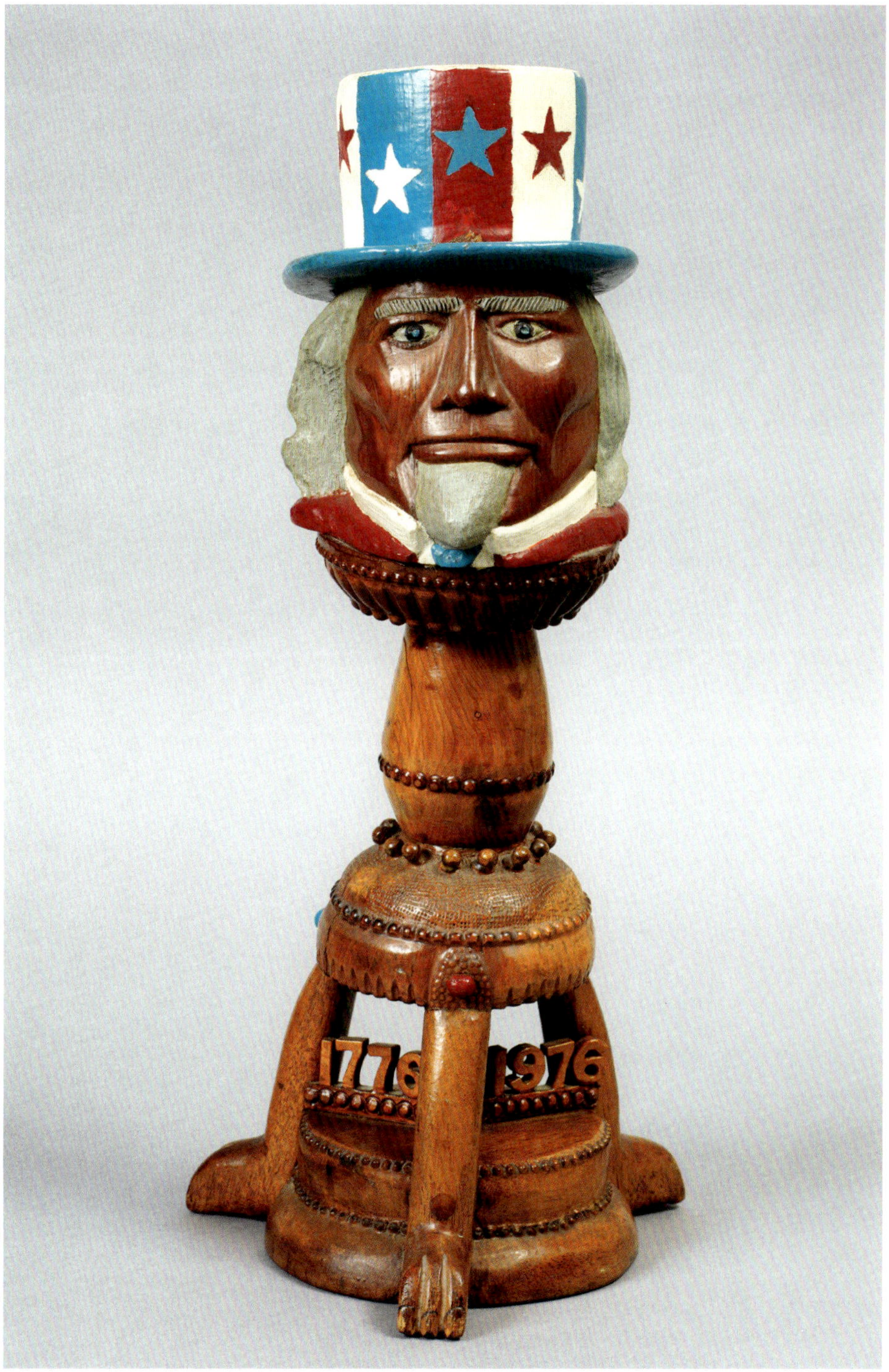
1776
1976

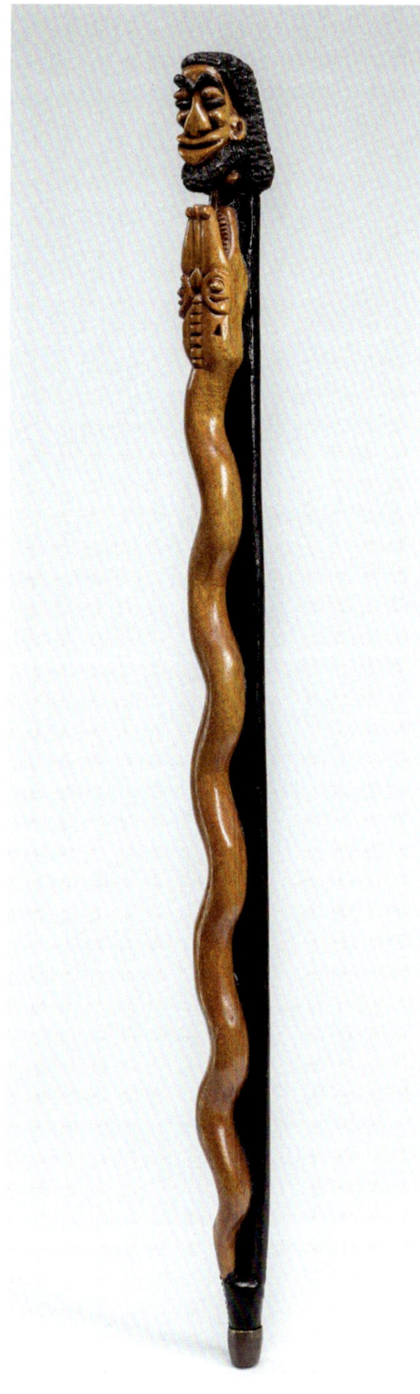

including mahogany, cedar, and poplar.[115] One reviewer believed it was Davis's intention to present the presidents as Black, or, as he problematically phrased it, "in blackface."[116] Yet Davis's portraits of Martin Luther King Jr. and Frederick Douglass argue against this notion, as his depictions of African Americans are given a deeper color in the polish, and his careful attention to each individual's facial features indicates the seriousness with which he took the task of representation. One bas-relief carving, paying tribute to revered figures on a piece he called *Immortality Board*, shows King with John F. Kennedy, Robert Kennedy, Abraham Lincoln, and George Washington.[117] King takes the foremost position, and is clearly given, by Davis, a darker skin tone than his peers; Lincoln's dark hair and beard—akin to similar treatments in his early carving of Lincoln (see **CAT. 7**)—and the very pale hair color given to Washington further argue for Davis's careful treatment of such details. The ambiguity remains interesting, however, particularly as Davis might have sought lighter woods for the presidential series if this had been a critical point of clarification in his mind.

Without a doubt, Davis was, like Doyle, fiercely patriotic. Local Savannah art teacher Virginia Kiah became an advocate for Davis's work in the late 1950s; she saw to his inclusion in the 1976 exhibition *Missing Pieces: Georgia Folk Art, 1770–1976*. The show traveled to the Library of Congress in 1978, where Davis presented First Lady Rosalynn Carter with a bust of President Jimmy Carter (Fig. 35).[118] Four years later he met another first lady, Nancy Reagan, at the preview for the *Black Folk Art in America* show. Mrs. Reagan told Davis she had recognized his portrait of her husband, and Davis would look back on this as "one of the proudest moments" of his lifetime.[119] Arguably the premier patriotic work in Davis's oeuvre is his *Uncle Sam* from 1976; made in celebration of America's bicentennial, the piece shows a regal male bust wearing a polychrome, star-spangled top hat (**CAT. 55**). Uncle Sam—another figure in which race, despite the figure's blue eyes and straight gray hair, acquires some ambiguity through the wood's russet tone—gazes straight ahead, perhaps toward the nation's future. On the lower section, Davis frames Uncle Sam with dates celebrating the bicentennial of the republic: 1776–1976. In this sculpture, Davis took time to show his array of skills, with spherical beadwork encircling the bust in several places, texturing, painted details, and the remarkably elegant face itself. In a detail that nods to the Black vernacular aesthetic, Davis set the bust atop a "footed" pedestal, using a visual pun in which the structure's feet are shaped like animal feet.[120]

Davis was an artist of encompassing vision, and his patriotic works were only one facet of his vivid pantheon. His carvings drew on a deep wellspring of Christian spirituality, animals and mythological creatures, historical and celebrity figures, philosophical musings and spiritual abstractions given physical form, and a smaller number of items such as canes, tables, and

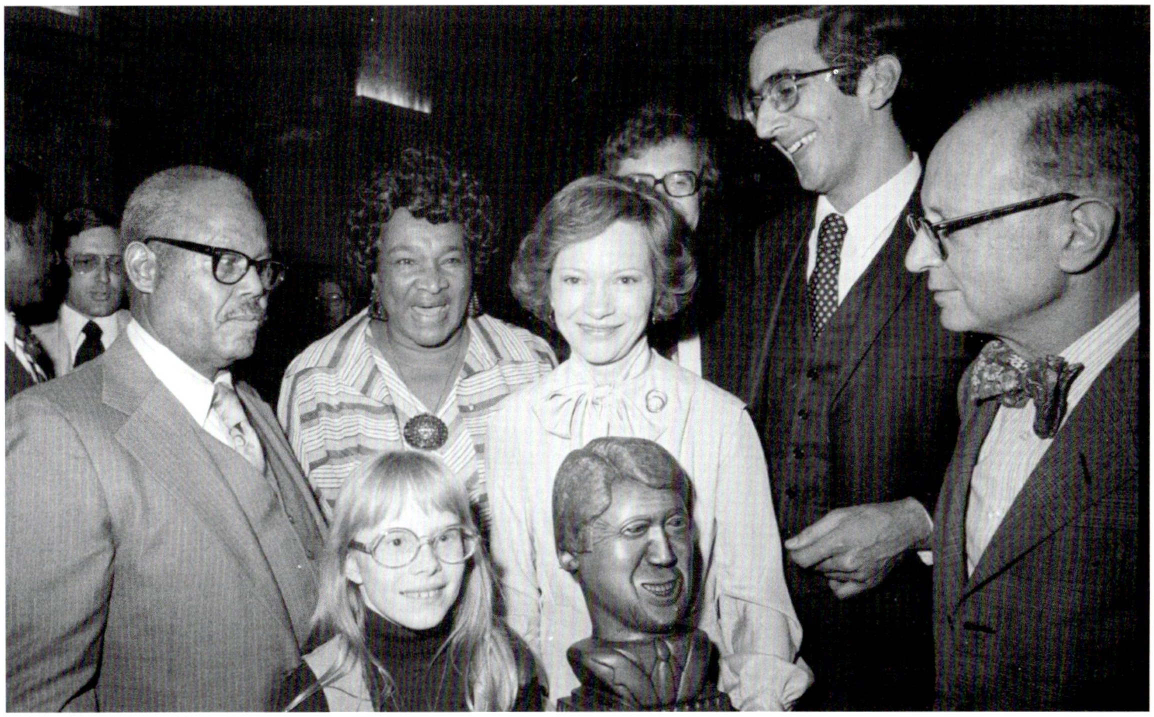

Fig. 35. Ulysses Davis presenting his portrait bust of President Jimmy Carter to First Lady Rosalynn Carter and her daughter, Amy, with Elizabeth Davis, American Folklife Center Director Alan Jabbour, and Librarian of Congress Daniel J. Boorstin, 1978. Library of Congress Manuscript Division

embellished household or personal items. He favored African and African-inspired subjects—kings and queens, warriors, and tribesmen, whose images he reportedly studied at the local library.[121] A number of African-inspired but imaginatively rendered figures draw on the theme of Lost Tribes, stories of exile that resonate across the Black Atlantic for the connections they offer between biblical figures and people uprooted or displaced from their ancestral lands. A cane Davis carved shows a serpent crawling up toward a bearded figure with dark, wavy hair and thick eyebrows: a Moses figure that Davis has endowed with distinctly Black features (**CAT. 56**). In the Book of Exodus, God sends poisonous snakes to punish those who complained about his judgment of their sins with a fatal bite. Yet he also showed his mercy, by giving Moses the power to heal those who had been bitten: "Then the Lord said to Moses, 'Make a snake image and mount it on a pole. When anyone who is bitten looks at it, he will recover.' So Moses made a bronze snake and mounted it on a pole. Whenever someone was bitten, and he looked at the bronze snake, he recovered.'"[122] Davis's carving expertise garnered respect and acclaim, and his array of subjects made him harder to encapsulate as an artist. By a number of accounts, Davis was a highly intelligent man who educated himself as he could and put his knowledge to work in an unparalleled body of carved sculpture.

ANCESTRAL LEGACY

As self-taught Black artists in America increasingly asserted their right to be creative on their own terms, a concomitant groundswell of visibility arose amid the larger context of American art. The artists discussed in this section were the enslaved or their progeny, makers for whom painful family memories backdropped a threatening present but never determined their path forward. The art they made did not fade from a trending moment as some predicted. Instead, it stood the test of time, and a younger generation of artists followed in their footsteps.

In 1989, another important exhibition picked up on what *Black Folk Art in America* had begun, but also served as a corrective for some of the framing errors in the Corcoran show. For the Dallas Museum of Art, curators Alvia J. Wardlaw and Regenia A. Perry dedicated *Black Art, Ancestral Legacy: The African Impulse in African-American Art* to African American artists and the ways in which their creative vision had enriched the world.[123] That both curators are African American gave the project an inherently different grounding, and the contrast in exhibition titles alone is telling. They highlighted unifying themes of legacy, personal visions, and reclamations, along with festival and ritual, and, with the help of prominent scholars including David C. Driskell and Robert Farris Thompson, foregrounded the connectivity among Africa, the Caribbean, and North America. *Black Art, Ancestral Legacy* was intentionally broader in scope, giving adjacency to trained and self-taught American artists who drew on their Black roots; it gave these artists equal respect and treatment, crossing the boundaries of class in a groundbreaking way and conferring historical significance on the practices of a number of artists whose work might otherwise have gone unappreciated, or have been silenced by the white mainstream. Importantly, the installation demonstrated that the art was not simply a moon shining with reflected light but casts its own artistic incandescence. In the wake of the exhibition, other African American artists working in vernacular modes were noticed and valued, contributing to entire bodies of work being recognized and saved.

LEROY PERSON (1907–1985) / SIMON SPARROW (ca. 1925–2000)

One such maker was **LEROY PERSON**, who lived near Albemarle Sound in North Carolina (Fig. 36). Person worked at a sawmill, which might have fostered his affinity for saw-blade cuts on wood, a visual effect that Paul Arnett describes as a defining feature of the body of work Person made in retirement.[124] Person had built his own house, and his sculptural foray may have begun with carving its windowsills and doors. He subsequently made an array of incised sculptural objects and pieces of furniture that came to encompass his property, including a fence from

CAT. 57.
Leroy Person
Untitled
ca. 1975

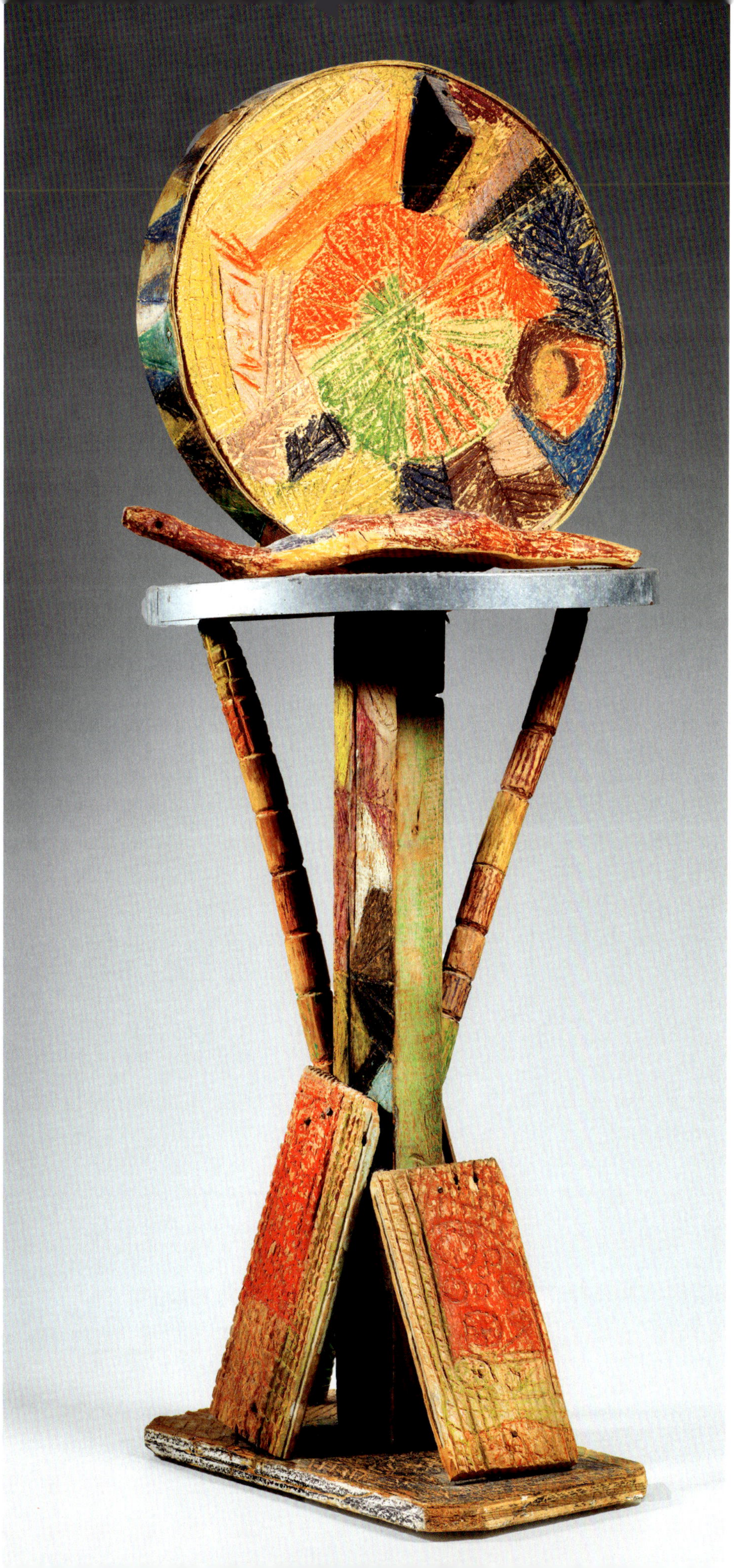

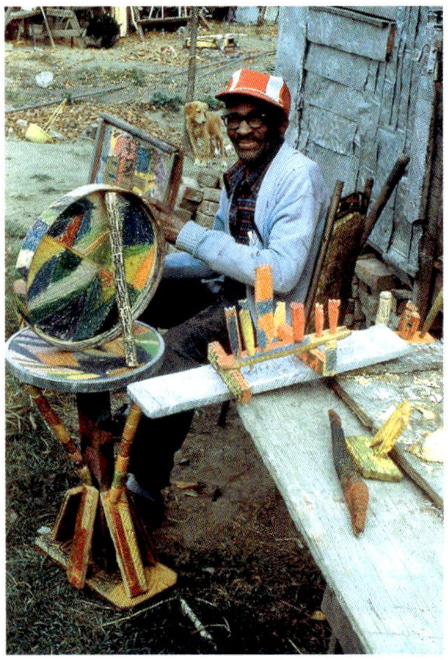

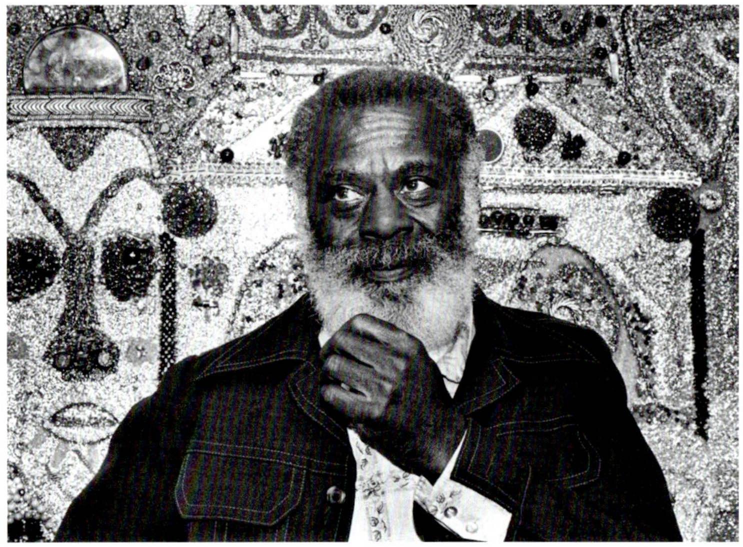

Fig. 36. Leroy Person, shown with his carved wooden table (**CAT. 57**), 1981; photograph by Roger Manley

Fig. 37. Minister Simon Sparrow; photograph by Glenn Trudel. Wisconsin Historical Society

carved tree limbs. Some pieces pay homage to the woodland creatures from his region such as snakes and birds, but Person became best known for his chairs and small tables, patterned with cross-hatching and rubbed with crayon for color (**CAT. 57**). Folklorist Roger Manley has described Person as "paraliterate," having a conventional literacy that was rudimentary, but supplementing English with his own invented system of writing—a code-like script that those who knew him well could interpret.[125] Arnett has ruminated on the degree to which Person's geometric and circular forms might have been intentionally rooted in his cultural heritage or ancestral belief systems, discussing the ways in which his practice read as protective, even if Person did not specifically describe it this way. Sadly, Person is among the artists whose beliefs and thoughts regarding the art they made were insufficiently documented and thus, to a large degree, lost to any permanent record.[126] Art historian Jenifer P. Borum called Person's aesthetic "a powerfully raw brand of figuration," noting, "Person unselfconsciously demonstrated a level of authenticity that has been the holy grail of mainstream twentieth-century artists who tried repeatedly—and in vain—to effect a willed forgetting of the dictates of Western culture."[127]

SIMON SPARROW was born in West Africa, to a Yoruban father and Native American mother (Fig. 37).[128] When Sparrow was two, they moved to the Qualla Boundary land trust in the Great Smoky Mountains, home of the Eastern Band of Cherokees and where his maternal grandfather lived. Like Edmondson and Pierce, Sparrow believed that spiritual visions had guided his path. He was seven when he experienced a visitation from God, who told Sparrow to go out and speak on his behalf. Sparrow went to the woods and spoke to the animals. "The birds would stop their

CAT. 58.
Simon Sparrow
Untitled
ca. 1968–83

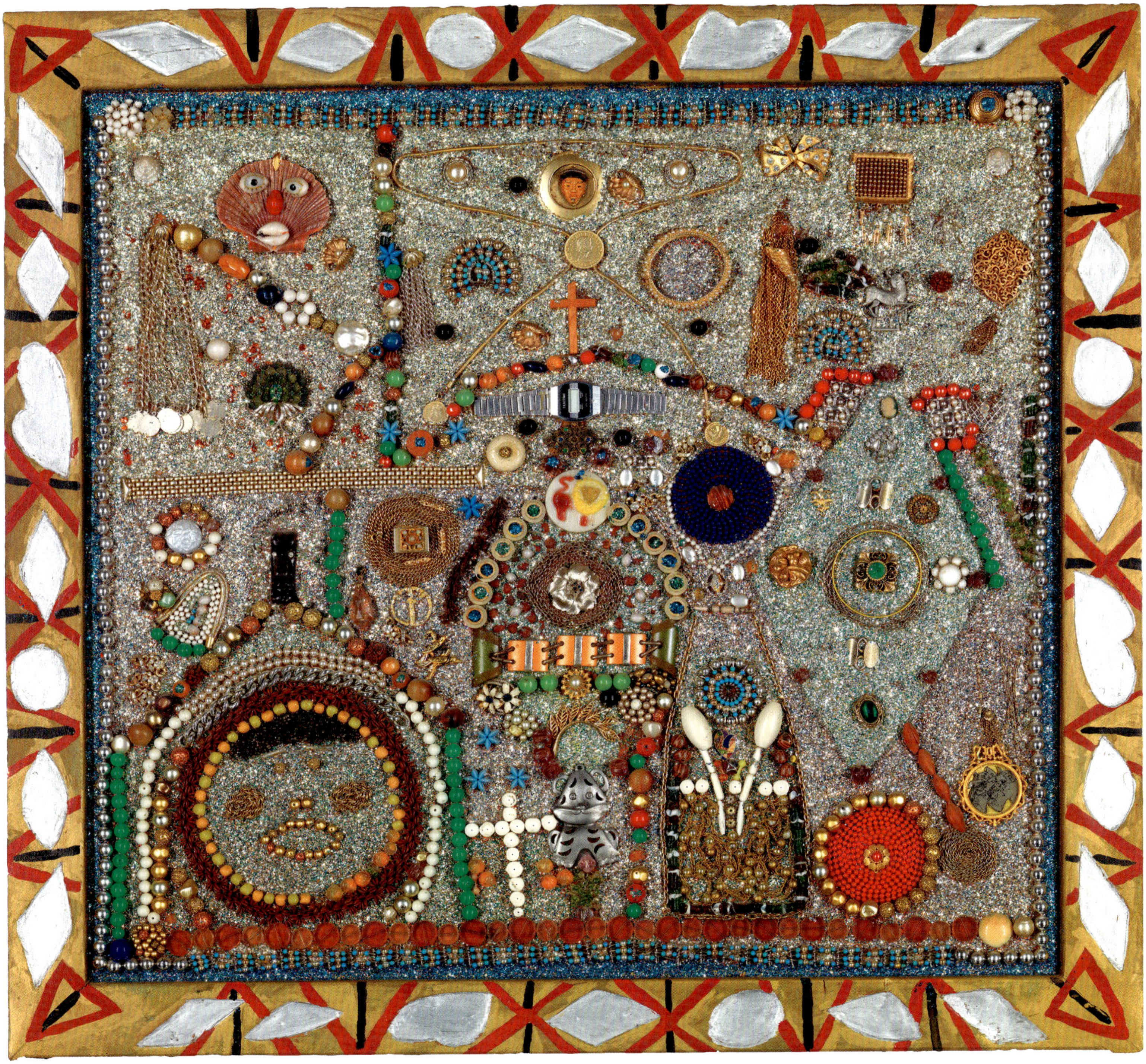

twittering, and the squirrels would stop chattering. They'd all just sit there quietly, listening to me."[129] It was the beginning of a spiritual journey for Sparrow, who began preaching at his family's Pentecostal church and making works of art. In keeping with that faith, Sparrow believed that the Holy Spirit descended into his body and effected an altered state of consciousness and the spiritual gift of speaking in tongues. He called himself a child of God rather than a Christian, saying, "When you come to be saved, you is saved by God, by the Son, by the Holy Ghost. Not by no religion. Religion is man-made."[130]

The hard facts of Sparrow's life have only been loosely documented, but by his own account he ran away when he was about twelve and lived for periods in Philadelphia and New York before eventually settling in Madison, Wisconsin, near his second wife's family. There, Sparrow preached the Pentecost on the streets and, starting in the 1970s, made dazzling mosaic collages from glitter, costume jewelry, toys, and other found objects (**CAT. 58**). He spoke about the spiritual nature of his images and how the Holy Spirit possessed him during their making. Sparrow's shimmering works center on faces and creatures surrounded with geometric forms, and which, in his description, give form to the spiritual essences of those who lived long ago. They evoke, directly or indirectly, Sparrow's Yoruban heritage and traditions of representing the spirit world in art. As Robert Farris Thompson has detailed in *Flash of the Spirit* and other volumes, the supreme Yoruban deity is Olorun, "master of the skies . . . neither male nor female, but a vital force... the supreme quintessence of áshe," which he translates as spiritual command, or the "power to make things happen."[131] Sparrow was proud to identify as a living connection between Africa and America, and as a preacher of the Pentecost, saw himself and his artworks as conduits of the Holy Spirit. Not unlike James Hampton and other artists whose work comingled African roots with American Christianity, Sparrow used objects and materials that captured and reflected light to symbolize the shining radiance of God and create a sense of spiritual movement and vitality.[132]

PHILADELPHIA WIREMAN (active 20th century)

Within the uneven record of makers who came to the attention of the art world only obliquely, an artist known only by an assigned moniker, the **PHILADELPHIA WIREMAN**, remains among the most mysterious. It is a story of an art survival more against the odds than most: around a thousand bound-up bundles of wire, wrappers, reflectors, lost possessions, trash-treasures—intentionally encompassed and shaped items—found in a South Philadelphia alley in the late 1970s (**CATS. 59–73**). Each cocooned sculpture is unique but related in size—give or take a bit—to the palm of a human hand, more specifically that of their maker. These objects have no designated front, back, top, or bottom, no title, and in and of themselves challenge notions of both art and artist. They were seen and gathered in a historically Black neighborhood by Robert Leitch, who saved the objects for a time before sharing them with local gallerist John Ollman, who took an interest and acquired a number of them around 1985. They made their public debut that year at Cavin-Morris Gallery in New York, after co-owner/director Randall Morris shared them with art historian Robert Farris Thompson, whose influential book (mentioned above) *Flash of the Spirit* had come out two years earlier.[133]

Morris posited that the consistent strength evidenced in the objects' formation suggested a male maker working primarily with his hands. Thompson made a connection between the bundles and the Kongo *nkisi* (plural *minkisi*)—a protective charm or power bundle tracing back over a thousand years. Thompson has shown that the Bakongo believe such bundles to be imbued with a protective life force, an energy that can help the holder remain safe, heal, or feel empowered.[134] Morris and Thompson's combined theories on the maker being an African American male jelled some years later, when visitors at Fleisher/Ollman saw some of the pieces and recalled seeing such an individual making bundles like these near the place they had been found.[135] Although the identity and intention of the maker cannot be known, the objects carry messages and traces of a life within them. Their weblike forms function as memory bottles or keepsakes, entrapping and distilling vestiges of time, place, and human life. The carefully shaped forms are designed to cradle the traces of others within them; silently, they share the maker's enigmatic perspective through castaway items deemed potent and talismanic—or at least worth saving.

Morris has drawn frequently, in his writing, on the concept of "the One and the Many," a Jamaican vernacular phrase referring to a person balancing culture and tradition with a personal trajectory in a contemporary world, and African diasporic tenets of balance. He describes the Wireman objects as a meeting point between African American vernacular practice, a cultural wellspring, and something deeply personal—an autonomous language in physical form:

> *The cultural connection is inherent, but the concept and intention is idiosyncratic and unique; "The One and the Many" at the same time. A lot of vernacular art is about the performance; the act of making the work was more important, or as important, as the final outcome. This gives the work an intense immediacy and personal meaning. When I first saw these pieces, there was no doubt in my mind as to their non-whimsicality, that there was something compressed within them that was part of, if not an alternate universe, at least an interior one, and that they were the ultimate examples of how Art Brut and cultural art can coincide.*[136]

The urbanity of the so-called Wireman's work, made with cigarette packages, broken glass, nails, bike reflectors, and numerous other street finds, pulls them into their own reality, even if the sense

following pages

CATS. 59–73.
Philadelphia Wireman
Untitled (15 individual artworks)
ca. 1970–75

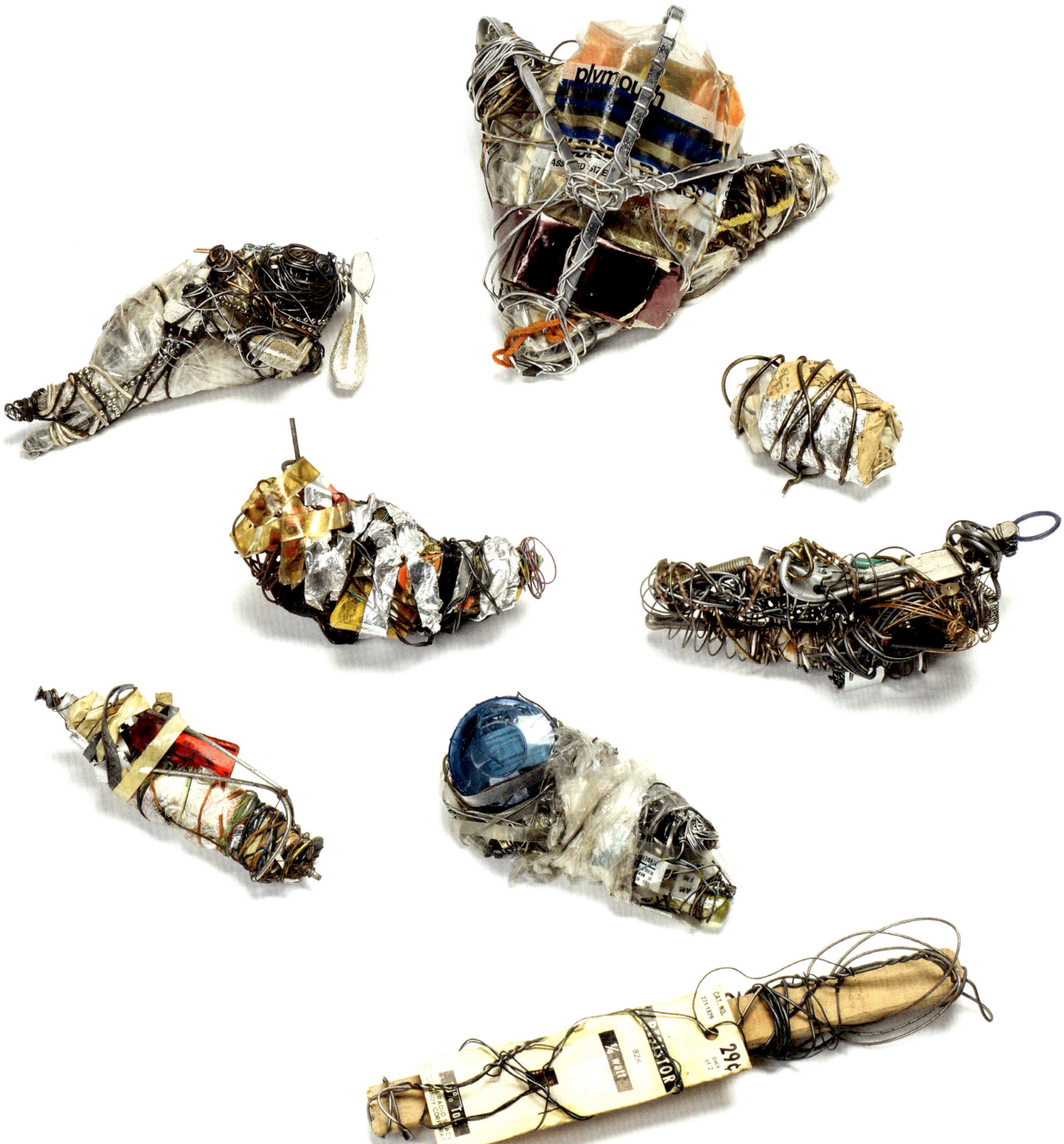
plymouth
29¢

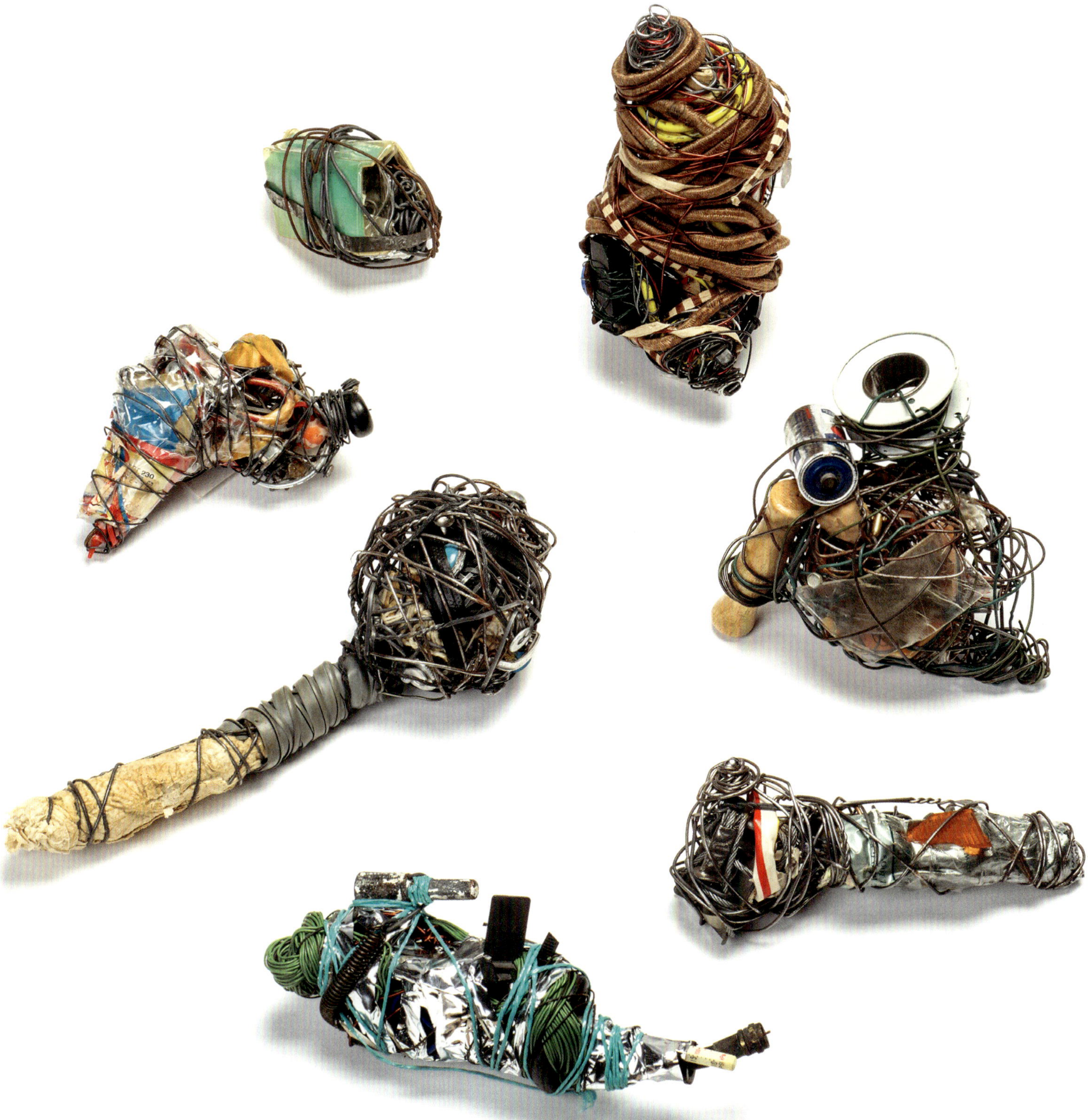

of talismanic force they radiate is hard to ignore. It is critical to consider, as Morris observes, that the very act of making, of defining oneself through enacting reclamation and transformation, is also a survival mechanism. Abstraction, particularly as it takes shape here, further confers importance on the act over the result. Gathering the objects to encompass, the wires required for the task, sorting and uniting the trash-treasures, and, finally, shaping each piece, forms a cyclical ritual unto itself. Collectively, the pieces shape a calendar of sorts—a day's or a week's labor, the passing of time, the chronicle of a life.

CATS. 74, 75.
Bessie Harvey
Untitled (Root Figures)
1988

BESSIE HARVEY (1929–1994)

BESSIE HARVEY saw her sculptural forms as revelations of indwelling spirits in roots and branches, identities that she brought to life with found objects and paint (Fig. 38). Harvey believed that she was creating artworks as God directed her to—not determining form herself, but listening to and following the forms suggested by the organic materials she used (**CATS. 74, 75**). Her works were often painted in dark colors, and frequently expressed emotional or spiritual anguish, sometimes related to her own struggles coming from a poor family in rural Tennessee. Her pieces are fierce, raw, and edgy. "I know that my art is a peculiar kind of art," Harvey acknowledged. But she believed her sculptures faithfully conveyed God's vision: "What I do is what He lets me see."[137]

As Nellie Mae Rowe's experience reveals, the challenges of being an African American woman from the southern underclass were myriad and often extreme. Also like Rowe, Harvey's creativity was often positioned as something threatening, related to dark magic or folk religion. Although Rowe's artworks, in her day, were often perceived as overly boisterous and eccentric, their bright colors and joyous tone ultimately won over many skeptics. By contrast, Harvey's pieces were more often seen by the mainstream as raw or primitive—her aesthetic a direct challenge to white middle-class conventions, her personal faith an animistic departure from Christian norms. But Harvey was determined to articulate her personal vision whether or not she had the support of the art world, or anybody else. She spoke in a language of forms that came naturally to her, and, like a number of artists discussed in the following section, "Gamechangers," used art as a means of understanding her own identity and surviving in a world that was only slowly coming to regard different kinds of practices as worth seeing and saving.

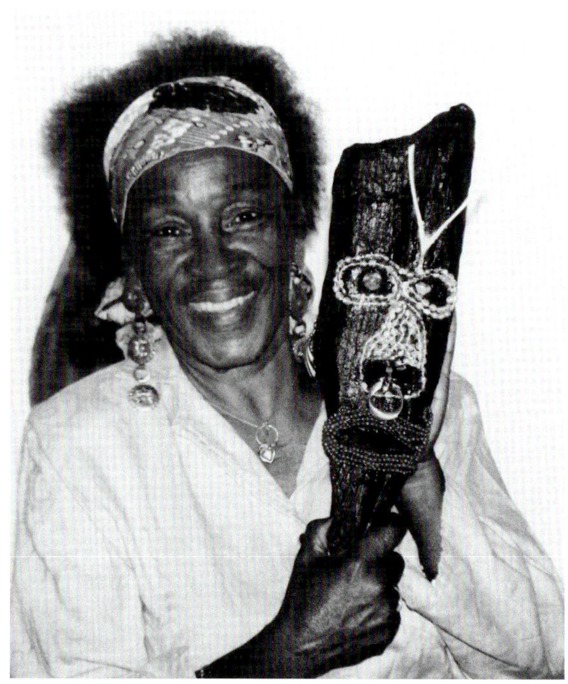

Fig. 38. Bessie Harvey with artwork, 1991; photograph by Charles Russell

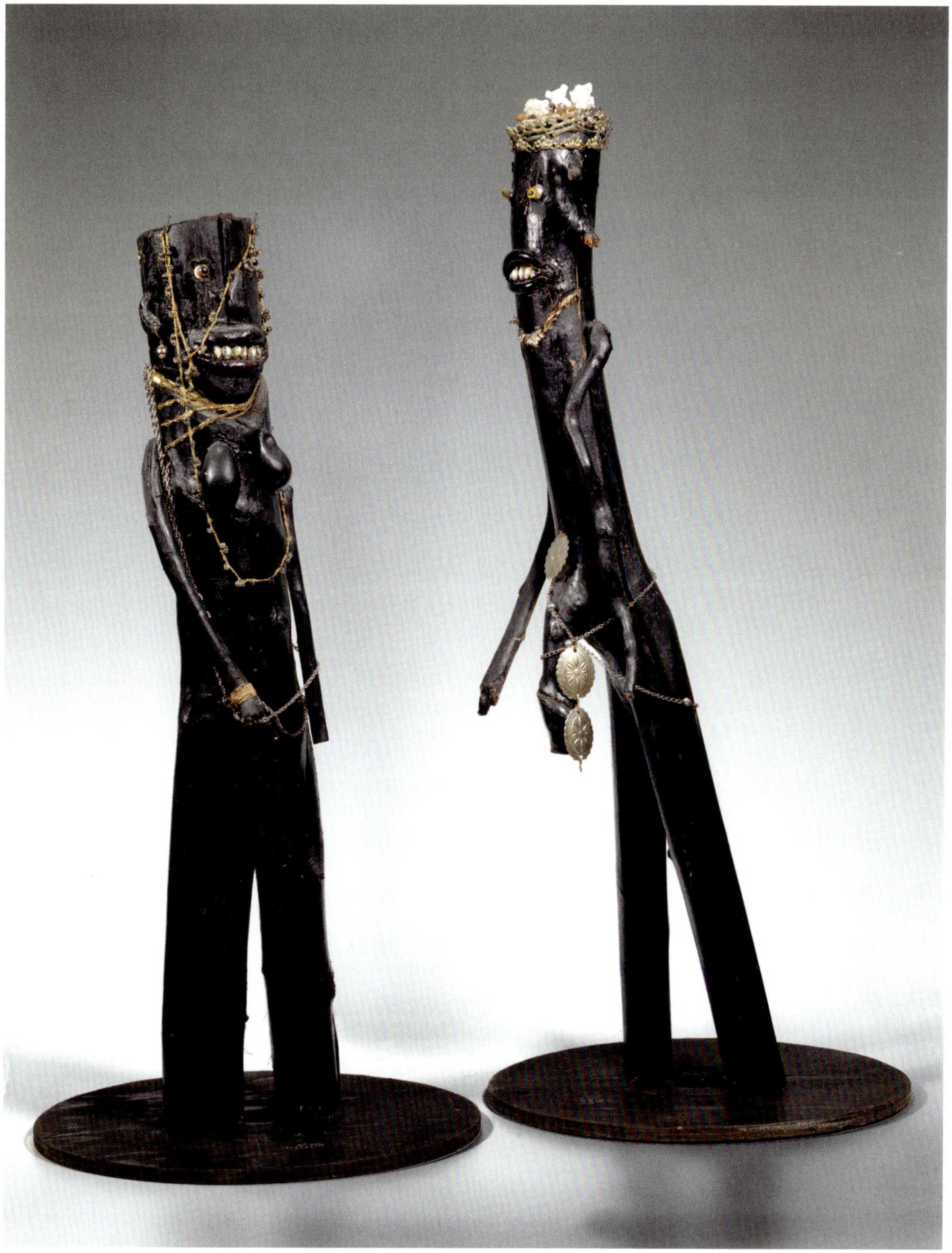

PURVIS YOUNG (1943–2010)

Among the youngest African American self-taught artists to move into the spotlight in the waning years of the twentieth century was **PURVIS YOUNG** (Fig. 39). Young lived his entire life in a segregated district of Miami known as Overtown, often called "Colored Town" until the late 1960s, when an overpass for Interstate 95 was constructed straight through its heart. Young witnessed firsthand the ways in which neighborhoods of immigrants and people of color came last in the United States. Young's grandmother came to the United States from the Bahamas, and told her grandson that America had made Black immigrants feel doubly unwelcome. His mother eschewed education in her youth and did not impart its importance to her own children; Young dropped out before high school and found his way to trouble.

In the first half of the twentieth century, Overtown was a thriving Black diaspora community of southern African Americans and Caribbean immigrants, many of whom had come to work on the rail lines in the century's early years.[138] In the late 1950s, Overtown began an economic decline, driven in large part by the decimation of the community by the construction of new highways right through it. Overtown and Coconut Grove were the two oldest neighborhoods in Miami, but the State of Florida saw the less affluent Overtown as dispensable; the highway projects displaced forty thousand residents and their businesses, making the once vibrant community a food desert and ghetto.[139] Young himself got into trouble with the law as a teenager and spent time in prison for breaking and entering. While incarcerated, he became interested in art—and was particularly inspired by the African American activist murals in Chicago and Detroit. He began painting as a form of activism, a visible display of his community's voice, a record that they saw, understood, and remembered—where they had come from, and where they needed to go.

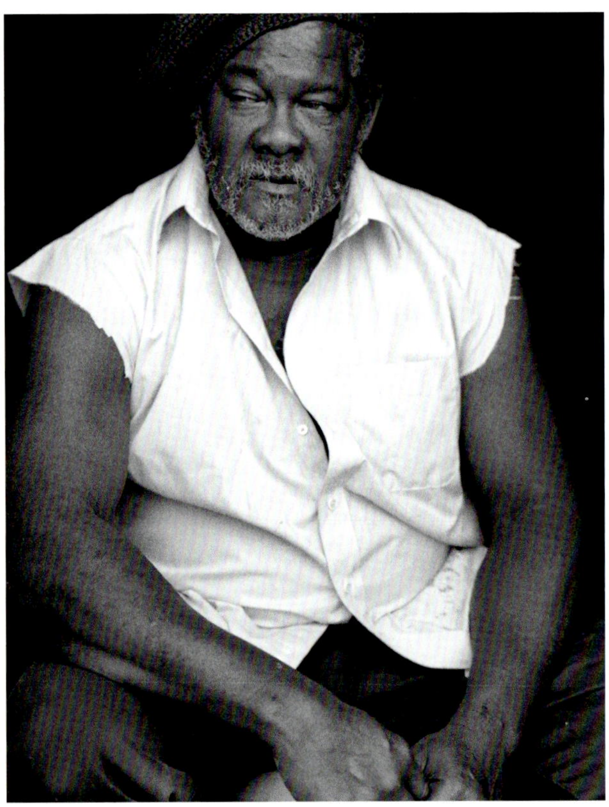

Fig. 39. Purvis Young, 2008; photograph by David Raccuglia

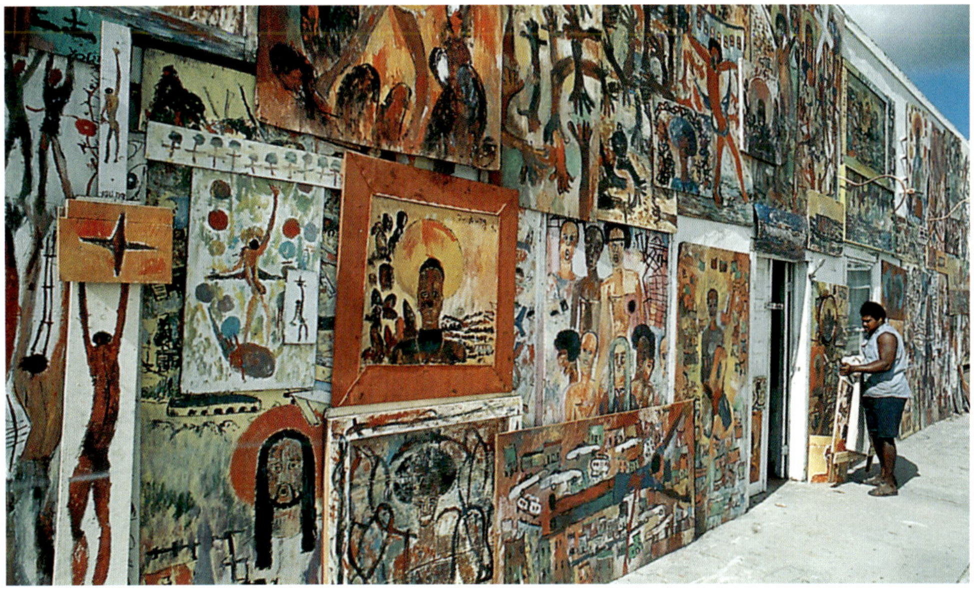

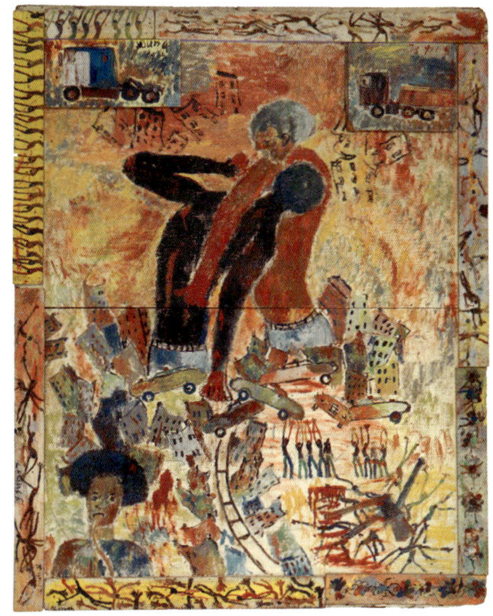

Fig. 40. Purvis Young with his paintings in Goodbread Alley, Miami, 1972

Fig. 41. Purvis Young, *The Struggle*, 1973–74, acrylic on wood, 88 × 77 in. Smithsonian American Art Museum, Gift of the Grumbacher-Viener Collection in memory of Nancy Grumbacher, 2014.15

In 1971, Young determined to make a statement of his own. In a vacant alley of boarded-up storefronts, Young saw a blank slate. He began to paint, directly on the plywood window coverings, a record of the people who once composed a vibrant community. What followed was an intense period of creativity in which Young transformed the alley into a mural-clad environment celebrating and historicizing his place. "There's alleys all around that neighborhood," Young explained of his choice of a spot once known for the uplifting scent of baking bread, before the Jamaican bakeries were pushed out. "Goodbread Alley was just another alley. But it was a hell of an alley. Police wouldn't go into that place back then. They wasn't taking no chances.... It was up to me to put up how I feel about stuff, like the [civil rights] protesters did."[140]

Young's themes spanned an array of topics but focused on the perils of being poor and Black in the United States, and the particular trials of immigrants and displaced persons and communities (**CAT. 76**). He became a local celebrity and the alley a tourist attraction. But as Miami's urban renewal project advanced, city officials dismantled Goodbread Alley (Figs. 40, 41). Young was able to sell some of the paintings. Other pieces were scavenged, and some were lost in the destruction. Subsequently, Young was given materials and working spaces by various dealers, and he continued to paint and gain prominence and stature until his death in 2010. His symbolic and expressive work always honored suffering while persistently offering hopes for joy and a brighter future.

/ / /

In the 1990s, some scholars considering Black American visual traditions critiqued heavy-handed "retentionist" arguments, which, they feared, risked prioritizing Old World connections over lived experience and the fluency required for life in an inequitable society. In 1994, Lynda Roscoe Hartigan expressed this concern: "Ironically, one of the key factors in advancing the study [of African American

CAT. 76.

Purvis Young

On the March

1996

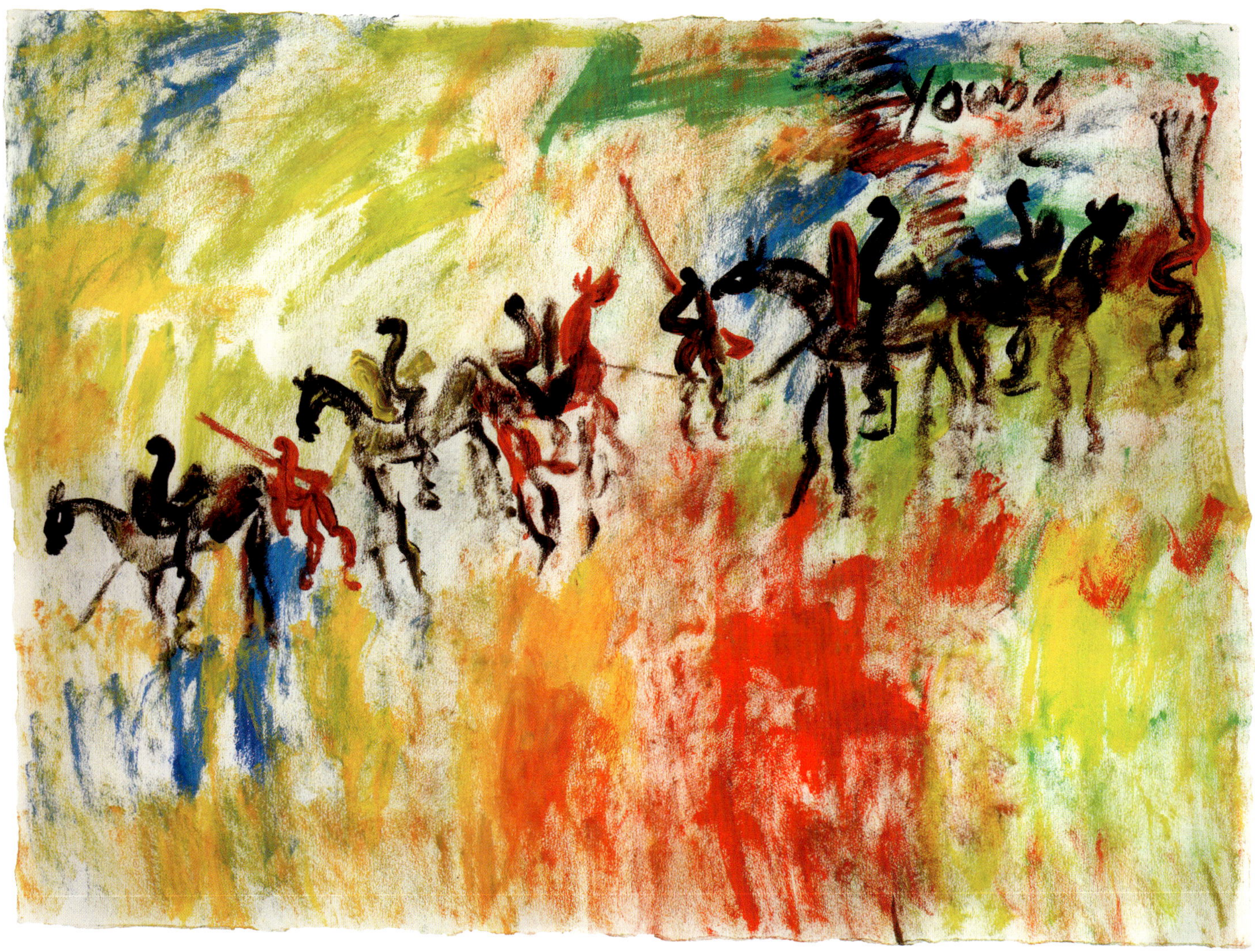

folk art] has also begun to impede it, and that is the pursuit of African influences in black American art, to the exclusion of other similarly enlightening considerations and approaches. To assert an influence where an artist would reject or not identify with it runs the risk of reinforcing a relationship of intellectual colonialism in the name of efforts to undo it."[141] Such concerns are especially relevant when the artist's voice went largely unheard, as happened with Leroy Person, or when their identity remains unknown, as in the case of the so-called Philadelphia Wireman, but these issues are most problematic when posthumous interpretations are expressed as known truths, rather than as illuminating possibilities, informed by the objects themselves.

Concerns of overinterpretation are, in turn, complicated again by the frequency with which Black American artists, particularly those for whom memories of Jim Crow lived in them all their years, who had less education and social agency, felt unable to speak openly about their work—regardless of opportunities to do so. Hartigan's view that "other enlightening considerations and approaches" must be factored into the interpretation of any art is on point, and yet, far too often, the tendency has been to underread the work of non-white self-taught artists, rather than the opposite. Charles Shannon, the white artist who saved the lion's share of Bill Traylor's artworks, captured fragmented remarks from Traylor about his drawings, but then failed to reconcile those remarks, made within the constraints of an inherently hierarchical social relationship in a segregated community, with what the images actually conveyed.[142] While it is critical not to overstep the limits of contemporary readings and cultural difference, the graver danger is to underestimate the intelligence, intentionality, and cultural nimbleness of African American artists working in a vernacular mode.

Today, the collective power and validity of Black vernacular practice has become unquestionable. The encompassing sphere of African American vernacular art is rooted in the American experience and shaped by the multicultural syncretisms that vary from region to region. Broadly and fluidly, this vein of creative production embodies and reflects the present while reaching back in time and across oceans. Independent from larger and more organized art movements, drawing on oral culture and folkways, and speaking visually through languages of time and place including unique conceptions of spirituality, these artists made bodies of work in the lingua franca of the Black Atlantic: autonomous, self-affirming expressions that charted struggle and persistence, and ultimately defined a distinct, visibly vocal realm within the larger sphere of American art. The artists considered in "Becoming Visible" refuted invisibility; they steadily asserted and effected, through unique visions and powerful creativity, a visible presence within and among their larger society, on their own terms, and in so doing brought a world of change.

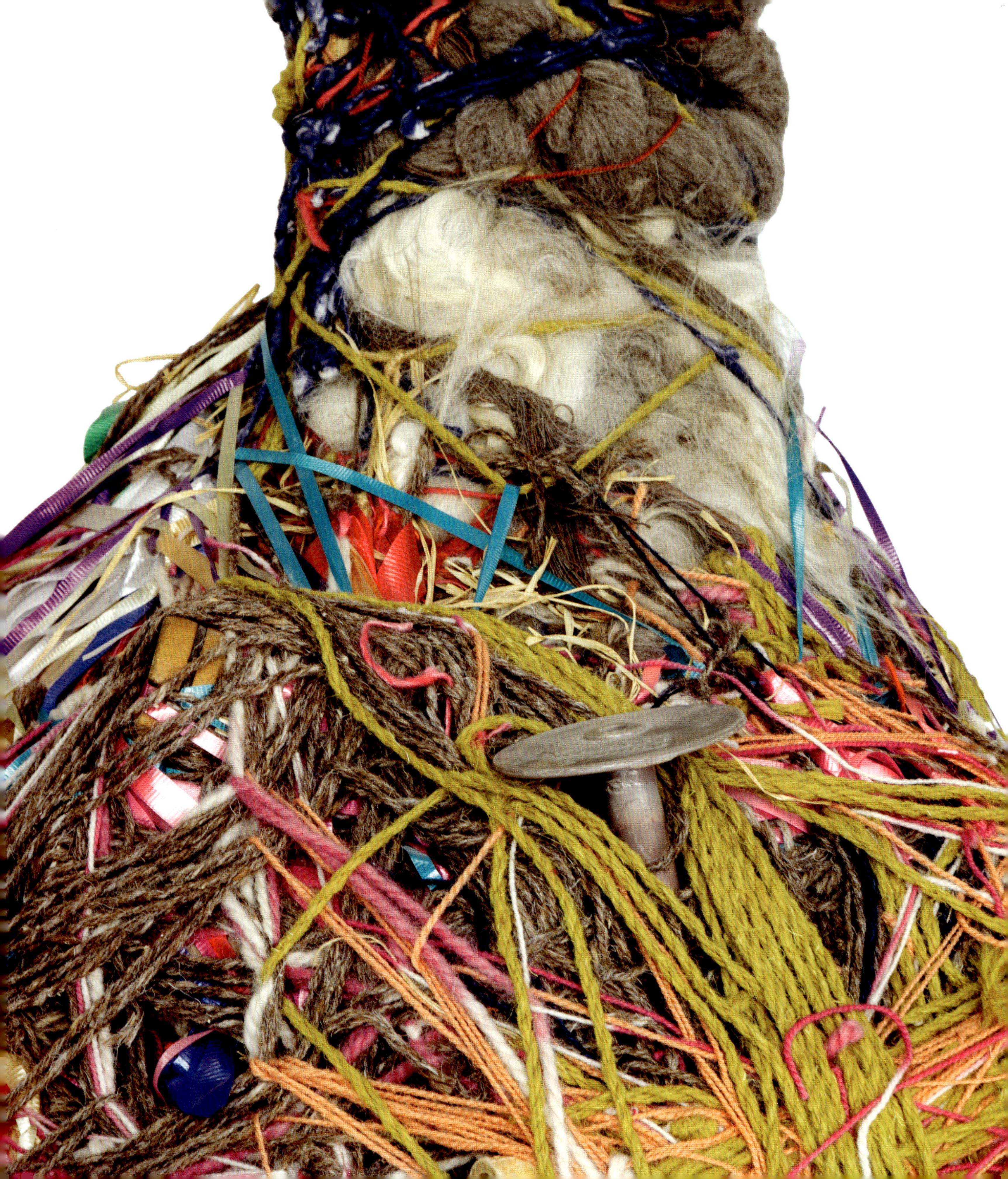

GAME-CHANGERS / PIVOTAL ARTISTS WITHIN A SHIFTING PARADIGM

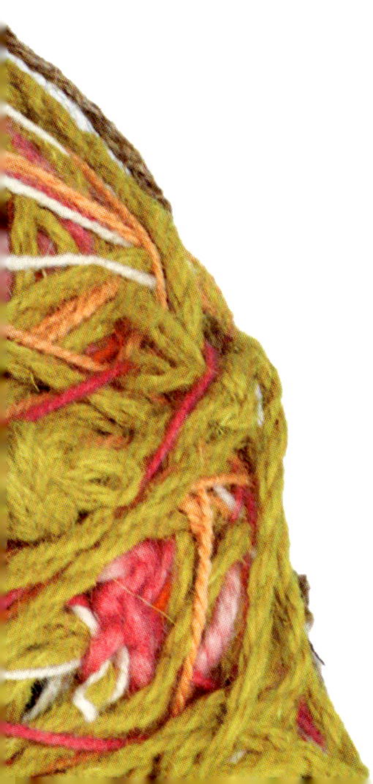

Without any doubt, the impact of African American artists working in a vernacular vein has been immeasurable. The fraught history of racial inequity in the United States, inextricably intertwined with the Black Atlantic tradition, sets this distinctive sector of American art history apart from related frameworks for "self-taught art and artists" around the world. The 1982 exhibition at the Corcoran Gallery of Art had a ripple effect that piqued interest in self-taught artists across the board — from a younger generation of Black vernacular artists to a more diverse, less definable array of creative individuals. But this interest writ large went significantly more mainstream in the late twentieth century, in Europe and in North America.

Historians find the steady rise in interest in untrained artists rooted in many moments and places, but curator and author Jane Kallir has connected it with a more overarching obsession with "otherness," especially as art became increasingly challenged as the de facto purview of the ruling class. Ultimately, this was fallout from the readjustment of class boundaries and sudden comingling of people across racial, ethnic, and economic strata—spurred by both industrialization and global migrations. "The simultaneous need and inability to deal with the 'other' became a leitmotif of twentieth-century history, contributing to its many genocides," Kallir explains. "The crumbling of once stable aristocratic empires touched off World War I, which in turn triggered Hitler's retaliatory quest for European domination and World War II. And for each world war, there was a concomitant surge of interest in self-taught art, the art of the 'other,' on the part of the cultural elite."[1]

In the first decade of the twentieth century, Pablo Picasso and Wassily Kandinsky celebrated the childlike innocence and naivete in Henri Rousseau's work, and the art historian and dealer Wilhelm Uhde promoted a number of naive painters, Rousseau among them. In 1921, Swiss psychiatrist Walter Morgenthaler wrote a book on the art of a schizophrenic patient he was caring for, Adolf Wölfli. The following year, German psychiatrist Hans Prinzhorn wrote a more sweeping assessment on the connection between mental illness and creativity, *Bildnerei der Geisteskranke* (Artistry of the Mentally Ill), based on his work with and collection of artworks by patients at the Heidelberg Psychiatric Clinic.[2] Prinzhorn's groundbreaking book attracted the attention of European artists including Paul Klee, Max Ernst, André Breton, and other surrealists who often linked notions of insanity to a Romantic model essentializing mental illness as a kind of liberation from reality.[3] Jean Dubuffet became the artist most often associated with what he would term "art brut"; he further romanticized a wide range of makers in a 1959 essay, casting "schizophrenics, rogues, hermits, innocents, tramps, and eccentrics" as artists who had escaped the tyranny of society.[4]

"Art Brut does not seek approval," wrote Roger Cardinal, who attempted to find a more user-friendly English counterpart to Dubuffet's term, which more directly translated to "raw art." Cardinal's 1972 book, titled with the help of editors *Outsider Art*, corralled an array of disparate makers who had little in common beyond defying the confines of the Western canon. What art-world figures from Holger Cahill to Cardinal were gravitating toward was a quest for authentic vision, the original over the derivative. But there was a chasm between artists like Adolf Wölfli, the Swiss inmate at the Waldau Mental Asylum in Bern, whose drawn worlds presented an alternative realm and self-crafted persona (see **CAT. 9**), and working-class and racially oppressed artists in America, where the personal and symbolic identity of self-taught artists was entangled in ideas of national identity and an "up from nothing" spirit. And as Kallir concludes, "something was literally lost in translation and in the transplantation of the genre from Europe to the United States."[5]

In 1979, Cardinal and Victor Musgrave cocurated *Outsiders: An Art without Precedent or Tradition*, at London's Hayward Gallery, bringing together European artists who adhered to Dubuffet's notions of extremely marginalized makers, with American artists, some of whom were, in fact, grounded in tradition.[6] As art brut followed its own trajectory in Europe, Cardinal's term took on a life of its own in America, dovetailing as it did with Bert Hemphill's advocacy for "Twentieth Century Folk Art," and an array of artists that were connected solely by ties of non-belonging—from the socially isolated or disenfranchised to the mentally ill. As collector enthusiasm picked up, the market responded, collectively shaping an ad hoc field that built itself around a cluster of remarkable artists that defied easy definition and art-world conformity.[7] When John Maizels founded the London-based *Raw Vision* magazine in 1989, and Sanford L. Smith established the Outsider Art Fair in New York in 1993, awareness and appreciation of nonmainstream artists grew, even as the illogical and often offensive framework of "outsider" was critiqued by scholars and critics.

In a 1994 volume of essays entitled *The Artist Outsider: Creativity and the Boundaries of Culture*, editors Michael D. Hall and Eugene W. Metcalf Jr. asked important questions about a field that had, by then, become a Frankenstein's monster of sorts—thrilling for bringing astonishing art and artists to light, horrifying for the ways in which it capitalized on marginality and misfortune. Cardinal contributed an essay, defending "outsider" as a pragmatic umbrella term—even if inherently flawed. Others begged to differ, effectively dissecting how the term had become a euphemistic dog whistle for race and class, a coded reference to the artist, not the art, a category defined by and imposed upon the disempowered by the empowered. At best, "outsider" was never a description that meaningfully positioned or illuminated the art itself, and in the case of Black artists—enslaved, persecuted, and degraded from their first moments in America—this kind of marginalization pressed far beyond casual issues of professional versus nonprofessional or rural versus urban; it tapped into deeply fraught issues of power and humanity.[8]

A number of self-taught artists came perforce into focus in the 1980s and 1990s who forever changed the game. As the art world fought over labels and terms and reluctantly made room for them in exhibitions and in permanent collections, these artists unmasked the core issues of inside versus outside and, in turn, the validity of the Western art canon and its hierarchies. One by one, they revealed a myriad of histories, personal stories, and insights into who we are, collectively, as a nation. Although this "Gamechangers" section could detail ten times as many artists, six in particular, in tandem with key figures discussed in the preceding section, such as Bill Traylor, William Edmondson, and Nellie Mae Rowe, serve as a microcosm of a field in which diversity has been both central tenet and perpetual quagmire.

HENRY DARGER (1892–1973)

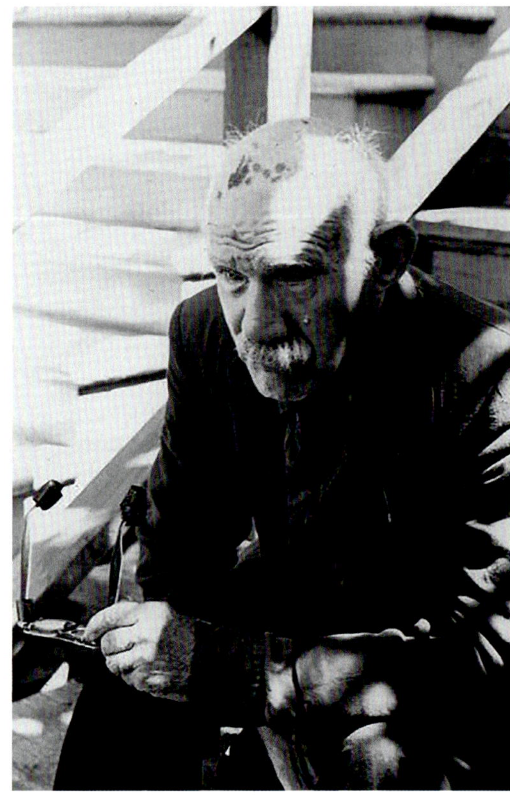

Fig. 42. Henry Darger, 1971; photograph by David Berglund

In many ways, the Chicagoan **HENRY JOSEPH DARGER JR.** became the ultimate icon of the American artist outsider (Fig. 42). Fitting Dubuffet's framework for creatives at the extreme margins of culture, Darger lived in relative isolation and made an extensive body of work that was little known until shortly before his death. When it was first shown, at Chicago's Hyde Park Art Center in 1977, the vast scope of the oeuvre, technicolor content read as disturbing, and an agonizing biography synthesized into sensational identity construct. Neither Darger nor his art was easily quantifiable, and debates about his personal character and the content of his imagery coalesced into a persistent framework, within which many still malign Darger as "infamous."[9]

Darger expert Michael Bonesteel describes the artist as a reclusive janitor with a tortured past; his opus is an array comprising two epic novels, a five-thousand-page autobiography, extensive journals, diaries, notebooks, and scrapbooks, and three giant albums of painted narratives.[10] "While all of Darger's visual art centers around and sometimes depicts specific episodes from his fifteen-thousand-page novel, *The Story of the Vivian Girls, in What Is Known as the Realms of the Unreal, of the Glandeco-Angelinnian War Storm, Caused by the Child Slave Rebellion (The Realms of the Unreal)*," Bonesteel explains, "most of his carbon-traced watercolor drawings are more like loose improvisations on activities taking place in the novel's imaginary world, where the Christian nation of Abbieannia is at war with the satanic empire of Glandelinia over child slavery."[11]

Darger's provocative imagery — beatific and brutal in equal measure — has invited a wide array of interpretation. His narratives feature a complex presentation of self-portraiture, a constellation of male Dargers playing roles, some good, some evil, within the narrative. John M. MacGregor, author of an in-depth study on Darger, argues that *The Realms* is, overarchingly, "an infinitely detailed self-portrait, with every character, every event, each battle and aspect of nature, functioning as a dynamic fragment of his enormously complex and conflicted self."[12] Darger's heroic Vivian Girls, seven sisters who bravely battle the evil child-enslaver Glandelinians, are depicted as angel-faced children, often drawn naked, comprehensively feminine yet featuring male genitalia (**CAT. 77**).[13] In the written narrative that accompanies his painted epic, Darger explained that the heroes are girls because their bravery surpasses that of both boys and men:

> *Although, dear readers, in this big story, boys and men play usual and principal roles in the dreadful battles, and during the great war encounter many terrible adventures by land, sea, fire, water, and so forth, the reason the story runs so much with little girls as the actual heroes in this warfare is because, under most circumstances, women are braver than men. I go to show that by putting little girls in this story as the real heroines, that little girls do and are brave enough, for a fact, to be able to play and show any amount of nerve and courage, full equal or moreso than boys or men or women who may take part in active warfare.*[14]

Art historian and curator Leisa Rundquist reads the ambiguously sexed Vivian cohort as emblematic of mutability and adaptation, noting: "Darger positions these little *girls* somewhere between male and female, both biologically and socially. The Vivian girls' ambiguous gender and shifting anatomy speak broadly, and with rich complexity, to American culture's polarizing constructions of child/adult and male/female. Darger plays with these polarities and fabricates an extraordinary child beyond nature—capable of defeating bloodthirsty Glandelinians on one hand and rebelling against conventional girlhood on the other."[15]

Darger's graphically violent battle scenes stand in stark contrast to those in which the girls frolic, accompanied by their horned and winged allies, the Blengigomeneans (also called Blengins), amid lush floral landscapes. The violent images are undeniably charged, triggering internal alarms even as they thwart a clear understanding of what is taking place. The monstrous violence Darger depicted has prompted many to question the artist's morality. Accusatory questions were given oxygen by MacGregor's authoritative volume, in which a wealth of valuable scholarship was muddied by speculations about Darger's mental health, sexual interests, and possible criminality—based on a body of work that openly pitched a traumatic reality against a victorious fantasy.[16] Ellen Handler Spitz, a professor specializing in the links between aesthetics and psychology, argued for a more empathetic interpretation, observing, "Darger's *Realms of the Unreal*, as he named it, makes the beholder into a witness of a panorama of pain. A delegitimized witness, however, condemned to watch without understanding." Spitz asserted a view that is more commonly held about Darger today: that he made art as "a private pictorial tent for his own survival," observing that what we project onto his imagery has little bearing on Darger's intentions or reality.[17]

Those who have studied this massive body of work agree that Darger's personal losses and challenges inherently structured his personality, and that the degree to which factors including his mental health were in play remain unclear. When Darger was four, his mother died from complications following childbirth and his newborn sister was given up for adoption, compound losses

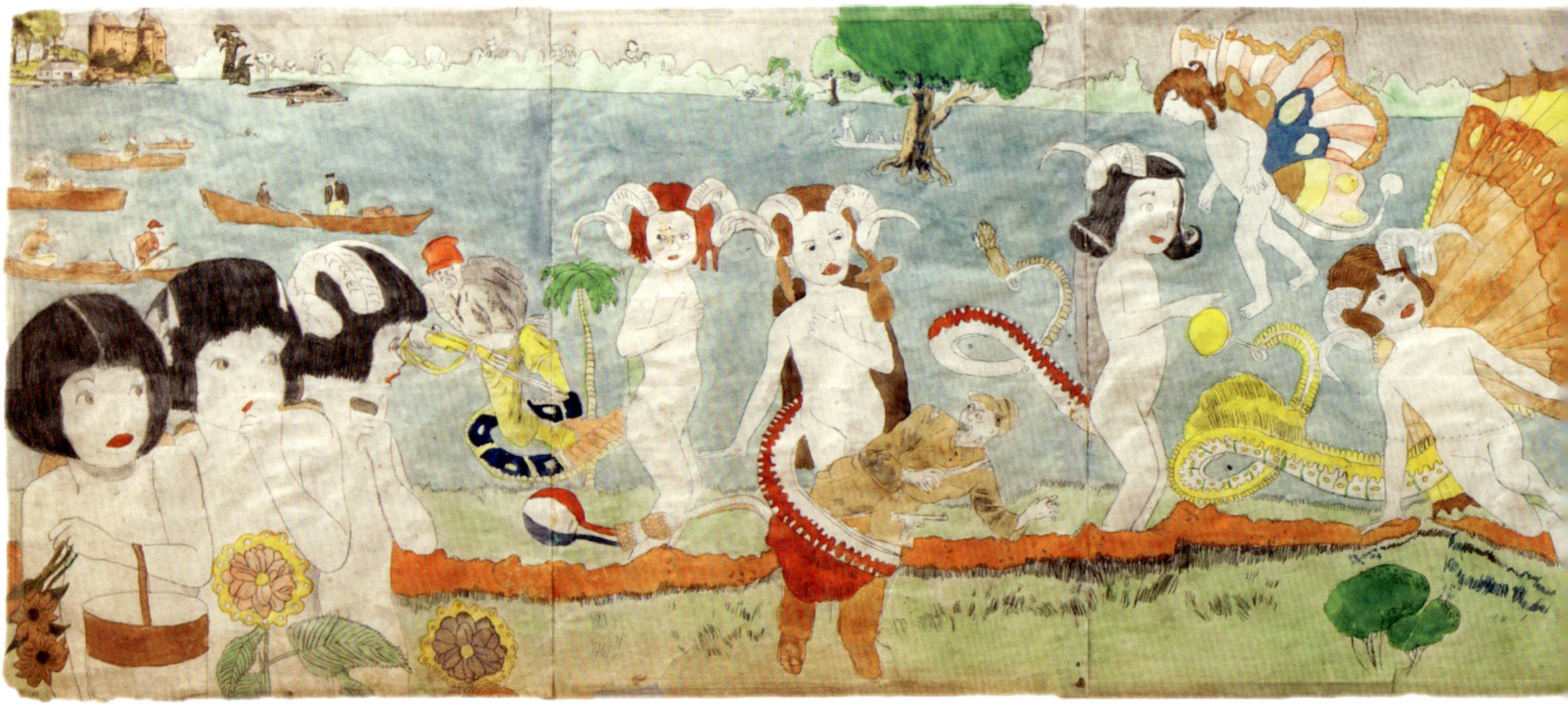

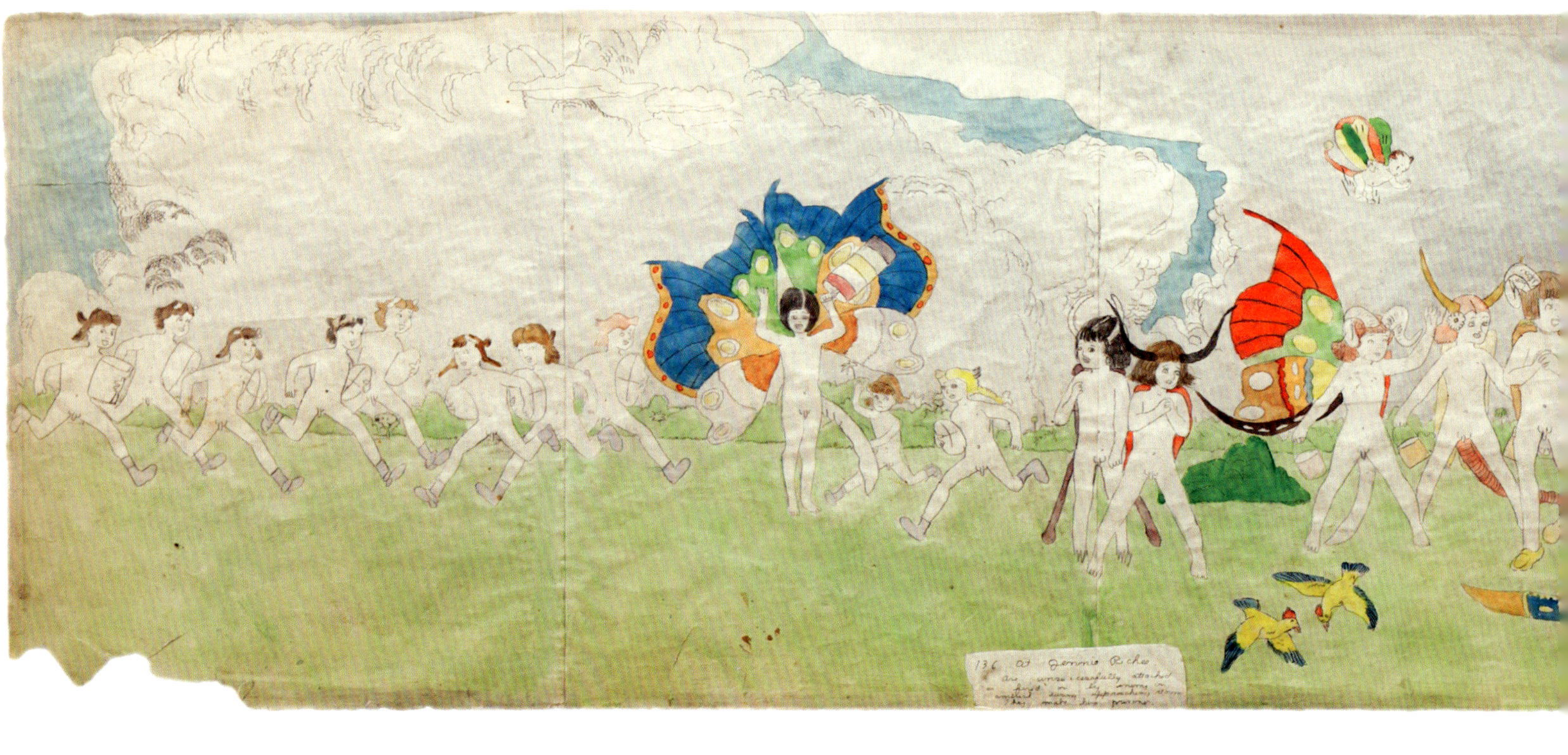
136 At Jennie Richee

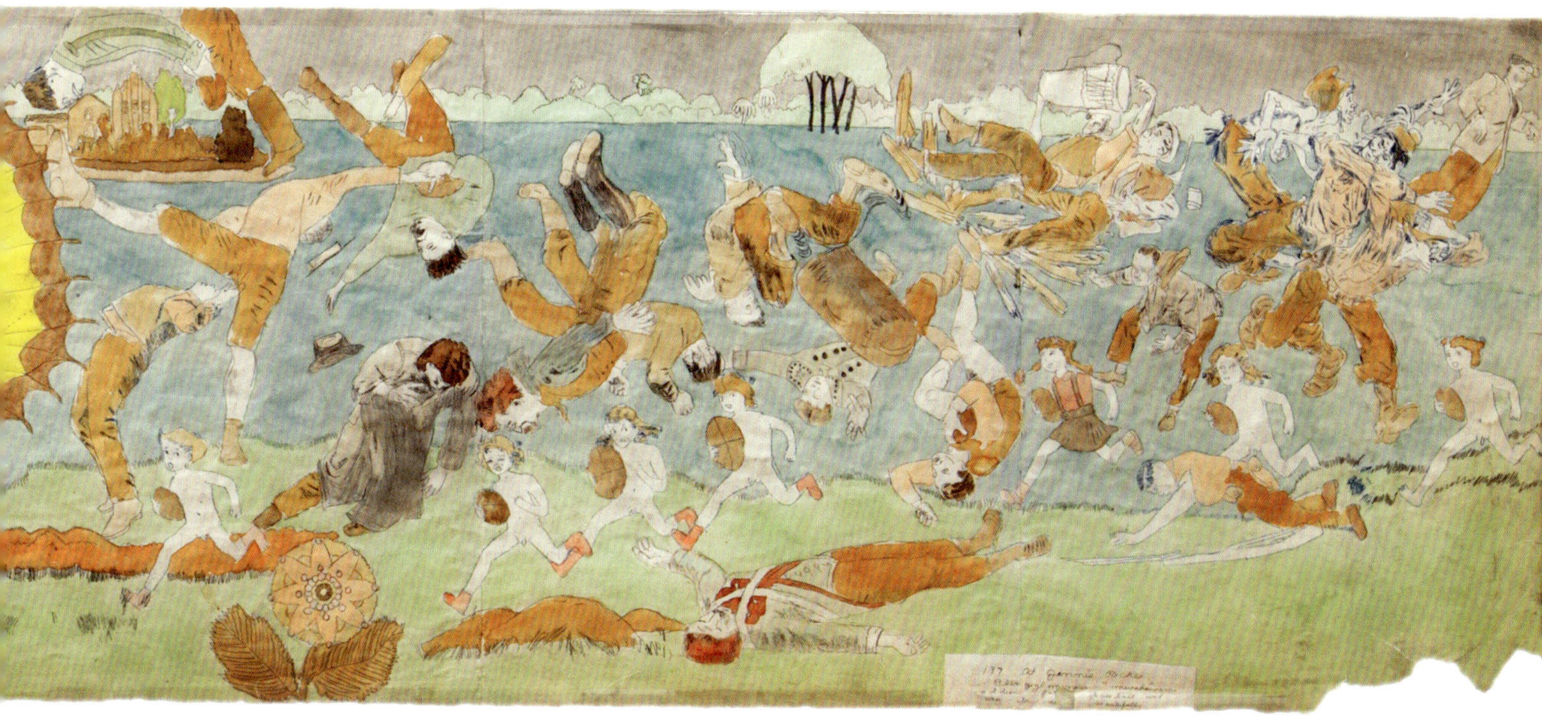

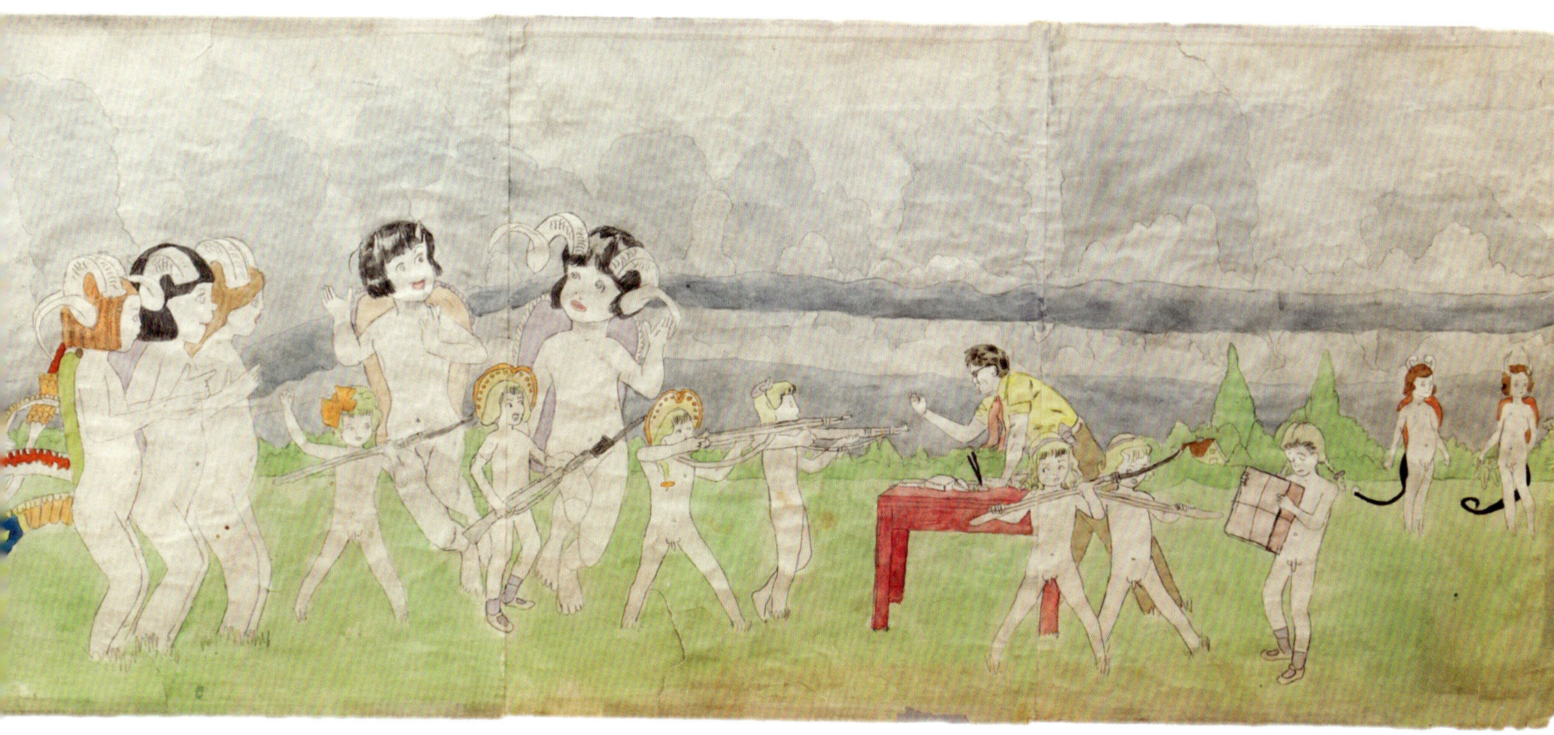

which had profound impact. Several years later, his father was no longer able to work and moved into an assistance home for the poor, delivering what was likely the ultimate blow to Darger's sense of security and belonging. He was sent first to a boys' home and remained in public school. Things worsened yet again when he was expelled for behavior problems and sent to live at the Illinois Asylum for Feeble-Minded Children, despite having learned to read and write at a young age and skipping the second grade entirely.[18] The asylum became enmeshed in scandal during Darger's time there, for unspeakable abuses and neglect, which, in several cases, resulted in death. After several attempts, Darger successfully escaped when he was sixteen.[19]

Darger was a devout Catholic and attended Mass multiple times daily while also supporting himself with custodial work and other menial jobs. Sometime around 1912, when he was about twenty, Darger began writing his epic tale and creating portraits of its characters; in the ensuing years he began to paint scenes from *The Realms*, with scale, style, and depictions evolving over time.[20] In the 1930s the artworks became increasingly larger, as the artist learned to conjoin sheets of paper. In the mid-1940s, Darger learned how to have the images he used as source material enlarged, which allowed greater flexibility in the scale of the figures, and resulted in scenes that were more complex and heavily populated. In the later decades, Darger's paintings were often massive, as long as 113 inches.[21]

Darger's written texts indicate a pained yearning for his lost family and ongoing confusion about why the God he loved and feared could allow his life to be so agonizing. Jane Kallir has observed that Darger's challenges with accepting the duality of good and evil in the world is a theme underlying his entire body of work, and that his struggle to understand a God who could remain silent in the face of suffering and inhumanity was as universal and timeless as it was endemic to the era:

> *The period during which Darger created his watercolors spans the age of Shirley Temple to that of* Leave It to Beaver*: an era when children, even naughty ones, were always ineffably cute, and the nuclear family was sacrosanct. The images of childhood innocence that were ubiquitous in American pop culture—and that Darger copied into his watercolors—belied the sometimes horrific realities of child neglect and abuse that the artist had experienced at first hand during a boyhood spent largely in custodial institutions. After all, while Darger was creating his pictures of child torture, real children were being gassed in Nazi Germany. This was an era when difference (including Darger's apparent "craziness") was brutally stigmatized; when even in the U.S., discrimination on racial or religious grounds was not only condoned, but legally enforced.*[22]

preceding pages

CAT. 77.

Henry Darger

137 At Jennie Richee (recto)

136 At Jennie Richee (verso)

ca. 1950–70

Detail, Cat. 77

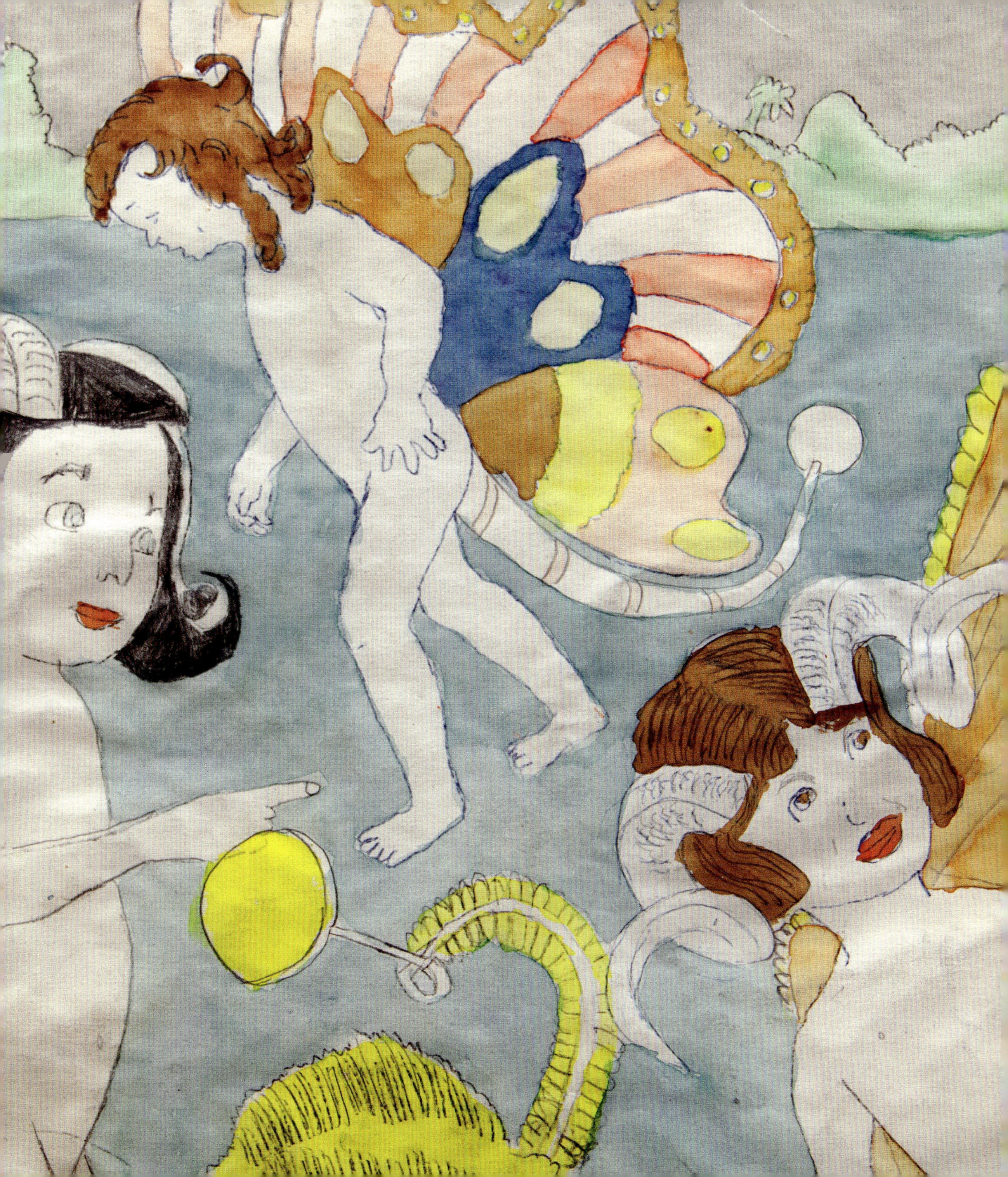

Many have conjectured that Darger's fantasy involvement with girls is inextricably connected to the loss of his sister, or perhaps the larger unraveling of his own childhood following the simultaneous loss of his mother and sibling. It is also difficult to separate the compounded trauma of being orphaned and incarcerated from the imagery and texts that describe, in obsessive detail, child torture and enslavement. Bonesteel is among the scholars who characterize Darger's project as a survival mechanism: "He did not do this to make 'art' or 'literature.' He did not do this to gain fame or make money. He did it to save his life. And though he fought with God over it and risked losing his soul in the process, it worked."[23] This assessment situates Darger's body of work in meaningful dialogue with the practices of artists Martín Ramírez, Nellie Mae Rowe, and Bill Traylor —who similarly used art as a tool of transformation, self-definition, and endurance. It is not being an outcast or "outsider" that unites them but, rather, their use of art as a strategic mechanism.

MARTÍN RAMÍREZ (1895–1963)

When making up a short list of artists failed by mainstream structures of interpretation, **MARTÍN RAMÍREZ** frequently joins Henry Darger near the top (Fig. 43). And, not unlike Darger, Ramírez created a body of work in which the role of "outsider" becomes relative, as the world he depicted is one in which the viewer is held at a permanent remove from Ramírez's internal perspective. Nevertheless, as a number of twenty-first-century projects have borne out, even partially decoding arcane visual texts demands that the work be situated amid the knowable facts of a life and the holistic context of history, era, place, and culture.[24] "We cannot adopt the man but reject or ignore his roots, smugly designating his utterances as garble because they are not in our tongue," Michael D. Hall asserted in 1988.[25] But until more recently, voices like this were the minority, and, from the earliest days when "outsider" makers moved into the spotlight, dominant presentation models favored fanfare, with reductive, partially factual biographies that played up marginalizing factors and avoided or minimized the complex, culturally grounded frameworks that truly honor bodies of work too often backdropped by anguish.

The drawings that survive Ramírez and define his known body of work were made after he was institutionalized in 1931, in a California mental hospital where he was declared a "catatonic schizophrenic" despite his insistence that he did not speak English and was not insane. "In those years," explains sociologist and Ramírez biographer Víctor M. Espinosa, "for somebody in his situation, his diagnosis meant a life sentence. He was never released."[26] Ramírez's tragic confinement is compounded by the fact that he had migrated to the United States to find work in 1925, and, like thousands of Mexicans in similar circumstances, never returned to the wife and family he left behind.

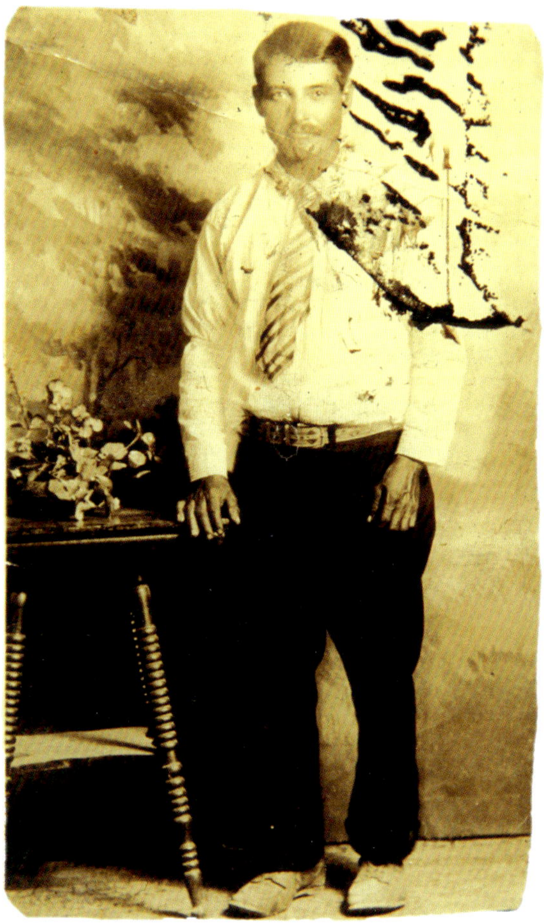

Fig. 43. Studio portrait of Martín Ramírez, 1920s. Courtesy of Estate of Martín Ramírez

Ramírez's American experience began in 1925, when he left his home in Los Altos de Jalisco and traveled by train to El Paso, Texas. He came from a Catholic family of farm laborers and had a rudimentary literacy. His family was poor, but he had managed to acquire land, a home, and animals, increasing both his stature and pride. His farm, however, likely did not produce enough to both provide for basic needs and pay off the property debt, driving him in search of additional income in the United States. In California he worked the rail lines and possibly the mines, moving as the work demanded. Less than a year after he left home, a devastating civil war broke out between the Mexican government and the Catholic Church. The peril of becoming enmeshed in the Cristero Rebellion, in tandem with the heightened need for the income they were sending home, forced many migrants to stay in the States for far longer than planned.

Ramírez kept in touch with his family to the extent it was possible. Since his wife could not read, he exchanged letters with his brother, who was only partially literate. A complex array of events and miscommunications led to Ramírez feeling estranged and disinclined to return. When the Great Depression caused many migrants to lose the work they had in America, unemployed Mexicans were deported in great numbers. Ramírez, however, refused to go back. Without reliable work, shelter, or food, Ramírez fell prey to the police, who were on the lookout for "vagrants." Espinosa has given in-depth attention to the factors that led from this detention to lifelong institutionalization, and notes that Ramírez was likely hospitalized illegally, without a trial or a court hearing, or any certainty of a significant mental health condition.[27] Randall Morris interviewed James Durfee, a caretaker on Ramírez's ward, who said that Ramírez had received shock treatments as a matter of course, and opined that in today's society he might have been treated for mild depression, as an outpatient.[28] Ramírez was confined at California's Stockton State Hospital until he was diagnosed with tuberculosis in 1948, when he was transferred to the DeWitt State Hospital in Auburn, where he remained until his death in 1963.[29]

The images Ramírez drew speak of a yearned-for homeland, and seemingly chart the selfhood and identity he feared losing hold of in a place that had stripped him of everything (**CAT. 78**). In later works, abstraction increasingly pushes to the fore (**CAT. 79**). As Morris puts it, "Ramírez has taken from his experiences the dream sense the surrealists so avidly sought. His is the real surreal. He took the objects of a local mundane and blew them up to mythic proportions."[30]

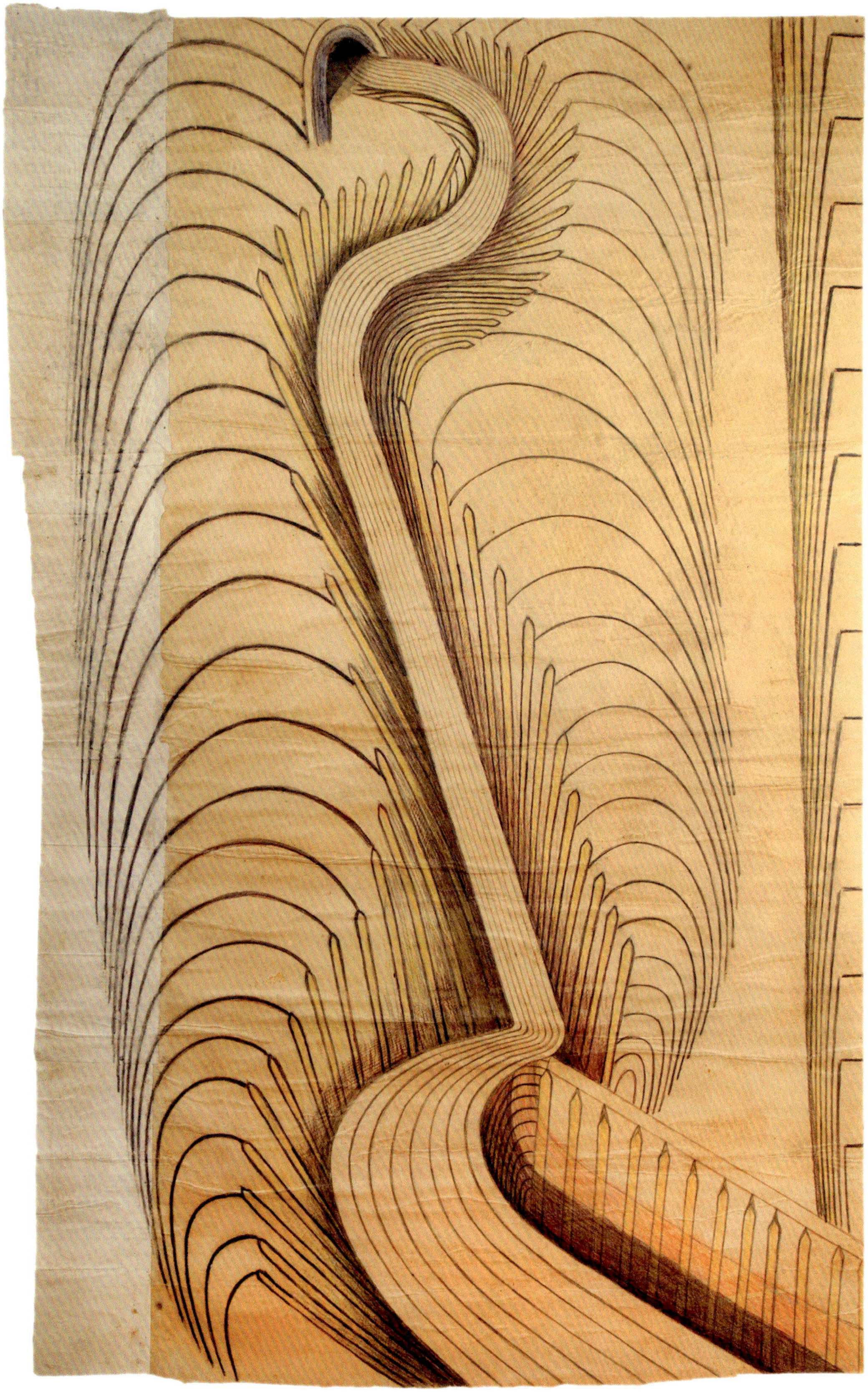

CAT. 78.
Martín Ramírez
Untitled (Vertical Landscape)
ca. 1948–63

CAT. 79.
Martín Ramírez
Untitled (Semi-Abstract Landscape with Birds, Tunnels, and Blue Teardrop Clusters)
ca. 1960–63

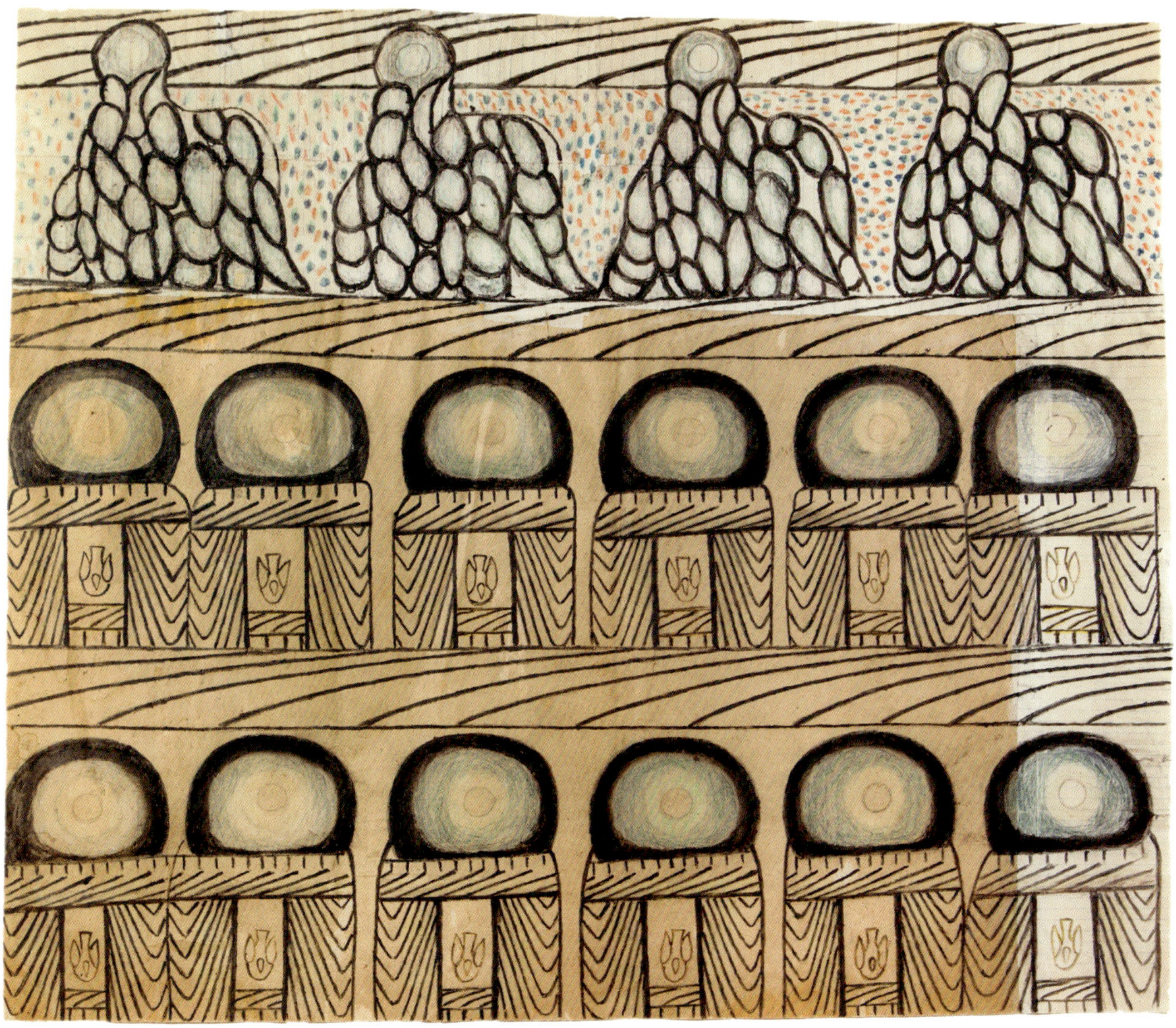

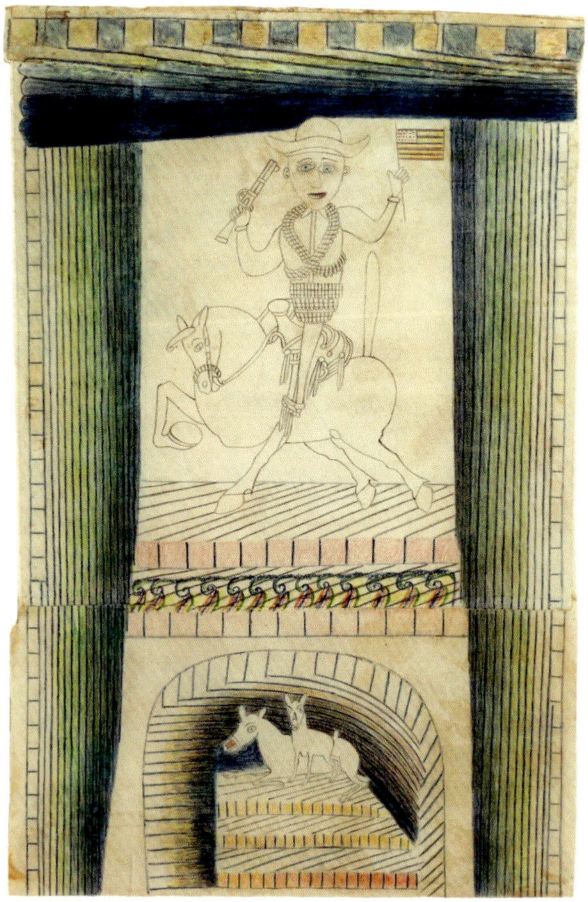

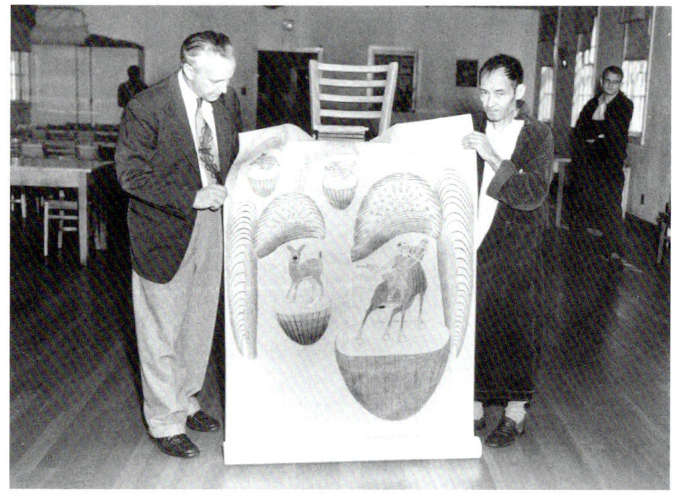

Fig. 44. Martín Ramírez, *Soldado with American Flag*, ca. 1950–53, crayon, watercolor, and pencil on various papers, 40 × 25 ⅝ in. Smithsonian American Art Museum, Gift of Herbert Waide Hemphill Jr. and museum purchase made possible by Ralph Cross Johnson, 1986.65.194

Fig. 45. Martín Ramírez (right) with Tarmo Pasto at the DeWitt State Hospital, Auburn, California, 1954; photograph by Percel Followell. Courtesy of the Estate of Martín Ramírez and Ricco/Maresca Gallery

And indeed, Ramírez's world reveals a somnambulist's search for lost normalcy; he depicts churches and villages from homeland locales, the flora and fauna of Mexico and his own farm, mounted riders as he himself had been (Fig. 44), and trains snaking northward, crossing a boundary that had amounted to tremendous consequence.

These works, ranging in scale from modest to epic, were made on whatever paper Ramírez was given or could find and patch together, with makeshift materials. Family stories indicate that Ramírez had a creative inclination and made drawings before his hospitalization, but no such works were retained. Ramírez's time at Stockton and DeWitt coincided with an era in which arts and crafts activities were increasingly implemented as therapy in psychiatric hospitals, which facilitated interactions with art teachers or therapists in varying degrees, in some cases with artists sent from the Federal Art Project.[31] Artist, psychiatrist, and professor Tarmo Pasto became interested in art by mentally ill patients and began visiting DeWitt (Fig. 45). He became aware of Ramírez's creative output, and beginning in 1948 started to nurture him as an artist and save his work.[32] In 1952, Ramírez's art was first shown in a gallery setting, when Don R. Birrell mounted a show at the Crocker Art Gallery in Sacramento.[33] He was only a niche interest then, but Pasto managed to organize subsequent Bay Area shows in the coming years. With the 1954 exhibition at Mills College Art Gallery, *The Art of a Schizophrene*, Ramírez came to wider attention than he had before—particularly after the museum's director, Alfred Neumeyer, called him "a sort of Mexican Rousseau."[34]

After that, Pasto put greater effort into promoting Ramírez; he reached out to the Museum of Modern Art and the Guggenheim in New York, but neither mounted a show.[35] He had better luck at smaller venues, but, during Ramírez's lifetime, interest remained minimal. By 1958, Pasto had stopped visiting Ramírez. Dr. Max Dunievitz began volunteering at DeWitt not long after, however, and took a similar interest in Ramírez. He brought Ramírez materials and kept most of the artworks he made.[36] The bodies of work Pasto and Dunievitz saved compose the bulk of the extant work.[37]

In the late 1960s, Jim Nutt and Gladys Nilsson saw images of Ramírez's art during a teaching stint at Sacramento State College, where Nutt was also running the art gallery. They went to see Pasto's collection of what he called "psychotic art." Nutt and Nilsson were among the Chicago artists who had taken keen interest in Joseph Yoakum, and by then had become interested in other art brut artists, such as Adolf Wölfli, as well. Ultimately, the meeting took on historic importance, as Pasto was retiring and wanted to sell his collection. Nutt, in conjunction with his own art dealer, Phyllis Kind, acquired the whole collection, setting in motion the commercial advocacy that would propel Ramírez from unknown patient to "outsider" icon. As Espinosa's 2015 book amply illustrates, Ramírez's complex story—from peasant farmer to paradoxical art star—is an epic tale, as illuminating as it is tragic.

Over time, Ramírez's art and legendary status escalated into the blue-chip market, climbing steadily throughout the 1980s and 1990s, and especially after the major exhibition put on by the American Folk Art Museum in New York in 2007.[38] His work has been increasingly seen in international settings, but for Ramírez, the multifaceted stigmas of mental illness and being a non-English-speaking, transnational migrant prevented easy categorization or interpretation for his work, and even the Latinx/Chicanx communities held him at a remove. "Ramírez is a cross-border artist who produced all his work in a transnational third space, that is, far away from his homeland, completely marginalized from society in California, without being part of any immigrant or Latino artistic community," Espinosa explains. "Only in recent years has Ramírez become a symbol of the Mexican immigrant experience and a source of inspiration for many Latino and Latina artists and writers in the United States."[39] Today Ramírez, like Traylor, Edmondson, and a handful of others, is counted among the key shifters of the mainstream canon in America.

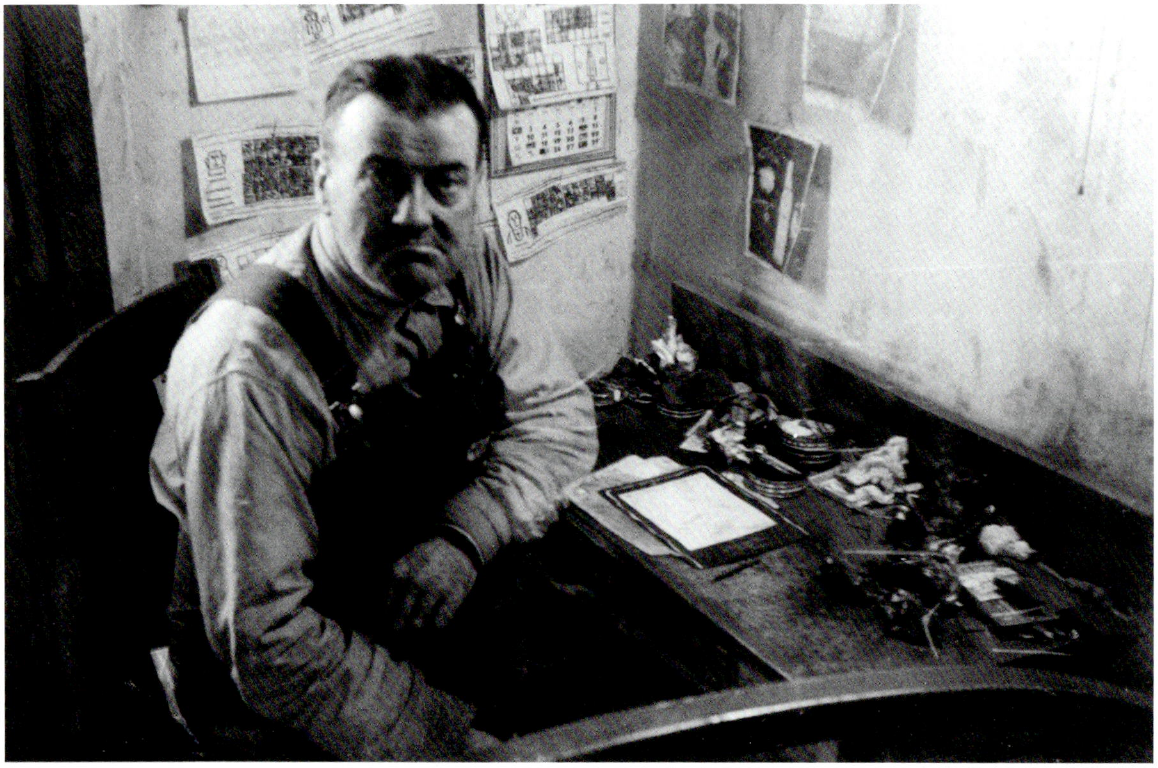

Fig. 46. James Castle at desk in shed, ca. 1955; photograph by Robert Beach. Tom Trusky Papers, Special Collections and Archives, Boise State University

JAMES CASTLE (1899–1977)

Born in 1892, 1895, and 1899, respectively, Henry Darger, Martín Ramírez, and **JAMES CASTLE** paint a distinctively different picture of untrained artists born at the end of the nineteenth century than do their African American counterparts (Fig. 46). While Black artists were finding dignity and visibility through community, faith, and ancestral continuums, marginalized white artists who attracted art-world interest most often did so through other strong filters of difference—isolation, mental challenge, and degrees of sensory or neural difference.[40] While Castle's specific challenges were a world apart from those of Darger and Ramírez, they were no less nuanced or complex. The body of work he made—drawings and constructed paper sculptures—would make Castle one of the rare self-taught artists to become the focus of a full-scale retrospective at a major art museum.[41]

Castle was born and lived his whole life in the Boise Basin of Idaho. He was acutely deaf from infancy and, despite some schooling, never became fluent in any alternative means of communication (lipreading, signing, reading, or writing), a reality that positions him differently than a person who lost hearing after some years of full-sensory engagement with other people and communicated with relative ease.[42] Deafness from birth is considered neurological rather than medical, which stems from later illness or injury. Individuals with neurological deafness are neurodivergent; their brains function differently than that of a neurotypical individual, rerouting auditory pro- cessing resources toward other strengths.[43] The neurodivergent world is wide-ranging, and describing Castle as such is not meant to diagnose him or describe his specific way of thinking and functioning but, rather, to give important context to the ways in which his creative pathway was unique. Castle's art reveals his profound ability to observe and interpret the visual world; that his interpretations were extralinguistic and singular in ways we can only imagine makes the imagery all the more powerful.[44]

Castle used art expansively, beginning as a child. He was born in Garden Valley and, apart from the five years he spent at the Idaho School for the Deaf and Blind, lived at home with his family.[45] His parents, Frank and Mary Castle, were farmers who supplemented the family income by serving as local postmasters and selling goods such as coffee and sugar from the living room of their home.[46] In 1923 the family moved to Star, and in 1931 to the outskirts of Boise. In the moves to Star and Boise, Castle's family discarded his accumulated artistic output from that place; with the exception of a few annotated books, the only surviving art Castle made dates between 1931 and his death in 1977.[47] He was prolific, however, both in his own drawing and in the amount of printed material he looked at and interpreted on a daily basis. Curator Nicholas R. Bell has observed that, as postmasters and minor grocers, Castle's parents processed a great deal of the printed matter that was delivered to their home. "Castle clearly enjoyed early access to this material, and was influenced by it—revealing a man deeply connected to the paper tide inundating his home."[48]

Castle's imagery draws deeply on the Idaho landscape that comprised all he ever saw firsthand. He also drew himself, people he knew, his home, and things that populated his life, from clothing to ducks (**CATS. 80–83**). He made text-based images and booklets that variously decipher and recipher the written world through the eyes of someone endlessly seeking their arcane meanings; he often worked on both sides of a piece of paper, and made enigmatic scenes of totem-like structures (**CAT. 84**). Among Castle's most intimate-feeling works are string-bound paper constructions of people, animals, and objects such as chairs or water pitchers. In rooms at home, he would surround himself with installations of his paper people, and sometimes make drawings showing them in attendance (Fig. 47, **CAT. 85**). Castle's artworks reveal not just a world but a worldview, an autotopography, which cultural theorist Mieke Bal has described as a "spatial, local, and situational 'writing' of the self's life in visual art."[49] Castle charted his experience via a personally

CAT. 80.
James Castle
Untitled
ca. 1931–77

CAT. 81.
James Castle
Untitled
ca. 1931–77

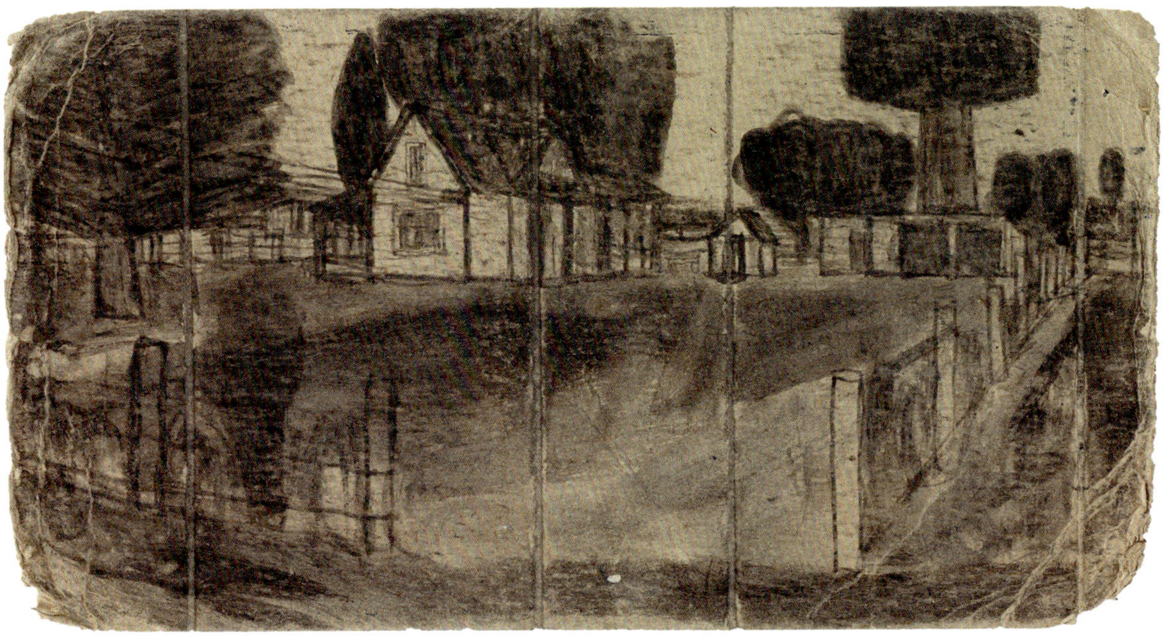

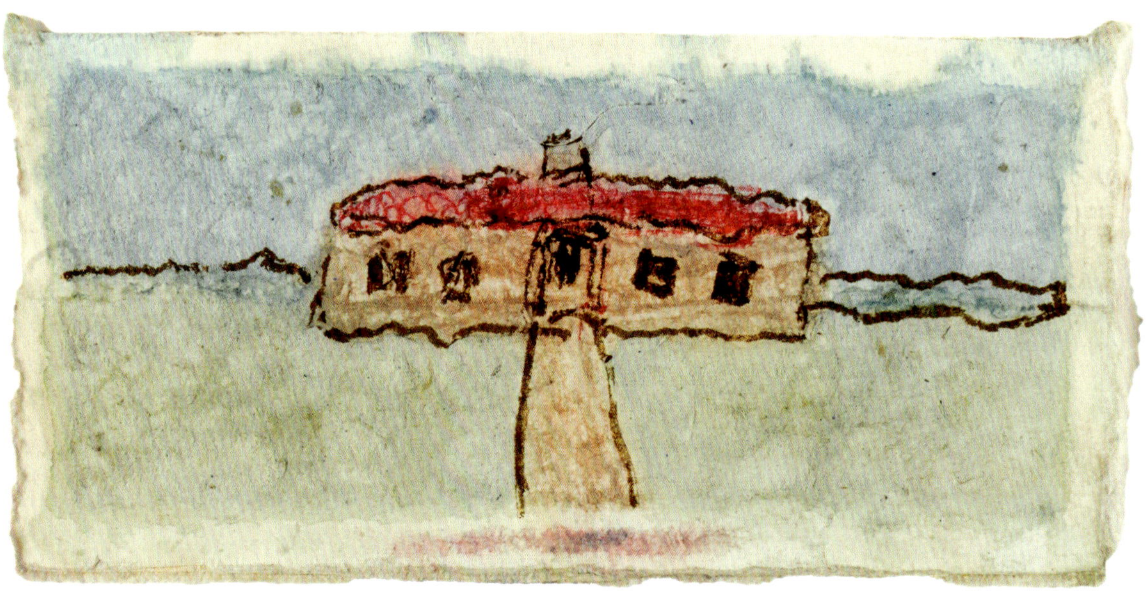

CAT. 82.
James Castle
Untitled
ca. 1931–77

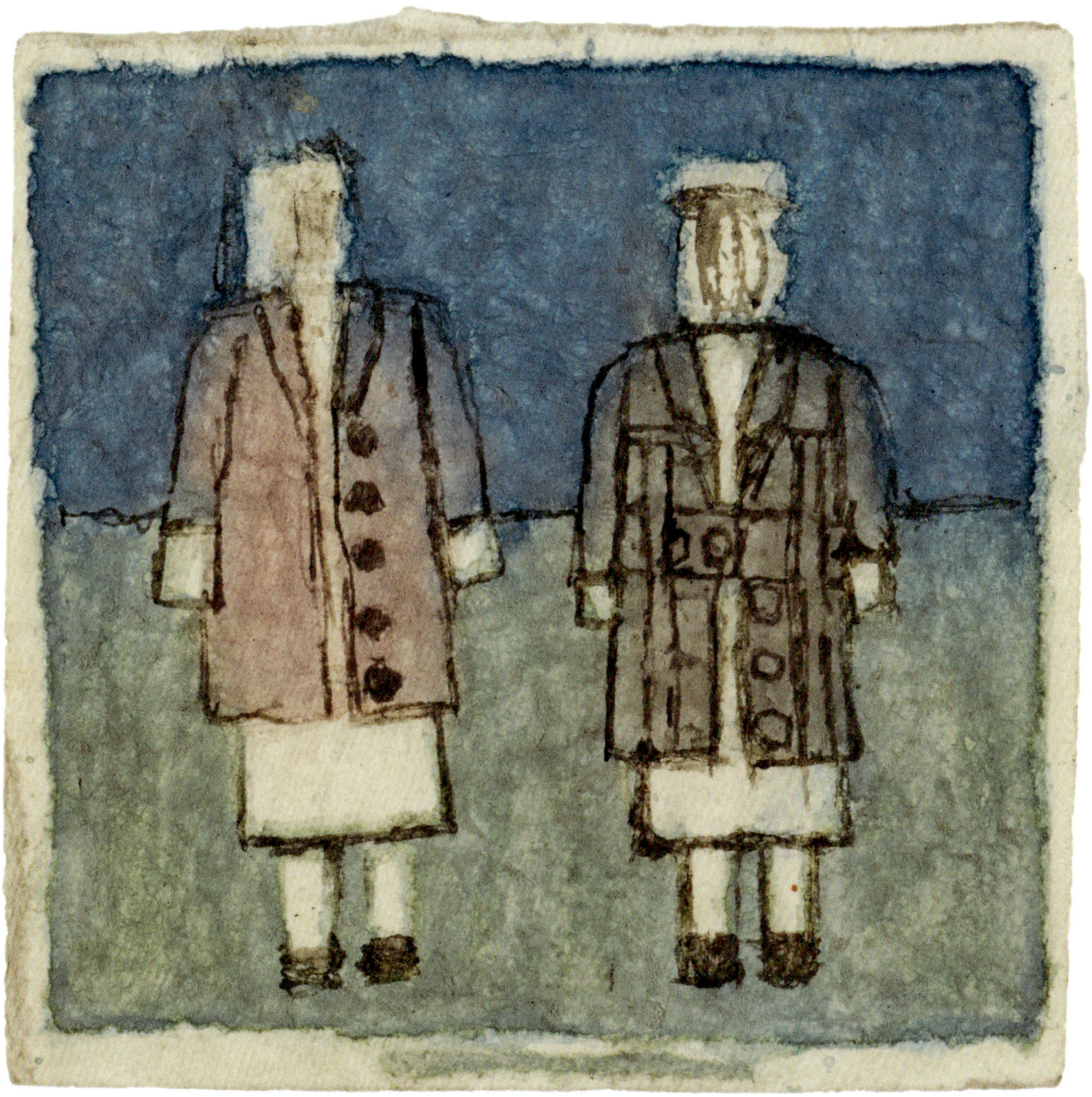

CAT 83.
James Castle
Untitled (recto/verso)
ca. 1931–77

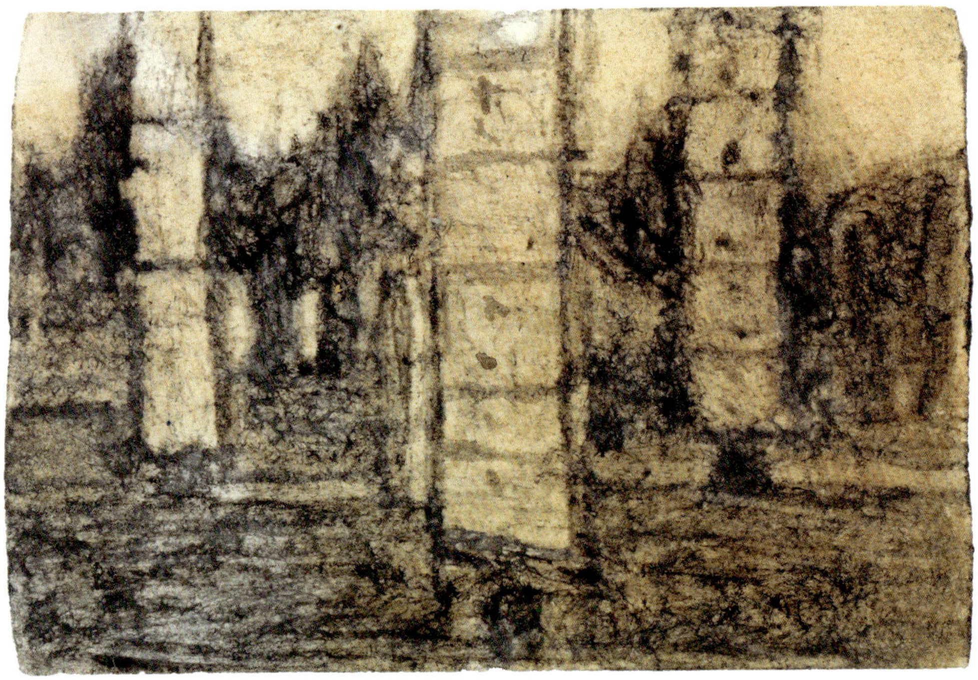

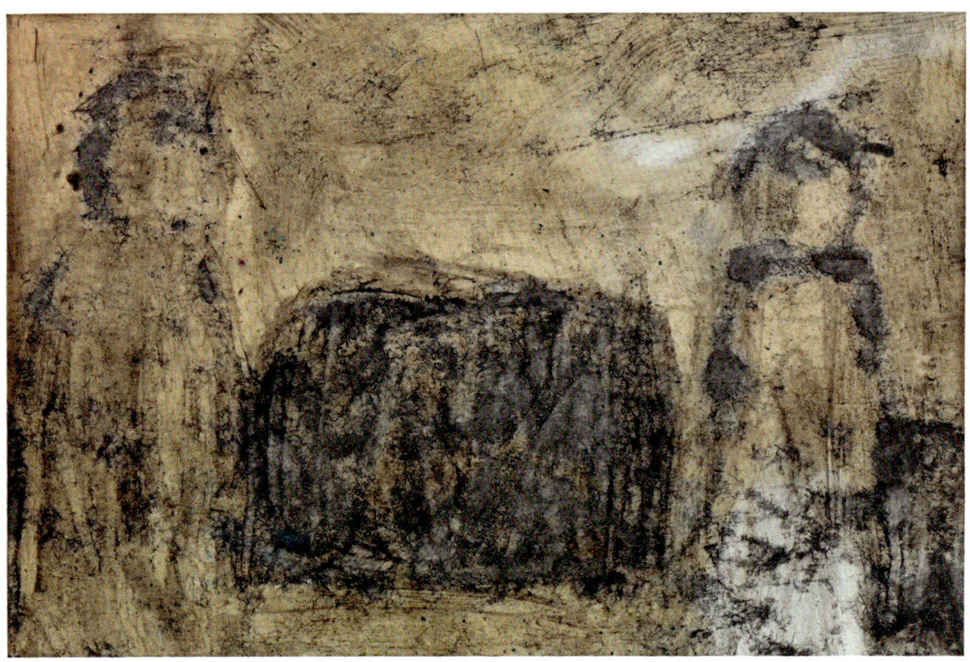

CAT. 84.
James Castle
Untitled
ca. 1931–77

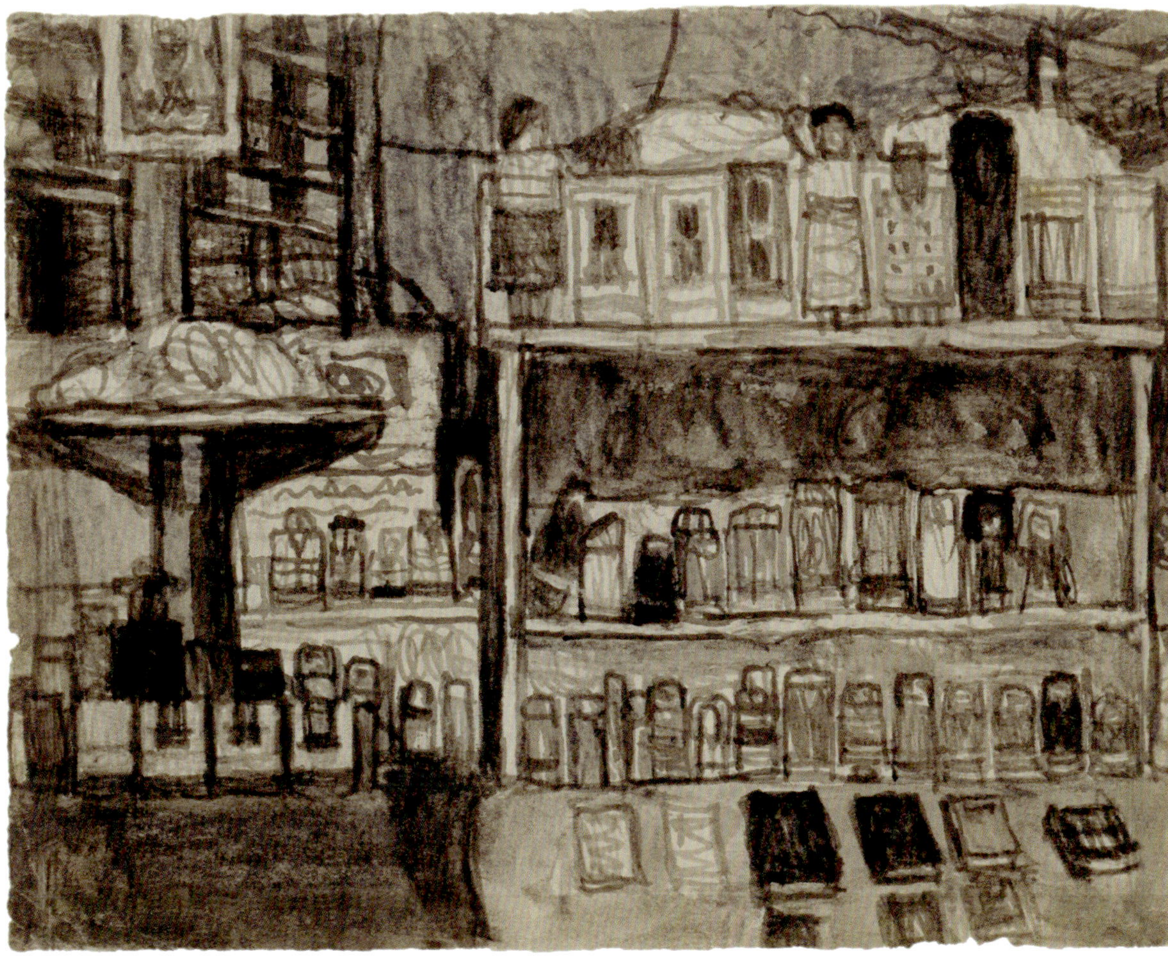

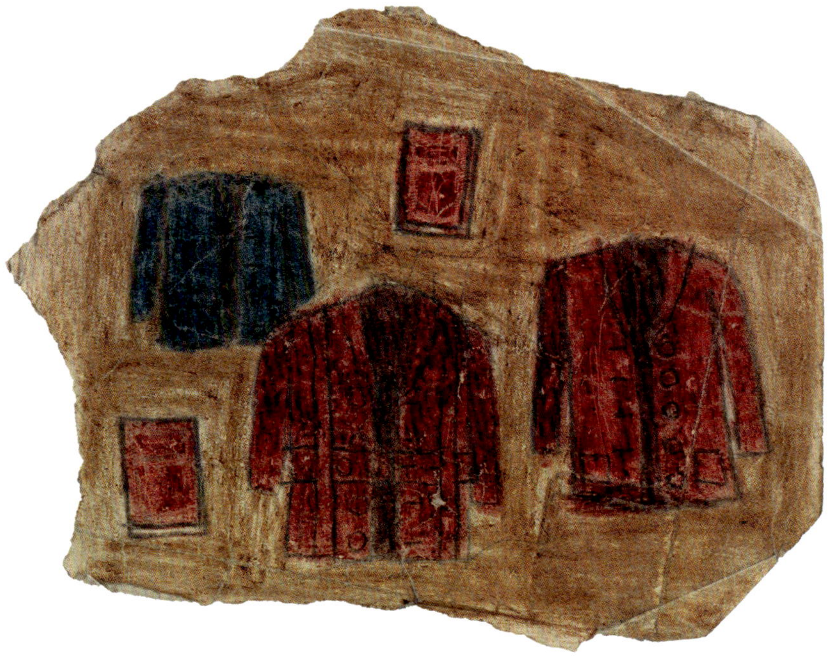

CAT. 85.
James Castle
Untitled
ca. 1932

invented pictorial language and made as unique a body of art as any. His art, as with certain other game-changing artists, brought the thorny issue of "otherness" to the fore in a very particular way, while simultaneously underscoring the ways in which biographical specificity plays a critical role in the work of certain artists.[50] Castle's innate grasp of perspective alone drew questions pertaining to ability and disability, challenging conventional wisdom about how linear perspective could be learned and implemented without formal artistic training.

Akin to Ramírez being packaged as a maker of "psychotic art," Castle, when his work came into art-world view, first in the 1950s and 1960s and with more fervor in subsequent decades, was routinely described as a "deaf mute" artist, as though his productivity were most remarkable only in the context of his life's challenges, rather than as a body of work that revealed a profound world beyond the boundaries of sound and language. Herein lies the historical significance and critical complexity of Castle—as with other artists who cannot articulate their own practice in, as Michael D. Hall put it, "our tongue": the images he made revealed an identity that the art world could not reconcile with preconceived notions of an isolated, neurodivergent person of unconventional literacy. Castle's identity was central to both the work he made and its reception, but for entirely different reasons. In his art, his life experience was the informative universe. For the art world, his images were too representational and grounded to be art brut, too complex and sophisticated to be "modern primitive," too haunting and arcane to be "folk," and too isolated to be mainstream.

Castle had been dead for twenty years by the time his work was first seen at the Outsider Art Fair in New York, but, ultimately, the ways in which Castle remained an outsider among "outsiders" was arguably to his benefit. The power of his work and the complexity of his story captured the

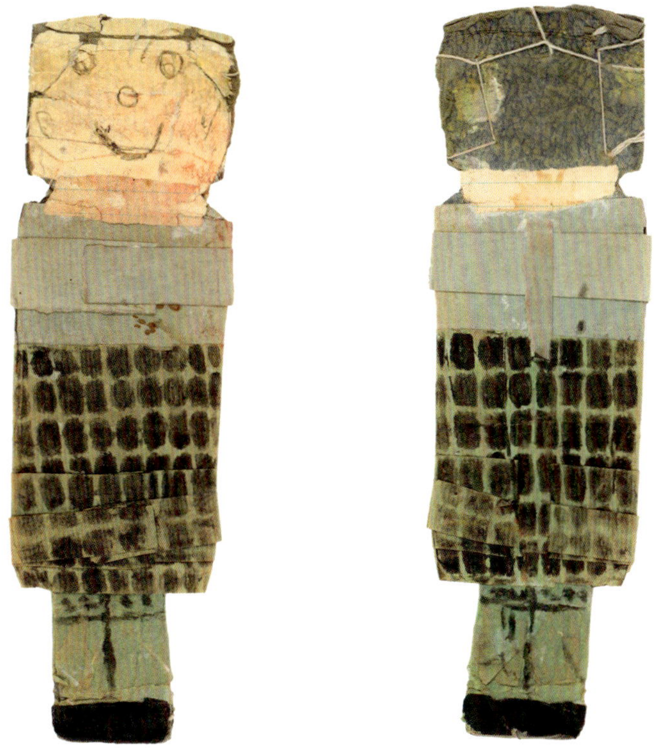

Fig. 47. James Castle, *Untitled* (recto/verso), ca. 1931–77, soot, color of unknown origin, wheat paste, and string on found paper, 11 ½ × 3 ½ in. Smithsonian American Art Museum, Gift of the James Castle Collection and Archive and museum purchase through the Luisita L. and Franz H. Denghausen Endowment, 2013.27.10

attention of museums and scholars interested in deeply engaged investigations. It resisted the sensational treatment of the exotic "other," but offered itself for meaningful, long-term contemplation. In 2008, Ann Percy of the Philadelphia Museum of Art organized *James Castle: A Retrospective*, with a title that boldly declared the scope and gravity afforded to this artist. Never before had a major, encyclopedic East Coast art museum so fully acknowledged the value of a self-taught artist in a temporary exhibition. Percy positioned Castle among poets, bricoleurs, and all manner of iconoclastic individualists. Catalogue contributor, curator, and folklorist Brendan Greaves addressed the slippery issue of Castle's artistic nomadism as a positive, calling him "representative of an alternative multivalent modernity," and demanding that museums move beyond field-based frameworks of apprehension. He argued that consideration of Castle requires "a kind of analytic parallax that can combine sociolinguistics, performance theory, folkloristics, cultural anthropology, cultural studies, art history, literacy, deaf studies, and hopefully other, heretofore untapped approaches for the examination of the phenomenology of everyday expressive life."[51]

Percy effectively positioned Castle as an inflection point for the treatment of marginalized and differently abled artists in the context of the traditional museum—the very places that had long been ground zero in their marginalization.[52] Castle became emblematic of an insider/outsider endgame; his body of work demanded that difference be reconciled rather than admired or ignored from a distance.

HOWARD FINSTER (1916–2001)

In the early 1980s, **HOWARD FINSTER** became the most highly visible self-taught artist of his era: not only an art star of sorts but a popular-culture celebrity in his own right (Fig. 48).[53] By then he had come a long way from his humble beginnings, growing up as he had in a family of meager means in Appalachian Alabama and Georgia. But a childhood vision may have revealed a path to Finster, who looked back at the moment as indelible: "At three years old I had a vision of my sister, and she was telling me I would be a billionaire artist. And then I pastored churches for about forty years, and that was to get me acquainted with Earth people."[54]

Finster was moved, after these decades of preaching, to take up painting and sculpting after a vision he had in 1976, in which God appeared to him and directed: "paint sacred art." At the polar extreme from Ramírez and Castle, Finster's own words are extensively on record—written, painted, recorded, and filmed—all entirely in keeping with his calling as a Southern Baptist preacher and a man on a mission to get the Word of God out, by any means possible. Hal Fulmer, a professor

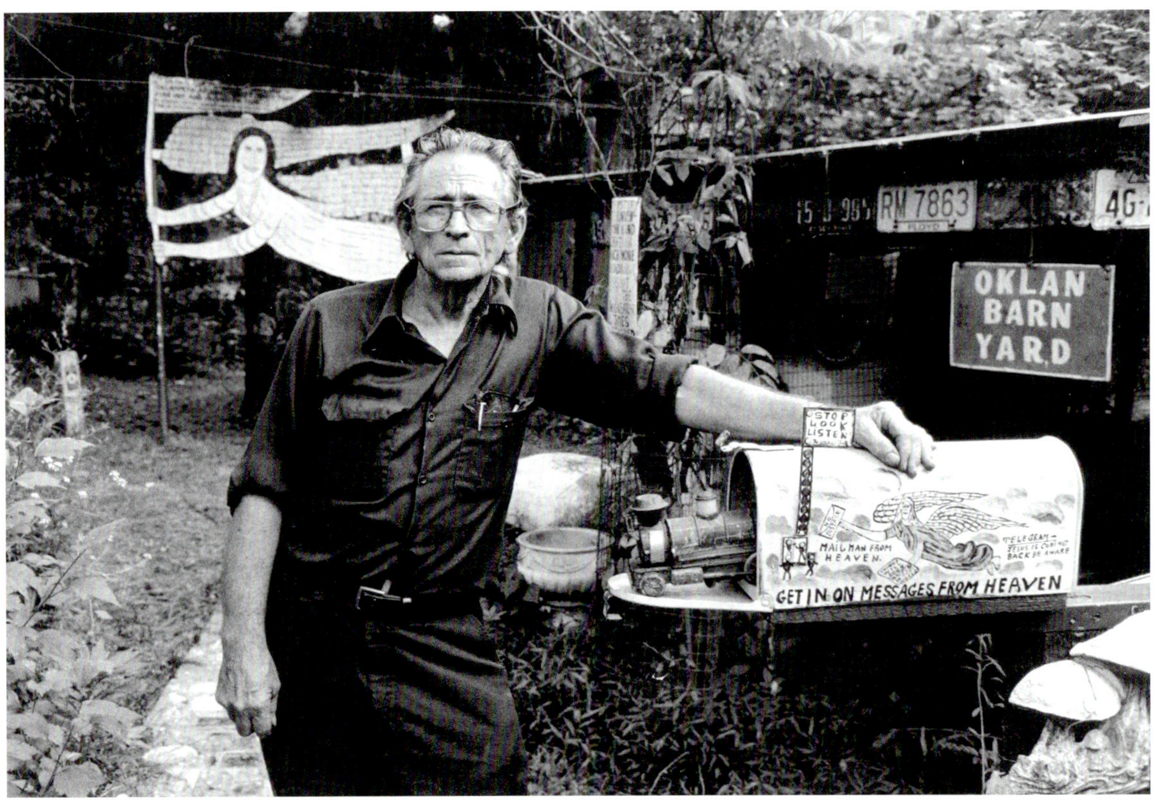

Fig. 48. The Reverend Howard Finster, Paradise Garden, Summerville, Georgia, 1987–88; photograph by Guy Mendes

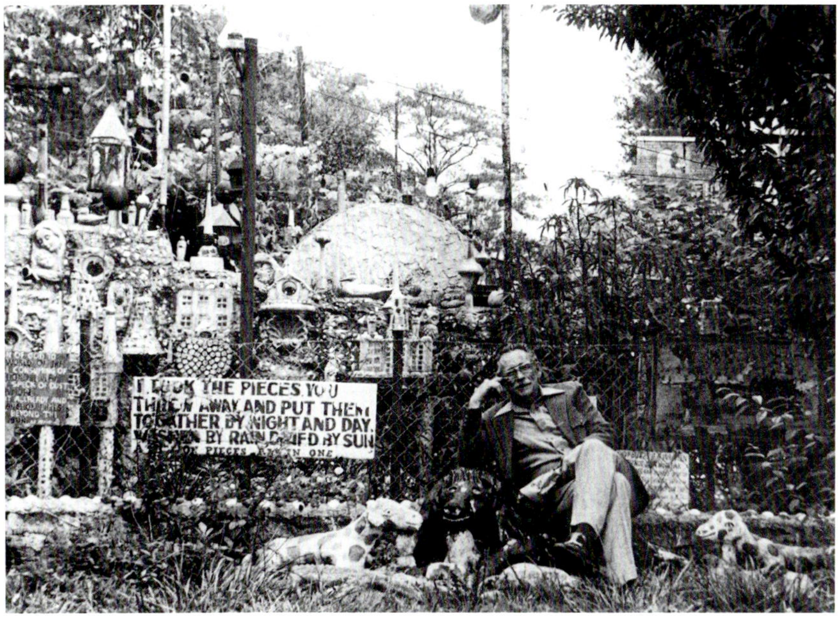

Fig. 49. Howard Finster at Paradise Garden, ca. 1981, Summerville, Georgia; photograph by Tom Patterson

who has studied southern oratory, has observed, “In the South, first and foremost, there is the Word. There are other books and other authors, to be sure, but only one text is empowered with a capital letter, and it is the Bible, divinely inspired, inerrant, and literal.”[55]

Katherine Jentleson has noted that Finster’s vision may have been sparked by the disappointment he felt one Sunday when he discovered that his congregation could not recall the sermon he had given just the week before. As powerful as the word of God might be, he realized he needed better tools for sharing it. His idea to employ art as visual evangelism invigorated his mission. His sermons in paint became, as he called them, “signposts to salvation,” affixed to the fence, trees, and buildings in what became “Paradise Garden,” a four-acre environment at his home in Summerville, Georgia (Figs. 49, 50). “Over the next two and a half decades, Finster would generate more than 46,900 works of art,” Jentleson explains. “Painted on everything from sneakers and decommissioned motel telephones to wooden boards cut into squares and rectangles as well as irregular shapes, like angels and human figures. Finster maintained detailed records, not only numbering each work, but also keeping running ledgers on all manner of surfaces he used, from scrap wood to the sides of filing cabinets.”[56]

Inspired by things as wide-ranging as the Ave Maria Grotto in Cullman, Alabama, and the admirably efficient production lines of Henry Ford, Finster set about reaching as many souls as he could—sinners and saved alike. His eclectic beliefs included extraterrestrial life, and that he had been reincarnated on earth to help save the doomed. Liza Kirwin, archivist at the Smithsonian’s Archives of American Art, has recounted that it wasn’t long before collectors and the curious alike were beating a path to visit Finster and buy his art. “They’d come here and just blow up on it,” Finster told her. “So, I’d just take a crowbar and start pulling [the art] off [the fence].”[57] His art, in tandem with his boundless energy and gregarious nature, propelled him into a reach far beyond the local. Kirwin, who interviewed Finster in 1984, described his personality as a fusion of “fire-and-brimstone swagger” and sweetness, noting: “One could say that all artists are visionaries, but Finster was tuned to a special frequency. He took on the big topics—life and death, redemption and salvation.

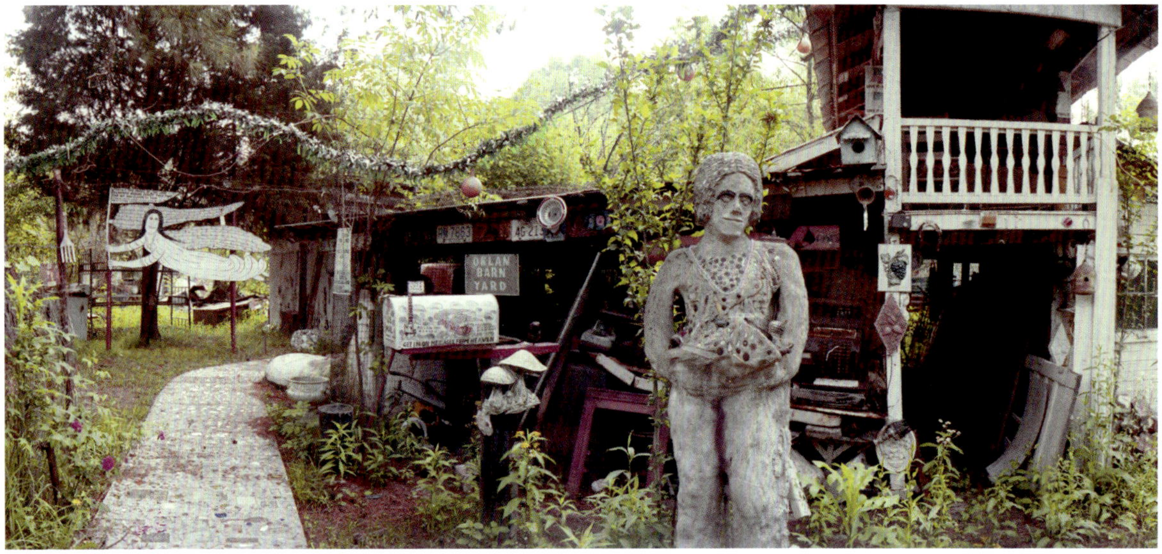

Fig. 50. View of Howard Finster's Paradise Garden, 1987–88; photograph by Roger Manley

In the 1970s and 1980s, that angst-ridden era of few certainties, here was a man of solid convictions, pointing the way. It's no wonder he was a hero to hipsters."[58]

And at the height of his appeal, it was hard to say whether it was the art or the man that attracted more attention (**CAT. 86**). His art was shown at New York's Phyllis Kind Gallery in the late 1970s, but it was in 1983, after the Athens, Georgia, band R.E.M. filmed a music video at Paradise Garden and featured a Finster painting on the cover of their album, *Reckoning*, the following year, that Finster and his project began to really attract attention. Also in the mid-1980s, Finster had artworks included in the Venice Biennale and made his first appearance on Johnny Carson's *Tonight Show*, pushing self-taught art, in the highly particular form of Howard Finster, into the mainstream spotlight. Recalling Finster's grand, open-armed television entrance, one journalist described the moment "when the pomade-slicked folk artist picks up a banjo and begins to sing in front of Carson's desk, and all of a sudden the roles reverse, and Finster is the showbiz superstar, and Carson is just trying to stay in the frame."[59] In 1985, Finster's work was featured on another album cover, the Talking Heads' *Little Creatures*, which was awarded best album and best album cover of the year by the *Village Voice* and *Rolling Stone*, respectively, and sold over two million copies.

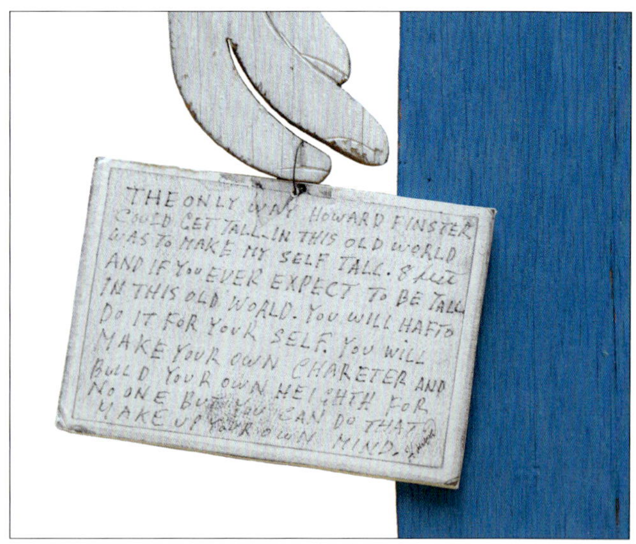

CAT. 86.
Howard Finster
Self-Portrait
1975

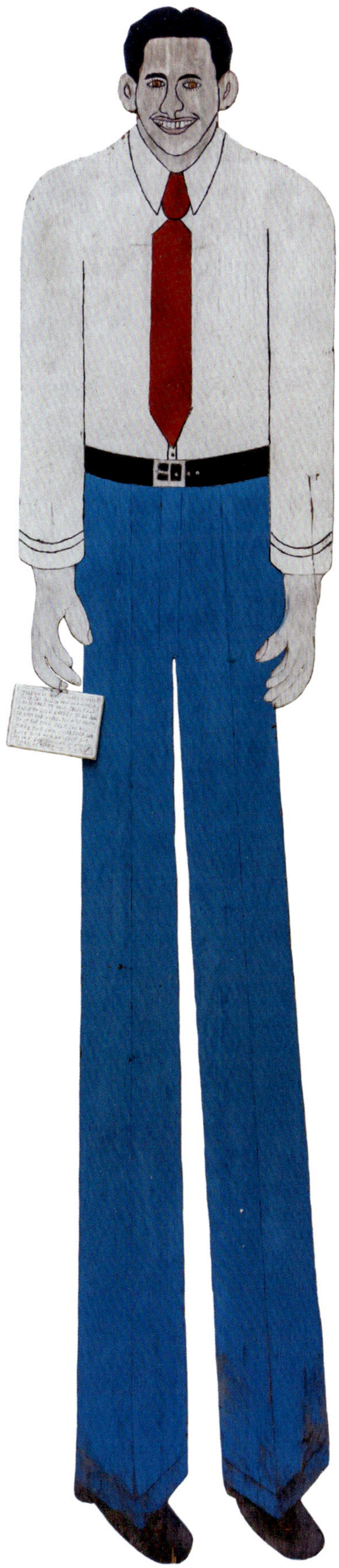

The sheer number of artworks he produced prompted critics to question Finster's validity as an artist, revealing an inherent clash between his missionary intentions and the art world's attempt to clarify the inferiority of art by interlopers. In 1987, Finster said, "I've done six thousand, nine hundred and eight works of art and I think two or three hundred of them would be pretty perfect. Eighty-five percent of the paintings are okay and the rest of them sells as third-class art."[60] He confessed to trying every shortcut he could to keep up with demand but remained clear that—as it was for Sister Gertrude Morgan—the message was the point. Finster's artworks spanned fully realized paintings of biblical scenes, to portraits (and self-portraits), to painted items that seem to translate and make portable the sculpted and painted faces and forms that dwell like omnipresent resident spirits throughout Paradise Garden (Figs. 51, 52; **CATS. 87–91**). Some understood that Finster's aim was not that of mainstream fine artists, but the taint of marginalization touched the artist as well as the art. In the secular art world, he was viewed as varying degrees of crazy, from "lovingly peculiar" to "pathological," while others criticized him as a pawn of gallerists eager to package and sell his colorful character as, in the words of Daniel Wojcik, "an authentic and rustic astronaut of outsider realms."[61]

American art historians including Sally M. Promey, Erika Doss, and Carol Crown agree that the intersections of art and religion, especially with regard to modern and contemporary artists, have not been sufficiently considered and respected by scholars and critics. Promey asserts that religion has been routinely marginalized on various fronts of modernist intellectual assumptions, including its "restriction of creative individuality, its responsibility for an inferior aesthetic or taste culture, and its presumed universal proclivity toward conservative, sectarian, and ideological obsessions." But she also notes that, in the late twentieth century and after, wide-ranging publications from John Beardsley's *Gardens of Revelation: Environments by Visionary Artists* (1995) to David Morgan's volume of essays *Icons of American Protestantism: The Art of Warner Sallman* (1996) have encouraged more considered treatment of religious thought, experience, and practice as "an integral part of the complicated cultural fabric of artistic production and reception in the United States."[62] Doss maintains that, in different ways, American artists of all varieties are engaged in visualizing faith: "Artists who are labeled 'modern' and 'contemporary,' like Rothko, Tobey, Warhol, and Weisberg, and those called 'self-taught' or 'outsider,' such as Rowe,

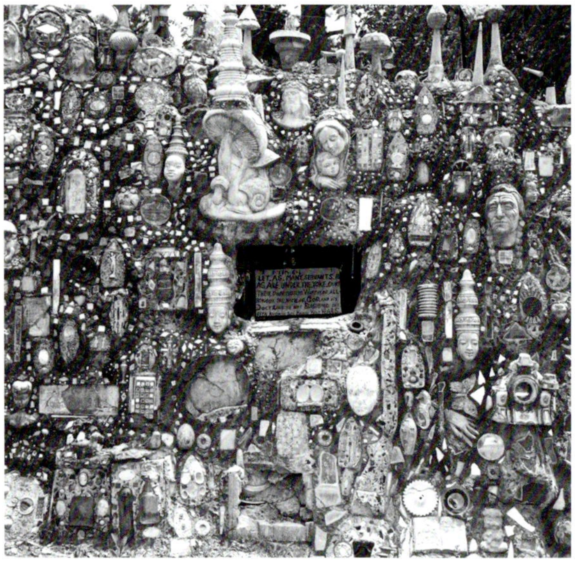

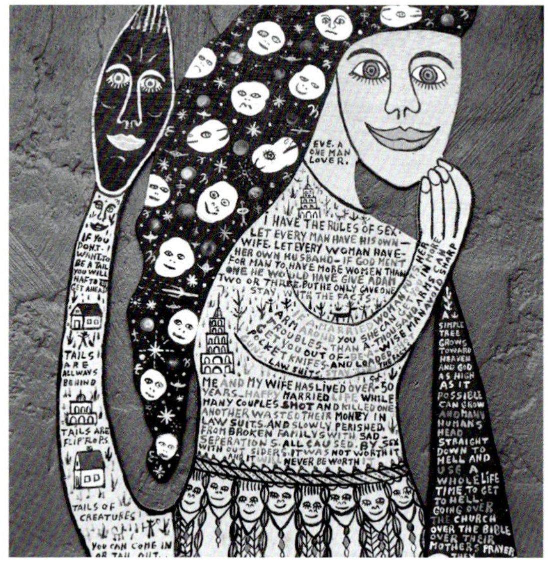

Figs. 51, 52. Howard Finster's Paradise Garden (details), 1987–88; photographs by Roger Manley

Murray, Morgan, and Finster, share interests in faith and spirituality and express them in visually diverse strains."[63] And Crown has argued that apocalyptic themes and prophecy-belief traditions, in the context of life experiences, demand serious consideration instead of provoking, as they more often do, characterizations of mental instability.[64]

Finster's buoyant disposition may have belied the psychic searching that led him first into preaching, and subsequently to be "a man of visions." Wojcik underscores the significance of trauma in Finster's childhood, which was greatly impacted by the deaths of five of his twelve siblings.[65] Like millions of born-again Christians, Finster's conversion experience redirected him toward spiritual light in a manner completely aligned with survival and self-preservation.

Propelled by his existential worries, Finster refused to be powerless in a world that seemed increasingly grim, and for a humankind that seemed increasingly doomed—from nuclear annihilation to environmental destruction to global suffering, and countless other problems streaming into the living room with the evening news. "This world's just an awful place, when you get to studyin' about it," he told writer Tom Patterson in 1989. "This world is in trouble. The poor people gettin' poorer, and there's gettin' to be more and more jobless people, and they're doin' ever'thing they can, but they don't know what to do."[66] Ultimately, Finster highlighted the ways in which tradition, folk culture, and personal spirituality transform and in turn are transformative through the vehicle of creative practice. His art-world reception revealed how foregrounding marginalization was, in the 1980s and 1990s, the sole framework for presenting artists that did not conform to mainstream norms.

CATS. 87–91.
Howard Finster
Untitled (Bottles)
1988

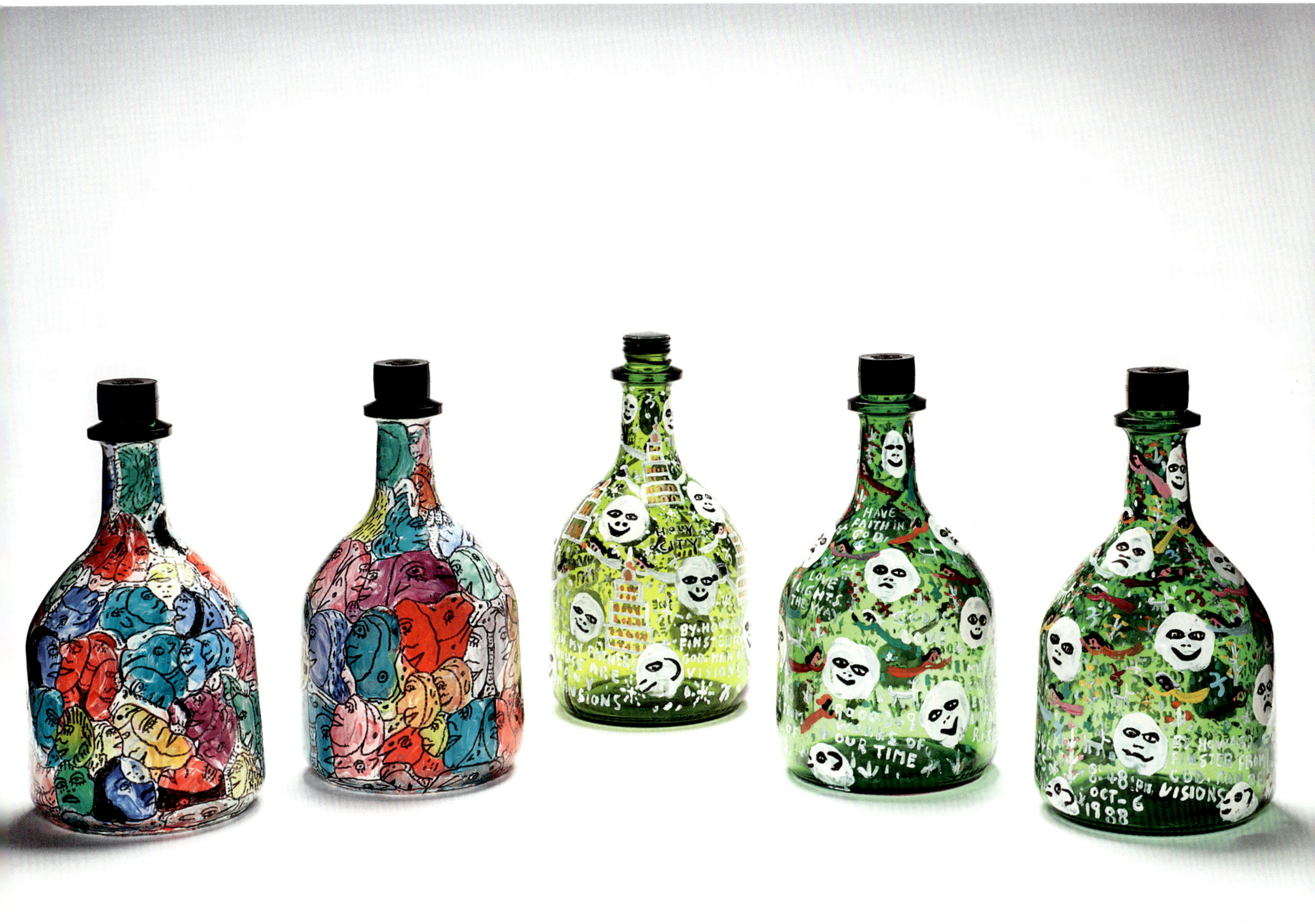
HOLY CITY
HAVE FAITH IN GOD
OUR TIME
VISIONS
OCT-6
1988

THORNTON DIAL SR. (1928–2016)

THORNTON DIAL SR. became a powerful voice among artists working in the Black vernacular tradition—closing the circle between nineteenth-century-born artists like Bill Traylor, quilters who had never been recognized as artists, and a younger generation seeking to find their way forward in a racist society where progress has been both tremendous and insufficient (Fig. 53). Dial was born into a sharecropping family in rural Alabama on the eve of the Great Depression. Like other artists from the Black Atlantic South, he experienced Jim Crow segregation and the civil rights movement in a crisis-driven landscape. Profoundly influenced by Dr. Martin Luther King Jr., Dial used art to openly confront issues of racial oppression in America, developing an allegorical style that balanced narration with abstraction and the personal with the universal. He lived to see his work acquired by some of the most revered museums in the United States and became relevant to the mainstream art world in ways that were unprecedented, pressing the urgency of questioning qualifying labels that constrain the reception of an artist rather than illuminating the art.

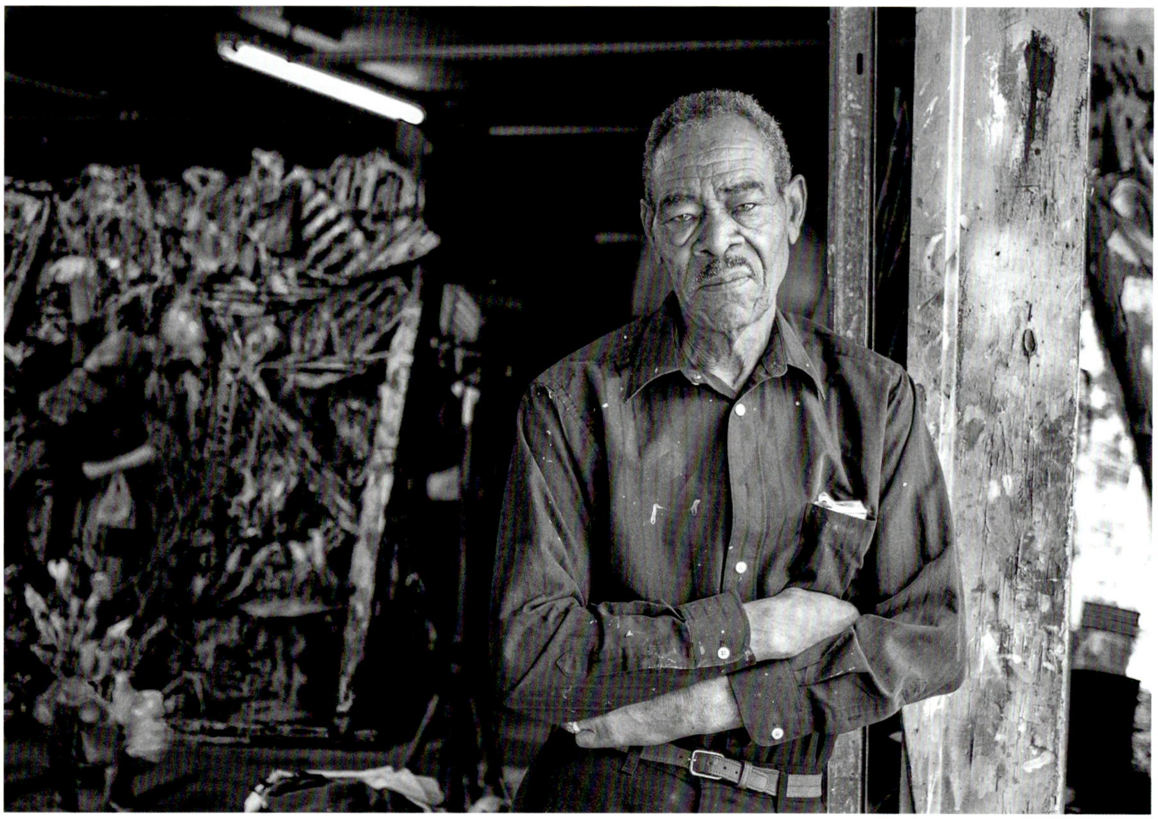

Fig. 53. Thornton Dial Sr., 2007; photograph by Jerry Siegel

Dial was sent to live with relatives in Bessemer, Alabama, when he was about thirteen. He had little formal education, and his community was impoverished and deeply segregated. He grew up knowing little about his rights as an American and had little interaction with white people, other than those for whom he had worked, before he was in his sixties. In the late 1980s, Dial was noticed for making expressive, large-scale sculptures and painted assemblages, densely composed with found materials. A younger artist from the area, Lonnie Holley, introduced Dial to William Arnett, mentioned in the preceding section, who had increasingly turned his attention from African art to African American art from the rural South in the 1970s.

Arnett understood the ways in which Black vernacular practice had survived, often covertly, over the centuries, and recognized and preserved artworks that others dismissed or overlooked. He noted that music and oral stories, which could be shared in private and transmitted from person to person, had a better chance of survival. Given its physicality, art has greater challenges. "Abstraction and disingenuous explanations could safeguard it but could not totally conceal it. To be protected it needed to be placed where it would not likely be seen," he explained. "So the cultural heritage contained within the visual arts survived by being put in the graveyard. As art gradually made its way from the cemeteries to the woods to the backyards and ultimately to the front yards, it became larger and more overt, but maintained its secrecy by seeming to be unstructured, being composed of unattractive materials, and being characterized by a strange aesthetic, at least, strange for its time and place."[67]

For Dial, raised on folktales and oral tradition, allegory was his native language. Like Bill Traylor, he used animals and the natural world as stand-ins for people and challenging environments (**CATS. 92, 93**), and, like Traylor, he was trepidatious about his views being openly known. Speaking about Dial's initial refusal to admit that his works had underlying meaning, curator and gallerist Phillip March Jones has said, "This was, of course, patently false. Indeed, Dial had found yet another way to redirect the attention of too-eager eyes, shielding his thoughts and actions through abstraction and visual misdirection. There would be grave consequences for someone like Dial making bold critiques of the entrenched structures of power."[68] And art historian Paul Arnett concurs, noting that Dial later admitted he had been effecting survival strategies that served him first as a Black boy, and later as a Black man, in the Jim Crow South. "The imperative had always been to shield one's thoughts from outside curiosity," Arnett explains. "And when circumstances required, perform ignorance, or even emptiness of mind."[69]

But as Dial gained confidence, he spoke eloquently about the content of his mind and his art. He had learned to make do, but he had also developed his own visual language, and his art fully embodied a Depression-era way of creating something from nothing. It went beyond recycling;

CAT. 92.
Thornton Dial Sr.
The Movie Star and the Tiger Need One Another
March 1992

CAT. 93.
Thornton Dial Sr.
Tiger Colored Lady
1994

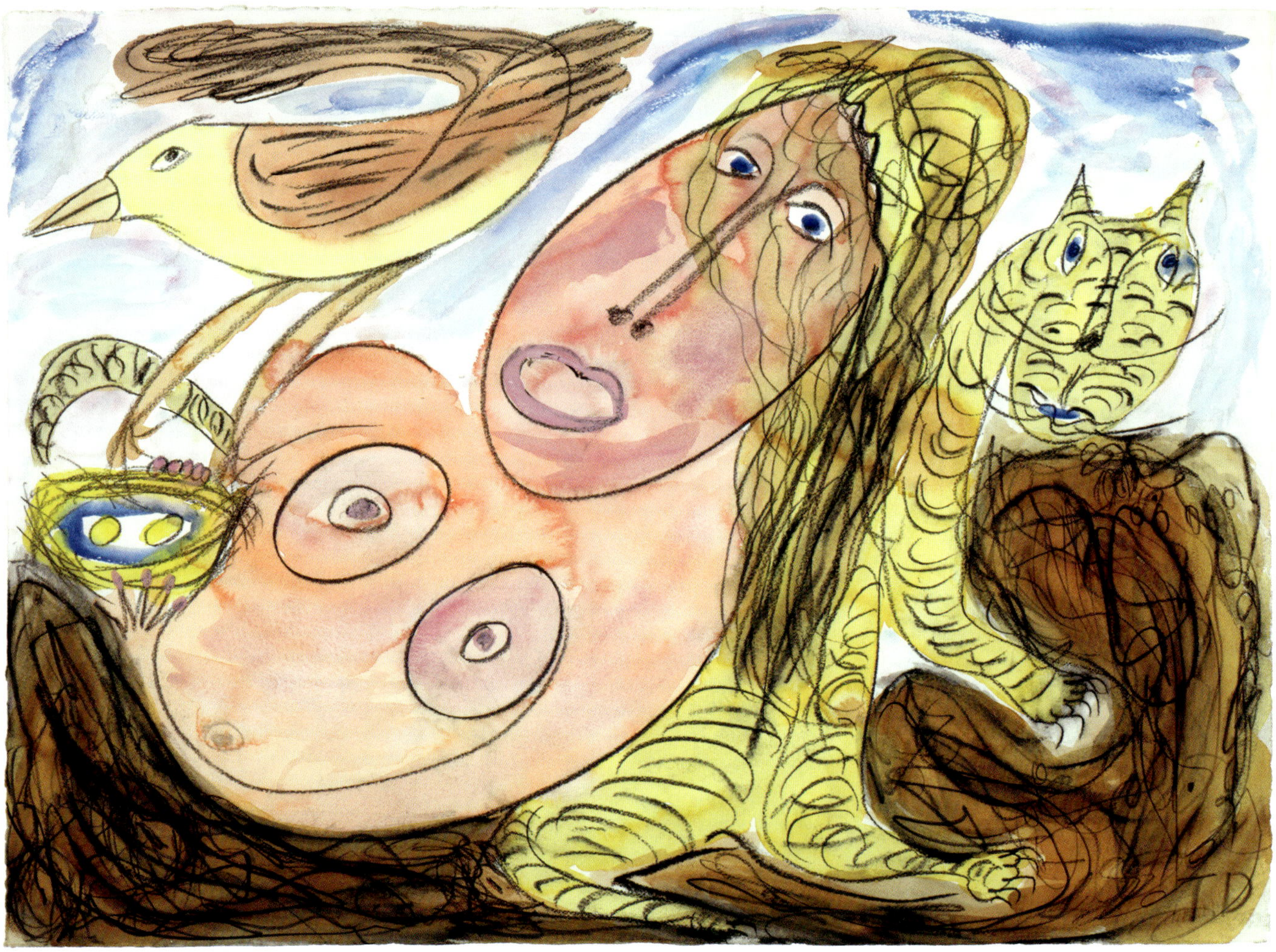

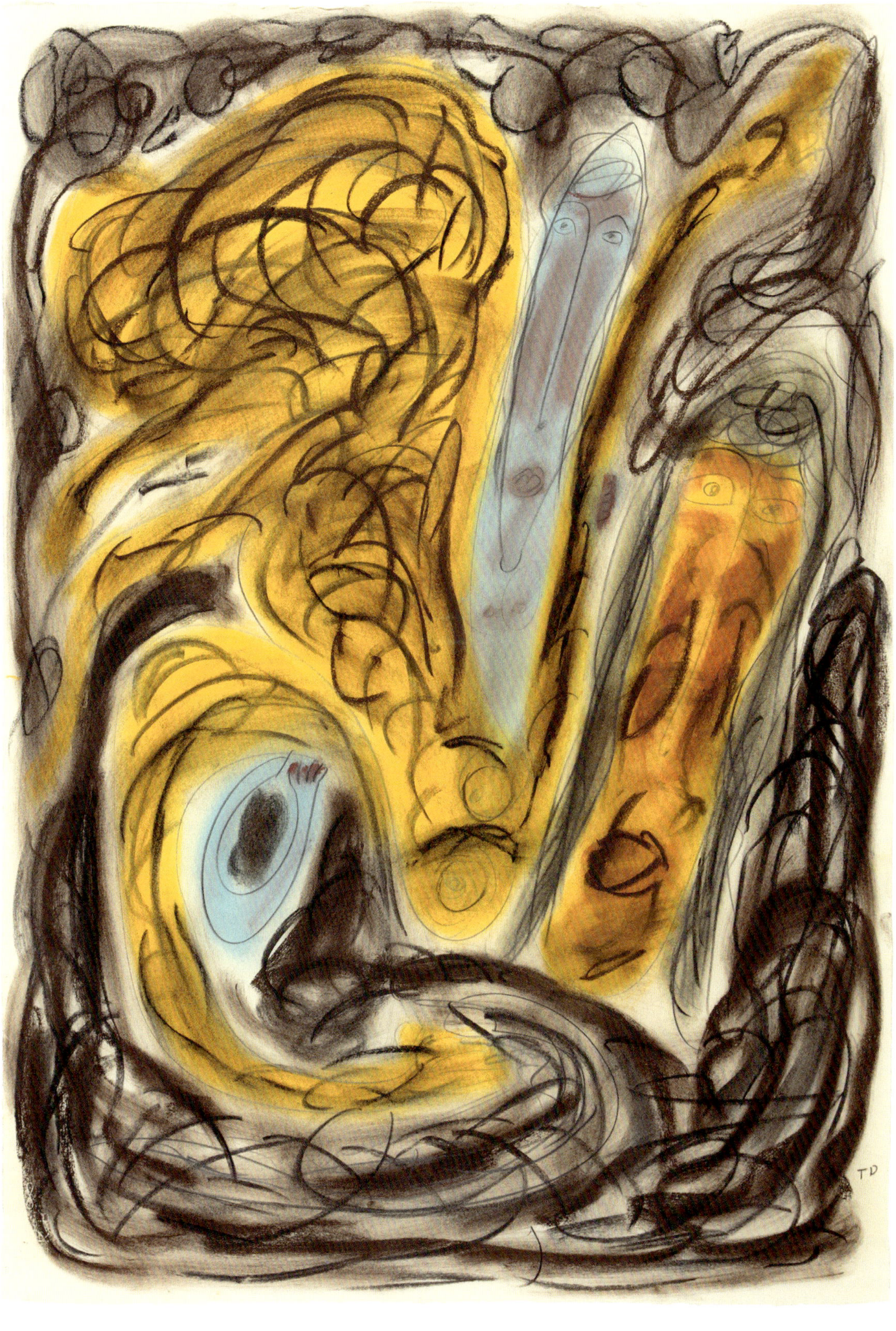
TD

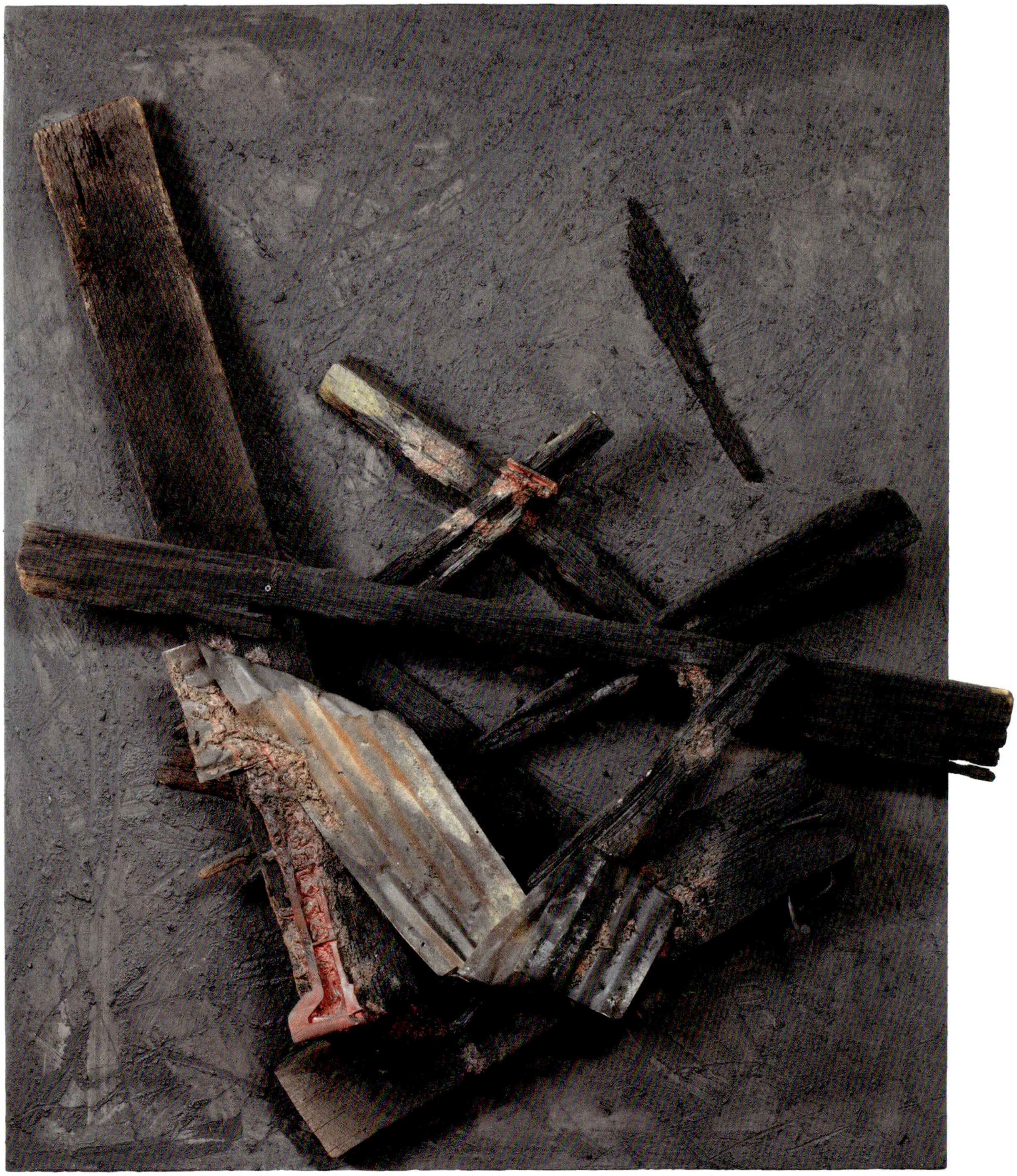

in Dial's hands, the cast-off goods of a community spoke powerfully about poverty and struggle in one of the richest countries on earth. He was a quiet man, raised in a place where his views and voice were not often welcome. But Dial's artworks disgorged a torrent of philosophy and politics—from the global to the personal, as the artist explained:

> *It is exactly the truth that the Negro has been mistreated in the United States. But we got to look at what we have had to use, what we have built, after what he been through. I come through it myself, and I know what life was like at that time, and I can respect myself and the Negro for what we have did. We was captured and brought over here to the United States. That was the Negro family, captured to do work on the farms. We had to work, and we also had to pay attention. We had to learn surviving. We had to learn that everything you want to do, you got to struggle for it.*[70]

By the early 1990s, Dial's art was garnering international acclaim. His first solo exhibition took place in 1993, presented simultaneously in New York at the New Museum of Contemporary Art and the American Folk Art Museum, and a number of museums, the Smithsonian American Art Museum among them, added his work to their collections and celebrated the strength of his vision. But Dial arguably came into his creative florescence in the twenty-first century, when he increasingly produced monumentally scaled, painted assemblages that synthesized force and poetics, that confounded imposed boundaries, and were likened to the major works of Anselm Kiefer and Robert Rauschenberg (**CAT. 94**). Dial was included in the Whitney Biennial in 2000, and in 2005 and 2011 was the focus of two major solo exhibitions.[71] But whenever the spotlight shone on him, Dial advocated for other southern, vernacular artists and the traditions and motives that drove and united them. His large bold works, with incisive titles and themes troubling race and class, captivated the art world with their sophisticated content and an aesthetic that defied stereotypes of "folk." As the art world increasingly embraced him, Dial used his voice to raise serious questions about its long-standing hierarchies and inequities, and became emblematic of a shifting southern landscape in the early twenty-first century, when African Americans transitioned from concealing their creative natures and personal views to asserting their freedom of self-expression.

Dial became a pivotal figure, a mentor to a younger generation of southern Black artists like Lonnie Holley (born 1950), Bessie Harvey, and Purvis Young, who came of age during the civil rights era and saw their artistic roots in elders like William Edmondson and Bill Traylor—but who saw Dial stand among them and succeed in the world of contemporary American art, embodying what was possible. Perhaps even more significantly, Dial bridged the worlds of Black vernacular

CAT. 94.
Thornton Dial Sr.
Recalling the Pain
2011

self-taught artists and the contemporary mainstream. He unhesitatingly conferred his own cachet upon a southern rural aesthetic previously seen as shabby and impoverished, and used his spotlight to advocate for the traditions and motives that drove and united artists across the Black Atlantic South. In so doing, he prompted scholars and institutions everywhere to ask themselves a harder set of questions and confront problematic imbalances in their collections.[72]

CAT. 95.
Judith Scott
Untitled
ca. 1990–2005

JUDITH SCOTT (1943–2005)

Against the odds, **JUDITH SCOTT** became an artist of great renown (Fig. 54), known for fiber and mixed-media sculptures, made with webbed and bound yarn encasing forever-softened objects, muted and stripped of their former identities to serve instead as the heart and bones of compelling organic forms. Scott's sculptures captured attention for their visual power and sense of mystery. Although her works are not autobiographical in a traditional sense, they embody an alternate language sought and found, and their nuanced ways of speaking benefit from the context of her experience. Scott was beset with physical and mental disabilities from birth, but it was arguably the era's severe stigma and inhumane handling of persons with such conditions that had the most profound impact on her early life. In this respect, her challenges have commonalities with those of Henry Darger and Martín Ramírez, but it is the contrast between her formative experiences and a radical change of physical and emotional environments in adulthood that both allowed her creativity to emerge and her output to redefine the measure and transcendence of neurodivergent creativity.

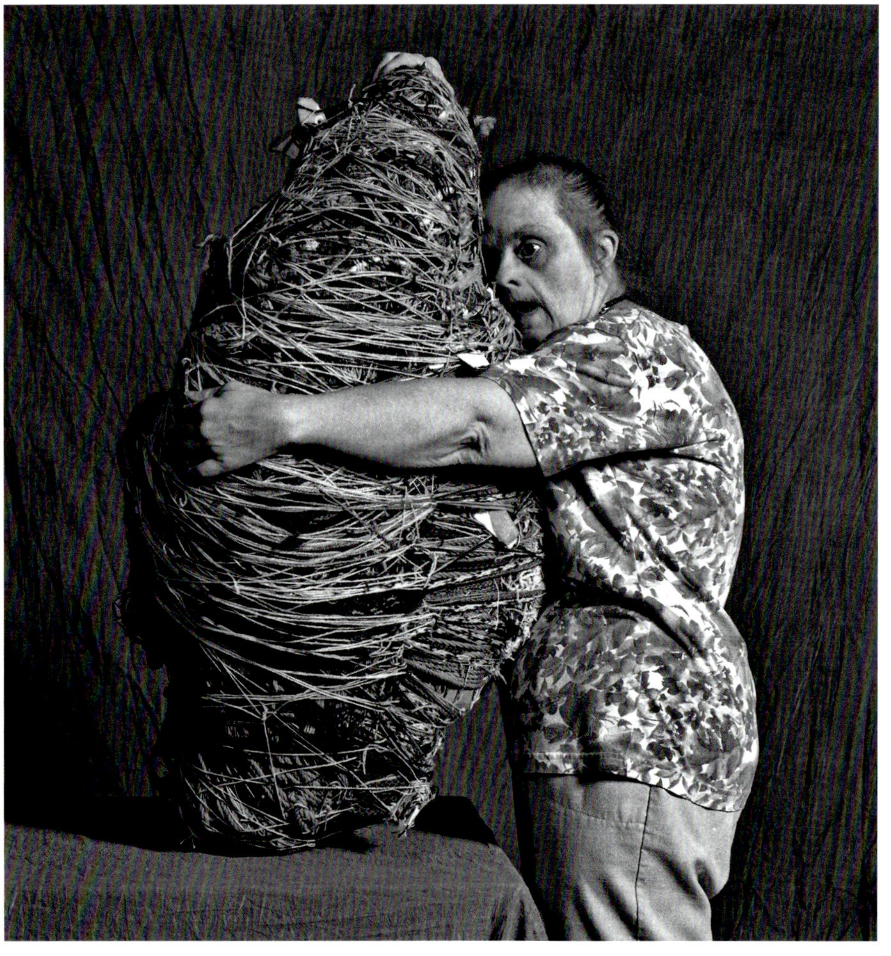

Fig. 54. Judith Scott, 1999; photograph by Leon Borensztein

In 1957 the US Department of Justice established a section devoted to civil rights. The South was resistant to such measures,

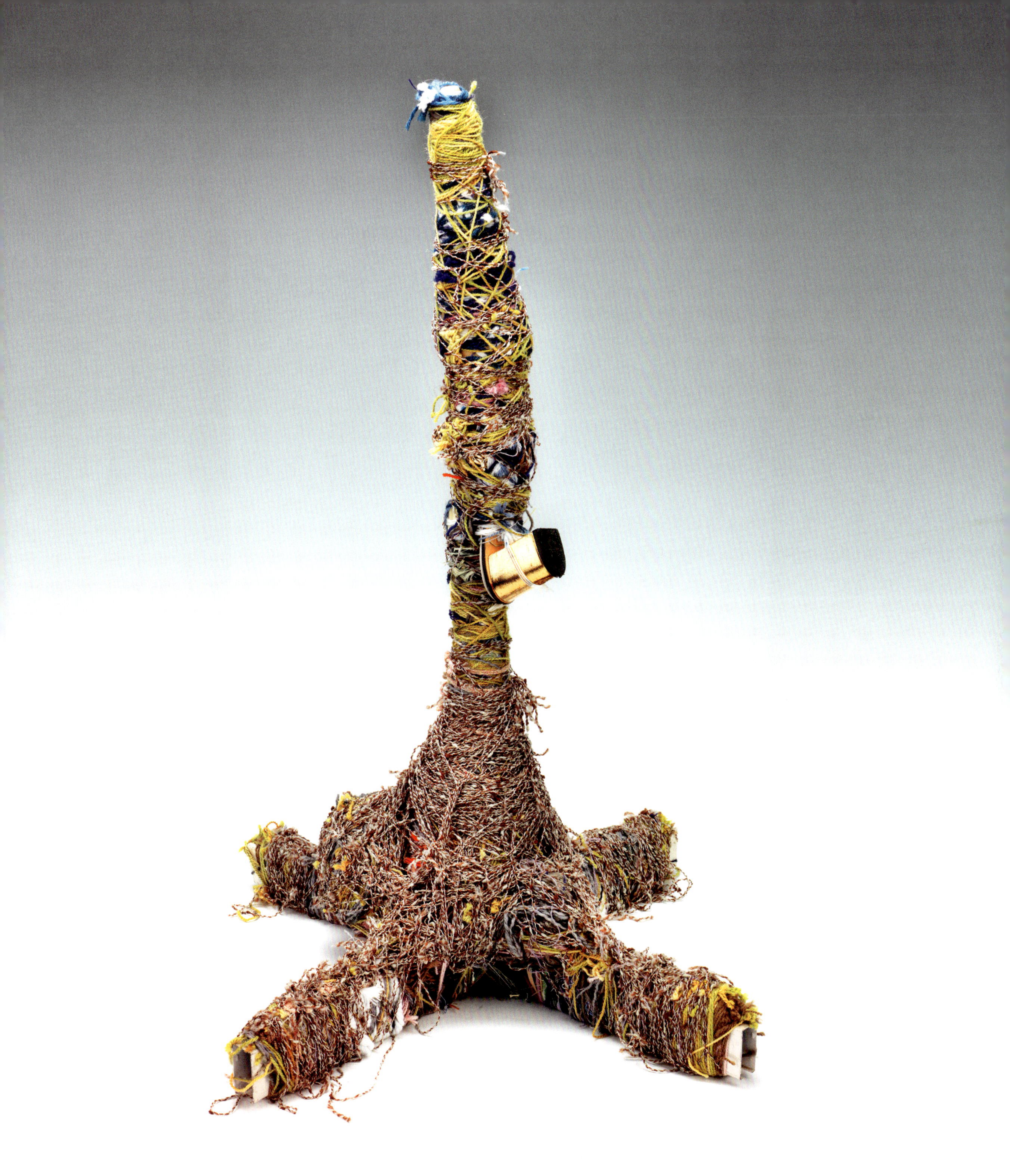

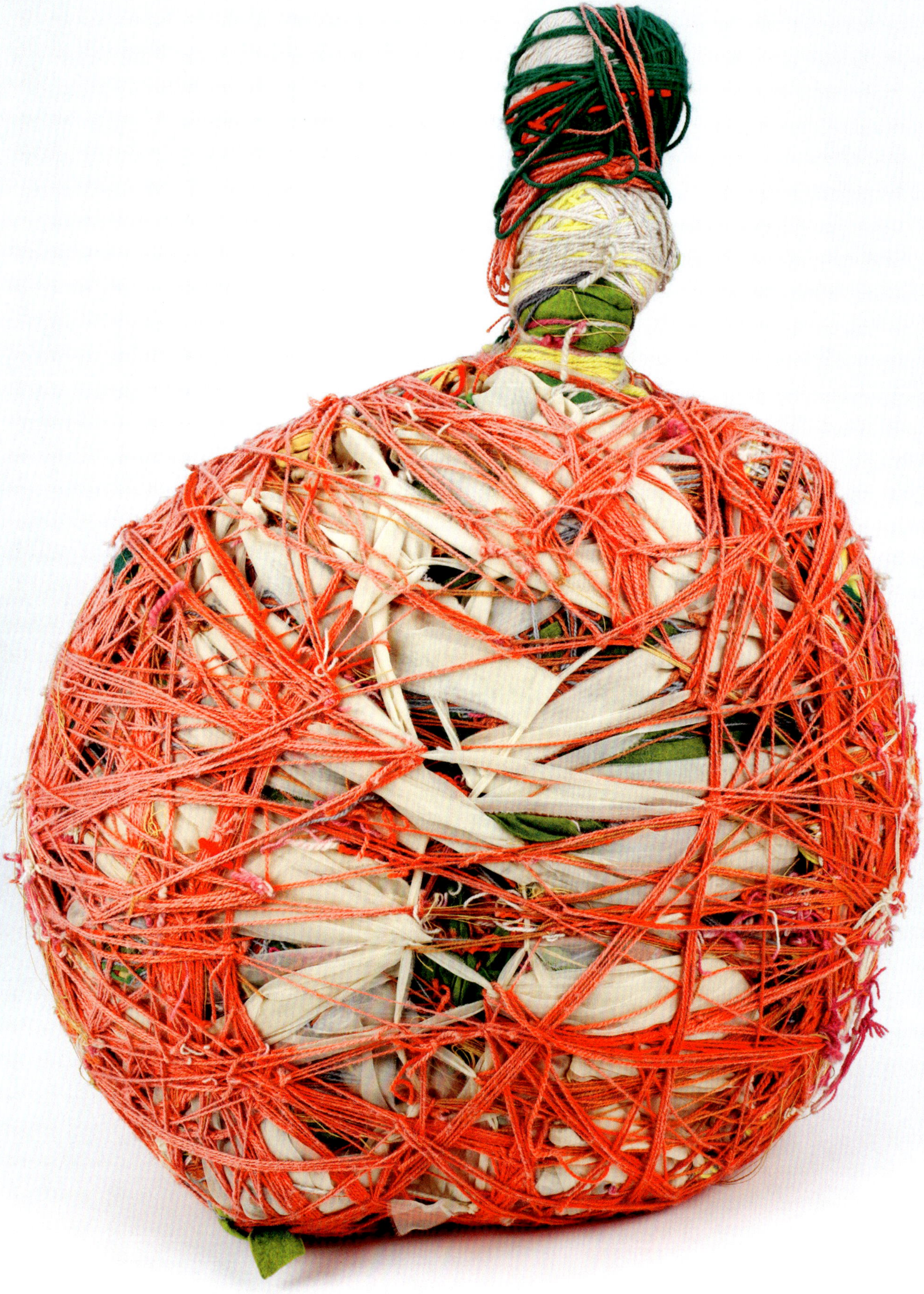

and, in the long stretch between Reconstruction and the midcentury, there had been little progress toward an equitable society. In the summer of 1963, President John F. Kennedy proposed sweeping civil rights legislation, and the following year, after Kennedy was assassinated and Lyndon Johnson became president, Congress passed the Civil Rights Act. The act ended segregation in public places and banned discrimination on the basis of race, sex, religion, and national origin. These were major milestones, but they ignored the plight of Americans with disabilities. At age seven, Scott was abruptly parted from her family and sent to an Ohio institution at the recommendation of doctors and clergy. Scott had Down syndrome, a chromosomal abnormality that would not be medically understood for another nine years.[73] The trauma of moving from the rural outskirts of Cincinnati into a bleak clinic filled with the sounds, sights, and smells of despair is itself unimaginable, but the separation from her parents, three brothers, and twin sister make the enormity profound. Because Scott did not speak conventionally, the hearing loss she had suffered following a bout of scarlet fever in infancy would go unnoticed for some time during her institutionalization, exacerbating her mental isolation. She remained in the asylum for the next thirty-six years.

Reflecting on Scott's release, into her twin sister Joyce Scott's custody at age forty-three, clinical psychologist Amelia Rachel Hokule'a Borofsky notes, "Across the United States in the 1970s and '80s, institutions like Judy's shut down. Their Hitchcock-esque legacy, the arrival of psychotropic medications, the financial burden of their maintenance, and a new, enlightened philosophy of integration encouraged the shift." Joyce Scott and her two daughters lived in Berkeley, California, when they brought Judith to live with them. Judith Scott's story becomes thereafter entwined not only with that of her twin, but with the Creative Growth Art Center.[74]

In the postwar era, people with developmental disabilities were being deinstitutionalized across the United States. In California, this dovetailed with a progressive view on civil rights that was more encompassing than legal mandates. In 1974, Florence Ludins-Katz, an artist and educator, and her husband Elias Katz, a clinical psychologist, founded a nonprofit space where artistic activity could help people with developmental, mental, or physical disabilities adjust and flourish. The Creative Growth Art Center opened in their Oakland garage, and broke new ground with its mission and vision. Joyce enrolled Judith in the studio art program in 1987.[75] Joyce recalls, "'When Judy first arrived at Creative Growth, they couldn't get her to do much of anything.' Judy did not like painting, sewing or sculpture class. Then she found her medium in a fiber arts class taught by textile artist Sylvia Seventy. She started wrapping. Yarn disappeared. Magazines disappeared. Even chairs and bike wheels disappeared. All of it would emerge later in colorfully woven sculptures. She even created pieces that looked like twins reaching towards one another."[76]

CAT. 96.
Judith Scott
Untitled
(Medicine Bottle)
1996

Scott began her fiber practice in 1988 and remained dedicated to it until her death in 2005. Her earliest works were bundles of sticks wrapped with fabric and knotted and interwoven strands of yarn, with subsequent pieces becoming more considered in coloration and strategy, growing into what curator Matthew Higgs has called "a coherent and recognizable sculptural methodology."[77] Her work became ever larger—more approximate to the scale of the human body—and her manner of weaving evolved into a signature style (**CAT. 95**; see also **CAT. 11**, p. 32). "In these and subsequent works, she invariably started out with the selection of a found object, an item that she typically scavenged, or occasionally appropriated from an unsuspecting source in the Creative Growth studio," Higgs has explained. "The significance of the objects she chose, which were generally commonplace and of no discernible value, remains unknown, yet they clearly meant something to Scott, functioning both as an armature and as a catalyst for her subsequent creative interventions."[78] Scott had a clear understanding of being finished with a given piece, indicating to Creative Growth staff when she was ready for them to take one away and let her begin on the next.

Florence Ludins-Katz and Elias Katz were prescient in their shared belief that the work of differently abled artists should be seen in tandem with that of other kinds of artists, then a radical view which they articulated in a 1990 book about their efforts.[79] Scott's work first appeared in an exhibition at Creative Growth, organized by Seventy, that showed established fiber artists alongside the work of Creative Growth artists. "Discussing someone's diagnosis in relationship to their art is a delicate balance. You shouldn't like it just because it is made by someone with Cerebral Palsy or Down's Syndrome. You should love it and then find out who the artist is and their story," Tom di Maria has explained. Di Maria, who was Creative Growth's executive director from 2000 to 2018, has pointed out that artists, not psychologists, guide the program, and that collectively they eschew qualifying terms to distinguish one type of artist from another; most of the artists' biographies do not mention disabilities. "I don't call such artists 'outsider,'" he explains. "As people with disabilities, they have already been pushed to the margins of society, and there is nothing positive about reinforcing that idea. So, I prefer 'contemporary artists'; they exhibit a unique voice and vision not always seen by other makers. This is what makes the work particularly interesting."[80]

Scott's work was shown in incrementally larger and more significant settings, first in the Bay Area, then nationally, and internationally. Today, her work is in museum collections around the world.[81] A 2014 exhibition at the Brooklyn Museum situated Scott in a feminist context, and in 2017 her work was included at the Venice Biennale. Catherine Morris, who cocurated the exhibition at the Brooklyn Museum with Matthew Higgs, ruminated on the "long,

CAT. 97.
Judith Scott
Untitled (JS 39)
1997

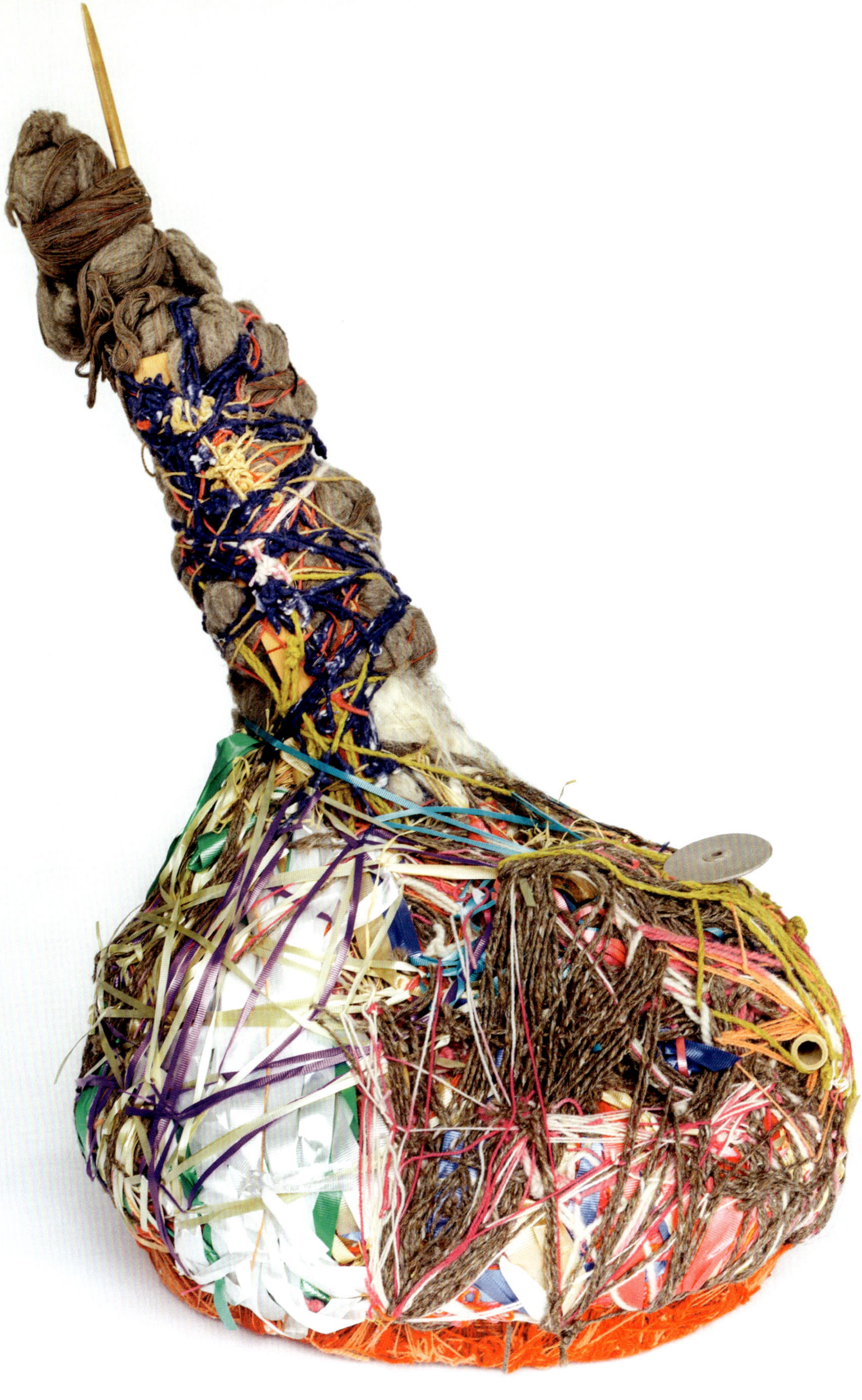

unresolved, and losing struggle to categorize and quantify art by people with disabilities into its own school, movement, or practice, which extracted these artists from the general context of the cultures we all live within."[82] Importantly, Morris acknowledges the delicate and tricky issues that plague curators endeavoring to share the work of an artist who did not, or was not able to, speak about the art they made, indicate preferences for particular works or their installation details, or even convey how to orient a given artwork (**CATS. 96, 97**). "Why all this hand-wringing in order to implement these fairly anodyne display structures?" she asks. "Because one of the biggest challenges to presenting the work of an artist whose voice was sharply circumscribed by her life experience is to avoid adding layers of interpretation that can calcify into a narrow fable."[83]

The era encompassing Scott's life and practice overlaps with a national movement toward better care—medically, physically, emotionally—for people of different physical and mental abilities. Although President Kennedy had not included the disabled in the Civil Rights Act, he had established the Community Mental Health Act, which would lead to models of community support with smaller, more personal facilities over large institutions. Advances in pharmaceutical treatments and new approaches in psychotherapy made life more manageable and enjoyable for many. Less widely known than the civil rights movement, the disability rights movement was similarly hard-won over time, by a number of concerned parties. The movement fought presumptions that issues of unemployment and lack of education were inherent results of disability, and showed they were, instead, directly related to societal barriers and prejudices. These arguments effectively repositioned a wide array of people with disabilities as collectively having class status, which warranted protections from discrimination by the government. The Americans with Disabilities Act was passed into law in 1990 under President George H. W. Bush.[84]

In positioning Scott's work within a feminist discourse, Morris reminds us of the feminist adage "the personal is political": the notion that one's personal experience is connected to one's location within the larger power structures of society.[85] This is not only applicable, of course, to women or the disabled, but in Scott's case provides a particularly sobering framework for the decades of institutionalization and psychic alienation she endured.[86] The most lasting legacy of Scott's body of work, some two hundred pieces, is arguably the way in which it evidences art as an alternate language, an extralinguistic way of conveying emotion and self-situation. In this respect, Scott paved a path for other neurodivergent artists to be similarly framed and appreciated. Her success, hand in glove with the transformative model embodied in Creative Growth, has shifted the paradigm for artists of different abilities the world over.[87]

/ / /

There was no single moment when the scales tipped in favor of including nonmainstream artists in an art hierarchy that was inherently disinclined to accept them. But in specific ways, each of these six "gamechanger" artists revealed an art-world blind spot. They were not the only ones who had an impact, of course. Nellie Mae Rowe can rightly be called a gamechanger for the ways in which her radical determination to use pride and joy as weapons of defense helped her win the legacy long game, and allowed her to transition from this world to the next having experienced a better moment for Black women than the one she was born into. Anna Mary Robertson "Grandma" Moses also turned the art establishment on its ear and is historically significant as a gamechanger as well. Moses, who is not encompassed in the Robson Family Collection but will be explored in depth in a major 2025 exhibition at SAAM, locked horns with the art world in many ways. She not only contested the midcentury's gold standard of artistic identity—a diminutive, rural granny type in contrast to the macho white men of the New York avant-garde—but by doggedly narrating the stories of her life in pictures, rejected both modern abstraction and those who critiqued her choices. Artists like Jon Serl, who has yet to be the focus of a comprehensive study or retrospective, challenged conventions of lifestyle, gender identity, even anthropocentrism—posing trenchant questions about individualism, and what it meant to be an "American" in the late twentieth century. Lonnie Holley, another artist beyond the scope of this project but central to the SAAM collection and to the history of self-taught American artists, took a page from the book of the Black vernacular and transfigured a childhood of abuse and neglect into an international multimedia artistic practice that continues to defy all categories.

For art lovers, the powerfully moving stories, emotional candor, and the depth of experience poured into and radiating outward from the works of artists who were simultaneously excluded and liberated from the art-world mainstream increasingly felt revelatory. By comparison, fairly or not, the work of mainstream artists often felt contrived or homogenized—the backfire of professionalism. Self-taught artists bucked the rules and overturned assumptions: from studio practice to survival tool, from parlor pictures to asemic texts, from philosophy, training, and theory to animal instinct, guttural response, and megaphone.[88] Jokes and headlines fully exhausted the juxtaposition of outside/inside, but, in a global-media society, they also relentlessly pressed questions about power structures and overly narrow definitions of "diversity," rejected all the same old answers, and demanded that the art world keep pace with a changing society.

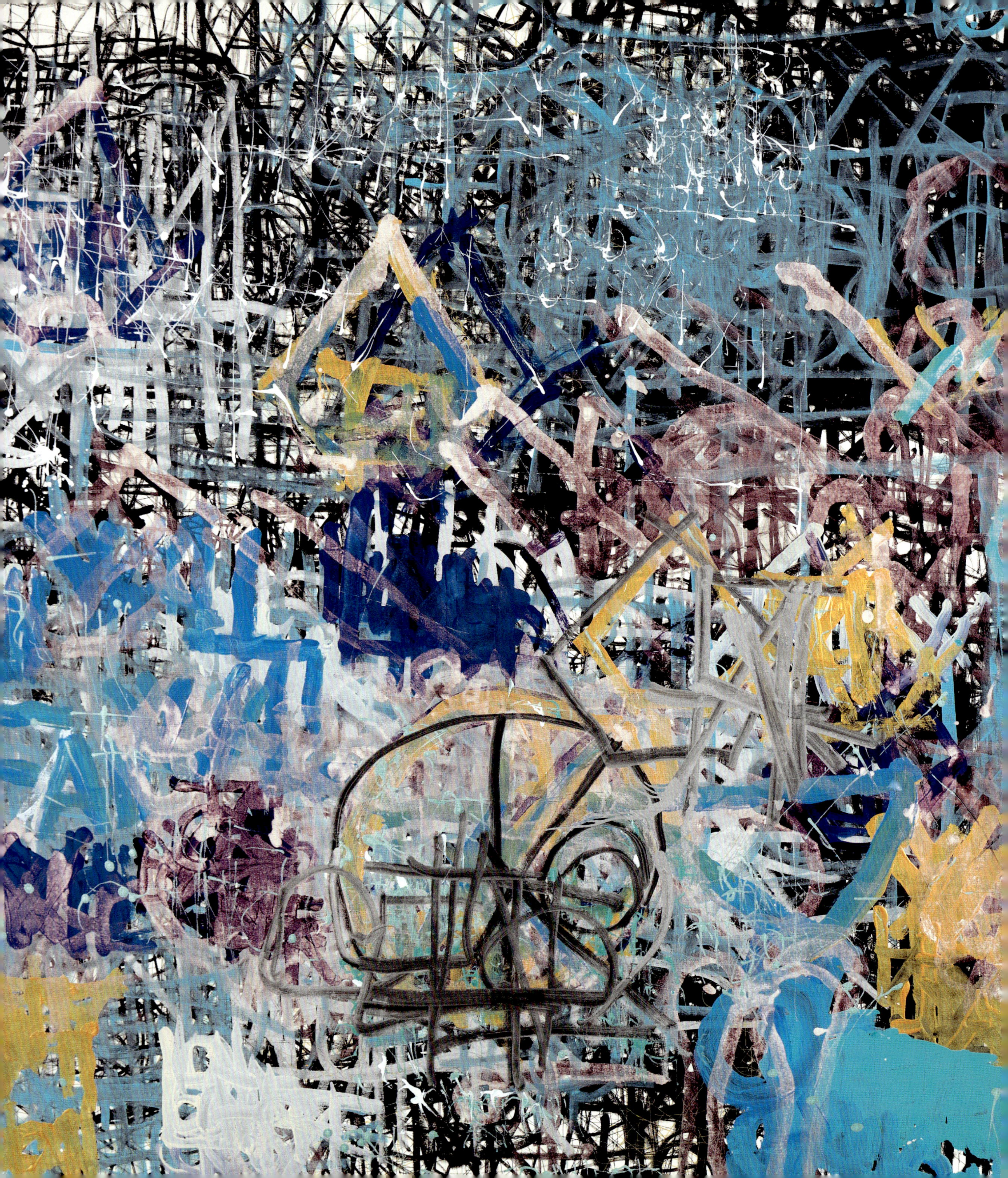

A BREAKING WAVE

"The Encyclopedic Palace" was the theme of the 2013 Venice Biennale. Its curator, Massimiliano Gioni, made interrogating the tenets and boundaries of the mainstream art canon a subtheme—less overt but not less important. The Encyclopedic Palace concept was borrowed from an Italian American self-taught artist, Marino Auriti (1891–1980), who in 1955 filed a patent for a museum that could house—on the National Mall of Washington, DC—all the world's greatest discoveries. Auriti's grand plan never came to fruition, but Gioni fixed upon the metaphorical power contained within that idea, noting that "personal cosmologies, with their delusions of omniscience, shed light on the constant challenge of reconciling the self with the universe, the subjective with the collective, the specific with the general, and the individual with the culture of her time."[1] And indeed, the urgent and abiding need to reconcile oneself with or within an expansive universe is a thread that runs throughout the art and artists that Margaret Z. Robson supported and collected in her lifetime, and that her son Doug continues to support and collect today.

Gioni's Biennale was not the first exhibition or venue to situate the work of self-taught artists alongside that of mainstream contemporary artists, or to interrogate the arbitrary and malleable boundaries of the art world.[2] It did, however, signal that a wave had perhaps finally broken, that the tide had shifted in an irrevocable, permanent way. Gioni's project moved beyond isolated instances of inclusion with a wide array of makers, and, importantly, it sidestepped hierarchical tropes, most notably the mainstream artist flowering amid a *Wunderkammer* of inspirational, untutored muses. He presented alternative worlds through the eyes of

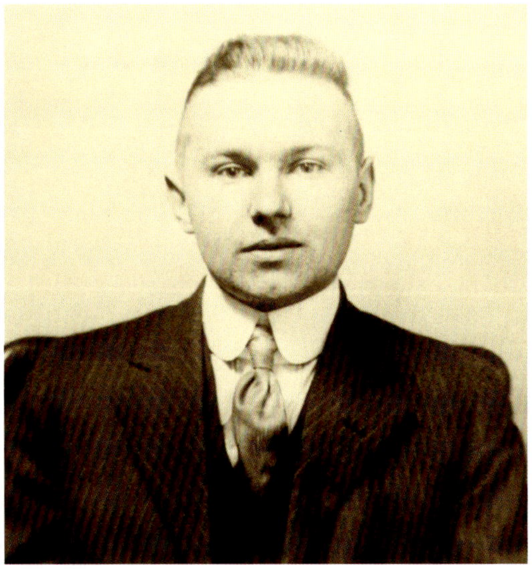

Fig. 55. Achilles G. Rizzoli, 1918. Collection of the estate of the artist

James Castle and California artist **ACHILLES G. RIZZOLI** (1896–1981; Fig. 55), whose symbolic portraits of people (his mother foremost among them) took the astonishing form of intricately conceived architectural elevations and floor plans (**CATS. 98, 99**). There were ecstatic gift drawings from Shaker communities, the cosmographies of Chinese artist Guo Fengyi, and botanical dreamscapes by Czech artist Anna Zemánková. Critic Sarah Boxer, in a somewhat mockingly toned review, said that outsider artists had been "invited into the Star-On Machine" in Venice, suggesting they were momentarily in fashion à la Dr. Seuss and his Star-Bellied Sneetches.[3] But this simplistic take missed a deeper, more abiding reality: that even at the sometimes glacial pace of the art world, change comes.

BE THE CHANGE

Both collectively and individually, each maker's experience and body of work shifts the narrative, a little or a lot, over time. In the years she spent making art at Creative Growth, Judith Scott effected seismic change. Whatever her practice meant to her, the ripple effect it ultimately had on larger art-world spheres cannot be underestimated. The challenges for self-taught and communally taught artists in America have been great, but for women of color and people of disability the added layers are unique, and their advances have been exceedingly slow. Scott's clear and consistent vision manifested a number of truths, most significantly that art is a personal language and tool for anchoring oneself in a world that offers no secure footholds, and that such personal worldviews must matter to us all. In 2017, Scott, who had died in 2005, and her junior colleague at Creative Growth, Dan Miller, had artworks included in the Venice Biennale. Its organizer, curator Christine Macel, explained that her project was grounded in humanism: "Today, in a world full of conflicts and shocks, art bears witness to the most precious part of what makes us human. Art is the ultimate ground for reflection, individual expression, freedom, and for fundamental questions.... Art is the last bastion, a garden to cultivate above and beyond trends and personal interests."[4] Macel's remarks have felt even more relevant throughout 2021 and 2022, in the wake of profound global trauma. Although the dual pandemics of COVID-19

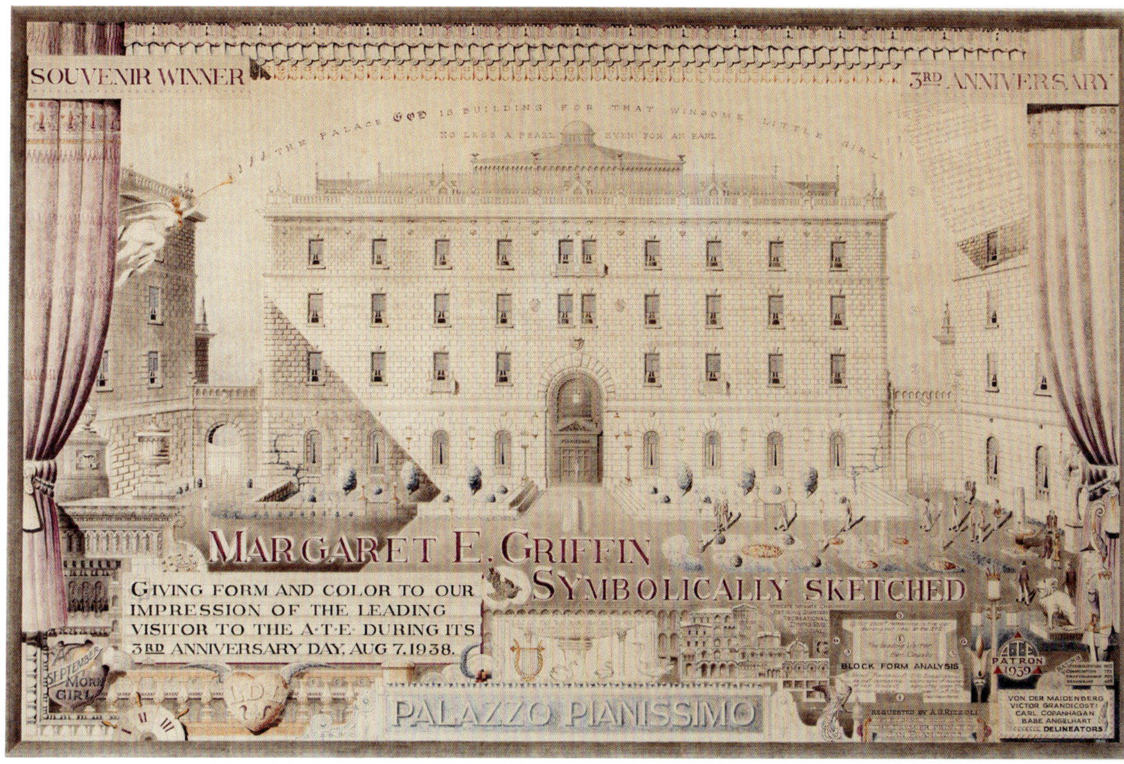

CAT. 98.
Achilles G. Rizzoli
Margaret E. Griffin Symbolically Sketched / Palazzo Pianissimo
1939

and racism remain far from resolved, optimism is finding toeholds as vaccinations and social responsibility help on one frontier, and as community activism and increased self-reflection among police departments, the US Department of Justice, and the cultural sector respond to the urgency of meaningful diversity.

In a moment when humanism feels paramount, and trends and personal interests assume diminished importance, the stories that describe and contain our collective existence and experience are more meaningful than ever. It is worth reiterating Ruchi Mital's insights: "We are made of stories. It's the story that matters, the story that reveals," and appreciating how her views dovetail with Macel's frameworks for art as a garden to endlessly cultivate, an organic testimonial to experiences that make us human.[5] Underscoring the power of this framework still further, Māori artist George Tamihana Nuku spoke of stories on similarly important terms in 2021. "We carry our stories with us everywhere we go.... And that's probably the last landscape left to Indigenous peoples. It's that landscape between their ears; that's probably the last territory that belongs to them that can't be taken from them, is their stories.... Let's own the good and the bad parts of the stories... so that we're no longer victims of change but agents of change."[6]

CAT. 99.

Achilles G. Rizzoli

Marina Row Houses,

Office of O. A. Deichmann

1932

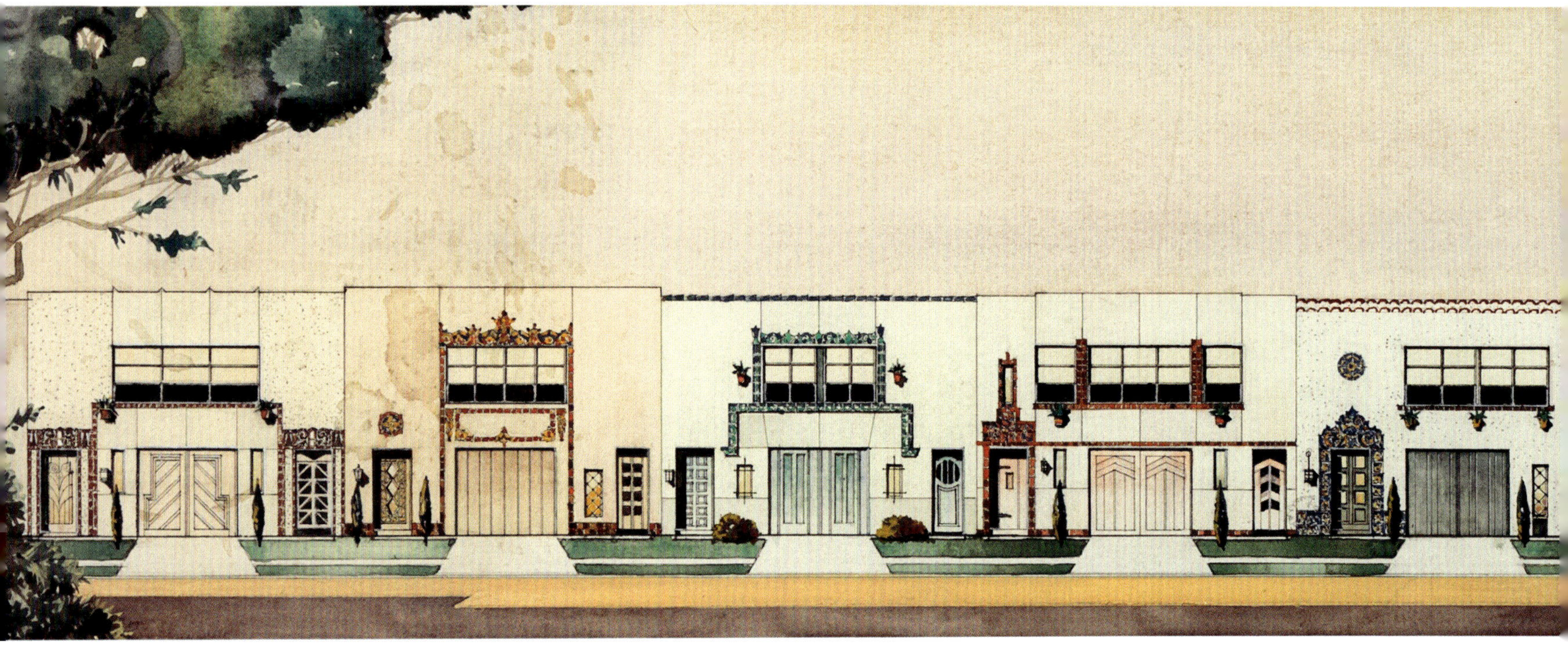

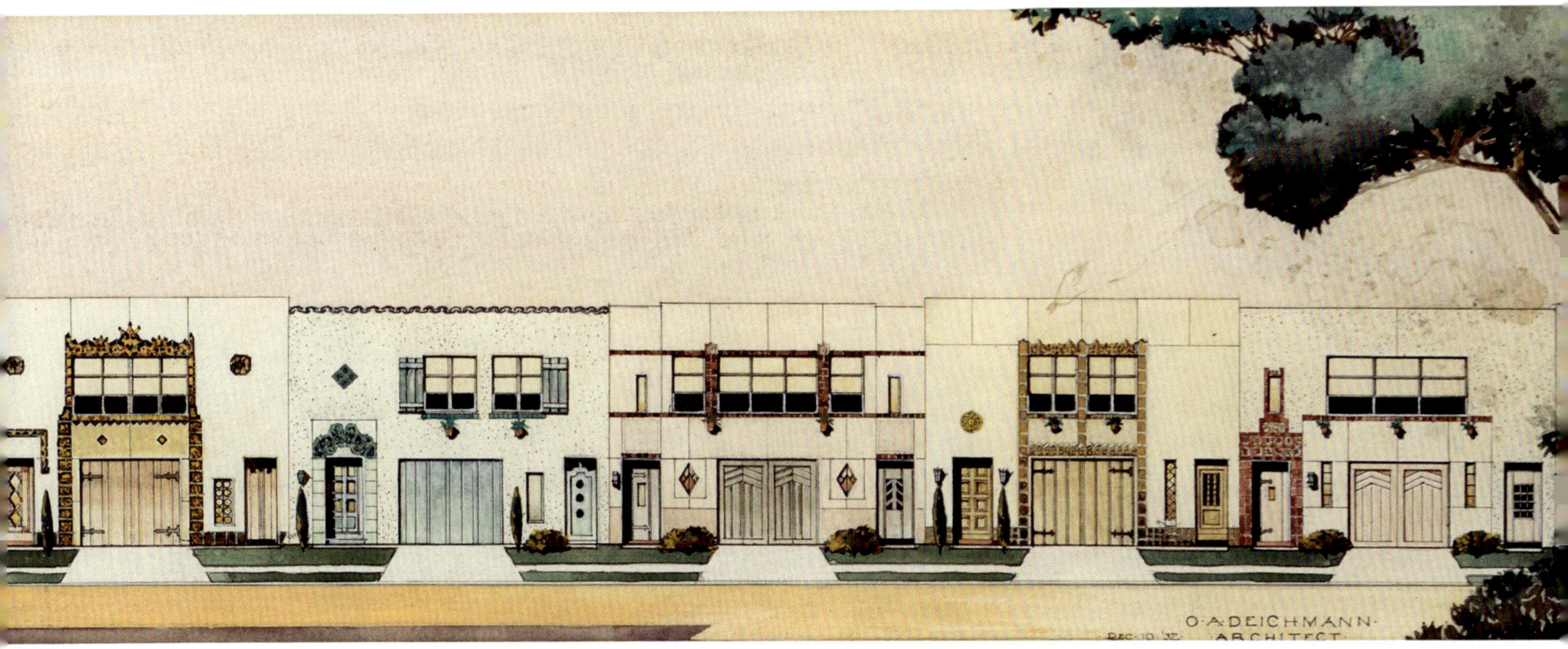
O·A·DEICHMANN·
DEC·10·'32·
·ARCHITECT·

Perhaps ironically, it is the stories of self-taught artists that have both drawn people to them and provoked disdain within the art world. In the 1980s and 1990s especially, museums and galleries implemented biographies of difference as an exoticizing tool for marketing. The practice remains common today, with marginalizing headlines and labels preceding the artists and their work. But equally damaging are curatorial overcorrections, which divorce art from the meaningful experiences that informed and drove it. Just as identity and experience can be the weapons of the gatekeepers, so too can they be the tools of change.

As noted in this essay's first section, over half of the forty-three artists in this exhibition were born in the nineteenth century and close to half of them were African American. Roughly a third of them lived with a cognitive difference that put them at some degree of remove from mainstream society. The relatively few women represented (seven) evidence how male preferencing manifests in an imbalanced history—what was not appreciated did not survive to stake a claim. In some cases, objects survived but the makers' identities did not. Some of the artists lived to witness the appreciation of their work and earn a living from it; too many died before seeing how their work chipped away at the central tenets of the Western art canon. All of the individuals represented in the Robson Family Collection faced challenges in being recognized as artists, raised important questions about hierarchy and control, and embodied the countless ways in which individuality resists classification. Whether they did so with intention, or the results their art achieved were incidental to personal aims, these artists collectively became the change that defines American art today. Although some of their stories are less well documented and researched, the following artists are no less important than those in the preceding sections.

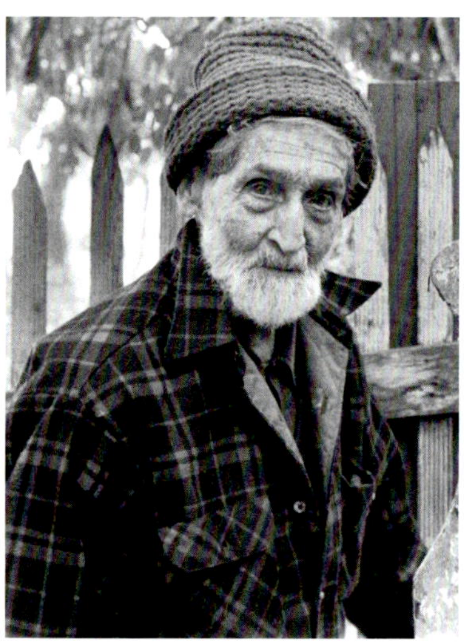

Fig. 56. Jon Serl; photograph by William Jamison

MORE TO THE STORY

The story of California painter **JON SERL** (1894–1993) illustrates how rich and substantial bodies of work have led to moderately scaled books and exhibitions and widespread museum representation, but how legacies were ultimately left adrift in a sea of identity politics—too eccentric to be an insider, too savvy to be an outsider (Fig. 56). Serl's theatrically colorful imagery recalls a "traveling carny-cum-vaudeville" upbringing, ruminations on gender binaries, personal sexuality, mutable identity, and a life circuitously mapping the hardships of underclass marginalization.[7] Serl drew art-world attention in the 1980s when the "outsider" paradigm, for many, had as

CAT. 100.
Jon Serl
Texas Scene
1975

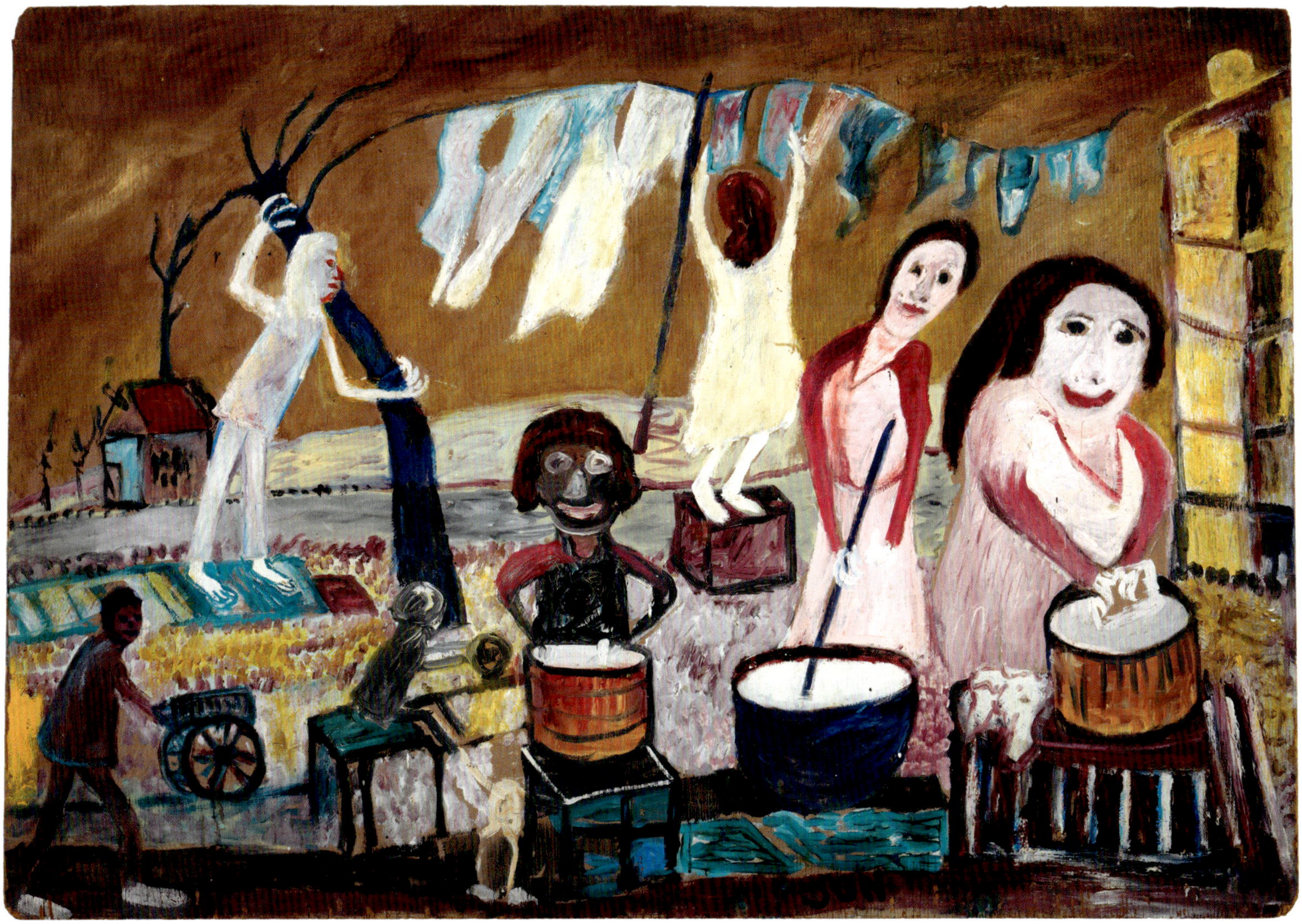

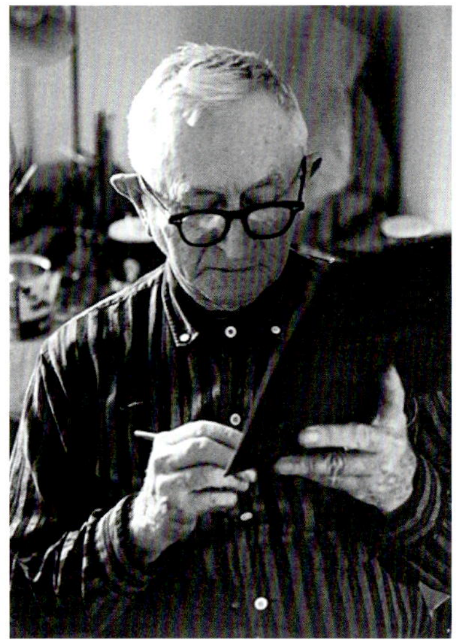

Fig. 57. Justin McCarthy; photograph by Leonard J. Ross

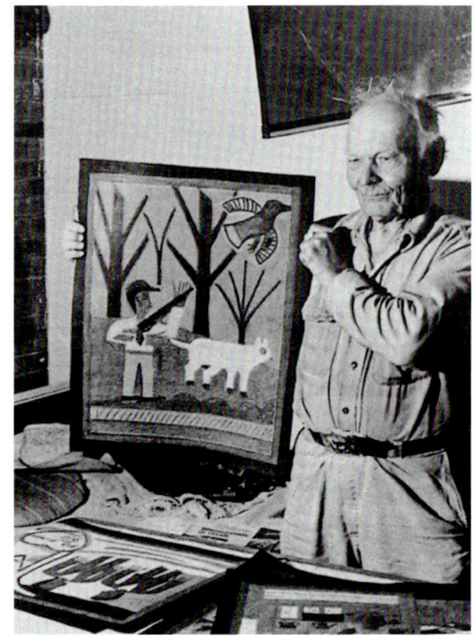

Fig. 58. Eddie Arning; photographer unknown

much to do with eccentric characters as it did the art. But Serl's paintings are sophisticated, with compelling spatial organization and deep, sensuous coloration that evoke ever-present tensions between the pleasures of life and existential alienation (**CAT. 100**). Serl became popular enough to appear on Johnny Carson's *Tonight Show* twice, arguably more for being a nonagenarian "folk artist" and colorful character than in recognition of his art. His "white trash past," as Serl himself called it, was both subtext in his imagery and imprint on the role he was allowed to occupy in a stratified art world.[8] Of Serl's paintings, Randall Morris has said, "They are great enough ultimately that it no longer matters how we define them, or the man who made them. Like Joseph Cornell or Forrest Bess and others of that ilk, they are the sounds of trees falling, whether we hear them or not."[9]

JUSTIN MCCARTHY (ca. 1891–1977) and **EDDIE ARNING** (1898–1993) (Figs. 57, 58) both made large and richly sourced bodies of work inspired by magazine pictures and popular culture, and suffered from mental health problems in the early part of the twentieth century (**CATS. 101–4**; see **CAT. 1**, p. 24). Like Martín Ramírez and Judith Scott, they likely would have lived altogether different lives if not for an era that socially stigmatized them for needs that were ill-addressed and misunderstood by the medical world.[10] In other instances, fewer extant works and scant facts leave only a partial picture. **PETER "CHARLIE" ATTIE BESHARO** (1899–1960) made paintings about space travel, alien and supernatural life forms, and futuristic intergalactic battles (Fig. 59, **CAT. 105**). Besharo immigrated to the United States in 1912 when he was a teenager, departing the Mount Lebanon area of Syria, possibly to escape military conscription under the Ottoman Empire. In the United States, he led a solitary life and faced social challenges that often accompany the immigrant experience. Besharo was a devout Catholic, but being an ethnic Arab in his predominantly white adopted hometown of Leechburg, Pennsylvania, created an inherent strain between his desire to assimilate and to also retain his Syrian identity. He often went only by "Peter Charlie," and few knew his given surname. Besharo worked as a housepainter, and while some knew that he painted pictures on occasion, no one realized that his identity was fully enmeshed in a creative practice; his body of work came to light only after his death.[11] Individually, the subjects of Besharo's paintings are hard to interpret, with themes spanning space travel, immigrant struggle and American

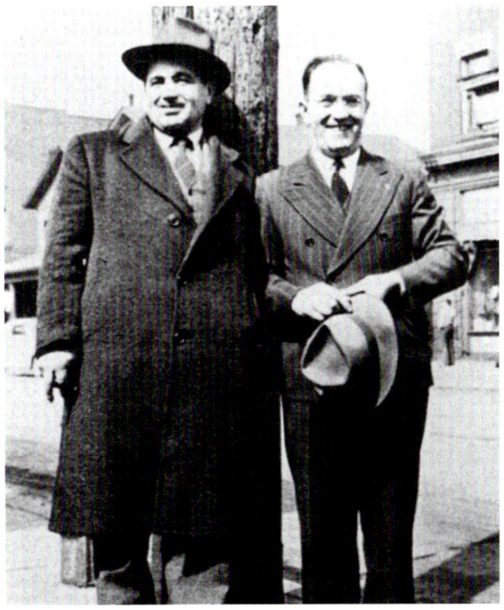

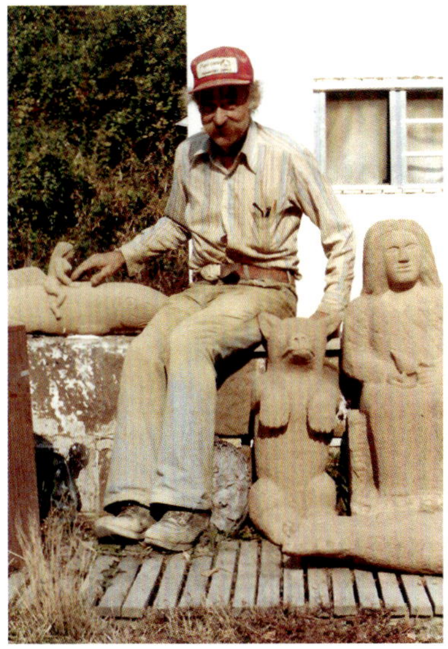

Fig. 59. Peter Attie Besharo and friend Joe Zana on the corner across from Penn Lee Hotel, Leechburg, Pennsylvania, late 1930s

Fig. 60. Ernest "Popeye" Reed, ca. 1980; photograph by Michael Noland

patriotism, Christianity and Eastern mysticism, and concerns from atomic weaponry to ghosts, demons, and the afterlife. Collectively, however, they convey the trauma of leaving one's homeland, and ongoing struggles of alienation and non-belonging in United States.

Ohio carvers **STEPHAN POLAHA** (1891–1977) and **ERNEST "POPEYE" REED** (1919–1985; Fig. 60) were both only regionally and locally known during their lifetimes. Polaha was born in Cleveland, Ohio, and later moved to Reading, Pennsylvania. He loved dogs and made carvings of them with sweet comical faces or the wings of angels (**CAT. 106**). Reed grew up in the Appalachian hill country of southeastern Ohio, earning the nickname "Popeye" for the strong arms he built carving wood and stone. His father was a second-generation Irish immigrant, his mother a member of the Miami tribe. Reed had a natural flair for carving and found he could earn a modest living selling his works at flea markets during the Depression. He carved native hardwoods like walnut, and stone including flint, limestone, and sandstone. Reed made thousands of pieces over some five decades, from tobacco pipes to large figural works drawing on themes from myth, the Bible, literature, and lore (**CATS. 107, 108**). His distinctive style earned him a loyal local and regional following, but wider recognition of Reed's carvings did not come during his lifetime.

Margaret Robson collected artworks that drew her attention, regardless of whether the maker's identity had been lost to time or grown to iconic status. From memory jugs that held and unified the mementos of a life to elegant decoys or weathervanes, the works that attracted her notably inspired empathy, inviting one to see the world through the eyes of another—if only for a moment. One such figure was **EDWIN LAWSON** (1911–1980), an artist about whom little is known, and whose work invites questions about the afterlife of artworks and the stories that live within them after the artist is gone. Artist and professor Colin Rhodes has theorized that Lawson made drawings as private negotiations with an inner self, an identity he was unprepared to share with the world, not even with his wife. The artworks, found by his widow not long after his death, show a figure, consistent in looks and presentation throughout the body of work, that is believed to be the artist himself. They present a moment in which empathy becomes an imaginative act, a foray into the soul-searching of a person whose outer visage and existence seemed at odds with an interior identity.

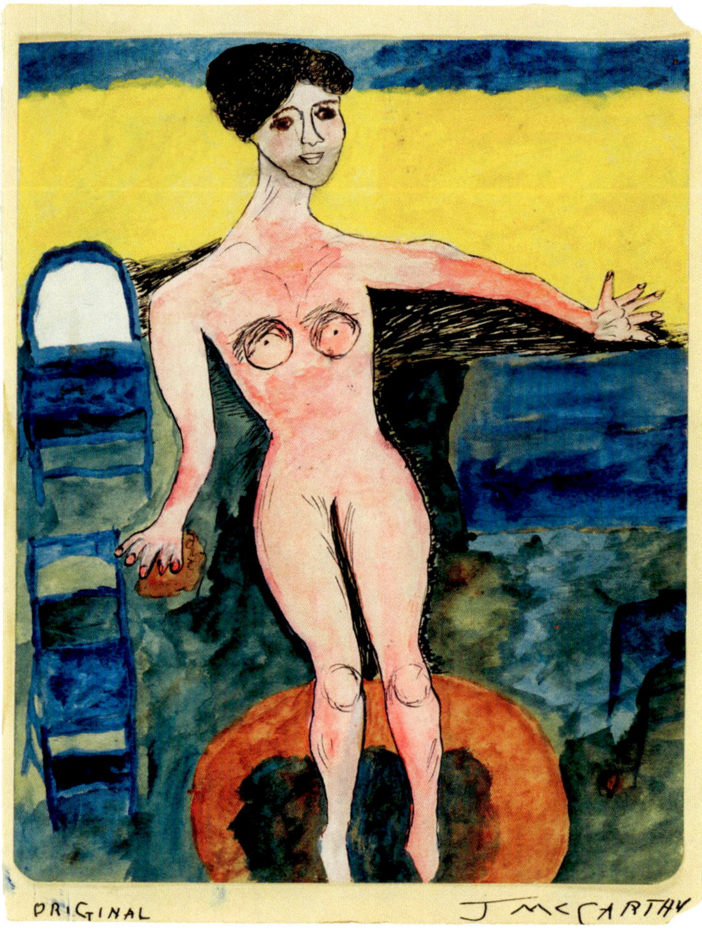

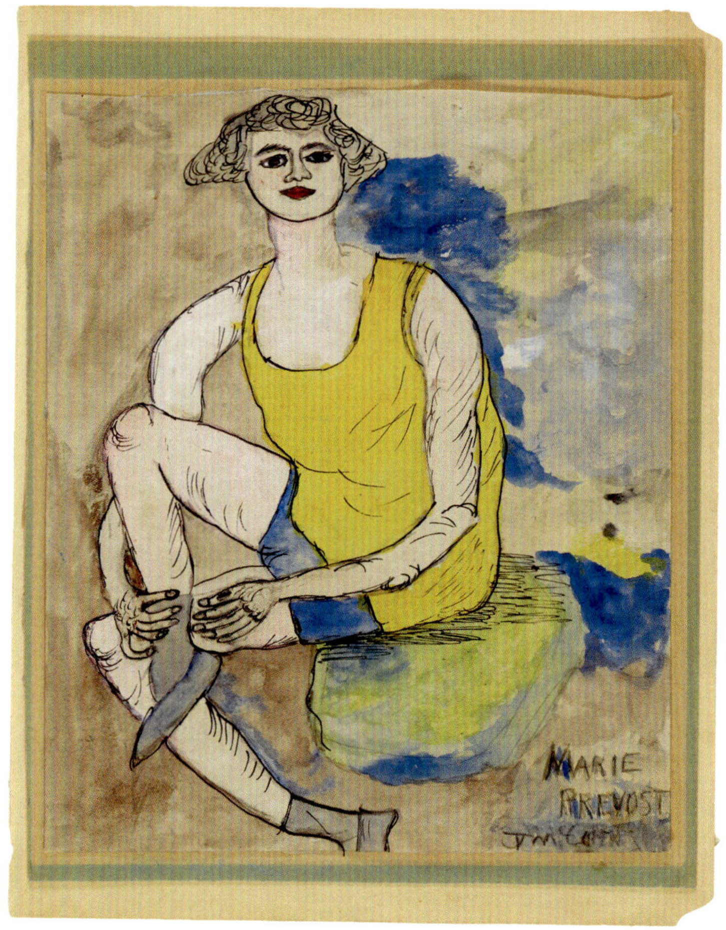

CAT. 101.
Justin McCarthy
Original
ca. 1930–70

CAT. 102.
Justin McCarthy
Marie Prevost
ca. 1930–60

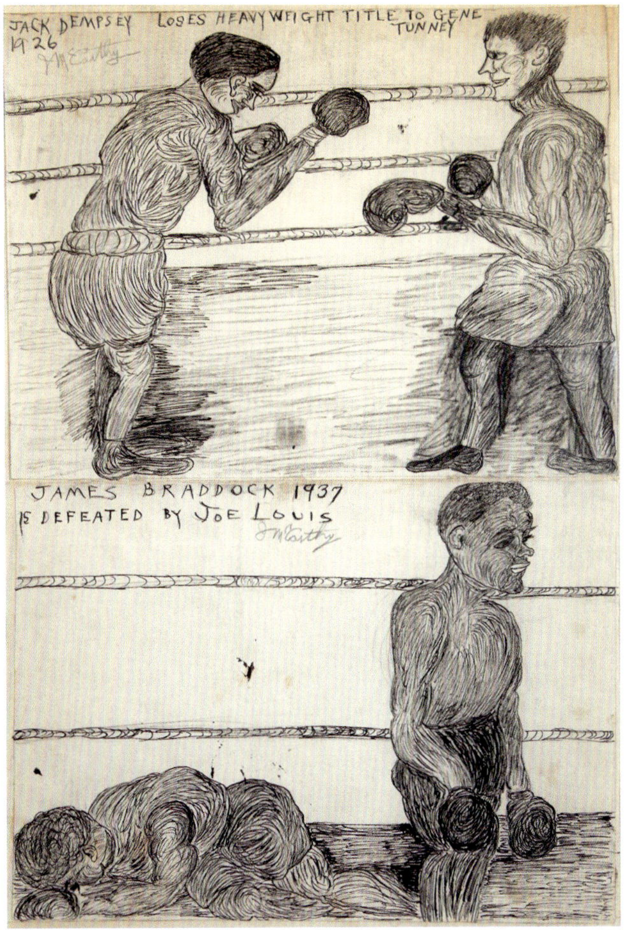

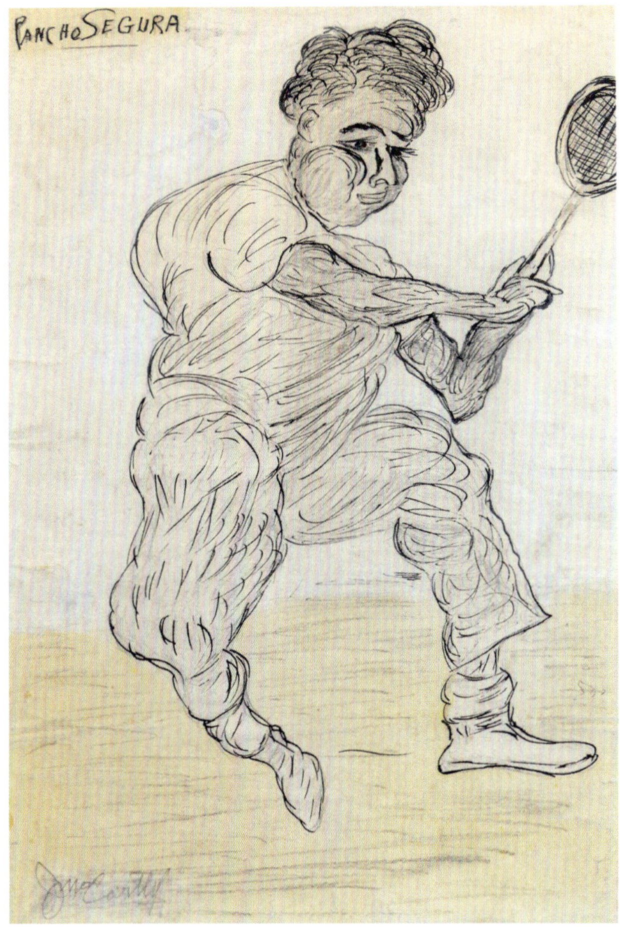

CAT. 103.
Justin McCarthy
Jack Dempsey Loses Heavyweight Title to Gene Tunney 1926/ James Braddock 1937 Is Defeated by Joe Louis
ca. 1930–60

CAT. 104.
Justin McCarthy
Pancho Segura
ca. 1930–60

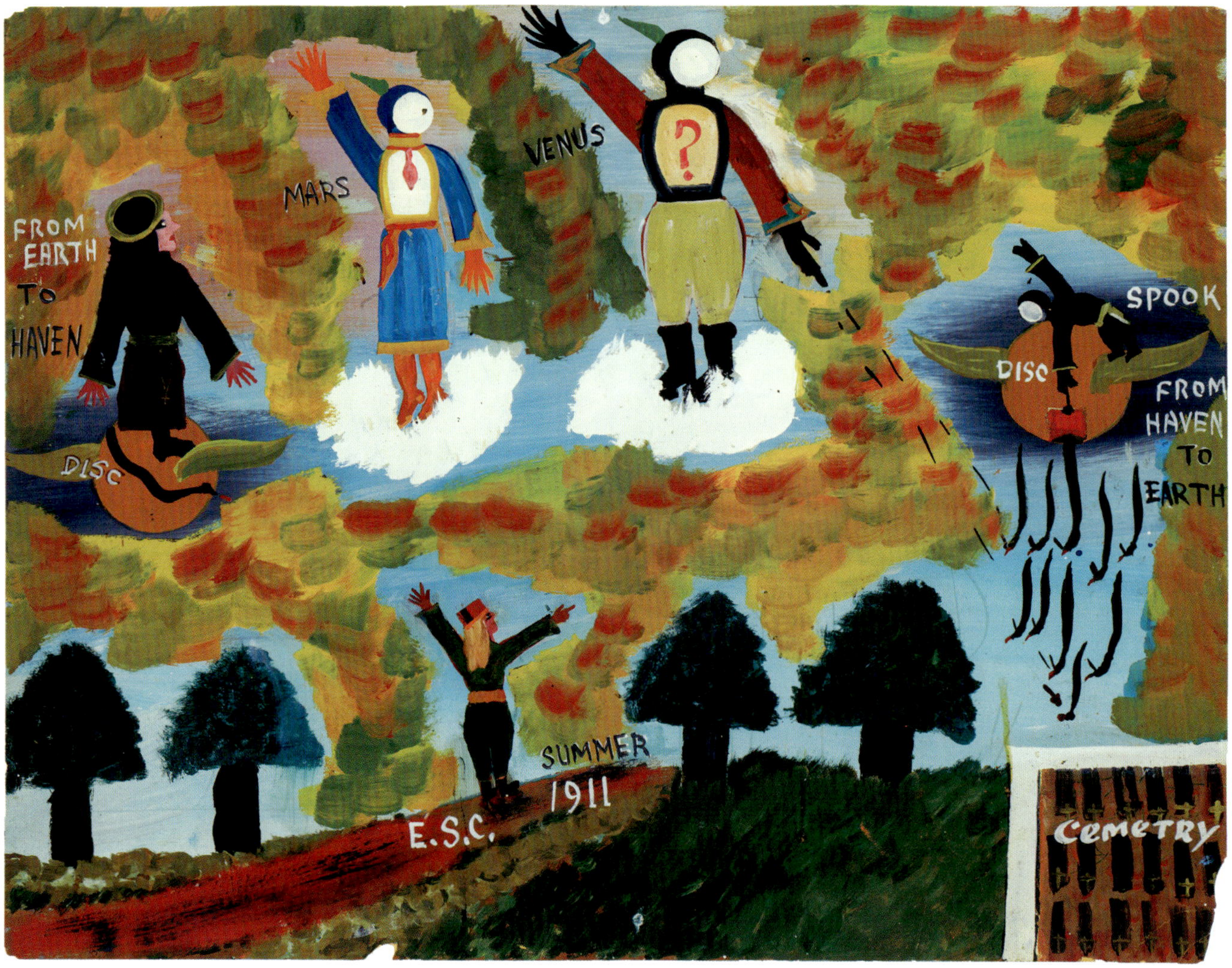

CAT. 105.
Peter "Charlie" Attie Besharo
Untitled (From Earth to Haven/From Haven to Earth)
ca. 1950–60

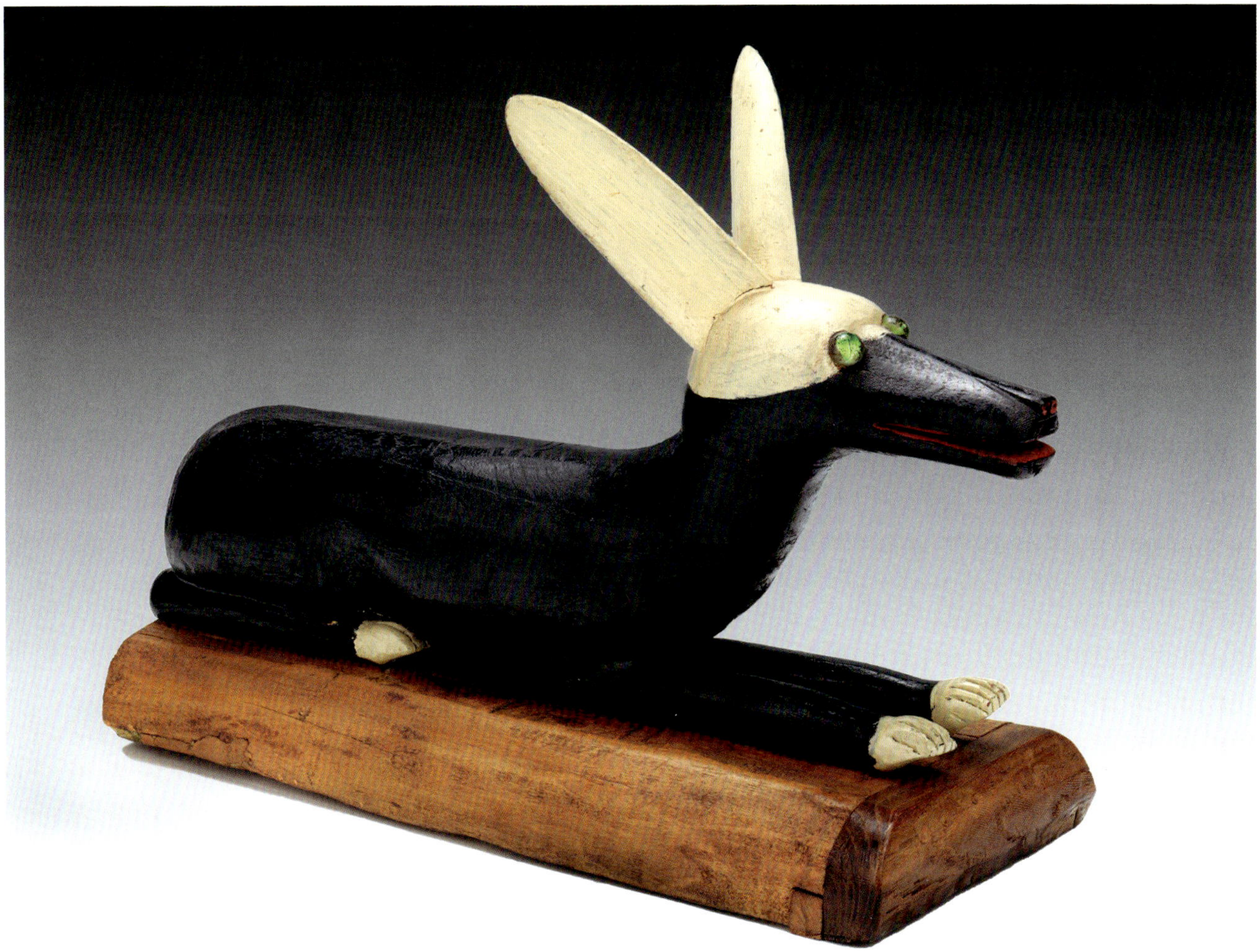

CAT. 106.
Stephan W. Polaha
Green Eyed Dog
ca. 1975

CAT. 107.
Ernest "Popeye" Reed
Venus
1980

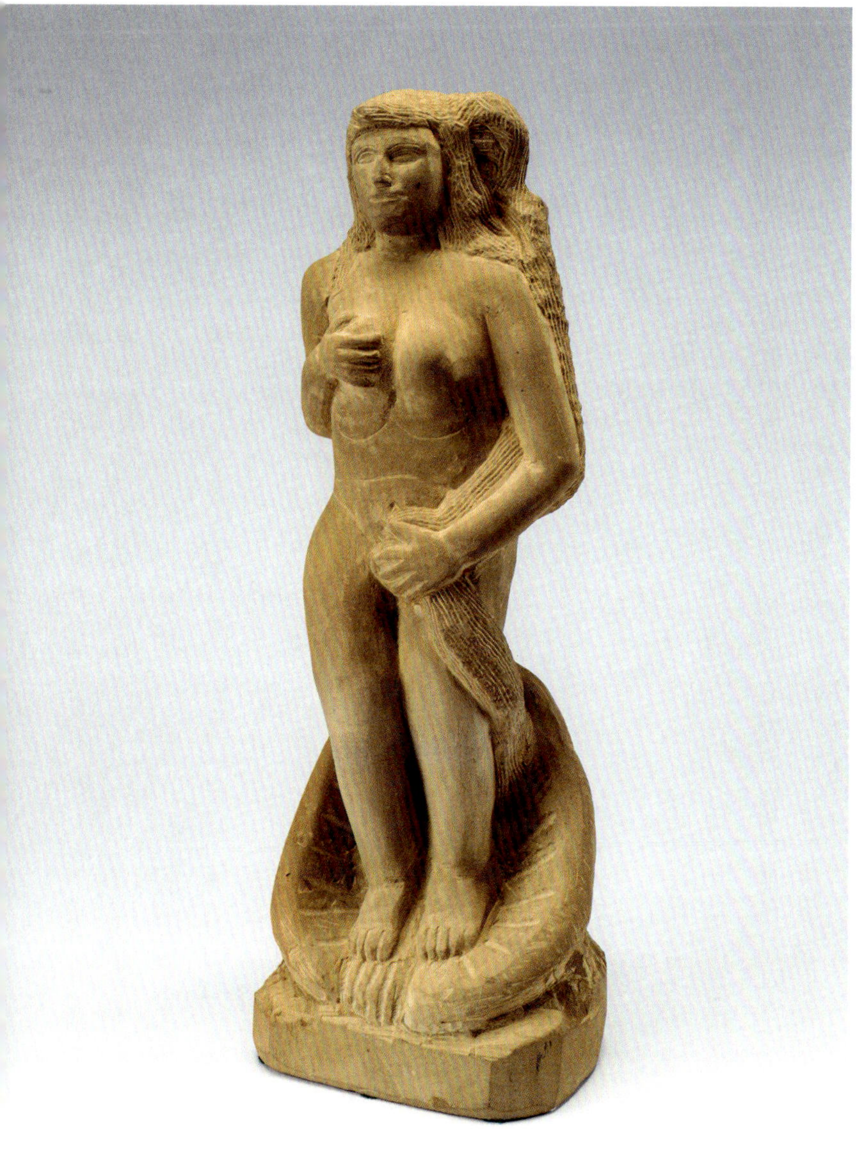

CAT. 108.
Ernest "Popeye" Reed
Woman and Child
ca. 1980–85

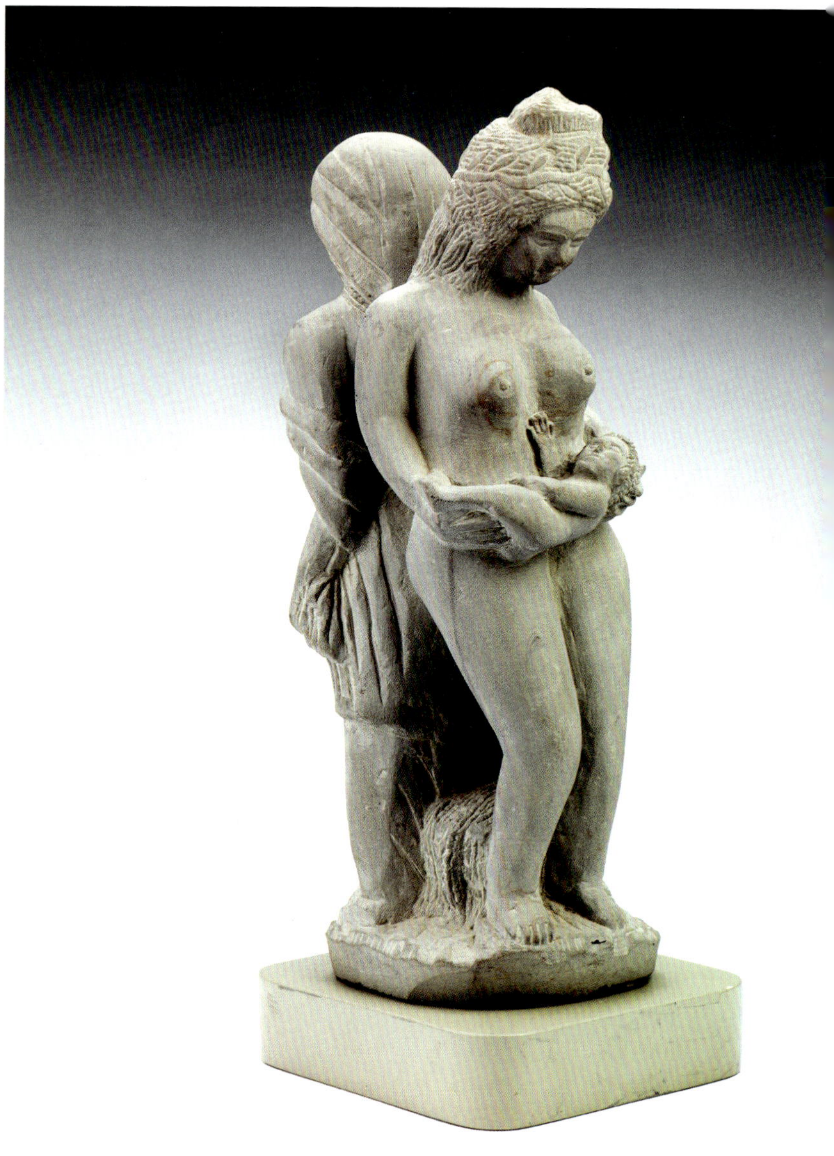

Lawson's drawn figures, one per page, confront the viewer from a central position; each comes dressed in glamorous feminine attire, coiffured and made-up but in a manner that does not fully transform the figure's masculinity (**CATS. 109, 110**). Interestingly, in drawings such as the innocuously titled *Fashions 1899*, Lawson embellished the gown with winglike sleeves—possibly a reference to the butterfly, a time-honored symbol of transformation; the truncated arms, however, may suggest feelings that contradicted transformation—a powerlessness to actualize his innermost needs. "At a time when society frowned upon alternative gender identities and cross-dressing in both opinion and law, it would have been immensely damaging for Lawson to have publicly revealed such fantasies and urges," Rhodes notes. "It seems likely that Lawson chose to play this out only in these secret drawings. He makes no attempt to fully feminize his figure. The musculature, heavy makeup, awkward poses and unfeasibly large, stuck-on breasts repeatedly corroborate that this is a man playing a part—as though confirming, at least to himself, his natural state. It is instructive and poignant that today we are able to share Lawson's images without judging their maker."[12]

Over the past century, time, place, and happenstance have played significant roles in bodies of work by self-taught artists being appreciated and cared for, underscoring the important role of artists and collectors who noticed and valued such production. Another significant factor, however, is that self-taught artists were often driven by goals and concerns that were a world apart from those of their professional peers. These goals and concerns critically inform the afterlife of the artworks themselves and create instances in which severing the story of the maker—the context that backdropped its making—would diminish the surviving object in profound ways. We are ultimately left to wonder if Lawson intended his drawings to be found, a postscript from the beyond. Bill Traylor knew, as people purchased his drawings from him for a dime or quarter, that he was relinquishing their fate to the buyer. But he could scarcely have imagined the degree to which they would live on, being seen internationally and held by some of the world's most prestigious museums. But each case is unique, and the ways the artists used or intended their work to be seen or engaged with become an inherent part of the work's survival story. For Sam Doyle, it was essential to his project that the paintings be on view around his property as an outdoor history museum. On his South Carolina Sea Island home, this meant the pieces were exposed to extreme weather year-round, which took a toll on the portraits he painted on roofing tin. Doyle steadfastly repainted them, keeping them from fading or washing away, and their visage is variously rusted, refreshed, painted, and overpainted—their journey imprinted upon and baked into the artwork over time.

CAT. 109.
Edwin Lawson
Fashion 1955
1973

CAT. 110.
Edwin Lawson
Fashions 1899
1974

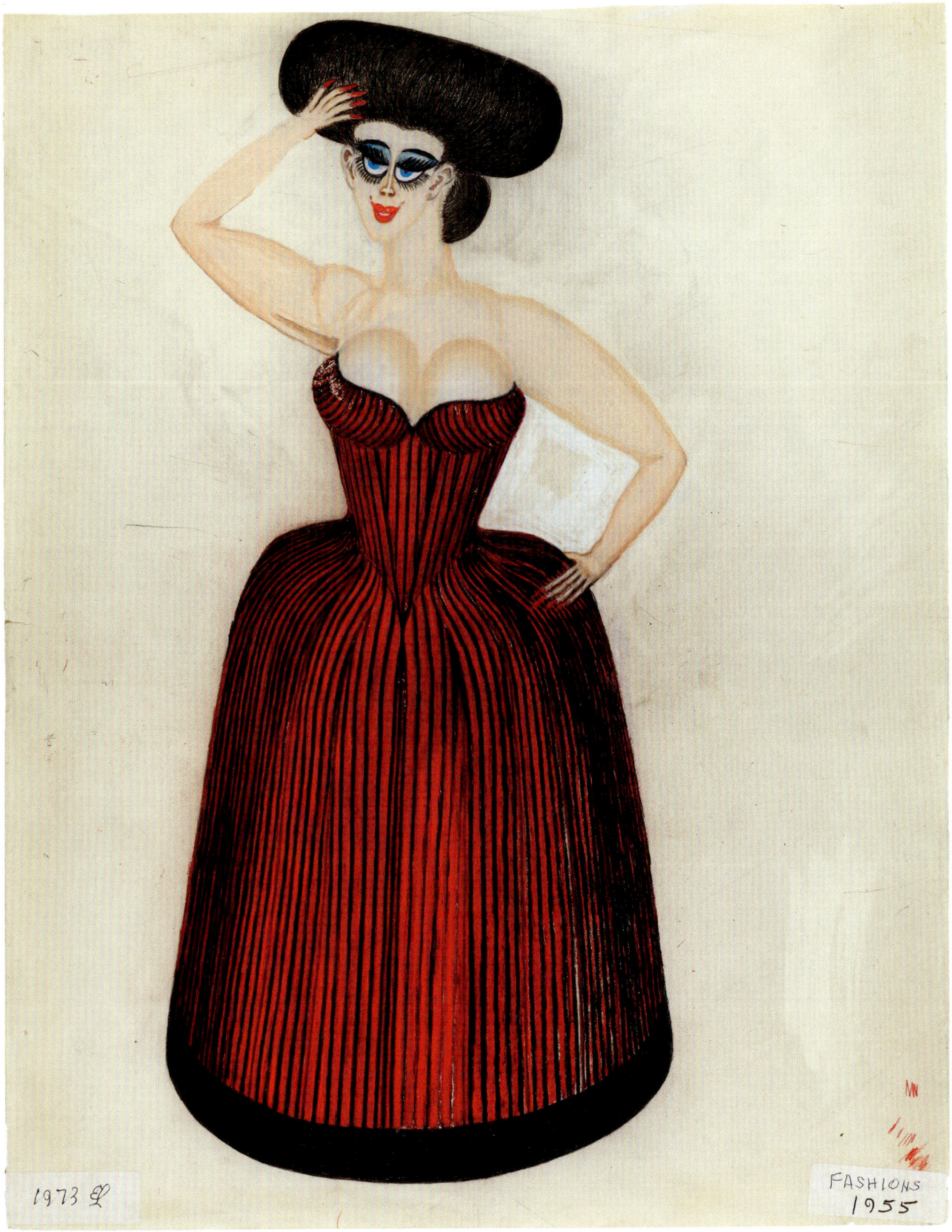

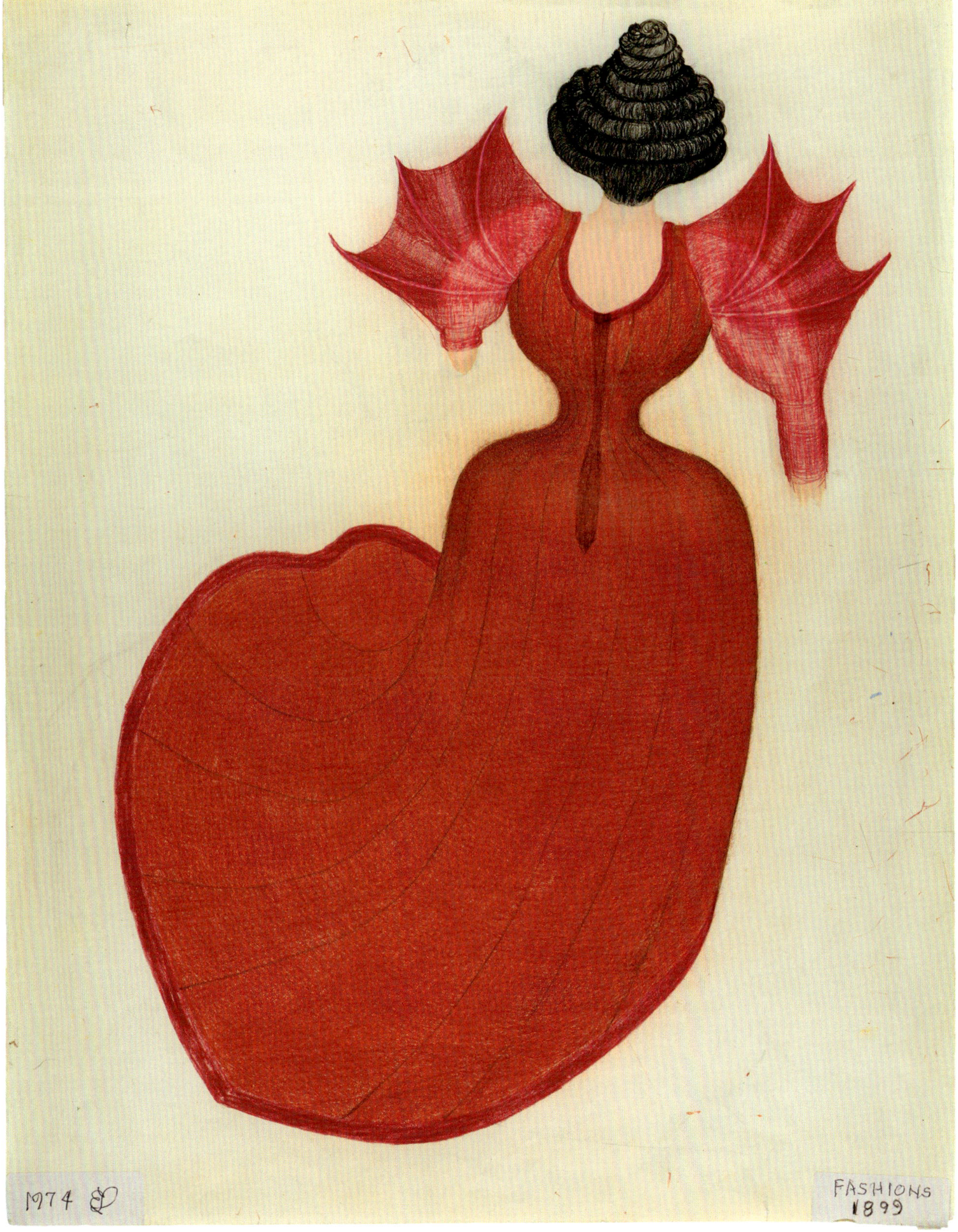
1974
FASHIONS
1899

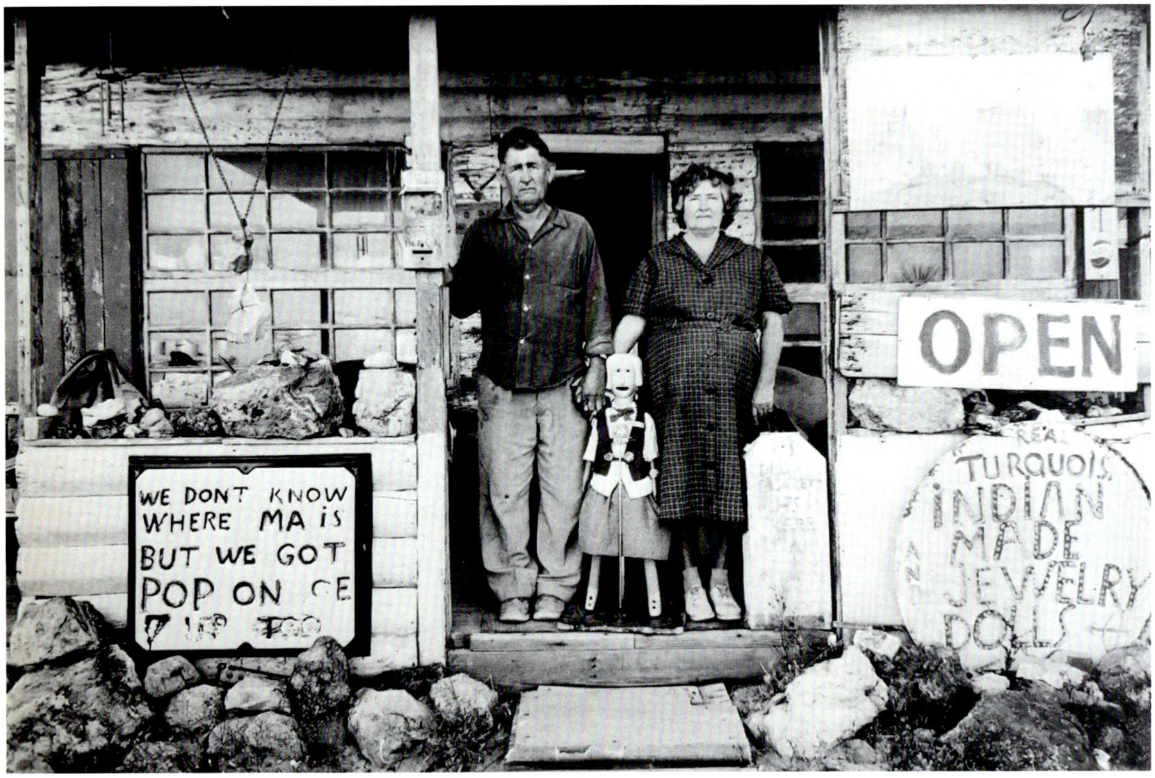

Fig. 61. Calvin Black and Ruby Black, ca. 1970–71; photograph by Tim Brehm

The almost life-size figures that **CALVIN BLACK** (1903–1972) carved and painted and that his wife, **RUBY BLACK** (1913–1980), sewed clothes for and dressed with care, similarly wear the ravages of Possum Trot, their desert environment/roadside attraction (Figs. 61, 62). Calvin Black was from Tennessee, and Ruby from Georgia. They met as pen pals and married in 1933, moving to California in hopes of working for the movies or striking it rich panning for gold. In 1953, they moved to Yermo, where they believed the arid climate would be beneficial for Calvin's fragile health. They bought land and dubbed it "Possum Trot," which art historian Jeffrey R. Hayes has explained as "highland slang for a remote and backward settlement, the shortest route between two farms, or a style of house with a central breezeway, also known as a dog trot."[13] The Blacks aimed to earn their living with a homemade rock shop and roadside attraction located along the route to Calico Ghost Town. The heart of the attraction became about eighty half-life-size dolls, mostly female, modeled on friends and celebrities (**CATS. 111, 112**). Calvin determined and carved their characters; Ruby fashioned their attire. In the late 1960s, when their doll population swelled beyond the confines of the shop, Calvin built the Birdcage Theater (Fig. 63), where he staged the "Fantasy

CAT. 111.
Calvin Black and
Ruby Black
Gladys (Possum Trot Doll)
ca. 1953–72

CAT. 112.
Calvin Black and
Ruby Black
Untitled (Possum Trot Doll)
ca. 1953–72

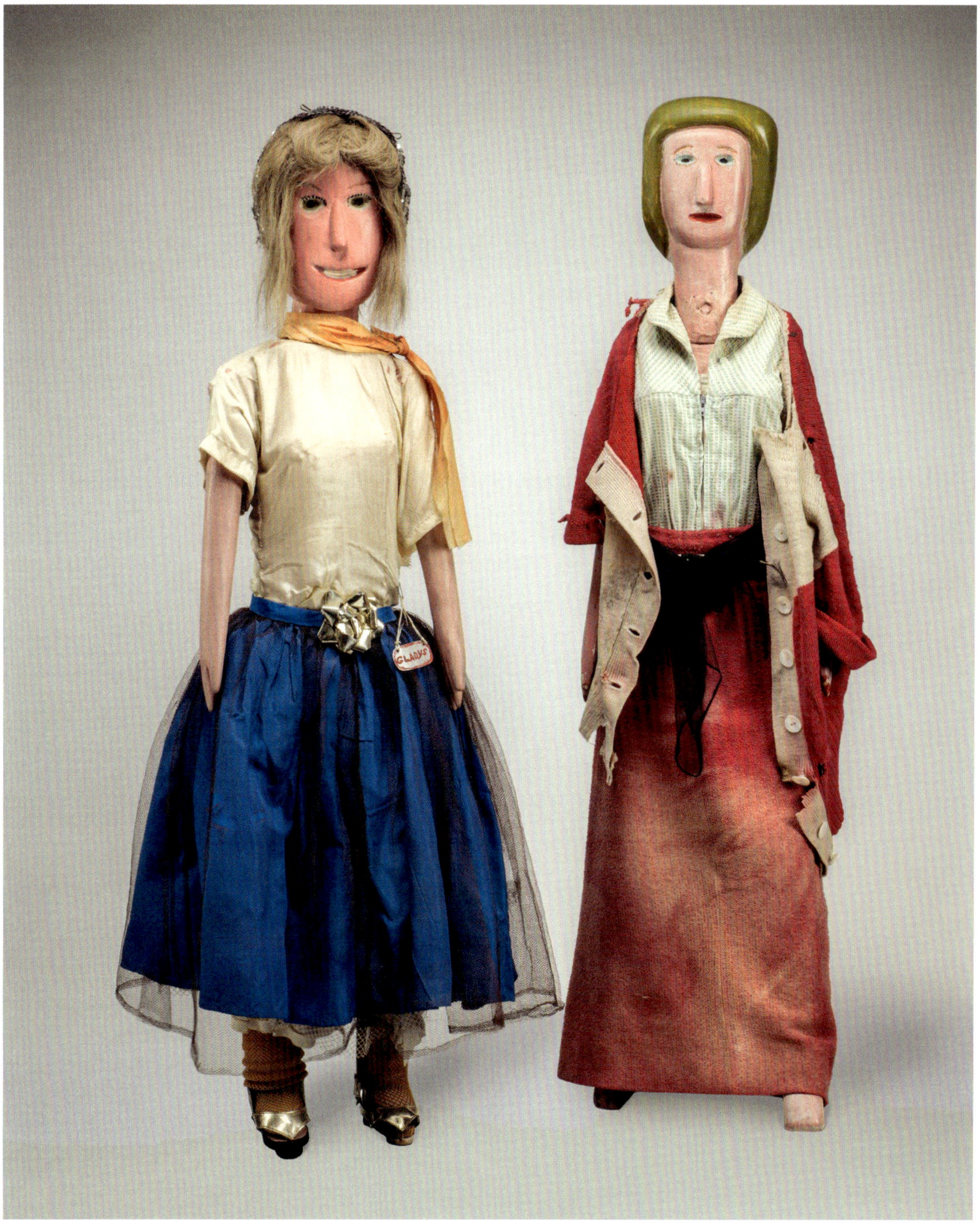
GLADYS

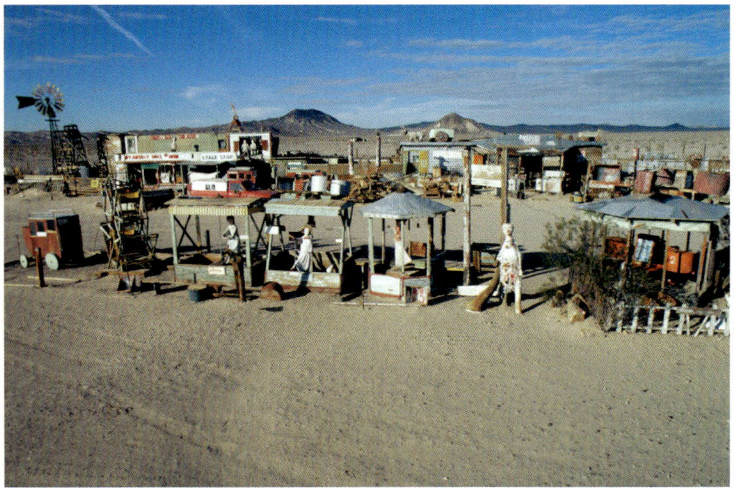

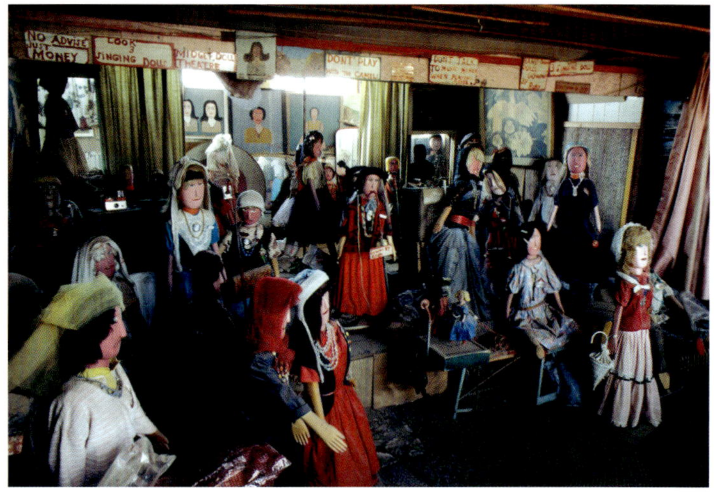

Fig. 62. Possum Trot, ca. 1975–82; photograph by Seymour Rosen

Fig. 63. Interior view of Calvin and Ruby Black's Birdcage Theater, ca. 1975–82; photograph by Seymour Rosen

Doll Show."[14] Both Calvin and Ruby had homegrown theatrical backgrounds not unlike that of Jon Serl. Ruby had worked for circuses and carnivals; Calvin too had a carny background and had learned ventriloquism working for a puppet show. He played guitar and used his nine different falsetto voices to provide audio tracks for the dolls, broadcast through speakers positioned near the backs of their heads.

Between the time Calvin died and the end of Ruby's life, the state of the site declined. The condition of the surviving dolls directly corresponded to their sheltered or exposed location around the property. Objects that serve functional roles for their makers become, in the absence of those makers, artwork and artifact in equal measure, and demand the context of their creation in ways that differ from discrete works. Significant in this case are the audio recordings that Calvin made, as well as photographs documenting the site and its sculptural inhabitants during its heyday. Director and producer Allie Light visited Possum Trot not long after Calvin had passed away. With Irving Saraf, she made a film documenting the site in 1976, which went on to become a finalist at the American Film Festival, and in tandem with photographs of the site taken by Seymour Rosen and others substantiates the Blacks' project and reveals the fullness and vitality of a lived art environment.[15]

ALBERT "KID" MERTZ (1905–1988) surrounded his home space with the sculptures and paintings he made, but he did not layer it with a performative function, or necessarily view all of his artworks as pieces of a conceived whole (Fig. 64). While tourists flocked to Howard Finster's Paradise Garden, Mertz's home, which he called, in turn, "Owl's Rest," "Owl's Roost," and "Al's Roost," was off the beaten path in Bitely, Michigan. Mertz was born Albert Marcincavage

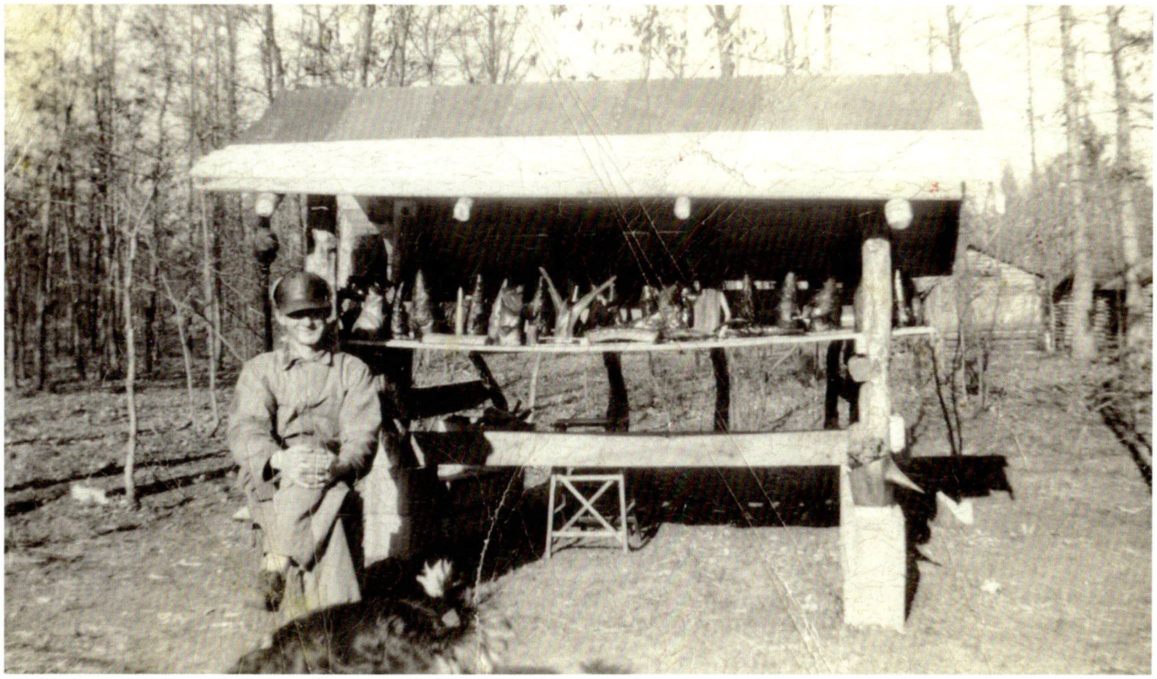

Fig. 64. Albert "Kid" Mertz in front of his "souvenir stand" along highway M-37, Baldwin, Michigan. Courtesy of William Eugene May, Lawrence Douglas May, Garth Andrew May, and Clare Alexander May

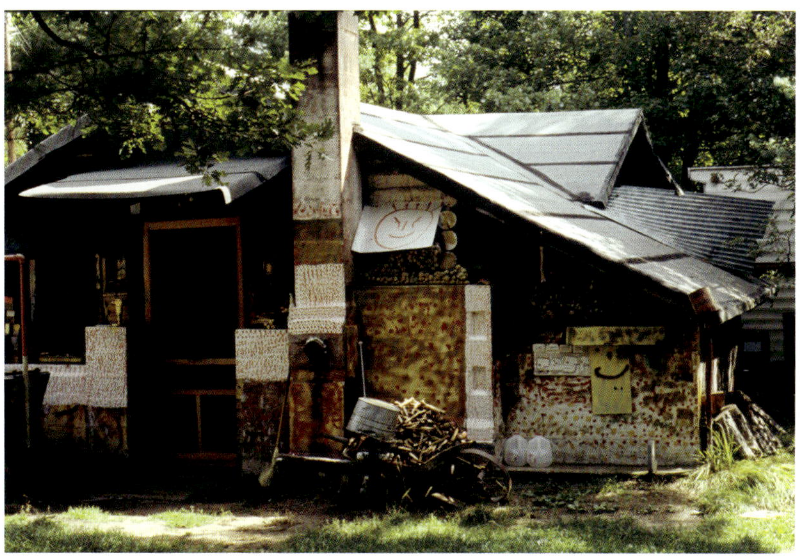

Fig. 65. Albert "Kid" Mertz's home in Michigan, 1986; photograph by David Kargl

in Pennsylvania, in 1905.[16] On the eve of World War II, perhaps concerned about his Russian Jewish heritage, Albert legally anglicized his family's surname to Mertz.[17] When he retired in 1967 from a career as a die cutter in the automotive industry, he turned to painting and sculpting. He covered his modest home with polka dots, stripes, and colorful embellishments (Fig. 65). He painted objects as well, including hundreds—possibly thousands—of railroad spikes that he collected from tracks near his property, giving each individual spike a tiny painted face (**CAT. 113**). In contrast to David Butler, who was reluctant to sell his personally protective artworks to interested collectors, and Howard Finster, who eagerly imparted his painted sermons to anyone willing to hear and spread his word, Mertz was delighted to have people visit and take an interest in what he viewed as a personal drive to stay busy and create a fun, cheerful environment.

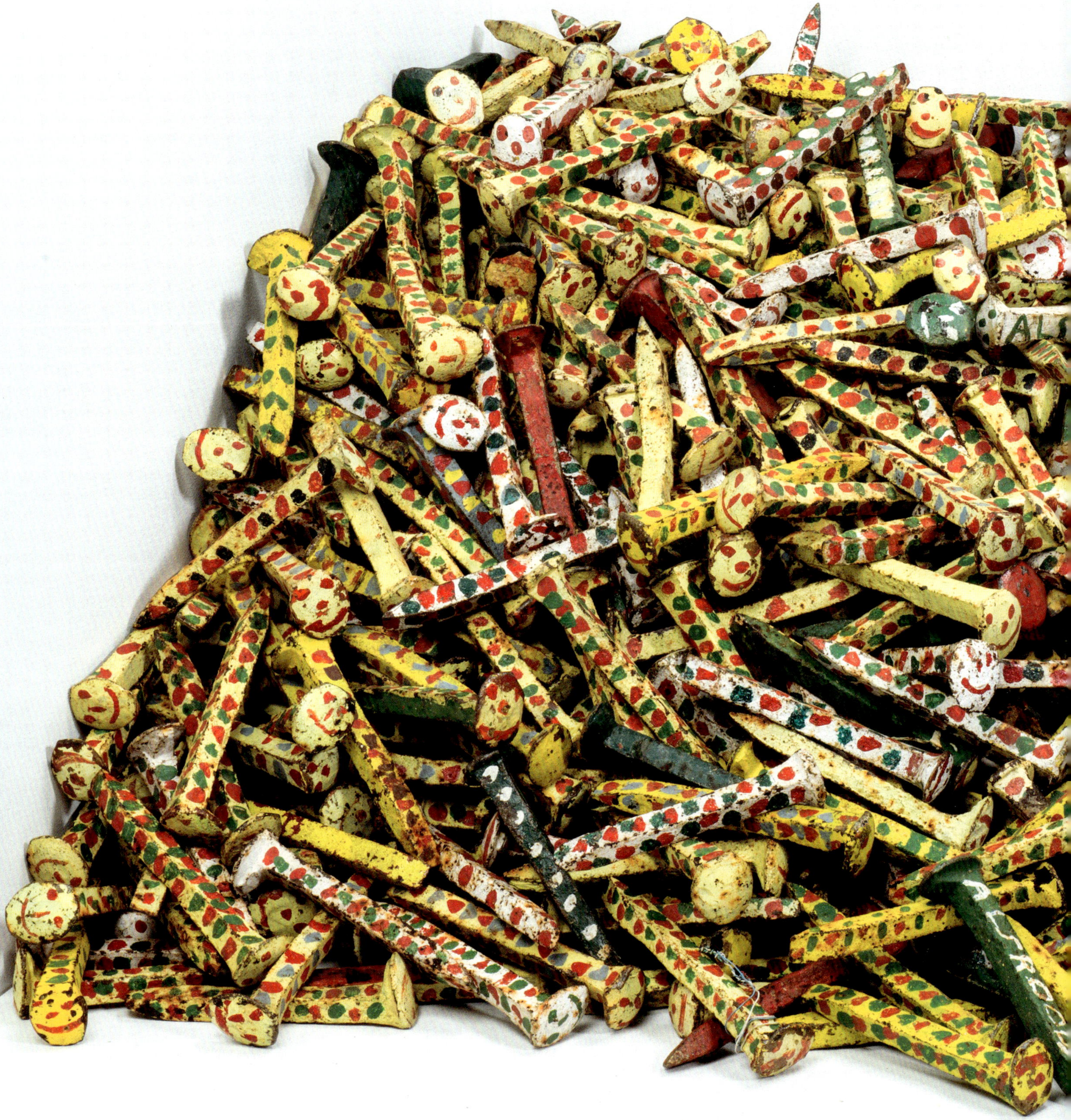

CAT. 113.
Albert “Kid” Mertz
Untitled
ca. 1980

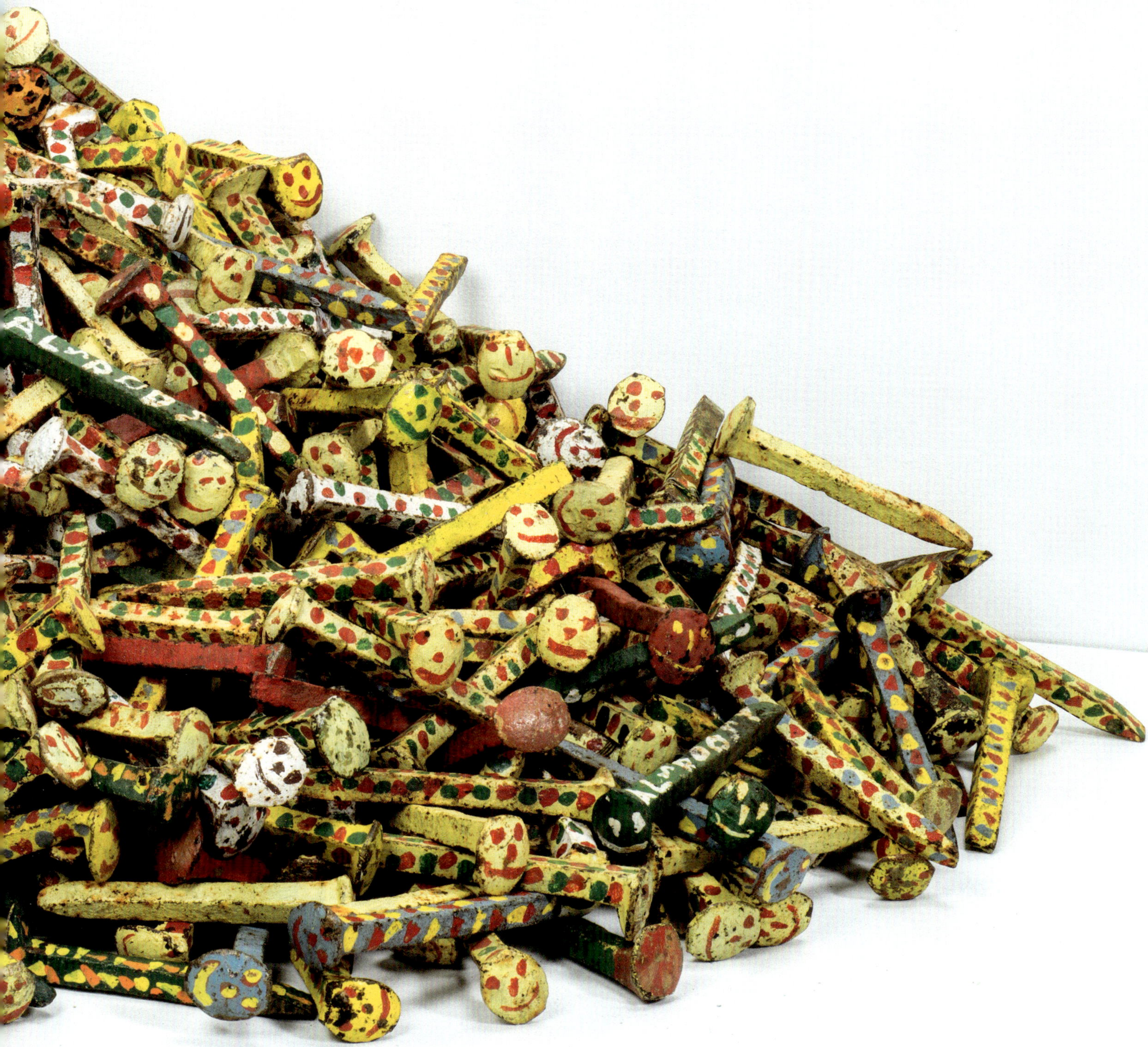

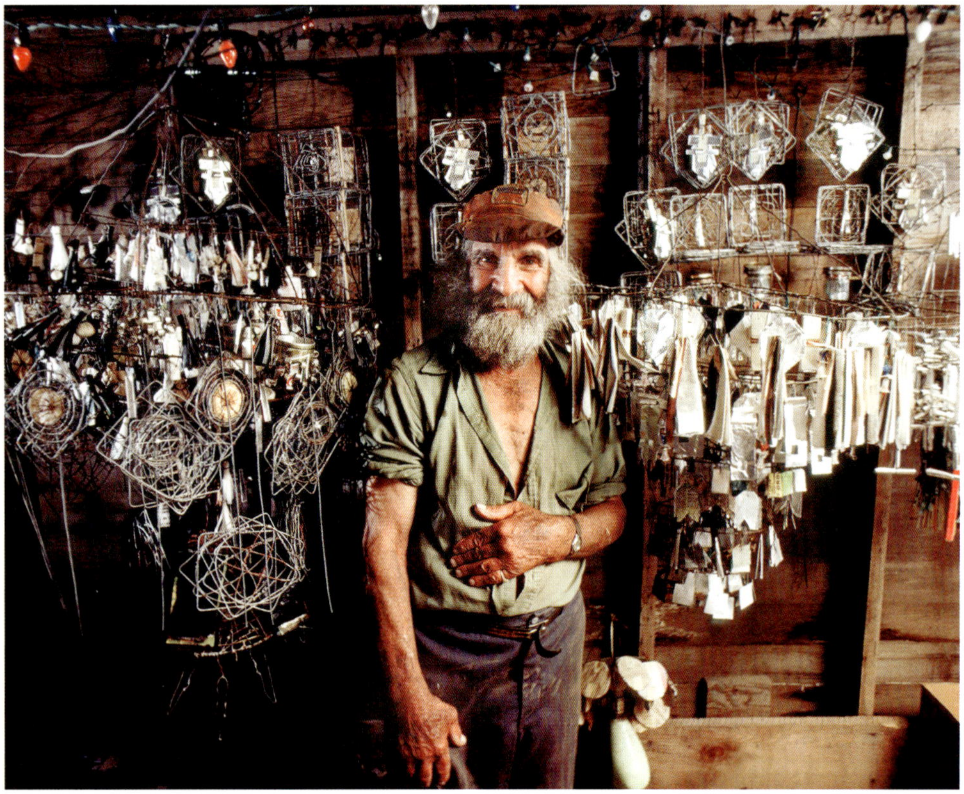

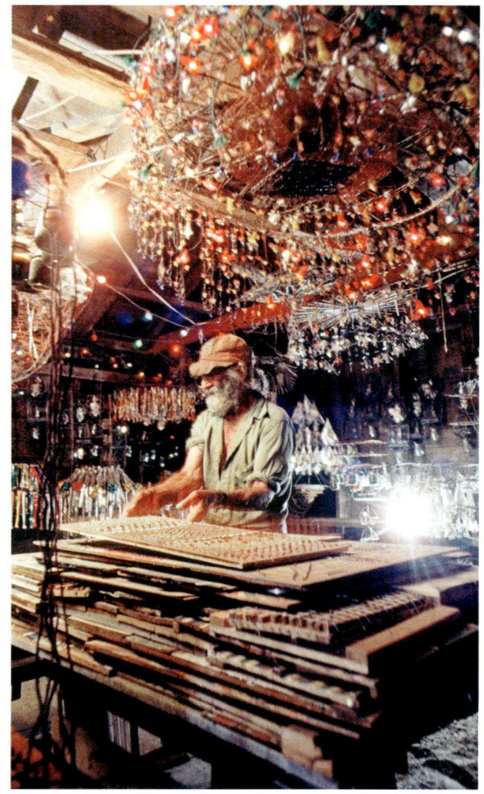

In still another unique flavor of art environment, Nebraska artist **EMERY BLAGDON** (1907–1986) created an interactive site with truly distinct aims (Fig. 66). In the late 1950s, Blagdon began a project on his farm that would consume his next three decades.[18] He envisioned his shed-environment as a machine to create and distribute the earth's healing energies into the body. Blagdon was profoundly troubled by his mother's death from cancer in 1936 and his father's, also from cancer, in 1951. His own arthritis and abiding concerns about disease and suffering drove him to channel his interests in science, the natural world, and medical advances with electricity and radiation into the creation of a space wherein healing energies could flourish and abound. He made paintings on board—abstract shapes and forms of bold, bright paints discovered at yard sales—and created woven and bent wire sculptures that variously cascaded down, formed a battery-like bundle, or had a shape that he felt could direct magnetic or electrical energy around the space. His materials were primarily salvaged, magnets and copper wire, baling twine, aluminum foil, and other found objects (**CATS. 114–17**). He incorporated earth elements when he could, believing that ingredients like

Fig. 66. Emery Blagdon and his Healing Machine, 1979; photograph by Richard Greenhill

Fig. 67. Emery Blagdon and his Healing Machine, 1979; photograph by Richard Greenhill, Museum of Nebraska Art

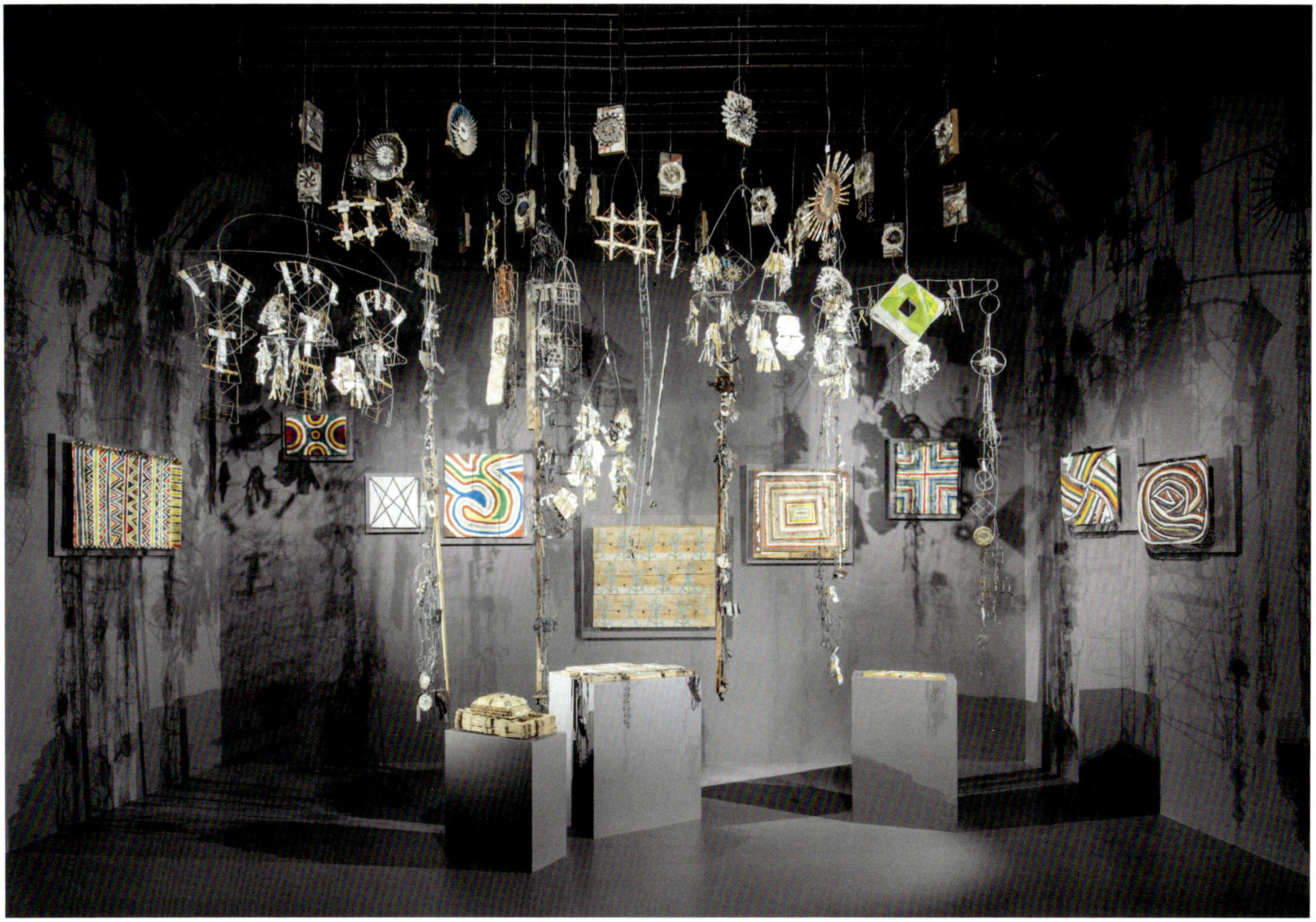

Fig. 68. Individual elements from Emery Blagdon's *Healing Machine*, ca. 1955–86, mixed media. Smithsonian American Art Museum, Museum purchase through the Luisita L. and Franz H. Denghausen Endowment and gift of Dan Dryden, friend of Emery Blagdon, the Kohler Foundation, Inc., and John E. and Douglas O. Robson, from the Margaret Z. Robson Collection, VR.2014.49.GRP

sodium, and certain minerals found in paints, were critical to the functional role of his aesthetically powerful space. By the 1970s, the space that Blagdon called "The Healing Machine" was a complex array of interrelated sculptures, illuminated with colored Christmas lights, and geometric paintings (Fig. 67), all installed in a shed on Blagdon's property. He reorganized the components regularly and refashioned them as he saw fit. Blagdon invited passersby who needed pains alleviated or spirits lifted to sit in the Healing Machine and experience the combined benefits of the earth's energies and the transformative powers of delight and wonder (Fig. 68).

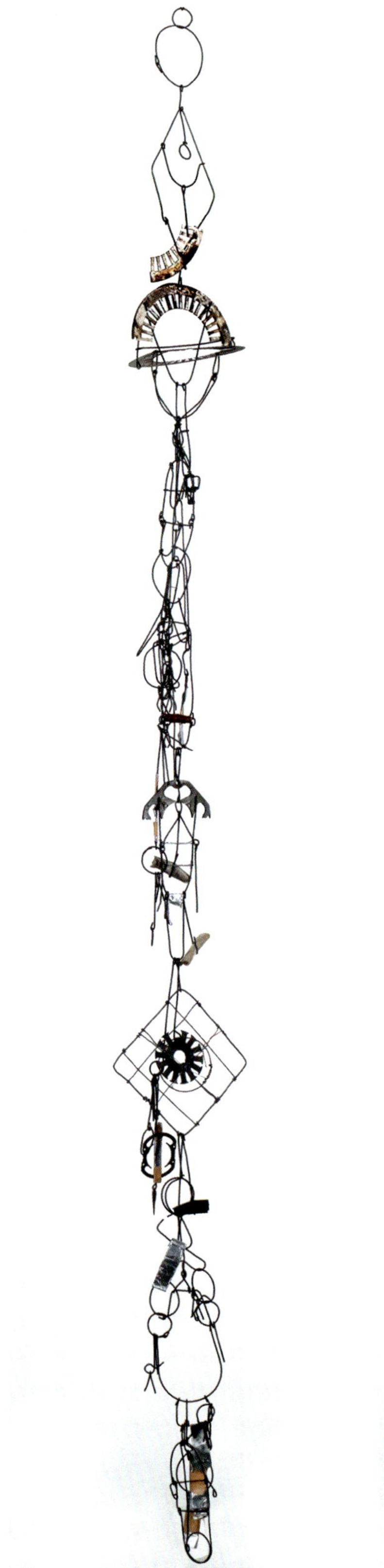

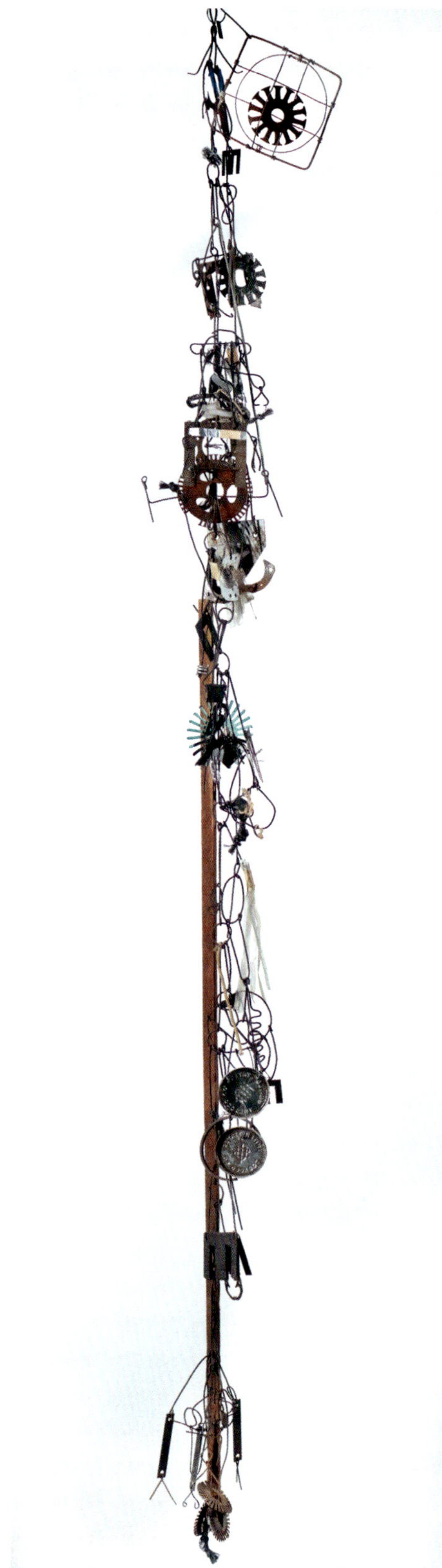

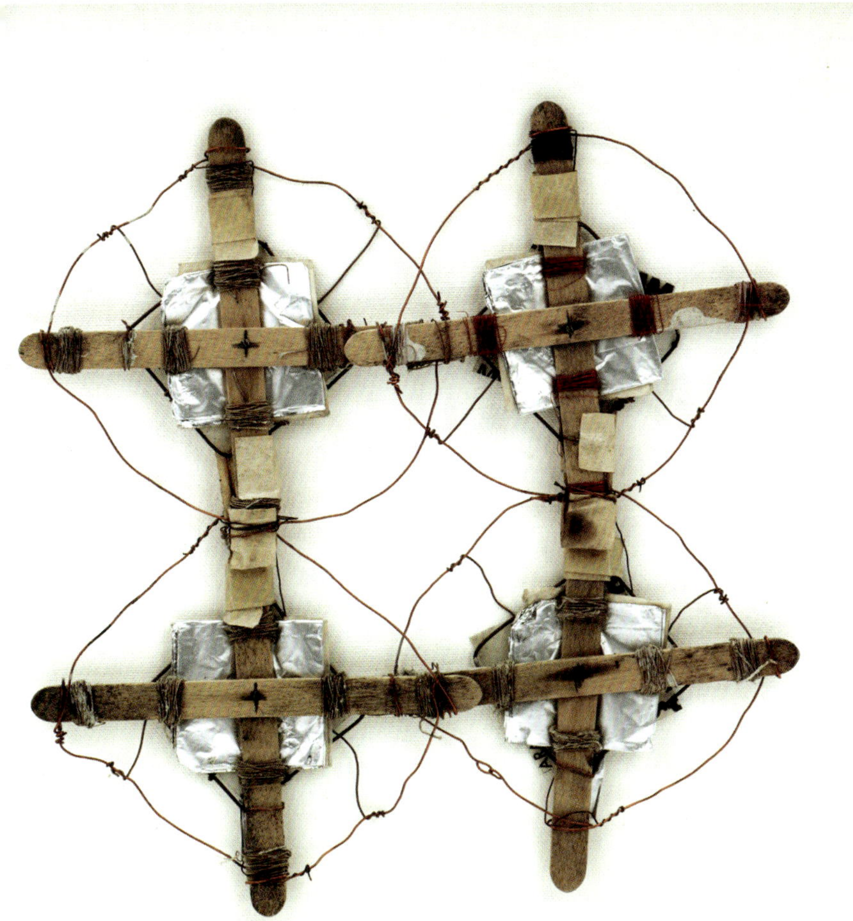

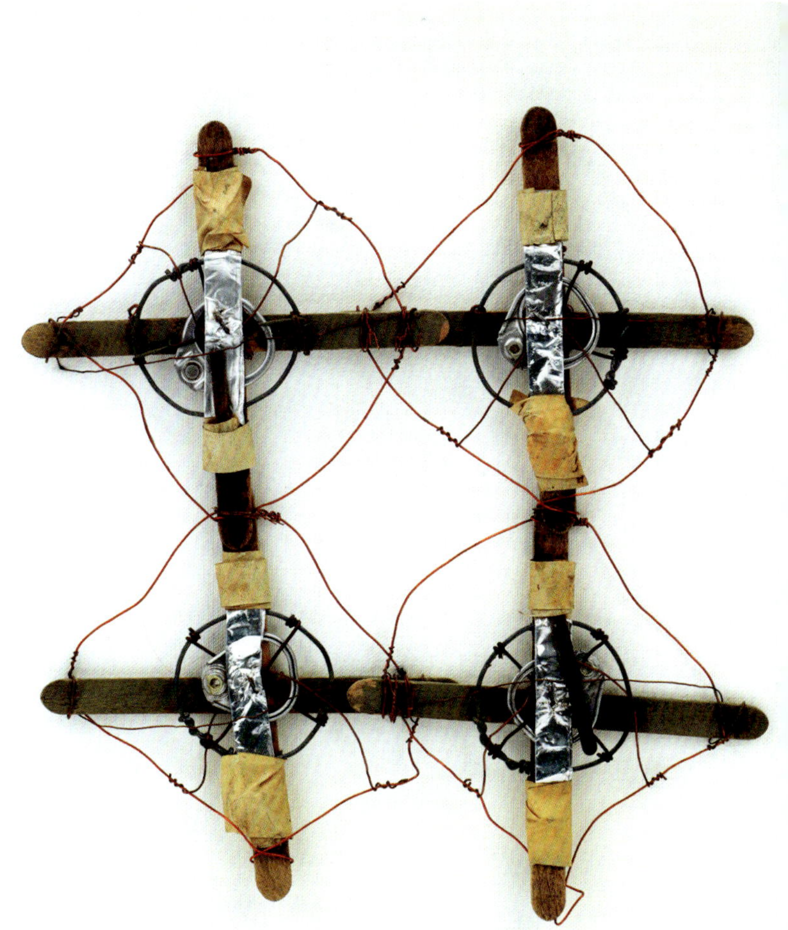

CATS. 114–117.

Emery Blagdon

Untitled (Individual elements from *The Healing Machine)*

ca. 1956–84

California artist **DAN MILLER** (born 1961) was already garnering meaningful attention when his work appeared in Venice alongside that of Judith Scott (Fig. 69). Years earlier, his art had been featured in exhibition projects at New York's White Columns and the Museum of Modern Art, and acquired by major museums including MoMA and the Smithsonian American Art Museum.[19] Miller's art is a graphic communication made in the moment (**CATS. 118, 119**). His paintings and drawings convey words and thoughts, recorded and repeatedly overdrawn until the imagery coalesces into a visual cloud that vibrates and hovers with an almost audible presence. Miller's graphic works, made in the same Oakland studio where Scott worked, are communiqués in a language he has shaped for himself, with moments of legibility amid a linguistic abstraction that a viewer can get lost in. Miller is on the autism spectrum; his art provides a forum for what he wants to convey but is unable to express verbally. Tom di Maria describes autism as a syndrome in which communication challenges are central, noting, "Miller addresses this obstacle by having words come out of his hands, rather than from his mouth."[20]

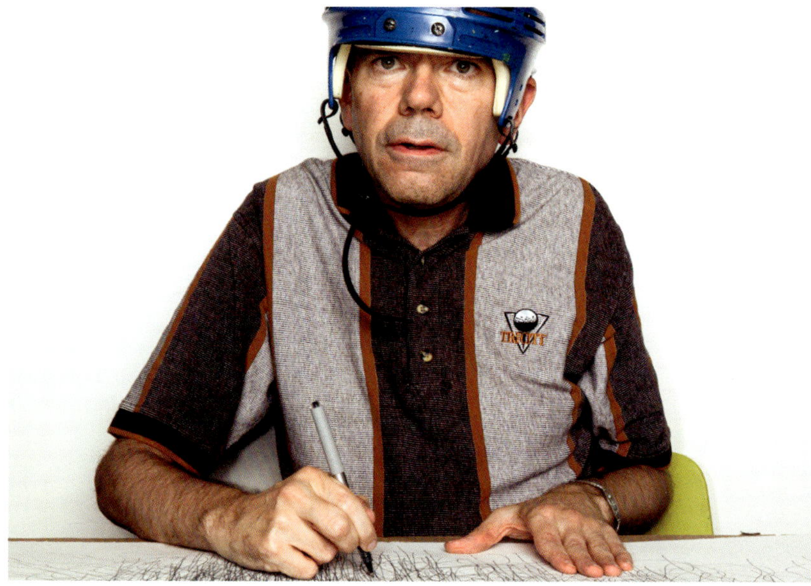

Fig. 69. Dan Miller at Creative Growth Art Center in Oakland, California, 2015; photograph by Jeff Minton

Miller was born in California's Castro Valley in 1961 and joined Creative Growth in 1992. Until the COVID-19 pandemic interrupted the status quo in 2020, he attended daily. In a 2015 essay, di Maria reflected on Miller's journey. "At the time of Miller's birth, children born on the autistic spectrum received little understanding or early intervention. Yet Miller's grandmother proved to be a prescient and positive influence on his development," he explains. "A schoolteacher herself, she would spend evenings with the young boy at home, teaching him to read or spell, repeating letters and words over and over again.... Her work proved to be a large influence on what was to become a large and significant body of work built upon obsessive overlays and repetitions of words, letters, and numbers."[21] Miller's family has given context to some of his more legible imagery—names of teachers, and objects or moments recalled from his uncle's hardware store, where he used to spend time, that are inscribed into nests of memories. But overall, Miller's images do not need interpretation. Matthew Higgs agrees: "Dan's work speaks—I think literally in many ways—on its own terms and for itself. Despite his interest in layering, there is a clarity to his work that I think 'translates' to almost any viewer. What initially appears

CAT. 118.
Dan Miller
Untitled (283_2016)
2016

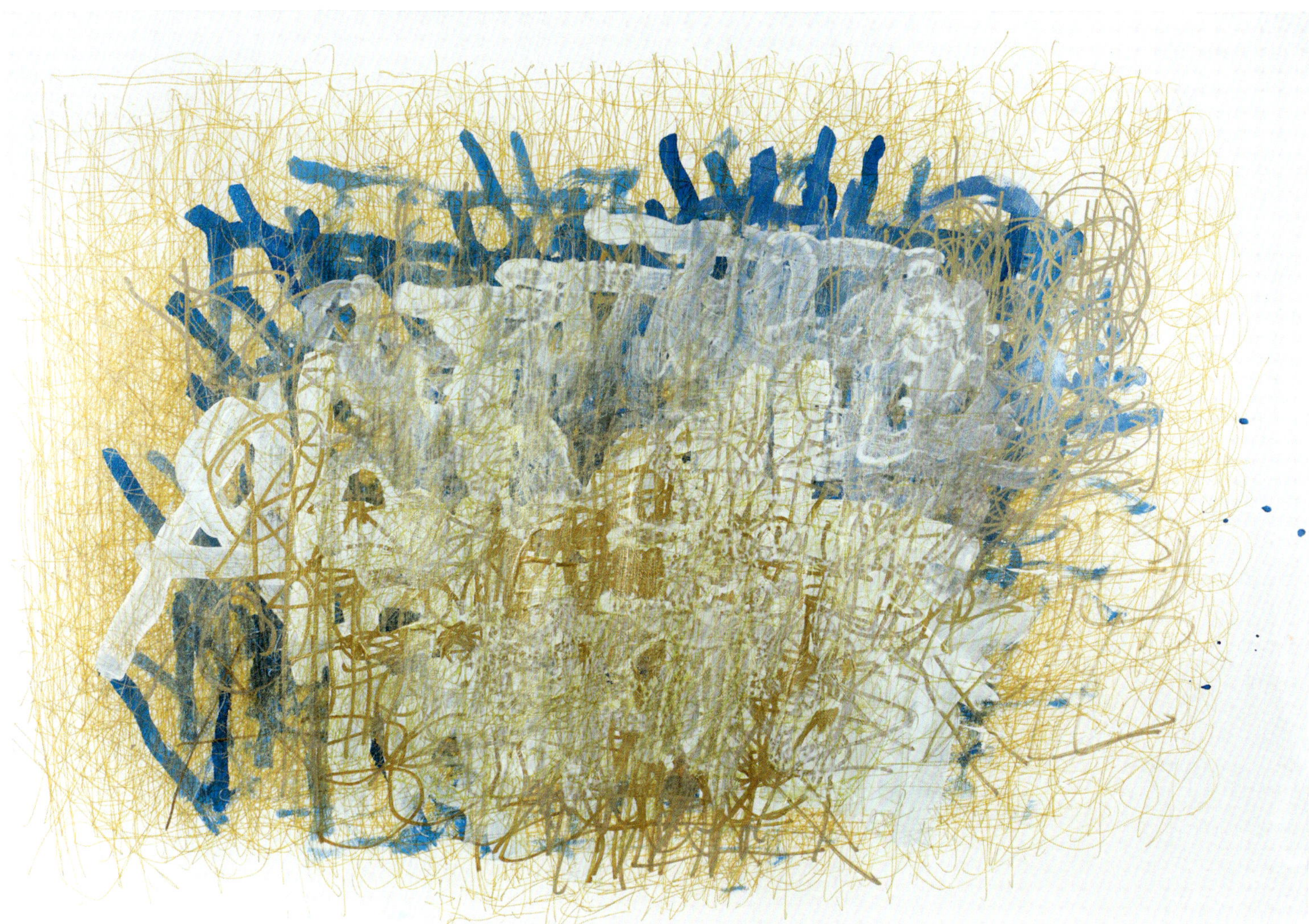

CAT. 119.

Dan Miller

Untitled (DM 1024)

2018

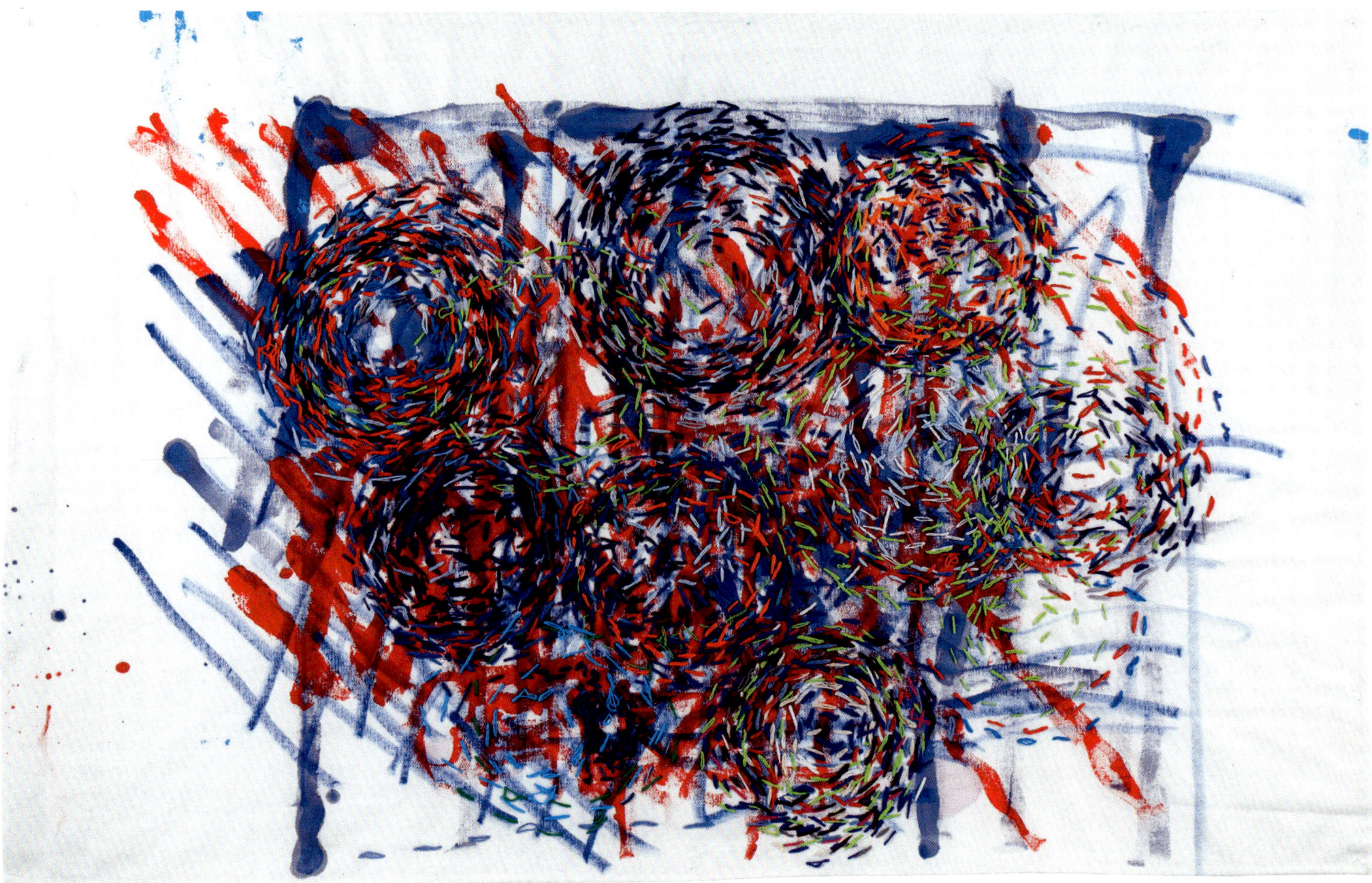

to be chaotic is in fact a very measured accumulation of ideas and experiences" (**CAT. 120**). Higgs offers another perspective on Miller's work that is particularly valuable today—that his biography is not mandatory for appreciating his imagery, but that it provides a critically enriching context. "Dan's circumstances and his development as an artist at Creative Growth is an extraordinary story—and one I personally think people should be aware of. The complexity in Dan's work mirrors the complexity of his life, which in turn amplifies the complexity of Creative Growth's profoundly radical mission."[22]

"The grounds crackle with life, vacillating between centrifugal and centripetal forces. The simplest drawings in pencil or black pen are not simple at all," Professor Claire Daigle says of Miller's work.[23] Daigle has traced Miller's development over time, describing in detail his quest for an ever-expanding visual vocabulary. Miller's artworks range from intensely rich color weavings to monotone hurricanes of marks; they are sometimes skyward-reaching scrolls, other times horizontal expanses. He makes occasional forays into other media, exploring how materials such as ceramic, textiles, and wood can activate his ideas. Regardless of the media, Miller's themes draw on deeply embedded memories—linguistic and physical. Light bulbs are among his recurring subjects, related to a childhood experience of having shattered one. In the papier-mâché pair in the Robson Family Collection, Miller overlaid his handmade forms with painted script, words forming a "skin" over the skeletal frame, a memory made manifest (see **CATS. 15, 16**, p. 37). Using a typewriter as both tool and medium, he crafts pieces that are part poem, part word painting, evoking John Cage or Samuel Beckett in the way these pieces effectively call into question convention and rationale, and make abstraction seem like the most viable logic.[24] Beckett in particular sought, as Miller seems to, an elusive sense of selfhood, or, as drama professor Martin J. Esslin described, "to capture the essence of the stream of consciousness that is one's being."[25] Miller's fragments—held, offered, and reoffered across the years—indicate a critical self-locating or existential record that in turn reveals the humanity in valuing uniquely personal languages and the exchanges they enable. He reminds us that memories can have tangible form, that communication is always a subjective volley between sender and receiver, and that the complexities inherent to interpreting the experience and emotional life of another being are profound.

Scott, and subsequently Miller, became iconic artists in the increasingly recognized sector of neurodivergent creativity.[26] As Doug Robson recounts in the preceding essay, Margaret became aware of Creative Growth after moving to the Bay Area in 1993 and began to support the work of several artists working there, including Scott and Miller. Di Maria has credited Margaret for recognizing early on that the efforts of differently abled artists were important, undervalued and

CAT. 120.

Dan Miller

Untitled (239_2016)

2016

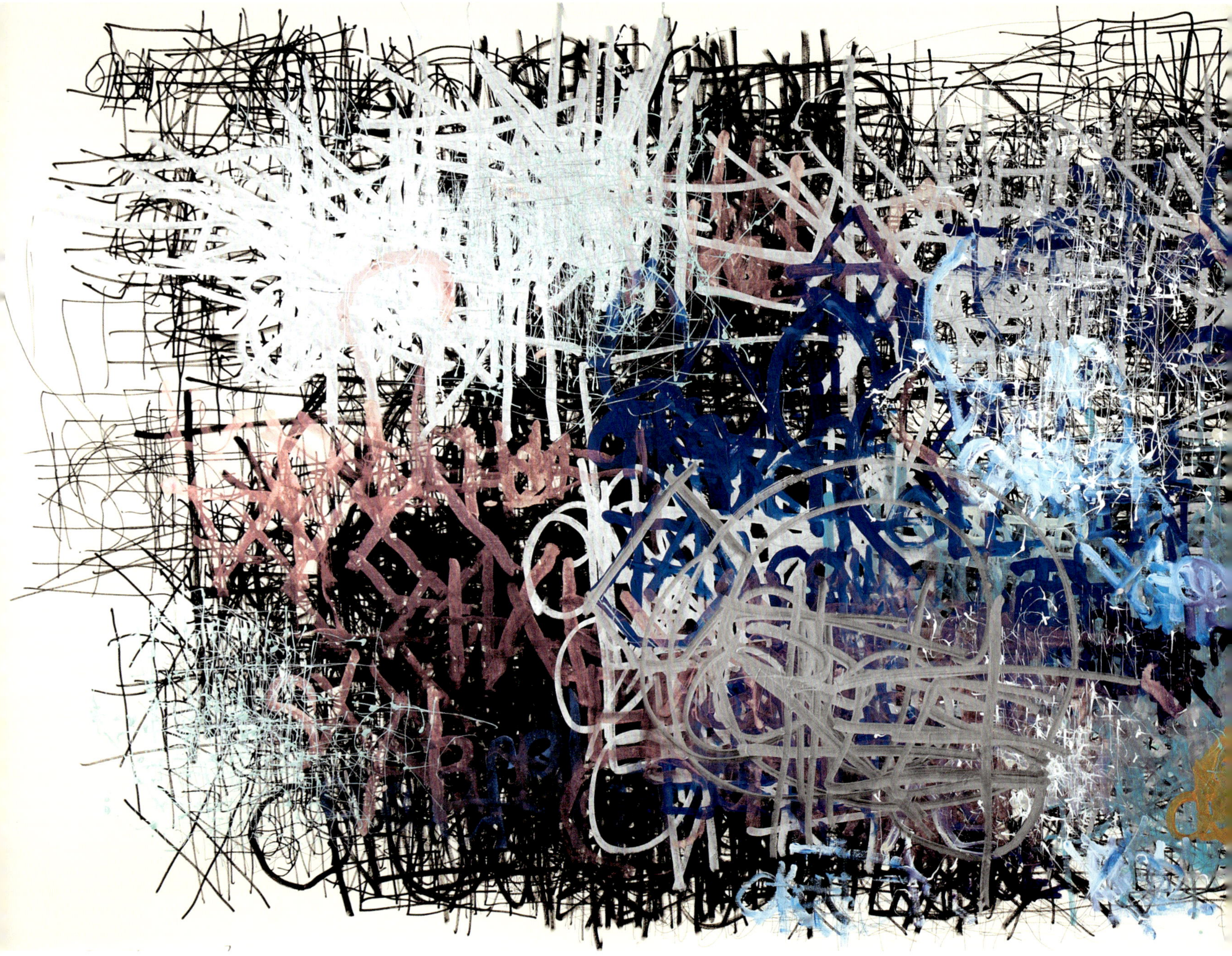

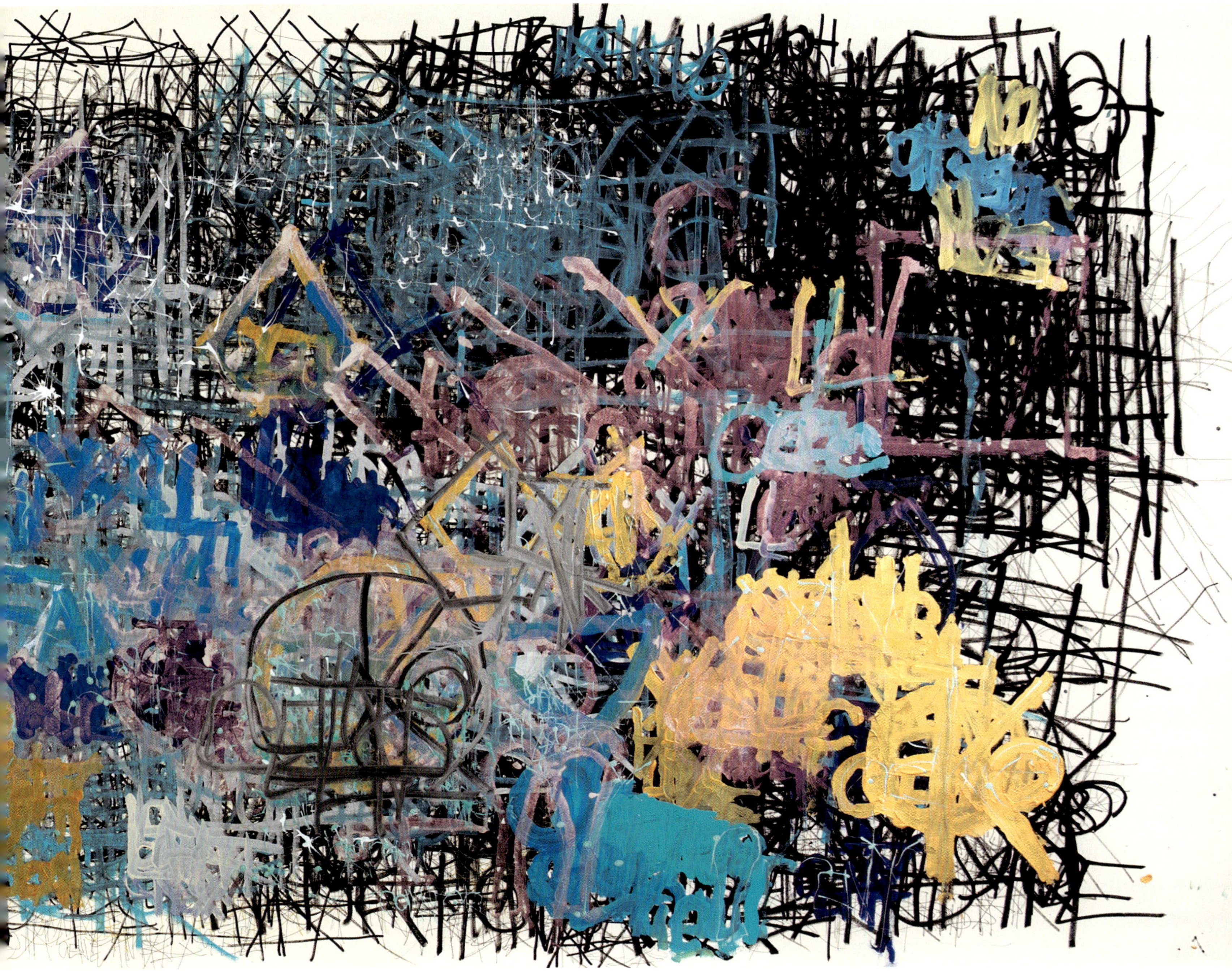

misunderstood, and inappropriately excluded from widespread art appreciation. She knew that what they were making was deeply personal, and that their practice was a critical vehicle for connecting with the people in their life and sharing the world as only they could. Margaret was resolute in her view that the art world's unattended blind spots and troubling array of presumptions revealed ignorance and required remedying; these artists needed and deserved champions. Her advocacy was, like that of other supporters mentioned throughout this text, of inestimable importance. Today, Doug carries this effort forward, working to support artists, preserve their art as well as their legacies at cultural institutions, and support the much-needed scholarship surrounding art that poses difficult questions and demands the time and resources of numerous researchers.

TIPPING THE BALANCE

As Catherine Morris keenly observed, biography is complicated. It requires great care to present nonmainstream artists, particularly those whose work has been under-documented or -collected and whose lives have been insufficiently researched—resulting too often in an overly narrow, "calcified" partial truth.[27] For younger or emerging artists, their stories must be heard and valued in tandem with the art they make. Among the most difficult questions in a large, collection-based exhibition is how to evenly represent the array of artists therein. The frustrating but honest answer is that we cannot. Not all of these artists had their works cared about or preserved equitably, and too many of them died without having their thoughts or insights preserved along with the images and objects they made. While artists including Castle, Dial, Ramírez, Scott, Traylor, and Yoakum have had major solo exhibitions and monographic publications dedicated to their lives and output, they are the exceptions in a pantheon of artists whose records are more commonly uneven, scant, or nonexistent. Sometimes, their identities were severed from the things they made and lost to the living world, marooning artworks as enigmatic artifacts.

Some art historians have asserted that artists like Blagdon, Miller, and Scott—artists whose projects utterly defy fine art conventions—did not view their own work as "art." Such presumptions, often emanating from entrenched mainstream perspectives, clip and constrain a more generous concept of "art," positioning it as a prescribed form of creativity instead of a personally defined practice or exploratory realm.[28] They undercut autonomous projects in which the generative act of creativity, the visual and physical stimuli of making images and objects, and outcomes that permeate the boundaries of daily life and intellectual intrigue define art and practice on entirely different frontiers. Awe and beauty played significant if ambiguous roles in Blagdon's art environment, and the artist was not alone in the conviction that spending time in the space alleviated pain.[29] Projects that redefine art practice and art object, as wide-ranging in result as the Blacks', Blagdon's, Butler's, and Finster's, reveal the need for a multiplicity of canons and more flexible means of measure.[30]

When interest in the art of nonmainstream artists began to grow exponentially in the early twentieth century, the spate of names and proposed frameworks casually attached to types of makers and their assigned niches failed to envision the magnitude of a diverse and expansive art world. Over time, the proposition that nonmainstream production could be reduced to a tidy category of Others was better understood as the foundation of an elitist canon meant to endure and exclude in perpetuity. In the late 1970s and early 1980s, collective events including a conference on folk art at the Winterthur Museum in Delaware, the *Black Folk Art in America* show, and a meeting at the American Folklife Center at the Library of Congress revealed a philosophical divide along disciplinary lines.[31] The labels for American self-taught artists flagged disagreements that were not merely semantic, but demanded a reckoning between outmoded models with valuable vestiges, and ways of encompassing living makers and personal experiences—as well as practices that inherently thwart standard categorization. Central to the battles of the late twentieth century were the folklorists' and cultural anthropologists' perspective that culture and context were foremost considerations, while curators and collectors prioritized visual intrigue and originality. A reconciliation of these concerns became key to a path forward.

Terms have nuance and meaning that is alternately as valuable, useless, or manipulative as the person who wields them. When "Outsider" was implemented as a double-edged category—both simplistic and strategic—ongoing "term warfare" continued to embody a battle that cut more deeply than mere word choices.[32] Outsider is, at the end of every day, a term that describes the artist, not the art—a euphemism for the identity politics of race, class, and social agency. As noted earlier in this volume, Arthur C. Danto has observed that being part of the art world has long required savvy in the "language game," and astutely warns that descriptive qualifiers unfailingly signal disparity.[33] Art historian Kenneth L. Ames agrees, noting that classification is a means of control that spans the gamut of useful, mischievous, and pernicious. When misused, "it reduces human complexity and diversity to a few oversimplifying words. It conceals authentic ambiguity and fluidity behind a rigid and reductionist mask. It dehumanizes."[34] Labels and meaningful context should never be conflated; the art should provoke interest in the artist's story, not the other way around.

Today, it is clear that experience, context, and individualized expressive modes can carry equal weight. And at a moment when museums are grappling with the full meaning and gravity of diversity and effecting allyship that is transformative rather than performative, varied voices and perspectives are key. Comprehensively, the artists in the Robson Family Collection have approached art as a means of existence, a tool for survival, and a testament of perspective and worth in a world that did not always make room for them. In 2019, *New York Times* art critic Roberta Smith wrote: "What made the 2010s the most thrilling of all the decades I've spent in the New York art world was the rising presence of black artists of every ilk, on every front: in museums, commercial galleries, art magazines, private collections and public commissions. During this exhilarating sea change new talent emerged, older talent was newly appreciated and the history of American art was suddenly up for grabs—and in dire need of rewriting."[35] Smith is not alone in her relish for the richness of cultural diversity, and has been ahead of her peers in demanding real change in our nation's art-historical narrative. The rise of Black American artists, both self-taught and professional, has demanded more honesty about a nation built on racial inequity, but that overlooks other frontiers of oppression, including the ongoing positioning of self-taught artists of all races as inferior to their trained counterparts, and ignoring compound inequities that reach across class, sex, ability, and other measures of dominant norms.

When two advocates who chose to remain unnamed acquired and donated James Hampton's *Throne of the Third Heaven* to SAAM, they effected meaningful change in addressing the fact that museums in the United States had, for too long, bought into and promoted a national narrative that was reductive and problematically biased. They became emblematic of the critical role collector-advocates played at a transitional moment when most museums were reluctant to expand a canon rooted in exclusion. Bert Hemphill became known as a pioneer, hailed by Howard Finster as a "collector of the lone and forgotten," and a great many collectors followed in his footsteps.[36] As noted in section two, collectors with greater social agency sometimes overshadowed the artists they supported, and today narratives juxtaposing empowered heroes with makers in need of rescue have been displaced by models aiming for greater balance, transparency, and respect.

Margaret Robson understood and honored personal journeys; her own road from a midwestern childhood of little means to the empowered circles of DC society surely inspired her to reflect deeply on the American Democratic Project—from its lofty ideals to its profound flaws. She not only valued the art and the artists, but also understood the need to push beyond simple frameworks for classifying makers and what they made. She traveled her own road, and as she reconciled herself within the universe, she increasingly valued the ways in which others did the same. Margaret recognized that in spite of the hope and freedom signaled in nostalgic works of Americana, "America" had never been a truly inclusive enterprise; too many of its citizens were not merely lone and forgotten—but oppressed and dehumanized. Margaret's path was often private, but much can be gleaned from the things she chose to live with. Over the years, her collection progressed from objects that wore the patina of a bygone age to things that revealed the stories and experience of a living maker. If her endeavor increasingly blurred the lines between art collecting and active empathy, her son has picked up where she left off.

When Margaret died in 2014, Doug grappled, as he has noted, with the art she left and the ways in which the images and objects with which she had surrounded herself and their family had, over time, impacted his worldview. Margaret certainly saw the tides shifting in her lifetime, but she did not live to see a day when flexing the Western canon in collections, exhibitions, and programming was an urgent social mandate for major institutions. Doug has worked to better understand the art, the artists, and the importance of advocacy and philanthropy. Today, he serves on the board of Creative Growth and is an active supporter of self-taught artists, particularly those from the Bay Area. His gift to SAAM continues with this project and will extend into an ongoing partnership with the Museum for advancing scholarship on underrecognized artists and their work, promoting empathy and transformative allyship in collecting and multivocal exhibition practices, and preserving and sharing artworks that evidence a paradigm of "many canons." Doug's gift of his mother's collection to SAAM in 2016 was the largest expansion of the Museum's folk art collection in twenty years, and, in tandem with works donated or promised in 2022 and the endowment of the Margaret Z. Robson Symposium Series, constitutes one of the most impactful outright gifts of art and program support in this area in SAAM's history.[37] For Doug, this project propelled his own drive to support a wide array of artists and be instrumental, as his mother had been, in tipping the balance of art-world representation toward a fuller, more authentic picture of our nation.

The artists explored in this exhibition and catalogue reveal the limitless range of humanity and perspective encompassed in the art of our time. The project underscores a heightened need not only to honor artists and their stories, but to relinquish top-level labels and the drawbacks that increasingly outweigh their use. Language and categories should describe—with care and specificity—artists and what they made, and employ relevant context to reveal the challenges and triumphs carried within the art. We must value varied ways of seeing and self-identifying and reject myopic views of America and Americans. *We Are Made of Stories* traces the historical rise of artists in the United States whose visions and actions embodied living change and charts some of the place- and era-specific hurdles along the road. It highlights the ways in which what we, as a society, see, value, and preserve ultimately becomes the visual text of an age, and how what we forget or leave out makes an equally indelible mark.

Each artist encompassed in this catalogue has earned an unrestricted place in the story of American art and paved the way for a future in which the boundaries of class and agency will become increasingly less apparent and defining. The historical moments, the framing receptions, and the marginalization most of the artists herein endured cannot be unwritten; these realities are indelible upon the individuals and the art they made. Journalist Heidi Stevens recently reflected on all that has changed since the long year of 2020, concluding, "More lenses get us closer to the truth. More lenses broaden and deepen our understanding of who we are and who we want to become; who has been heard and who has been harmed."[38] Artworks are lenses. Through them, we become more closely attuned to the makers and their journeys; they are experience distilled and offered as urgent communiqués, in the favored, if not only, language that the artist had. Collectively they lend us the ability to see more clearly who's been heard and who's been harmed, and to become connected with the most precious part of what makes us human. Significant societal change plays out over generations. From Bill Traylor—the earliest-born of the known artists in this project—to the two living artists, Laura Craig McNellis and Dan Miller, the power of art as a tool for change is evident. The determination of artists, hand in glove with the empathy and vision of their allies and advocates, has allowed us to witness, in this moment more than any before, a tide that has definitively changed.

NOTES

ROBSON FAMILY COLLECTION

(pp. 45–51)

1. I am grateful to Ruchi Mital for the phrase "we are made of stories," which inspired this exhibition title; it is drawn from her essay, "This World Is Not My Own: A Creative Treatment of Actuality," in *Really Free: The Radical Art of Nellie Mae Rowe*, ed. Katherine Jentleson, exh. cat. (Atlanta: High Museum of Art in partnership with DelMonico Books, 2021), 44. Mital's essay on Rowe accompanies a documentary film she has been working on, *This World Is Not My Own*, to be released in 2022. To learn more about the film and where you can see it, visit www.thisworldisnotmyown.com. Mital's essay is published in conjunction with a major exhibition, *Really Free: The Radical Art of Nellie Mae Rowe*, which opened at the High Museum of Art in 2021 and is scheduled to tour nationally.
2. Smithsonian Institution, "Statement from Secretary Lonnie G. Bunch," news release, May 31, 2020, https://www.si.edu/newsdesk/releases/statement-secretary-lonnie-g-bunch.
3. Bunch, "Statement from Secretary."
4. Bystanders awaiting the verdict of police officer Derek Chauvin in George Floyd Square, Minneapolis, gave comments to John Eligon, a *New York Times* correspondent covering race; oral testimonies included in Michael Barbaro's podcast, *The Daily (New York Times)*, "Guilty of All Charges," April 21, 2021, https://podcasts.apple.com/us/podcast/the-daily/id1200361736?i=1000518027800. On April 29, 1992, a jury acquitted four police officers of the assault on Rodney King, an African American from California. University of Southern California law professor Jody David Armour commented, "When the verdict came out, it was a stunner for people coast to coast. My jaw dropped. There was ocular proof of what happened. It seemed compelling," he says of the videotape. "And yet, we saw a verdict that told us we couldn't trust our lying eyes. That what we thought was open and shut was really 'a reasonable expression of police control' toward a black motorist." Rodney King survived but suffered permanent brain damage, and Los Angeles erupted in violent riots. See Karen Grigsby Bates, "When LA Erupted in Anger: A Look Back at the Rodney King Riots, NPR, April 26, 2017; https://www.npr.org/2017/04/26/524744989/when-la-erupted-in-anger-a-look-back-at-the-rodney-king-riots. A week after the guilty verdict was returned in the case against Chauvin, three white men in Georgia were indicted for federal hate crimes in the death of Ahmaud Arbery, an African American man who was shot to death while jogging in his South Atlanta neighborhood on February 23, 2020; Katie Benner and Will Wright, "3 Indicted on Federal Hate Crime Charges in Ahmaud Arbery Shooting," *New York Times*, April 28, 2021, https://www.nytimes.com/2021/04/28/us/politics/ahmaud-arbery-shooting.html.
5. Margaret Renkl, "The Picassos of the American South," *New York Times*, April 26, 2021, https://www.nytimes.com/2021/04/26/opinion/picasso-nashville-southern-art.html.
6. *Black Folk Art in America* toured to seven venues and elicited a sweeping rise of collectors, enthusiasts, and scholars. It is unclear where or at what point the Robsons saw the exhibition, nor is it even certain that they did. With the buzz the exhibition and publication made in folk art circles, however, it is probable that the event precipitated their purchase of an artwork by Bill Traylor in May 1983. *Black Folk Art* opened in Washington, DC, where the Robsons sometimes visited and may have seen it; in 1984 the exhibition traveled to Chicago, where they lived at the time. Another possibility is that the Robsons discovered Traylor's work prior to seeing the exhibition or catalogue, at the Carl Hammer Gallery in Chicago.
7. The National Gallery of Art announced the first addition of self-taught art (forty works) to their collection on December 28, 2020. The Metropolitan Museum of Art in New York announced the acquisition of fifty-seven works by self-taught artists on November 24, 2014, and organized its first exhibition drawn from this body of work in 2018. The Smithsonian American Art Museum acquired its first major work by a self-taught artist in 1970, *The Throne of the Third Heaven of the Nations' Millennium General Assembly*, by DC artist James Hampton (see figs. 1, 2, pp. 63, 64 in this volume). SAAM acquired over five hundred works by self-taught artists from the collection of Herbert Waide Hemphill Jr.in 1986, and today has one of the leading collections of this material of any institution. Other longtime, major art museum supporters include the High Museum of Art in Atlanta and the Milwaukee Art Museum.
8. The artists in *We Are Made of Stories* are discussed in the section in which they are most significant, in the context of the histories in which they are key. In many cases, an artist might be appropriately discussed in multiple sections; Bill Traylor, for example, was as much of a "gamechanger" as any, but his importance is still greater in the preceding narrative, "Becoming Visible."

MOMENTUM (pp. 53–65)

1. This is not meant to reduce either the empowered or the underclass to a homogenous entity but rather, to posit an overarching truth about who is heard and seen, and who is suppressed.
2. Only two artists featured in *We Are Made of Stories* are living, Dan Miller and Laura Craig McNellis; both have been impacted by art-world presumptions about disability.
3. Arthur C. Danto, "The Art World Revisited: Comedies of Similarity," in *Beyond the Brillo Box: The Visual Arts in Post-Historical Perspective* (New York: Farrar, Straus and Giroux, 1992), 46. See also Leslie Umberger, "Housewives, Witches, Beauty Queens, and Conjure Women: Locating the Practice of Self-Taught Women Artists," in *Boundary Trouble: The Self-Taught Artist and American Avant-Gardes*, ed. Lynne Cooke (New Haven, CT: Yale University Press, forthcoming).
4. For a concise history of untrained artists in Europe, see Jane Kallir, "Art Brut and 'Outsider' Art: A Changing Landscape," introduction to *Accidental Genius: Art from the Anthony Petullo Collection*, by Margaret Andera and Lisa Stone, exh. cat. (Milwaukee, WI: Milwaukee Art Museum in association with DelMonico Books, 2012), 23–27.
5. See "U.S. Immigration Timeline," History, updated April 20, 2021, https://www.history.com/topics/immigration/immigration-united-states-timeline; and "Colonial History of the United States," Wikipedia, updated June 26, 2021, https://en.wikipedia.org/wiki/Colonial_history_of_the_United_States.
6. Charles Sheeler, quoted in Wanda M. Corn, *The Great American Thing: Modern Art and National Identity, 1915–1935* (Berkeley: University of California Press, 1999), 319; originally cited in Constance Mayfield Rourke, *Charles Sheeler: Artist in the American Tradition* (New York: Harcourt, Brace, 1938), 183.
7. It is worth noting that a fair portion of the material culture being collected in the 1920s and 1930s had origins in trades and utility, and the names of the people who made things could have been lost long before these collectors began to celebrate them. Yet this was nonetheless an era in which the distinction between upper-class fine artists and any creative maker from the working class was stark, and almost all the folk artists whose names did remain associated with their art were white and male painters or sculptors. See also "Identities Once Known," in the section "Becoming Visible" in this volume, p. 69.
8. See also Umberger, "Housewives, Witches."
9. Other government art programs included the Public Works of Art Project (1933–34), the Department of the Treasury's Section of Painting and Sculpture (1934–42; renamed the Section of Fine Arts in 1938), and its Treasury Relief Art Project (1935–38); see Library of Congress, "New Deal Programs: Selected Library of Congress Resources: Federal Art Project," accessed April 29, 2021, accessed April 28, 2021, https://www.loc.gov/rr/program/bib/newdeal/fap.html. The Holger Cahill papers, 1910–1993, are held at the Smithsonian Archives of American Art, accessed April 28, 2021, https://www.aaa.si.edu/collections/holger-cahill-papers-6730. Records of the Works Progress Administration (renamed Work Projects Administration in 1939) are on file at the National Archives and Records Administration, August 15, 2016, https://www.archives.gov/research/guide-fed-records/groups/069.
10. Lynne Cooke, "Boundary Trouble: Navigating Margin and Mainstream," in *Outliers and American Vanguard Art*, by Lynne Cooke, et al., exh. cat. (Washington, DC: National Gallery of Art in association with University of Chicago Press, 2018), 9.
11. The exhibition was titled *Sculpture by William Edmondson* and opened at the Museum of Modern Art in New York in October 1937; https://www.moma.org/calendar/exhibitions/2094.
12. Katherine Jentleson, *Gatecrashers: The Rise of the Self-Taught Artist in America* (Oakland: University of California Press, 2020), 91; and Bridget R. Cooks, *Exhibiting Blackness: African Americans and the American Art Museum* (Amherst: University of Massachusetts Press, 2011), 30.
13. The Museum of Modern Art, "Sculpture by William Edmondson," press release, October 18, 1937, https://assets.moma.org/documents/moma_press-release_333062.pdf; and Jennifer Jane Marshall, "Find-and-Seek: Discovery Narratives, Americanization, and Other Tales of Genius in Modern American Folk Art," in Cooke et al., *Outliers and American Vanguard Art*, 59.
14. See Richard Meyer, "How to Make a Modern Primitive," in Cooke et al., *Outliers and American Vanguard Art*, 43–51.
15. Researching the responsibilities of individuals for various MoMA projects, Lynne Cooke found conflicting information on the curation of the show *Masters of Popular Painting* (1938). She concludes that Barr was its primary organizer, but that work was shared by Dorothy C. Miller, and Cahill, whom Barr credits, in his catalogue preface, for organizing the American section of it. See Cooke, "Boundary Trouble," 25n3. For a copy of MoMA's exhibition catalogue, *Masters of Popular Painting*, which includes Cahill's essay, see https://assets.moma.org/documents/moma_catalogue_2090_300061927.pdf?.
16. Jentleson, *Gatecrashers*, 91; and Cooks, *Exhibiting Blackness*, 30.

17. Jentleson and Cooke both note that Barr and Cahill were in agreement only to a degree, and that Barr preferred to promote "modern primitives" as an international phenomenon, whereas Cahill presented a nationalistic idea centered on American individualism and American Dream heroes. Jentleson, *Gatecrashers*, 12–13; and Cooke et al., *Outliers and American Vanguard Art*, 10–11.

18. Sidney Janis, *They Taught Themselves: American Primitive Painters of the 20th Century* (New York: Dial Press, 1942), 13.

19. Corn, *Great American Thing*, 326–27.

20. Herbert W. Hemphill Jr. and Julia Weissman, *Twentieth-Century American Folk Art and Artists* (New York: E. P. Dutton, 1974), 9–10.

21. This history is also detailed in Umberger, "Housewives, Witches."

22. Umberger, "Housewives, Witches."

23. All but a few pieces of Hampton's *Throne of the Third Heaven* are in the collection of the Smithsonian American Art Museum. A very small number of individual artworks from *The Throne* were purchased by collectors before patrons acquired and donated the full array to SAAM; several of these individual works are in the collection of the Milwaukee Art Museum.

24. SAAM uses the term Latinx as a gender-neutral and nonbinary alternative to Latina/Latino, and Chicanx as a similar alternative to Chicana/Chicano.

BECOMING VISIBLE (pp. 67–149)

1. Patricia Phillips Marshall and Jo Ramsay Leimenstoll, *Thomas Day: Master Craftsman and Free Man of Color* (Chapel Hill: University of North Carolina Press in association with the North Carolina Museum of History, 2010), esp. 1–2, 9. In Tim Barringer and Tom Flynn, eds., *Colonialism and the Object: Empire, Material Culture and the Museum* (New York: Routledge, 1998), essayist Rachel E. C. Layton points out that in cases such as Bentzon's, birth and situation placed him in an elite class of free Blacks known as "mustice"; Bentzon was the child of a white father and free "mulatto" mother and lived dually in Philadelphia and in a "free coloured" community on the Caribbean island of St. Croix; see https://www.smpub.com/ubb/images/18/Bentzon1-ocr.pdf.

2. At the time of this publication, Dave Drake's pottery survives as the earliest extant signed and dated expressive works by an enslaved artist. "Dave," sometimes given the objectifying sobriquet "Dave the Slave," had no last name during his enslavement. He adopted the name Drake as his own after Emancipation. Dave's first enslaver, Harry Drake, is believed to have taught some of those he enslaved to read and write, in hopes they could better learn the Bible. Harry Drake was unusual in this, as facilitating literacy for the enslaved was condemned throughout the South. Between 1841 and 1858, Dave stopped inscribing his vessels, perhaps because threatened uprisings on Georgia and Virginia plantations had heightened the peril of drawing attention to himself or his owner, as both could have been severely punished for such a breach. He began inscribing his pieces again around 1858, and the latest of these dates to 1864—at the height of the Civil War. The free Black artisans Peter Bentzon and Thomas Day are distinguished herein as craftsmen who earned their livings from skilled trades, rather than as artists that made personally driven, expressive artworks. For examples of their work, see National Museum of African American History and Culture, Smithsonian Institution, https://nmaahc.si.edu/object/nmaahc_2010.14; and NCpedia (North Carolina), https://www.ncpedia.org/biography/day-thomas.

3. Between 1740 and 1834, Alabama, Georgia, Louisiana, Mississippi, North and South Carolina, and Virginia all passed anti-literacy laws; see Janet Duitsman Cornelius, *When I Can Read My Title Clear: Literacy, Slavery, and Religion in the Antebellum South* (Columbia: University of South Carolina Press, 1991). For an in-depth discussion of conventional, institutionally backed Roman script literacy and a broader view of African American vernacular/visual literacy, see Grey Gundaker, "'Without Parse of Script': The Interaction of Conventional Literacy and Vernacular Practice in African American Expressive Culture" (PhD diss., Yale University, 1992).

4. SAAM acquired a major signed, dated, and poem-inscribed stoneware jar by Dave Drake in 2021, as this publication was in process; see https://americanart.si.edu/artwork/untitled-verse-jar-118734.

5. The curatorial team for *Striking Iron* was led by artist Tom Joyce, a MacArthur Fellow originally trained as a blacksmith, with cocurators Allen F. Roberts, UCLA Professor of World Arts and Cultures/Dance; Marla C. Berns, Shirley & Ralph Shapiro Director, Fowler Museum; William J. Dewey, director, African Studies Program, and associate professor of African Art History at Pennsylvania State University; and Henry J. Drewal, Evjue-Bascom Professor of Art History and Afro-American Studies at the University of Wisconsin–Madison; see https://africa.si.edu/exhibitions/current-exhibitions/striking-iron-the-art-of-african-blacksmiths/irons-empowering-roles/.

6. For more information on snakes and conjure culture in the American South, see Leslie Umberger, *Between Worlds: The Art of Bill Traylor*, exh. cat. (Washington, DC: Smithsonian American Art Museum in association with Princeton University Press, 2018), 147, 419n127. See also Donald J. Waters, "Snakes and Conjure Doctors,"

in *Strange Ways and Sweet Dreams: Afro-American Folklore from the Hampton Institute*, ed. Donald J. Waters (Boston: G. K. Hall, 1983), 297.

7. The makers of the snake-inspired artworks in the Robson collection are not identified, and may have been African American or European American, as snakes played a role in the lives of all, and making sculptures, toys, or canes from available materials was commonplace throughout rural America in the early twentieth century and prior. Snakes do play a prominent role in African American folklore and their forms are frequently evoked by self-taught artists.

8. The Victorian-era fashion for memory work stemmed from Queen Victoria's loss of her husband, Prince Albert, and her extended period of mourning that followed.

9. Robert Farris Thompson, *Flash of the Spirit: African and Afro-American Art and Philosophy* (New York: Vintage Books, 1983), 134. See also Robert Farris Thompson and Joseph Cornet, *The Four Moments of the Sun: Kongo Art in Two Worlds*, exh. cat. (Washington, DC: National Gallery of Art, 1981).

10. For additional examples of Traylor's many depictions of African Americans living, but not working, see Umberger, *Between Worlds,* plates 149 (p. 312), 150 and 151 (p. 313), and 169 (p. 327).

11. A young white artist in Montgomery, Jay Leavell, first saw Bill Traylor making pictures on the streets of Montgomery's Black Business District sometime in 1938; in 1939, Leavell introduced Traylor to John Lapsley and Charles Shannon, more established local white artists. These three men, along with other white artists in a liberal cohort self-named the New South, would save works by Bill Traylor and collectively be to thank for the survival of his art. The largest collection of Traylor's work was gathered by Charles Shannon and his first wife, Blanche Balzer Shannon, and he became possessive about the discovery narrative of Bill Traylor. Although segregated Montgomery society would have had no tolerance for imagery deemed critical of whites on any level, the members of the New South all would have been far more tolerant. Whether any members of this group did read Traylor's imagery as subversive is ultimately unknown, but no written or oral accounts given by New South artists indicate that any of them grasped Traylor's images as layered or coded; notes and accounts do evidence an appreciation of Traylor's style as unintentionally modern, and general understandings of the images as anecdotal, funny, and nostalgic, at least in part, for a rural past, during which Traylor's family labored in bondage and in poverty. See Umberger, *Between Worlds*, 88–96.

12. See note 3, in this section.

13. Edward M. Puchner, "'A Tried Stone': Community, Conversion, and Christ in the Sculpture of William Edmondson," in *Beholding Christ and Christianity in African American Art*, ed. James Romaine and Phoebe Wolfskill (University Park: Penn State University Press, 2017), 129.

14. Puchner, "'A Tried Stone,'" 129.

15. Robert Farris Thompson, "Edmondson's Art," in *The Art of William Edmondson*, by Robert Farris Thompson et al. (Nashville, TN: Cheekwood Museum of Art in partnership with the University Press of Mississippi, 1999), 11.

16. Puchner, "'A Tried Stone,'" 131, 133.

17. See Katherine Jentleson, *Gatecrashers: The Rise of the Self-Taught Artist in America* (Oakland: University of California Press, 2020), 93; and Bobby L. Lovett, "From Plantation to the City: William Edmondson and the African American Community," in Thompson et al., *Art of William Edmondson*, 24. See also Liz Hager, "Doin' the Lord's Work," Archive for Louise Dahl-Wolfe, March 11, 2009, https://venetianred.wordpress.com/tag/louise-dahl-wolfe/.

18. For a detailed account of Edmondson's relationship with prominent African Americans in Nashville, see Lovett, "From Plantation to the City." Kinshasha Holman Conwill has asserted that Black self-taught artists created a problematic situation for African American artists in that "training diminished desirability"; see Kinshasha Holman Conwill, "In Search of an 'Authentic' Vision: Decoding the Appeal of the Self-Taught African-American Artist," *American Art* 5, no. 4 (Autumn 1991): 7. Lowery Stokes Sims, scholar and former director at the Studio Museum in Harlem, has opined that the African American community believed self-taught artists thrived only with the support of the white art establishment; see Lowery Stokes Sims, "The Self-Taught among Us: William Edmondson and the Vanguardist Dilemma," in Thompson et al., *Art of William Edmondson*, 74; and Lowery Stokes Sims, "Bill Traylor and William Edmondson and the Challenges to African American Artists Between the World Wars," in *Bill Traylor, William Edmondson, and the Modernist Impulse*, ed. Josef Helfenstein (Urbana, IL: Krannert Art Museum and Kinkead Pavilion, 2004), 38. And Bridget R. Cooks has argued that southern, untrained Black artists were positioned as relics of antebellum America and used to counter positions of the midcentury American "New Negro"; see Bridget R. Cooks, "Bill Traylor in Context: African American Artists and Modern Primitives," in *Bill Traylor: Beyond the Figure, Symposium, American Folk Art Museum, New York, 2013*, ed. Valérie Rousseau (New York: American Folk Art Museum, forthcoming); and Bridget R. Cooks, *Exhibiting Blackness: African Americans and*

the *American Art Museum* (Amherst: University of Massachusetts Press, 2011), 27–30. Although a number of Black scholars and artists have contended that Black self-taught artists were pawns in an art-world game, it is important to note that the Black art establishment was not and is not a single entity of like-minded individuals.

19. Puchner, "'A Tried Stone,'" 127. Puchner cites Romare Bearden and Harry Henderson, *A History of African-American Artists: From 1792 to the Present* (New York: Pantheon Books, 1993), 351–54. Bearden and Henderson asserted that Edmondson's stories "simply conform to the southern stereotypes of the ignorant, superstitiously religious black man" (p. 353). Bearden died in 1988 before the collection of essays could be published; Henderson finished the project and published their book, with the aid of Bearden's estate, in 1993. The essays are not individually dated.

20. Katherine Jentleson conducted extensive research on the support networks of William Edmondson and Horace Pippin, and produced a chart that visually manifests these connections. She notes that African American scholars Alain Locke (*The Negro in Art*, 1940) and James A. Porter (*Modern Negro Art*, 1943) both wrote about Edmondson and his art, and that Edmondson was featured in exhibitions on Black American artists including one at New York's Downtown Gallery (1941), and an exhibition at the Newark Museum (1944); see Jentleson, *Gatecrashers*, 79, 95–96. Jentleson and Charles Russell have both pointed out that Locke still confined Edmondson and other self-taught African American artists to a subcategory of primitive/folk artists, and Jentleson notes that Porter included Edmondson in his 1943 book, but used undermining language to discuss his work; see also Charles Russell, "On the Absence and Presence of Bill Traylor in Euro-American and African American Modernist Thought" (paper presented at Bill Traylor: Beyond the Figure, American Folk Art Museum, New York, September 16, 2013).

21. John Michael Vlach, "From Gravestone to Miracle: Traditional Perspective and the Work of William Edmondson," in *By the Work of Their Hands: Studies in Afro-American Folklife* (Charlottesville: University Press of Virginia, 1991), 109–26. See also Jennifer Jane Marshall, "Nashville, New York, Paris, and Nashville: William Edmondson, Mobilized and Unmoved," *American Art* 31, no. 2 (Summer 2017): 69–76. Marshall is a professor of art history at the University of Minnesota; she is currently working on a book on William Edmondson.

22. Puchner, "'A Tried Stone,'" 129.

23. Stacy Morgan, "Clementine Hunter and Melrose Plantation," *American Art* 19, no. 1 (Spring 2005): 25–27, https://doi.org/10.1086.429972. According to Morgan, "From the time her [Hunter's] family moved to Melrose around the turn of the century until the late 1920s, she worked in the plantation's cotton fields and pecan groves; later she assumed full-time domestic work as its primary cook, maid, and laundress."

24. Art Shiver and Tom Whitehead discuss the history and names of the buildings at Melrose in *Clementine Hunter: Her Life and Art* (Baton Rouge: Louisiana State University Press, 2013). Tuliza Fleming, curator of American art at the Smithsonian's National Museum of African American History and Culture, notes that the "so-called African House" was "so named because it was thought to have Congolese origins to its design (when actually it traced to the French)." Fleming, quoted in Roger Catlin, "Self-Taught Artist Clementine Hunter Painted the Bold Hues of Southern Life," *Smithsonian Magazine*, October 18, 2018, https://www.smithsonianmag.com/smithsonian-institution/self-taught-artist-clementine-hunter-painted-bold-hues-southern-life-180970572/.

25. Shiver and Whitehead, *Clementine Hunter*, 30–45. The authors reveal that François Mignon lived much of his life under a false identity; nevertheless, it was he who had promoted Hunter and her work, and narrated tales—a mixture of truth and fiction—about both Hunter and Melrose, which contributed greatly to the reputation of both. Mignon organized the first exhibition of Hunter's work in African House for a group of visiting African American teachers, in 1949. The authors also credit James Pipes Register, who met Mignon and Hunter at Melrose, as working with Mignon to promote Hunter's career.

26. Lee Kogan, quoted in Shiver and Whitehead, *Clementine Hunter*, 45; originally from Lee Kogan, "Clementine Hunter: Self-Taught Louisiana Artist," in *Louisiana Women: Their Lives and Times*, ed. Janet Allured and Judith F. Gentry (Athens: University of Georgia Press, 2009), 175–94.

27. Shiver and Whitehead, "The African House Murals," in *Clementine Hunter*, 68–75.

28. For additional notes on Hunter's Melrose Plantation murals, see "Clementine Hunter Murals," Louisiana State Museum, accessed April 28, 2021, https://www.crt.state.la.us/louisiana-state-museum/exhibits/clementine-hunter-murals; and "Portfolio: Clementine Hunter African House Murals," South Writ Large, accessed April 28, 2021, https://southwritlarge.com/articles/portfolio-murals/.

29. Alice Rae Yelen, "The Setting, the South," in *Passionate Visions of the American South: Self-Taught Artists from 1940 to the Present* (New Orleans, LA: New Orleans Museum of Art Museum, 1993), 45–53.

30. Elaine Y. Yau, email message to author, July 19, 2021. Yau, curator at the UC Berkeley Art Museum and Pacific Film Archive, has researched and written on Clementine Hunter. For additional information on Marie Thérèse Coincoin (1742–1816), see Elizabeth Shown Mills, "Demythicizing History: Marie Thérèse Coincoin, Tourism, and the National Historical Landmarks Program," *Louisiana History: The Journal of the Louisiana Historical Association* 53, no. 4 (2012): 402–37, https://www.jstor.org/stable/24396547.

31. Alice Rae Yelen, "Daily Life," in Yelen, *Passionate Visions,* 95; and Yau, email.

32. Nick Sacco, "Louisiana's 'Uncle Jack' Statue and the Problem of Interpreting Iconography in History Museums," *Exploring the Past* (blog), October 1, 2015, https://pastexplore.wordpress.com/2015/10/01/louisianas-uncle-jack. See also "Uncle Jack," The Historical Marker Database, September 6, 2015, https://www.hmdb.org/m.asp?m=88234.

33. Sacco, "Louisiana's 'Uncle Jack' Statue."

34. The recovered sculpture was put in storage until Jo Bryan Ducournau, daughter of the man who funded its creation, eventually found a home for it, in 1974, at the Louisiana State University Rural Life Museum, where it remains today. See also Sacco, "Louisiana's 'Uncle Jack' Statue."

35. General information on David Butler is drawn from Leslie Umberger et al., *Sublime Spaces & Visionary Worlds: Built Environments of Vernacular Artists* (New York: Princeton Architectural Press, 2007), 189–201; William A. Fagaly, *David Butler*, exh. cat. (New Orleans, LA: New Orleans Museum of Art, 1976); and David Butler, untitled artist's statement, 1983, reproduced in *It'll Come True: Eleven Artists, First and Last* (Lafayette, LA: Artists' Alliance, 1992).

36. For more information about yard shows, see Dallas Museum of Art, *Black Art, Ancestral Legacy: The African Impulse in African-American Art* (Dallas, TX: Dallas Museum of Art, 1989); Thompson, *Flash of the Spirit*; Thompson and Cornet, *Four Moments of the Sun*; Gundaker, "'Without Parse of Script'"; and Theophus H. Smith, *Conjuring Culture: Biblical Formations of Black America* (New York: Oxford University Press, 1994).

37. Richard Gasperi, cited in Umberger et al., *Sublime Spaces & Visionary Worlds*, 192 (letter to Leslie Umberger and Jane Bianco, December 6, 2005, on file in the John Michael Kohler Arts Center Artist Archives, and interviewed in *The Magic of David Butler*, a documentary film on David Butler, produced by Rancy Boyd-Snee, 1985; https://www.aaa.si.edu/collections/magic-david-butler-director-writer-producer-rancy-boydsnee-7217). *Untitled (Reindeer)* and *Untitled (Three Wise Men and a Goat)* are in keeping with Butler's "window screen" forms and were acquired by John and Margaret Robson via Richard Gasperi but have not been identified in the extant images of the Butler property. Butler's window screens were often larger, rectangular pieces, but some slimmer panels, such as these, interspersed the top and bottom panels. Butler expert and former New Orleans Museum of Art curator William A. Fagaly notes that these pieces may have been repainted (by Butler or by an unknown party) at a later date; phone call with author, January 18, 2021.

38. Gasperi, cited in Umberger et al., *Sublime Spaces & Visionary Worlds*, 192. See also Fagaly, *David Butler*; and William A. Fagaly, interview by Leslie Umberger, November 8, 2005, conducted in conjunction with *Sublime Spaces & Visionary Worlds*; on file in the John Michael Kohler Arts Center Artist Archives. (Additional citation for this is in Umberger et al., *Sublime Spaces & Visionary Worlds*, 200n9.)

39. In the era when Butler drew widespread notice, his yard show/art environment was little understood as a cohesive entity by collectors, and the individual artworks spread far and wide during Butler's remaining years and after his death. Today, the connectivity of the artworks and the power they lend one another is more commonly apprehended, and the strongest collections of Butler's work show his pieces in groups, often accompanied by images from the original site. Many have argued that, given the heat and intense weather where Butler's environment was made, his painted metal pieces would have deteriorated beyond survival if they had remained in situ, and many of the surviving works indeed show extreme fading, peeling, and loss of paint and added embellishments. Butler's story is complex and cautionary and demands careful consideration, not only of Butler's artistic vision, but of the cultural time and place in which it existed. The three Butler works in the Robson collection were acquired on the secondary market in 1998 and 2003 and join six others in the SAAM collection.

40. For further information on the theme of creative play in Hawkins's art, see Susan Mitchell Crawley, "The Ecstatic Play of William Hawkins," in *William L. Hawkins: An Imaginative Geography*, ed. Susan Mitchell Crawley (Milan: Skira, 2018), 21–32.

41. Records showing the year of birth for Joseph Elmer Yoakum (spelled Yocum at birth) are unclear; in recent research conducted for a major exhibition organized by the Art Institute of Chicago, Emily Olek concludes that 1891 is the most likely. See Emily Olek, "The Fantastical Reality of Joseph Yoakum: A Chronology," in *Joseph E.Yoakum: What I Saw*, ed. Mark Pascale, Esther Adler, and Édouard Kopp, exh. cat. (Chicago: Art Institute of Chicago, 2021), 28–33.

42. Olek, "Fantastical Reality."

43. Multiple sources explore Yoakum's art and identity, the most recent and deeply researched being Pascale, Adler, and Kopp, *Joseph E. Yoakum*. Other sources include Derrel B. DePasse, *Traveling the Rainbow: The Life and Art of Joseph E. Yoakum* (Jackson: University Press of Mississippi in conjunction with the Museum of American Folk Art, 2001); Nancy Thebaut, Christina Ramberg, and Norman Mark, *Joseph Elmer Yoakum*, exh. cat. (New York: Venus Over Manhattan Gallery, 2019); and an authoritative but unpublished manuscript by Whitney Halstead, "Joseph E. Yoakum," ca. 1977, located in the Whitney Halstead Papers, Art Institute of Chicago, AIC Archives 4809-0000, Box One, 1977.

44. Pascale writes: "In 1962 a seventy-one-year-old veteran has a dream that inspires him to draw every day for the rest of his life. His storefront apartment on Chicago's South Side doubles as his studio—a world away from galleries popping up in gentrifying neighborhoods across the city, the flourishing Black Arts Movement, and a new museum dedicated to contemporary art and artists. Then, in 1967, a chance encounter leads to his first exhibition, and soon after he gains gallery representation, begins selling work and meeting Chicago artists, and eventually has work acquired by major museums in Chicago and New York—all within the span of five years." Mark Pascale, "Revisiting Joseph E. Yoakum's Chicago Legacy," in Pascale, Adler, and Kopp, *Joseph E. Yoakum*, 16. Pascale details the chain of events and people involved in the aforementioned chapter, pp. 16–23.

45. Pascale, "Revisiting Joseph E. Yoakum's Chicago Legacy," 17. I attended the School of the Art Institute of Chicago as an undergraduate from 1985 to 1990, a point at which Helen Gardner (1878–1946) still loomed large; her book *Art Through the Ages* was the standard for comprehensive art history, and the outlook that she, Blackshear, Halstead, and by then a cohort of professors instilled in students was grounded in a reverence for the unconventional, "trash-treasures," and the validity of all points of view.

46. Pascale, "Revisiting Joseph E. Yoakum's Chicago Legacy," 23.

47. Thebaut, Ramberg, and Mark, *Joseph Elmer Yoakum*, 14–15.

48. Yoakum described his work as "a spiritual unfoldment" to journalist Norman Mark, who used the quote in the title of his article "My Drawings Are a Spiritual Unfoldment," *Panorama—Chicago Daily News*, November 11, 1967. Esther Adler explores Yoakum's spirituality, particularly that statement and how it relates to the foundational text of Christian Science, and how that theology may be reflected in Yoakum's landscapes. Esther Adler, "Unfolding Joseph E. Yoakum: Christian Science and Life on the South Side," in Pascale, Adler, and Kopp, *Joseph E. Yoakum,* 45–57.

49. Adler, "Unfolding," 50.

50. Elijah Pierce married Zetta Palm while still living in Baldwyn; about a year into their marriage, she died in childbirth; see Columbus State Community College, "Biography: Elijah Pierce," accessed April 28, 2021, https://www.cscc.edu /elijahpierce /bio.htm. Nancy Ireson, "'Your Life Is a Book, and Every Day Is a Page': Elijah Pierce's Storytelling," in *Elijah Pierce's America*, ed. Nancy Ireson and Zoé Whitley, exh. cat. (Philadelphia: Barnes Foundation in association with Paul Holberton, 2020), 24.

51. Jeffrey Wolf, "Elijah Pierce: An American Journey," Folk Art Society of America, accessed March 3, 2021, https://folkart.org /mag/elijah-pierce-american-journey. The elephant figure that Wolf photographed Pierce carving and had this recollection about was acquired by Margaret Z. Robson and is part of the Margaret Z. Robson Collection at SAAM.

52. Wolf, "Elijah Pierce." Jeffrey Wolf and Jeany Nisenholz Wolf hold a personal archive of photographs, films, and records on Elijah Pierce.

53. Betsa Marsh, "The Woodcarver of Long Street," *Columbus Monthly* (June 1975): 55.

54. Ireson, "'Your Life Is a Book,'" 24.

55. In 2020, Nancy Ireson and Zoé Whitley cocurated *Elijah Pierce's America* for the Barnes Foundation in Philadelphia; the accompanying catalogue (see note 50 in this section) provides more information on Pierce's *Book of Wood*. See also Michael D. Hall, ed., *Legacy in Wood: Elijah Pierce at the Columbus Museum of Art* (Columbus, OH: Columbus Museum of Art, 2013).

56. Ireson, "'Your Life Is a Book,'" 26. Cornelia Pierce was Elijah's second wife and was instrumental in his project. Cornelia died in 1943, and in 1953 Pierce married his third and final wife, Estelle Greene, who also became dedicated to helping Pierce promote his work.

57. Michael D. Hall, "The Pierce Effect: One Artist's Impact on Museum Practice in Columbus, Ohio," in Ireson and Whitley, *Elijah Pierce's America*, 15. Hall details the magnitude of Pierce's effect on the Columbus Museum of Art and, by extension, the larger sphere of American art history. The Columbus Museum organized the first retrospective of Pierce's work in 1993: *Elijah Pierce: Woodcarver.*

58. Sampada Aranke, "Written in the Wood: Black Life Made Visible," in Ireson and Whitley, *Elijah Pierce's America*, 34. In 1982, Pierce also was featured in a solo exhibition, *Elijah Pierce: Messages in Wood*, at the Smithsonian American Art Museum's Renwick Gallery; that same year the National Endowment for the Arts awarded him a National Heritage Fellowship.

59. Proverbs 18:16, "Your gifts will make room for you and bring you into the presence of great people" is an often-quoted biblical passage, discussed by AME bishop Vashti Murphy McKenzie on the PBS series *The Black Church*, 2021, https://www.pbs.org/show/black-church/.

60. Hawkins identified as mixed race, claiming to have Black, Native American, and white European ancestry.

61. Barbara R. Nicholson and Deidre Hamlar, "Roads Diverged: William L. Hawkins and Elijah Pierce in Columbus," in Crawley, *William L. Hawkins,* 50. Nicholson and Hamlar cite Gary J. Schwindler, "William L. Hawkins: A Biography" (unpublished manuscript, after 1990), 77, William Hawkins Collection, Ohio History Connection Archives, Columbus.

62. Jenifer P. Borum, "The Golden Book of William Hawkins," in Crawley, *William L. Hawkins,* 59. Schwindler, a contributor to this same volume, is a Hawkins biographer who conducted and compiled audio interviews with the artist from 1987 to 1989 and has written an unpublished book-length study of the artist's life, which is on file in the William Hawkins Collection of the Ohio State University.

63. Crawley, "Ecstatic Play," 32.

64. In 1983, Ricco-Johnson Gallery in New York began representing Hawkins, who gained increasing notice thereafter. Gary J. Schwindler, "Popular Images—Personal Visions: The Art of William Hawkins," in Crawley, *William L. Hawkins,* 13–14.

65. Nicholson and Hamlar, "Roads Diverged," 49. Barbara R. Nicholson was executive director of the King Arts Complex in Columbus, Ohio, and served on the District of Columbia Commission on the Arts & Humanities; Deidre Hamlar has been an arts advocate, lawyer, curator, and educator for over thirty years.

66. Nicholson and Hamlar, "Roads Diverged," 49–55. Hawkins and Pierce met when Garrett invited Roger Ricco, of New York's Ricco/Maresca Gallery, to come to Columbus to meet them both. They met at Pierce's barbershop gallery, but, by all accounts, the meeting was tense, as Hawkins was wary of competition; Nicholson and Hamlar, "Roads Diverged," 53–54.

67. Michael Noland notes that the impact these artists had on his own trajectory was inestimable. Noland, interview with Nannette Maciejunes, November 2, 2017, cited in Nicholson and Hamlar, "Roads Diverged," 55n31.

68. Inez Nathaniel-Walker has remained less recognized than the other women artists mentioned herein, perhaps because, for her, the challenges of being an undereducated Black woman were exacerbated by being imprisoned for manslaughter in the death of an abusive man in her life. Although her work is not represented in the Robson Family Collection, she is represented in the SAAM collection by four artworks; see https://americanart.si.edu/artist/inez-nathaniel-walker-3497.

69. See also Leslie Umberger, "Housewives, Witches, Beauty Queens, and Conjure Women: Locating the Practice of Self-Taught Women Artists," in *Boundary Trouble: The Self-Taught Artist and American Avant-Gardes*, ed. Lynne Cooke (New Haven, CT: Yale University Press, forthcoming).

70. Book-length discussions of Black, female, self-taught artists have increased since 2000, but few existed before then. A slender volume, *Minnie Evans: Artist* (Charles M. Lovell and Erwin Hester, eds.) was published by the Wellington B. Gray Gallery at East Carolina University in 1993; the Morris Museum of Art in Augusta, Georgia, published a fifty-five-page book of essays, *Nellie Mae Rowe* (J. Richard Gruber, ed.) in 1996; and Lee Kogan's exhibition catalogue *The Art of Nellie Mae Rowe: Ninety-Nine and a Half Won't Do* was published by the American Folk Art Museum in 1998. For the present publication, I am indebted to Katherine Jentleson's 2021 exhibition catalogue, *Really Free: The Radical Art of Nellie Mae Rowe*, and Elaine Y. Yau's dissertation on Sister Gertrude Morgan, "Acts of Conversion: Sister Gertrude Morgan and the Sensation of Black Folk Art, 1960–1982" (University of California, Berkeley, 2015), https://escholarship.org/uc/item/3f5660xh.

71. Ruchi Mital, "This World Is Not My Own: A Creative Treatment of Actuality," in *Really Free: The Radical Art of Nellie Mae Rowe*, ed. Katherine Jentleson, exh. cat. (Atlanta: High Museum of Art in partnership with DelMonico Books, 2021), 44. Speaking about her current film project on Nellie Mae Rowe, Mital notes: "In our documentary, we don't seek to determine what year she was really born. We don't interrogate family members to a consensus nor put the census record on the screen to expose or belie Nellie Mae Rowe's self-proclaimed birthday. That's history as a timeline." Her film, *This World Is Not My Own,* will be released in 2022; see https://thisworldisnotmyown.com/.

72. Katherine Jentleson, "Born on the Fourth of July," in Jentleson, *Really Free,* 17; Jentleson discusses the historical timeline of Rowe's life and practice throughout her essay, and confirmed in personal correspondence with

the author that, while Rowe made art far earlier, it seemed to be following the deaths of her last employers in 1968–69 that she stopped working for pay and became entirely self-directed.

73. The Civil Rights Act of 1964 prohibited discrimination in public accommodations, facilities, schools, and in federally funded projects; the Civil Rights Act of 1968 prohibited discrimination in the rental or sale of housing. Jentleson points to Chisholm's work as a likely source of inspiration for Rowe. Shirley (St. Hill) Chisholm (1924–2005) was of Guyanese and Bajan descent; she served as the congresswoman of the 12th District of New York, and, because of her family roots in Barbados and her time studying there as a girl, she considered herself a Barbadian American; see Barbara Winslow, *Shirley Chisholm: Catalyst for Change* (New York: Routledge, 2018), 5.

74. Jentleson, "Born on the Fourth of July," 15; Rowe said, "This is the talent he gave me, and I have to use it." Jentleson cites the original source as Linda Connelly Armstrong, dir., *Nellie's Playhouse* (Memphis, TN: Center for Southern Folklore, 1983), 7:19, a film that features rare recordings of Rowe working, speaking, and singing while working on her yard environment.

75. Rowe, quoted in William Arnett, "Nellie Mae Rowe: Inside the Perimeter," in *Souls Grown Deep: African American Vernacular Art of the South,* vol. 1, *The Tree Gave the Dove a Leaf*, ed. William Arnett and Paul Arnett (Atlanta: Tinwood Books, 2000), 293. Arnett notes that the quotations from Nellie Mae Rowe in his essay were drawn from interviews conducted by Maude Southwell Wahlman and Judith Alexander in 1981 and 1982, respectively. Writer and art collector William Arnett (1939–2020) founded the nonprofit Souls Grown Deep Foundation in 2010.

76. Jentleson, "Born on the Fourth of July," 17. Susan Mitchell Crawley also discusses the nature of play as a serious component of art rooted in self-preservation and pride in Crawley, "Ecstatic Play," 20–39.

77. The first photographs showing Rowe's property as a site of transformation date to 1971; Jentleson, "Born on the Fourth of July," 21.

78. Kinshasha Holman Conwill, "Something That Hasn't Been Born Yet: Nellie Mae Rowe and the Southern Imagination," introduction to Kogan, *Art of Nellie Mae Rowe,* 11; Conwill quotes Houston A. Baker Jr., *Blues, Ideology, and Afro-American Literature: A Vernacular Theory* (Chicago: University of Chicago Press, 1984), 2. Conwill, a native of Atlanta, Georgia, was director of the Studio Museum in Harlem from 1988 to 1999; today she serves as the deputy director of the Smithsonian's National Museum of African American History and Culture in Washington, DC.

79. Rowe, quoted in Arnett, "Nellie Mae Rowe: Inside the Perimeter," 1:296–97.

80. Cathy Yarbrough, "All I Got Out There Is Junk," *Atlanta Constitution*, May 13, 1973.

81. Jentleson concludes that Hemphill must have purchased work at this time, as he loaned several artworks to the exhibition *Missing Pieces: Georgia Folk Art, 1770–1976*; Jentleson, "Born on the Fourth of July," 39n40.

82. Arnett, "Nellie Mae Rowe: Inside the Perimeter," 1:297.

83. Jentleson, "Born on the Fourth of July," 35.

84. Jentleson discussed this reciprocity in an online gallery talk at the High Museum of Art, August 19, 2021, https://youtu.be/TnySTGrOkSA; she has also discussed their relationship in Jentleson, "Born on the Fourth of July," 35.

85. Rowe died in the fall of 1982. Jentleson notes that the things Rowe lived to enjoy that year included receiving the Jubilee Award, which celebrated contributions to Black culture in Atlanta; seeing her artwork featured in one-woman shows at both the world's fair in Knoxville, Tennessee, and at Spelman College; and being included in *Black Folk Art in America, 1930–1980* at the Corcoran Gallery of Art. Rowe experienced the Spelman show firsthand, but she was not well enough to travel to Washington, DC, for *Black Folk Art*, nor to accept the invitation of First Lady Nancy Reagan to design that year's White House Christmas card. Jentleson, "Born on the Fourth of July," 41, cites Catherine Fox, "Renown Came Late in Life for Gifted Folk Artist," *Atlanta Journal-Constitution*, October 24, 1982.

86. William A. Fagaly, "Chronology," in William A. Fagaly, Jason Berry, and Helen M. Shannon, *Tools of Her Ministry: The Art of Sister Gertrude Morgan* (New York: American Folk Art Museum; Rizzoli International, 2004), 95–97.

87. Morgan, quoted in Fagaly, Berry, and Shannon, *Tools of Her Ministry*, 12. Fagaly notes the artwork referred to with this text is called *DR JESUS AND HIS NURS*, collection of Rod McKuen.

88. Fagaly, Berry, and Shannon, *Tools of Her Ministry*, 18. See also Elaine Y. Yau, "Acts of Conversion: Sanctification and the Senses of Race in the Art of Sister Gertrude Morgan," in *Sensational Religion: Sensory Cultures in Material Practice*, ed. Sally M. Promey (New Haven, CT: Yale University Press, 2014), 403–12.

89. Yau, email.

90. The text here appears as written in Morgan's letter, dated September 6, 1972; cited in Fagaly, Berry, and Shannon, *Tools of Her Ministry*, 18.

91. Fagaly, quoted in Michael Kimmelman, "With an Ear for God and an Eye for Art," Art Review, *New York Times*, February 27, 2004, https://www.nytimes.com/2004/02/27/arts/art-review-with-an-ear-for-god-and-an-eye-for-art.html.

92. Elaine Y. Yau, "The Love in Labor: Reconsidering Amateurism in Sister Gertrude Morgan's Performances and Paintings," *Panorama: Journal of the Association of Historians of American Art* 5, no. 1 (Spring 2019), https://doi.org/10.24926/24716839.1684. For a more in-depth discussion of Sister Gertrude Morgan's artistic practice and cultural milieu, see Yau, "Acts of Conversion"; and Elaine Y. Yau, "Sister Gertrude Morgan and the Materials of Visionary Art," in *Beholding Christ and Christianity in African American Art*, ed. James Romaine and Phoebe Wolfskill (University Park: Penn State University Press, 2017), 113–24.

93. Yau, "Love in Labor."

94. Yau, "Love in Labor."

95. Ben Ratliff, "Critic's Choice: Singing with Power, Citing the Bible," *New York Times*, August 2, 2004, https://www.nytimes.com/2004/08/02/arts/critic-s-choice-jazz-cd-s-singing-with-power-citing-the-bible.html.

96. Kimmelman, "With an Ear for God."

97. Fagaly, Berry, and Shannon, *Tools of Her Ministry*, 26; and Yau, "Acts of Conversion," 81n254.

98. Yau, email.

99. General facts on Doyle's life and art are drawn from Gordon W. Bailey, multiple sources: "Sam Doyle," in *The Hidden Art: 20th- & 21st-Century Self-Taught Artists from the Audrey B. Heckler Collection*, by Valérie Rousseau (New York: Skira Rizzoli in association with the American Folk Art Museum, 2017), 182–85; "Sam Doyle," in *The New Encyclopedia of Southern Culture*, ed. Carol Crown, Cheryl Rivers, and Charles Reagan Wilson, vol. 23, *Folk Art* (Chapel Hill: University of North Carolina Press, 2013), 264–66; "Sam Doyle: Haints and Saints," *Raw Vision* 61 (Winter 2007): 29–35; "Sam Doyle: Heart and Soul," *New Orleans Museum of Art (NOMA) Arts Quarterly*, 23 (2001): 11; and "Sam Doyle: A Biographical Essay," 2013, http://selftaughtgenius.org/reads/sam-doyle-a-biographical-essay. See also Regenia Perry, "Sam Doyle, St. Helena Island's Native Son," *Raw Vision* 23 (Summer 1998), 28–35, and Joseph E. Holloway, "A Biography of Sam Doyle," The Slave Rebellion, accessed January 29, 2022, http://slaverebellion.info/index.php?page=a-biography-of-sam-doyle.

100. Bailey, "Sam Doyle: A Biographical Essay."

101. For a number of years, Doyle worked in the laundry at the Marine Corps Recruit Training Depot on nearby Parris Island. Bailey notes that Doyle was deemed "unfit" for service in the Second World War due to a childhood foot injury, a matter that dispirited him; Bailey, "Sam Doyle: Haints and Saints," 33, and ibid.

102. Bailey, "Sam Doyle: Haints and Saints," 35.

103. Sam Doyle, quoted in Bailey, "Sam Doyle: A Biographical Essay," and Lynne E. Spriggs, *Local Heroes: Paintings and Sculpture by Sam Doyle* (Atlanta: High Museum of Art, 2000), 25. Spriggs draws on an audio interview Barbara Archer conducted with Doyle, recorded on St. Helena in August and September of 1985.

104. See Clarence Major, ed., *Juba to Jive: A Dictionary of African-American Slang* (New York: Puffin, 1994, reprint ed.).

105. Gordon W. Bailey has theorized that Doyle's painting may have been inspired by the trailblazing Harlem Renaissance–era singer Gladys Bentley (1907–1960), who performed in male attire and pushed the boundaries of gender conformity in her day; email to author, January 27, 2022; see also National Museum of African American History and Culture, Smithsonian Institution, https://music.si.edu/object/nmaahc_2011.57.25.1; "Gladys Bentley: Blues Singer," Smithsonian Institution, https://womenshistory.si.edu/spotlight/gladys-bentley; and Haleema Shah, "The Great Blues Singer Gladys Bentley Broke All the Rules," *Smithsonian Magazine*, March 14, 2019, https://www.smithsonianmag.com/smithsonian-institution/great-blues-singer-gladys-bentley-broke-rules-180971708/. I am grateful to Dr. Richard J. Powell, the John Spencer Bassett Professor of Art and Art History at Duke University, for sharing his thoughts on this artwork with me; phone conversation with author, February 9, 2022.

106. Dr. Sharon Patricia Holland is the Townsend Ludington Distinguished Professor in the Department of American Studies at the University of North Carolina, Chapel Hill; her focus includes feminism, sexuality, and critical ethnic/critical race studies; email exchange with author, February 10, 2022. See also Sharon P. Holland, "Put Honey in the Sky Where It Could Drip and Make the World Sweet: Looking for Purvis Young and Thomas Samuel Doyle but Seeing Something Else; Meditations on the *Matter* of Black Freedom," in *The Unfinished Business of Unsettled Things: Art from an African American South*, ed. Bernard L. Herman (Chapel Hill: University of North Carolina Press, forthcoming).

107. William Arnett, "Sam Doyle: The News from Frogmore," in Arnett and Arnett, *Souls Grown Deep: African American Vernacular Art of the South*, 1:322, and https://www.soulsgrowndeep.org/artist/sam-doyle.

108. Hylan Booker, "A World Made Visible," *Unframed*, Los Angeles County Museum of Art, August 18, 2014, https://unframed.lacma.org/2014/08/15/a-world-made-visible. See also "Outsider Art Fair Lectures: J M Basquiat + Sam Doyle" (panel discussion with Brooke Davis Anderson, Eric Fretz, Lenore Schorr, and Xaviera Simmons), Inside Outsider Art, May 29, 2014, https://www.outsiderart.me/outsider-art-fair-lectures-j-m-basquiat/.

109. Marquetta L. Goodwine, interview with Lynne Spriggs, St. Helena, South Carolina, November 12, 1999, High Museum of Art curatorial files, Atlanta, Georgia; Spriggs, *Local Heroes*, 9.

110. Susan Mitchell Crawley, *The Treasure of Ulysses Davis: Sculpture from a Savannah Barbershop* (Atlanta: High Museum of Art in association with the King-Tisdell Cottage Foundation of Savannah, GA, 2008), 13.

111. Quincy T. Mills, *Cutting Along the Color Line: Black Barbers and Barber Shops in America* (Philadelphia: University of Pennsylvania Press, 2013), 3.

112. Mills, *Cutting Along the Color Line*, 9.

113. Crawley, *Treasure of Ulysses Davis*, 11.

114. The 1970s bust of George Washington is in the collection of the King-Tisdell Cottage Foundation, Savannah, Georgia; it can be seen in Crawley, *Treasure of Ulysses Davis*, 33. According to the Mount Vernon Ladies' Association, which preserves and maintains the Virginia estate of the first president, although wigs were fashionable at the time, Washington did not wear a wig but powdered his own hair, giving it the white color seen in iconic portraits of him; see "Ten Common Misconceptions About George Washington," George Washington's Mount Vernon, accessed July 26, 2021, https://www.mountvernon.org/george-washington/facts/myths/ten-misconceptions-about-washington/.

115. Crawley, *Treasure of Ulysses Davis*, 18, 112n24, notes that Davis collected wood from many sources, including pieces from the woods and scraps from lumberyards, from a banjo maker, and from friends who worked on the Savannah docks and saved pieces used in packing the shipping freighters. Her information was drawn from Virginia Kiah, "Ulysses Davis: Savannah Folk Sculptor," *Southern Folklore Quarterly* 42 (1978): 275, and confirmed by the Davis family.

116. Crawley notes that, in his review of Davis's work at the Beach Institute in 1996, Darryl Lorenzo Wellington asserted that Davis's presidents are depicted as African American, but that the more recent presidents were depicted in "blackface." See Crawley, *Treasure of Ulysses Davis*, 9, citing Darryl Lorenzo Wellington, review of *Ulysses Davis* at the Beach Institute African-American Cultural Center, Savannah, *Art Papers* 20, no. 5 (September/October 1996): 53.

117. Ulysses Davis's artwork *Immortality Board* (1968–85) is in the collection of the King-Tisdell Cottage Foundation, Savannah, Georgia; it is pictured in Crawley, *Treasure of Ulysses Davis*, 49.

118. *Missing Pieces: Georgia Folk Art, 1770–1976* opened at the Atlanta Historical Society in 1976, traveling to Savannah's Telfair Academy of Arts and Sciences and the Columbus (GA) Museum of Arts and Crafts in 1977 and to the American Folklife Center at the Library of Congress, Washington, DC, in 1978; Crawley, *Treasure of Ulysses Davis*, 14.

119. Crawley, *Treasure of Ulysses Davis*, 14, originally cited in Tony Brown, "Whittling Barber Works on Display," *Savannah Morning News*, January 24, 1982.

120. This is an example of metonymy, a wordplay in visual form that is commonly used in Black vernacular art. Robert Farris Thompson connects this practice to African folkways in his book *Flash of the Spirit*, and with Joseph Cornet in *Four Moments of the Sun*.

121. For additional information on Davis's themes and practices, see Crawley, *Treasure of Ulysses Davis*, 11–32; and James E. Allen papers, 1921–1949, Archives of American Art, Smithsonian Institution.

122. Biblia, "Numbers 21:8–9," *The Bible (English Standard Version)*, https://biblia.com/bible/csb/numbers/21/8-9.

123. Dr. Regenia A. Perry is professor emerita of art history at Virginia Commonwealth University in Richmond; Alvia J. Wardlaw is an expert on African American art and curator and director of the University Museum at Texas Southern University in Houston. *Black Art, Ancestral Legacy: The African Impulse in African-American Art* was organized by the Dallas Museum of Art in 1989 and traveled to the High Museum of Art, the Milwaukee Art Museum, and the Virginia Museum of Fine Arts, Richmond. Perry had also served as an essayist for the Corcoran's *Black Folk Art in America, 1930–1980*.

124. Paul Arnett, "Leroy Person: Chipping Away," in Arnett and Arnett, *Souls Grown Deep*, 2:104.

125. Roger Manley, *Signs and Wonders: Outsider Art Inside North Carolina* (Raleigh: North Carolina Museum of Art, 1989), 80. Today this notion might be better understood as an alternate literacy, not necessarily a subordinate one.

126. Everett Mayo Adelman, "The Thrones and Chairs Leroy Person Made," *Folk Art* 19, no. 3 (Fall 1994): 48–50.

127. Jenifer P. Borum, "Review: Leroy Person: Luise Ross Gallery," *Artforum* 38, no. 9 (May 2000): 181, https://www.artforum.com/print/reviews/200005/leroy-person-559.

128. The year of Sparrow's birth is unverified. His headstone states he was born in 1915, his obituary 1914; 1925 has most frequently been noted as the year Sparrow believes he was born. He noted lying about his age in 1942 when he enlisted in the army. See Paul Schmelzer, "The Mystery Art and Ministry of Simon Sparrow," *Raw Vision* 34 (Spring 2001): 35. See also Joanne Cubbs, *Religious Visionaries*, exh. cat. (Sheboygan, WI: John Michael Kohler Arts Center, 1991); and Ann Percy, ed., *"Great and Mighty Things": Outsider Art from the Jill and Sheldon Bonovitz Collection*, exh. cat. (Philadelphia: Philadelphia Museum of Art, 2013), 150–55.

129. Schmelzer, "Mystery Art," 32–38; and Paul Schmelzer, "The Seen and the Unseen: The Life, Death, and Mystery Art of Simon Sparrow," *Outsider* 5, no. 2 (Winter 2001): 14–16. Schmelzer ("Seen and the Unseen," 16) notes that Sparrow dictated some of his thoughts to his friend Darryl Markowitz in the late 1970s, calling the two-hundred-page book *The Standard of the Foundation of the Understanding of Life* and inscribing the title page with his name as Minister Simon Sparrow.

130. Simon Sparrow, quoted in Schmelzer, "Seen and the Unseen," 15.

131. Thompson, *Flash of the Spirit*, 5.

132. Schmelzer, "Mystery Art," 36.

133. Information on the Philadelphia Wireman's exhibition history can be found at "Philadelphia Wireman," Fleisher Ollman Gallery, accessed April 28, 2021, https://www.fleisher-ollmangallery.com/artists/philadelphia_wireman. Fleisher/Ollman Gallery, formerly Janet Fleisher Gallery, notes inaugural exhibitions in 1985 at Cavin-Morris Gallery, New York, and at Janet Fleisher Gallery, Philadelphia, with subsequent exhibitions in 1986 at Cavin-Morris Gallery; Lawrence Hall Gallery, Rosemont College, Rosemont, Pennsylvania; Janet Fleisher Gallery; and Acme Art, San Francisco.

134. Thompson, *Flash of the Spirit*, 117.

135. The objects were found in the late 1970s, saved and kept by the man who found them for some additional years before they were acquired by John Ollman of Janet Fleisher Gallery (later Fleisher/Ollman Gallery) in 1985. Ollman notes this report from gallery guest Robert Leitch occurred around 1999, a considerable time later. Ollman recollects that the visitor named the street where he had seen a Black man making similar bundles, and it was close to where the objects had been located; John Ollman, emails with author, July 6, 2021.

136. Randall Morris, email exchange with author, February 26, 2021, and March 6, 2021. Morris notes that conjure culture draws heavily on African ideas of balance: the cultural with the personal, the physical with the mental, the one with the many. Per "idiosyncratic," Morris specifically refers to the genre of art brut, a term for "raw" art that is explained further in the following section in this volume, "Gamechangers." The term was coined by French artist Jean Dubuffet and is especially associated with art made by mentally isolated artists. Dubuffet was of the mind that art brut was anti-cultural, or made utterly apart from history and culture. Morris argues that a creative practice can draw on history and culture and still be profoundly autonomous. For additional thoughts from Morris on "the One and the Many," see Randall Morris, "Martín Ramírez: Master of Los Altos," in *Vernacular Visionaries: International Outsider Art*, ed. Annie Carlano (New Haven, CT: Yale University Press in association with the Museum of International Folk Art, 2003), 55.

137. Bessie Harvey, quoted in Stephen C. Wicks, *Awakening the Spirits: Art by Bessie Harvey*, (Knoxville, TN: Knoxville Museum of Art, 1997), 18. Wicks drew Harvey's quotations from a videotaped interview with the artist conducted on April 2, 1991. This citation also appears in Umberger, "Housewives, Witches," 84. See also Jenifer P. Borum, "Bessie Harvey," in Arnett and Arnett, *Souls Grown Deep*, 1:168; and Shari Cavin, "Bessie Harvey: The Spirit in the Wood," *Clarion* 12, no. 2/3 (Spring/Summer 1987): 44.

138. Many worked on the rail lines built by American industrialist Henry Morrison Flagler (1830–1913): "[Flagler] was responsible for building the Florida East Coast Railway from Daytona to Key West.... In 1905, he began constructing what would be called 'Flagler's Folly,' a railroad that would span seven miles of open water on its way to Key West.... Almost 4,000 men built the railroad bridge in seven years. They had to contend with mosquitoes, sand flies, and hurricanes. Hundreds of workers died in the storms. The railroad was finished but it proved to be a failure. It never earned the expected money and was destroyed by a 1935 Labor Day hurricane." See "Famous Floridians: Henry Morrison Flagler," Exploring Florida: A Social Studies Resource for Students and Teachers (Tampa: Florida Center for Instructional Technology, College of Education, University of South Florida, 2002), https://fcit.usf.edu/florida/lessons/flagler/flagler.htm.

139. Coconut Grove has been historically populated by Afro-Caribbean immigrants as well, although the East and West sections are marked by dramatic differences in socioeconomic status. "The dichotomy that still exists between East and West Coconut Grove is one of economics, progress, and resources," notes Alex Plasencia in "A History of West Coconut Grove from 1925: Slum Clearance, Concrete Monsters, and the Dichotomy of East and West Coconut Grove" (master's thesis, Clemson University, 2011), https://tigerprints.clemson.edu/all_theses/1117.

140. Purvis Young, "This Is the Life I See," in Arnett and Arnett, *Souls Grown Deep*, 2:393.

141. Lynda Roscoe Hartigan, "Recent Challenges in the Study of African American Folk Art," *International Review of African American Art* 11, no. 3 (June 1994): 27–29, 60–63.

142. This concern—striking a balance between reading artworks as texts, in cases where the artist had spoken little about those images in his life, and the comments he did make had to be parsed in the context of the fraught social strata of segregated, midcentury Montgomery, Alabama—was central to my 2018 exhibition and monograph, *Between Worlds: The Art of Bill Traylor*. The poles I navigated between were decades of racially biased readings of Traylor's images as simplistic, humorous, culturally disconnected, and benignly naive, with the overdetermined interpretations put forth by Mechal Sobel in her book *Painting a Hidden Life: The Art of Bill Traylor* (Baton Rouge: Louisiana State University Press, 2009). Sobel's research offered numerous relevant connections and sociohistorical factors that shed light on a body of work made in a time and place for which expressions of Black pride or white critique could have cost the artist his life. But her book was justifiably critiqued for consistently stating opinion and possibility as fact, and for drawing conclusions based on one or two artworks rather than on a comprehensive study of the full oeuvre. While artists such as Sister Gertrude Morgan left, in addition to their images, considerable writings and oral expressions of their beliefs and goals, Traylor was among a sizable group who left only visual texts. Although he could not safely express his views openly, Traylor's abiding themes, colors, portrayals, and story lines, recurring in over a thousand images, vividly attest to his core concerns and memories.

GAMECHANGERS (pp. 151–93)

1. Jane Kallir, "Art Brut and 'Outsider' Art: A Changing Landscape," introduction to *Accidental Genius: Art from the Anthony Petullo Collection*, by Margaret Andera and Lisa Stone, exh. cat. (Milwaukee, WI: Milwaukee Art Museum in association with DelMonico Books, 2012), 23.

2. Allan Beveridge notes that the first book on art and the mentally ill, *Art by the Mad* (1907), was written by Paul Meunier, a psychiatrist, under the pseudonym Marcel Reja. Allan Beveridge, "A Disquieting Feeling of Strangeness? The Art of the Mentally Ill," *Journal of the Royal Society of Medicine* 94, no. 11 (November 2001): 595–99, https://www.ncbi.nlm.nih.gov/pmc/articles/PMC1282252/.

3. Beveridge, "Disquieting Feeling." See also Joanne Cubbs, "Rebels, Mystics, and Outcasts: The Romantic Artist Outsider," in *The Artist Outsider: Creativity and the Boundaries of Culture*, ed. Michael D. Hall and Eugene W. Metcalf Jr. (Washington, DC: Smithsonian Institution Press, 1994), 77–93.

4. Jean Dubuffet delivered the impactful lecture "Anticultural Positions" at the Arts Club of Chicago in 1951, https://www.austincc.edu/noel/writings/Anticultural%20Positions.pdf. He began collecting the work of mentally ill patients in 1945, and his collection of five thousand works by 133 artists now composes the Collection de l'Art Brut in Lausanne, Switzerland. In 1959, he wrote the essay "Art Brut," which Joanne Cubbs draws from in "Rebels, Mystics, and Outcasts," 85.

5. Kallir, "Art Brut and 'Outsider' Art," 24.

6. The exhibition was framed largely around Dubuffet's category for the mentally ill, spiritual mediums, and extreme eccentrics, but muddied the waters by including American artists such as Joseph E. Yoakum, Clarence Schmidt, and Sabato Rodia, who were drawing on vernacular traditions that were not well understood at the time.

7. For information about influential art dealers of the time, see note 10 in Douglas Robson's essay in this volume.

8. I have addressed this idea in several publications, including "Housewives, Witches, Beauty Queens, and Conjure Women: Locating the Practice of Self-Taught Women Artists," in *Boundary Trouble: The Self-Taught Artist and American Avant-Gardes*, ed. Lynne Cooke (New Haven, CT: Yale University Press, forthcoming); and *Between Worlds: The Art of Bill Traylor*, exh. cat. (Washington, DC: Smithsonian American Art Museum in association with Princeton University Press, 2018).

9. The Hyde Park Art Center website says this about the 1977 exhibition *In the Realms of the Unreal: The Life and Work of Henry Darger*: "This exhibition introduced the now infamous works on paper by the posthumously discovered outsider artist Henry Darger (1892–1973) alongside paraphernalia from the artist [*sic*] studio"; see https://www.hydeparkart.org/exhibition-archive/in-realms-of-the-unreal-the-life-and-work-of-henry

-darger/. In a 2020 interview with Michael Bonesteel, interviewer Jennifer Lauren posed the following question: "You have written a couple of books about the infamous outsider artist Henry Darger. Can you explain to us what drew you to him in the first place and why you have written so many things on this great artist?"; see https://www.jenniferlaurengallery.com/projects/michael-bonesteel-interview. In *Henry Darger: Art and Selected Writings* (New York: Rizzoli, 2000), 15, Bonesteel ruminates on why Darger's early reception was so powerful, and why many retain a negative association with him and his work.

10. A website detailing Darger's art, life, and posthumous art-world history and bibliography was organized by Michael Bonesteel, Mary Trent, and Yukiko Koide; for the biography written by Michael Bonesteel, see http://officialhenrydarger.com/about/. The American Folk Art Museum Archives in New York hold the Henry Darger Papers; see https://folkartmuseum.libraryhost.com/resources/henry_darger_papers. Intuit: The Center for Intuitive and Outsider Art in Chicago holds the Henry Darger Room Collection; see https://www.art.org/henry-darger-room-collection/.

11. Michael Bonesteel, "Henry Darger," in *The Hidden Art: 20th- & 21st-Century Self-Taught Artists from the Audrey B. Heckler Collection*, by Valérie Rousseau (New York: Skira Rizzoli in association with the American Folk Art Museum, 2017), 136. In another publication, Bonesteel explores Darger's method of tracing his figures from source material such as catalogues, magazines, and comics and then adapting them. This method allowed him to create anatomically proportionate imagery beyond his own rendering skills, and enabled Darger to weave a complex and epic tale. See Bonesteel, *Henry Darger: Art and Selected Writings*, 26–31. Leisa Rundquist also explores Darger's use of source material in *Betwixt and Between: Henry Darger's Vivian Girls*, online exh. cat. (Chicago: Intuit: Center for Intuitive and Outsider Art, 2018), 7–8, https://issuu.com/intuitart/docs/darger_catalog_final_issuu_7a96c7d2fda871/6?ff. See also Michael Moon, *Darger's Resources* (Durham, NC: Duke University Press, 2012).

12. Male Darger story characters include the artist himself, his father (who shared the name Henry Joseph Darger), and two of his uncles. John M. MacGregor, *Henry Darger: In the Realms of the Unreal* (New York: Delano Greenidge, 2002), 114, 248–49. MacGregor trained in art history, psychiatry, and psychoanalysis and has studied the art of the mentally ill. While records indicate that Darger had significant personal/emotional challenges, the degree to which trauma was at the core of them remains unclear. Leisa Rundquist has noted: "The 2002 study by MacGregor remains the most informative text on Darger's art and life, however, scholarly interest in relying on psycho-biographical methods have waned in recent years, in favour of research that considers cultural influences in tandem with the artist's resources and other methodologies." She credits Michael Bonesteel for pioneering this shift in direction, making connections to children's literature and newspaper clippings that Darger kept, and for proposing that giving the girls male genitalia might be Darger's way of indicating their warrior status. See Leisa Rundquist, "Vivam! The Divine Intersexuality of Henry Darger's Vivian Girl," *Elsewhere: The International Journal of Self-Taught and Outsider Art*, no. 2 (May 2014): 27, http://stoarc.com/journals/ELSEWHERE_Journal_Issue_2_May_2014.pdf.

13. Darger depicted both girls and boys with male genitalia; the reasons for this remain unverified. Speculations have included sexual perversion, a lack of understanding of male/female anatomy, and an intentional duality of roles or identities. As noted above (note 12), Michael Bonesteel was the first to raise important questions, in his 2000 book, *Henry Darger: Art and Selected Writings*, about sexual dualism in Darger's imagery and possibly in his own identity: downtrodden laborer by day, fantastic artist by night. Bonesteel observes that the Vivian Girls often disguise themselves as boys: a character called Rattlesnake Boy is secretly a girl; the girls are preadolescent but speak like adults and fight like warriors; and he discusses literature that Darger drew upon, including L. Frank Baum's Oz series; and the character Tip, a girl who is transformed into a boy by a witch. Michael Bonesteel, *Henry Darger: Author/Artist*, exh. cat. (Chicago: Intuit: The Center for Intuitive and Outsider Art, 2017), 10, https://issuu.com/intuitart/docs/aa_catalog_v18_final; Bonesteel, *Henry Darger: Art and Selected Writings*, 22. Leisa Rundquist has furthered this area of scholarship, similarly considering Darger's nonbinary depictions in relation to his collection of children's books featuring girl heroines. She contrasts Darger's depictions with the gender/sex-conforming source material he regularly used and notes that scholarly approaches assuming perversion or confusion "selectively deny or downplay the multivalent potential of the Vivian body, a rich and effusive fictional representation." Rundquist, *Betwixt and Between,* 7; see also Rundquist, "Vivam!"; and Leisa Rundquist, *The Power and Fluidity of Girlhood in Henry Darger's Art* (New York: Routledge, 2021).

14. Henry Darger, *The Story of the Vivian Girls, in What is Known as the Realms of the Unreal, of the Glandeco-Angelinnian War*

Storm, Caused by the Child Slave Rebellion (unpublished, ca. 1911–39), 6:262–63. This passage appears here as the artist wrote it; cited in Rundquist, *Betwixt and Between*, 14.

15. Rundquist, *Betwixt and Between*, 4–5.

16. John MacGregor has conjectured that Darger may have been a pedophile and possibly a murderer, but also concedes that neither can be proven. In common with other scholars, MacGregor views the severe distress caused by Darger's having lost his mother and sister when he was just shy of four, losing his father a few years later, and living thereafter in an abusive/non-nurturing environment as central to a significant personality disorder.

17. Ellen Handler Spitz, "Henry Darger," in *Self-Taught Artists of the 20th Century: An American Anthology*, ed. Elsa Longhauser and Harald Szeeman, exh. cat. (San Francisco: Chronicle Books in association with the Museum of American Folk Art, 1998), 102–3. Some of Darger's writings do indicate an awareness of a reader or viewer or muse, although detangling the degree to which a fictive audience played into a fictitious narrative may be impossible; Michael Bonesteel quotes from a Darger text (*The Realms of the Unreal*, vol. 1): "Editors of great experience will in due time be allowed to go over the whole work most carefully," and comments, "Whether [Darger] really expected it or not, this is exactly what is happening." Bonesteel, *Henry Darger: Art and Selected Writings*, 16, 18.

18. Bonesteel, *Henry Darger: Art and Selected Writings*, 8. Bonesteel explains that Darger's father reported his son as being both exceptionally intelligent and "peculiar"; see Bonesteel, Trent, Koide, *Henry Darger*.

19. Bonesteel, *Henry Darger: Art and Selected Writings*, 9. When Darger was twelve, his father and Dr. Otto Schmidt signed papers that sent him to the Illinois Asylum for Feeble-Minded Children in Lincoln; see Bonesteel, Trent, Koide, *Henry Darger*.

20. For a timeline of Darger's life, see Bonesteel, Trent, and Koide, *Henry Darger*. Darger resided in a number of places in Chicago over the course of his life but lived and worked for the longest period of time in rented rooms on West Webster Avenue. A leg injury in 1969 precipitated his final move, in 1972, from these rooms, then owned by Nathan Lerner, into a nursing home. Shortly before Darger's death, the day after his eighty-first birthday, his trove of art was discovered by Lerner and another tenant, David Berglund. Lerner recognized the artistic value of Darger's work and became, with his wife, Kiyoko Lerner, instrumental in its preservation, exhibition, and placement.

21. In his assessment of Darger's artistic evolution, Michael Bonesteel notes that the artist may have painted aspects of the *Realms* from the time he began writing it around 1912 (and typing it in 1916), but likely began painting full scenes from the story in the 1920s and 1930s, on sheets of paper roughly 19 × 24 in. Sometime around 1930, Darger stopped writing *Realms* but kept illustrating it; he began to join multiple sheets of paper for larger paintings, and by the 1940s, the artworks were often over seventy inches in length. In the 1930s and 1940s, Bonesteel points to an increased depiction of violence and stylistically changing imagery: the Vivian Girls wear a wider range of clothing and were increasingly depicted nude; the Glandelinians become clean-shaven and sometimes dress like cowboys. In 1944, Darger discovered he could have his source material clippings photographically enlarged, and thus make tracings at different scales. This drove increasingly complex narrative sequences. Bonesteel concludes that Darger's last works were his longest, some up to 113 inches. During the 1950s and 1960s, he observed a decrease in violent scenes and an increase in number of figures, sometimes dozens in a single scene. The Blengins were featured less frequently in the 1930s and 1940s but resurge in the work in the 1950s and 1960s and often appear unclothed, and much like the other children in appearance, except for their wings and horns. In 1971, Darger became increasingly ill; he moved into a nursing home in 1972 and died in 1973. See Bonesteel, *Henry Darger: Art and Selected Writings*, 26–30, 34n31, 35n51.

22. Jane Kallir, "Henry Darger: Art and Myth," Galerie St. Etienne, 2004, https://www.gseart.com/exhibitions-essay/1005.

23. Bonesteel, *Henry Darger: Art and Selected Writings*, 7.

24. Most of the in-depth projects on individual artists mentioned as sources in this book draw on models that include a multifaceted, sociocultural history. For examples specific to Ramírez, see Randall Morris, "Martín Ramírez," *Folk Art* 20, no. 4 (Winter 1995/96): 36–45; Randall Morris, "Martín Ramírez: Revisited," *Folk Art* 27, no. 4 (Winter 2002/3): 52–59; Randall Morris, "Martín Ramírez: Master of Los Altos," in *Vernacular Visionaries: International Outsider Art*, ed. Annie Carlano (New Haven, CT: Yale University Press in association with the Museum of International Folk Art, 2003), 50–63; Michael D. Hall, "The Problem of Martín Ramírez: Folk Art Criticism as Cosmologies of Coercion," in *Stereoscopic Perspective: Reflections on American Fine and Folk Art* (Ann Arbor, MI: UMI Research Press, 1988), 231; and Víctor M. Espinosa, *Martín Ramírez: Framing His Life and Art* (Austin: University of Texas Press, 2015), 9.

25. Hall, "Problem of Martín Ramírez," 231.

26. Espinosa, *Martín Ramírez*, 1. Espinosa is a sociologist and ethnographer who focuses on the intersection of art and transnational migration. He notes that, after thirty-two years of seclusion, Ramírez died in 1963, at the age of sixty-eight. He explains that Ramírez was a ranchero in Los Altos de Jalisco (1895–1925), a migrant worker in California (1925–30), an "exile of consequence of a Mexican religious war" (1926–29), detained for vagrancy and subsequently confined at the Stockton State Hospital (1931–48), and lived his last years at the DeWitt State Hospital (1948–63). Espinosa (p. 57) also points out that the American Psychiatric Association publicly decried the immigrant population as harboring a number of "mental defectives"; a 1912 editorial from the *Journal of the American Medical Association* asserted that some 30 percent of the "feeble-minded children in the general population of the United States" were the progeny of aliens or naturalized citizens.

27. For a summary of Ramírez's circumstances, see Espinosa, *Martín Ramírez*, 1–12.

28. Morris, "Martín Ramírez: Revisited," 55; and Morris, "Martín Ramírez: Master of Los Altos," 55.

29. See note 26, in this section. Espinosa also notes that Ramírez's thirty-two-year incarceration overlapped with a grim period in the history of California's psychiatric institutions; by 1934, the hospitals had "reached an overcrowding rate of 86%," resulting in insufficient clothing, beds, food, cleanliness, and doctors per patient, and an environment that one visitor to Stockton in this period said "would seem enough to drive a normal person insane." Espinosa, *Martín Ramírez*, 76–77, 88.

30. Morris, "Martín Ramírez: Revisited," 55; and Morris, "Martín Ramírez: Master of Los Altos," 50.

31. Espinosa, *Martín Ramírez*, 99–123, specifically 101n94. Espinosa addresses art therapy as another context in which art brut advocates downplayed cultural context in favor of a romanticized myth of genius blooming in isolation, and he cites John M. MacGregor's influential but fraught book *The Discovery of the Art of the Insane* as central to this problem. Espinosa critiques MacGregor's assertion that input from physicians and art therapists might "have destructive effects" on the purity of art made by insane patients. Espinosa notes that arguing against art therapy "imagines an ideal situation of complete isolation," which prioritizes the art over the health and well-being of the artist. See John M. MacGregor, *The Discovery of the Art of the Insane* (Princeton, NJ: Princeton University Press, 1989), 213.

32. Tarmo Pasto was a professor of art at Sacramento State University, his own university training having been in fine art and psychology. Before Pasto showed an interest, the staff burned Ramírez's drawings, possibly owing to fear that they were infectious, as he used saliva to paste sheets of paper together. By the time Pasto met Ramírez, it is estimated that Ramírez had been making drawings for fifteen years; the staff at Stockton said Ramírez drew regularly and gave his drawings to interested parties. Espinosa, *Martín Ramírez*, 108, 112, 152.

33. Pasto's interest, at least at first, largely pertained to his own work on what he called "psychotic art." It was DeWitt volunteer Gail Northe who, with her husband, Charles Muskavitch, a conservator at the Crocker Art Gallery in Sacramento, convinced curator/director Don R. Birrell to mount a show. When Birrell discovered that Pasto had interest in Ramírez and a collection of his work, they collaborated on the effort. Espinosa, *Martín Ramírez*, 127–28.

34. Alfred Neumeyer and Miss Williams, "Art Gallery, Current Exhibition," press release, February 15, 1954, Mills College Art Museum Archive, referenced in Espinosa, *Martín Ramírez*, 139–40.

35. Pasto sent James Johnson Sweeney, then director of the Guggenheim, ten original artworks after he expressed interest in Ramírez. These languished in storage until the 1990s, when they were recognized as the work of a known artist and accessioned. Espinosa, *Martín Ramírez*, 150. Espinosa refers also to Jon Ippolito, "Recognition and Rescue: The Martín Ramírez Drawings at the Guggenheim," *Guggenheim Magazine* 13 (1999): 6–9.

36. Espinosa gives a detailed account of the ways in which Ramírez's art was variously kept, lost, and sold, including works that Max Dunievitz sent to the Ramírez family in Mexico after he died. The works Tarmo Pasto saved were sold to Jim Nutt and Phyllis Kind, heralding Ramírez's entry into the art world. Espinosa, *Martín Ramírez*, 156–91.

37. Ownership of Ramírez artworks saved by Pasto and Dunievitz has been disputed by the artist's descendants but remains unresolved; see National Public Radio, https://www.npr.org/templates/story/story.php?storyId=96004813; LA Times, https://www.latimes.com/archives/la-xpm-2008-aug-13-et-ramirez13-story.html; and Providentia, https://drvitelli.typepad.com/providentia/2017/09/immigrant-who-died-in-psychiatric-hospital-now-honoured-as-master-artist.html.

38. Brooke Davis Anderson organized the *Martín Ramírez* project for the American Folk Art Museum, bringing together a number of scholars to tackle the magnitude of this complex story and body of work. The project led to the discovery of the "late works" held by the Max Dunievitz family. Víctor M. Espinosa's 2015 book, *Martín Ramírez*, grew out of this project.

39. Espinosa, *Martín Ramírez*, 3, 15; Espinosa specifies Ramírez's race as white criollo.

40. See Leslie Umberger "James Castle: Vanishing Point," in *Untitled: The Art of James Castle* by Nicholas R. Bell and Leslie Umberger (Washington, DC: Smithsonian American Art Museum in association with D Giles, 2014), 51n28.

41. The thresholds of "full-scale retrospective" and "major art museum" make this list exceedingly short: *James Castle: A Retrospective*, organized by the Philadelphia Museum of Art (2008–9), and *Between Worlds: The Art of Bill Traylor*, organized by the Smithsonian American Art Museum (2018–19). Other significant and recent solo exhibitions at prominent institutions include: *William L. Hawkins: An Imaginative Geography* (Columbus Museum of Art, 2018), *Elijah Pierce's America* (Barnes Foundation, 2020–21), *Joseph E. Yoakum: What I Saw* (Art Institute of Chicago, 2021), and *Really Free: The Radical Art of Nellie Mae Rowe* (High Museum of Art, 2021–22).

42. Castle's family noted that he was unresponsive to auditory input from infancy and was unhealthy in other unspecified ways, including being unable to walk until he was four. He was not biologically mute but did not learn to converse fluently in any conventional or alternative spoken, written, or signaled language; his family maintains that he did know some signs and used various gestures to communicate with those he knew well. See Ann Percy, "Unfolding the Familiar: James Castle Reintroduced," in *James Castle: A Retrospective*, ed. Ann Percy (Philadelphia: Philadelphia Museum of Art in association with Yale University Press, 2008), 20; Jeffrey Wolf, interviews with Eleanor Scanlon Thompson, Geraldine Garrow, and Byron Johnson, September 13, 2006 (tapes 30–32) for the film *James Castle: Portrait of an Artist* (New York: Foundation for Self-Taught American Artists and Breakaway Films, 2008), transcripts courtesy of Jeffrey Wolf; and Bell and Umberger, *Untitled: The Art of James Castle*.

43. Some reasons for deafness are medical, i.e., brought about by disease or injury. Deafness from birth is neurological, not medical, and the individual with neurological deafness is considered neurodivergent, not neurotypical. A neurologically deaf person may or may not also be autistic; Castle was never diagnosed during his lifetime, so this detail about his specific neurodisability is unknowable.

44. In a 2021 publication on James Castle, John Beardsley considered a question I posed in 2014: "So how, then, is the internal world of someone lacking such structures [thoughts framed around words and shared language] organized?"; Bell and Umberger, *Untitled: The Art of James Castle*, 37–38. Beardsley asserted that this rhetorical question positioned Castle's thought processes as having "an implicit deficit in the capacity to shape or organize thoughts." His characterization misinterprets my original point, which described Castle's ability to shape and organize thoughts as being rooted in a unique, entirely visual interpretation of the physical world, rather than an interpretation organized via words and language. See John Beardsley, *James Castle: Memory Palace* (Boise, ID: James Castle Collection and Archive in association with Yale University Press, 2021), 217.

45. See Percy, "Unfolding the Familiar," 20–24; Nicholas R. Bell, "Being James Castle," in Bell and Umberger, *Untitled: The Art of James Castle*, 20; and Nicholas R. Bell, *The James Castle Primer* (Boise, ID: James Castle Collection and Archive, 2018), 10–11.

46. Bell, *James Castle Primer*, 10. Unless otherwise noted, all general information about James Castle is drawn from the three sources listed in note 45 in this section.

47. Bell explains that in the 1970s, a cache of material from the farm in Garden Valley was found in an outbuilding on the property, a number of books with drawings in the pages. This collection of early material differs from the mature drawings Castle became widely recognized for and are known as the "icehouse books." Bell, *James Castle Primer*, 12.

48. Bell, *James Castle Primer*, 14.

49. Mieke Bal, "Autotopography: Louise Bourgeois as Builder," *Biography* 25, no. 1 (Winter 2002), cited and explored as related to Castle in Bell and Umberger, *Untitled: The Art of James Castle*, 20. See also Bell, *James Castle Primer*, 35–50.

50. See also Umberger, "James Castle: Vanishing Point," 40; and Bell, *James Castle Primer*, 35–50.

51. Brendan Greaves, "'Characters More Comely to the Eye': Text and Intention in the Art of James Castle," in Percy, *James Castle*, 154.

52. For the artist's full exhibition history, see "James Castle Selected Exhibitions," James Castle Collection and Archive, accessed April 28, 2021, https://jamescastle.com/selected-exhibitions/.

53. It is difficult to say whether Howard Finster or Anna Mary Robertson "Grandma" Moses ultimately loomed larger in American popular culture, although their moments came at different times and impacted different sectors. Moses hit her stride with a white, middle-class mainstream audience between the 1940s and her death in 1961. Finster became famous in the 1980s and 1990s, and enjoyed widespread admiration, but perhaps most remarkable was the degree to which his followers included members of the creative class and counterculture groups. Moses is absolutely a "gamechanger" artist in her own right, but is not encompassed in the scope of this project.

54. Norman Girardot, Ricardo Viera, and Howard Finster, "Howard Finster" (interview, Summerville, Georgia, June 12–13, 1992), *Art Journal* 53, no. 1 (1994): 48–50, https://doi.org/10.2307/777533. Finster's sister was deceased at the time of the revelation; this is also referenced in Roger Manley and Mark Sloan, "Reverend Howard Finster: Paradise Garden and Plant Farm Museum," in *Self-Made Worlds: Visionary Folk Art Environments* (New York: Aperture, 1997), 58.

55. Hal Fulmer, "The Word and the World: Evangelical Christianity, the Bible, and the Secular South," in *Coming Home! Self-Taught Artists, the Bible and the American South*, ed. Carol Crown (Oxford: University Press of Mississippi in association with the Art Museum of the University of Memphis, 2004), 55.

56. Katherine L. Jentleson, "Howard Finster," in Rousseau, *Hidden Art*, 186.

57. Liza Kirwin, "Appreciation: The Reverend Howard Finster, the Last Red Light before the Apocalypse," *American Art* 16, no. 2 (Summer 2002): 92.

58. Liza Kirwin interviewed Finster for the Smithsonian's Archives of American Art oral history project in 1984, and filmed him at Paradise Garden for a *Smithsonian World* television program in 1988. She noted that Finster had a special regard for the Smithsonian, "which mirrored his mission to collect the wonders of the world," and that he archived his papers there, making them available to the public. See "Howard Finster," Smithsonian American Art Museum, accessed April 28, 2021, https://americanart.si.edu/artist/howard-finster-1543; and "Howard Finster papers, 1932–1987," Archives of American Art, Smithsonian Institution, https://www.aaa.si.edu/collections/howard-finster-papers-8596.

59. Laura Hutson, "Howard Finster Exhibit Is Filled with Prophetic Visions of Spaceships and Henry Ford," *Nashville Scene*, December 1, 2011, https://www.nashvillescene.com/arts-culture/article/13040876/howard-finster-exhibit-is-filled-with-prophetic-visions-of-spaceships-and-henry-ford.

60. J. F. Turner, "Howard Finster: Man of Visions," *Clarion* 14, no. 4 (Fall 1989): 43, https://issuu.com/american_folk_art_museum/docs/clarion_14_4_fall1989.

61. Daniel Wojcik, *Outsider Art: Visionary Worlds and Trauma* (Jackson: University Press of Mississippi, 2016), 105, 107; see also Wojcik, "Outsider Art, Vernacular Traditions, Trauma, and Creativity," *Western Folklore* 67, no. 2/3 (2008): 178–98, http://www.jstor.com/stable/25474913.

62. Sally M. Promey, "The 'Return' of Religion in the Scholarship of American Art," *Art Bulletin* 85, no. 3 (2003): 581–603, https://doi.org/10.2307/3177387.

63. Erika Doss, "Visualizing Faith: Religious Presence and Meaning in Modern and Contemporary American Art," in Crown, *Coming Home!*, 42–43. The artists Doss mentions are Howard Finster, Sister Gertrude Morgan, J. B. Murray, Mark Rothko, Nellie Mae Rowe, Mark Tobey, Andy Warhol, and Ruth Weisberg.

64. Carol Crown, ed., *Wonders to Behold: The Visionary Art of Myrtice West* (Memphis, TN: Mustang, 1999); Crown, *Coming Home!*; and Carol Crown and Charles Russell, eds., *Sacred and Profane: Voice and Vision in Southern Self-Taught Art* (Jackson: University Press of Mississippi, 2007).

65. Wojcik, *Outsider Art*, 107–8. Wojcik cites Howard Finster and Tom Patterson, *Howard Finster: Stranger from Another World: Man of Visions Now on This Earth* (New York: Abbeville Press, 1989), 28–30.

66. Finster and Patterson, *Howard Finster*, 183–84.

67. William Arnett, "The Tradition," Souls Grown Deep, 2012, https://soulsgrowndeep.org/tradition. In 2010, Arnett formed the Souls Grown Deep Foundation, which remains dedicated to documenting, researching, preserving, and exhibiting the work of African American artists from the rural South. The foundation has been instrumental in placing artworks at museums across the country and changing the face of American art. It has rightly argued that education in the United States has been unevenly accessible to citizens of different agency, and that communal and traditional training is no less valuable than that of the academy—which in and of itself has been defined arbitrarily throughout history. Moreover, it has asked museums to consider why white artists without formal training, especially those aligned with other mainstream norms, often elude labels like "self-taught" or "outsider." This passage from Arnett was also cited in Leslie Umberger, "Appreciation: Thornton Dial (1928–2016)," *American Art* 30, no. 2 (Summer 2016): 111.

68. Phillip March Jones, introduction to *Thornton Dial: The Earliest Years, 1987-1989,* ed. Phillip March Jones, exh. cat. (Los Angeles: Parker Gallery, 2021), 1.

69. Paul Arnett, "Artistic License," in Jones, *Thornton Dial*, 6.

70. Thornton Dial Sr., "Mr. Dial Is a Man Looking for Something," in *Souls Grown Deep: African American Vernacular Art of the South,* vol. 2, *Once That River Starts to Flow*, ed. William Arnett and Paul Arnett (Atlanta: Tinwood Books, 2001), 196–98.

71. In 2005 the Museum of Fine Arts in Houston organized *Thornton Dial in the 21st Century*; a second major solo exhibition, *Hard Truths: The Art of Thornton Dial*, was organized by the Indianapolis Museum of Art in 2011, and traveled to the High Museum of Art in Atlanta, Georgia; the Mint Museum, Charlotte, North Carolina; and the New Orleans Museum of Art. Both exhibitions were accompanied by major publications.

72. In 2014 the Souls Grown Deep Foundation donated fifty-seven works of art, all by African American artists from the southern United States, to the Metropolitan Museum of Art, including ten by Thornton Dial Sr. A catalogue accompanied the exhibition of the collection: Cheryl Finley, Randall R. Griffey, Amelia Peck, and Darryl Pinckney, *My Soul Has Grown Deep: Black Art from the American South* (New York: Metropolitan Museum of Art, 2018).

73. According to Dr. Ananya Mandal, "Down syndrome or Down's syndrome is a congenital condition caused by the presence of an additional copy of chromosome 21 in a person's cells. This is also referred to as trisomy 21....Historically, many individuals with Down's syndrome were killed, abandoned or ostracized from society. In the 20th century, it was common for these individuals to be institutionalized and they did not receive appropriate treatment for the associated medical complications such as heart disorders, vision defects and intestinal problems. Many children with Down's syndrome therefore used to die during infancy or early adulthood. As the eugenics movement came into being, the forced sterilization of individuals with Down's syndrome was introduced to 33 of the 48 states that then existed in the United States. The sterilization programs reached large proportions until protests from the general public led to their discontinuation. At this point in history, the cause of Down's syndrome was not understood. It was assumed that several genetic factors, older maternal age, birth injuries, and injury during pregnancy caused the illness. It was only in the mid-twentieth century (the 1950s) that karyotype techniques were discovered, which could be used to help identify the shape and number of chromosomes. This led to the understanding that trisomy 21 was the cause of Down's syndrome." Ananya Mandal, MD, "Down Syndrome History," News Medical Life Sciences, last updated February 26, 2019, https://www.news-medical.net/health/Down-Syndrome-History.aspx. See also Down's Syndrome Association, https://www.downs-syndrome.org.uk/about/history-of-downs-syndrome-2/.

74. Amelia Rachel Hokule'a Borofsky, "Where Great Art Transcends Disability," *Atlantic*, December 13, 2012, https://www.theatlantic.com/health/archive/2012/12/where-great-art-transcends-disability/266184/. Joyce Wallace Scott tells the story of her and her sister's life in *Entwined: Sisters and Secrets in the Silent World of Artist Judith Scott* (Boston: Beacon Press, 2016).

75. Creative Growth is a nonprofit based in Oakland, California, that serves artists with disabilities by providing a professional studio environment for artistic development, gallery exhibition, and representation. The sale of each artwork is split equally between the artist and Creative Growth, which uses the proceeds to purchase materials and keep the program running. A cooperative agreement creates a pool of funds, so that even artists who do not sell artwork still receive a monthly check and identify as working artists. Artwork made at Creative Growth, including Judith Scott's, has been acquired by prominent collections worldwide, including the Museum of Modern Art, San Francisco Museum of Modern Art, Smithsonian American Art Museum, Studio Museum in Harlem, Collection de l'Art Brut, American Folk Art Museum, and the Museum of Everything. See "About—Creative Growth Art Center," https://creativegrowth.org/about.

76. Joyce Wallace Scott, quoted in Hokule'a Borofsky, "Where Great Art Transcends Disability."

77. Matthew Higgs, "Judith Scott: Creative Growth," in *Judith Scott: Bound & Unbound*, ed. Catherine Morris and Matthew Higgs, exh. cat. (Brooklyn, NY: Brooklyn Museum in association with DelMonico Books-Prestel, 2014), 32.

78. Higgs, "Judith Scott," 33.

79. Florence Ludins-Katz and Elias Katz, *Art and Disabilities: Establishing the Creative Art Center for People with Disabilities* (Cambridge, MA: Brookline Books, 1990).

80. Tom di Maria, quoted in Hokule'a Borofsky, "Where Great Art Transcends Disability"; and email correspondence with author, August 12, 2021.

81. See note 75, in this section.

82. Catherine Morris, "Judith Scott and the Politics of Biography," introduction to Morris and Higgs, *Judith Scott: Bound & Unbound*, 9. Catherine J. Morris is the Sackler Family Curator at the Brooklyn Museum's Elizabeth A. Sackler Center for

Feminist Art; Matthew Higgs is director and chief curator of White Columns, New York.

83. Morris, "Judith Scott," 10.

84. See Disability Rights Education & Defense Fund, accessed August 2, 2021, https://dredf.org/about-us/publications/the-history-of-the-ada/; and OlmsteadRights.org, "The Americans with Disabilities Act of 1990—ADA," accessed August 2, 2021, https://www.olmsteadrights.org/about-olmstead/item.6460-The_Americans_with_Disabilities_Act_of_1990_ADA.

85. Morris, "Judith Scott," 12; see also Christopher J. Kelly, "The Personal Is Political," *Encyclopedia Brittanica*, May 1, 2017, https://www.britannica.com/topic/the-personal-is-political and https://isreview.org/issue/92/personal-and-political.

86. Lynne Cooke, curator of special projects in modern art at the National Gallery of Art in Washington, DC, has noted that Scott "provides one of the most remarkable instances of an individual overcoming psychic alienation." Lynne Cooke, "Orthodoxies Undermined," in *"Great and Mighty Things": Outsider Art from the Jill and Sheldon Bonovitz Collection*, ed. Ann Percy, exh. cat. (Philadelphia: Philadelphia Museum of Art, 2013), 209.

87. The importance of the work that Florence Ludins-Katz and Elias Katz began at Creative Growth, and that Tom di Maria has continued for over twenty years, is immeasurable. Today arts centers for individuals with disabilities exist the world over; they include La Tinaia in Italy; Studio Herenplaats in the Netherlands; Gateway Arts in Brookline, Massachusetts; Arts Project Australia; Art Enables in Washington, DC; Atelier Incurve in Japan; Riera Studio in Cuba; Atelier Goldsteinin Frankfurt; Project Onward in Chicago; Project Ability and Outside In, both in the United Kingdom, and many others.

88. Asemic texts are script-like abstract calligraphies that appear word-like but have no semantic meaning; their meaning is either known only to the maker, or left to the viewer to ascribe.

A BREAKING WAVE (pp. 195–232)

1. Massimiliano Gioni, "A Universal, All-Embracing Knowledge," introduction, 55th International Art Exhibition, 2013, https://www.labiennale.org/en/art/2013/introduction-massimiliano-gioni.

2. It is important to note that none of the artists celebrated in this project would have gained greater recognition without first being supported and noticed at community and regional venues, many of which are mentioned throughout this text. Other such places include Intuit: The Center for Creative and Outsider Art in Chicago, and the Milwaukee Art Museum. Important groundwork for preserving the work of self-taught and vernacular artists, and especially for integrating the work of self-taught artists into the larger scheme of American art, has taken place over the years at the John Michael Kohler Arts Center in Wisconsin, where I served as curator from 1998 to 2012, picking up work begun by my predecessor, Joanne Cubbs, and carried on after me by Karen Patterson, Laura Bickford, and others.

3. Sarah Boxer, "The Rise of Self-Taught Artists: Out Is the New In," *Atlantic*, September 2013, https://www.theatlantic.com/magazine/archive/2013/09/out-is-the-new-in/309428/. In this article Boxer noted a number of concurrent goings-on for self-taught artists, including the exhibitions *The Alternative Guide to the Universe* at London's Hayward Gallery and *"Great and Mighty Things"* at the Philadelphia Museum of Art, and an acquisition of work by James Castle at the National Gallery of Art, Washington. In 2013 the Smithsonian American Art Museum also acquired a major body of Castle's art, which was featured in a solo show in 2014.

4. Christine Macel, "The Exhibition: Focus on Art and Artists," introduction, 57th International Art Exhibition, 2017, https://www.labiennale.org/en/art/2017/introduction-christine-macel.

5. Ruchi Mital,"This World Is Not My Own: A Creative Treatment of Actuality," in *Really Free: The Radical Art of Nellie Mae Rowe*, ed. Katherine Jentleson, exh. cat. (Atlanta: High Museum of Art in partnership with DelMonico Books, 2021), 44.

6. George Tamihana Nuku, "Past and Present," session 3, People: A Global Dialogue on Museums and Their Publics (webinar), Metropolitan Museum of Art, New York, May 19, 2021, https://www.youtube.com/watch?v=ACzk-2XnSY4.

7. Randall Morris, "The Hawk King of Elsinore: A Memoir of Jon Serl," in *Jon Serl: The Mutability of Being*, by Jo Farb Hernández, Randall Morris, and Cara Zimmerman, exh. cat. (San Jose, CA: Natalie and James Thompson Art Gallery, 2013), 9. In the same volume, pp. 27–33, Zimmerman notes that Serl went by a number of names, among them Joseph Searles, Ned Palmer, Jerry Palmer, and "Slats." He was born in upstate New York, possibly on an Indian reservation, to a large family of vaudeville performers. He spent his youth performing and traveling, often playing female roles.

8. Morris, "Hawk King," 15. Morris notes that Serl appeared on *The Tonight Show* with Johnny Carson on December 14, 1989; his second appearance was on February 7, 1990.

9. Morris, "Hawk King," 25.

10. Justin McCarthy was institutionalized in his home state of Pennsylvania for five years following what was loosely called "a nervous breakdown"; a fuller diagnosis was never made. N. F. Karlins, "Four from Coal Country: Friendships and the Contemporary Folk Artist," *Clarion* 12, no. 2/3 (Spring/Summer 1987): 58. Eddie Arning spent most of his adult life in a mental institution in Austin, Texas. Pamela Jane Sachant completed her dissertation, "The Art and Life of Eddie Arning," in 2003 at the University of Delaware. See also Pamela Jane Sachant, "Evidence of Abridgment in Eddie Arning's Art, and Its Importance," *Folk Art* 29, no. 3 (Fall, 2004): 48–55; and Pamela Jane Sachant, "Eddie Arning's American Dream," *Raw Vision* 28 (1999): 28–33.

11. Besharo's known body of work comprises sixty-nine paintings found in a rented garage where the painter stored his belongings. Lee Kogan, "New Museum Encyclopedia Shatters Myths," *Clarion* 15, no. 5 (Winter 1990–91): 55, a review of Chuck and Jan Rosenak, *Museum of American Folk Art Encyclopedia of Twentieth-Century American Folk Art and Artists* (New York: Abbeville Press, 1990). See also Lynda Roscoe Hartigan et al., *Made with Passion: The Hemphill Folk Art Collectionin the National Museum of American Art* (Washington, DC: Smithsonian Institution Press, 1990), 140. Hartigan's text, which predated the location of his death certificate and World War II draft card, listed Besharo under the surname "Boshegan"; other early sources listed him as "Boshero."

12. Colin Rhodes, biography on Edwin Lawson for Ricco/Maresca Gallery, email with author, December 15, 2020.

13. Jeffrey R. Hayes, "Black, Calvin and Ruby," in *The New Encyclopedia of Southern Culture*, ed. Carol Crown, Cheryl Rivers, and Charles Reagan Wilson, vol. 23, *Folk Art* (Chapel Hill: University of North Carolina Press, 2013), 226, https://www.jstor.org/stable/10.5149/9781469607993_crown.

14. The Possum Trot environment was dismantled after Ruby's death. A section of the theater with original dolls is now in the collection of the Milwaukee Art Museum; individual dolls from the site are held in numerous public and private collections. See William Keyse Rudolph, "Possum Trot," *From the Collection* (blog), Milwaukee Art Museum, February 12, 2012, https://blog.mam.org/2012/02/22/from-the-collection-possum-trot/.

15. For information on the Blacks, see "Calvin & Ruby Black, Possum Trot," SPACES, accessed April 29, 2021, http://www.spaces-art-environments.org/explore/collection/environment/possum-trot/.

16. Albert Mertz's grandson Garth Andrew May has explained that the artist called his home art environment "Owl's Rest" in the early to mid-1980s, and later changed it to "Owl's Roost," finally naming it for himself as "Al's Roost." Garth Andrew May, Albert Mertz's grandson, interview by SAAM curatorial assistant Maria R. Eipert, September 25, 2020, and text exchange with Maria R. Eipert, March 12, 2021, notes on file in the SAAM curatorial office.

17. May notes that Albert's family was from Lithuania, but he identified as a Russian Jew. Other papers on file include Mertz's court documents for his name change and orphan court certificate. May lives on the property that once belonged to his grandfather. May, interview.

18. Leslie Umberger, "Emery Blagdon: Properly Channeled," in *Sublime Spaces & Visionary Worlds: Built Environments of Vernacular Artists*, by Leslie Umberger et al., (New York: Princeton Architectural Press, 2007), 203–23. All information on Emery Blagdon, his life, and his art is drawn from this author's primary research on Blagdon for the 2007 exhibition *Sublime Spaces & Visionary Worlds: Built Environments of Vernacular Artists*, at the John Michael Kohler Arts Center, Sheboygan, Wisconsin, and book of the same title noted above. Blagdon has been more thoroughly researched than other artists in this section, although relatively few photographs chart his project during Blagdon's active years.

19. Miller was featured in a solo exhibition at White Columns in 2007 and a group exhibition at the Museum of Modern Art, New York, in 2008, and his art was acquired by MoMA in 2007 and by SAAM in 2015.

20. Tom di Maria, email correspondence with author, August 12, 2021.

21. Tom di Maria, "When Words Write Pictures," *Raw Vision* 88 (Winter 2015/16): 16.

22. Matthew Higgs, quoted in Di Maria, "When Words Write Pictures," 18–19.

23. Claire Daigle, quoted in Di Maria, "When Words Write Pictures," 18. Daigle is also a contributor to Tom di Maria, ed., *The Creative Growth Book: From the Outside to the Inside with Disabilities Today* (Milan: 5 Continents Editions, 2015). Daigle is a professor at the San Francisco Art Institute.

24. For examples of Miller's typewriter works, see Smithsonian American Art Museum, https://americanart.si.edu/artwork/untitled-116919 and https://americanart.si.edu/artwork/untitled-116918.

25. Martin J. Esslin, "Samuel Beckett: Irish Author," *Encyclopedia Britannica*, December 18, 2020, https://www.britannica.com/biography/Samuel-Beckett.

26. Individuals whose neurology differs substantially from dominant norms are "neurodivergent." Other abilities/disabilities (sensory, physical, learning) may require additional or nuanced language. The "neurodiversity paradigm" advocates that diverse minds are equally valuable; this contrasts with ethnology models that promoted normative ideals versus inferior beings. Ableism, a critique increasingly cast at museums, refers to discrimination of anyone with physical, intellectual, or psychiatric disabilities.

27. Catherine Morris, "Biography Is Complicated," *Art 21 Magazine*, October 30, 2018, https://magazine.art21.org/2018/10/30/biography-is-complicated/.

28. Even in cases where self-taught artists made statements regarding whether they considered themselves an artist or their work "art," such statements demand a careful consideration of semantic interpretations and word-use disparities between the subjects and those who subsequently recorded and interpreted such statements. They more likely pertain to a conceptual conversation about mainstream notions of "fine art" as a rarefied realm they were excluded from, rather than a true measure of self-regard.

29. See accounts given in Umberger, "Emery Blagdon," 203–23.

30. Artworks from interrelated environments function best, when off-site, in cohesive groupings. The SAAM collection contains four Blagdon sculptures from the Margaret Z. Robson Collection; they are on long-term view with other components of his Healing Machine. During my tenure at the Kohler Arts Center (1998–2012), I orchestrated the preservation and acquisition of the primary body of Blagdon's oeuvre.

31. See John Michael Vlach and Simon J. Bronner, *Folk Art and Art Worlds* (Logan: Utah State University Press, 1992). These events took place, respectively, in 1979, 1982, and 1983. See also Gerald Pocius, "Material Culture Worlds: A Report on Three Conferences," *Material Culture Review* 46, no. 1 (Fall 1997), https://journals.lib.unb.ca/index.php/MCR/article/view/17754/22235.

32. The debate at Winterthur became so heated that it became known colloquially as the "Shootout at Winterthur"; see Pocius, "Material Culture Worlds."

33. See note 3, "Momentum" section, above.

34. Kenneth L. Ames, "Outside Outsider Art," in *The Artist Outsider: Creativity and the Boundaries of Culture*, ed. Michael D. Hall and Eugene W. Metcalf Jr. (Washington, DC: Smithsonian Institution Press, 1994), 264.

35. Roberta Smith, "A Sea Change in the Art World, Made by Black Creators," *New York Times*, November 24, 2019, updated November 30, 2019, https://www.nytimes.com/2019/11/24/arts/design/black-artists.html.

36. For Finster's tribute to Herbert Hemphill, see Smithsonian American Art Museum, https://americanart.si.edu/artwork/herbert-wade-hemphill-jr-collection-founder-american-folk-art-man-who-preserves-lone-and; see also Lynda Roscoe Hartigan, "Collecting the Lone and Forgotten," in Hartigan et al., *Made with Passion*, 1–80.

37. Thirty-three artworks promised and one donated in 2022, in tandem with ninety-three donated in 2016, make the Robson Family Collection the largest outright donation of art by self-taught makers at SAAM, to date. This extraordinarily important gift of art, in conjunction with the endowment of the Margaret Z. Robson Symposium Series, is collectively among the most major gifts of self-taught art and program support in SAAM's history. The Herbert Waide Hemphill Jr. collection was a partial gift/partial purchase (1986), followed by a bequest that funded the Herbert Waide Hemphill Jr. American Folk Art Fund at SAAM. The Chuck and Jan Rosenak collection was also a partial gift/partial purchase (1987; 1997).

38. Heidi Stevens, "What a Woody Allen Reckoning Can Teach Us about Lincoln Statues, Dr. Seuss and the British Royal Family," *Chicago Tribune*, March 8, 2021, https://www.chicago tribune.com/columns/heidi-stevens/ct-heidi-stevens-rethinking-woody-allen-manhattan-harry-meghan-0308-20210308-l5lqx4hxdvbelcnqudsmbxnkei-story.html.

CATALOGUE OF WORKS

Artworks are in the collection of the Smithsonian American Art Museum (The Margaret Z. Robson Collection, Gift of John E. and Douglas O. Robson, 2016), unless delineated as promised gifts from the Robson Family Collection.

Life dates are presented to the best of our knowledge, as documentation for many artists is either scant or insufficient and may not be verified. In keeping with oral tradition, preference has been given, in some cases, to the life dates used by the artists or their families. Works marked with an asterisk (*) are not in the exhibition but can be seen at americanart.si.edu/art; those marked with a dagger (†) are not illustrated or discussed in the text. Dimensions are object-only (unless noted otherwise) and are presented in inches; height precedes width and depth.

EDDIE ARNING
1898–1993

Untitled (American Flag)
ca. 1964

crayon and graphite on paper
22 × 17 in.

SAAM 2016.38.1

CAT. 1

PETER "CHARLIE" ATTIE BESHARO
1899–1960

Untitled (From Earth to Haven/ From Haven to Earth)
ca. 1950–60

oil on paper
22 ⅝ × 28 ¾ in.

SAAM 2016.38.2

CAT. 105

CALVIN BLACK
1903–1972

RUBY BLACK
1913–1980

Gladys (Possum Trot Doll)
ca. 1953–72

carved and painted wood, fabric, sequins, and foil bow
41 ⅜ × 16 ½ × 12 ⅛ in.

SAAM 2016.38.3

CAT. 111

Untitled (Possum Trot Doll)
ca. 1953–72

carved and painted wood, fabric
46 ½ × 11 ¾ × 10 ½ in., with base

SAAM 2016.38.4

CAT. 112

EMERY BLAGDON
1907–1986

Untitled (Individual element from *The Healing Machine)**
ca. 1956–84

steel, copper wire, tinfoil, paper, and plastic
76 × 7 × 6 in.

SAAM 2016.38.5

CAT. 114

Untitled (Individual element from *The Healing Machine)**
ca. 1956–84

steel wire, plastic, tinfoil, wood, paper tape, and mixed media
86 × 7 × 3 in.

SAAM 2016.38.6

CAT. 115

Untitled (Individual element from *The Healing Machine)**
ca. 1956–84

popsicle sticks, tinfoil, paper tape, copper wire, and steel
8 × 7 ⅝ × ½ in.

SAAM 2016.38.7

CAT. 116

Untitled (Individual element from *The Healing Machine)**
ca. 1956–84

popsicle sticks, tinfoil, paper tape, copper wire, and steel
7 ⅞ × 8 ½ × ⅝ in.

SAAM 2016.38.8

CAT. 117

DAVID BUTLER
1898–1997

Untitled (Reindeer)
1965

paint on cut and pieced sheet metal
12 ¼ × 42 ¾ in., irregular

SAAM 2016.38.9

CAT. 35

Untitled (Three Wise Men and a Goat)
1965

paint on cut sheet metal
13 ¾ × 42 ⅛ × 2 ⅛ in.

SAAM 2016.38.10

CAT. 36

Untitled (Mary with Baby Jesus)
ca. 1970–80

paint on articulated cut sheet metal
38 ¼ × 18 ¼ × 7 ¾ in.

SAAM 2016.38.11

CAT. 37

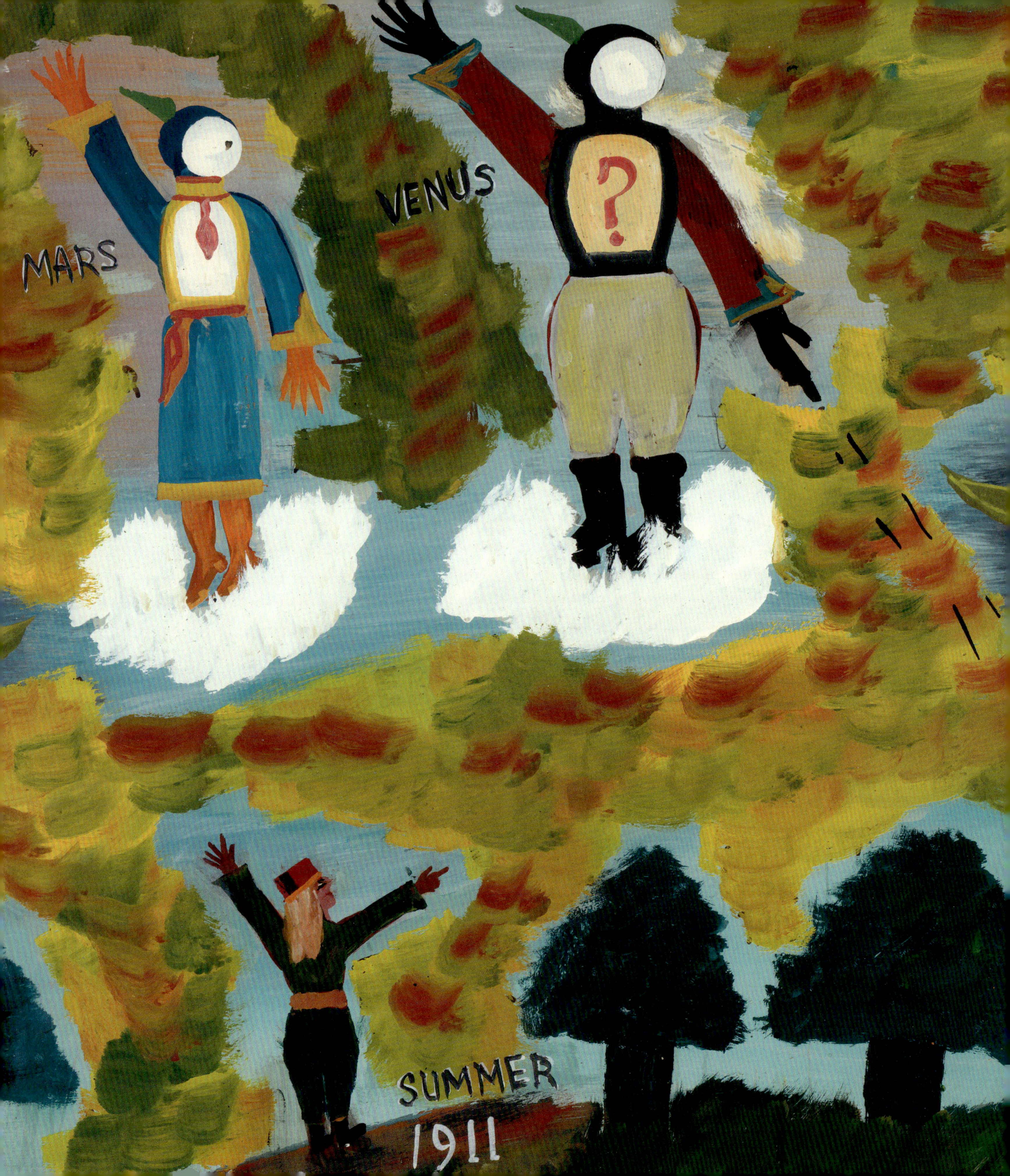
MARS
VENUS
?
SUMMER
1911

Peter "Charlie" Attie Besharo, detail, Cat. 105

JAMES CASTLE
1899–1977

Untitled
ca. 1931–77
soot on found paper
sheet and image: 4 ¾ × 8 ¾ in.
SAAM 2016.38.14
CAT. 80

Untitled
ca. 1931–77
color of unknown origin and soot on found paper
3 ½ × 6 ⅞ in., irregular
SAAM 2016.38.12
CAT. 81

Untitled
ca. 1931–77
color of unknown origin and soot on found paper
sheet and image: 4 ¾ × 4 ¾ in.
SAAM 2016.38.16
CAT. 82

Untitled
ca. 1931–77
soot on found paper
recto: 3 ¼ × 4 ¾ in.
verso: 2 ⅞ × 4 ¼ in. (sight)
SAAM 2016.38.13R-V
CAT. 83

Untitled
ca. 1931–77
soot on found paper
sheet and image: 4 ¾ × 5 ⅞ in.
SAAM 2016.38.15
CAT. 84

Untitled
ca. 1932
crayon on found paper
4 ¾ × 5 ⅞ in., irregular
SAAM 2016.38.17
CAT. 85

HENRY DARGER
1892–1973

137 At Jennie Richee
(verso: *136 At Jennie Richee*)
ca. 1950–70
watercolor, carbon transfer, and graphite on pieced paper
23 ½ × 109 ¼ in.
Collection of Douglas O. Robson from the Robson Family Collection, Promised gift to the Smithsonian American Art Museum
CAT. 77

ULYSSES DAVIS
1913–1990

George Washington
ca. 1940s
carved and stained wood
9 ¼ × 7 ¼ × 3 ½ in.
Collection of Douglas O. Robson from the Robson Family Collection, Promised gift to the Smithsonian American Art Museum
CAT. 6

Lincoln
1940
carved and stained wood
9 ¾ × 7 ¼ × 3 ½ in.
Collection of Douglas O. Robson from the Robson Family Collection, Promised gift to the Smithsonian American Art Museum
CAT. 7

Where Life Comes From
ca. 1950–90
carved and stained wood
11 ¾ × 2 ¾ × 4 ¾ in.
SAAM 2016.38.23
CAT. 8

Sputnik
ca. 1957
carved and stained wood
8 × 2 ½ × 2 ⅜ in.
SAAM 2016.38.22
CAT. 50

Untitled
1942
carved and painted wood, inlaid with sand
10 ¼ × 20 ½ × 2 in.
SAAM 2016.38.24
CAT. 51

Strong Man
ca. 1950–90
carved and stained wood
11 × 5 × 2 ⅛ in.
SAAM 2016.38.18
CAT. 52

Headhunter
ca. 1950–90
carved and painted wood and rhinestones
19 ⅞ × 3 ⅞ × 3 ⅝ in.
SAAM 2016.38.20
CAT. 53

Untitled
ca. 1950–90
carved and painted wood and rhinestones
19 ½ × 5 × 3 ¾ in.
SAAM 2016.38.19
CAT. 54

Uncle Sam
1976
painted and carved wood
18 ⅝ × 7 ¾ × 7 ¾ in.
Collection of Douglas O. Robson from the Robson Family Collection, Promised gift to the Smithsonian American Art Museum
CAT. 55

Untitled (Cane)
ca. 1950–90
carved and stained wood
34 ⅞ × 2 ½ × 2 ⅛ in.
SAAM 2016.38.21
CAT. 56

THORNTON DIAL SR.
1928–2016

The Movie Star and the Tiger Need One Another
March 1992
charcoal, graphite, and watercolor on paper
sheet and image: 22 ½ × 30 in.
SAAM 2016.38.25
CAT. 92

Tiger Colored Lady
1994
charcoal, graphite, chalk, and pastel on paper
43 ½ × 29 ½ in.
Collection of Douglas O. Robson, Promised gift to the Smithsonian American Art Museum
CAT. 93

Recalling the Pain
2011
charred wood, metal, corrugated tin, plastic, nails, and enamel on wood
60 × 51 ⅛ × 10 in.
Collection of Douglas O. Robson, Promised gift to the Smithsonian American Art Museum
CAT. 94

SAM DOYLE
1906–1985

F. Capers
ca. 1970–83
paint on repurposed tin siding
40 ⅜ × 26 ½ in.
Collection of Douglas O. Robson, Promised gift to the Smithsonian American Art Museum
CAT. 48

Bull Dager
ca. 1980
paint on sheet metal
39 ⅛ × 25 ½ × 2 ⅜ in., irregular
SAAM 2016.38.26
CAT. 49

WILLIAM EDMONDSON
1874–1951

Untitled (Bird Bath with Figures)
ca. 1932–40
carved limestone
32 ½ × 26 ⅞ × 12 ¾ in., with base
SAAM 2016.38.87A-C
CAT. 31

Untitled (Bird)
ca. 1937
carved limestone
8 ⅛ × 11 ⅛ × 3 ¾ in.
SAAM 2016.38.89
CAT. 32

Untitled (Teacher)
ca. 1932–40
carved limestone
12 × 3 ⅞ × 7 ⅝ in.
SAAM 2016.38.88
CAT. 33

HOWARD FINSTER
1916–2001

Self-Portrait
1975
paint on cut plywood; ink on foamcore
94 ½ × 19 in.
Collection of Douglas O. Robson from the Robson Family Collection, Promised gift to the Smithsonian American Art Museum
CAT. 86

Untitled
1988
paint and marker on glass bottle
12 ¼ × 6 ½ in. (diam.)
SAAM 2016.38.27
CAT. 87

Untitled
1988
paint and marker on glass bottle
12 ¼ × 6 ½ in. (diam.)
SAAM 2016.38.28
CAT. 88

following pages: William Hawkins, detail, Cat. 44

Untitled
1988
paint on glass bottle
12 ¼ × 6 ½ in. (diam.)
SAAM 2016.38.29
CAT. 89

Untitled
1988
paint on glass bottle
12 ⅛ × 6 ½ in. (diam.)
SAAM 2016.38.30
CAT. 90

Untitled
1988
paint on glass bottle
12 ¼ × 6 ½ in. (diam.)
SAAM 2016.38.31
CAT. 91

SELDEN CONNOR GILE
1877–1947

*Church, Rancho de Taos**†
1931
watercolor on paper
17 ⅝ × 14 ⅛ in. (sight)
SAAM 2016.38.32
CAT. 121

FLOYD GRABER
1911–2003

*Untitled (The Fields Are White for to Harvest; and the Storms of Judgment Are Threatening)**†
n.d.
mixed media on board
48 × 88 in.
SAAM 2016.38.33
CAT. 122

BESSIE HARVEY
1929–1994

Untitled (Root Figure)
1988
painted root, beads, turkey bones, metal, plastic, and fabric
37 ¼ × 17 ¾ in. (diam.)
SAAM 2016.38.34
CAT. 74

Untitled (Root Figure)
1988
painted root, beads, turkey bones, metal, and plastic
42 ½ × 17 ⅝ × 18 ⅝ in.
SAAM 2016.38.35
CAT. 75

WILLIAM HAWKINS
1895–1990

Demolition of St. Mary's Church, Boston
1986
enamel paint on Masonite and collaged elements
40 × 48 ⅛ in.
Collection of Douglas O. Robson from the Robson Family Collection, Promised gift to the Smithsonian American Art Museum
CAT. 43

White Dog
1988
enamel, cornmeal, and collaged paper on Masonite
48 × 56 ¾ in.
Collection of Douglas O. Robson, Promised gift to the Smithsonian American Art Museum
CAT. 44

CLEMENTINE HUNTER
ca. 1886/7–1988

Untitled (Magi Bearing Gifts)
ca. 1970–80
paint on Albany slip whiskey jug
9 ¼ × 7 ⅝ in. (diam.)
SAAM 2016.38.36
CAT. 34

EDWIN LAWSON
1911–1980

Fashion 1955
1973
colored pencil and graphite on paper
23 ⅝ × 18 in.
SAAM 2016.38.37
CAT. 109

Fashions 1899
1974
colored pencil and graphite on paper
23 ⅝ × 18 in.
SAAM 2016.38.38
CAT. 110

ERMA "JUNIOR" LEWIS
1948–1999

*Last Supper**†
1993
painted and carved wood
23 × 9 ½ × 6 ⅛ in.
SAAM 2016.38.39
CAT. 123

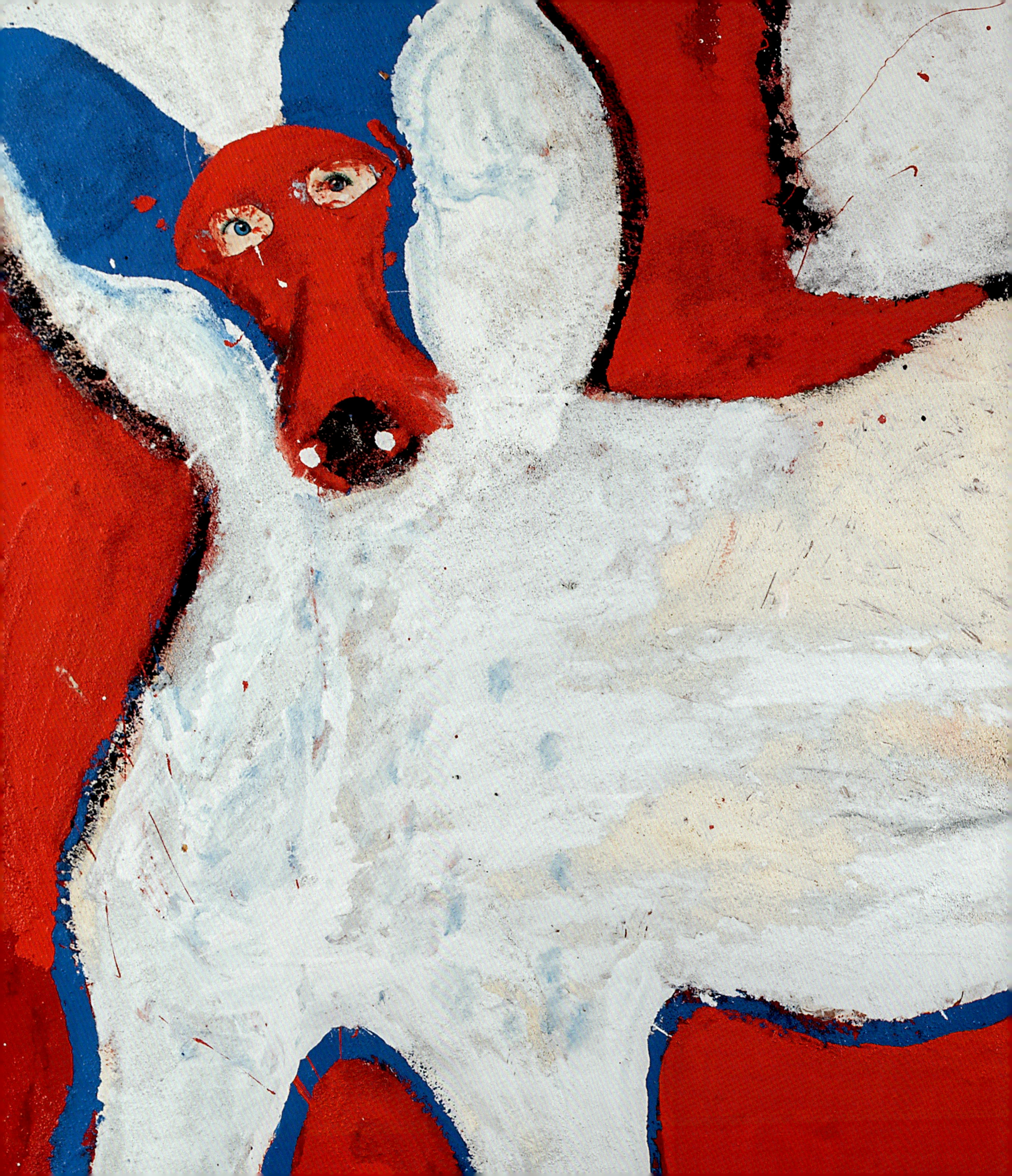

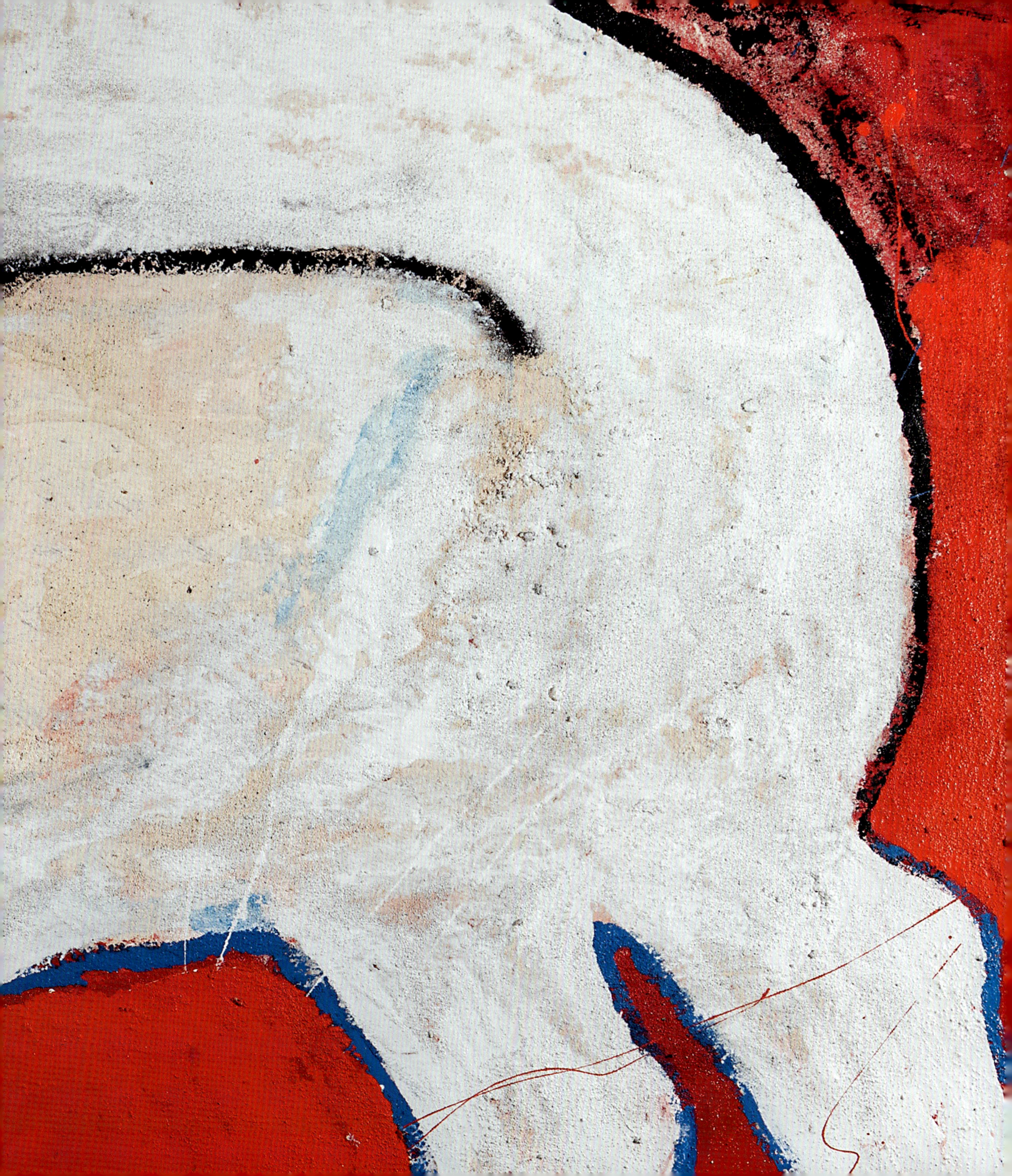

Philadelphia Wireman, Cat. 70

JUSTIN McCARTHY
ca. 1891–1977

Original
ca. 1930–70
watercolor and ink on paper mounted on manila folder
overall: 11 ¾ × 9 ⅛ in., irregular
SAAM 2016.38.40
CAT. 101

Marie Prevost
ca. 1930–60
watercolor, ink, and graphite on paper mounted on manila folder
overall: 11 ¾ × 9 in., irregular
SAAM 2016.38.41
CAT. 102

Jack Dempsey Loses Heavyweight Title to Gene Tunney 1926/James Braddock 1937 Is Defeated by Joe Louis
ca. 1930–60
ink and pencil on paper
18 ⅝ × 12 ¼ in.
Collection of Douglas O. Robson, Promised gift to the Smithsonian American Art Museum
CAT. 103

Pancho Segura
ca. 1930–60
ink and pencil on paper
17 ⅜ × 11 ½ in.
Collection of Douglas O. Robson, Promised gift to the Smithsonian American Art Museum
CAT. 104

LAURA CRAIG McNELLIS
b. 1957

Untitled (Fudgesicles)
ca. 1982
mixed media on newsprint
21 ¼ × 26 in.
Collection of Douglas O. Robson, Promised gift to the Smithsonian American Art Museum
CAT. 13

Untitled (White Plate with Sandwich)
ca. 1982
mixed media on newsprint
20 ¼ × 30 ½ in.
Collection of Douglas O. Robson, Promised gift to the Smithsonian American Art Museum
CAT. 14

ALBERT "KID" MERTZ
1905–1988

Untitled
ca. 1980
painted railroad spikes
dimensions variable
SAAM 2016.38.42
CAT. 113

DAN MILLER
b. 1961

Untitled (DM 847)
2016
papier-mâché and tin can
13 × 9 × 8 in.; diam. at smallest point: 2 ⅞ in.
Collection of Douglas O. Robson, Promised gift to the Smithsonian American Art Museum
CAT. 15

Untitled (DM 848)
2016
papier-mâché and tin can
15 × 11 × 8 in.; diam. at smallest point: 2 ⅞ in.
Collection of Douglas O. Robson, Promised gift to the Smithsonian American Art Museum
CAT. 16

Untitled (283_2016)
2016
acrylic and ink on paper
28 ¾ × 41 ½ in.
Collection of Douglas O. Robson, Promised gift to the Smithsonian American Art Museum
CAT. 118

Untitled (DM 1024)
2018
acrylic and embroidery on fabric, mixed media 24 ½ × 38 ½ in.
Collection of Douglas O. Robson, Promised gift to the Smithsonian American Art Museum
CAT. 119

Untitled (239_2016)
2016
acrylic and ink on paper
52 × 142 in.
Robson Family Collection,
Gift of Douglas O. Robson, 2022.3
CAT. 120

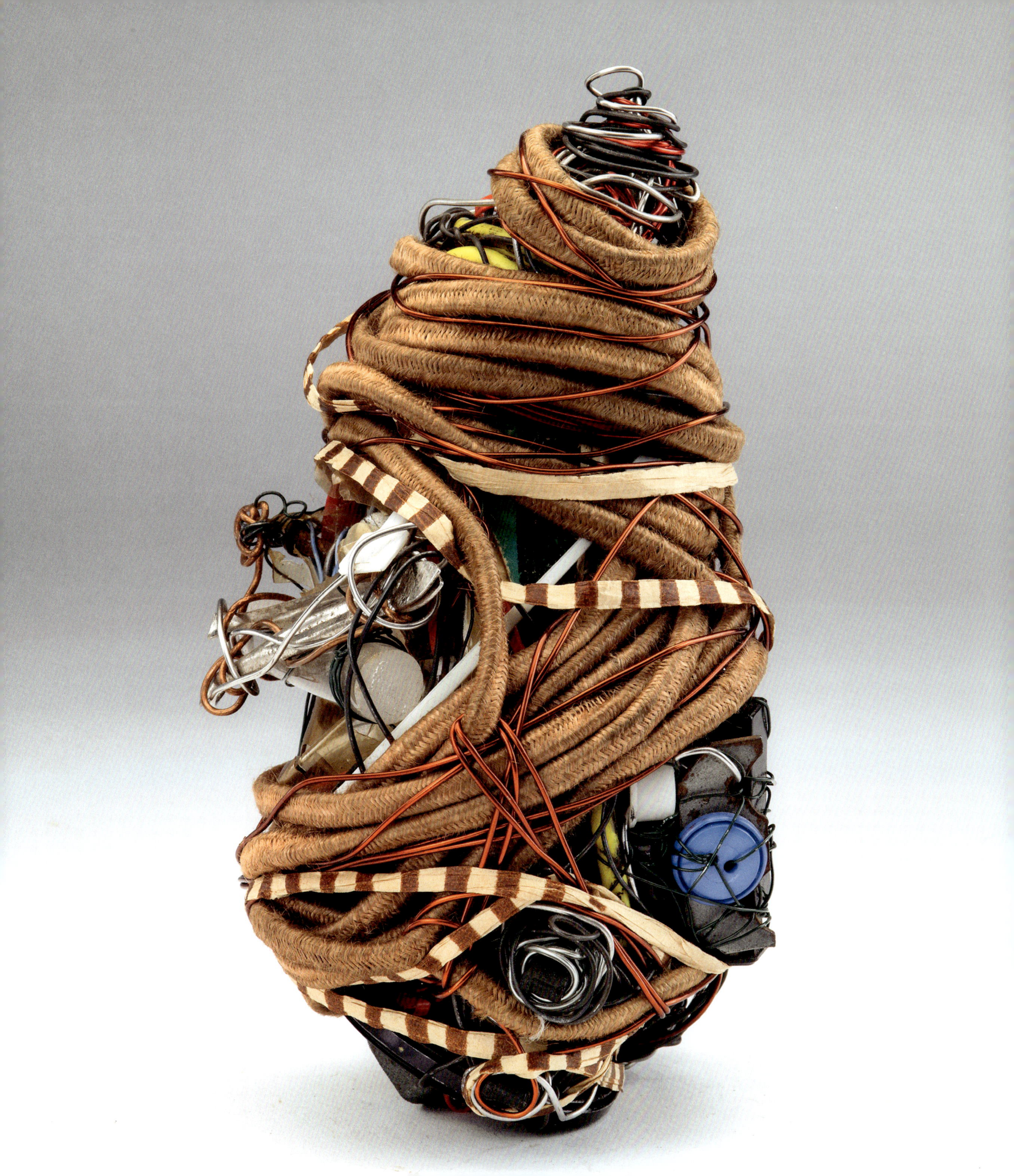

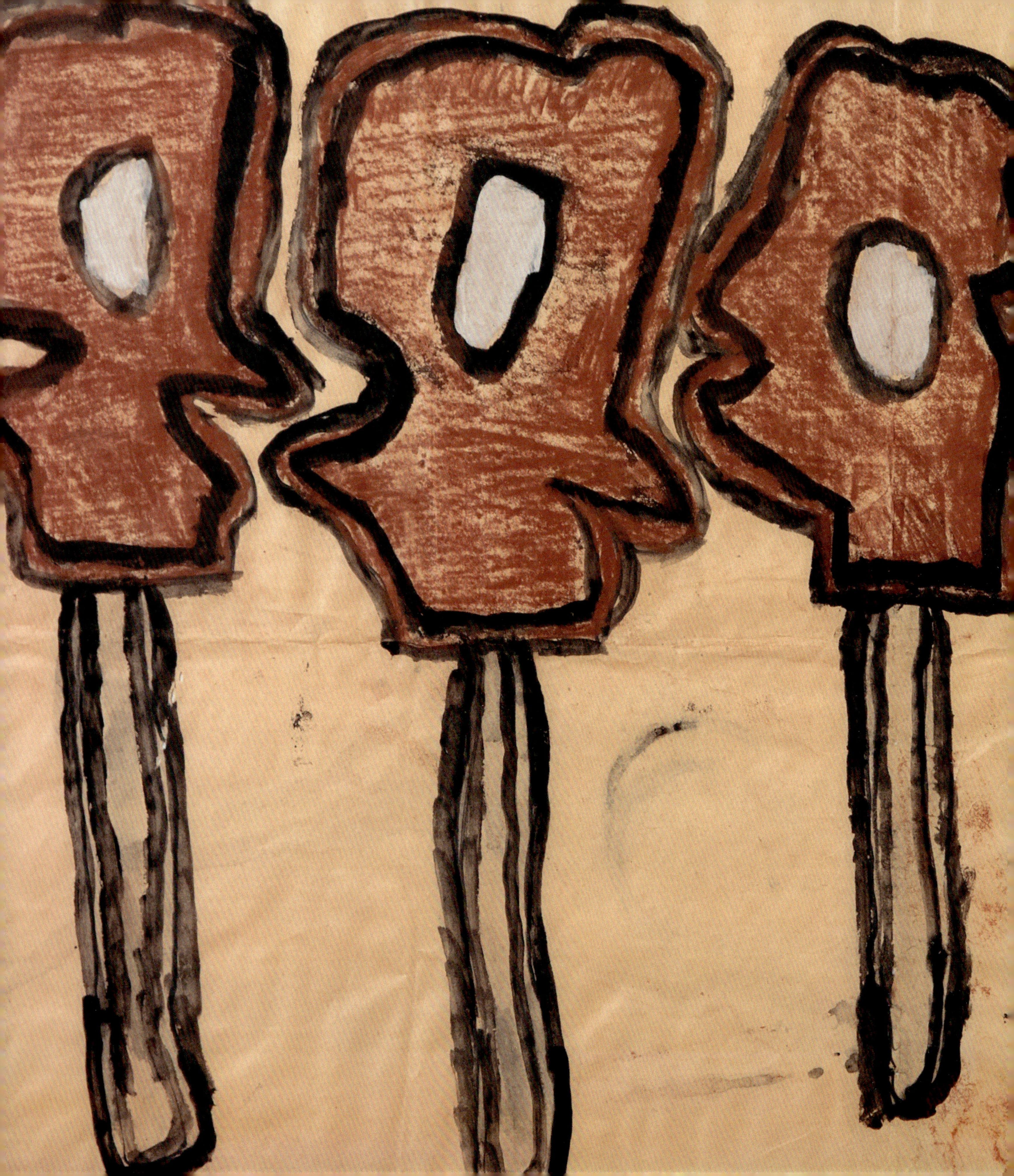

Laura Craig McNellis, detail, Cat. 13

SISTER GERTRUDE MORGAN

1900–1980

Fan
ca. 1970
paint and ink on card
9 ¾ × 8 ½ in.; irregular, double-sided
SAAM 2016.38.43R-V
CAT. 47

LEROY PERSON

1907–1985

Untitled
ca. 1975
polychrome carved wood and metal
38 ⅞ × 17 × 16 ¼ in.
SAAM 2016.38.44
CAT. 57

PHILADELPHIA WIREMAN

active 20th century

Untitled
ca. 1970–75
can opener, wire, and mixed media
7 ⅞ × 3 × 2 ⅜ in.
SAAM 2016.38.45
CAT. 59

Untitled
ca. 1970–75
found objects and wire
2 ⅝ × 3 ½ × 2 ⅜ in.
SAAM 2016.38.46
CAT. 60

Untitled
ca. 1970–75
bottle cap, paper towel, mixed media, and wire
10 ⅛ × 4 × 3 ⅝ in.
SAAM 2016.38.47
CAT. 61

Untitled
ca. 1970–75
found objects and wire
5 ⅜ × 4 ⅛ × 2 ¼ in.
SAAM 2016.38.48
CAT. 62

Untitled
ca. 1970–75
copper, wood, and wire
10 ⅞ × 2 ¼ × 1 ¼ in.
SAAM 2016.38.49
CAT. 63

Untitled
ca. 1970–75
plastic bag, plastic cup, and wire
6 × 3 × 1 ⅞ in.
SAAM 2016.38.50
CAT. 64

Untitled
ca. 1970–75
found objects and wire
6 ½ × 6 ½ × 3 ¼ in.
SAAM 2016.38.51
CAT. 65

Untitled
ca. 1970–75
piano keys, beads, chain, plastic, and wire
8 × 3 ¾ × 2 ¾ in.
SAAM 2016.38.52
CAT. 66

Untitled
ca. 1970–75
tinfoil, plastic, rubber, steel, and wire
7 ⅞ × 8 ⅛ × 5 ⅜ in.
SAAM 2016.38.53
CAT. 67

Untitled
ca. 1970–75
found objects and wire
8 ⅛ × 3 ⅜ × 2 ½ in.
SAAM 2016.38.54
CAT. 68

Untitled
ca. 1970–75
found objects and wire
6 ⅜ × 2 ¼ × 1 ⅛ in.
SAAM 2016.38.55
CAT. 69

Untitled
ca. 1970–75
tweezers, electrical cord, button, and wire
7 ¼ × 3 ⅝ × 3 ¾ in.
SAAM 2016.38.56
CAT. 70

Martín Ramírez, detail, Cat. 79

Untitled
ca. 1970–75
found objects and wire
3 ½ × 3 × 2 ⅝ in.
SAAM 2016.38.57
CAT. 71

Untitled
ca. 1970–75
found objects and wire
6 ⅜ × 4 ⅛ × 2 in.
SAAM 2016.38.58
CAT. 72

Untitled
ca. 1970–75
cigarette wrappers, found objects, and wire
6 ¾ × 3 × 2 in.
SAAM 2016.38.59
CAT. 73

ELIJAH PIERCE
1892–1984

Elephant
ca. 1978
painted and carved wood, pebbles, plastic, and rhinestone
17 ½ × 4 × 11 ⅞ in.
SAAM 2016.38.60
CAT. 42

STEPHAN W. POLAHA
1891–1977

*Eagle**
ca. 1975
carved and painted wood and glass
height: 15 ½ in.
SAAM 2016.38.62
CAT. 4

Green Eyed Dog
ca. 1975
carved and painted wood and glass
13 ⅝ × 18 ⅞ × 6 ⅞ in.
SAAM 2016.38.61
CAT. 106

MARTÍN RAMÍREZ
1895–1963

Untitled (Vertical Landscape)
ca. 1948–63
pencil and crayon on pieced paper
overall: 48 × 30 in.
Collection of Douglas O. Robson from the Robson Family Collection, Promised gift to the Smithsonian American Art Museum
CAT. 78

Untitled (Semi-Abstract Landscape with Birds, Tunnels, and Blue Teardrop Clusters)
ca. 1960–63
mixed media on paper
27 ½ × 31 ⅝ in.
Collection of Douglas O. Robson from the Robson Family Collection, Promised gift to the Smithsonian American Art Museum
CAT. 79

ERNEST "POPEYE" REED
1919–1985

Venus
1980
carved sandstone
17 5/16 × 6 ⅛ × 5 ¼ in.
SAAM 2016.38.63
CAT. 107

Woman and Child
ca. 1980–85
carved sandstone
14 ⅛ × 4 ⅞ × 6 ¼ in.
SAAM 2016.38.64
CAT. 108

WILLIAM CARLTON "W. C." RICE
1930–2004

*Jesus**†
ca. 1960–80
paint on rusted sheet metal
15 ¼ × 23 in., irregular
SAAM 2016.38.65
CAT. 124

ACHILLES G. RIZZOLI
1896–1981

Margaret E. Griffin Symbolically Sketched / Palazzo Pianissimo
1939
ink on paper
24 × 35 ⅝ in. (sight)
framed: 31 ½ × 43 ⅛ × ¾ in.
Collection of Douglas O. Robson, Promised gift to the Smithsonian American Art Museum
CAT. 98

Marina Row Houses, Office of O. A. Deichmann
1932
graphite, ink, and watercolor on paper
6 ⅜ × 32 ¼ in. (sight)
Collection of Douglas O. Robson, Promised gift to the Smithsonian American Art Museum
CAT. 99

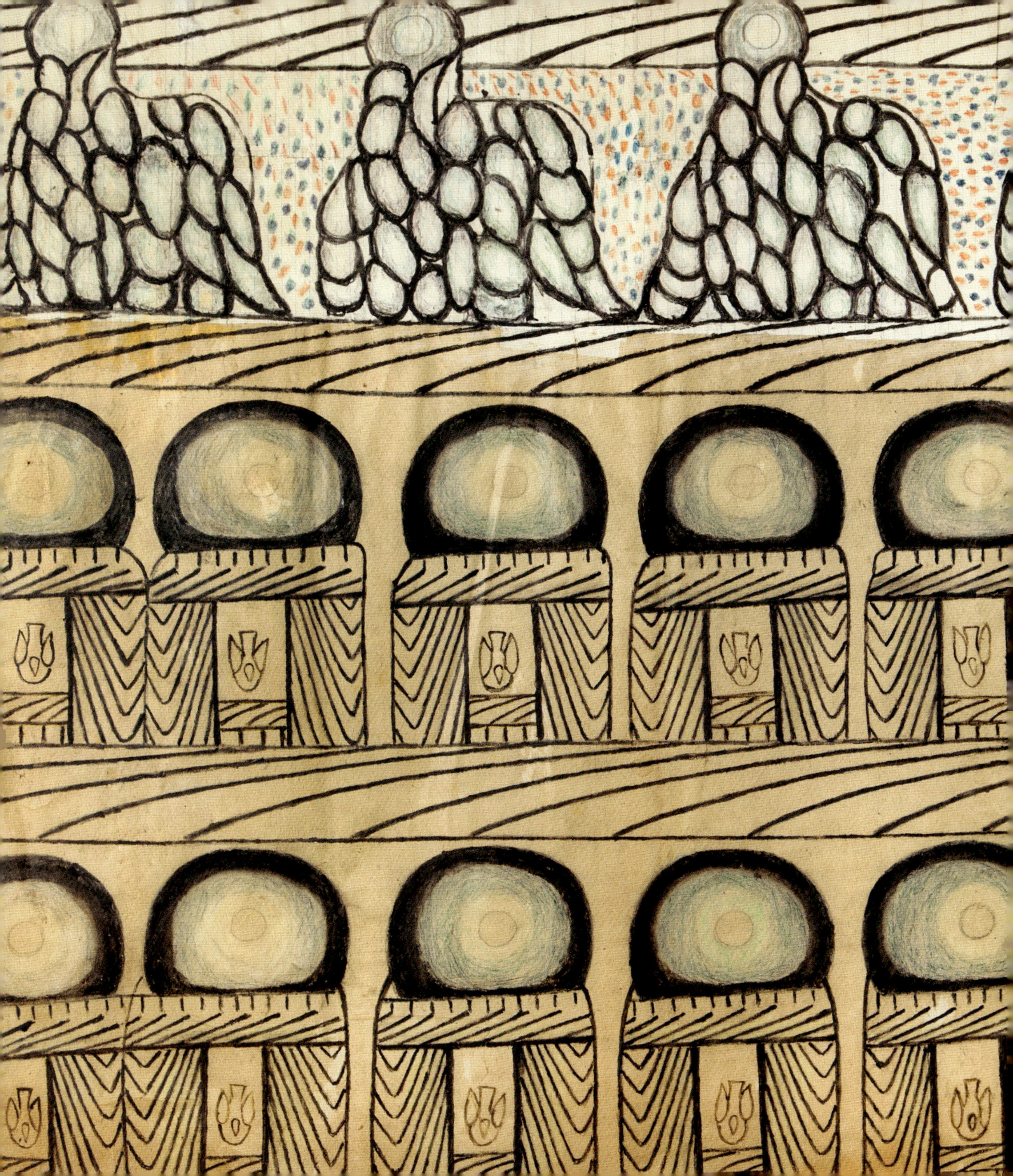

NELLIE MAE ROWE

1900–1982

Nellie on Blue
ca. 1978–82
paint and pastel on mounted photograph
9 ⅞ × 8 in.
Collection of Douglas O. Robson, Promised gift to the Smithsonian American Art Museum
CAT. 45

Nellie Mae Seated on Bench
ca. 1980
mixed media on photograph
11 ⅞ × 15 ¼ in.
Collection of Douglas O. Robson, Promised gift to the Smithsonian American Art Museum
CAT. 46

JUDITH SCOTT

1943–2005

Untitled
1994
mixed media and string
65 ⅛ × 14 ⅞ × 9 ¼ in.
SAAM 2016.38.67
CAT. 11

Untitled
ca. 1990–2005
mixed media, shoe section, and thread
33 ⅞ × 18 ¼ × 18 ¼ in.
SAAM 2016.38.66
CAT. 95

Untitled (Medicine Bottle)
1996
mixed media and string
32 × 24 × 15 in.
Collection of Douglas O. Robson from the Robson Family Collection, Promised gift to the Smithsonian American Art Museum
CAT. 96

Untitled (JS 39)
1997
mixed media
41 × 20 × 18 in.
Collection of Douglas O. Robson, Promised gift to the Smithsonian American Art Museum
CAT. 97

JON SERL

1894–1993

Texas Scene
1975
oil on board
34 ⅜ × 48 in.
SAAM 2016.38.68
CAT. 100

SIMON SPARROW

ca. 1925–2000

Untitled
ca. 1968–83
glitter, molded plastic, jewelry, shell, beads, and found objects on wood; artist-made painted wood frame
33 × 35 ⅛ in.
SAAM 2016.38.69
CAT. 58

BILL TRAYLOR

ca. 1853–1949

Untitled (Mule, Dog, and Scene with Chicken)
July 1939
pencil on paperboard
23 × 14 in.
SAAM 2016.38.93
CAT. 5

Untitled (Mule)
December 1939
opaque watercolor and pencil on paperboard
15 × 14 in.
SAAM 2016.38.90
CAT. 19

Untitled (Seated Woman)
ca. 1940–42
opaque watercolor and pencil on paperboard
14 ½ × 8 in.
SAAM 2016.38.92
CAT. 26

Untitled (Man in Blue and Brown)
ca. 1940–42
opaque watercolor and pencil on paperboard
15 × 11 ½ in.
SAAM 2016.38.91
CAT. 27

Untitled (Drinker in Chair)
ca. 1939–42
pencil and poster paint on cardboard
11 × 8 ¼ in.
Collection of Douglas O. Robson from the Robson Family Collection, Promised gift to the Smithsonian American Art Museum
CAT. 28

Untitled (Spotted Cat with Two Eyes)
ca. 1939–42
opaque watercolor and graphite on beige card
15 × 12 ½ in.
Collection of Douglas O. Robson from the Robson Family Collection, Promised gift to the Smithsonian American Art Museum
CAT. 29

Untitled (Brown Pig)
April 1940
opaque watercolor and pencil on paperboard
10 × 23 in.
SAAM 2016.38.70
CAT. 30

UNIDENTIFIED ARTIST
*Untitled (Cast Iron Eagle from White Eagle Oil Company)**
ca. 1920
cast iron
33 ⅛ × 13 ½ × 19 ½ in.
SAAM 2016.38.71
CAT. 2

UNIDENTIFIED ARTIST
*Untitled (Cast Iron Eagle from White Eagle Oil Company)**
ca. 1920
cast iron
33 ⅛ × 13 ½ × 19 ½ in.
SAAM 2016.38.72
CAT. 3

UNIDENTIFIED ARTIST
*Untitled (Twenty Mule Team)**
20th century
carved and painted wood
10 ¼ × 63 ⅛ × 5 ¾ in.
SAAM 2016.38.74
CAT. 12

UNIDENTIFIED ARTIST
Untitled (Eagle Weathervane)
ca. 1875
painted sheet iron
21 ⅛ × 24 ¾ × 1 ⅛ in.
SAAM 2016.38.75
CAT. 17

UNIDENTIFIED ARTIST
Untitled (Figure with Hat)
late 19th or early 20th century
cast iron
15 × 7 ½ × 6 ¼ in.
SAAM 2016.38.81
CAT. 18

UNIDENTIFIED ARTIST
Untitled (Swan Decoy from Delaware)
ca. 1920
carved wood
9 × 41 ⅛ × 7 ¾ in.
SAAM 2016.38.79
CAT. 20

UNIDENTIFIED ARTIST
Untitled (Snake Trivet)
late 19th or early 20th century
hand-forged metal
1 ⅝ × 13 ¼ × 6 ½ in.
SAAM 2016.38.83
CAT. 21

UNIDENTIFIED ARTIST
Untitled (Root Snake)
20th century
painted wood
2 ¾ × 17 ⅝ × 29 ¼ in.
SAAM 2016.38.82
CAT. 22

UNIDENTIFIED ARTIST
Untitled (Articulated Snake)
20th century
painted wood
1 ⅛ × 47 ⅞ × ⅞ in., variable
SAAM 2016.38.76
CAT. 23

UNIDENTIFIED ARTIST
Untitled (Snake)
20th century
painted wood
5 × 37 × 6 in.
SAAM 2016.38.78
CAT. 24

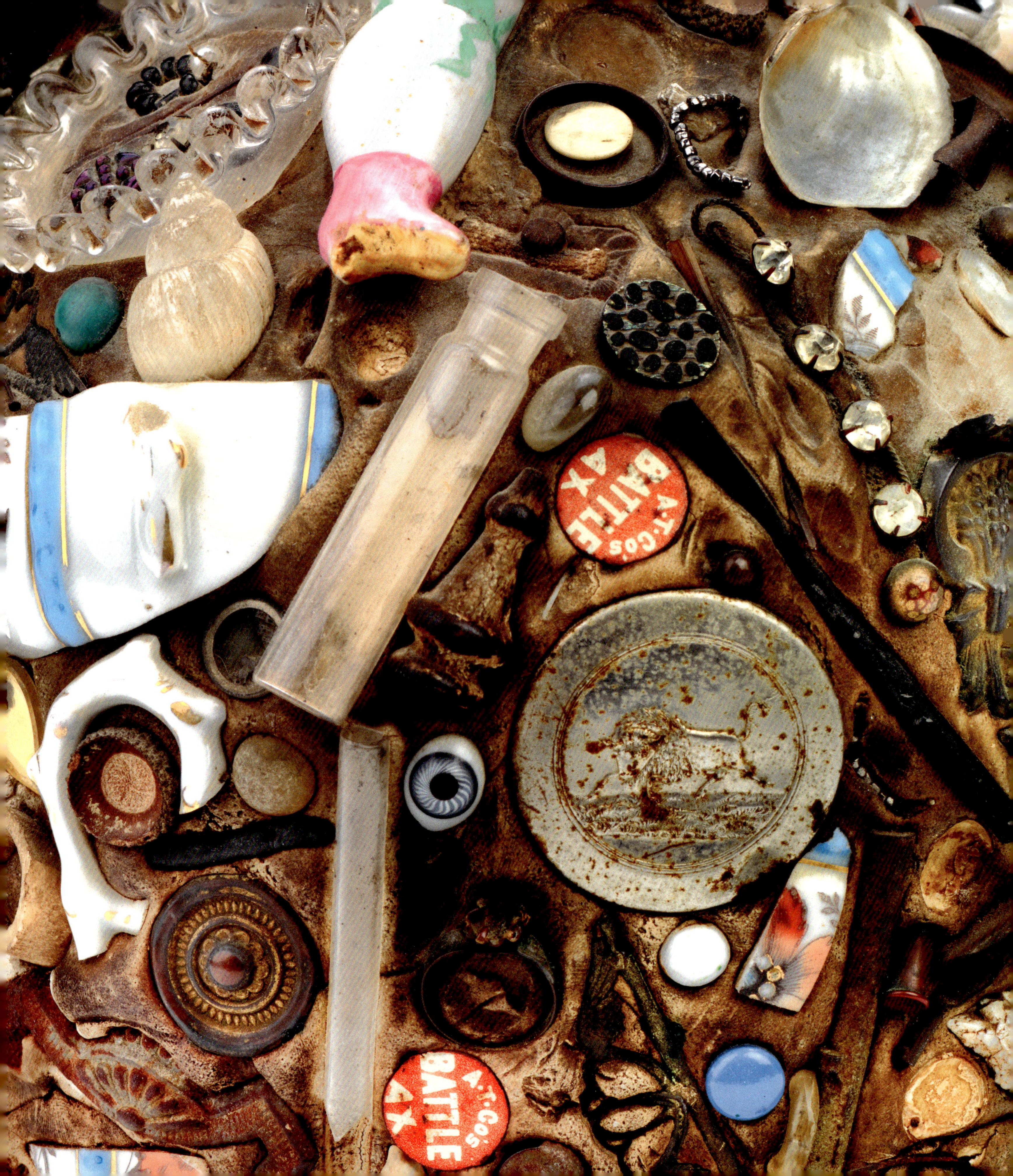
A.T.Co's
BATTLE
4X
A.T.Co's
BATTLE
4X

Unidentified artist, detail, Cat. 25

UNIDENTIFIED ARTIST

Untitled (Memory Jug)
ca. 1890–1920

clay and found objects
9 ½ × 9 ½ × 10 ¼ in.

SAAM 2016.38.80

CAT. 25

UNIDENTIFIED ARTIST

*Untitled (Feeding Curlew)**†
20th century

painted and carved wood
6 ¾ × 16 ¼ × 3 ¼ in.

SAAM 2016.38.73

CAT. 125

UNIDENTIFIED ARTIST

*Untitled (Architectural Angel, Chicago)**†
late 19th century

wood and silver leaf
42 × 26 × 16 in.

SAAM 2016.38.77

CAT. 126

ADOLF WÖLFLI
1864–1930

*Blatt Aus Heft #15**
1917

pencil, pastel, and colored pencil on paper

recto: 16 ½ × 11 ¼ in. (sight)
verso: 15 ⅞ × 10 ¾ in. (sight)

SAAM 2016.38.84R-V

CAT. 9

JOSEPH E. YOAKUM
1891–1972

Mt Jemel in Medicen Mtn Range Near Cheyenne Wyoming on Larime River

ca. 1960

ballpoint pen ink, colored pencil, and pastel on paper

17 ¾ × 23 ½ in.

Collection of Douglas O. Robson from the Robson Family Collection, Promised gift to the Smithsonian American Art Museum

CAT. 38

Devils Back Bone, in Mt Messa Near Trinadad Colorado
1966

ballpoint pen ink, colored pencil, and pastel on paper
11 ⅞ × 17 ¾ in.

Collection of Douglas O. Robson from the Robson Family Collection, Promised gift to the Smithsonian American Art Museum

CAT. 39

West Face Grand Prairy Near McCook Nebraska
1966

ballpoint pen ink, colored pencil, and pastel on paper
12 × 17 ¾ in.

Collection of Douglas O. Robson from the Robson Family Collection, Promised gift to the Smithsonian American Art Museum

CAT. 40

Mt. Baden Powell Near Pasadena California.
1969

ballpoint pen ink, colored pencil, and pastel on paper
17 ⅜ × 22 ⅞ in.

Collection of Douglas O. Robson from the Robson Family Collection, Promised gift to the Smithsonian American Art Museum

CAT. 41

PURVIS YOUNG
1943–2010

On the March
1996

paint on paper
30 × 40 in.

SAAM 2016.38.85

CAT. 76

CARLO ZINELLI
1916–1974

*Untitled**
September 26, 1968

opaque watercolor on paper
recto/verso: 27 × 19 ⅛ in. (sight)

SAAM 2016.38.86R-V

CAT. 10

BIBLIOGRAPHY

Adelman, Everett Mayo. "The Thrones and Chairs Leroy Person Made." *Folk Art* 19, no. 3 (Fall 1994): 48–50.

Adler, Esther. "Unfolding Joseph E. Yoakum: Christian Science and Life on the South Side." In Pascale, Adler, and Kopp, *Joseph E. Yoakum*, 45–57.

Ames, Kenneth L. "Outside Outsider Art." In Hall and Metcalf, *Artist Outsider*, 253–72.

Aranke, Sampada. "Written in the Wood: Black Life Made Visible." In Ireson and Whitley, *Elijah Pierce's America*, 34–41.

Armstrong, Linda Connelly, dir. *Nellie's Playhouse*. Parts I & II. Memphis, TN: Center for Southern Folklore, 1983. https://www.judithalexander.org/about-nellie-mae-rowe/nellie-s-playhouse-video-parts-i-ii/.

Arnett, Paul. "Artistic License." In Jones, *Thornton Dial*, 3–9.

———. "Leroy Person: Chipping Away." In *Once That River Starts to Flow*, 104–11. Vol. 2 of Arnett and Arnett, *Souls Grown Deep*.

Arnett, Paul, and William Arnett, eds. *Souls Grown Deep: African American Vernacular Art of the South*. 2 vols. Atlanta: Tinwood Books, 2000–2001.

Arnett, William. "Nellie Mae Rowe: Inside the Perimeter." In *The Tree Gave the Dove a Leaf*, 290–307. Vol. 1 of Arnett and Arnett, *Souls Grown Deep*.

———. "Sam Doyle: The News from Frogmore." Souls Grown Deep, n.d. https://www.soulsgrowndeep.org/artist/sam-doyle.

———. "The Tradition," 2012. Souls Grown Deep. http://soulsgrowndeep.org/tradition.

Bailey, Gordon W. "Sam Doyle." In Rousseau, *Hidden Art*, 182–85.

———. "Sam Doyle." In *Folk Art*, 264–66. Vol. 23 of Crown, Rivers, and Wilson, *The New Encyclopedia of Southern Culture*.

———. "Sam Doyle: A Biographical Essay," Self-Taught Genius, 2013. http://selftaughtgenius.org/reads/sam-doyle-a-biographical-essay.

———. "Sam Doyle: Haints and Saints." *Raw Vision* 61 (Winter 2007): 29–35.

———. "Sam Doyle: Heart and Soul." *New Orleans Museum of Art (NOMA) Arts Quarterly*, 23 (2001): 11.

Baker, Houston A., Jr. *Blues, Ideology, and Afro-American Literature: A Vernacular Theory*. Chicago: University of Chicago Press, 1984.

Bal, Mieke. "Autotopography: Louise Bourgeois as Builder." *Biography* 25, no. 1 (Winter 2002): 180–202.

Barbaro, Michael (Host). "Guilty of All Charges." *The Daily* (*New York Times*), April 21, 2021. https://podcasts.apple.com/us/podcast/guilty-of-all-charges/id1200361736?i=1000518027800.

Barringer, Tim, and Tom Flynn, eds. *Colonialism and the Object: Empire, Material Culture and the Museum*. New York: Routledge, 1998. https://www.smpub.com/ubb/images/18/Bentzon1-ocr.pdf.

Bates, Karen Grigsby. "When LA Erupted in Anger: A Look Back at the Rodney King Riots." NPR, April 26, 2017. https://www.npr.org/2017/04/26/524744989/when-la-erupted-in-anger-a-look-back-at-the-rodney-king-riots.

Beardsley, John. *James Castle: Memory Palace*. Boise, ID: James Castle Collection and Archive in association with Yale University Press, 2021.

Bell, Nicholas R. "Being James Castle: Experiencing Place, Time, and Memory." In Bell and Umberger, *Untitled: The Art of James Castle*, 19–34.

———. *The James Castle Primer*. Boise, ID: James Castle Collection and Archive, 2018.

Bell, Nicholas R., and Leslie Umberger. *Untitled: The Art of James Castle*. With an introduction by Alexander Nemerov. Exh. cat. Washington, DC: Smithsonian American Art Museum in association with D Giles, 2014.

Benner, Katie, and Will Wright. "3 Indicted on Federal Hate Crime Charges in Ahmaud Arbery Shooting." *New York Times*, April 28, 2021. https://www.nytimes.com/2021/04/28/us/politics/ahmaud-arbery-shooting.html.

Beveridge, Allan. "A Disquieting Feeling of Strangeness? The Art of the Mentally Ill." *Journal of the Royal Society of Medicine* 94, no. 11 (November 2001): 595–99. https://www.ncbi.nlm.nih.gov/pmc/articles/PMC1282252/.

Bonesteel, Michael. "Henry Darger." In Rousseau, *Hidden Art*, 134–43.

———. *Henry Darger: Art and Selected Writings*. New York: Rizzoli, 2000.

———. *Henry Darger: Author/Artist*. Exh. cat. Chicago: Intuit: The Center for Intuitive and Outsider Art, 2017. https://issuu.com/intuitart/dors/aa_catalog_u18_final.

Bonesteel, Michael, Mary Trent, and Yukiko Koide. Henry Darger (website). Accessed July 2021. http://officialhenrydarger.com/about/.

Booker, Hylan. "A World Made Visible." *Unframed*, Los Angeles County Museum of Art, August 18, 2014. https://unframed.lacma.org/2014/08/15/a-world-made-visible.

Borum, Jenifer P. "Bessie Harvey." In *The Tree Gave the Dove a Leaf*, 158–71. Vol. 1 of Arnett and Arnett, *Souls Grown Deep*.

———. "The Golden Book of William Hawkins." In Crawley, *William L. Hawkins*, 56–61.

———. "Review: Leroy Person: Luise Ross Gallery." *Artforum* 38, no. 9 (May 2000): 181. https://www.artforum.com/print/reviews/200005/leroy-person-559.

Boxer, Sarah. "The Rise of Self-Taught Artists: Out Is the New In." *Atlantic*, September 2013. https://www.theatlantic.com/magazine/archive/2013/09/out-is-the-new-in/309428/.

Brown, Patricia Leigh. "42,000 Miles a Year on the Antiques Track." *New York Times*, November 9, 1995.

Brown, Tony. "Whittling Barber Works on Display." *Savannah Morning News*, January 24, 1982.

Cahill, Holger. "Holger Cahill papers, 1910–1993." Archives of American Art, Smithsonian Institution. Accessed April 28, 2021. https://www.aaa.si.edu/collections/holger-cahill-papers-6730.

Cardinal, Roger. *Outsider Art*. New York: Praeger, 1972.

Catlin, Roger. "Self-Taught Artist Clementine Hunter Painted the Bold Hues of Southern Life." *Smithsonian Magazine*, October 18, 2018. https://www.smithsonianmag.com/smithsonian-institution/self-taught-artist-clementine-hunter-painted-bold-hues-southern-life-180970572/.

Cavin (Morris), Shari. "Bessie Harvey: The Spirit in the Wood." *Clarion* 12, no. 2/3 (Spring/Summer 1987): 44–49.

Columbus State Community College. "Biography: Elijah Pierce." Accessed April 28, 2021. https://www.cscc.edu/elijahpierce/bio.htm.

Conwill, Kinshasha Holman. "In Search of an 'Authentic' Vision: Decoding the Appeal of the Self-Taught African-American Artist." *American Art* 5, no. 4 (Autumn 1991): 2–9.

———. "Something That Hasn't Been Born Yet: Nellie Mae Rowe and the Southern Imagination." Introduction to Kogan, *Art of Nellie Mae Rowe,* 11–13.

Cooke, Lynne. "Boundary Trouble: Navigating Margin and Mainstream." In Cooke et al., *Outliers and American Vanguard Art*, 9–11.

———. "Orthodoxies Undermined." In Percy, *"Great and Mighty Things,"* 204–14.

Cooke, Lynne, with Darby English, Richard Meyer, Jennifer Jane Marshall, John Beardsley, Katherine Jentleson, Faheem Majeed. *Outliers and American Vanguard Art*. Exh. cat. Washington, DC: National Gallery of Art in association with University of Chicago Press, 2018.

Cooks, Bridget R. "Bill Traylor in Context: African American Artists and Modern Primitives." In *Bill Traylor: Beyond the Figure, Symposium, American Folk Art Museum, New York, 2013*, edited by Valérie Rousseau. New York: American Folk Art Museum, forthcoming.

———. *Exhibiting Blackness: African Americans and the American Art Museum*. Amherst: University of Massachusetts Press, 2011.

Corn, Wanda M. *The Great American Thing: Modern Art and National Identity, 1915–1935*. Berkeley: University of California Press, 1999.

Crawley, Susan Mitchell. "The Ecstatic Play of William Hawkins." In Crawley, *William L. Hawkins,* 20–39.

———. *The Treasure of Ulysses Davis: Sculpture from a Savannah Barbershop*. Atlanta: High Museum of Art in association with the King-Tisdell Cottage Foundation of Savannah, GA, 2008.

———, ed. *William L. Hawkins: An Imaginative Geography*. Milan: Skira, 2018.

Creative Growth. "About—Creative Growth Art Center." Accessed April 28, 2021. https://creativegrowth.org/about.

Crown, Carol, ed. *Coming Home! Self-Taught Artists, the Bible, and the American South*. Oxford: University Press of Mississippi in association with the Art Museum of the University of Memphis, 2004.

———, ed. *Wonders to Behold: The Visionary Art of Myrtice West*. Memphis, TN: Mustang, 1999.

Crown, Carol, and Charles Russell, eds. *Sacred and Profane: Voice and Vision in Southern Self-Taught Art*. Jackson: University Press of Mississippi, 2007.

Crown, Carol, Cheryl Rivers, and Charles Reagan Wilson, eds. *Folk Art*. Vol. 23 of *The New Encyclopedia of Southern Culture*, edited by Charles Reagan Wilson. Chapel Hill: University of North Carolina Press, 2013.

Cubbs, Joanne. "Rebels, Mystics, and Outcasts: The Romantic Artist Outsider." In Hall and Metcalf, *Artist Outsider,* 77–93.

———. *Religious Visionaries*. Exh. cat. Sheboygan, WI: John Michael Kohler Arts Center, 1991.

Dallas Museum of Art. *Black Art, Ancestral Legacy: The African Impulse in African-American Art*. Dallas, TX: Dallas Museum of Art, 1989.

Danto, Arthur C. "The Art World Revisited: Comedies of Similarity." In *Beyond the Brillo Box: The Visual Arts in Post-Historical Perspective*, 33–54. New York: Farrar, Straus and Giroux, 1992.

DePasse, Derrel B. *Traveling the Rainbow: The Life and Art of Joseph E. Yoakum*. Jackson: University Press of Mississippi in conjunction with the Museum of American Folk Art, 2001.

Dial, Thornton, Sr. "'Mr. Dial Is a Man Looking for Something.'" In *Once That River Starts to Flow*, 192–225. Vol. 2 of Arnett and Arnett, *Souls Grown Deep*.

Di Maria, Tom, ed. *The Creative Growth Book: From the Outside to the Inside with Disabilities Today*. Milan: 5 Continents Editions, 2015.

———. "When Words Write Pictures." *Raw Vision* 88 (Winter 2015/16): 14–19.

Doss, Erika. "Visualizing Faith: Religious Presence and Meaning in Modern and Contemporary American Art." In Crown, *Coming Home!,* 41–54.

Dubuffet, Jean. "Anticultural Positions." Lecture presented at the Arts Club of Chicago, December 20, 1951. https://www.austincc.edu/noel/writings/Anticultural%20Positions.pdf.

Ellis, Estelle, Caroline Seebohm, and Christopher Simon Sykes. *At Home with Art: How Art Lovers Live with and Care for Their Treasures*. New York: Clarkson Potter, 1999.

Espinosa, Víctor M. *Martín Ramírez: Framing His Life and Art*. Austin: University of Texas Press, 2015.

Esslin, Martin J. "Samuel Beckett: Irish Author." *Encyclopedia Britannica*, December 18, 2020. https://www.britannica.com/biography/Samuel-Beckett.

Exploring Florida. "Famous Floridians: Henry Morrison Flagler." Exploring Florida: A Social Studies Resource for Students and Teachers. Tampa: Florida Center for Instructional Technology, College of Education, University of South Florida, 2002. https://fcit.usf.edu/florida/lessons/flagler/flagler.htm.

Fagaly, William A. *David Butler*. Exh. cat. New Orleans, LA: New Orleans Museum of Art, 1976.

Fagaly, William A., Jason Berry, and Helen M. Shannon. *Tools of Her Ministry: The Art of Sister Gertrude Morgan*. New York: American Folk Art Museum; Rizzoli International, 2004.

Finster, Howard. "Howard Finster papers, 1932–1987." Archives of American Art, Smithsonian Institution. https://www.aaa.si.edu/collections/howard-finster-papers-8596.

Finster, Howard, and Tom Patterson. *Howard Finster: Stranger from Another World: Man of Visions Now on This Earth*. New York: Abbeville Press, 1989.

Fleisher/Ollman Gallery. "Philadelphia Wireman." Accessed April 28, 2021. https://www.fleisher-ollmangallery.com/artists/philadelphia_wireman.

Fox, Catherine. "Renown Came Late in Life for Gifted Folk Artist." *Atlanta Journal-Constitution*, October 24, 1982.

Freiman, Jane Salzfass. "A Strategy for Entertaining: With Organized Planning and Informal Style, Chicago's Margaret and John Robson Produce a Convivial Dinner for 12 Friends." *Cuisine*, May 1982.

Fulmer, Hal. "The Word and the World: Evangelical Christianity, the Bible, and the Secular South." In Crown, *Coming Home!,* 55–60.

Gates, Henry Louis, Jr., exec. producer. *The Black Church*. 2021. Two-part series, PBS Studios. https://www.pbs.org/show/black-church/.

Gioni, Massimiliano. "A Universal, All-Embracing Knowledge." Introduction, 55th International Art Exhibition, 2013. https://www.labiennale.org/en/art/2013/introduction-massimiliano-gioni.

Girardot, Norman, Ricardo Viera, and Howard Finster. "Howard Finster." *Art Journal* 53, no. 1 (1994): 48–50. https://doi.org/10.2307/777533.

Goldstein, Richard. "Charles L. Bartlett, Journalist and a Kennedy Matchmaker, Dies at 95." *New York Times*, February 20, 2017. https://www.nytimes.com/2017/02/19/us/charles-l-bartlett-dead-journalist-kennedy.html.

Greaves, Brendan. "'Characters More Comely to the Eye': Text and Intention in the Art of James Castle." In Percy, *James Castle,* 118–55.

Gruber, J. Richard. *Nellie Mae Rowe*. Augusta, GA: Morris Museum of Art, 1996.

Gundaker, Grey. "'Without Parse of Script': The Interaction of Conventional Literacy and Vernacular Practice in African American Expressive Culture." PhD diss., Yale University, 1992.

Hall, Michael D., ed. *Legacy in Wood: Elijah Pierce at the Columbus Museum of Art*. Columbus, OH: Columbus Museum of Art, 2013.

———. "The Pierce Effect: One Artist's Impact on Museum Practice in Columbus, Ohio." In Ireson and Whitley, *Elijah Pierce's America*, 12–17.

———. "The Problem of Martín Ramírez: Folk Art Criticism as Cosmologies of Coercion." In *Stereoscopic Perspective: Reflections on American Fine and Folk Art*, 227–36. Ann Arbor, MI: UMI Research Press, 1988.

Hall, Michael D., and Eugene W. Metcalf Jr., eds. *The Artist Outsider: Creativity and the Boundaries of Culture*. Washington, DC: Smithsonian Institution Press, 1994.

Halstead, Whitney. "Joseph E. Yoakum." Unpublished manuscript, ca. 1977. Whitney Halstead Papers, Art Institute of Chicago, AIC Archives 4809-0000, Box One, 1977.

Hartigan, Lynda Roscoe. "Collecting the Lone and Forgotten." In Hartigan et al., *Made with Passion*, 1–80.

———. "From the Sahara of the Bozart to the Shoe That Rode the Howling Tornado: Collecting Folk Art in the South." In *Let It Shine: Self-Taught Art from the T. Marshall Hahn Collection*, 43–61. Atlanta: High Museum of Art, 2001.

———. "Recent Challenges in the Study of African American Folk Art." *International Review of African American Art* 11, no. 3 (June 1994): 27–29, 60–63.

Hartigan, Lynda Roscoe, Andrew L. Connors, Elizabeth Tisdel Holmstead, and Tonia L. Horton. *Made with Passion: The Hemphill Folk Art Collection in the National Museum of American Art*. Washington, DC: Smithsonian Institution Press, 1990.

Hayes, Jeffrey R. "Black, Calvin and Ruby." In *Folk Art*, 226–27. Vol. 23 of Crown, Rivers, and Wilson, *The New Encyclopedia of Southern Culture*.

Hemphill, Herbert W., Jr., and Julia Weissman. *Twentieth-Century American Folk Art and Artists*. New York: E. P. Dutton, 1974.

Henry Darger Research Archive of the Contemporary Center of the American Folk Art Museum. "Henry Darger: Writings." Accessed April 28, 2021. https://folkartmuseum.libraryhost.com/resources/henry_darger_papers.

Higgs, Matthew. "Judith Scott: Creative Growth." In Morris and Higgs, *Judith Scott: Bound & Unbound*, 28–35.

The Historical Marker Database. "Uncle Jack." September 6, 2015. Last modified January 1, 2018. https://www.hmdb.org/m.asp?m=88234.

History. "U.S. Immigration Timeline." Updated April 20, 2021. https://www.history.com/topics/immigration/immigration-united-states-timeline.

Hokule'a Borofsky, Amelia Rachel. "Where Great Art Transcends Disability." *Atlantic*, December 13, 2012. https://www.theatlantic.com/health/archive/2012/12/where-great-art-transcends-disability/266184/.

Holland, Sharon P. "Put Honey in the Sky Where It Could Drip and Make the World Sweet: Looking for Purvis Young and Thomas Samuel Doyle but Seeing Something Else; Meditations on the *Matter* of Black Freedom." In *The Unfinished Business of Unsettled Things: Art from an African American South*, edited by Bernard L. Herman. Chapel Hill: University of North Carolina, forthcoming.

Hutson, Laura. "Howard Finster Exhibit Is Filled with Prophetic Visions of Spaceships and Henry Ford." *Nashville Scene*, December 1, 2011. https://www.nashvillescene.com/arts-culture/article/13040876.

Ireson, Nancy. "'Your Life Is a Book, and Every Day Is a Page': Elijah Pierce's Storytelling." In Ireson and Whitley, *Elijah Pierce's America*, 24–33.

Ireson, Nancy, and Zoé Whitley, eds. *Elijah Pierce's America*. Exh. cat. Philadelphia: Barnes Foundation in association with Paul Holberton, 2020.

It'll Come True: Eleven Artists, First and Last. Lafayette, LA: Artists' Alliance, 1992.

James Castle Collection and Archive. "James Castle Selected Exhibitions." Accessed April 28, 2021. https://jamescastle.com/selected-exhibitions/.

Janis, Sidney. *They Taught Themselves: American Primitive Painters of the 20th Century*. New York: Dial Press, 1942.

Jentleson, Katherine. "Born on the Fourth of July." In Jentleson, *Really Free*, 14–41.

———. *Gatecrashers: The Rise of the Self-Taught Artist in America*. Oakland: University of California Press, 2020.

———. "Howard Finster." In Rousseau, *Hidden Art*, 186–91.

———, ed. *Really Free: The Radical Art of Nellie Mae Rowe*. Exh. cat. Atlanta: High Museum of Art in partnership with DelMonico Books, 2021.

Jones, Phillip March, ed. *Thornton Dial: The Earliest Years, 1987–1989*. Exh. cat. Los Angeles: Parker Gallery, 2021.

Kallir, Jane. "Art Brut and 'Outsider' Art: A Changing Landscape." Introduction to *Accidental Genius: Art from the Anthony Petullo Collection*, by Margaret Andera and Lisa Stone, 23–27. Exh. cat. Milwaukee, WI: Milwaukee Art Museum in association with DelMonico Books, 2012.

———. "Henry Darger: Art and Myth." Galerie St. Etienne, 2004. https://www.gseart.com/exhibitions-essay/1005.

Karlins, N. F. "Four from Coal Country: Friendships and the Contemporary Folk Artist." *Clarion* 12, no. 2/3 (Spring/Summer 1987): 54–61.

Kelly, Christopher J. "The Personal Is Political." *Encyclopedia Britannica*, May 1, 2017. https://www.britannica.com/topic/the-personal-is-political.

Kiah, Virginia. "Ulysses Davis: Savannah Folk Sculptor." *Southern Folklore Quarterly* 42 (1978): 275.

Kimmelman, Michael. "With an Ear for God and an Eye for Art." Art Review, *New York Times*, February 27, 2004. https://www.nytimes.com/2004/02/27/arts/art-review-with-an-ear-for-god-and-an-eye-for-art.html.

Kirwin, Liza. "Appreciation: The Reverend Howard Finster, the Last Red Light before the Apocalypse." *American Art* 16, no. 2 (Summer 2002): 90–93.

Knoch, Joanne. "Women in Business." *Chicago Daily Tribune*, October 25, 1958.

Kogan, Lee. *The Art of Nellie Mae Rowe: Ninety-Nine and a Half Won't Do*. New York: Museum of American Folk Art in association with University Press of Mississippi, 1998.

———. "Clementine Hunter: Self-Taught Louisiana Artist." In *Louisiana Women: Their Lives and Times*, edited by Janet Allured and Judith F. Gentry, 175–94. Athens: University of Georgia Press, 2009.

———. "New Museum Encyclopedia Shatters Myths." *Clarion* 15, no. 5 (Winter 1990–91): 53–56.

Library of Congress. "New Deal Programs: Selected Library of Congress Resources: Federal Art Project." Accessed April 29, 2021. https://www.loc.gov/rr/program/bib/newdeal/fap.html.

Louisiana State Museum. "Clementine Hunter Murals." Accessed April 28, 2021. https://www.crt.state/la.us/louisiana-state-museum/exhibits/clementine-hunter-murals.

Lovell, Charles M., and Erwin Hester, eds. *Minnie Evans: Artist*. Greenville, NC: Wellington B. Gray Gallery, East Carolina University, 1993.

Lovett, Bobby L. "From Plantation to the City: William Edmondson and the African American Community." In Thompson et al., *Art of William Edmondson*, 15–32.

Ludins-Katz, Florence, and Elias Katz. *Art and Disabilities: Establishing the Creative Art Center for People with Disabilities*. Cambridge, MA: Brookline Books, 1990.

Macel, Christine. "The Exhibition: Focus on Art and Artists." Introduction, 57th International Art Exhibition, 2017. https://www.labiennale.org/en/art/2017/introduction-christine-macel.

MacGregor, John M. *The Discovery of the Art of the Insane*. Princeton, NJ: Princeton University Press, 1989.

———. *Henry Darger: In the Realms of the Unreal*. New York: Delano Greenidge, 2002.

Major, Clarence, ed. *Juba to Jive: A Dictionary of African-American Slang*. New York: Puffin, 1994, reprint ed.

Mandal, Ananya, MD. "Down Syndrome History." News Medical Life Sciences. Last updated February 26, 2019. https://www.news-medical.net/health/Down-Syndrome-History.aspx.

Manley, Roger. *Signs and Wonders: Outsider Art Inside North Carolina*. Raleigh: North Carolina Museum of Art, 1989.

Manley, Roger, and Mark Sloan. "Reverend Howard Finster: Paradise Garden and Plant Farm Museum." In *Self-Made Worlds: Visionary Folk Art Environments*, 58–59. New York: Aperture, 1997.

Marsh, Betsa. "The Woodcarver of Long Street." *Columbus Monthly* (June 1975): 55–58.

Marshall, Jennifer Jane. "Find-and-Seek: Discovery Narratives, Americanization, and Other Tales of Genius in Modern American Folk Art." In Cooke et al., *Outliers and American Vanguard Art*, 52–63.

———. "Nashville, New York, Paris, and Nashville: William Edmondson, Mobilized and Unmoved." *American Art* 31, no. 2 (Summer 2017): 69–76.

Marshall, Patricia Phillips, and Jo Ramsay Leimenstoll. *Thomas Day: Master Craftsman and Free Man of Color*. Chapel Hill: University of North Carolina Press in association with the North Carolina Museum of History, 2010.

Mayerson, Arlene. "The History of Americans with Disabilities Act: A Movement Perspective." Disability Rights Education & Defense Fund, 1992. https://dredf.org/about-us/publications/the-history-of-the-ada/.

Meyer, Richard. "How to Make a Modern Primitive." In Cooke et al., *Outliers and American Vanguard Art*, 43–51.

Mills, Quincy T. *Cutting Along the Color Line: Black Barbers and Barber Shops in America*. Philadelphia: University of Pennsylvania Press, 2013.

Mital, Ruchi. "This World Is Not My Own: A Creative Treatment of Actuality." In Jentleson, *Really Free*, 42–49.

Morgan, Stacy. "Clementine Hunter and Melrose Plantation." *American Art* 19, no. 1 (Spring 2005): 25–28. https://doi.org/10.1086/429972.

Morris, Catherine. "Biography Is Complicated." *Art 21 Magazine*, October 30, 2018. https://magazine.art21.org/2018/10/30/biography-is-complicated/.

———. "Judith Scott and the Politics of Biography." Introduction to Morris and Higgs, *Judith Scott: Bound & Unbound*, 8–17.

Morris, Catherine, and Matthew Higgs, eds. *Judith Scott: Bound & Unbound*. Exh. cat. Brooklyn, NY: Brooklyn Museum in association with DelMonico Books-Prestel, 2014.

Morris, Randall. "The Hawk King of Elsinore: A Memoir of Jon Serl." In *Jon Serl: The Mutability of Being*, by Jo Farb Hernández, Randall Morris, and Cara Zimmerman, 9. Exh. cat. San Jose, CA: Natalie and James Thompson Art Gallery, 2013.

———. "Martín Ramírez." *Folk Art* 20, no. 4 (Winter 1995/96): 36–45.

———. "Martín Ramírez: Master of Los Altos." In *Vernacular Visionaries: International Outsider Art*, edited by Annie Carlano, 50–63. New Haven, CT: Yale University Press in association with the Museum of International Folk Art, 2003.

———. "Martín Ramírez: Revisited." *Folk Art* 27, no. 4 (Winter 2002/3): 52–59.

The Museum of Modern Art. "Exhibition: Sculpture by William Edmondson (1937)." Accessed April 28, 2021. https://www.moma.org/calendar/exhibitions/2094.

———. "Sculpture by William Edmondson." Press release, October 18, 1937. https://assets.moma.org/documents/moma_press-release_333062.pdf.

National Archives and Records Administration. "Records of the Work Projects Administration (WPA): Record Group 69." August 15, 2016. https://www.archives.gov/research/guide-fed-records/groups/069.

National Museum of African American History and Culture, Smithsonian Institution. "Teapot Made by Peter Bentzon." Accessed April 28, 2021. https://nmaahc.si.edu/object/nmaahc_2010.14.

Nicholson, Barbara R., and Deidre Hamlar. "Roads Diverged: William L. Hawkins and Elijah Pierce in Columbus." In Crawley, *William L. Hawkins,* 49–55.

Nuku, George Tamihana. "Past and Present." Session 3, People: A Global Dialogue on Museums and Their Publics (webinar), Metropolitan Museum of Art, New York, May 19, 2021. https://www.youtube.com/watch?v=AC2k-2XnSY4.

Olek, Emily. "The Fantastical Reality of Joseph Yoakum: A Chronology." In Pascale, Adler, and Kopp, *Joseph E. Yoakum,* 27–34.

Olmstead Rights. "The Americans with Disabilities Act of 1990—ADA." Accessed August 2, 2021. https://www.olmsteadrights.org/about-olmstead/item.6460-The_Americans_with_Disabilities_Act_of_1990_ADA.

Pascale, Mark. "Revisiting Joseph E. Yoakum's Chicago Legacy." In Pascale, Adler, and Kopp, *Joseph E. Yoakum,* 15–25.

Pascale, Mark, Esther Adler, Édouard Kopp, eds. *Joseph E. Yoakum: What I Saw*. Exh. cat. Chicago: Art Institute of Chicago, 2021.

Percy, Ann, ed. *"Great and Mighty Things": Outsider Art from the Jill and Sheldon Bonovitz Collection*. Exh. cat. Philadelphia: Philadelphia Museum of Art, 2013.

———, ed. *James Castle: A Retrospective.* Philadelphia: Philadelphia Museum of Art in association with Yale University Press, 2008.

———. "Unfolding the Familiar: James Castle Reintroduced." In Percy, *James Castle: A Retrospective*, 1–75.

Perry, Regenia. "Sam Doyle: St. Helena Island's Native Son." *Raw Vision* 23 (Summer 1998): 28–35.

Plasencia, Alex. "A History of West Coconut Grove from 1925: Slum Clearance, Concrete Monsters, and the Dichotomy of East and West Coconut Grove." Master's thesis, Clemson University, 2011. https://tigerprints.clemson.edu/all_theses/1117.

Pocius, Gerald. "Material Culture Worlds: A Report on Three Conferences." *Material Culture Review* 46, no. 1 (Fall 1997): 77–81. https://journals.lib.unb.ca/index.php/MCR/article/view/17754.

Promey, Sally M. "The 'Return' of Religion in the Scholarship of American Art." *The Art Bulletin* 85, no. 3 (2003): 581–603. https://doi.org/10.2307/3177387.

Puchner, Edward M. "'A Tried Stone': Community, Conversion, and Christ in the Sculpture of William Edmondson." In Romaine and Wolfskill, *Beholding Christ and Christianity in African American Art*.

Ratliff, Ben. "Critic's Choice: Singing with Power, Citing the Bible." *New York Times*, August 2, 2004. https://www.nytimes.com/2004/08/02/arts/critic-s-choice-jazz-cd-s-singing-with-power-citing-the-bible.html.

Renkl, Margaret. "The Picassos of the American South." *New York Times*, April 26, 2021. https://www.nytimes.com/2021/04/26/opinion/picasso-nashville-southern-art.html.

Rich, Nathaniel. "A Training Ground for Untrained Artists." *New York Times Magazine*, December 16, 2015. https://www.nytimes.com/2015/12/20/magazine/a-training-ground-for-untrained-artists.html.

Riner, Duane. "Newcomer Appointed to State Boxing Board." *Atlanta Constitution*, March 29, 1987.

Ringbom, Petter, dir. *This World Is Not My Own: The Life & Times of Nellie Mae Rowe*. Postproduction, 2021. https://thisworldisnotmyown.com/.

Romaine, James, and Phoebe Wolfskill, eds. *Beholding Christ and Christianity in African American Art*. University Park: Penn State University Press, 2017.

Rosenak, Chuck, and Jan Rosenak. *Museum of American Folk Art Encyclopedia of Twentieth-Century American Folk Art and Artists*. New York: Abbeville Press, 1990.

Rourke, Constance Mayfield. *Charles Sheeler: Artist in the American Tradition*. New York: Harcourt, Brace, 1938.

Rousseau, Valérie, with Jane Kallir and Anne-Imelda Radice. *The Hidden Art: 20th- & 21st-Century Self-Taught Artists from the Audrey B. Heckler Collection*. New York: Skira Rizzoli in association with the American Folk Art Museum, 2017.

Rudolph, William Keyse. "Possum Trot." *From the Collection* (blog). Milwaukee Art Museum, February 22, 2012. https://blog.mam.org/2012/02/22/from-the-collection-possum-trot/.

Rundquist, Leisa. *Betwixt and Between: Henry Darger's Vivian Girls*. Online exh. cat. Chicago: Intuit: Center for Intuitive and Outsider Art, 2018. https://issuu.com/intuitart/docs/darger_catalog_final_issuu_7a96c7d2fda871/6.

———. "Vivam! The Divine Intersexuality of Henry Darger's Vivian Girl." *Elsewhere: The International Journal of Self-Taught and Outsider Art,* Issue 2 (May 2014): 24–42. http://stoarc.com/journals/ELSEWHERE_Journal_Issue_2_May_2014.pdf.

Russell, Charles. "On the Absence and Presence of Bill Traylor in Euro-American and African American Modernist Thought." Paper presented at Bill Traylor: Beyond the Figure, American Folk Art Museum, New York, September 16, 2013.

Sacco, Nick. "Louisiana's 'Uncle Jack' Statue and the Problem of Interpreting Iconography in History Museums." *Exploring the Past* (blog), October 1, 2015. https://pastexplore.wordpress.com/2015/10/01/louisianas-uncle-jack-statue-and-the-problem-of-interpreting-iconography-in-history-museums/.

Sachant, Pamela Jane. "Eddie Arning's American Dream." *Raw Vision* 28 (1999): 28–33.

———. "Evidence of Abridgment in Eddie Arning's Art, and Its Importance." *Folk Art* 29, no. 3 (Fall 2004): 48–55.

Scanlon, Bette. "How One Woman Carves Bank Career." *Chicago Sun-Times*, February 7, 1959.

Schmelzer, Paul. "The Mystery Art and Ministry of Simon Sparrow." *Raw Vision* 34 (Spring 2001): 32–38.

———. "The Seen and the Unseen: The Life, Death, and Mystery Art of Simon Sparrow." *Outsider* 5, no. 2 (Winter 2001): 14–16.

Schwindler, Gary J. "Popular Images—Personal Visions: The Art of William Hawkins." In Crawley, *William L. Hawkins*, 13–14.

———. "William L. Hawkins: A Biography." Unpublished manuscript, after 1990, located in the William Hawkins Collection, Ohio History Connection Archives, Columbus.

Scott, Joyce Wallace. *Entwined: Sisters and Secrets in the Silent World of Artist Judith Scott*. Boston: Beacon Press, 2016.

Shiver, Art, and Tom Whitehead. *Clementine Hunter: Her Life and Art*. Baton Rouge: Louisiana State University Press, 2013.

Sims, Lowery Stokes. "Bill Traylor and William Edmondson and the Challenges to African American Artists Between the World Wars." In *Bill Traylor, William Edmondson, and the Modernist Impulse*, edited by Josef Helfenstein, 35–43. Urbana, IL: Krannert Art Museum and Kinkead Pavilion, 2004.

———. "The Self-Taught among Us: William Edmondson and the Vanguardist Dilemma." In Thompson et al., *Art of William Edmondson*, 71–78.

Smith, Roberta. "A Sea Change in the Art World, Made by Black Creators." *New York Times*, November 24, 2019. https://www.nytimes.com/2019/11/24/arts/design/black-artists.html.

Smith, Theophus H. *Conjuring Culture: Biblical Formations of Black America*. New York: Oxford University Press, 1994.

Smithsonian American Art Museum. "THE HERBERT WADE HEMPHILL J.R. COLLECTION FOUNDER OF AMERICAN FOLK ART THE MAN WHO PRESERVES THE LONE AND FORGOTTEN. THE UNKNOWN COLLECTION." Accessed April 29, 2021. https://americanart.si.edu/artwork/herbert-wade-hemphill-jr-collection-founder-american-folk-art-man-who-preserves-lone-and.

———. "Howard Finster." Accessed April 28, 2021. https://americanart.si.edu/artist/howard-finster-1543.

———. "Inez Nathaniel-Walker." Accessed April 28, 2021. https://americanart.si.edu/artist/inez-nathaniel-walker-3497.

Smithsonian Institution. "Statement From Secretary Lonnie G. Bunch." News release, May 31, 2020. https://www.si.edu/newsdesk/releases/statement-secretary-lonnie-g-bunch.

Smithsonian National Museum of African Art. "Striking Iron: The Art of African Blacksmiths." Accessed April 28, 2021. https://africa.si.edu/exhibitions/current-exhibitions/striking-iron-the-art-of-african-blacksmiths/irons-empowering-roles/.

South Writ Large. "Portfolio: Clementine Hunter African House Murals." Accessed April 28, 2021. https://southwritlarge.com/articles/portfolio-murals/.

SPACES. "Calvin & Ruby Black, Possum Trot." Accessed April 29, 2021. http://www.spaces-art-environments.org/explore/collection/environment/possum-trot/.

Spitz, Ellen Handler. "Henry Darger." In *Self-Taught Artists of the 20th Century: An American Anthology*, edited by Elsa Longhauser and Harald Szeeman, 102–3. Exh. cat. San Francisco: Chronicle Books in association with the Museum of American Folk Art, 1998.

Spriggs, Lynne E. *Local Heroes: Paintings and Sculpture by Sam Doyle*. Atlanta: High Museum of Art, 2000.

Stevens, Heidi. "What a Woody Allen Reckoning Can Teach Us about Lincoln Statues, Dr. Seuss and the British Royal Family." *Chicago Tribune*, March 8, 2021. https://www.chicagotribune.com/columns/heidi-stevens/ct-heidi-stevens-rethinking-woody-allen-manhattan-harry-meghan-0308-20210308-l5lqx4hxdvbelcnqudsmbxnkei-story.html.

Thebaut, Nancy, Christina Ramberg, and Norman Mark. *Joseph Elmer Yoakum*. Exh. cat. New York: Venus Over Manhattan, 2019.

Thompson, Robert Farris. "Edmondson's Art." In Thompson et al., *Art of William Edmondson*, 3–14.

———. *Flash of the Spirit: African and Afro-American Art and Philosophy*. New York: Vintage Books, 1983.

Thompson, Robert Farris, and Joseph Cornet. *The Four Moments of the Sun: Kongo Art in Two Worlds*. Exh. cat. Washington, DC: National Gallery of Art, 1981.

Thompson, Robert Farris, et al. *The Art of William Edmondson*. Nashville, TN: Cheekwood Museum of Art in partnership with the University Press of Mississippi, 1999.

Turner, J. F. "Howard Finster: Man of Visions." *Clarion* 14, no. 4 (Fall 1989): 38–43. https://issuu.com/american_folk_art_museum/docs/clarion_14_4_fall1989.

Umberger, Leslie. "Appreciation: Thornton Dial (1928–2016)." *American Art* 30, no. 2 (Summer 2016): 110–14.

———. *Between Worlds: The Art of Bill Traylor*. Exh. cat. Washington, DC: Smithsonian American Art Museum in association with Princeton University Press, 2018.

———. "Emery Blagdon: Properly Channeled." In Umberger et al., *Sublime Spaces & Visionary Worlds*, 203–23.

———. "Housewives, Witches, Beauty Queens, and Conjure Women: Locating the Practice of Self-Taught Women Artists." In *Boundary Trouble: The Self-Taught Artist and American Avant-Gardes*, edited by Lynne Cooke. New Haven, CT: Yale University Press, forthcoming.

———. "James Castle: Vanishing Point." In Bell and Umberger, *Untitled: The Art of James Castle*, 35–51.

Umberger, Leslie, et al. *Sublime Spaces & Visionary Worlds: Built Environments of Vernacular Artists*. New York: Princeton Architectural Press, 2007.

Vlach, John Michael. "From Gravestone to Miracle: Traditional Perspective and the Work of William Edmondson." In *By the Work of Their Hands: Studies in Afro-American Folklife*, 109–26. Charlottesville: University Press of Virginia, 1991.

Vlach, John Michael, and Simon J. Bronner. *Folk Art and Art Worlds*. Logan: Utah State University Press, 1992.

Waters, Donald J. "Snakes and Conjure Doctors." In *Strange Ways and Sweet Dreams: Afro-American Folklore from the Hampton Institute*, edited by Donald J. Waters, 297. Boston: G. K. Hall, 1983.

Wicks, Stephen C. *Awakening the Spirits: Art by Bessie Harvey*. Knoxville, TN: Knoxville Museum of Art, 1997.

Winslow, Barbara. *Shirley Chisholm: Catalyst for Change*. New York: Routledge, 2018.

Wojcik, Daniel. "Outsider Art, Vernacular Traditions, Trauma, and Creativity." *Western Folklore* 67, no. 2/3 (2008): 179–98. http://www.jstor.org/stable/25474913.

———. *Outsider Art: Visionary Worlds and Trauma*. Jackson: University Press of Mississippi, 2016.

Wolf, Jeffrey. "Elijah Pierce: An American Journey." Folk Art Society of America. Accessed March 3, 2021. https://folkart.org/mag/elijah-pierce-american-journey.

———. Interviews with Eleanor Scanlon Thompson, Geraldine Garrow, and Byron Johnson. Tapes 30–32, September 13, 2006. Collection of Jeffrey Wolf.

Wrenn, Tony P. "Day, Thomas" (1986). In NCpedia, from the *Dictionary of North Carolina Biography*, 6 vols., edited by William S. Powell. University of North Carolina Press, 1979–96. https://www.ncpedia.org/biography/day-thomas.

Yarbrough, Cathy. "All I Got Out There Is Junk." *Atlanta Constitution*, May 13, 1973.

Yau, Elaine Y. "Acts of Conversion: Sanctification and the Senses of Race in the Art of Sister Gertrude Morgan." In *Sensational Religion: Sensory Cultures in Material Practice*, edited by Sally M. Promey, 403–12. New Haven, CT: Yale University Press, 2014.

———. "Acts of Conversion: Sister Gertrude Morgan and the Sensation of Black Folk Art, 1960-1982." PhD diss., University of California, Berkeley, 2015.

———. "The Love in Labor: Reconsidering Amateurism in Sister Gertrude Morgan's Performances and Paintings." *Panorama: Journal of the Association of Historians of American Art* 5, no. 1 (Spring 2019). https://doi.org/10.24926/24716839.1684.

———. "Sister Gertrude Morgan and the Materials of Visionary Art." In Romaine and Wolfskill, *Beholding Christ and Christianity in African American Art*, 113–24.

Yelen, Alice Rae. *Passionate Visions of the American South: Self-Taught Artists from 1940 to the Present*. New Orleans, LA: New Orleans Museum of Art, 1993.

Young, Purvis. "This Is the Life I See." In *Once That River Starts to Flow*, 388–427. Vol. 2 of Arnett and Arnett, *Souls Grown Deep*.

INDEX

Page numbers in *italics* indicate illustrations. Artworks and book titles will be found under the artist's or author's name.

H

I

J

K

L

O

P

Q

R

T

U

V

W

Y

Z

IMAGE CREDITS

Unless otherwise specified, all photographs were provided by the owners/collections of the works of art noted in the captions and are reproduced with permission. Every effort has been made to obtain permissions for all copyright-protected images.

All photographs of artworks in the collection of the Smithsonian American Art Museum by Mildred Baldwin, Mindy Barrett, and Gene Young, unless otherwise noted.

FAR & WIDE / INSIDE & OUT

Photomontage, pp. 14–15 (clockwise from top left): Margaret Z. Robson, early 1950s; Robson home, Santa Fe, NM, 2011; on her wedding day, 1960; Chicago, 2013; with son Douglas, mid-1990s; Margaret (center) watches as husband John E. Robson is sworn in as Undersecretary of Transportation for the Johnson administration, 1967; Douglas's brother, Matthew, 1967; background text: Sargent Shriver to Margaret, May 24, 1961: all photos courtesy of Douglas O. Robson.

All figures courtesy of Douglas O. Robson, except: **FIG. 4** From *Chicago Sun-Times*. © 1959 Sun-Times Media. All rights reserved. Used under license; and **FIG. 14** Photo by Libba Gillum.

A CHANGING TIDE

Photomontage, pp. 42–43 (clockwise from top left): Sister Gertrude Morgan, ca. 1974, photo by Joshua Horwitz; Howard Finster, 1987–88, photo by Guy Mendes; Nellie Mae Rowe, 1971, photo by Melinda Blauvelt; Thornton Dial Sr., 2007, photo by Jerry Siegel; Sam Doyle, 1985, photo by Roger Manley; Dan Miller, 2018, Courtesy of Creative Growth.

FIG. 4 © 1994, Bill Traylor Family Trust; **FIG. 5** Series 9, box # EL1982.01-.02, COR5.1: Corcoran Gallery of Art registrar's office records, Special Collections Research Center, George Washington University Libraries, Washington DC; **FIG. 6** © Center for Creative Photography, Arizona Board of Regents; **FIG. 8** © British Pathé; **FIG. 9** Courtesy of Gilley's Gallery; **FIGS. 10, 11** Library of Congress, Prints and Photographs Division, Historic American Buildings Survey Collection, HABS LA-2-69-B; **FIG. 12** © Grandma Moses Properties Co., New York; **FIG. 13** © Cane River Art Corporation; **FIGS. 18, 19** The Art Institute of Chicago / Art Resource, NY; **FIG. 21** Photo by Jeffrey Wolf; **FIG. 23** © Chas Ray Krider; p. 43 (Nellie Mae Rowe, detail) and **FIGS. 25, 34** © Melinda Blauvelt; **FIGS. 27, 28** © 2022 Estate of Nellie Mae Rowe / Artists Rights Society (ARS), New York; **FIG. 29** From Guy Mendes, *Light at Hand: Photographs, 1970–85* (Frankfort, KY: Gnomon Press, 1986); p. 42 (Sam Doyle, detail) and **FIGS. 31, 32, 36** Photo © Roger Manley; **FIG. 33** Photo by Lee Stalsworth–Fine Art Through Photography; **FIG. 35** File 800: Container 52: Library of Congress Archives: Photographs, Illustrations, and Objects Series: Manuscript Division: Library of Congress; **FIG. 37** Wisconsin Historical Society, WHS-122526; **FIG. 38** © Charles Russell; **FIG. 40** From *The Miami Herald*. © 1972 McClatchy. All rights reserved. Used under license; **FIG. 41** © Larry T. Clemons / Gallery 721 / Artists Rights Society (ARS), New York, photo by Gene Young; **FIG. 44** © Estate of Martín Ramírez; **FIG. 45** Photo by Percel Followell; **FIG. 47** © James Castle Collection and Archive; p. 43 (Howard Finster, detail) and **FIG. 48** © Guy Mendes; **FIGS. 50–52** Artwork © 2022 Howard Finster / Artists Rights Society (ARS), New York, photo © Roger Manley; p. 43 (Thornton Dial Sr., detail) and **FIG. 53** © jerrysiegel.com; **FIG. 54** © Leon Borensztein; **FIG. 56** Courtesy Jeffrey Thomas Fine Art; **FIG. 57** Courtesy Estate of Leonard J. Ross and Grey Carter-Objects of Art; **FIG. 59** from Lee Kogan, "New Museum Encyclopedia Shatters Myth," *Clarion* 15, no. 5 (Winter 1990/91): 53; **FIGS. 62, 63** Photo by Seymour Rosen, © SPACES–Saving and Preserving Arts and Cultural Environments; **FIG. 64** Courtesy William Eugene May, Lawrence Douglas May, Garth Andrew May, and Clare Alexander May; **FIGS. 66, 67** Sally and Richard Greenhill / Alamy Stock Photo.

CATALOGUE *of* WORKS

CATS. 5, 19, 26, 27, 30 © 1994, Bill Traylor Family Trust; **CATS. 6, 7, 44, 48** Photo by Scott Saraceno; **CATS. 11, 95** © 2005, Creative Growth; **CATS. 13, 14** © Laura Craig McNellis, photo by Scott Saraceno; **CATS. 15, 16** Courtesy of Creative Growth, photo by Scott Saraceno; **CATS. 24, 37, 51, 56, 59–73, 111, 112** Photo by Lee Stalsworth–Fine Art Through Photography; **CATS. 28, 29** © 1994, Bill Traylor Family Trust, photo by Scott Saraceno; **CAT. 34** © Cane River Art Corporation; **CATS. 38–41, 43, 45, 46, 55** Photo: Matt Flynn © Smithsonian Institution; **CAT. 76** © Larry T. Clemons / Gallery 721 / Artists Rights Society (ARS), New York; **CAT. 77** © 2022 Kiyoko Lerner / Artists Rights Society (ARS), New York, photo by Scott Saraceno; **CATS. 78, 79** © Estate of Martín Ramírez, photo by Scott Saraceno; **CATS. 80–85** © James Castle Collection and Archive, photo by Mindy Barrett; **CAT. 86** © 2022 Howard Finster / Artists Rights Society (ARS), New York, photo by Scott Saraceno; **CATS. 87–91** © 2022 Howard Finster / Artists Rights Society (ARS), New York, photo by Lee Stalsworth–Fine Art Through Photography; **CAT. 92** © 2022 Estate of Thornton Dial / Artists Rights Society (ARS), New York; **CATS. 93, 94** © 2022 Estate of Thornton Dial / Artists Rights Society (ARS), New York, photo: Matt Flynn © Smithsonian Institution; **CATS. 96, 97** Courtesy of Creative Growth; **CAT. 100** © 8/7/2000, Randall Morris; **CATS. 118, 119** Courtesy of Creative Growth, photo by Scott Saraceno; **CAT. 120** Courtesy of Creative Growth, photo: Matt Flynn © Smithsonian Institution.